ENGLISH, IRISH AND SUBVERSIVES AMONG THE DISMAL SCIENTISTS

RESEARCH IN THE HISTORY OF ECONOMIC THOUGHT AND METHODOLOGY

Founding Editor: Warren J. Samuels

Series Editors: Jeff E. Biddle, Ross B. Emmett and Marianne Johnson

Recent Volumes:

Volume 26A:	Research in the History of Economic Thought and Methodology: A Research Annual Warren J. Samuels, Jeff E. Biddle and Ross B. Emmett; 2008
Volume 26B:	Research in the History of Economic Thought and Methodology: Further Documents from F. Taylor Ostrander; 2008
Volume 26C:	Research in the History of Economic Thought and Methodology: Further Documents from and on the History of Economic Thought; Warren J. Samuels, Marianne Johnson and Kirk Johnson; 2008
Volume 27A:	Research in the History of Economic Thought and Methodology: A Research Annual: Warren J. Samuels, Jeff E. Biddle and Ross B. Emmett; 2009
Volume 27B:	Henry George, the Transatlantic Irish, and Their Times; Kenneth C. Wenzer; 2009
Volume 27C:	Documents from Glenn Johnson and F. Taylor Ostrander; Warren J. Samuels and Marianne Johnson; 2009
Volume 28A:	Research in the History of Economic Thought and Methodology: A Research Annual; Jeff E. Biddle and Ross B. Emmett; 2010

RESEARCH IN THE HISTORY OF ECONOMIC THOUGHT
AND METHODOLOGY VOLUME 28-B

ENGLISH, IRISH AND SUBVERSIVES AMONG THE DISMAL SCIENTISTS

EDITED BY

NIGEL F. B. ALLINGTON

Downing College, University of Cambridge,
CB2 1DQ, UK and
Ecole de Management Grenoble University,
38000 Grenoble, France

NOEL W. THOMPSON

Professor of History and Pro-Vice-Chancellor,
Swansea University, Swansea, SA2 8PP, Wales, UK

Emerald

United Kingdom – North America – Japan
India – Malaysia – China

Emerald Group Publishing Limited
Howard House, Wagon Lane, Bingley BD16 1WA, UK

First edition 2010

British Library Cataloguing in Publication Data
A catalogue record for this book is available from the British Library

ISBN: 978-0-85724-061-3
ISSN: 0743-4154 (Series)

Printed and bound in Great Britain by
CPI Antony Rowe, Chippenham and Eastbourne

CONTENTS

LIST OF CONTRIBUTORS

Nigel F. B. Allington	Downing College and Centre for Economic and Public Policy Research, University of Cambridge, UK and Ecole de Management, Grenoble University, France
Giancarlo de Vivo	Department of Economics, University of Naples Frederico II, Italy
G. M. Ditchfield	School of History, University of Kent, UK
James P. Henderson	Department of Economics, Valparaiso University, USA
Samuel Hollander	Department of Economics, Ben-Gurion University, Israel
G. C. G. Moore	School of Business, University of Notre Dame Australia, Fremantle, Australia
Alan O'Day	Modern History at Greyfriars, University of Oxford, UK
Renee Prendergast	Management School, Queen's University, Belfast, Northern Ireland, UK
Jan S. Prybyla	Department of Economics, Penn State University, USA
John Pullen	School of Business, Economics and Public Policy, University of New England, Australia
Noel W. Thompson	Swansea University, Wales, UK

Richard van den Berg Faculty of Business and Law, Kingston University, London, UK

Michael V. White Department of Economics, Monash University, Australia

EDITORIAL BOARD

EDWIN ROBERT ANDERSON SELIGMAN: CHAMPION OF THE NEGLECTED BRITISH EPIGONES

Nigel F. B. Allington and Noel W. Thompson

1. INTRODUCTION

Seligman is an important and ironically somewhat neglected figure today in the history of American economic thought. However, an examination of his scholarly achievements reveals that he had a considerable impact on the development of professional economics in America and could count the most influential economists in Europe as personal friends and collaborators (Moss, 2003; Rutherford, 2004; Mehrotra, 2005). Asso and Fiorito (2006), in their introduction to Seligman's autobiography (1929) argue that 'his personal influence as an academic economist, as a teacher and as a central figure in the dissemination of economic knowledge was second to none and perhaps more meaningful than any single work he wrote' (p. 1). They also record (quoting his student, Alvin Johnson) that 'with Seligman…American economics began to acquire a distinctive professional reputation, some very high scholarly standards and a sort of "moral magnificence"' (p. 2). What this means is that through Seligman's work and guidance economics came to encompass a moral dimension that fed through into social policies, many of which were adopted by American legislatures. The major influences on his method included the German Historical School and a number of heterodox

English, Irish and Subversives Among the Dismal Scientists
Research in the History of Economic Thought and Methodology, Volume 28-B, 1–35

ISSN: 0743-4154/doi:10.1108/S0743-4154(2010)000028B004

Continental writers that informed Seligman's in great Whig interpretation of the development of economics. He also engaged critically with the more abstract methods of contemporary economic analysis of the early twentieth century.

Thus, Seligman endorsed a more pluralistic approach, preferring historo-deductive methods that gave a direct input into policy while more mathematical methods, with their high level of abstraction and unrealistic assumptions, were more likely to 'disregard elements of friction or complexity' (Asso & Fiorito, 2006, p. 4; Rutherford, 2004). This position garnered him little intellectual support from major neoclassical scholars like Edgeworth, who, in a critical review of his analysis of the incidence of taxation, nevertheless wrote 'it is an ungrateful task to contradict his judgements. One would almost rather prove inferior in argument than in courtesy' (1899, p. 286). Although he accepted the application of marginal methods he did not explain them systematically in the view of some of his critics, suggesting that he had little real understanding or sympathy for this approach.

Seligman's international reputation began with the widely read and acclaimed *Economic Interpretation of History* (1902) that split Marx's economic determinism from normative social theory. Reviewing the book, Higgs (1902) wrote '[the] economic interpretation of history means, not that the economic relations exert an exclusive influence, but that they exercise a preponderant influence in shaping the progress of society' (p. 520): a view that Higgs thought most English economists would then accept. To a lesser extent this reputation rested with his *Principles of Economics* (1905) that analysed specific 'American problems' by synthesising historical and comparative approaches to the subject. It went through 12 editions. When first published, however, the *Principles* attracted a critical review from the American economist Taussig (1906) because of the alleged textbook's 'illogical' ordering of the subject matter, its methodological approach, and the ill-judged support for the capital theory of John Bates Clark and the theory of distribution that rested upon it. Seligman protested in a reply, an unusual event even at that date, by claiming that:

> It is not primarily intended to be anything of the kind [a textbook]. My objective... was to give in compact shape a survey of the entire field of Economics (as distinct from Finance) for the average intelligent reader... who might be interested in the general subject and to restate the principles of the science in a form that might be in harmony with recent progress in economic thought ... it is far better to lead the student up to an appreciation of the fact that in economics, as in all social sciences, the present is a child of the past, and that no economic analysis is worth having unless it is an outgrowth of

actual rather than hypothetical phenomena and unless it is applicable to conditions as they really exist. This is the justification for prefacing the discussion of principles by a presentation of the historical development and by a consideration of the general framework of society within which the specific tendencies known as economic laws are at work. 1906, pp. 151–153)

But in England, Price (1906) was enthusiastic 'it would be difficult, if it were not impossible, to find any other single economist more thoroughly equipped for the task which he has undertaken and achieved in this new volume' (p. 231).

The two articles on neglected British economists that appeared in the *Economic Journal* of 1903 also received favourable reviews and helped to establish his reputation as one of the leading historians of economic theory of his generation. Edgeworth commissioned the articles and in correspondence with Seligman noted that he took the opportunity 'of expressing my sense of the great interest attaching to your literary finds. I am particularly impressed by what you reveal concerning my predecessor in the Oxford chair' (letter of 27 September 1903, Seligman Collection, Columbia University). The articles were ultimately collected with others in the same *genre* into a volume entitled *Essays in Economics* (1925a). Reviewing that volume, Higgs (1926) wrote that 'the essays…will permanently adorn this branch of inquiry, and puts to shame the neglectful British economists who leave unquarried the vast resources of the British Museum and Goldsmiths' library' (p. 613).

But Seligman himself believed that he had failed to rekindle interest in these epigones. In the Lectures of 1928/9 he refers to the group of independent writers whose contributions were written over the period 1820 to about 1848–1850, a period he now referred to as 'the dark ages in political economy' (Allen, 1992, p. 157). And he continued, 'I have no doubt that further study of these minor English writers at this time will bring out a great deal more' (*Ibid.*). However, he is mistaken when he argues that these economists were ignored in Palgrave's *Dictionary of Political Economy*, because there are entries for Bailey, Gray, Longfield, Ramsay, Read and Torrens in the first, 1899 edition. Indeed the success of his articles in the *Economic Journal* can be best judged by the appendix to the 1908 edition of the third volume.[1] In the Introduction to that appendix, Inglis Palgrave writes:

In the notices of the lives of the Economists, some have been commemorated whom we have lost since the last volume of the *Dictionary* was completed. In other cases an effort has been made to chronicle the work of the less known Economists of this country who laboured during the days when the teaching of Ricardo and James and John Stuart Mill

> was supreme, and who have been, in some instances, but imperfectly recognised, owing to the fact that their opinions were not in harmony with the orthodox teaching of the day. In arranging these I have had the assistance of Professor E. R. A. Seligman's papers 'On Some Neglected British Economists' in the *Economic Journal*, London, 1903. Such scattered notices are almost the only recognition that many of these writers have received. Those who are interested in Economics have much for which to thank Professor Seligman. There is much work of the same class to be done to which I trust our younger scholars will turn their attention. (Palgrave, 1908, p. 694)

Palgrave makes it much clearer here than Seligman ever did that the majority of the neglected economists shared an anti-Ricardian stance.

Finally, his work on public finance and taxation, which would be a continuous theme in his research and published output, probably gained him the largest number of admirers and disciples both at home and abroad and led to his appearance on a number of government inquiries. Here he opposed the single tax of Henry George and applied marginal analysis to tax theory to promote moderately progressive income taxes based on the ability to pay (Seligman, 1903c). His books on the subject of taxation went through many editions, *The Shifting Incidence of Taxation* (1892a) five, *Progressive Taxation* (1894), Seligman, 1895 two and *Essays in Taxation* (1895) three and all were translated into two or more languages. Finally, *The Income Tax* (1911b) that became a *locus classicus* considered principles that were 'put into practice by Congress in the income tax law of 1913' (Mitchell, 1939, p. 912).

In most of his research, Seligman was keen to use theory and empirics to underpin a specific policy and this can be seen most readily in his contributions to public finance. He was also able to garner financial support for his research. For example, General Motors financed his analysis of consumer behaviour and consumer credit (specifically instalment sales) representing an early example of industry/university collaboration. Given that his work came to be regarded as 'relevant and accessible', the press often published his articles and solicited his views on major policy issues such as progressive income taxation (Seligman, 1893). As Mitchell (1939) appositely noted in concluding his obituary notice for the *American Economic Review*, 'what he did will long intrigue the minds of men, either because of its curious interest or because of its continuing importance' (p. 913).

The structure of this Introduction is as follows. Section 2 provides a biographical sketch of Seligman's life. The third section assesses the contributions of the economists that appeared in Seligman's 1903 articles, although detailed analysis is reserved for those that do not receive a full treatment in this volume. Section 4 discusses the whole issue of neglect in political economy using Seligman's economists as a basis for that analysis.

A synopsis of the major findings from the individual chapters in this volume follows in Section 5. Section 6 concludes the Introduction, and an appendix provides a *dramatis personae* of the anonymous and named authors found in Seligman's articles.

2. BIOGRAPHY OF SELIGMAN

Edwin Robert Anderson Seligman, born on April 1861 in New York, was the son of the wealthy financier Joseph Seligman, co-founder with his brothers of the merchant banking house of J. & W. Seligman. Educated at home until the age of 11 and with a special aptitude for foreign languages, Seligman attended Columbia Grammar School in preparation for undergraduate studies. He entered Columbia University at the precocious age of 14, graduated in 1879 at just 18 and then continued his education abroad. His particular spread of intellectual skills meant that he soon made contact with some of the leading continental thinkers and economists. Initially he seemed more inclined towards the study of political science than economics *per se*, having been inspired by Columbia's constitutional lawyer John Burgess. In fact, Seligman followed a wide range of subjects during his *sojourn* in Europe: political science, history and law at Berlin, economics (particularly the history of economic theory and socialism) at Heidelberg, French at Geneva and the history of art and economics at the Sorbonne (although he found the instruction in politics and economics more rewarding at the Ecole des Sciences Politiques). While holidaying in Italy, Seligman met the economists Pareto and Pantaleoni and then in England Edgeworth, Sidgwick and Marshall.

In his autobiography, Seligman reveals that it was the German Historical School and the lectures of Karl Knies and his distinctive methodology (at Heidelberg where Böhm-Bawerk was a fellow pupil) that swayed him towards political economy as it did a number of contemporary American economists, including R. T. Ely and J. B. Clark. In a critical aside, however, he revealed that the Historical School in his view had made few 'real' contributions to economic theory so that as his professional work proceeded, he began to act more and more as a mediator between the old and new economics:

> I appreciated the shortcomings of the old deductive method in its applications to practical life; but I realised from the outset that the deductive method is an indispensable tool in all the social sciences...in considering any problem I deemed it important both to study the particular institution and the explanation in the light of the historical

> environment; but I realised that if by economic law we mean, as Montesquieu put it, a statement of the necessary relations between phenomena, the only fruitful way of ascertaining those relations is through the hypothetical and deductive method with a testing out of the tentative conclusions through the aid of statistics and inductive verification… I believed not so much that the orthodox classical school was wrong as that its results were incomplete; and that while the Economics of the future would assume a very different aspect from that elaborated by Ricardo and his followers, it would have to be built on foundations laid by them. (Seligman, 2006, pp. 34–35)

And he went on the record that 'I have never had sympathy with Economics, whether mathematical or otherwise, as a mere logical legerdemain. I have always conceived of economics as a science which should attempt to explain actual conditions from the point of view of affording a starting point for improving actual conditions. An economic theory which is of no use in practical life never appealed to me' (*Ibid.*, p. 36).

Seligman returned to Columbia in 1882 completing a bachelors degree in law in 1884 (and admittance to the bar) and a doctorate in economics (on the English mediaeval guilds) a year later *cum laude*. This secured him immediately a prize lectureship followed by promotion to Adjunct Professor of Political Economy in 1888 and full Professor of Political Economy and Finance in 1891. (Having rejected a career in banking, finance became one of his core research interests.) When memorial chairs were established at Columbia in 1904, Seligman became McVickar Professor of Political Economy and recruited a galaxy of rising stars to the faculty, including J. B. Clark and Wesley Mitchell, the first women lecturer (Evelyn Burns) and attracted many able students who went on to have successful academic careers (Rozwadowski, 1993). These included J. M. Clark, Paul Douglas and Alvin Johnson. He retired in 1931 and died eight years later.

As a teacher, the first course he taught was the History of Political Economy that became the core of the department's curriculum and led to a number of early publications including articles on Owen and the Christian Socialists (1886), Bastable and public finance (1892b) and the rightly celebrated essays on neglected British economists (1903a, 1903b). These were to have been preliminary studies, along with that on the History of American Economics and Curiosities of Early Economic Literature, for an 'elaborate history of the science' projected to be three or four volumes that never materialised (Seligman, 2006, p. 32). Not entirely giving up on the project, however, he remarked as late as 1929 that 'there are many unpublished contributions, which I hope some day to put together in a history of economics on which I have been working for many years' (Seligman, 1929, pp. 32–33).

In 1887, he introduced a novel course on the economics of transportation with a particular focus on railroads, followed by a course on the financial and tariff history of America that morphed into fiscal and financial history and then into a much grander-sounding science of finance that he taught for the rest of his career. It was during this period that Seligman quickly established himself as the leading American economist on the subject of public finance.

Outside the classroom he championed academic freedom, writing an important report on the subject in 1898 following the dismissal of a Leland Stanford University professor over issues connected with monometallism, bimetallism and government control over municipal monopolies. And then from 1915 he became the Chairman (later President) of the American Association of University Professors in which capacity he acted as an authority on the appeals process for immigrant economists and others seeking employment in America. His report on Academic Freedom in the same year in which he vigorously opposed academic censorship was regarded by academic friends as a Magna Carta for American academia.

Beyond the University, Seligman played an important role in the professionalisation of economics. He was co-founder in 1885 with Richard Ely of the American Economic Association becoming Treasurer (while Ely served as Secretary and Francis Walker became the first President) and President himself for 1902 and 1903. He set up the Political Economy Club, a dining club that brought together academics, businessmen, industrialists, politicians and financial journalists modelled on its earlier London namesake. The Social Reform Club similarly included economists, editors, clergymen, labour leaders and more socially 'enlightened' employers and formulated policies on a number of social issues, but more importantly campaigned for social reform including the building of model tenements, cooperative relations in the garment industry as well as social settlements based on Toynbee Hall in London. Seligman also acted as editor for several publications including being economics editor for Columbia's *Political Science Quarterly* and for the series of some 450 Columbia doctoral dissertations published in the fields of economics, history and public law (Mitchell, 1939, p. 913). As Chairman of the Government's Committee on Education, he oversaw the education of Russian immigrants escaping political persecution in a pioneering organisation that became the model for similar programmes of 'Americanisation' for other displaced peoples.

Seligman served with distinction as advisor on many commissions in America, for the League of Nations and the Cuban government, taking quite literarily Irving Fisher's plea that economists should offer themselves for public service where their technical expertise would be most useful. He also helped to shape a number of legislative instruments enacted by both Federal and State legislatures in America.

At the outbreak of the First World War, Seligman turned his attention to war finance steering a middle course between loans and taxation. In 1917, he became Chairman of the American Economic Association's Committee on War Finance and after the war focussed on sovereign debt and led a campaign to delay the repayment of loans to the Allies to avoid pushing their economies into recession. As the world depression deepened, he joined a Conference on Unemployment that produced a number of influential reports, the last of which, had it been taken up, might have prevented any repeats of 1929 *debacle*.

After the war, issues connected with taxation again took centre stage and Seligman fought against sales taxes and taxes on securities, but was less successful in his opposition to certain aspects of income tax and inheritance taxes (Mehrotra, 2005). His essays and addresses on these subjects were eventually collected together as *Studies in Public Finance* (1925b), Seligman, 1925b. As the world edged closer towards a new apocalypse with the political and military upheavals of the 1930s, Seligman broke off relations with academics in Europe who blindly supported oppressive regimes like Mussolini's in Italy particularly where *il Duce ha sempre ragione*.

Perhaps his greatest publishing legacy was the 15 volume *Encyclopaedia of the Social Sciences* compiled between 1930 and 1935 and for which he secured funding of three quarters of a million dollars. This monumental endeavour represented a grand synthesis of the social sciences with Seligman as Editor in Chief assisted by his former pupil, Alvin Johnson. The encyclopaedia represented the culmination of years spent collecting the prerequisite literature, some 40,000 volumes, most of which were published before 1875. The collection was eventually sold to Columbia University and forms the core of the renowned Seligman Library. Reminded of Adam Smith's remark to Smellie when the latter was perusing Smith's library, Shirras (1939) records in his obituary of Seligman that he too was 'a beau in nothing but my books' (p. 588).

3. SELIGMAN ON THE NEGLECTED ECONOMISTS

Seligman praises the depth and importance of the literature on economics in Britain from the end of the sixteenth century to the middle of the nineteenth, but at the same time deplores the fact that, apart from the 'masters' within the classical school, so many others are neglected in the secondary literature. The books of Foxwell (1884) and Cannan (1893) are regarded as exceptions that provide a rich diet of critical, although by no means encyclopaedic analysis, of the second division writers. In his two articles on neglected British economists, however, Seligman aimed to draw attention to a group of innovative thinkers over the 20-year period following the publication of Ricardo's *Principles*. Many of these are unsympathetic if not hostile to the Ricardian model. He was also acutely aware of the neglect of many writers between the publication of Smith's *Wealth of Nations* and Ricardo's early publications on money and profits. Many of these contributions had been a response to contemporaneous economic conditions and covered topics such as commercial relations, agriculture, taxation and public debt, poor relief and inflation. Adam Smith's work may have dominated intellectual exchanges and also parliamentary debate (Gordon, 1979), but Seligman is keen to draw attention to the writing during this period of Godwin, Malthus and Lauderdale.

Beyond these three, he draws particular attention to writers sympathetic to Physiocracy and issues connected with taxation. Two anonymous works are singled out for assessment under the first heading. The 1797 work, *The Essential Principles of the Wealth of Nations Illustrated, in Opposition to some False Doctrines of Adam Smith and Others* now attributed to John Gray (and discussed below) and the 1809 volume, *Sketches on Political Economy Illustrative of the Interests of Great Britain; Intended as a Reply to Mr Mill's Pamphlet Commerce Defended, with an Exposition of some of the Leading Tenets of the Economists* thought to be the work of Sharp (but see the essay below) who also came close to identifying value with utility and argued that Smith's distinction between productive and unproductive labour was 'futile'.

Moving on to public finance, Seligman refers to a remarkable book, *Enquiry into the Principles of Taxation Chiefly Applicable to Articles of Immediate Consumption* published in 1790 and identified as the first volume devoted to taxation in English (if William Petty's work in the previous century is ignored) which he tentatively suggests might have been written by Andrew Hamilton. This work recognised the concept of the incidence of taxation within a supply and demand framework that Seligman (1892) was to make his own just over a 100 years later. The anonymous author also rejects certain aspects of Smith's theory of taxation: that taxes on wages lower profits, that this has nothing to do with the peculiarities of wages and, finally, that when a commodity is taxed and subsequently incorporated into others as an input to commodities within the final price, the accumulated tax burden will have increased. In dismissing this last argument, the author maintained that technological improvements and enhanced labour productivity would actually reduce the total tax burden that 'becomes lighter in proportion to the number of hands through which they [commodities] pass, in a thriving society' (p. 340).

Turning to the contemporaries of Ricardo, Torrens is dealt with in this volume. Craig, however, has not found a champion here, although Thor Bruce published an article on him in the *Quarterly Journal of Economics* in 1938. This is a curious piece because it does not refer to Seligman's article and yet rather obviously uses his phraseology in several places. Craig only gained a single sentence in Palgrave's *Dictionary* although he published a three volume *Elements of Political Economy* in 1814 (with one volume devoted to public finance that Seligman remarked was the first time a single volume had been devoted to the subject in England) and a shorter *Remarks on Political Economy* in 1821.

Seligman records two points worthy of note in the *Elements*, namely the author's rejection of Smith's distinction between productive and unproductive labour (having been preceded in this attack by Lauderdale) and secondly problems connected with public finance. Surprisingly, Seligman says nothing more on this subject, but Thor records that he defended progressive taxation on the equality of sacrifice doctrine. Given that proportional taxes penalise the poor, the burden could be mitigated 'not only progressive taxation, but by making the rate depend partly on property and partly on income, that is by capitalising income' (Bruce, 1938, p. 706). Thus, all property should be taxed, otherwise if the tax were applied to only one type of capital, it would fall disproportionately on the owner of that capital with the fall in the value of the property equivalent to the capitalised value of the tax.

In the *Remarks*, Seligman notices that Craig makes a distinction between value in exchange and value in use claiming that the latter forms the basis of all value, although the two concepts are not in opposition. Using the example of a coat, Craig argues that if the value halved, then two coats would now have the exchangeable value that one had before, but that their use value would not increase 'perceptibly'. 'New purchasers indeed will appear in proportion to the reduction of price; because at every step of the decline it is brought down to the estimate which an additional number of persons had formed of its power of gratification, or, in other words, to their estimate of its use value' (*Ibid.*, p. 348). In this extract value depends on utility, but every fall in price brings forward a new group of marginal purchasers 'whose lower estimate of utility is now available for disposing of the increased supply' (*Ibid.*, p. 349). As Bruce and Seligman both note, Craig is on the verge of the theory of marginal utility.[2] The lower price also frees up income to be spent on other commodities so that the expanded supply of one commodity does not have a depressing effect on general values. However, he goes on to confuse total and marginal utility when he writes that 'value in use whether viewed in reference to any single commodity, or to the aggregate possession of a nation, must be very accurately measured by value in exchange' (*Ibid.*).

Craig did not accept many of the central tenets of Ricardo's economics. This included rejection of the labour theory of value; that exchange value depends upon the relationship between demand and supply with tastes, fashion and prosperity as well as the quantity of labour and capital and the 'fertility of the seasons' having an impact. Cost of production is therefore rejected as the determinant of value or price. Rejection of subsistence wages; here he adheres to a wage fund theory and in not accepting that a tax on them raises wages he invokes the empirical evidence to the contrary and argues that only if the tax upsets the balance between the demand (which is the major factor) and the supply of labour will the tax have any impact on the wage. Taxes, in fact, were more likely to have an effect on levels of poverty and privation in Britain. Finally, he rejects the view that wages and profits are inversely related, the so-called core theorem of Ricardo. Here the empirical evidence convinced Craig that wages and profits often rise simultaneously 'a new demand for a commodity at first enriched those, who, being in possession of this commodity, are enabled to raise its price; the desire to participate in their gains soon directs new capital to its production, and a rise in wages speedily ensues' (quoted in Bruce, p. 703). And he also sees congruence between the returns to land and that to fixed capital with land differentiated from fixed capital only in so far as land can be improved, whereas fixed capital depreciates and requires new investment to maintain the stock. Craig disputed the dynamic element in Ricardo's theory of rent that cultivation proceeded from the most fertile to the least which Henry George picked up much later.

In concluding his assessment, Seligman draws attention to Craig's failure to distinguish between interest and profits, but nevertheless acknowledges that many of his points were ultimately incorporated into modern economic doctrine so that his contribution deserves more than a cursory footnote. And Bruce wrote that epigones like Craig, whom he described as 'an original thinker of considerable power' and 'in the twilight zone between the Classical and the Austrian School' were worth recording even if they made a small contribution because 'a study of their life and writings enriches the science by the increased knowledge of what these writers thought and wrote' (Bruce, 1938, pp. 697 and 707). He was overlooked and neglected 'because most of his views were not in accord with the theories of the dominant school. The edifice erected by Ricardo and others of this school became so solid and so stable that it could not be shaken by any contemporary current of criticism or opposition' (*Ibid.*, p. 701).

Seligman goes on to note that with the appearance of Malthus's *Principles* in 1820 much discussion ensued between him, Ricardo and Say. The debate also spawned a number of anonymous pamphlets including *Observations on Certain Verbal Disputes on Political Economy, particularly relating to Value and Demand and Supply* (1821) that drew attention to some inconsistencies in the theories of Malthus et al. and in the same year *An Inquiry into those Principles Respecting the Nature of Demand and the Necessity of Consumption, lately advocated by Mr Malthus, from which it is concluded that Taxation and the Maintenance of Unproductive Consumers can be Conducive to the Progress of Wealth* that advanced the argument that gluts would only be avoided if unproductive consumption (of luxury goods) could be encouraged. A further pamphlet published in the following year *Considerations on the Accumulation of Capital and its Effects on Profits and on exchangeable Value* made a similar point and was actually penned by Cazenove who is considered in this volume so that no further commentary is necessary here.

A number of further works with 'attractive titles' but ultimately disappointing content are also recorded. These are the anonymous *An Essay on the Political Economy of Nations, or a View of the Intercourse of Countries as Influencing their Wealth* also published in 1821 devoted to domestic trade and an equally bulky volume by Thomas Smith entitled *An Attempt to Define Some of the First Principles of Political Economy* (1821). The book is highly critical of Ricardo, but most of its analysis relates to the relationship between the issue of bank notes and prices. The other works noted at this juncture by Seligman, namely those by Rogers (E. R.), Bailey, Cotterill and Lloyd, are all dealt with in this volume and can be passed over here.

In the second article published by Seligman in the *Economic Journal* he considers those authors who instead of focussing mainly on the issue of value covered virtually the whole field of political economy. What united them was their opposition to Ricardo, the significance of their individual contributions and the unifying fact that they were more or less neglected in their lifetime and beyond. The first to be resurrected is Rooke followed by Ravenstone and both of these authors are dealt with in this volume. Samuel

Read, who was to have been reviewed here, does not have a chapter in this volume because the designated author failed to deliver the manuscript. Therefore Read's contribution is reviewed through the lens provided by Seligman, there having been no full-scale review of his work over the intervening period.

Read's early work focussed on currency and banking issues, works such as, *Exposure of Certain Plagiarisms of J. R. McCulloch, Esq., Author of two Essays on Reduction of the Interest of the National Debt, committed in the last published of these Essays, the Scotsman Newspaper and Edinburgh Review. By Samuel Read, author of a Tract on Money and the Bank Restriction Laws. In recto decus* and published in 1819. As the title indicates, this challenged McCulloch over the changes he made to the second of his two *Essays on the National Debt* (both of which were published in 1816). Read claimed that the changes incorporated into the second essay contained ideas extracted from his *Tract on Money* (that had been published in between McCulloch's two publications) without due acknowledgement. The two major elements 'borrowed' were that when the currency is readjusted following inflation, justice requires that debts should be discharged by an equal weight of bullion, and secondly that the interest on debt after depreciation of the currency should reflect the actual amount of bullion lent in the first instance.

Two years later, Read published a *General Statement of an Argument on the Subject of Population in answer to Mr Malthus's Theory* in which he claimed that any increase in population would be tempered by the increased demand for luxuries and refinements that could only be achieved by some limit on population growth in the absence of increases in wages. In a more substantial work, *An Inquiry into the Natural Grounds of Right to Vendible Property or Wealth* (1829), inspired by the publications of the so-called Ricardian Socialists, Read moved from what is now called positive economics to normative economics – in this case 'the right to wealth' (meaning the moral right) rather than a simple consideration of the production and distribution of wealth (*Ibid.*, p. 516). This conception owes much in Seligman's view to Sismondi, although he does not report whether Read would have recognised the connection. The 'what is' follows quite closely the theory laid down by Smith, but not entirely of his distinction between productive and unproductive labour since he claimed that authors, for example, should be regarded as productive labour. His definition of capital 'consists of accumulated wealth, which is or may be applied to assist in the work of production, which is nearly equivalent to saying that it consists of all wealth whatever' (*Ibid.*, p. 517).

Labour is rejected as the sole cause of value mainly because of the use to which this has been put by the early socialists, although he fails to point out that Smith had made the first statement to the effect that labour creates everything and is therefore entitled to everything produced. He only notes the use of this conception by Hodgskin (*Labour Defended Against the Claims of Capital*)[3]. Wealth, in fact, consist of both labour and capital for Read, and some of his arguments are less than clear on this matter, and he does caution against claiming too much for capital and therefore too much for the capitalist.

Although private ownership of land is defensible, Read argues that there is some justification for the view that 'common rights' exist to the uncultivated and unimproved land. On this basis he therefore justifies the imposition of land taxes (at the rate of 12 percent) that in his view might be sufficient to meet all the needs of Government short of 'exceptional circumstances'. He also argues from a moral perspective that the privileged rich should support the aged, infirm and the unemployed. On rent he does not support Ricardo's argument that it is due to the indestructible powers of the soil, a position that even he acknowledges Ricardo himself later relaxed. More importantly, he presses the need to accommodate 'situation' in the determination of rent and argues that while determined by price, rent can in certain circumstances be a component part of price. Equally, he does not accept Ricardo's iron law of wages, arguing instead that under a system of liberty or good government, wages naturally rise because of the increasing productivity of capital. Of course he neglects to mention here the changes that Ricardo introduced to the third edition of the *Principles*. Neither does Read accept Ricardo's core theorem.

Perhaps one of the most interesting features of Read's volume is the discussion of profits that he links to interest. When he refers to 'business gains', Read noted that where these exceeded the ordinary rate of interest, this is due to the reward for labour or industry or skill in the application of capital. Alternatively, these gains may arise from 'fortune or accident' and should therefore be regarded as compensation for risk. Seligman claims at this juncture that Read has introduced for the first time 'the modern "risk theory" and the modern "entrepreneur theory" of profit' (*Ibid.*, p. 520). Finally, Read's discussion of public finance and the incidence of taxation finds him supporting the Smithian view that all factors of production should be taxed in contradistinction to the reviews of the Physiocrats and the Ricardians.

Ironically in the circumstances of continued neglect, Seligman forcefully argues that Read 'merits further study', but this appears to have fallen on deaf ears over the intervening generations. He concludes that he deserves recognition for his astute criticisms of Ricardian economics and for linking the school to the rise of the so-called Ricardian Socialists. More specifically, he deserves priority for the introduction of risk and entrepreneurial theories of profits and for pointing out that capitalists may have earned their privileges (rights), but that they most certainly had reciprocal duties emphasising the normative aspects of political economy.

Less original than Read, Ramsay, who Seligman discusses next, is dealt with in this volume. That leaves two economists whom Seligman refers to as the 'most remarkable of all [the neglected economists]' (*Ibid.*, p. 525). They are Mountifort Longfield, appointed first Professor of Political Economy at Trinity College, The University of Dublin in 1832 and Isaac Butt, who succeeded Longfield to the Archbishop Whately Professorship of Political Economy in 1837. Both receive a full examination in this volume. Suffice to mention, however, Seligman's conclusion to his *tour de force* where he records that 'The theory of marginal productivity as applied to capital and labour, Butt tells us, "seems obvious and simple enough, but until the appearance of Dr. Longfield's lectures it was not thought of. With the exception of the discovery of the theory of rent – and, perhaps, even the propriety of this exception is questionable – no such important service has been rendered to the science since the days of Adam Smith." When we reflect that the whole current of modern theory [was] setting in the direction indicated by Longfield and Butt, these encomiums do not appear to be altogether unmerited' (*Ibid.*, p. 533).

4. THE THEME OF NEGLECT

The first important question to ask here is why did these economic writers suffer neglect, or in some cases relative neglect, until Seligman's *Economic Journal* articles? This, of course, raises a prior question as to what is meant by neglect. At a prosaic level the answer might be the simple absence of citation, although nineteenth century authors did not make citations in a systematic way except when they were specifically targeting the work of a political economist with whom they disagreed; as Schumpeter (1954, p. 474) notes, Ricardo was an exception in this respect. And even then it was more likely to be a major name like Smith or Ricardo rather than an unknown commentator without the benefit of a platform such as parliament.

Yet neglect must surely imply more than this and certainly even in this regard there are at least two kinds of neglect. There is the neglect of a writer's theoretical or policy insights by contemporaries and subsequent generations of economists and there is what might be termed scholarly neglect; the latter having significance in relation to the sophistication and substance of the former, but not exclusively so. Thus, from the perspective of the discipline, neglect may be an inappropriate term when insight, sophistication and novelty are absent, but wholly legitimate where the work of a political economist can be seen as yielding a historical understanding of a period, either in terms of its intellectual or broader history particularly when it subsequently proves not to be ephemeral. Nor can the latter category of neglect be seen as a simple function of the former. Neglect by historians, even historians of economic thought, is not the same as neglect by economists. In assessing Seligman's neglected, some clearly fall into both of these categories, but some into only one.

That said, for Seligman the primary reason for neglect was not the intrinsic worth – theoretical or practical – of the authors or the work that they had produced. Indeed he makes it clear that there was considerable theoretical insight and sophistication in the political economy of the authors he discusses. Rather, their fate was a function of the emergence of an orthodoxy that was intolerant of, or at least unreceptive to, the heterodoxy of others who in the main had no followers or proselytisers to do their bidding. More specifically, Seligman saw neglect as a consequence of the dominance of Ricardianism; a dominance that amongst other things precluded the emergence at this time of a marginalist school of economics, although key elements of it were to be found in the political economy of some of the neglected economists:

> The practical issues of the time were so momentous that the economic science which taught a doctrine in harmony with these practical demands was accepted as infallible. The economists in England, indeed, were not responsible for free trade and industrial development. Those would have come almost as quickly had economics never existed; for practical policies are the result for the most part of actual interests and not of abstract considerations. But when the demands of the dominant social and political interests were reinforced by the teachings of the scientists, economics leaped with abound into the position not only of a popular, but almost of a sacrosanct, science. The edifice erected by Ricardo, and elaborated by McCulloch and Mill, became so solid and so stable that it could not be shaken by any current or gust of criticism or opposition. (Seligman, 1903b, p. 534)

Culpability here lays with contemporaries and in particular those defensive of a particular theoretical paradigm; subsequent historians are then the victims of the vices or mindset of others. Thus, the fact that Bailey's proto-marginalist economics that Seligman identified, 'should have been enunciated in 1825 and then seemingly forgotten is eloquent testimony to the power of a few great names in silencing for all time all criticisms however sound they may be' (Seligman, 1903a, p. 355). A similar view of things was repeated by subsequent authorities, but most notably by Schumpeter, 'so brilliant a light [Ricardo] will attract moths... moreover many people, noneconomists included, will profess themselves votaries of the light even though they have but a dim perception of it – just as today [1954] there are many Keynesians and Marxists who have never read a line of Keynes or Marx' (1954, p. 475). And he also records that in some cases the dissenters (in this case Torrens) will show respect for those they are attacking (Ricardo) and 'quite readily use phrases and propositions of his whenever they feel they can' (*Ibid.*).

However, this explanation of neglect is challenged by many of the contributors to this volume. As Hollander makes clear, Bailey's *Critical* dissertation did not represent a significant challenge to Ricardianism. Rather, 'in many cases, Bailey's criticisms constitute misunderstandings of Ricardo's position, while others would have been considered wholly acceptable by Ricardo'. Moreover, Bailey was even taken to task for his criticism of Ricardo by Malthus, who would be placed by Seligman and has been placed by others (most notably Keynes, [Corry, 1959]), in the dissenting tradition.

Similarly, the view that a writer such as Butt was confined to the shadows because he failed to conform to the prevailing economic orthodoxy is seen by O'Day as 'not quite accurate as far as [he] is concerned'. As to Torrens, de Vivo again finds Seligman's explanation wanting and also that of Schumpeter 'who accepted his judgment on the "neglected economists" *in toto* and completely deferred to what Seligman had written on these authors, whom he often knew at second hand'.[4] As de Vivo sees it 'Torrens was deeply entrenched in classical theory and it would be difficult to maintain that the reason why he came to be neglected was that of not belonging to the "Ricardian orthodoxy"'. In any case the categorisation of Torrens as neglected is simply not warranted from either a theoretical or a policy perspective, leaving aside the fact that few economists have achieved the notoriety of having a lake named after them. But in the case of Ravenstone and the misnamed Ricardian Socialists in general, it is easier to make the case that neglect on account of their being crowded out by the dominant paradigm.

Yet if Seligman's explanation of neglect does not hold as far as many of these writers are concerned it may nonetheless be opined that authors, political economists amongst them, may have suffered from that predilection for the canonical that has over the years inhibited scholarship in other areas – most notably that of English literature. So that the history of economic thought, like the history of literature, progresses by moving from one giant's shoulders in Newtonian fashion on to the next: a history of perhaps ten great economists or whatever number is more manageable. That said, intellectual history in recent decades has largely moved on from this perspective and post-1945 scholarship and the articles in this volume make abundantly clear the densely imbricated texture of political economy in the late eighteenth and early nineteenth centuries and, consequently, the importance of the contributions that 'lesser' writers have made to it.

The erosion of the authority of the canonical approach has in itself militated against neglect. However, to create and convey that texture requires the sensitive historical contextualisation of political economists and the interchanges between them; in the absence of this, their significance is still likely to be misunderstood or lost altogether and neglected. Thus, as Moore and White show, the importance of the work of Lloyd cannot be appreciated 'outside the context of the intellectual tradition established by the Oriel Noetics' and specifically the tensions that existed between the Lloyd–(Robert) Peel–Christ Church axis and the Oriel Noetic axis of Coplestone–Whately-Senior in early nineteenth century Oxford.

The contributions to this volume also suggest other possible reasons for neglect, where the appropriateness of this categorisation is not itself challenged. Thus, in a number of instances, it has been a consequence of the difficulty of identifying authorship. Anonymity can be embraced for many reasons, but it can militate against due recognition being given to a piece of work. Most obviously, anonymity inhibits contextualisation in a body of work and such deracination in turn denies that understanding of significance which comes with a sense of intellectual trajectory. As Pullen makes clear, Cazenove's preference for anonymity probably contributed to his neglect during his lifetime and beyond. Seven of his eleven books and pamphlets were anonymous. Even Seligman is guilty of relative neglect and again 'if Seligman had been aware of the number and range of Cazenove's publications and of his standing amongst the political economists of the time, he would surely have given him more than an eight line comment'.

The same charge of continued neglect applies in the case of Rooke in the view of Allington, where Seligman noted his contribution to the theory of rent and marginal cost in particular, but completely overlooked his work on a tabular standard that has brought him some belated degree of recognition in the last 20 years.[5] In this case the veil of neglect has been lifted as a result of the renewed interest in problems connected with indexation illustrating the point that fashionable subjects can exert a fascination for those scholars compelled to find earlier expositors or progenitors. Similarly, Rooke adds another dimension to the decision of an author to choose anonymity. By publishing his *Free Trade in Corn and the True Policy of the State* (1828) under the imprimatur of a 'Cumberland Landowner', and consequently its being mistaken for the work of Sir James Graham, the landed Tory MP, Rooke for a short time accelerated somewhat the case for repeal of the Corn Laws that garnered far more publicity inside and outside Parliament than it otherwise would have done under his name.

Anonymity by definition also prevents biographical contextualisation with all the insights which that could yield. Indeed it is often only when the veil of anonymity has been lifted or, from another perspective, once the curtain of false attribution has been removed, that historical scholarship can begin the work of rescuing an author from neglect; something that is made all too evident in Ditchfield's article on the authorship of *Sketches on Political Economy* (1809); a work which is usually attributed to Granville Sharp. Van den Berg's article on John Gray's *Essential Principles of the Wealth of Nations* (1797) also demonstrates that one of the most effective ways of repairing a work's neglect is to rescue its author's life from obscurity. Moreover, it can be said that many of those anonymous works noted by Seligman that have remained in this category have not received the scholarly attention which he intimated they deserved.

In addition, while acknowledging the dangers of economic determinism it can also surely be argued that authors came to be neglected because the economic reality they sought to explain, or more accurately their perceptions of that reality, what they saw as significant within it, and what they conceived as being of significance for the future, was rendered redundant by the course of economic events/developments. At the turn of the eighteenth century, agriculture was the dominant sector of the British economy in terms of the employment it generated and its contribution to national income. Moreover, land and rental income were still the basis of political power with the landed interest dominant in Parliament. For a short period in the late eighteenth and early nineteenth century a Physiocratic conception of wealth generation was sufficiently empirically rooted to give currency to the political economy of those who articulated it. However, during the course of that period such ideas had ceased to mesh with the realities of an economy where manufacturing activity was clearly the driver of growth. From the perspective of the theoretical development and practical relevance of the discipline, therefore, it was always likely that the work of writers such as Ravenstone and Gray would come to be neglected even if for a time they enjoyed some limited currency. As van den Berg sees it, even if Gray was not simply a faithful expositor of Physiocratic doctrine, his work nonetheless 'signalled the beginning of a short period during which the views of the French Economists exercised a certain belated influence on a number of British authors'; most obviously William Spence, but also writers such as Charles Hall whose *Effects of Civilization* (1805), like Gray's work, used Physiocratic doctrine to radical effect.

Factors other than economic circumstance or developments can also mediate and determine the degree of notoriety or neglect. The political economy of William Cobbett had its atavistic qualities that looked to the retrieval of a socio-economic world which even by the early nineteenth century was irrevocably lost. Nor did his thinking possess merit in terms of its sophistication, coherence or consistency. Yet his work was not neglected even if it ceased to have the kind of impact it had in the first three decades of the nineteenth century. In part this was due to his remarkable qualities as a proselytizer, not least through newspapers and periodicals such as *Cobbett's Weekly Political Register*. But, Cobbett was also fortunate in that there were those, not least his sons, who would keep the Cobbettian flame alive, at least in terms of circulating his writings.

What many, if not all, of Seligman's neglected lacked was a medium, or an immediate following, for the dissemination of their ideas. This is not true of Torrens, but it is the case with most of the other writers. Put another way they lacked a School; followers who would take and develop their ideas. This of course raises the question of whether their ideas had sufficient coherence and sophistication to warrant such development and that in turn raises a related and more fundamental possible reason for their neglect, namely that as thinkers neglect was warranted. As Prybyla makes it clear Ramsay's work strove to incorporate into English political economy ideas that were not native to it, and the curious blend of classicism and anti-classicism failed to impress his contemporaries and later generations despite 'a note of refreshing dissent from the growing complacency of the Ricardians who at the time were riding high on the prestige of Ricardo'. Also, as O'Day's article on Butt makes clear, notoriety of a kind unrelated to an author's economic writings can distract attention from his political economy. For Butt is a figure whose subsequent career after his tenure of the Whately Chair at Trinity College Dublin overshadowed his work as a political economist. As O'Day indicates, Butt has proved to be a contested figure in the history of Irish nationalism and that very contest would appear to have generated a historiography that militates against a focused and more serious consideration of his political economy. It might be added that the focus on practical policy issues may have precluded the kind of recognition that comes from theoretical originality and limited notice to the currency of the issues which Butt addressed.

Yet, whatever the reasons for neglect, some of the salient points to remember have surely been made by Schumpeter (1954) who wrote that 'historical performances are rarely like erratic blocks in a plain. They are more like peaks that rise from clusters of small eminences. In other words, a science develops by small accretions that create a common fund of ideas from which, by chance as well as merit, emerge the works that enter the hall of fame. Therefore we must add at least a few of those writers [to the *History of Economics*] who, though they failed to achieve historic fame, yet did important work and exerted an influence upon developments in analysis that are anonymous, but not negligible' (p. 480). But perhaps the last judgement should rest with Seligman, who ended his review of the minor troops by claiming that 'From these newer thinkers we must indeed not withhold our tribute of appreciation for their solidity and their originality; but we must likewise not begrudge a generous recognition to the predecessors, whose lot was cast in less fortunate times. When such recognition is accorded, it will be seen that Great Britain is the real mother, not only of classical political economy, but also of that series of newer ideas which is at the present time slowly transforming the face of economic science' (Seligman, 1903b, p. 535).

5. THE CONTRIBUTIONS OF THE ENGLISH, IRISH AND SUBVERSIVES TO SCHOLARSHIP[6]

Whether Seligman's neglected merit such a sobriquet or not, the articles in this volume consider the scholarship that has appeared since the publication of his *Economic Journal* articles in 1903. In assessing their theoretical work and policy prescriptions, it is clear that most have elicited scholarly attention and in some cases this has been sustained with full-length intellectual biographies of Bailey (Rauner, 1961), Longfield (Moss, 1976) and Torrens (Robbins, 1958). Certainly in passing it should be noted that there will be less justification for the use of this adjective after this volume has been published than there might have been before.

Seligman regarded Bailey as one of Ricardo's more acute critics and someone who had an impact on the other dissenters from the Ricardian cannon. In this regard, his range included value (he opposed the labour theory); rent (it should be part of price); time (it was an important element of value); productivity (has an impact on value) as well as imperfect competition and barriers against the entry of new firms. But whether this all adds up to a (partial?) paradigmatic breakthrough has divided subsequent historians of economic theory. Following Viner's (1937) advice to treat dissent with caution and of the need to reflect carefully on the responses of the Ricardians (McCulloch and the Mill's, James and John Stuart) to the critics, Hollander's masterful reassessment of Bailey shows convincingly that he misunderstood Ricardo's position. Yet other nostrums of Bailey would have been accepted by Ricardo and the Ricardians alike, even by Malthus. Put simply, Bailey was a Ricardian even if not a thoroughbred one. As to his influence on other dissenters (Cotterill, Read, Senior, Lloyd, Torrens and Malthus) Hollander, unlike Seligman, finds little substantive evidence for this. He quotes approvingly the judgement of James Mill to the effect that 'Bailey's analysis of the "nature of value makes profession, or rather ostentation, and parade, of being a controversy with Mr Ricardo", while it contained nothing of substance with which Ricardo would not have assented; and it provides the justification for Halévy's (1904) judgement that "all the elements of [Bailey's] criticism are borrowed from Ricardo's book"'.

In the case of Isaac Butt, as O'Day makes apparent, there has been significant post-Seligman scholarly discussion of his work, in particular, since the publication of Collison Black's (1960) *Economic Thought and the Irish Question 1817–1870* and the publication of a four-volume edition of Irish writings on political economy that has made some of Butt's work more accessible. That said it has been and may well remain the case, that scholarly attention will continue to be focused more on Butt as a contested figure in the history of Irish nationalism and that might favour a historiography that militates against a sustained consideration of him as a political economist.

Pullen's article on John Cazenove focuses on two aspects of his thought: his view of Say's Law and his work on bank credit. For over 50 years he 'maintained a persistent attack on the idea that production or supply would of itself generate sufficient demand' and did so in a manner markedly similar to Malthus, focusing on the concept of proportions in relation to consumption, savings and investment. So for Pullen, Cazenove has an honoured place in Keynes's (1936) 'brave army of heretics' alongside Mandeville, Malthus, Gesell, Hobson and Major Douglas.

As for his thinking on bank credit, Pullen sees this as 'significant and radical because of his insistence that when banks issue credit they are in effect creating money (or money substitutes) just as surely as they minted coins or printed notes'. However, while he recognised the potentially destabilising consequences of this he did not draw any radical policy conclusions, believing that the personal morality of bankers would ensure a self-correction for any over-issue of currency. Of course such thoughts have a contemporary resonance and political economists would be hard put in present circumstances to be as sanguine as Cazenove was on this matter.

In the case of John Gray, van den Berg's conclusion that 'his main contribution...did neither contain many truly original views, nor did it exercise any lasting influence on the development of economic thinking in Britain' would seem both to explain previous neglect and point to its continuation. Yet, while Gray's work has not received the focused discussion which van den Berg's article provides, and while it is true to say that 'the neglect of this author, signalled by Seligman over a century ago, continues', it is nonetheless the case that he has maintained a presence, however shadowy, in the secondary literature that has dealt with that 'short period during which the views of the French *Economistes* exercised a certain belated influence on a number of British authors'. Thus, for example, Gray's *Essential Principles* has received notice in the work of Meek (1962) and other commentators.

The case of Lloyd is similar to that of Gray. While there is a post-Seligman secondary literature that has been mostly concentrated in the last quarter of the twentieth century and while Lloyd makes the cut as regards inclusion in the *New Palgrave Dictionary of Economics* (Eatwell, Milgate, & Newman, 1987), there is nothing substantial on his contribution to the evolution of political economy, certainly nothing comparable to the sustained scholarly treatment of his work by Moore and White in this volume. Amongst other things they consider Seligman's contention that Lloyd made two major contributions to the conceptual structure of modern, mainstream economics: namely using the concept of diminishing marginal utility to derive a 'modern labour theory of value' and being one of the earliest scholars to recognise what is now termed 'the tragedy of the commons'. As to the former, they conclude that Lloyd worked with a 'surplus value theory' and did not anticipate, as Seligman and others have suggested, the marginalist framework that was produced by neoclassical economists later in the century. As to the latter, Lloyd did argue that because the larger social costs of incontinent breeding were spread over the entire population, they were likely to be 'imperceptible to the individuals making the decision to reproduce'.

If Lloyd was neglected before, this chapter removes the legitimacy of such a categorisation for the future, the more so once Moore and White have published their forthcoming intellectual biography. In a forensic analysis of his work informed by a nuanced historical contextualisation, Moore and White make clear that Lloyd's work must be understood within the context of the intellectual tradition established by the Oriel Noetics and that his political economy emerged out of the contest between the Whately-Senior and (Charles) Lloyd–Peel axes that dominated economic and political thinking in early nineteenth century Oxford. For Moore and White it is because 'the role of the Lloyd–Peel axis as a counter to the Oriel Noetic axis of Coplestone–Whately-Senior has been overlooked in the secondary literature' that to Lloyd has been written out of history.

Prendergast's essay provides a detailed consideration of the post-Seligman literature on Longfield and in particular the contribution to an understanding of his political economy made in the late twentieth century by Black (1984), Bowley (1978), Hollander (1979) and Moss (1976). This is also reviewed in relation to Seligman's argument that Longfield's work evinced a clear articulation of the marginal productivity doctrine of interest, usually ascribed to von Thünen as well as a productivity theory of wages. As Prendergast points out, Seligman also credited Isaac Butt with having generalised Longfield's marginal productivity theory by extending it to other factor inputs.

As Prendergast points out, Bowley (1978) like Schumpeter (1954) and most scholars in the earlier part of the twentieth century subscribed to the notion of Longfield having grasped the essentials of roundaboutness in production and having made it the basis of an analysis of capital that anticipated the work of Böhm-Bawerk. Also as having developed a reasonably correct marginal-cost approach to the theory of distribution. Black (1984) too, though there has been a shift of thinking over time, still believed that it was reasonable to categorise Longfield as a marginal utility theorist and that while 'it would be wrong to represent Longfield's analysis as a complete anticipation of neoclassical pricing and distribution theory' it was a fundamentally different analysis from that of Ricardo and arrived at different conclusions about the impact of the social division of the social product on economic growth.

Yet in Moss's (1976) view, Longfield was in the business of modifying rather than replacing the Ricardian model. Thus, his supply and demand theory of market price did not preclude him from being willing, in principle, to retain the Ricardian labour quantity theory for the analysis of secular changes in relative values. Similarly, Hollander (1979) has seen Longfield as following classical orthodoxy while developing it to some extent, although White (2009) has not only challenged the reading of Longfield as a marginal utility theorist, but even the notion of him as a marginalist precursor, furnishing an explanation for downward sloping individual and market demand curves. Clearly in this instance, as Prendergast's contribution makes clear, controversy has been a strong antidote to neglect.

Ramsay has remained a neglected figure except for a handful of historians of economic theory and some more recent writers who linked him to developments in the corn model and recognised his early use and incorporation of the entrepreneur into his analysis. Although Ramsay dissented from the Ricardian orthodoxy he nevertheless used the deductive method and his preoccupations were the usual ones of growth and distribution. Prybyla reports that he eschewed an analysis of the utility of commodities in favour of determining their natural value, using an opportunity cost rather than a scarcity conception. Interestingly, Ramsay introduced time into his analysis of value and although it was not fully integrated he clearly predates Knies's similar tripartite distinction between form, place and time in the determination of value. And while value is determined by labour and capital inputs, Ramsay also uses a demand and supply apparatus and has a clear idea of the concept of elasticity.

Turning to distribution, Ramsay argues for a social wage rather than any physical minimum and of course incorporates the entrepreneur as another factor of production that must be rewarded. While accepting Ricardo's core theorem, he nevertheless recognises that enhancements to productivity can raise both profits and wages. Finally, the controversy over the Sraffian corn model finds Skourtos (1991) taking a novel approach by trying to determine whether contemporaries of Ricardo used it and Ramsay emerges as an important exponent. Prybyla, not unreasonably, argues that in the light of his reassessment, Ramsay deserves more than a cursory glance today from historians of economic theory.

Thompson shows that Ravenstone is another author who has attracted a trickle of scholarship throughout the twentieth century. Though the categorisation of 'anti-capitalist' is one that needs to be adjectivally qualified and circumspectly used, it has, nevertheless, guaranteed Ravenstone a minor, if sometimes inappropriate, place in literature dealing with the history of socialist thought; inappropriate in the sense that his political economy has sometimes been wrongly categorised as socialist. Thus, he has been noted in the work, amongst others, of Beer (1921), Cole (1953), Stack (1998), Thompson (1984), Claeys (1986), Dorfman (1966) and Dobb (1973). Again, though, he falls into the category of those whose work has not been the subject of any sustained scholarly treatment.

Uncharacteristically Seligman, as Allington records, failed to notice the important contributions that Rooke made to the debate over free trade and his development of a tabular standard that attracted Irving Fisher's attention in the 1920s and that of some macroeconomists in the late 1990s. Thus, in keeping with his emphasis on those aspects of Ricardian economics that had been pre-empted or contradicted by earlier authors, Seligman chose first to discuss Rooke's analysis of rent, where he had priority in the literature around 1814/5 given that Anderson's work on the subject in the eighteenth century had been forgotten (see Seligman, 1911a). Secondly, Seligman praised his analysis of the determination of price and the role of demand and supply, particularly his consistent use of the concept of marginal cost: price depends on the cost of production at the margin and demand.

However, Seligman missed the fact that Rooke published anonymously *Free Trade in Corn* (1828) (the author was given as a 'Cumberland Landowner') that for some time was assumed to have been authored by Sir James Graham who did not contradict the attribution. That such a prominent member of the Government could have changed his view on the subject served to advance the debate over the repeal of the Corn Laws in a way that Rooke never could have done. In fact, Graham did eventually change his mind on the subject switching his support in favour of the abolitionist case and the circumstantial evidence suggests that Rooke played some part in this.

Seligman also failed to draw attention to Rooke's attempt to eliminate the impact of changes in the value of money on the value of commodities. He proposed a convertible currency with the rate of exchange determined by a tabular standard based on an index of agricultural wages, but, as an additional check, a comparison with wages in the export sector that are more sensitive to fluctuations in the value of the currency. Beyond these two contributions, Rooke took a major interest in economic growth and his analysis of consumption and savings had a remarkably Keynesian flavour. The analysis of growth also framed his discussion of taxation and Rooke favoured the establishment of a real sinking fund to repay the national debt.

Henderson's article on 'E. R.', the alias of Edward Rogers, confirms him as one of those authors in the Cambridge Whewell group who published mathematical tracts in Britain between 1820 and 1850. More specifically, he shows how Rogers, William Whewell (1850) and John Tozer (1838, 1840) translated several of Ricardo's doctrines into mathematical models. They also used mathematics to uncover and iterate the logical flaws in Ricardo's *Principles*. Henderson contends that Seligman's discovery of Edward Roger's mathematical pamphlet was crucial to an understanding of 'how William Whewell came to apply the tools of mathematics to economics'.

Thus, Roger's *Essay on Some General Principles of Political Economy* (1822) influenced Whewell's mathematical model in his 'Mathematical Exposition of some Doctrines of Political Economy' (1829).

In Seligman's opinion, the anonymous pamphlet subsequently attributed to Granville Sharp, demonstrated that economic ideas connected with policy issues found in Ricardo's *Principles* were in circulation well before its publication in 1817. The attribution to Sharp fitted in with his public *persona* as a prolific author with a particular focus on colonial issues and the slave trade where he supported the abolitionist case, not on the grounds of its economic bankruptcy, but rather its moral, legal and religious illegitimacy. He followed, in fact, what Hilton (1995) has called a model of 'free-trade individualism' with a strong evangelical dimension. From his review of the evidence for Sharp as the author, Ditchfield concludes that it is circumstantial at best, there being no reference to the *Sketches on Political Economy* in either biography of Sharp plus the rather telling verdict of his contemporaries that he chose to ignore strictly economic subjects in his writing. Finally, Sharp's published work exhibits a prolix and inaccessible style whereas the author of the *Sketches* has a fluent and engaging way of writing.

Only resort to the most recent statistical textual analysis can settle the issue once and for all, but in its absence, Ditchfield provides compelling evidence that Walter Thom is the more likely author. In his *History of Aberdeen* (1811), Thom is actually described on the title page as the author of the *Sketches* and the reviews of the *History* in the *Scots Magazine* and the *Monthly Review* appear to confirm Thom as the author of this work. Both of these publications of Thom take a Physiocratic perspective on the British economy and this dimension in the *Sketches* had impressed itself on Seligman. While the authorship of the *Sketches* remains in doubt, the volume will continue to be neglected unless Seligman's original thesis gathers renewed support. Either way, it would not be lost on Seligman that Ditchfield and de Vivo (see below) have each uncovered one further neglected economist both of whom deserve better treatment from the profession.

Seligman grouped Torrens and Craig together as the two most neglected economists, but as de Vivo notes, Torrens was far from neglected in his own lifetime. He was elected a Fellow of the Royal Society, Chairman of the Political Economy Club (where he took an active role) and became a leading member of the Currency School. His 1837 letter to Melbourne, for example, led to the separation of the Issue and Banking Departments of the Bank of England under the 1844 Act, even though Ricardo could claim intellectual priority for the idea. As an MP, Torrens was appointed Chairman of the Colonisation Committee in 1835, although he was rather ignominiously sacked for misconduct. He received a Civil List pension for his services to political economy. Nonetheless, de Vivo argues that the epithet neglected might still be explicable since with the eclipse of classical economics (and Torrens had moved from being anti-Ricardian in 1810 to accepting Ricardo's theory of value in the 1830s and was thus thoroughly classical) those associated with it were no longer read. In the second half of the nineteenth century only Marx and Cannan discussed Torrens work, but in the twentieth century Viner (1937) and Robbins (1958) did revive interest in his many contributions.

De Vivo singles out six areas where Torrens made a contribution, although each receives some measure of qualification. The subjects were the law of rent (really only the surplus version with a less impressive account of the differential aspect); a theory of wages adopted by Ricardo (true, but the theory was eclipsed by the wage fund theory) and the theory of profit (it was actually Ricardo's and the argument that wages and profits could both rise was made earlier by McCulloch). That leaves two. Priority over the theory of comparative advantage (his only claim to immortality), but his exposition is sadly now regarded as only 'satisfactory' and, in the view of Viner (1937) 'not an integral part of his thinking'. Moreover, de Vivo finds, rather ironically in the circumstances, that another neglected economist who anonymously published a pamphlet entitled *Considerations on the Importation of Foreign Corn* (the abbreviated version of a much longer title) in 1814 actually deserves priority. Finally, Torrens suggested a national insurance fund to alleviate the condition of the unemployed, but again Relief Works had been discussed before and Torrens had no contextual theory to support this policy intervention.

6. CONCLUSIONS

Seligman was a revered and energetic economist who, even if he failed to establish a school, did have a major impact on the professionalisation and formal structure of economics in America (Laughlin, 1892). He co-founded the discipline's pre-eminent society that now publishes the world's pre-eminent journal. Columbia University's reputation and that of the successor economics department to Seligman's, has produced more Memorial Nobel Prize-winners in Economic Science than any other institution and this legacy owes much to his foresight and ability to establish an intellectual tradition in which others would want to share in. The Seligman Library is another wonderful memorial (Anon, 1939).

Seligman's *oeuvre* covered a wide spectrum of disciplines and as his rapid mind darted from one subject to another he could draw on a rich reservoir of experience to freshen his intellectual thinking. In some cases, such as public finance, this meant being a *de facto* translator of several continental texts and monographs into English that led to a lifetime's engagement with the subject and the production of numerous original and scholarly contributions of his own. These were not simply confined to pure theory either, because Seligman was keen to see his new ideas turned into government policy and ultimately into law. In championing 'progressive' capitalism, Seligman supported the trade union movement and collective bargaining and, rather like New Labour in the United Kingdom, believed that capitalism could and should be combined with social responsibility. As Mehrotra (2006) remarked, 'his sense of social responsibility and citizenship spilled over into the civic arena' and led to his establishing many forums for debate as well as applying his considerable scholarship and expertise to numerous government commissions and enquiries. Thus, Seligman was, and remained a true advocate of the underdog.

Mirroring his public life, Seligman was also an enthusiastic champion of the underdog in political economy. Although he never produced the monumental history of economic theory and policy that he repeatedly promised, which in all probability would have surpassed Schumpeter's *History of Economic Analysis*, the only possible comparator in terms of its scope, analytical acumen and depth of coverage, he nonetheless drew attention to the supporting cast in the development of the subject. Although Seligman himself is now a relatively neglected economist, apart from his pioneering work on taxation and public finance, incorporated into the history of the subject, the fact that this book is being published in 2010, more than a hundred years after his justly famous articles, bears testimony to his work and will have succeeded if more of his neglected find a permanent place in the history of the development of the subject.

NOTES

1. Volume 1 of the *Dictionary of Political Economy A–E* was published in 1894, the second volume *F–M* in 1896, which was reprinted in 1900, and the third volume *N–Z* in 1899, with the reprint containing the Appendix in 1908. In subsequent printings the preface was dropped and the appendix incorporated into the main text.

In the 1908 edition there were intellectual biographies of varying lengths of Butt, Cotterill, Craig, Lloyd, Longfield, Ravenstone and Rooke, but none for Cazenove, Gray, Ramsay, Rogers or Sharp. In the first edition only: Bailey, Longfield, Read and Torrens could be found. When Eatwell et al. produced a 'new' edition in 1987, now called *The New Palgrave: A Dictionary of Political Economy*, only the following still warranted entries (with the authors in brackets): Bailey (Rauner); Cazenove (Pullen); Lloyd (Gordon); Longfield (Black); Ravenstone (O'Brien); Read (Rauner) and Torrens (Corry).

2. Bruce (1938, p. 699) records that 'in thus emphasising the utility theory he was the forerunner of the Austrian school of the latter half of the nineteenth century'.

3. In Read's book, the author of this title is shown as being 'a Labourer' throughout. Later indentified as Thomas Hodgskin, Seligman incorrectly gives the author as (John Francis) Bray (1903b, p. 518).

4. The exception here is Rooke, whom 'so far as I can see, he has no case at all' with respect to originality over the theory of rent (Schumpeter, 1954, p. 475n8).

5. Irving Fisher (1922) had drawn attention to Rooke's contribution on this subject somewhat earlier, but thereafter he disappeared from the radar until renewed interest in the problems associated with indexation in the 1990s.

6. Within the title of this volume, English, Irish and Subversives now becomes appropriate since the Union of The United Kingdom and Ireland was dissolved in 1922 to become the United Kingdom of Great Britain and Northern Ireland. When Seligman wrote his articles the designation of neglected British economists would have been correct.

REFERENCES

Allen, P. S. (1992). Notes from Edwin R. A. Seligman's Lectures on the History of Economics, 1927–1928. *Research in the History of Economic Thought and Methodology*, Archival Supplement 3, 19–206.

Anon. (1939). In memoriam: Edwin Robert Anderson Seligman. *Political Science Quarterly*, *54*(3), 489–491.

Asso, P. F., & Fiorito, L. (2006). Edwin Robert Anderson Seligman. Autobiography (1929). In: W. J. Samuels (Ed.), *Research in the history of economic thought and methodology* (Vol. 24-C) (documents from and on economic thought) England: Emerald.

Beer, M. (1921). *History of British socialism*. London: Bell and Sons.

Black, R. D. C. (1960). *Economic thought and the Irish question 1817–1870*. Cambridge University Press.

Black, R. D. C. (1984). The Irish dissenters and nineteenth-century political economy. In: A. Murphy (Ed.), *Economics and the Irish economy from the eighteenth century to the present day*. Dublin: Irish Academic Press.

Bowley, M. (1978). Review of: Mountifort Longfield: Ireland's first professor of political economy by L. S Moss. *Economic Journal*, *88*(349), 176–178.

Bruce, T. W. (1938). The economic theories of John Craig, a forgotten English economist. *Quarterly Journal of Economics*, *54*(4), 697–707.

Cannan, E. (1893). *A history of theories of production and distribution in English political economy from 1776 to 1848*. London.

Claeys, G. (1986). *Machinery, money and the millennium.* Cambridge: Polity Press.
Cole, G. D. H. (1953). *Socialist thought: The forerunners, 1789–1850. Vol. 1, A history of socialist thought.* London: Macmillan.
Corry, B. (1959). Malthus and Keynes – a reconsideration. *Economic Journal, 69*(276), 717–724.
Dobb, M. (1973). *Theories of value and distribution.* Cambridge: Cambridge University Press.
Dorfman, J. (1966). *'Introduction' to P. Ravenstone, a few doubts on the correctness of some opinions generally entertained on the subjects of population and political economy, [1821].* New York: A. M. Kelley.
Eatwell, J., Milgate, M., & Newman, P. (1987). *The new Palgrave: A dictionary of political economy.* London: Macmillan.
Edgeworth, F. Y. (1899). Professor Seligman on the mathematical method in economics. *Economic Journal, 34*(9), 286–313.
Fisher, I. (1922). *The making of index numbers: A study of their varieties, tests and reliability.* Boston: Houghton Mifflin.
Foxwell, H. S. (1884). *'Introduction' to W. S. Jevons, investigations in currency and finance.* London: Macmillan.
Gordon, B. (1979). *Economic doctrine and Tory liberalism, 1824–1830.* London: Macmillan.
Halévy, E. (1904). *The growth of philosophic radicalism.* Boston: The Beacon Press.
Higgs, H. (1902). Review: The economic interpretation of history. *Economic Journal, 12*(48), 520–521.
Higgs, H. (1926). Review: Essays in economics. *Economic Journal, 36*(144), 613–614.
Hilton, B. (1995). *The age of atonement: The influence of evangelicalism on social and economic thought 1785–1865.* Oxford University Press.
Hollander, S. (1979). *The economics of David Ricardo.* Toronto: Toronto University Press.
Keynes, J. M. (1936). *The general theory of employment, interest and money.* London: Macmillan.
Laughlin, J. T. (1892). The study of political economy in the United States. *Journal of Political Economy, 1*(1), 1–19.
Meek, R. L. (1962). *The economics of physiocracy: Essays and translations.* London: George Allen & Unwin.
Mehrotra, A. K. (2005). *Edwin R. A. Seligman and the beginnings of the US Income Tax.* Indiana Legal Studies Research Paper 56.
Mitchell, W. C. (1939). Edwin Robert Anderson Seligman, 1861–1939. *American Economic Review, 29*(4), 911–913.
Moss, L. S. (1976). *Mountifort Longfield: Ireland's first professor of political economy.* Ottawa, IL: Green Hill Publishers.
Moss, L. S. (2003). The Seligman–Edgeworth debate about the analysis of tax incidence: The advent of mathematical economics. *History of Political Economy, 35*(2), 205–240.
Palgrave, R. H. I. (1908). *Dictionary of political economy, Volume III.* London: Macmillan.
Price, L. L. (1906). Review: Principles of economics. *Economic Journal, 16*(62), 230–235.
Rauner, R. (1961). *Samuel Bailey and the classical theory of value.* Cambridge: Harvard University Press.
Robbins, L. (1958). *Robert Torrens and the evolution of classical economics.* London: Macmillan.
Rozwadowski, F. (1993). From recitation room to research seminar: Political economy at Columbia University. In: W. J. Barber (Ed.), *Economists and the higher learning in the nineteenth century* (pp. 188–197). Cambridge University Press.
Rutherford, M. (2004). Institutional economics at Columbia University. *History of Political Economy, 36*(1), 31–78.

Schumpeter, J. A. (1954). *History of economic analysis*. London: George Allen & Unwin.

Seligman, E. R. A. (1886). Owen and the Christian socialists. *Political Science Quarterly, 1*, 206–249.

Seligman, E. R. A. (1892a). *On the shifting incidence of taxation*. Baltimore: Publications of the American Economic Association, Monographs, Vol. 7.

Seligman, E. R. A. (1892b). Bastable's public finance. *Political Science Quarterly, 7*, 708–720.

Seligman, E. R. A. (1893). *Theory of progressive taxation*. Baltimore: Publications of the American Economic Association, Monographs, Vol. 8.

Seligman, E. R. A. (1894). *Progressive taxation in theory and practice*. American Economic Association, Monographs, Vol. 9.

Seligman, E. R. A. (1895). *Essays in taxation*. New York: Macmillan.

Seligman, E. R. A. (1902). *An economic interpretation of history*. New York: Columbia University Press. Published first in (1901–1902), *Political Science Quarterly*. Vol. 16, pp. 612–640 and in continuation Vol. 17, pp. 284–312.

Seligman, E. R. A. (1903a). On some neglected British economists – I. *Economic Journal, 13*(51), 333–363.

Seligman, E. R. A. (1903b). On some neglected British economists – II. *Economic Journal, 13*(52), 511–535.

Seligman, E. R. A. (1903c). The theory of progressive taxation. *Political Science Quarterly, 8*, 220–251.

Seligman, E. R. A. (1905). *Principles of economics, with special reference to American conditions*. New York: Longmans, Green & Co.

Seligman, E. R. A. (1906). Seligman's *principles of economics*, a reply and a rejoinder. *Quarterly Journal of Economics, 21*(1), 151–160.

Seligman, E. R. A. (1911a). Ricardo and Torrens. *Economic Journal, 21*(83), 448–455.

Seligman, E. R. A. (1911b). *Income tax: A study in the history, theory and practice of income taxation at home and abroad*. New York: Macmillan.

Seligman, E. R. A. (1925a). *Essays in economics*. New York: Macmillan.

Seligman, E. R. A. (1925b). *Studies in public finance*. New York: Macmillan.

Seligman, E. R. A. (1929). Edwin Robert A. Seligman. In: *Die Volkswirtschaftslehre der Gevenwart Selbstdarstellungen* (Vol. II, pp. 117–160). Leipzig.

Shirras, G. F. (1939). Obituary, Edwin Robert Anderson Seligman. *Economic Journal, 49*(195), 577–589.

Skourtos, M. (1991). Corn models in the classical tradition: P. Sraffa considered historically. *Cambridge Journal of Economics, 15*, 215–228.

Stack, D. (1998). *Nature and artifice, the life and thought of Thomas Hodgskin, 1787–1869*. London: Boydell.

Taussig, F. W. (1906). Seligman's principles of economics. *Quarterly Journal of Economics, 20*(4), 622–633.

Thompson, N. W. (1984). *The people's science. The popular political economy of exploitation and crisis 1816–34*. Cambridge University Press.

Tozer, J. E. (1838). Mathematical investigations of the effect of machinery on the wealth of a community in which it is employed and on the fund for the payment of wages. *Cambridge Philosophical Transactions, I*, 502–507.

Tozer, J. E. (1840). On the effect of the non-residence of landlords, etc., on the wealth of a community. *Cambridge Philosophical Transactions, VII*, 189–196.

Viner, J. (1937). *Studies in the theory of international trade*. London: Allen and Unwin.

Whewell, W. (1850). Mathematical exposition of some doctrines of political economy. Second and third memoir. *Cambridge Philosophical Transactions, IX*, 128–149 and Part ii, pp. 1–7.

White, M. V. (2009). Hunting a pre-cursor: The limits of Mountifort Longfield on utility and value. *The European Journal of the History of Economic Thought, 16*(1), 65–96.

APPENDIX. DRAMATIS PERSONAE IN SELIGMAN'S NEGLECTED ECONOMISTS

Generation that Intervened Between the Wealth of Nations *and Ricardo's Earliest Tracts Included in the First Seligman Article*

John Gray (?): (1797), The Essential Principles of the Wealth of Nations illustrated, in Opposition to some False Doctrines of Adam Smith and Others.

Granville Sharp (?): (1809), Sketches on Political Economy Illustrative of the Interests of Great Britain; intended as a Reply to Mr Mill's Pamphlet Commerce Defended, with an Exposition of some of the Leading Tenets of the Economists.

Andrew Hamilton (?): (1790), Enquiry into the Principles of Taxation chiefly applicable to Articles of Immediate Consumption.

Contemporaries of David Ricardo

Robert Torrens: (1815) (and fourth edition 1827), An Essay on the External Corn Trade; (1821), An Essay on the Production of Wealth; (1834), On Wages and Combinations.

John Craig: (1814), Elements of Political Science; (1821), Remarks on some Fundamental Doctrines in Political Economy illustrated by a Brief Inquiry into the Economical State of Britain since the year 1815.

After the Publication of Robert Malthus' Principles of Political Economy *in 1820 active Discussion on Special Points of Theory*

Anon: (1821), Observations on certain verbal Disputes on Political Economy, particularly relating to Value and Demand and Supply.

Anon: (1821), An Inquiry into those Principles respecting the Nature of Demand and the Necessity of Consumption, lately advocated by Mr Malthus, from which it is concluded that Taxation and the Maintenance of unproductive Consumers can be conducive to the Progress of Wealth.

John Cazenove: (1822), Considerations on the Accumulation of Capital and its Effects on Profits and on exchangeable Value.

Anon: (1821), An Essay on the Political Economy of Nations, or a View of the Intercourse of Countries as influencing their Wealth

Thomas Smith: (1821), An Attempt to define some of the First Principles of Political Economy.

Edward Rogers [E. R (?)]: (1822), An Essay on some General Principles of Political Economy on Taxes upon Raw Produce, and on Commutation of Tithes.

Samuel Bailey: (1825), A Critical Dissertation on the Nature, Measures, and Causes of Value, chiefly in reference to the Writings of Mr. Ricardo and his followers, By the Author of Essays on the Formation and Publication of Opinions, etc. etc; (1826), A Letter to a Political Economist.

Charles Foster Cotterill: (1831), An Examination of the Doctrines of Value as set forth by Adam Smith, Ricardo, McCulloch, Mill, the author of 'A Critical Dissertation etc.', Torrens, Malthus, Say etc. being a Reply to those Distinguished Authors.

William Foster Lloyd: (1834), A Lecture on the Notion of Value as distinguishable not only from Utility, but also from Value in Exchange. Delivered before the University of Oxford in the Michaelmas Term, 1833.

Authors Who Attempted to Cover the Whole Field and Included in the Second Seligman Article

John Rooke: (1824), An Inquiry into the Principles of National Wealth, Illustrated by the Political Economy of the British Empire; (1825), Claim to the original Publication of certain new Principles in Political Economy addressed in a Letter to E. D. Davenport, Esq. By John Rooke, author of An Inquiry into the Principles of National Wealth.

Percy Ravenstone: (1821), A Few Doubts as to the Correctness of some Opinions generally entertained on the Subjects of Population and Political Economy.

Samuel Read: (1829), An Inquiry into the Natural Grounds of Right to Vendible Property or Wealth; (1819), Exposure of certain Plagiarisms of J. R. McCulloch, Esq., Author of two Essays on Reduction of the Interest of the National Debt, committed in the last published of these Essays, the Scotsman Newspaper and Edinburgh Review. By Samuel Read, author of a Tract on Money and the Bank Restriction Laws. In recto decus; (1821), General Statement of an Argument on the Subject of Population in answer to Mr Malthus's Theory.

Sir George Ramsay: (1836), An Essay on the Distribution of Wealth.

Mountifort Longfield: (1833), Lectures on Political Economy, delivered in Trinity and Michaelmas Term, 1833.

Isaac Butt: (1837), Rent Profits and Labour. A Lecture delivered before the University of Dublin in Michaelmas Term, 1837; (1837), Introductory Lecture delivered before the University of Dublin in Hilary Term, 1837.

JOHN GRAY'S ESSENTIAL PRINCIPLES OF THE WEALTH OF NATIONS

Richard van den Berg

The earliest writer highlighted by E.R.A. Seligman, in his article 'On Some Neglected British Economists' was the author of a pamphlet, published anonymously in 1797, with the title *The Essential Principles of the Wealth of Nations, Illustrated, in opposition to some false doctrines of Dr. Adam Smith, and Others* (Seligman, 1903, pp. 336–337). The work is noteworthy mainly for containing a defence by a British author of the theories of the French physiocrats against the critical discussion of the 'agricultural system' by Adam Smith in book IV, chapter ix of his *Inquiry Into the Causes of the Wealth of Nations*. As such the pamphlet was something of an exception. By the last decade of the 18th century Smith's great work had long achieved a solid reputation in Great Britain as an influential text containing a profound new economic philosophy. As Dugald Stewart put it, in the 15 years after the publication of the *Wealth of Nations* in 1776, Smith had 'not only the satisfaction of seeing the opposition to it at first excited, gradually subside, but to witness the practical influence of his writings on the commercial policy of his country' (quoted in Ross, 1998, p. 120).

The pamphlet, however, published seven years after the Scotsman's death, contained some strongly worded criticism of a number of Smith's views. It was particularly dismissive of his discussion of what constituted 'productive' economic activity: '[Smith's] verboseness and ambiguity' the author

English, Irish and Subversives Among the Dismal Scientists
Research in the History of Economic Thought and Methodology, Volume 28-B, 37–72

ISSN: 0743-4154/doi:10.1108/S0743-4154(2010)000028B005

asserted, 'clearly shew how a man of ability, when overlooking fundamental principles, may speculate upon the surface of things, without ever getting at the kernel' (Gray, 1772, 1777, 1797, 1780, 1786, 1789a, 1802, p. 15). What Smith had failed to see, but what had been 'very systematically' demonstrated by 'the French Economists', was that '[t]he principal and most essential cause of the prosperity of a state is the ingenuity and labour of its inhabitants exercised upon the fertility of its soil' (1797, p. 4).

The argument of the pamphlet shows that, at least in the minds of some British writers, Smith's dismissal of the distinctive physiocratic doctrine that agriculture must be considered as the only 'productive' economic activity in a nation had not been decisive. Indeed, for a decade or so after the publication of the *Essential Principles* a number of British authors seriously continued to consider the merits of the views of Quesnay and his followers about the 'exclusive productivity' of the agriculture. While the lingering influence of physiocratic ideas on authors such as Dugald Stewart, Thomas Malthus and William Spence has been discussed by modern commentators (see especially, Spengler, 1945; Meek, 1962; Delmas & Demals, 1995; Hollander, 1995), the *Essential Principles* and its author have rarely been studied closely in their own right. Thus the 'neglect' of this author, signalled by Seligman over a century ago, continues.

This chapter attempts to shed some new light on this curious pamphlet. One of the most intriguing questions connected to it is simply who was the man who wrote the work that Karl Marx (1969, p. 382) judged to be 'the *only important* English work directly supporting the Physiocratic teaching'? The biographical sketch in the next section provides an answer to this question. Then we examine the contents of the author's library and his literary production prior to the *Essential Principles* in order to answer the question how the author arrived at his peculiar adherence to the physiocratic theory. Some distinctive ideas put forward in the pamphlet are discussed in the third section, and the last section examines the influence of the work, such as there may have been.

LIFE OF JOHN GRAY, LL.D. (1724–1811)

From well before the mid-19th up to the mid-20th century those scholars who read and commented on *The Essential Principles of the Wealth of Nations*, including Marx and Seligman, seem to have been unaware of the very name of its author. Since then it has become accepted knowledge (again) that the work was written by one John Gray. Beyond the name, however, biographical details about Gray have remained extremely sparse until the present day. If one were to use a measure of obscurity, something which perhaps is appropriate in a work devoted to 'neglected economists', then one may use the fact that neither the *Oxford Dictionary of National Biography* (old or new editions), nor the *Palgrave Dictionary of Economics* (any edition), nor any other biographical dictionaries devote an entry to Gray. The modern authors who discuss his economic writings contend themselves with the statement that 'little biographical information is available about Gray' (Delmas & Demals, 1995, p. 119, n. 5).[1] This is unfortunate because at least some knowledge about the personal background and career of an author is often useful in arriving at a better understanding of his or her ideas. This, as will become clear shortly, is the case too for John Gray.

In order to start piecing together a brief outline of Gray's life one has to go back to 19th century sources. A few interesting details can be gleaned from an obituary note that appeared in the *European Magazine* of June 1811. It reads, in full:

> John Gray, esq. LL.D., at Paddington in his 88th year, for many years one of the commissioners of the lottery; a very worthy, benevolent and scientific man.

The mention of his age at death is consistent with his year of birth being 1724, which is adopted in the Goldsmith's library catalogue for the author of some of Gray's other publications.[2] Another obituary note in the *Gentleman's Magazine* omits Gray's age and place of residence at death. It does however add that he was 'a frequent correspondent for many years in Mr. Urban's Miscellany' (i.e. the *Gentleman's Magazine*).

There is nothing in these two obituary notes that allows us to identify this particular John Gray, which is after all not an uncommon name,[3] as the author of *Essential Principles*. However, another scrap of information in the *Gentleman's Magazine*, namely the October 1797 issue that carried a review of that work, establishes a link between the *Essential Principles* and the John Gray 'esq. LL.D.' who died on 9 May 1811. This review starts: 'Mr. Grey [*sic*], of the lottery-office, Somerset-place, flatters himself that, in this essay on the fundamental principles of politicks and finance, he has refuted some very misleading doctrines of Dr. Adam Smith and Mr. Arthur Young' (Anon., 1797a, pp. 858–859) The reference in both pieces to his involvement with the state lottery (about which more below), suggests that we are dealing with the same John Gray 'LL.D.'

Gray, it seems, had been reluctant to put his name to his critical discussion of Adam Smith and Arthur Young. As much is suggested in a comment written soon after the publication of the *Essential Principles*. There Gray is described as 'a most respectable member of society [who] from prudential motives has concealed his name' (Mortimer, 1801, p. 438). However, if Gray did indeed intend his identity to remain a secret, then it was not a very jealously guarded one. In subsequent years, perhaps due to the mention of his name in the *Gentleman's Magazine*, various authors correctly identified him as the author.[4]

Apart from the single-line obituary notices, next to nothing seems to have been published about the man in the nearly two centuries since his death; there is fortunately an unpublished source that provides new leads from which a fuller, though still sketchy, picture of John Gray's life begins to emerge. This source is his will (National Archives, prob. 11/1522). It reveals that, apparently without (surviving) wife or children towards the end of his life,[5] Gray left money and other possessions to several persons and institutions who played a significant role in his life. First, he left £500 to the 'provost, clergyman and schoolmasters' of Cupar for the establishment of a girl's school in that town and, in a later addition to his will, he also left 'my small collection of books' to the subscription library of Cupar (for a discussion of this collection see the next section). These charitable donations to Cupar suggest an attachment of Gray to the small Scottish market town and indeed it turns out to be the place where he grew up. One local historian confirms that Gray was 'the son of one of the masters at Cupar grammar school' (Martin, 2001, p. 11),[6] and he will most probably have attended this school as a boy.

Gray continued his education at St. Andrews University where he graduated in Greek (Lloyd, 2003, p. 2) presumably sometime in the 1740s. His gratitude to his *alma mater* is evident from another legacy he left in his will, the grant of a sum of £2,000 for the establishment of a chair in chemistry at St. Andrews. Perhaps this grand gesture was partly motivated by the fact that later in life Gray had been awarded an honorary doctorate in civil law by the university, allowing him to add 'LL.D.' to his name (Hirsch, 1952, p. 276).

What career Gray embarked upon after leaving St. Andrews is not quite clear. An unconfirmed source mentions him as an assistant private secretary to the Duke of Northumberland in the period 1763–1764. An acquaintance with Hugh Smithson (1714–1786), later Percy, the first Duke of Northumberland, is indeed confirmed by Gray himself in an aside where he mentions dining with the nobleman (see Gray, 1780, p. 1). The connection may be quite significant for the understanding of several of Gray's writings, since not only was Percy Lord Lieutenant of Ireland during the period 1763–1765 (various of Gray's pamphlets deal with proposals for constitutional and economic reforms with respect to Ireland), the duke was also known as an active agricultural improver. Hence it is possible that Gray's later conviction that agricultural development was the surest route to economic prosperity was due in part to the influence of one of his patrons.[7]

Some other significant details about Gray's career are related in the memoirs of John Campbell (1779–1861).[8] Born in Cupar, John Campbell was the son of the Reverend George Campbell who was a parish minister in that town for fifty years and, as it turned out, was also an old friend of John Gray. When, in 1798, the 18-year-old son came to live in London, Gray became something of a mentor.[9] Interestingly, Campbell relates that earlier in his life Dr. Gray 'had been in the profession, now obsolete, of travelling tutor, [and] had repeatedly made the grand tour with young English noblemen' (Hardcastle, 1881, p. 32). This would have meant that Gray had spent time in Italy, France and possibly other European countries.[10] Campbell further states that Gray's 'last pupil' had been 'Lord Fortescue', that is Hugh Fortescue (1753–1841). This implies that, if Fortescue had been in his late teens or early twenties when he made his Grand Tour, as was the customary age for pupils, Gray would have given up his employment as travelling tutor by the early to mid-1770s.[11] Furthermore, Campbell states that it had subsequently been Fortescue on whose recommendation Gray 'had been made Secretary to the Lottery, with handsome apartments in Somerset House' (Hardcastle, 1881, p. 32).

Reportedly Gray kept his position at the lottery office 'for many years' (*Gentleman's Magazine*, 1811, p. 601). It should be noted that in the last decades of the 18th century the lottery office had a reputation of being badly administered. Little government control was exercised and the commissioners were 'widely mistrusted' (Raven, 1991, p. 381). Perhaps Gray's worth at death of £5,000 was not unrelated to the opportunities for enrichment that his position would have offered.[12] Some years before his death Gray had to give up his residence at Somerset House and moved to an address at Paddington Green.[13] He had kept up his friendship with John Campbell, judging by the fact that the latter was a witness at the signing of his will and that it was he who was given the task of sending Gray's personal library to Cupar. His attachment to the Fortescue family also persisted, something that can be deduced from the fact that Gray left in his will sums of money to several Fortescues.

From this short sketch Gray emerges as a man with an academic schooling who via a career of personal tutor achieved lucrative public office and social standing, and who successfully cultivated contacts with some influential political patrons. It also allows us to note some parallels between the life of this obscure critic of Adam Smith and that immeasurably more famous author. Both were Scotsmen; they were born less than 20 miles and about one year apart; and both made, at approximately the same time, the Grand Tour as tutors of wealthy noblemen. Whether their paths ever crossed is unknown, but Gray only picked up his pen against Smith in his early 70s, seven years after his adversary had died.

ORIGINS OF THE INFLUENCE OF PHYSIOCRACY ON GRAY'S THINKING

The Essential Principles of the Wealth of Nations was not Gray's first publication. During the last three decades of the 18th century, he frequently intervened in public debates publishing pamphlets on subjects as varied as financial reforms in Ireland, Scottish fisheries, the American tax revolt and slavery.[14] In addition, as we saw, he was a regular contributor to the *Gentleman's Magazine*, and perhaps other periodicals, although it is difficult to ascertain what topics he covered. It is only in some of his later writings that Gray explicitly endorsed and tried to give further developments to some of the doctrines of the French *Economistes*.[15] The aim of the present section is to establish how this influence of physiocratic ideas on Gray's thinking may have come about.

A first question to address is what textual sources Gray may have had at his disposal from which he would have learned about the ideas of Quesnay and his followers. This is not as trivial a question as it may seem. Some doubts have been raised about the depth of knowledge amongst British political economists at the turn of the 19th century about the ideas of their French colleagues from a generation before. As Groenewegen (in Torrens, [1808] 1984, p. xiv, n. 27) has observed, there is a 'lack of real knowledge of Physiocracy in [such authors as] Spence and Torrens, … Malthus and even James Mill'.[16] To an important extent the understanding of physiocratic theory may have come to these and other authors second hand, that is for example through Adam Smith's influential discussion of the 'agricultural system' in the *Wealth of Nations*.[17] This indirect apprehension of ideas may have been the cause of a certain degree of distortion. Therefore one may ask what evidence can be found for a first-hand study of key physiocratic texts in John Gray's case.

One source of evidence that suggests itself is Gray's library. As was explained in the previous section, in his will Gray made the fortunate decision to leave his personal library to the subscription library of Cupar. What he describes as 'my small collection of books' in fact comprised over 630 volumes that were catalogued in 1813.[18] This allows a good impression to be formed of his intellectual interests generally and his reading on economic subjects more specifically.

Out of 638 titles, 550 were more or less easily classifiable in one of the 11 categories given in Table 1. Works devoted exclusively to economic subjects (defined widely) form the third largest category after 'history and geography' and 'language'. This last category, which contains a high proportion of books about the classical languages, betrays Gray's background as a classically schooled linguist. Of the modern languages, books on the French language (books about grammar, style, dictionaries etc.) are the most numerous. It seems to indicate an acquaintance with French at the very least, even though it is of course impossible to say from this evidence how good Gray's French was. Of all categories, the category 'economic subjects' contains the highest proportion of books published in French (22 titles, or about a quarter). The works contained in this group confirm Gray's specific interest in French economic thought: included are works by authors such as Casaux, Dufour, Dufrane, Dutot, Gournay, Goyon de Plombanie, Herrenschwand, Melon, Necker and Vauban. Of more immediate relevance to the ideas expressed in the *Essential Principles* is that three important physiocratic texts were present in Gray's library. They are Mirabeau's *l'Ami des hommes*, *Théorie de l'impôt* (either the 1760 or 1761 edition), and *Philosophie rurale*. In addition, Gray owned three works by (or reproducing the ideas of) Turgot, namely *Théorie de l'intérêt de l'argent*,[19] *Des Administrations Provinciales* (Dupont de Nemours, 1788), and *Reflections on the Formation and Distribution of Wealth* (the English edition of 1793 or 1795). While Gray does therefore not appear to have owned a large number of physiocratic works, he possessed some crucial titles and perhaps it may be conjectured that *Théorie de l'impôt* and *Philosophie rurale* were his main direct sources of physiocratic thought. In addition Turgot's *Reflections* may have been influential in formulating his reply to Smith (a point further discussed in the next session).

The content of Gray's library also lends support to Seligman's observation that he 'had some acquaintance with the earlier English economic literature' (Seligman, 1903, p. 336). Many British authors of the 17th and 18th centuries are represented in his book collection: Briscoe, Cantillon, Cary, Child, Culpeper, Defoe, Davenant, Gee, King, Law, Petty, Pollexfen, Temple, Yarranton, Young and others.

Table 1. A Classification of John Gray's Library.

	Category											
	Economics	History and geography	Language	Education	Politics	Philosophy and science	Religion	Periodicals and pamphlets	Architecture	Law	Literature	Total
English	66	61	44	9	48	15	43	39	9	3	6	343
French	22	7	12	1	9	6	1	0	5	0	1	64
Latin and/or Greek	2	38	37	1	1	26	14	0	1	10	7	137
Portuguese or Spanish	0	3	2	0	0	0	0	0	1	0	0	6
Total	90	109	95	11	58	47	58	39	16	13	14	550

Nevertheless, what is without a doubt most noteworthy about the economic theories put forward in the *Essential Principles* is the strong influence of physiocratic ideas on Gray's thinking. In addition to identifying which were the probable textual sources that Gray used, it is also possible to indicate *when* the Economists started to have a significant impact on his thinking. This can be deduced from the content of Gray's writings prior to the *Essential Principles*. Between 1768 and 1792 Gray published a dozen pamphlets, most of which dealt with or touched upon economic matters (for a full listing see the appendix). There is however very little suggestion in these writings of any substantial influence of Quesnay or his followers. A solitary reference is made to Mirabeau in a pamphlet that takes Richard Price to task over his support for the American tax rebellion (see Gray, 1777, p. 93).[20] All this reference suggests is that by the late 1770s Gray was at least familiar with some of the physiocratic literature.

More significant however are the views expressed in his pamphlet *The Policy of the Tax upon Retailers Considered* (Gray, 1786). In this short work Gray explicitly addresses the question of what should be considered 'productive' activities in economic life. While in 1797 he almost completely endorses the physiocratic position that only agricultural activities are truly productive (for a fuller discussion see the next section), just over a decade earlier his position is quite different. The 1786 pamphlet is an attempt to provide theoretical vindications for a proposal by William Pitt the younger to impose a new tax on retailers. Quoting both 'domestic and foreign authorities' (1786, p. 1), Melon being the most prominent among the latter, Gray argues that 'political writers have generally considered the activities of retailers as a low-skilled reselling business that adds nothing to goods but higher prices'. In contrast, *both* agriculture *and* manufacturing should be seen as requiring skilled labour that produces new goods, which can be consumed either within the country or exported. Since an increase in the number of farmers and craftsmen is accompanied by an increase in output while an increase in the number of retailers is not, Gray states as a general principle: 'That the increase of the number of husbandmen and manufacturers tends to make things cheap; but on the contrary, the increase of Retailers, beyond a certain number proper for competition, tends to make things dear' (1786, p. 33). This common sense distinction between men who only resell goods and those who produce them appears to owe little to Adam Smith: neither is the Scotsman mentioned as one of the 'domestic authorities', nor do Gray's arguments closely resemble the specific criteria Smith uses to distinguish between 'productive' and 'unproductive' activities.

There is also no obvious influence of physiocratic thinking in the 1786 pamphlet.[21] What is interesting to note, however, is the way Gray accounts for the profits made by retail merchants. Gray argues that, whilst retailers commonly earn profits, by selling dearer than they buy, 'it must be remembered that those profits [of retailers] are no profits to the nation' (1786, p. 31). Thus, if retailers earn profits without contributing to the produce of the nation, they must be earned at the expense of the incomes of other citizens: 'the more they [retailers] gain it is so much the worse for the nation, as those gains chiefly come out of the pockets of the industrious fellow-subjects, who are consequently less able to sustain other burdens' (1786, p. 10). This reasoning is noteworthy because in 1797 Gray extends it to explain the profits made by manufacturers.

Of course this extension only suggested itself to Gray after he changed his mind, sometime in the early 1790s about what economic activities must be considered truly 'productive'.[22] In 1797 he admits that 'among those who have been formerly mislead [to believe that the manufacturer increases the income of society], *I must include myself*' (Gray, 1797, p. 36; emphasis added). He describes his change of mind as a process by which 'frequent meditation on the subject [gave] me the clearest conviction that no augmentation of revenue of society arises from the labour of a manufacturer, except in the case of its being sold abroad' (1797, p. 36). These meditations resulted in quite a different outlook that is present in Gray's *Essential Principles*.

DISTINCTIVE IDEAS

Rather than considering the *Essential Principles* as a faithful exposition of physiocratic theory by a British follower of the doctrine, it should be seen as an attempt to borrow the authority of the French economists in support of a number of economic policies to be introduced in Britain. That is to say, despite the doctrinaire tone adopted in parts of the work, the author's purposes seem to be primarily practical. Gray adheres to several (but certainly not all) of Quesnay's positions because they confirm his vision of what should be the most vital concerns of the government in attempting to promote prosperity in the nation. This is probably also the main reason why he singles out Adam Smith (besides Arthur Young) for criticism. It should be remembered that Smith, despite his critique of Quesnay, also acknowledges in other parts of the *Wealth of Nations* the great importance of agriculture in economic development (e.g. see the first two chapters of book III). On the whole however, Smith strongly advocates a general stance by the government of not favouring any order or economic activity in society. In contrast, Gray stresses in various places that there should be clear priorities in economic policy. For example, the text starts with the admission that '[t]he causes of the wealth of nations are various, nay infinite' (Gray, 1797, p. 3). Nevertheless, in order to conduct an effective economic policy, one needs to understand what activities promote the wealth of a nation *the most*: 'The prudent statesman, sensible that it would be a presumptuous and vain attempt to trace out the million of small causes that contribute to the wealth of nations, applies his attention chiefly to *the principal and most essential causes*, and assiduously endeavours to render these causes as efficient as possible' (1797, pp. 3–4; emphasis added). In other words, by recognising that the various economic activities have different potentials for engendering economic growth, the statesman will understand where to focus his attention.[23]

In Gray's view it is obvious that '[t]he principal and most essential cause of the prosperity of a state is the ingenuity and labour of its inhabitants exercised upon the fertility of its soil' (1797, p. 4). This, at least, is the case for a country 'while it can with little labour draw a great revenue from its lands' (1797, p. 21), that is as long as gains in agricultural productivity can be made relatively easily. States go through what may be called developmental stages, according to Gray. Especially 'nascent states', such as America, will concentrate almost exclusively on developing its agriculture at the expense of manufacturing.[24] With time, however, the relative advantage of agricultural production becomes less: 'In adult states lands not yielding such a surplus of revenue after the expense of cultivation is deducted, the profit from handicrafts and the allurements of society attract in a greater degree the attention of men' (1797, p. 21).[25] Britain, while being certainly a more 'adult' state than the American States, has in Gray's opinion not yet arrived at a stage where the potential for further improvements in agricultural production is diminishing.

On the contrary, substantial growth in agricultural production can be achieved, since according to our writer, Britain suffers from both 'neglected lands' and 'neglected cultivators of those lands' (1797, p. 117). With regards to the 'neglected lands', of the estimated 56 million acres of 'fertile territory'[26] in Great Britain, Gray believes 'not much more than half [to be] cultivated'. Most of the neglected lands, an estimated 22 million acres (1797, p. 130), consist of commons and wastelands. Gray advocates further acts of parliament to enclose these fields (1797, p. 116), something which in his estimate 'would give employment to 200,000 new families, and subsistence to twice that number' (1797, p. 131).

Besides extending the area of land under the plough, even more important gains could be made through improvements in agricultural production. Rather than promoting the introduction of any particular new agricultural techniques, Gray emphasises that the key factor here is the motivation of cultivators. In many parts of the country, especially the north, he notes, cultivators are generally considered to be 'lazy and indolent'. While this may be true, he argues, it is not because these peasants are 'naturally indolent'. Instead, 'they are lazy and indolent for the same reason that slaves are lazy and indolent, from their daily experience that all their sweat and all their labour go only to fill another man's pocket, and turn to no account to themselves. Such a consequence damps their exertions' (1797, p. 121).[27] In Gray's opinion, many British farmers are held in a kind of servitude by the landowners and it is up to 'the legislature [to take] upon itself the noble occupation of exempting from thraldom the poor and industrious country labourers' (1797, p. 117). The oppression felt by many consists not only of the high rents they have to pay. More importantly, 'the want of security to the farmers in the possession of their farms' (1797, p. 117) acts as a serious disincentive to improvements in cultivation. If farmers 'were to be reproached with the miserable cultivation of their fields', Gray imagines the following reply:

> They may justly plead, we have no property in our farms; we are in continual dread of being dispossessed; were we to attempt improvements, some avaricious neighbour, who offered a small rise of rent, would be preferred to us. These are discouragements which sink us ... As the state, by our oppression, is a very great sufferer as well as ourselves, government is therefore, for its own sake as well as ours, bound to establish a law founded on the principles of justice, by which we may be secured, that the more we improve our farms, where we were born, and which we love to occupy, the more we shall enrich ourselves. Give us but such security, and the improvements of our farms, and the embellishment of the country will in a short time prove that we are neither lazy nor unintelligent. We will then willingly participate our gains with our landlords.... (Gray, 1797, pp. 122–123)

In other words, legal or institutional factors form the main obstacles to improvements in agricultural production. More specifically, in Gray's opinion, government should introduce penalties to landowners who refuse to let their land on long-term leases (1797, pp. 122–123). Leases should be devised so that 'the advantages arising from improvements [made by producers] may be shared proportionately between the tenant and the landlord' (1797, p. 124).[28]

All this shows what seems to be Gray's fundamental motivation in opposing Adam Smith and in siding with the Quesnay and his school. He sees policies that remove the causes of underdevelopment of the agricultural sector as the surest way to increasing economic prosperity of a country with a large territory such as Great Britain. In part Gray's recommendations for unlocking the great potential for economic growth of agriculture are also reminiscent of the physiocrats, especially his emphasis on the need for 'security' of farmers in order to give them proper incentives for investments in their farms.[29]

Of course the perception that one (or some) sectors of the economy have greater potentials for economic growth than others is not the quite the same as the more rigid conviction that all but one sector of the economy is 'productive'. Gray clearly also follows the physiocrats in this more dogmatic version of the championing of agriculture. Indeed the most well-known part of the *Essential Principles* (roughly the pages 8–30) is devoted to this doctrinaire disagreement between Adam Smith and the physiocrats. Gray acknowledges that Smith had 'in my opinion given, (except in one point) a fair and accurate view of the great outlines of that system, according to the French writers, with the purpose of objecting to some material parts of it' (1797, p. 4). As a matter of fact Gray's own short account of physiocratic theory (1797, pp. 4–8) owes more than a little to the outline in the *Wealth of Nations*. The one point where Smith had unfairly portrayed the Economists was his statement that they failed to distinguish between activities that resulted in products that could be resold (manufacture) and those that did not (services). Without giving a textual source, Gray maintains that the physiocrats did make this distinction, but that it was irrelevant to the question of which activities are and which are not productive (1797, pp. 11–12).

Similar to the physiocrats, in Gray's view a 'productive' activity is a production that yields a surplus above all expenses of production. This, according to him, is something only agriculture can do and consequently '[i]t is the mass of surplusses [*sic*] occasioned by the whole of the cultivators that forms the revenue of every other class in society' (1797, p. 43). At length Gray dismisses each of Smith's five objections to this position. Some of his defence of the physiocrats is not particularly strong (just like the points Smith raises against them are not all very insightful either). One line of argument Gray uses is worth highlighting however. It concerns his explanation of manufacturing profits. If the mass of agricultural surpluses constitutes the total sum of surplus incomes in a nation, then how does this square with the fact that manufacturing has become such a lucrative activity in various parts of Great Britain? Gray offers the following reasoning:

> But do we not see many manufacturers get rich? Yes certainly; and this very circumstance of their *acquiring a capital*, has led political and commercial writers into the false conclusion, that manufacturers *created a capital*. In a professed enquiry into the nature and causes of the Wealth of Nations, one would have expected to have found this error clearly refuted; but so far otherwise, Dr. Smith has interwoven it into the whole of his performance, which renders that performance worse than useless as a political treatise, a mere castle of cards, erected without a foundation, and affording no habitation for the politician. (1797, p. 37; emphasises added)

Capitals are accumulated out of profit, but in manufacturing this profit is not 'created' but 'transferred' from the truly productive sector:

> Whatever value is put upon any manufacture, it is resolvable into three other values; namely, the value of the raw material of which it is made, the value of the wages expended in its fabrication, and thirdly, the value of profit which the manufacturer superadds to the other two values, as a recompense to himself. Now none of these three values comprehends in it any increase of general revenue, consequently the three together cannot form any increase of general revenue. They only occasion *a commutation or transfer* of the revenue previously provided by the cultivator, by giving a permanency to that revenue under a new form. Nay, in some cases (which, indeed, rarely happen) they do not even do that.... (1797, p. 38; emphasis added)

A few things may be said about this conception. Firstly, as we saw, in 1786 before any clear influence of physiocratic thought is discernable, Gray used a similar argument to explain the profits made by retailers. Secondly, Gray's way of allowing for manufacturing profits in the *Essential Principles* as a 'transfer' out of the agricultural surplus is not commonly encountered before him. To be sure, in physiocratic theory any payments required for the production of goods and services outside agriculture (e.g. for raw materials and wages) were admittedly often portrayed as being 'paid out of' the *produit net*. In addition, some contractual payments such as pensions and house rents were sometimes described as 'false' revenues (as opposed to 'true' revenues in the form of rent payments). However, Quesnay and his closest followers did not commonly admit the existence of regular industrial profits. That is to say, if profits were admitted it was more like a transitory, 'disequilibrium' phenomenon.[30]

An exceptional position was defended, however, by A. R. J. Turgot in his *Reflections on the Formation and Distribution of Wealth* (1766). After clearly acknowledging the normal existence of profit in manufacturing and mercantile activities, Turgot nevertheless reasserted, in physiocratic fashion, that only agriculture was 'productive'. Thus, he suggested, profits made in trade and manufacture should be understood as being 'taken from' the incomes of landowners and farmers (1766, section 99).[31] This view soon found support from one of Turgot's lesser-known friends G. F. Le Trosne who expressed it even more explicitly:

> the entrepreneurs of the works of commerce and industry make great profits and enrich themselves. This is true but if one concludes from this that those profits are an increase of wealth for a nation, one could as well conclude that when a man wins the jackpot in the lottery, there is an increase of wealth for the nation. The entrepreneurs, in addition to [their] cares, contribute capitals and advances for which they have to receive a proportioned interest, because nobody makes advances but in the hope of a profit. They could have acquired landed properties that would have given them revenue.... But those profits are costs to those who pay for them, costs that are always paid for by [agricultural] production. They do not constitute an increase but an employment of the wealth of a nation.... (Le Trosne, 1770, pp. 23–24; author's translation)[32]

One imagines that, as a commissioner of the lottery, Gray would have appreciated Le Trosne's comparison of non-agricultural profits to winning money in the lottery. It neatly captured the image of gains obtained from a pool of a definite size, that is the 'mass of surpluses', originating from other, truly productive, activities. However, Gray very probably did not know Le Trosne's statement, since it occurred in a very little-known work. Turgot's *Reflections*, on the other hand, Gray did know; at least, this we may infer from the presence of the English edition of this work in his library. Perhaps he was actually indebted to Turgot for this distinctive argument with which to counter the opinion that the wealth of 'master manufacturers' sufficiently proved that their activities must be 'productive'. The fact that the English editions of the *Reflections* appeared in the same period as when Gray changed his mind on this point seems to lend some support to this suggestion as to Turgot's influence.[33] The reason to emphasise Gray's views about manufacturing profits as 'transfer' incomes is that, as we will see in the next section, it also figures in the writings of a small number of other British authors in the subsequent decade.

While Gray's way of accounting for manufacturing profits can be seen as an attempt to preserve the validity of physiocratic theory in the face of the emergence of Smith's third order of rich 'master manufacturers and merchants', there was another distinctive point on which he explicitly opposed Quesnay and his school. According to Gray, the physiocrats had misunderstood what he calls 'the political nature of rent paid by a cultivator for leave to cultivate the ground' (Gray, 1797, p. 60). In his opinion 'the fundamental error of the French Economists [is] ranking the proprietors of lands as a productive class in society' (1797, p. 49). While this is a somewhat odd reproach (the physiocrats did in fact rarely call the landowners a 'productive' class) what he seems to object to was the assumption of an unconditional right that landowners would have to rent payments. The physiocrats, and following them Adam Smith (see 1797, pp. 8, 60) and Arthur Young (1797, pp. 60–64), consider the rent of land as 'something sacred, indefeasibly appropriated to the landlords, who have a right to increase it as much as possible, and to dispose of it as they please' (1797, p. 61). In fact however, the right to payment for the use of land can be questioned since 'the rents of lands [are] a surplus income falling into the lap of the landowners, without their contributing to the production of that surplus' (1797, p. 61, see also, p. 52). Rent could indeed be considered as a tax, an imposition from which farmers in young nations such as the American states are exempt and 'which circumstance has been the very animating soul of the agriculture of the Americans' (1797, p. 52). Gray estimated the value of rents paid in Britain to amount to between a quarter and a third of total agricultural production, or 25 million pounds, and it was a payment to a largely idle class that is paid for doing nothing: 'The proprietors of land as mere receivers of land rents are not an essential class in society ... [they] render themselves one of the most unessential and most burdensome classes in society' (1797, p. 51).

This was strong political language, going well beyond Smith's isolated remark that landlords 'love to reap where they never sowed' (Smith, [1776] 1904, Book I, Chapter VI, para. 8) and it was to be noted approvingly by Marx (1969, Vol. I, p. 382).[34] Meek (1962, p. 355) too argues that 'Gray uses Physiocracy not to defend but to attack the landed interests' and as such made 'Physiocratic principles serve radical ends'. The twist Gray gave to the physiocratic conception of rent as an 'unearned' income, or a payment without a real counterpart, is indeed interesting. It is curious that an author with a respectable social position and probable connections with the landowning classes in Britain should be questioning the unconditional right of landlords to charge rent. This is true also in the light of events across the channel, since the most radical phase of the Revolution had only just subsided.[35]

It should be noted however that it is doubtful whether Gray's ends were 'radical' in any progressive sense. That is to say, he does not propose any revolutionary social solution. Instead he argues for a restoration of the link that existed in feudal times between landownership and military duty (see Gray, 1797, p. 91). Having over the last three centuries progressively 'shaken off their obligations to defend the state, [the landowners] had rendered themselves from an *essential class*, one of the most *unessential classes* of society' (1797, p. 98). By providing for defence of society landowners would resume an essential service and this was only just since 'reason requires that the land owners should do something for the community in return for the privilege of having this surplus [i.e., rent] secured to them by the community' (1797, pp. 61–62).

As stated earlier, Gray did certainly not adopt all aspects of physiocratic theory. Especially in view of the reception of his pamphlet, most notably by William Spence (see below), two important omissions are worth noting. They are the doctrine of the *bons prix* of agricultural products and Quesnay's circular flow analysis. The first doctrine, that is the persistent emphasis in the physiocratic literature on the necessity for 'high' prices of agricultural produce in order to stimulate more plentiful reproduction, is implicitly rejected in Gray's criticism of Arthur Young. While Gray considers Young a poor economic theorist generally, one of the points he singles out for criticism is the 'erroneous doctrine, fondly embraced by Mr. Young, [of] the importance of high price to the prosperity of agriculture, and even to the prosperity of the nation' (1797, p. 65). The second omission is not only clear from the fact that Gray does not even mention the *Tableaux Économiques*; more generally, in the *Essential Principles* the spending of the landlords, of prime importance in Quesnay's analysis of circular flow of income and reproduction, is not given any extended discussion.[36]

Finally, Gray also attributed a few ideas to the French Economists apparently without much justification. For example, he asserted that the French Economists 'exceedingly condemn the aggregating or crowding of men ... in towns and cities' (1797, p. 125). He used this alleged view in support of a peculiar proposal for 'proportionate distribution of the people over the territory' in smaller communities preferably near the coast (1797, p. 132). Another example is that he maintained that according to the Economists the production of manufactures *did* increase the income of the nation when they are exported abroad (1797, p. 22).[37] What these various developments, omissions and false embellishments of physiocratic theory indicate is not in the first place that Gray would not have fully understood the ideas of Quesnay and his school. Although this is likely to have been the case to some extent too, they are probably due more to the fact that Gray was a selective follower of the Economists using those ideas that served his purposes. As will be seen in the next section, it is especially the views by which Gray distinguished himself from more common physiocratic teachings that are useful for establishing what impact his work may have had.

RECEPTION

The impact of the *Essential Principles* was certainly not great. Nevertheless, as will presently be illustrated, the text may have had a certain influence on those British authors who in the decade after its publication re-examined Smith's arguments against physiocratic theory. After this period, however, Gray's publication seems to have been relegated to an almost complete obscurity.

The earliest responses to the *Essential Principles* consisted of two anonymous reviews (Anon., 1797a, 1797b), one in *The Gentleman's Magazine* the other in *The Monthly Review*. Both reviews adopted a studiously neutral tone, noting Gray's attack on the authority of Adam Smith with regards to the concept of productive activity but withholding a judgment as to which author may be correct.[38] In the following years, more unequivocal endorsements of Gray's views can be found in Mortimer (1801, pp. 36, 438) who refers to Gray as an 'intelligent writer' whose 'arguments are unanswerable' and Fraser (1802, p. 59n) who calls the *Essential Principles* 'an excellent publication'. Since, however, these endorsements came without any substantial discussion, they merely serve to show that Gray's pamphlet seems to have made some positive impression.

The first more extended discussion of the work can be found in David Wakefield's *An Inquiry into the Truth of the Two Propositions of the French Œconomists* (1799). This pamphlet was followed up five years later with a more ambitious and better-known work called *An Essay Upon Political Œconomy* (1804), which had the title of the first offering as subtitle. It was in fact a largely rewritten and enlarged 'second edition'.[39] It is useful to discuss the two works together especially in order to note that some significant changes in Wakefield's views occurred in the five years between the two editions. The earlier text, despite its title, betrays no clear first-hand knowledge of the writings of the physiocrats. It is in fact a defence of Adam Smith against Gray's attack, and only the works of these two authors are quoted. According to Wakefield, Smith after 'having exerted his full powers on the mercantile system, [had] hastily dismissed the agricultural: of this circumstance Doctor Gray has taken advantage' (Wakefield, 1799, pp. 5–6). Hence he took upon himself the task of defending Smith's views by stating them more precisely.

By 1804 however, Wakefield no longer considered himself the defender of Smith. Having become much more critical of Smith economic liberalism, he now held up Sir James Steuart as 'the great master of political science' (Wakefield, 1804, p. 3).[40] While Smith was for this reason given a less prominent role, Wakefield's demotion of John Gray was even more rigorous: he deleted all references to his *Essential Principles*.[41] A large part of Wakefield's argument was still devoted to the rejection of physiocratic theory, but where in 1799 Gray had been taken as a faithful exponent of this doctrine (see, e.g. Wakefield, 1799, p. 17), now Turgot was given this role.[42] The main point Wakefield made in both texts was that the production of manufactures, similar to agricultural production, also gives rise to 'surplus value or … surplus production' (1799, p. 8). That is to say, in both cases the value of the output was greater than costs of (a) 'the intermediate support' of the labourers during the production period, (b) 'the wear of his stock advances' and (c) 'the raw materials used' (1799, pp. 9–10). According to Wakefield the principal difference was that:

> [t]he surplus of the manufacturer, whether real or nominal, resolves itself into profits of stock and interest of capital; while that of the cultivator resolves itself into profits of stock and rent of land. (1799, pp. 14–15)

Without explaining why profits of stock and interest of capital were distinct categories in manufacture but not in agriculture, Wakefield concluded that 'an analogy subsists between interest of capital and rent of land' (1799, p. 15). This leads him into a discussion about the relations between the 'rate' of rent, that is the value of rent over the value of land, and the money rate of interest.[43] Wakefield's discussion of Turgot's *Reflections* is quite interesting. For example, he pointed out the inconsistency between the earlier sections in which artificers were said to be unproductive and to only receive incomes that just cover costs and later sections in which entrepreneurs in manufacturing and trade are said to receive 'proportionate profits' (Wakefield, 1804, p. 49n.). He hinted that he did not find Turgot's attempted reconciliation convincing, just as he had five years before rejected Gray's idea of a 'transfer' of surplus (Wakefield, 1799, p. 9).

A final thing to note about Wakefield's *Essay* is that it is possibly the earliest text suggesting a close link between the theories of Malthus and the physiocrats.[44] To be precise, Malthus was said to be the leader of a somewhat peculiar 'Chinese' branch of physiocracy according to which 'that part of society only can be considered as productive, whose labour and skill are devoted to the cultivation of the soil, in order to *the production of food*' (Wakefield, 1804, p. 2; emphasis added; see also, pp. 6n., 8–9).[45] This association between Malthus' conception of productive activity and that of the physiocrats has occasionally been made by students of his work ever since.[46] Rather than entering here into the wider question to what extent or in what sense one may consider 'Malthus as a physiocrat', we may briefly consider the possibility that Gray may have had some very precise, but also limited and brief, influence on Malthus.

The issue is not whether Malthus would have based his general understanding of physiocratic theory on Gray's exposition of it in his pamphlet of 1797. This is rather unlikely especially since it has been established that Malthus knew some of the physiocratic literature in the original French (see Hollander, 1992). Gray's work may however be relevant with regards to some striking alterations Malthus made to the second edition of his *Essay on the Principle of Population*, published in 1803. Although Gray is nowhere referred to in that text, the presence in Malthus' library of the *Essential Principles* (see Malthus, 1983, p. 54) suggests that it is likely that he knew that work.

This seems to be confirmed by some alterations in particular with regards to the explanation of manufacturing profits in view of the opinion that only agriculture is 'productive'. In the first edition of his *Essay*, Malthus had already asserted that the employment of capitals in agriculture 'may be unproductive [i.e., unprofitable] to the individual that employs it, and yet be productive to the society'; and that the reverse may be the case for a capital employed in trade (Malthus, 1798, p. 333). In the second edition, he somewhat adapted this view to render it more similar to the position of the physiocrats, namely that 'the proof of a net produce arising to individuals from manufactures, would not really invalidate the definition of the Economists' (Malthus, 1803, p. 431). This he then explained in the following manner:

> But manufactures, strictly speaking, are no new production, no new creation, but merely a modification of an old one, and when sold must be paid out of a revenue already in existence, and consequently the gain of the seller is the loss of the buyer. A revenue is transferred, but not created. (1803, p. 433)

It is in particular the wording of the last sentence that reminds of Gray, since the actual phrase 'transfer of revenue' had not been used by Turgot or apparently any other earlier writer. If this wording was indeed borrowed from Gray, then the very temporary popularity of the latter's pamphlet may also explain why Malthus dropped the passage again in the third edition of his *Essay* of 1806. In any case it should be noted that this particular tinkering with his text does not really seem to affect Malthus' principal reasoning, which continued to be his association of the alleged productive nature of agriculture with its unique position of supplying means of subsistence.[47]

While Gray's influence on Malthus may be limited to some temporary changes in wording, he arguably exercised a more substantial influence on another important figure of the same period, namely Dugald Stewart. It is obvious that Stewart knew Gray's contribution, since the former refers in his *Lectures on Political Economy* to 'the anonymous author of a pamphlet printed a few years ago, under the title of *The Essential Principles of the Wealth of Nations*' (Stewart, [1855] 1968, Vol. 1, p. 275).[48]

On a number of points Stewart's critique of Smith in the section 'Of Productive and Unproductive Labour' in his *Lectures* (Stewart, [1855] 1968, Vol. 1, pp. 253–308) were rather similar to that of Gray. As a general position, Stewart agreed with Gray that on balance it were the French Economists, rather than Smith, who upheld the correct notions when examining the issue of what constitutes 'productive labour'. Of course this does not by itself prove any direct influence of Gray on Stewart. It is important to note that the high esteem in which Stewart held the economic (though not the political) theories of Quesnay and his group was based on a first-hand study of their writings.[49] In his lectures he recommended a close study of their ideas,[50] an advice that was taken to heart by at least some of his pupils, including Brougham and Horner.

Rather than emphasising the differences between Smith and the physiocrats, Brougham and Horner ended up defending the somewhat surprising view that the famous Scot had not actually differed fundamentally from the view that agriculture was the only productive economic activity.[51] This attempt to emphasise the 'Physiocratic tendency within Smith's work' (Tribe, 1978, p. 110) was very probably inspired by their teacher and it differs strikingly from the confrontational tone of Gray's critique of Smith. Given the very high esteem in which Stewart held the author of the *Wealth of Nations*, it is not surprising that he is not very kindly disposed towards Gray's tone. But Stewart's lengthy rejection of a very minor point made by Gray (whether manufacturing and menial services can be compared to the cultivation of plots of land of different fertility)[52] is somewhat disingenuous since several other points he raises against Smith closely echo Gray's argument.

To be more precise, the main points of similarity are the following. Firstly, similar to Gray, Stewart highlighted that there was a single point on which Smith had misrepresented the doctrine of the Economists, namely that they would not have distinguished 'artificers and manufacturers' from 'menial servants'. Stewart noted that they had made such a distinction, but that this was not essential since it did not affect the truth of view of the Economists that both were unproductive.[53] Secondly, similar to Gray,

Stewart clearly rejected Smith's definition of productive labour according to which 'the true characteristic of productive labour is, that it fixes itself on some vendible commodity' (Stewart, [1855] 1968, Vol. 1, p. 265). The fact that an economic activity yielded durable products was important especially for the possibility of accumulating wealth, but this had little to do with the question whether or not such an activity was productive. With regards to that question Stewart sided with Quesnay according to whom only labour applied in agriculture was productive, because it alone 'reproduces a surplus in addition to its value' ([1855] 1968, Vol. 1, p. 264). A third similarity is that Stuart names Locke and Vanderlint as two British authors who before Quesnay had already advanced the proposition that all tax falls on the land.[54]

Fourth and most importantly, Stewart follows Gray in treating the profits made by merchants and manufacturers as surplus incomes transferred from the truly productive sector of the economy. Not only was it true that the 'wages of artificers are a mere *transference of wealth*' (Stewart, [1855] 1968, Vol. 1, p. 265), Stewart explicitly argued that

> [t]he same observations apply, with equal force, to the profits of merchants and master manufacturers. [they add a margin to the price as a compensation for their trouble and advances] This increase, evidently, is a salary, and the gains of the merchant are but *a transference, not a production of riches*. The same thing may be said of every species of industry, the object of which is to modify the productions of the earth, without increasing their quantity. ([1855] 1968, Vol. 1, pp. 266–267; emphasis added)

Taken together these various similarities between Stewart's *Lectures* and Gray's *Essential Principles* suggest that the former was more influenced by the latter than he let on. Or in any case, if the evidence for this influence can be doubted, Dugald Stewart is the economist whose exposition is closer than any other to Gray's discussion of the concept of 'productive labour' in Smith and the physiocrats.

The last author on whom Gray had a discernable influence was William Spence. Apparently as early as 1801 Spence defended 'all the main positions' of his pamphlet *Britain Independent of Commerce* (see Meek, 1962, p. 358), which upon its publication in 1807 achieved an instant, but short-lived, notoriety. Nowhere in *Britain Independent of Commerce* is Gray's work named and Spence only explicitly acknowledged its relevance in a reply to James Mill's attack published in 1808.[55] However, an attentive reading of Spence's pamphlet learns that Gray's *Essential Principles* is the unacknowledged source of a number of opinions expressed there.

It should be noted that Spence, unlike Malthus and Stewart, did not seem to have had any first-hand acquaintance with the physiocratic literature. His understanding of Quesnay's theory appears to have derived primarily from the accounts by Smith in the *Wealth of Nations* and Gray in his *Essential Principles*.[56] It is especially some of Spence's *misunderstandings* of physiocratic theory that suggest a reliance on Gray. The most important misunderstanding is Spence's opinion that the French economists had not understood that the increase in agricultural production depended on a sufficient effective demand. Since this demand had to come mainly from outside agriculture, the physiocrats had, according to him, been wrong to ignore the importance of the consumption of food by the class of manufactures. Indeed, Spence (1807, p. 22) alleged that the physiocrats' ignorance of the importance of effective demand for food and of the need for a balanced growth of both agriculture and manufacture was the principal way in which his own theory differed from theirs. This is peculiar since anyone who has read any of the main works of Quesnay or his closest followers recognises that the analysis of the circular flow of incomes and the notion of a demand for agricultural produce at prices that encourage increased reproduction is at the very heart of physiocratic theory. However, as was noted, these were the precise points on which Gray's account of that theory had been weak and it seems that Spence took this to be the case for physiocratic theory generally.[57]

Other views expressed by Spence which were more specifically reminiscent of Gray include an emphasis on the importance of modern, reliable contractual relations between farmers and landlords (1807, pp. 24–25); a reference to rent payments as being 'unnatural' and being merely the result of the political situation in feudal times (1807, p. 31); the view that it is appropriate for 'nascent' states such as the United States to concentrate exclusively on agriculture (1807, pp. 22, 26, 27) and the assurance that even if foreign trade would come to a standstill this would not spell ruin for a country such as Britain (Spence, 1807, pp. 9–10 and cf. Gray, 1797, p. 113). Finally the idea of a 'transfer' of surplus to explain the nature of manufacturing profits also figured prominently in Spence's pamphlet. He asserted that the price of any manufacture

> resolves itself into the amount of food consumed during their manufacture by the labouring manufacturer, and into the profit of the master manufacturer; the former ... is merely a conversion of one sort of wealth, into another sort of the same value, and the latter is in every case a transfer of wealth, merely, from the pocket of the buyer to that of the seller. (Spence, 1807, p. 19)

Thus the surplus income of the 'master manufacturer' was no proof that the activities he organised and directed were 'productive'. Instead this income was obtained as a deduction of the surplus incomes generated in agriculture: 'A transfer, then, not a creation of wealth, has taken place, whatever one gains, the other loses, and the national wealth is just the same' (1807, p. 19). Although Spence ascribed this view to the French Economists (see 1807, pp. 13–14), it seems, for reasons explained before, that Gray was a more direct source for this precise notion.

Having highlighted the similarities between the pamphlets of Spence and Gray, it must be emphasised that the former did of course develop a number of noteworthy ideas of his own. In particular Spence's analysis of circular flow, which is in some respects quite different from that of Quesnay, had no counterpart in Gray. The presumed underconsumptionist arguments Spence derived from that analysis historically form the most significant part of his contribution, if only because they called forth James Mill's classic formulation of the law of markets in his *Commerce Defended* (1808; see van den Berg, 2010).

But with regards to the more limited topic of Gray's influence it must be said that by the end of the first decade of the 19th century, after the controversy about Spence's pamphlet had subsided, references to the former's work became even rarer than they had already been before that time. Edward Wakefield's *An Account of Ireland Statistical and Political* (1812), which mentions Gray several times, is a rare exception.[58] Any resonance Gray's views may have had with British economic authors had by this time definitely come to an end.[59]

CONCLUSION

It would be an exaggeration to call John Gray an important British economist. His main contribution, *The Essential Principles of the Wealth of Nations*, neither contained many truly original views, nor did it exercise any lasting influence on the development of economic thinking in Britain. Nevertheless the neglect that befell his work in most of the 19th and 20th centuries is not entirely deserved. Perhaps the most significant thing about Gray's pamphlet is that it signalled the beginning of a short period during which the views of the French *Economistes* exercised a certain belated influence on a number of British authors. Of course these authors – Gray, Malthus, Stewart and Spence – cannot in any way be considered a coherent group. They were all sympathetic to physiocratic economics, or what they understood by that, but each developed their views in their own ways. What these authors had in common, however, was a certain bias in favour of agriculture production, seeing its expansion as essential for the growth of the wealth of the nation more generally. It is fundamentally this bias that made them subscribe to Quesnay's otherwise puzzling view that only agricultural labour was 'productive'.

John Gray was the author who was most explicit in spelling out the differences with Adam Smith's more even-handed approach to economic development. As we saw earlier, one of his arguments in particular, intended to account for the profits earned by Adam Smith's 'third order', found some following amongst the economists. This piece of reasoning, according to which the surplus incomes earned in manufacture and commerce did not originate in those activities but were deducted, or 'transferred', from the 'mass of surpluses' generated in agriculture, appears not to have survived in Britain beyond the first decade of the 19th century.[60] The reason why it found no further following was not perhaps that it was necessarily logically flawed, but that the unproven assumption that motivated it, namely that agriculture was the surplus generating engine of economic growth, became increasingly unfeasible. Within a few years this view of economic development was undermined by what Donald Winch has described as the ascendancy of 'Ricardian logic'. This logic, a combination of the principles of diminishing returns in agriculture and comparative advantage in international trade, 'pointed to the benefits an island with a rapidly rising population could derive from embracing a policy of paying for its food and raw materials by exporting the products of its new workshops and factories rather than by having recourse to increasingly inferior land at home' (Winch, 1996, p. 400). Manufacture rather than agriculture came to be seen as the engine of Britain's economic growth.

NOTES

1. The two other significant 20th century commentators on Gray's work, Spengler (1945) and Meek (1962) relate nothing about the man but his name.
2. Confusingly, however, the *Essential Principles* is ascribed to what the cataloguers seem to consider as a different John Gray for whom other vital dates are given (see appendix). I have not seen any other contemporary evidence to corroborate the birth date of 1724.
3. In the same period there were, for example the historian John Gray who contributed to the 12 volume work *A General History of the World, from the Creation*

to the Present Time (London, 1764) and another John Gray who published a treatise on *The Art of Land-Measuring* (Glasgow, 1757).

4. See D. Wakefield (1799, p. 6); Stewart ([1855] 1968, Vol. II, p. 229 n. 1); Fraser (1803, p. 67 n. 1); Spence (1808, p. 106); Edgeworth (1809, p. 402); E. Wakefield (1812, p. 18). In view of this it is a little surprising that subsequently his name appears to have been so thoroughly forgotten for such a long time.

5. While this does not conclusively prove that there were no familial connections with other economic authors of the time with the same surname, I have not come across any evidence to the contrary. This applies both to (yet another) John Gray (1799–1883), one of the so-called 'Ricardian socialists' and to Simon Gray, a critic of Malthus' theory of population.

6. The father was probably William Gray who taught at the Grammar school uninterruptedly between 1709 and 1737, apart from a short period between 13 September 1725 and 17 March 1726, when he was temporarily dismissed (Boyd, 1991, p. 43). There is no trace of the name of the mother.

7. An argument against this speculation would be however that Gray only developed a prejudice in favour of agricultural development after the Duke's death in 1786.

8. Campbell was set for a successful legal and political career, which culminated in being made the first Baron Campbell of St. Andrews in 1841 (see Jones & Jones, 2004).

9. When, for example in 1800 Campbell considered embarking on an (eventually very successful) legal career he turned to Gray for advice 'and the cold, the phlegmatic, the timid John Gray said that he thought the plan very rational, and that I was uncommonly well cut out to succeed at the bar' (Hardcastle, 1881, p. 49, see also pp. 72 and 356).

10. Gray (1792, p. 12) mentions that he had visited Rome, where he had witnessed people of different races worship together. The presence in his library of some guidebooks for Venice suggests that he visited that town. It also seems probable that he visited Paris, possibly during the period that the *Economistes* were an important intellectual group, but nothing suggests a personal acquaintance with any physiocratic author.

11. This is consistent with the fact that Gray's activities as a pamphleteer commence around this period. See appendix.

12. This unkind conjecture could perhaps be falsified by an examination of the surviving Lottery Office Papers (National Archives, IR 55).

13. Gray would presumably have moved to Somerset House in the early 1790s, when a large part of the building was completed. In 1789, he still lived in Gerard Street (see Gray, 1789a, p. 4). When the first part of his will was written, on 30 June 1808, Gray's address is given as Paddington Green.

14. For a list of Gray's publications see the appendix to this chapter. Beside Gray (1797), there does not seem to be a secondary literature on any of these works.

15. In addition to Gray (1797), Gray (1802), his proposal for a single tax on land, is clearly influenced by physiocratic ideas.

16. Groenewegen (in his introduction to Torrens, [1808] 1984) criticises Meek for lightly passing over the question of the actual sources on which British authors based their views about physiocracy. The same point may be raised against the more recent

discussion of the influence of physiocracy on British authors by Delmas and Demals (1995).

17. In contrast to these authors, as will be noted below, Dugald Stewart and his pupils Horner, Brougham and Lauderdale did possess first-hand knowledge of various physiocratic texts. Hollander (1992) makes the case, contradicting Groenewegen, that Malthus knew some crucial physiocratic works in the original.

18. In *The Laws and Catalogue of the Cupar Library* (1813, p. iii) it is noted that Gray's books take up the catalogue numbers 'from 800 to about 1450'. Among the volumes there are 32 that contain a collection of a total of about 270 pamphlets, including one volume with nine of Gray's own pamphlets (catalogue number 1437; see the Appendix).

19. This work, published in 1780 by P. Rulie and J.-L. Gouttes contained Turgot's *Sur les prêts d'argent*.

20. An estimate of Mirabeau's is quoted, most likely from *Théorie de l'impôt*, that in France only one-third of the tax on tobacco is appropriated by the king.

21. What reminds one most of the physiocrats is Gray's insistence that government taxation must be seen as a 'natural' claim on individuals' incomes for the support of society (primarily to pay for protection against foreign invasion): 'Government taxes are, in their principle, State necessities, imposed not by man, but by nature, though in general they are regarded by payers, as wanton exertions of legislative authority'. This same basic view on taxation appears in several of Gray's pamphlets, whether it is to justify taxes imposed on the Irish (Gray, 1772) or American colonies (Gray, 1777) or on British subjects (Gray, 1802).

22. Gray (1789a, p. 75) still maintains the same position about the productiveness of manufacture as in 1786.

23. For other clear statements to this effect see Gray (1797, pp. 114, 116): 'a state possessing an ample territory [is] exceedingly misled and ill advised, [if it] bestows more of its attention upon commerce than agriculture, since this last is a much more ample and more substantial support of national opulence and power than the former'.

24. Gray (1797, p. 28) approvingly quotes the 'enlightened politician' Jefferson's opinion that, 'Tis for the interest of the American States, that for a long time to come their manufacturers should reside in Europe'. Importantly, with regards to America, Smith had also taken this view (see Smith, [1776] 1904, Book III, Chapter 1, para. 5).

25. Note that there is in this reasoning an implicit assumption of diminishing returns in agriculture. The same is true in Spence (1807, pp. 28–29, 37), although this writer goes further by linking the same assumption to increasing agricultural prices and rents (without quite formulating a theory of differential rent).

26. Gray (1797, p. 83) notes that 'in Great Britain are reckoned 72 million of acres and upwards' and he then assumes '16 millions to be of little value'.

27. One of Gray's arguments in favour of the abolition of slavery is the disincentives to slaves that are the result of this institution. See Gray (1792), his contribution to the intensive public debate over slavery in the early 1790s.

28. Gray recognises that this is a difficult issue, which according to him had however been addressed satisfactorily by Lord Kaims, in a plan that was originally published in Anderson (1794). This plan was added as an appendix to the *Essential Principles*.

29. In physiocratic theory the introduction of fixed rents payable in money is an important aspect of the establishment of modern contractual relations between farmers and landlords. However, not following the analysis of the *Tableaux Economiques*, Gray does not discuss the perceived role of fixed (or sluggishly adjusting) rent payments in explaining disruptions to the circular flow (see Steenge & van den Berg, 2007).

30. As such these net incomes in manufacturing appeared in the 'dynamic' *Tableaux*. On these aspects of physiocratic theory, see Steenge and van den Berg (2007).

31. Turgot's attempt at reconciling the existence of regular profits outside agriculture with Quesnay's notion of agriculture as the sole surplus creating sector has often been noted. Some commentators have played down its importance. For example, Meek (1962, p. 312) argued that Turgot's acceptance of the physiocratic doctrine of the exclusive productivity of agriculture is 'purely formal', and a transitory position 'preparing the way for Adam Smith'. Others have pointed out that Turgot's 'transitory position' was persuasive enough for a number of French authors to keep defending basically the same position until the first decade of the 19th century. On this, see Faccarello (1990).

32. The original reads: '[...] les entrepreneurs des travaux du commerce & de l'industrie font de gros bénéfices, & s'enrichissent. Cela est vrai, mais si l'on en conclut que ces bénéfices sont un accroissement de richesses pour une nation, on est en droit de conclure que lorsqu'un homme gagne le gros lot de la loterie, il y a accroissement de richesses pour la nation. Les entrepreneurs, outré leurs soins, apportent des capitaux & des avances dont ils doivent retirer un intérêt proportionné; car personne ne fait des avances, que dans l'espérance d'un benefice; ils auroient pu acquérir des propriétés foncieres qui leur auroient donné un revenu; & il faut considérer que leurs benefices doivent leur servir à réparer les pertes auxelles ils sont exposés: mais ses bénéfices sont des frais pour ceux qui les payent, frais qui sont toujours payés par la production, qui ne forment pas dans une nation un accroissement, mais un emploi de richesses, & qu'il est de l'intérêt des deux classes propriétaires de la totalité de la reproduction, de réduire aux frais indispensables par la libre concurrence'. It are especially Le Trosne's reference to profit as a 'proportionate interest' on capital advanced and its explanation as a kind of 'opportunity cost' (i.e. the same capital 'could have been' invested in land giving a return in rent) which suggest a direct influence of Turgot.

33. It is even possible that Gray was the still unidentified English translator of the *Reflections*. Even though this puzzle has been addressed a number of times (most laboriously by Lundberg (1964) who most unconvincingly concludes the translator was none other than Adam Smith!), Gray has to my knowledge not been considered as a candidate before. However, this conjecture would require further investigation since any evidence in its favour is merely circumstantial.

34. Marx made quite extensive excerpts from Gray's pamphlet, first in a 'Beiheft H', which he subsequently used in preparation of notebook xxiii of his Manuscript 1861–1863. This part of the manuscript was posthumously edited for *Theories of Surplus Value*, Vol. 1 (Marx, 1969). Some of the excerpts were dropped in this process. Nevertheless Marx's positive appreciation of Gray as a faithful transmitter of various physiocratic ideas is still evident.

35. Gray does show no sympathy for the French Revolution in any of his later writings. What may be noted, however, is that one radical author, Mably, in whose work the 'accidental' historical nature of property rights is emphasised, is well represented in Gray's library. Another French author who at about the same time as Gray gave a similar political twist to the physiocratic notion of rent as an 'unearned' income was Germaine Garnier (1796, p. 27): 'the landowner receives rent for nothing [*gratuitement*] and only by virtue of a legal fiction that recognises and upholds the right of property of some individuals'.

36. Some hints at the importance of the spending of landlords are given (Gray, 1797, pp. 80, 118).

37. Meek (1962, p. 355) calls this 'a thorough-going mercantilist position' of Gray. Whilst it is true that Gray differs here from what is generally maintained by the physiocrats, he also confirms that 'the exportation of corn is of all other exportations the most profitable'.

38. The review in *The Monthly Review* (Anon., 1797b, pp. 24, 33) ends with the following observation: 'Without speaking decidedly on the principal point at issue between the present writer and the illustrious Adam Smith, we recommend the perusal of this judicious performance to those who turn their thoughts to the subject of political economy, persuaded that there are few readers who may not derive from it some useful information'. Similarly, *The Gentleman's Magazine* (Anon., 1797a, pp. 67, 859) finishes with the non-committal 'we recommend his book to general perusal'. A few years later, *The Monthly Magazine* retained a neutral position in a somewhat different manner by printing both a discussion that compared Gray's position favourably to that of Smith and one that compared it unfavourably (see, *Monthly Magazine*, [1800], Vol. 9, pp. 332–334, 621).

39. Both works appear in Gray's library (catalogue numbers 1423 and 1058 respectively).

40. In addition, he now referred favourably to Davenant. Although the mercantilist tendency of Wakefield's *Essay* has been recognised (see, e.g. Tribe, 1978, p. 112), the curious fact that this tendency was not yet present in the 1799 pamphlet has not. The 'retrograde' Wakefield accused Smith of borrowing much from Steuart while being 'entirely destitute of candour and gratitude'. Interestingly, Wakefield now rejected Smith's laissez-faire convictions on the grounds of their being dogmatic, arguing that the reasoning in the *Wealth of Nations* 'is trammelled with a *systême*' (Wakefield, 1804, p. 3n). His new position was best summed up in a footnote where he argued that personal economic freedom should not prevent the state from providing guidance: 'let each individual in his sphere, do the best he can do for himself, consistently with the law; but surely such exertions need the guide and protection of government, whose superior and extended knowledge, and elevated situation, enables it to combine all the component parts, which compose national prosperity, into one effective and harmonious effort' (1804, pp. 55–56).

41. A single, very minor, reference to Gray (1802) occurs in Wakefield (1804, p. 70).

42. The reason for this substitution may have been that Wakefield had recognised Turgot as a more worthy opponent. Calling Turgot 'the ablest advocate of the *systême* of the French œconomists' (Wakefield, 1804, p. 88), he quoted the *Reflections* throughout his *Essay* and discussed it more specifically in an appendix (1804, pp. 87–113). Wakefield (1804, pp. 113–114) explains that, unable to obtain an

original version either in Paris or Britain, he had relied on the English edition of 1795 and that only after finishing his work he had able to borrow a French version from the marquis of Lansdowne. While Wakefield had by now studied a number of other French economic authors, including Chastellux, Necker, Garnier and Canard, there still was no evidence that he studied any of the writings of Quesnay and his closest followers at first hand.

43. For a short discussion of this interesting but not very successful line of argument see Meek (1962, pp. 356–367). Wakefield (1804, pp. 15–19) noted that Locke, Turgot, Alexander Hamilton and Canard had also hinted at the analogy. This was perhaps more reasonable than his earlier claim (Wakefield, 1799, p. 12) that the same idea had been pursued by Smith.

44. Wakefield refers to both the first edition of Malthus' *Essay on Population* published in 1798 and the second edition of 1803.

45. As opposed to the more faithful 'Persian' branch, headed by Turgot, according to which it are productions of the earth generally (i.e. also raw materials) that form the basis of the wealth of a nation.

46. A recent lengthy contribution is by Hollander (1995), who also notes most of the other modern literature on the presumed nature of the relation. Further examples of early 19th century commentators who suggested such an association were Spence (1808, p. 108), E. Wakefield (1812, p. 437) and Foster (1815, p. 103ff).

47. For Gray, as for the physiocrats generally, the notion is not so directly bound up with the supply of food as it is for Malthus. It should be noted though that Hollander (1995, p. 85) reads significantly more into the same alterations to the second edition arguing that it signified a 'fundamentalist' physiocratic phase in Malthus' thinking.

48. Although this appears to suggest that Stewart did not know the author's identity, elsewhere he refers to 'Gray's Pamphlet. Becket, 1797' (Stewart, [1855] 1968, Vol. 2, p. 229 n. 1). The lectures date from the academic year 1800–1801 at earliest, but perhaps this last note is of a slightly later date.

49. Stewart ([1855] 1968, Vol. 1) referred to Mirabeau's *Philosophie Rurale* (on p. 274), Baudeau's *Exposition de la Loi Naturelle* (p. 278), Turgot's *Reflections* (p. 295), Le Trosne's *De L' Administration Provinciale* (p. 301), Mercier de la Rivière's *L'Ordre Naturel* (p. 308) and the physiocratic journal, *Ephémérides du Citoyen*.

50. Stewart ([1855] 1968, Vol. 1, p. 289) stated: 'That the writings of the authors by whom the system was first explained; those of Quesnai (in particular), of Turgot, and of the Marquis de Mirabeau, will amply repay the labour of a very diligent perusal to all who turn their attention to these studies, I can venture to pronounce with confidence: and it is only after examining the different parts of the system in their relation to each other and to the whole that a correct judgment can be formed of their scope and of their importance'.

51. This position is expressed most clearly in Horner's review of Canard's *Principes d'Economie Politique*' (1803, see esp., p. 447), and Brougham's review of Lauderdale's *Inquiry* (1804). It is worth noting that William Spence quoted both articles and supported his own view that Smith tended to the physiocrats' (and his own) position by quoting Brougham: 'The principles of Dr. Smith clearly carry him to the theory of the Economists; and in order to be consistent, he ought,

unquestionably, to have reckoned Agriculture the *only* productive employment of capital and labour' (Spence 1807, p. 12; emphasis in the original).

52. Although agreeing with Gray that both are unproductive, he rejected his comparison that was meant to illustrate that the former only produces an equivalent while the other produces less than an equivalent. See Stewart ([1855] 1968, Vol. 1, pp. 275, 278–279) and Gray (1797, pp. 11–12).

53. Stewart backs this claim up with a reference to Mirabeau's *Philosophie rurale* (p. 55 of the 1763 large edition) where the 'sterile class' was subdivided into a *classe sterile industrieuse* (manufacturers), a *classe sterile soudoyée* (menial servants) and a *classe oisive* (the leisurely class).

54. The reference to Vanderlint's *Money Answers All Things* (1734) is telling (Stewart, [1855] 1968, Vol. 1, pp. 298–299; see also, Gray, 1797, p. 4). Stewart indicated that that work was little known by this time with the remark: 'I was entirely unacquainted with them [i.e. Vanderlint's opinions] till his Essay was put into my hands a few years ago by Lord Lauderdale' ([1855] 1968, Vol. 1, p. 299). This suggests that Stewart became interested in that author when reading Gray whom he had equally read 'a few years ago'.

55. Spence (1808, p. 106) observed that 10 years earlier Dr Gray had published his work 'in which *every one* of the doctrines of the Economists (except that which regards the landowners as a *productive* class, a mere verbal difference) is insisted upon much more earnestly than I have done'.

56. The only other sources he mentions and from which he may have learned something about physiocratic theory are the reviews by Horner (1803) and Brougham (1804).

57. One passage in particular seems to point to Gray. In his pamphlet, Spence asserted that 'the followers of the Economists' had not understood the reason why much wasteland was not brought into cultivation (namely a lack of effective demand food). He next noted that in Great Britain 'it is calculated' that the total extent of this wasteland is 22 millions acres (Spence, 1807, p. 28). He does not provide a source for this estimate, but it was in fact Gray (1797, p. 130) who gave precisely that figure. Spence (1807, p. 16) did also adopt Gray's opinion that the physiocrats had believed that the sale of manufactures when exported would increase national income.

58. Edward appears more kindly disposed towards Gray than his younger brother David. Most references are however to Gray's *Income Tax Scrutinized* (1802). This is also the only work by Gray that McCulloch would mention in *The Literature of Political Economy* (see McCulloch, 1845, p. 336).

59. Outside Britain Gray's contribution seems to have been largely unknown. One exception was the anglophile French economist André Morellet, who apparently around the turn of the century critically discussed Gray's refutations of Smith in an unpublished manuscript (see van den Berg & Salvat, 2001, p. 156).

60. Faccarello (1990, p. 72) has argued that Marx's transformation problem is similar to the reconciliation Turgot proposed between the notion that only agriculture produces a surplus and the idea that regular net incomes are earned outside agriculture. He traces the same view in Condorcet and Roederer. In fact, Gray expressed the reconciliation more clearly than those writers. Of course Faccarello's suggestion is fascinating, since as Gehrke and Kurz (1995, pp. 76–77 n. 20) observe 'It may be conjectured that Marx got this idea [of the redistribution of a

predetermined aggregate surplus value in proportion to the capital advanced in the various spheres of production] from these authors [Turgot, Condorcet and Roederer] and that he generalized it to all spheres of production in which surplus labour is performed'. This is however a conjecture for which one would want to find textual evidence. Gray's case does not provide this evidence: although Marx was interested in his pamphlet he appears to have paid little heed to Gray's 'transfer problem'.

ACKNOWLEDGMENT

The author thanks Dr. Regina Roth of the Marx–Engels–Gesamtausgabe (Berlin – Brandenburgische Akademie der Wissenschaften) for information regarding Marx's use of, and appreciation for, Gray. He also wishes to thank Ms. Janice Wightman, the Adult Services Supervisor of Cupar Library for providing him with photocopies of the Library's *Laws and Catalogue*, and Dr. Craig Brown of St. Andrews University for helping him to establish contact with the Cupar library.

REFERENCES

Anderson, J. (1794). *Edinburgh General view of the agriculture and rural economy of the county of Aberdeen*. Edinburgh.

Anon. (1797a). Review of the essential principles of the wealth of nations. *The Gentleman's Magazine*, *67*(July–December), 858–859.

Anon. (1797b). Review of the essential principles of the wealth of nations. *The Monthly Review; or Literary Journal Enlarged*, *24*(September–December), 28–33.

Boyd, M. W. W. (1991). *Over 600 years of schooling in the royal & ancient Burgh of Cupar-Fife*. Cupar: Library Publication.

Brougham, H. (1804). Review of an inquiry into the nature and origin of public wealth, and into the means and causes of its increase, by the earl of Lauderdale. *Edinburgh Review*, *4*(8), 343–377.

Delmas, B., & Demals, T. (1995). La physiocratie en Grande-Bretagne au début du XIXe siècle: Errances ou déshérence. *Economies et Sociétés*, *22–23*, 1–2117–147.

Dupont de Nemours, P. S. (1788). *Des administrations provinciales*. Lausanne: Mémoire Présenté au Roi.

Edgeworth, R. L. (1809). *Essays on professional education*. London: J. Johnson.

Faccarello, G. (1990). Le legs de Turgot: Aspects de l'économie politique sensualiste de Condorcet à Roederer. *Economies et Sociétés*, *13*, 67–107.

Foster, R. (1815). *An address to the nation on the relative importance of agriculture and manufactures and the means of advancing them both to the highest degree of improvement of which they are capable: Together with remarks on the doctrines lately advanced by Mr. Malthus on the nature of rent and the relation it has to the amount of national income*. Wakefield: R. Hurst.

Fraser, R. (1802). *Gleanings in Ireland; particularly respecting its agriculture, mines and fisheries.* London: G and E. Nicol.

Fraser, R. (1803). A Letter to Charles Abbot, Speaker [of the House of Commons].

Garnier, G. (1796). *Abrégé Elémentaire des Principes de L'Économie Politique.* Paris: Agasse.

Gehrke, C., & Kurz, H. D. (1995). Karl Marx on physiocracy. *European Journal of the History of Economic Thought, 2*(1), 53–90.

Hardcastle, M. S. (1881). *Life of John, Lord Campbell, Lord High Chancellor of Great Britain.* London: Murray.

Hirsch, L. (1952). A note on John Gray (1724–1811). *Papers of the Bibliographical Society of America, 46,* 275–276.

Hollander, S. (1992). On Malthus's physiocratic references. *History of Political Economy, 24*(2), 369–380.

Hollander, S. (1995). Malthus as a physiocrat: Surplus versus scarcity. *Economies et Sociétés* (22–23), 1–2, 79–116.

Horner, F. (1803). Review of Principes d'Economie Politique, by N.F. Canard. *Edinburgh Review, 1*(2), 431–450.

Jones, G. H., & Jones, V. (2004). *"Campbell, John, first Baron Campbell of St. Andrews (1779–1861)", Oxford Dictionary of National Biography.* Oxford: Oxford University Press.

Le Trosne, G. F. (1770). *Les effets de l'impôt indirect prouvés par les deux examples de la gabelle et du tabac.* Paris.

Lloyd, D. (2003). *Chemistry in St. Andrews.* University of St. Andrews.

Malthus, T. R. (1798). *An essay on the principle of population.* London: J. Johnson.

Lundberg, I. C. (1964). *Turgot's unknown translator. The réflexions and Adam Smith.* The Hague: Martinus Nijhof.

Malthus, T. R. (1803). *An essay on the principle of population* (2nd ed.). London: J. Johnson.

Malthus, T. R. (1983). *The Malthus library catalogue.* New York: Pergamon.

Martin, P. (2001). *Cupar: A short history and guide.*

Marx, K. H. (1969). *Theories of surplus value.* London: Lawrence and Wishart.

McCulloch, J. R. (1845). *The literature of political economy.* London: Longman, Brown, Green and Longmans.

Meek, R. L. ([1962] 1993). *The economics of physiocracy.* New York: Augustus M. Kelley.

Mortimer, T. (1801). *Lectures on the elements of commerce.* London: Longman and Rees.

Raven, J. (1991). The abolition of the English state lotteries. *Historical Journal, 34*(2), 371–389.

Ross, I. (1998). *On the wealth of nations: Contemporary responses to Adam Smith.* Bristol: Thoemmes Press.

Seligman, E. R. A. (1903). On some neglected British economists. *Economic Journal, 13*(51 and 52), 335–363, 511–535.

Smith, A. ([1776] 1904). *An inquiry into the nature and causes of the wealth of nations.* In: E. Canaan (Ed.). London: Methuen.

Spence, W. (1807). *Britain independent of commerce.* London: Cadell and Davies.

Spence, W. (1808). *Agriculture the source of the wealth of Britain.* London: Cadell and Davies.

Spengler, J. J. (1945). The physiocrats and Say's law of markets, Part 2. *Journal of Political Economy, 53*(3), 317–347.

Steenge, A. E., & Van den Berg, R. (2007). Transcribing the Tableau Économique: Input–output à la Quesnay. *Journal of the History of Economic Thought, 29*(3), 331–358.

Stewart, D. ([1855] 1968). Lectures on political economy. New York: Augustus M. Kelley.

Torrens, R. ([1808] 1984). The economists refuted, and other early economic writings. In: P. D. Groenewegen (Ed.), *Reprints of economic classics*, Series 2 No. 3. University of Sydney, Department of Economics.

Tribe, K. (1978). *Land, labour and economic discourse*. London: Routledge.

Van den Berg, R. (2010). The Spence–Mill dispute: Some thoughts inspired by 'input–output analysis à la Quesnay'. In: A. Prinz, G.-J. Hospers, & B. Bünger (Eds), *Squaring the circle: Essays in honour of A.E. Steenge*, Forschung und Wissenschaft, No. 26 (pp. 22–49). Münster: LIT Verlag.

Van den Berg, R., & Salvat, C. (2001). Scottish subtlety: André Morellet's comments on the wealth of nations. *European Journal for the History of Economic Thought*, *8*(2), 146–185.

Wakefield, D. (1799). *An inquiry into the truth of the two positions of the French Œconomists etc.* London: F. and C. Rivington.

Wakefield, D. (1804). *An essay upon political economy: An inquiry into the truth of the two positions of the French Œconomists*. London: F. C. and J. Rivington.

Wakefield, E. (1812). *An account of Ireland, statistical and political, 2 vols*. London: Longman, Hurst, Rees, Orme and Brown.

Winch, D. (1996). *Riches and poverty: An intellectual history of political economy in Britain, 1750–1834*. Cambridge: Cambridge University Press.

APPENDIX. WORKS BY JOHN GRAY

All of John Gray's works are in the form of pamphlets. Several were published anonymously and the ones that do mention an author have either 'John Gray' or 'John Gray LLD'. Because of this, there exists ambiguity in the attribution of some of the works below. The most reliable source for attribution is the 1813 catalogue of Cupar library (indicated below with the letter C) because it records amongst the works donated to this library upon Gray's death a collection of his own pamphlets (catalogue number 1437). Additional pamphlets attributed to 'John Gray' or 'John Gray LLD' are in the British Library (B) and the Goldsmith's library (G). Whenever a pamphlet is present in one of those two libraries the author to whom it is attributed in the relevant catalogue is given.

1768 *Reflections on inland navigation: And a new method proposed for executing the intended navigation betwixt the Forth and the Clyde*, etc., 48pp.
Author: J. Gray
Publisher: London: T. Cadell
Collections: G: Gray, John (1724–1811)

1772 *A comparative view of the public burdens of Great Britain and Ireland, with a proposal for putting both islands on an equality*, etc.
Author: Anonymous

Publisher: London: G. Robinson
Collections: G: Gray, John (1724–1811)
Second edition: Dublin, 1779

1774a *An essay concerning the establishment of a National Bank in Ireland*, 56pp.
Author: Anonymous
Publisher: London: G. Robinson.
Collections: C, G: Gray, John (1724–1811)

1774b *The right of the British Legislature to tax the American colonies vindicated: And the means of asserting that right proposed*
Author: Anonymous
Publisher: London: T. Becket.
Collections: G: Gray, John (1724–1811); B: 'Gray, John, ca. 1724–1777'
Second edition: [1775] sl, sn, nd.

1775 *Remarks on the new essay of the Pennsylvanian farmer; and on resolves and instructions prefixed to that essay.*
Author: 'By the Author of The Right of the British Legislature Vindicated'
Publisher: London: T. Becket
Collections: B: 'Gray, John, ca. 1724–1777'

1777 *Doctor Price's notions of the nature of Civil Liberty, shown to be contradictory to reason and scripture.*
Author: John Gray
Publisher: London: T. Becket
Collections: B: 'Gray, John, Political Writer'

1780 *A letter to the Earl of Nugent, relative to the establishment of a National Bank in Ireland*, 33pp.
Author: John Gray (p. 31)
Publisher: London: John Donaldson
Collections: C; G: Gray, John (1724–1811)

1785 *A plan for finally settling the Government of Ireland upon constitutional principles; and the chief cause of the unprosperous state of that country explained*, 79pp.
Author: Anonymous
Publisher: London: J. Stockdale
Collections: C; G: Gray, John (1724–1811); B: 'Gray, John, Political Writer'
Other edition: Dublin, 1785

1786 *The policy of the tax upon retailers considered; or A plea in favour of manufacturers*, 48pp.
Author: Anonymous
Publisher: London: T. Becket; G. and T. Wilkie.
Collections: C.; G: Gray, John (1724–1811); B: 'Gray, John, LL.D.'

1789a *Some reflections intended to promote the success of the Scotch Fishing company. (Included in: George Dempster A discourse containing a summary*

of the proceedings of the society for extending the fisheries and improving the sea coast of Great Britain, pp. 40–87).
Author: John Gray esq. of London
Publisher: London: Wilkie and Debrett.
Collections: B: 'Gray, John, Political Writer'

1789b *Discourse and reflections on the British fisheries, and thoughts on emigration from the highlands.*
Author: ?
Publisher: ?
Collections: C

1792 *An essay on the abolition, not only of the African slave trade, but of slavery in the British West Indies*, 48pp.
Author: Anonymous
Publisher: London: T. Becket
Collections: C.; G.: Gray, John (1724–1811)

1797 *The Essential Principles of the Wealth of Nations, illustrated, in opposition to some false doctrines of Dr. Adam Smith, and others*, 142pp.; appendix, 8pp.
Author: Anonymous
Publisher: London: T. Becket.
Collections: C.; G.: Gray, John, LL.D. (1696–1782)

1798 *A proposal for supplying London with bread, at an uniform price from one year to another, according to an annual assize*, 42pp.
Author: Anonymous
Publisher: London: T. Becket
Collections: C.; G.: Gray, John, LL.D.

1800 *Practical observations on the proposed Treaty of Union of the Legislatures of Great Britain and Ireland, etc.*, 104pp.
Author: John Gray LL.D.
Publisher: London: T. Becket, J. Wright and H. D. Symonds
Collections: C; B: 'Gray, John, LL.D.'

1802 *The income tax scrutinized, and some amendments proposed to render it more agreeable to the British Constitution*, 86pp.
Author: John Gray, LL.D.
Publisher: London: H. D. Symonds
Collections: G: Gray, John, LL.D.; B: 'Gray, John'
B edition: np, nd., 84pp.

GRANVILLE SHARP: A NEGLECTED ECONOMIST?

G. M. Ditchfield

One of the first pamphlets to which E. R. A. Seligman (1903, p. 338) refers in his study of neglected British economists is the short book (or long pamphlet) entitled *Sketches on Political Economy* (Anon., 1809a; hereafter, *Sketches*). For Seligman, the significance of the pamphlet was twofold. Since it was published nine years before the appearance of David Ricardo's *Principles of Political Economy* in 1817 it supported his argument that many of the ideas credited to Ricardo were in circulation well before the publication of his best-known work. Secondly, since there was no doubt as to its British authorship – its tone was unmistakably nationalistic and it was published by Longmans in London – it could be invoked as a potential witness for Seligman's contention that many nineteenth-century British economists were theoretically and conceptually more sophisticated than many of their continental counterparts, notably over the question of marginal utility.[1]

Perhaps because many publications in the eighteenth and early nineteenth-century Britain did not carry the name of an author (or authors), Seligman did not attach any special importance to the anonymous nature of the *Sketches*, nor did he offer any speculation as to its authorship. The question of attribution, however, is clearly an important one; knowledge of an author's identity, political opinions and position in society can be central to an understanding of that author's text; to paraphrase E. H. Carr, 'Study the economist before you study the theory'.[2] The question of the authorship of

English, Irish and Subversives Among the Dismal Scientists
Research in the History of Economic Thought and Methodology, Volume 28-B, 73–88

ISSN: 0743-4154/doi:10.1108/S0743-4154(2010)000028B006

the *Sketches* becomes all the more urgent because a small but significant number of academic authorities have identified it as the work of the anti-slavery campaigner and philanthropist Granville Sharp (1735–1813).[3] This identification has considerable implications for Sharp's career and reputation, as well as for the *Sketches* themselves and the intellectual context in which they were composed. This essay will argue, however, that the attribution of this work to Sharp is erroneous; that Sharp did not and could not have written the *Sketches* and that a far stronger case can be made for the ascription of the work to the Scottish political and economic writer Walter Thom (1770–1824).

I

It is not difficult to understand why the *Sketches* would be credited to Sharp. His death four years before the publication of Ricardo's *Principles* placed him within the period under discussion by Seligman. Sharp possessed an extremely wide range of interests and was a prolific writer on a remarkable variety of topics. By 1809 he was a prominent public figure and had produced more than 40 separate works, several of which had reached second or third editions. He had established a reputation as a controversialist and his *oeuvre* is certainly consistent with Seligman's generalisation that the 'greater part of the economic literature' between 1776 (the year of *The Wealth of Nations*) and 1817 consisted of 'pamphlets dealing with current practical problems' (Seligman, 1903, p. 336). Sharp had published on the conditions in West Africa, the illegality of the press-ganging of sailors, parliamentary reform, colonial law, frankpledge, a popular militia and public charities.

Above all, Sharp had attracted much public admiration for his campaigns against the slave trade, which he had conducted since the late 1760s, and for his denunciations in print of slaveholding in all its forms. He had been a founding member of the London Committee of the Society for the Abolition of the Slave Trade in 1787, and the abolition by Act of Parliament of the British slave trade 20 years later had conferred upon him considerable prestige. More specifically, he had been a leading promoter of the establishment of a colony for freed slaves in Sierra Leone, and he became one of the first directors of the company that managed it. In 1786, he published his *Regulations for the New Settlement of Sierra Leone* and followed it up in 1790 with a descriptive account of the colony. Undeterred by the early disasters that it experienced, he made personal financial contributions to its sustenance, and could claim vindication when Sierra Leone was made a crown colony in 1808. The previous year he had become one of the first directors of the African Institution.

It is true that Sharp did not research deeply many of the most pressing social and economic questions of the end of the eighteenth century. He did not produce statistical studies of population, nor did he attempt the detailed survey of the poor law, the subject of increasing debate in his later years, in the manner essayed, for example, by Sir Frederick Morton Eden in *The State of the Poor* (1797). Nor did he publish any work comparable to Patrick Colquhoun's analysis of the social structure of Britain. On the other hand, he was the author of a *Plan of a Public Charity* (1790), while his *Letter to a Committee of the Corporation of London appointed to enquire into the State of the London Workhouses* (1791) contained a proposal for a 'general asylum' for unemployed men, women and children who were unable to support themselves. At the same time, he advocated the construction of what he called a 'College of Industry' near London, with 20 or 30 acres of land, for the poor who wanted work. Schemes of this nature, together with his leading role in the promotion of Sierra Leone, qualify him for inclusion in the category of 'projector', in the eighteenth-century sense of the term.[4]

Furthermore, at least three of Sharp's obsessions linked directly to major politico-economic themes of the late eighteenth and early nineteenth centuries. In each instance, he espoused an explicit, and sometimes aggressive, point of view and contributed notable controversial tracts to the public debate. Firstly, during the 1770s he sympathised very strongly with the American colonies in their disputes with the British government. So strongly did he feel about the government's policy of coercion that he resigned from his post in the Ordnance Office and, in lieu of the salary thereby foregone, relied on the financial support of his brothers (see Lascelles, [1928] 1969, Ch. 5). His pro-American arguments in print stressed natural rights, the illegality, as he saw it, of the taxation of the colonies from London, and the idea that the use of force would lead inescapably to divine retribution (see, in particular, Sharp, 1774). But although, with the exception of taxation (and even here his concerns were predominantly moral), he did not give priority to economic arguments, his opinions were entirely consistent with colonial protests against restrictions upon their commerce. Sharp, at least by implication, was an opponent of protectionism.

Secondly, Sharp took a leading part in the promotion of one of the most important economic decisions of the period, namely the ending of the British slave trade, 1806–1807. As early as 1769, long before the emergence of the popular movement for abolition, he had denounced the slave trade and the institution of slavery itself with his *A Representation of the Injustice of Tolerating Slavery* (1769). It was impossible to discuss the slave trade without some consideration of its economic implications. Critics and defenders of the trade alike discussed the issue in economic as well as moral and political terms; the value to the British economy of the trade at the time of abolition was, and indeed remains, a contentious issue. The claim that, rather than an act of altruism, British abolition merely reflected the declining profitability of the trade, a claim associated particularly with Eric Williams (1944), has been challenged in subsequent work by Roger Anstey (1975), Seymour Drescher (1977) and Howard Temperley (1977), amongst others. At the time, defenders of the trade stressed the damaging effects, as they saw them, of abolition upon the principal British slave ports – London, Liverpool, Bristol and Glasgow. That one of the most high-profile critics of the slave trade should pen a treatise on political economy would not, of itself, have appeared surprising.

Thirdly, Sharp, in common with William Wilberforce and many other abolitionists, belonged to the Evangelical tendency within the Church of England. By the time of the publication of the *Sketches*, evangelicalism within the Church, and outside it, had advanced considerably in terms of numbers and influence. Roger Anstey (1975, Chs. 7 and 8), indeed, interpreted abolition primarily as a triumph for the evangelical values of Christian benevolence and redemption for national (as well as personal) sins, manifest in the active promotion of 'vital' religion and individual conversion. And, as Boyd Hilton (1986) has convincingly demonstrated, evangelical religion in the early nineteenth century left a decisive imprint upon the prevailing economic, as well as moral and political, theory, offering, in Professor Hilton's words, a 'model of free-trade individualism' other than that provided by classical economics (1986, p. viii). Although he did not reside there, Sharp was associated with the Clapham Sect, and was personally acquainted with many of its members. One of them, the banker and MP Henry Thornton, was a noted economic thinker and author (in 1802) of a tract on paper credit (Thornton, 1802); he is included among the economists whose papers are listed by R. P. Sturges (1975, pp. 116–117). Sharp, then, kept company with evangelical economic thinkers, and was seen to do so.

Circumstantial evidence of this nature helps to explain why a possible attribution of the *Sketches* to Sharp could have been made.

II

Circumstantial evidence alone, however, must remain inconclusive, and there are sound reasons for non-attribution of this work to Sharp. In the first place, the *Sketches* are not included in the 61 separate works of Sharp listed in Prince Hoare's biography (1828, pp. 341–354), or in the 50 works enumerated by E. C. P. Lascelles ([1928] 1969, pp. 139–143) in his sympathetic study of Sharp and slavery. Moreover, a work such as the *Sketches* was not one that those who knew Sharp would have expected him to write. He was not regarded as an economic thinker by those of his contemporaries who were. Significantly, perhaps, the one surviving letter to Sharp from Richard Price, economist, statistician and authority on reversionary payments as well as a Dissenting minister, did not concern an economic matter (Letter of 30 March 1780, in Thomas & Peach, 1991, pp. 59–60). Price expressed admiration for Sharp because of his pro-Americanism and his work for parliamentary reform; both were members of the Society for Constitutional Information. But, as a measure of the differences between their respective priorities, Price – perhaps because of ill health and advancing age – declined to become a committee member of the British anti-slavery society. And Sharp's work made very little impression upon Jeremy Bentham, and none upon Ricardo.

Sharp, in fact, did not take a detailed, statistical, interest in the financial aspects of the British slave trade. His attacks on the trade depended much more upon moral, religious and legal considerations than upon economic arguments. He saw British abolition as the working of divine providence in human affairs and insisted repeatedly that the Bible condemned slavery. His 'Short Sketch' of temporary regulations for the settlement of Sierra Leone was most concerned with public order (sustained by frankpledge), free labour, protection for strangers and the provision of chaplains. Even the section on 'Public Revenue' was driven by moral considerations, with a proposal for a tax on 'pride and indulgence', while a lengthy appendix set out forms of prayer to be used in religious worship in the new colony (Sharp, 1788, pp. 54–88, and 129–178). On the eve of abolition, he published his 20-page pamphlet '*The System of Colonial Law*' *Compared with the Eternal Laws of God* (Sharp, 1807b), denouncing the West India planters' petition to the House of Lords protesting against abolition. But of that petition's 13 paragraphs, Sharp chose to attack only one, that which dealt with the claim that abolition would violate 'the system of colonial law'. Taking the contrary view, he declared that the 'system of colonial law' itself violated the 'whole system of English law' and the law of God (1807b, p. 4).

He gave pride of place to this argument over the need to refute arguments from defenders of the slave trade that abolition would damage the British economy. In doing so, he revealed his legal experience in London, acquired in securing the freedom of former slaves from attempts at recapture by their owners, and the humanitarianism inspired by his evangelical Christianity. Hence the obituary of Sharp in the *Gentleman's Magazine* described him as 'this venerable Philanthropist' (Anon., 1813a, p. 89), and, quite reasonably, made no mention of any contribution to economic theory.

'*The System of Colonial Law*' was far more representative of Sharp's work than were the *Sketches*, published only two years later. We do not find that Sharp ever concerned himself with the major economic issues of his time. He did not write about population, the national debt, the question of bullion, paper currency or agricultural rents. He did not analyse the relationship between value and utility, as the *Sketches* did. He did not dwell on the questions of profit, nor did he seek to evolve a theory of wages or a theory of rent. There is no evidence that he took any serious interest in the work of James Mill, to whom the *Sketches* were a response. He was neither a protectionist nor a critic of commerce, while the author of the *Sketches* inclined in both directions, a point dealt with below. Sharp, in fact, was an activist rather than a theorist. Passing judgment on the changing climate of opinion whereby the slave trade gradually came to be perceived as intolerable by the overwhelming majority of British public opinion, Leslie Stephen in *The English Utilitarians* (1900, Vol. 1, p. 115) noted that 'the honour of the first victory in the practical application must be given to Granville Sharp'. The qualification is significant, as is the way in which Sharp features far more prominently in Seymour Drescher's *Capitalism and Antislavery* (1986), which deals with the mobilisation of public opinion against the slave trade, than in Drescher's *Econocide* (1977), which deals primarily with the economics of British abolition in 1806–1807 and makes a decisive attack on the 'decline' theory.[5]

Sharp's main concern – one might even say his obsession – during the last ten years of his life was not economic theory but biblical scholarship. From 1806–1807, his known publications were exclusively devoted to theological, usually specifically to biblical, subjects. The fulfilment of prophecy, the Hebrew of the Old Testament, the precise etymology of key words in the Greek New Testament, and the promotion of evangelical Christianity had been among his interests from youth; from the time of the abolition of the slave trade they came to dominate his thinking. In 1804, he became the first chairman of the British and Foreign Bible Society, under the presidency of Lord Teignmouth; he assisted in the foundation of the Society for the

Conversion of the Jews in 1808, and his opposition to Catholic Emancipation led him to take the chair of the Protestant Union immediately before his death in 1813. He reserved much energy for publications that attacked the Unitarian perception of the pure humanity of Christ, a process begun with his *Remarks on the Uses of the Definite Article in the Greek Text of the New Testament* (Sharp, 1798). Despite his earlier collaboration with Unitarians such as John Jebb in the interests of parliamentary reform,[6] he believed strongly in the need to reinforce orthodox Trinitarian doctrine against the assertions of Socinianism. In 1806, he published *A Dissertation on the Supreme Divine Dignity of the Messiah*. He provoked controversy on the subject (see, for example, Anon., 1810). So apparently arcane were some of his theological interests that Sir James Stephen, writing in 1849, felt obliged to offer an explanation:

> [In old age] Granville Sharp was passing into a state which, in a nature less active and benevolent than his, would have been nothing better than dotage. In him it assumed the form of a delirium, so calm, so busy, and giving birth to whims so kind-hearted, as often to remind his young associate of Isaac Walton's saying, that the very dreams of a good man are acceptable to God. To illustrate by examples the state of a mind thus hovering on the confines of wisdom and fatuity, may perhaps suggest the suspicion that the old man's infirmities were contagious. (Stephen, 1849, Vol. 2, p. 319)

Stephen (1789–1859) was aware of Sharp's work through his career as an attorney and counsel to the colonial under-secretary. He was closely associated with the Clapham Sect and married the daughter of John Venn (1759–1813), Rector of Clapham. His father (also named James; 1758–1832) was a fellow anti-slavery campaigner with Wilberforce, whose widowed sister he married. In his character sketch of Sharp, therefore, Stephen was writing from personal knowledge, and possibly from direct personal acquaintance.

Sharp's eccentricities included a conviction that the iniquities of Babylon could be identified with those of Rome, and that the four beasts described in the Book of Daniel had a literal, and immediately relevant, significance (see Lascelles, [1928] 1969, Ch. 18). In 1806, he famously lectured a bewildered Charles James Fox, briefly serving as Foreign Secretary, on the state of Europe by invoking the 'Little Horn' (Daniel, Ch. 8) and maintaining that toleration of slavery placed Britain among the 'horns of the Beast' (Stephen, 1849, Vol. 2, pp. 320–321; Anstey, 1975, p. 161). When Benjamin Rush wrote to Sharp from Philadelphia on 20 June 1809, it was to thank Sharp for a copy of his book *The Case of Saul* (1807a; see Woods, 1967, pp. 36–37). James Stephen (1849, Vol. 2, p. 321) concluded that 'As the end drew nearer, he [Sharp] became less and less able of seizing the distinction between the prophecies and the newspapers'. This was hardly the mentality of a potential author of a sober, materialistic and decidedly down-to-earth exposition upon political economy. And although the question of literary style is necessarily problematical, involving subjective considerations, and although the entry on Sharp in the *Biographical Dictionary of British Radicals* exaggerates when it describes his prose style as 'practically unreadable', and observes that his success owed more to his 'forceful personality' than to his published work, it nonetheless had a point (Cooper, 1979, p. 436). Sharp's legal experience is evident throughout his work; he was apt to descend into jargon; and his sometimes convoluted sentence construction left an impression of turgidity. He was far from being an accessible writer and his manner of expressing himself in print contrasts markedly with the relative lucidity of the *Sketches*.

III

It is much easier to make a convincing case for Sharp's non-authorship of the *Sketches* than to make a positive identification of the real author. There are, however, strong indications that it was the work of Walter Thom. As with Sharp, we may begin by citing contemporary opinion. In 1811, Thom published, under his own name, a small octavo *History of Aberdeen*, in two volumes and on the title page of the first volume he was described as 'Author of *Sketches on Political Economy* ....' When this book was reviewed in the *Scots Magazine* and in the *Monthly Review*, the full title was given, together with the attribution of the *Sketches* to Thom, as if that authorship was an acknowledged fact (Anon., 1812, 1813b). Towards the end of its review, the *Monthly Review*, indeed, specifically referred to the *Sketches* as Thom's work and reminded its readers that it had reviewed that work in an earlier number (Anon., 1809b). In so doing, it rightly pointed to an intellectual consistency between the *History of Aberdeen* and the *Sketches* and had no doubt that the two works were the productions of the same author. The ascription of the *Sketches* to Thom was not challenged at the time, when the subject of the work was still topical.

Thom ended his chapter in the *History of Aberdeen* on the city's 'Manufactures–Commerce – Banks – Canal' with a resoundingly patriotic declaration:

> The resources of a great nation are founded on her agriculture and internal industry, and not on her foreign relations, which are liable to every change that may result from accident, or the caprice of invidious and unfriendly powers. To have said only a few years ago, that Britain could have defied the united efforts of all Europe to crush

> her – and, although deprived of the commerce of the continent – could still maintain her greatness and grandeur, would have been deemed the hallucination of a theorist; yet such a state of things has nearly occurred, and we still *exist* – not as a second-rate power, but – as a great, an opulent, and independent nation! (Thom, 1811a, Vol. 2, pp. 167–168)

Admittedly, Thom wrote at the height of the Napoleonic War and the consequent strains imposed on British overseas trade by the Continental System, and his utterance owed something to wartime defiance and anti-French sentiment. He appealed, nonetheless, to a more general series of principles, arguing strongly that agriculture, fishery and manufacture formed the true strength of a nation. These opinions corresponded, to a considerable extent, to the political economy of Physiocratic anti-commercialism that had been propounded in England by several authors immediately before Thom wrote.

Among them was John Gray (1724–1811), whom Seligman (1903, pp. 336–337) located firmly within the English Physiocratic tradition. Gray's *Essential Principles of the Wealth of Nations* ([Gray], 1797, p. 130) claimed that Britain had concentrated excessively upon manufactures and commerce, and insufficiently upon agriculture.[7,8] Perhaps better-known as an advocate of Physiocratic ideas was William Spence, author of *Britain Independent of Commerce* (1807), who, says Seligman (1903, p. 337), sought to 'recall the British public to the true path of honour and riches', which led to the soil rather than to commerce and industry. The *Sketches* adopted similar arguments, arguing that 'Commerce dissipates the resources of a country, and should be gradually restrained by the abandonment of external connections' (Anon., 1809a, p. 14). Autarchic in substance and in tone, it urged that increased agricultural production, so important to national survival, could be achieved only by the enlargement of farms and by the subordination of 'the efforts of several individuals' to 'the superintendence of one' (1809a, p. 8). The *Monthly Review* commented unfavourably upon the similarity between the *Sketches* and Spence's book and caustically dismissed the author's 'prejudices against commerce' (Anon., 1809b, p. 447). Seligman (1903, p. 339) regarded the *Sketches* as the last attempt to promote Physiocratic doctrines in Britain. The affinity between Thom's *History of Aberdeen* and the *Sketches* is indeed considerable, but to take the question further, we need a brief exploration of Thom's career.

We know regrettably little about Thom's upbringing and education. However, a significant clue may be found in the obituary of him printed by the *Aberdeen Journal* (on 30 June 1824):

> He was a native of Bervie, where he was a Manufacturer for some time; but not succeeding in this line of business, he repaired to Aberdeen to reside, in order that he might have greater facilities from Libraries of pursuing his literary avocations.

The obituary added that Thom subsequently moved to Edinburgh, 'as he had now adopted Literature as a profession' and then settled in Dublin, where he became editor and joint manager of the *Dublin Journal*. There is not much evidence that his later business career was significantly more successful than its predecessor, but his son Alexander Thom, who was born in 1810 and accompanied his father to Dublin 12 years later, became a distinguished printer and publisher. He began his career in conjunction with his father, who evidently continued to entertain commercial as well as literary ambitions (Falkiner & Benson, 2004).

Walter Thom has been credited with several other publications that support the possibility of his authorship of the *Sketches* and indicate that he had acquired some reputation as an economic writer. He contributed to Sir John Sinclair's *Statistical Account of Scotland* (1797), and the separately published *Sketch of the Second Chapter of the General Report regarding the Agricultural and Political State of Scotland ... by W.T., etc.* (1811b) has been authoritatively attributed to him.[9] In 1819, the publication of the third volume of William Shaw Mason's *Statistical Account of Ireland* (1814–1819) established Thom as a contributor to the introductory material of its first volume. In the preface to volume three, Mason wrote:

> Walter Thom, Esq. Author of the History of Aberdeen, and a contributor to the Edinburgh Encyclopaedia, and to Sir John Sinclair's great work, 'The general Report of Scotland', has enriched the first volume with a Synoptical View of the Principles of Political Economy – a branch of science, a correct and practical acquaintance with which, can only be attained through the medium of Statistics. (Mason, 1814–1819, Vol. 3, p. xii)

Thom's short outline of these principles, beginning with the primacy of agriculture, were published without his name (Mason, 1814–1819, Vol. 1, p. xvii–xxxi), but Mason obviously placed a high value on an introductory essay by someone of Thom's reputation before embarking on his own detailed survey of the parishes of Ireland which formed the substance of his volumes.

Equally revealing, perhaps, are the indications that Thom wrote the 32 page pamphlet entitled *A Synopsis of the Science of Political Economy*, published in Dublin – the scene of Thom's residence – in 1814.[10] Although much shorter than the *Sketches*, its general line of argument is quite consistent with the former work, and by 1814 it might be that Thom was sufficiently well known for his name to be seen by his publisher (J. Cumming) as advantageous for the work's success. Thom, however, was not the author of a work with a title similar, although not identical, to that which forms the subject of this essay, namely 'Sketches of political economy', by Anthony Dunlop (1818).[11]

This latter piece appeared in *The Pamphleteer* in 1818. Although not specifically a riposte to the *Sketches on Political Economy* (Anon., 1809a), it differed entirely in its argument; Dunlop was an advocate of free trade and acknowledged his debt to Adam Smith.

The other publication which has, without controversy, been deemed the work of Thom, *Pedestrianism* (1813), adds little to the question, except to demonstrate that Thom, while falling well short of Granville Sharp's literary versatility, had a fairly wide range of interests. But Thom has never been taken seriously as an economist by later scholars; he does not feature, for example, in Henry Higgs' *The Physiocrats* (1897) nor in Higgs's edition of *Palgrave's Dictionary* (1923–26), nor in the *New Palgrave* (Eatwell, Milgate & Newman, 1987; Durlauf & Blume, 2008). Neither Thom nor the *Sketches* has been discussed by recent leading historians who specialise in the study of economic thought in early nineteenth-century Britain: for example, Thom is not included in Sturges' Economists' Papers (1975), nor included for consideration in Berg (1980), Collini, Winch, and Burrow (1983) or Thompson (1984). Nonetheless, the likelihood is that the *Monthly Review* was correct in its identification of Thom as the author of the *Sketches*, and we may conclude with some confidence that it was amongst his earliest works.

IV

The solution to the question of attribution offered by this essay has removed at least one reason for the neglect of the *Sketches* as a contribution to economic theory. Anonymity tends by its very nature to be solitary. A work whose author remains unidentified may be of major significance, witness the 'Letters of Junius', of which the authorship remains a matter of conjecture (see Cannon, 1978, appendix 7). Such a work, however, lacks the intellectual hinterland that accompanies a treatise which can be placed conclusively within the *oeuvre* of a particular writer. Such has been the fate of the *Sketches*. The attribution to Walter Thom means that Thom himself merits, and may indeed receive, more serious consideration than he has hitherto been accorded. However, the significance of *Sketches* and the extent to which it remains a 'neglected' work will not depend only on the issue of Thom's authorship. It is clear that the work is a valuable prop to Seligman's thesis and that its embodiment of the anti-Ricardian, anti-classical tradition suited his own opinions. Crucial to its future recognition will be the acceptance or non-acceptance by historians of the economic thought of

Seligman's general argument that many ideas associated with Ricardo and his successors in Britain and continental Europe had been propounded and discussed well before the publication of Ricardo's *Principles* in 1817. It will depend, too, on the durability of the current fashion whereby historians eschew a 'great names' approach to the past, and turn their attention to the lesser-known, and less successful, without at the same time embracing a 'whiggish' search for origins and an anxiety to unearth unrepresentative evidence for the values of the present in previous eras.

Where, then, does this leave Granville Sharp? He has indeed been 'neglected' as an economist for the very good reason that he does not merit that designation. He was never perceived as such by his contemporaries, and was not a theoretical writer in the sense in which Adam Smith, Richard Price – and Edmund Burke or Francis Place – clearly were.[12] He cannot be placed easily into any compartment except that of an Evangelical activist with a moral imperative and a campaigning spirit. As Hilton and other historians have shown, Christianity, including Evangelical Christianity, has made important contributions to economic theory. Sharp, however, applied his religious values to politics, morality, ethics and theological polemic, not to economics. But if neglect of Sharp as an economist is justified, his relative neglect, especially in biographical terms, as philanthropist and public campaigner, is much more surprising. To be sure, recent historians of anti-slavery have accorded him a measure of recognition, but even the enhanced interest in the slave trade prompted by the bicentenary in 2007 of British abolition has not led to a biography of Sharp to supersede that of Lascelles, which was first published in 1928. Moreover, there is a substantial Sharp archive at Gloucestershire Record Office and, since like many campaigners he was an energetic letter writer, there is no shortage of his correspondence in the papers of many of his fellow campaigners and leading politicians of his day. It does Sharp's reputation no justice to regard him as the author of the *Sketches*, which he certainly was not, nor to judge his work by the standards which might be reasonably applied to that of political economists. His claim to the respect of posterity is a serious one, but it rests upon entirely different foundations.

NOTES

1. Seligman (1903, p. 535): 'It will be seen that Great Britain is the real mother, not only of classical political economy, but also of that series of newer ideas which is at the present time slowly transforming the face of economic science'.

2. Carr (1961, p. 17): 'Study the historian before you begin to study the facts'.
3. These authorities include Goldsmiths'-Kress Library of Economic Literature, no. 19781; the National Library of Australia; Edinburgh University Library and the National Library of Scotland. Other copyright libraries in Britain, including the British Library and Cambridge University Library, do not have a copy of the *Sketches*, and I have not been able to trace a copy either in the Bodleian Library or the National Library of Wales.
4. Samuel Johnson (1755) gives two definitions of 'projector': 'one who forms schemes or designs' and 'one who forms wild impracticable schemes'. The latter definition probably reflects Johnson's Tory suspicion of Whig commercial innovations; the former could well be said to include Sharp.
5. Compare Drescher (1986, Chs. 2 and 3), where Sharp's role is discussed fully, with Drescher (1977), where Sharp is mentioned only twice.
6. For Sharp's friendship and co-operation with Jebb in the Society for Constitutional Information during the early 1780s, see Page (2003, pp. 185–190).
7. The *Scots Magazine* review (Anon., 1812) is no more than a detailed summary of the contents of Thom's book; the Monthly Review (Anon., 1813b) provides a critical assessment of it.
8. Like the *Sketches* (Anon., 1809a), *Essential Principles of the Wealth of Nations* (Gray, 1797) appeared anonymously, although its accreditation to Gray has not been disputed. For more information, see the essay on Gray in this volume.
9. The attribution to Thom is made, *inter alia*, by the British Library catalogue.
10. The attribution comes from the National Library of Australia, citing Goldsmiths'-Kress Library of Economic Literature, no. 20897. The *Synopsis* is not in the British Library.
11. Dunlop's *Sketches* (1818) is in the British Library.
12. The papers of Burke, Place and Pitt's secretary to the treasury, George Rose, are included in Sturges, *Economists' Papers* (1975); those of Sharp, significantly and appropriately, are not.

ACKNOWLEDGMENT

The author is grateful to Professor Noel Thompson for his helpful comments on this essay.

REFERENCES

Anon. (1809a). *Sketches on political economy illustrative of the interests of Great Britain; Intended as a reply to Mr. Mill's pamphlet commerce defended, with an exposition of some of the leading tenets of the economists*. London: Longman, Hurst, Rees, and Orme.

Anon. (1809b). Politics. *Monthly Review (London)*, *59*(August), 446–447.

Anon. (1810). A letter to Granville Sharp, Esq., respecting his remarks on the two last petitions in the Lord's Prayer, from a country clergyman. *Monthly Review (London)*, *62*(August), 432.

Anon. (1812). Scottish review. *Scots Magazine and Edinburgh Literary Miscellany*, *74*(March), 207–213.
Anon. (1813a). Memoirs of Granville Sharp, esquire. *Gentleman's Magazine (London)*, *83*(July), 89–90.
Anon. (1813b). Review of the history of Aberdeen by W. Thom. *Monthly Review (London)*, *70*(February), 205–208.
Anstey, R. (1975). *The Atlantic slave trade and British abolition, 1760–1810*. London: Macmillan.
Berg, M. (1980). *The machinery question and the making of political economy 1815–1848*. Cambridge: Cambridge University Press.
Cannon, J. (Ed.) (1978). *The letters of Junius*. Oxford: Oxford University Press.
Carr, E. H. (1961). *What is history?* London: Penguin.
Collini, S., Winch, D., & Burrow, J. (1983). *That noble science of politics: A study in nineteenth-century intellectual history*. Cambridge: Cambridge University Press.
Cooper, R. A. (1979). Granville Sharp. In: J. O. Baylen & N. J. Gossman (Eds), *A biographical dictionary of modern British radicals* (Vol. I, pp. 1770–1830). Sussex: Harvester Press.
Drescher, S. (1977). *Econocide: British slavery in the era of abolition*. Pittsburgh: University of Pittsburgh Press.
Drescher, S. (1986). *Capitalism and antislavery: British mobilization in comparative perspective*. Oxford: Oxford University Press.
Dunlop, A. (1818). Sketches on political economy. *The Pamphleteer*, *9*, 403–441.
Durlauf, S., & Blume, L. (2008). 2nd ed. *The new Palgrave dictionary of economics* (Vol. 8). New York: Palgrave Macmillan.
Eatwell, J., Milgate, M., & Newman, P. (Eds). (1987). *The new Palgrave dictionary of economics* (Vol. 4). London: Macmillan.
Eden, F. M., Sir. (1797). *The state of the poor: Or, an history of the labouring classes in England from the conquest to the present period*. London: J. Davis.
Falkiner, C. L., & Benson, C. J. (2004). *'Thom, Alexander (1801–1879)', Oxford dictionary of national biography*. Oxford: Oxford University Press.
Gray, J. (1797). *The essential principles of the wealth of nations, illustrated, in opposition to some false doctrines of Dr. Adam Smith, and others*. London: T. Becket.
Higgs, H. (1897). *The physiocrats: Six lectures on the Économistes of the 18th century*. London: Macmillan.
Higgs, H. (1923–1926). *Palgraves' dictionary of political economy* (Vol. 3). London: Macmillan.
Hilton, B. (1986). *The age of atonement: The influence of evangelicalism on social and economic thought, 1785–1865*. Oxford: Oxford University Press.
Hoare, P. (1828). *Memoirs of Granville Sharp esq.: Composed from his own manuscripts, and other authentic documents in the possession of his family and of the African Institution* (2nd ed.). London: H. Colburn.
Johnson, S. (1755). *A dictionary of the English language: In which the words are deduced from their originals and illustrated in their different significations by examples from the best writers*. London: W. Strahan.
Lascelles, E. C. P. ([1928] 1969). *Granville sharp and the freedom of the slaves in England*. New York: Negro Universities Press.
Mason, W. S. (1814–1819). *A statistical account or parochial survey of Ireland: Drawn up from the Communications of the Clergy*. Dublin: J. Cummins.
Page, A. (2003). *John Jebb and the enlightenment origins of British Radicalism*. Westport, CT: Greenwood.

Ricardo, D. (1817). *On the principles of political economy and taxation.* London: John Murray.

Seligman, E. R. A. (1903). On some neglected British economists. *Economic Journal, 13*(51 and 52), 335–363 and 511–535.

Sharp, G. (1769). *A representation of the injustice and dangerous tendency of tolerating slavery: Or of admitting the least claim of private property in the persons of men, in England.* London: Benjamin White and Robert Horsfield.

Sharp, G. (1774). *A declaration of the people's natural right to a share in the legislature; against the attempts to tax America, and to make laws for her against her consent.* London: B. White.

Sharp, G. (1788). *A short sketch of temporary regulations (until better shall be proposed) for the intended settlement on the grain coast of Africa, near Sierra Leona* (3rd ed.). London: H. Baldwin.

Sharp, G. (1790). *Plan of a public charity.* London.

Sharp, G. (1791). Letter to a Committee of the Corporation of London appointed to enquire into the State of the London Workhouses, London.

Sharp, G. (1798). *Remarks on the uses of the definite article in the Greek text of the New Testament: Containing many new proofs of the divinity of Christ, from passages which are wrongly translated in the common English version, remarks on the uses of the definite article in the Greek text of the New Testament: Containing many new proofs of the divinity of Christ, from Passages which are wrongly Translated in the Common English Version,* Durham, Pennington.

Sharp, G. (1806). *A dissertation on the supreme divine dignity of the messiah: In reply to a tract.* London: J. Edwards.

Sharp, G. (1807a). *The case of Saul, showing that his possession was a real spiritual disorder.* London: W. Calvert.

Sharp, G. (1807b). *'The system of colonial law' compared with the eternal laws of God and with the indispensable principles of the English constitution.* London: Richard Edwards.

Sinclair, J., Sir. (1797). *The statistical account of Scotland, drawn up from the communications of the ministers of the different parishes.* Edinburgh: William Creech.

Spence, W. (1807). *Britain independent of commerce: Or, proofs, deduced from an investigation into the true causes of the wealth of nations, that our riches, prosperity, and power, are derived from resources inherent in ourselves, and would not be affected, even though our commerce were annihilated.* London: T. Cadell and W. Davies.

Stephen, J., Sir. (1849). *Essays in ecclesiastical biography* (Vol. 2). London: Longman, Brown, Green and Longmans.

Stephen, L. (1990). *The English Utilitarians.* Vol. 3. London: Duckworth & Co.

Sturges, R. P. (1975). *Economists' papers 1750–1950. A guide to archive and other manuscript sources for the history of British and Irish economic thought.* London: Macmillan.

Temperley, H. (1977). Capitalism, slavery and ideology. *Past and Present* (75), 94–118.

Thom, W. (1811a). *The history of Aberdeen, containing an account of the rise, progress and extension of the city, from a remote period to the present day* (Vol. 2). Aberdeen: D. Chalmers.

Thom, W. (1811b). *Sketch of the second chapter of the general report regarding the agricultural and political state of Scotland, Aberdeen.* Aberdeen: D. Chalmers & Co.

Thom, W. (1813). *Pedestrianism; or, an account of the performances of celebrated pedestrians during the last and present century.* Aberdeen: D. Chalmers.

Thom, W. (1814). *A synopsis of the science of political economy*. Dublin: J. Cumming.

Thomas, D. O., & Peach, W. B. (Eds). (1991). *The correspondence of Richard Price, Vol. 2: March 1778–February 1786*. Durham, NC: Duke University Press.

Thompson, N. W. (1984). *The people's science: The popular political economy of exploitation and crisis, 1816–34*. Cambridge: Cambridge University Press.

Thornton, H. (1802). *An enquiry into the nature and effects of the paper credit of Great Britain*. London: J. Hatchard.

Williams, E. E. (1944). *Capitalism and slavery*. Chapel Hill: University of North Carolina Press.

Winch, D. (1996). *Riches and poverty. An intellectual history of political economy in Britain 1750–1834*. Cambridge: Cambridge University Press.

Woods, J. A. (1967). The correspondence of Benjamin rush and Granville sharp 1773–1809. *Journal of American Studies*, *1*(1), 1–38.

ROBERT TORRENS AS A 'NEGLECTED ECONOMIST'

Giancarlo de Vivo

E. R. A. Seligman's 1903 article on 'Some neglected British economists' has had a great influence on authors who have dealt with the development of British (and not only British) economic thought and doctrine. Following that article, a whole stream of contributions over decades have tried to identify important authors, neglected because they allegedly moved in a direction contrary to the prevailing orthodoxy. This literature has in particular had the aim of unearthing precursors of marginalism who would have been crushed by the 'Ricardian orthodoxy'. It must however be noticed that in this anti-Ricardianism the literature inspired by Seligman went well beyond Seligman's own position. Although traces (or more than traces) of a position critical of Ricardo can be found in Seligman, it was only in authors who came after him, deriving their inspiration from his 1903 article, that the anti-Ricardian point is fully spelled out (as an example see Gordon, 1967).

Seligman targeted the treatment Torrens had recently received from Palgrave's *Dictionary* as proof of neglect ('only five lines'). An idea of Seligman's success can be gathered from the fact that five years after the appearance of his article, in 1908, Palgrave, issuing an Appendix to his *Dictionary*, wrote in the Preface:[1]

> an effort has been made to chronicle the work of the less known Economists of this country who laboured during the days when the teaching of Ricardo and James and John Stuart Mill was supreme, and who have been, in some instances, but imperfectly recognised, owing to the fact that their opinions were not in harmony with the orthodox

English, Irish and Subversives Among the Dismal Scientists
Research in the History of Economic Thought and Methodology, Volume 28-B, 89–110

ISSN: 0743-4154/doi:10.1108/S0743-4154(2010)000028B007

> teaching of the day. In arranging these I have had the assistance of Professor E.R.A. Seligman's papers 'On Some Neglected British Economists' in the *Economic Journal*, London, 1903. Such scattered notices are almost the only recognition that many of these writers have received. Those who are interested in Economics have much for which to thank Professor Seligman. There is much work of the same class to be done. (Palgrave, 1908, p. 694)[2]

Indeed for Torrens, as for most of the other economists on whose behalf Seligman had complained of 'neglect' by the dictionary, Palgrave felt bound to add a supplementary entry in the appendix, longer than the original one, basically made with extracts from Seligman's article. Another important (but much later) vehicle of Seligman's influence was Schumpeter, who accepted his judgement on the 'neglected economists' *in toto*, and completely deferred to what Seligman had written on those authors, whom he often only knew at second hand.

According to Seligman, Robert Torrens (together with John Craig) was the main 'neglected economist' among Ricardo's contemporaries. We may notice that although Torrens was certainly neglected and virtually ignored at the time Seligman came to write his article, this had not always been the case. Indeed, the question of Torrens's status as a 'neglected economist' is to be approached with some caution, because his position is not little different from that of many other economists discussed by Seligman, such as M. Longfield or W. F. Lloyd, whose work seems to have really been largely ignored in their lifetime[3] and for quite some time afterwards, being basically rescued from oblivion by Seligman.

Although Torrens never achieved a position as eminent as that of other economists who were more or less his contemporaries, like Malthus and Ricardo,[4] it would be wrong to say that in his lifetime he was 'neglected' (see Fetter, 1965a, pp. 137–138). Indeed, he was made a Fellow of the Royal Society in December 1818 (at age 38); three years later, in 1821, he took the chair at no less an occasion than the founding meeting (attended by Malthus, Ricardo and James Mill among others) of the Political Economy Club, the first economic society ever established, of which he was a very active and influential member for 30 years (he resigned in 1851 on grounds of ill health).[5] Nor could it be argued that his economic thought was at the time neglected, both from a theoretical and – even more – from a policy point of view. He was one of the leading members of the 'Currency School' of monetary thought, which triumphed with the 1844 Act (also known as 'Peel's Act')[6] redesigning the British monetary and credit system, basically ruling it until the first World War. Indeed, it was in Torrens's (1837) *Letter to Lord Melbourne on the Causes of the Recent Derangement in the Money*

Market, and on Bank Reform, that the proposal for the division of the Bank of England into an Issue and a Banking Department, the cornerstone of Peel's 1844 reform, was first put forward in print.[7] It could be affirmed that Torrens was one of the fathers of what F. W. Fetter has called 'British Monetary Orthodoxy'.[8] As for recognition of Torrens in public life, not only was he repeatedly returned as MP, but following his contributions to the colonisation debates of the late 1820s and 1830s, in which he basically followed in Edward Gibbon Wakefield's footsteps,[9] he was appointed (1835) Chairman of the Colonization Commission for South Australia, the body to which the task had been entrusted of carrying into execution the Act passed in August 1834, to establish the new province of South Australia. This Commission was superseded in 1840 by the Colonial Land and Emigration Commission, of which Torrens was also the chairman, thus becoming – even though briefly – 'the chief executive officer of the British Empire' (Moore, 2004, p. 56). The fact that in 1841 he was sacked from that body by the then Colonial Secretary Lord John Russell, on charges of misconduct,[10] and that the colony of South Australia had gone bankrupt shortly before, certainly did not do much good to Torrens's standing as an upholder of 'self-supporting colonization', and in general as a public man, but nonetheless a river and a lake in South Australia were and are still named after him. It can also be added that in 1851 he was given a Civil List pension of £200 *per annum* (about £15,000 at today's prices) 'in consideration of his valuable contributions to the Science of Political Economy' (Fetter, 1965b, p. 182n) – something hardly consistent with the status of a 'neglected economist'.

All this however is not meant to argue that Seligman's definition of Torrens in 1903 as a 'neglected economist' was unwarranted, but to stress that it is important to see this question in historical perspective: account must be taken of the changes that Torrens's standing as an economist underwent over time, which were significant. I think it can be said that Torrens's descent into oblivion only started in the 1850s (also due to his old age for which he more or less ceased participation in economic and political debates), and certainly it was more or less complete in the later decades of the nineteenth century,[11] so that, as Seligman lamented, in 1899 he was treated 'somewhat cavalierly' in Palgrave's *Dictionary*, which only devoted a very short and not well-informed entry to him, written by C. A. Harris, Chief Clerk of the Colonial Office (the fact that he was chosen to write the entry was an implicit statement that Torrens's main title to fame were his colonisation activities, not his contributions to economics). As Seligman recalls, Harris wrote (clearly without much knowledge of them)[12] that Torrens's economic works were 'as a rule, devoid of permanent merit'.

The period from 1850 to the triumph of marginalism, in which Torrens's demise took place, is one which has undergone little scrutiny in studies on the development of economic doctrine. It might be argued that this period, which was dominated by what Marx called 'vulgar economics', is well worth forgetting: as Foxwell (1899, p. lxxviii) wrote, in this period economists became 'men of one book' – John Stuart Mill's *Principles of Political Economy*, the 'bulky compendium' (Marx, 1969–1972, Vol. 3, p. 190) published in 1848. This is not the place to enter into a discussion of the economics of this period, or the relationship between J. S. Mill's *Principles* and Ricardo's thought,[13] but it can be affirmed that the neglect that Torrens then started to suffer was rather due to his being a Classical economist, and to the fact that the problems to which he had devoted himself – especially as far as the core of economic theory is concerned, value and distribution – made his position difficult to understand at a time when the structure of Classical economic theory was being 'submerged and forgotten' (Sraffa, 1960, p. v). Although known as a critic of Ricardo on value theory (but a critic however who later went back to the Ricardian fold)[14] Torrens was deeply entrenched in Classical theory, and it would be difficult to maintain that the reason why he came to be neglected was that of not belonging to the 'Ricardian orthodoxy'. It is not by chance that probably the only author who, before the recent reawakening of interest in Torrens,[15] discussed in depth his economic thought was Karl Marx, 'the last of the Classical economists', in his *Theories of Surplus Value*, written in 1862–1863.

The main claims put forward on behalf of Torrens by Seligman in his article (p. 341) are the following:

> He discovered, independently of Malthus and Ricardo, the law of rent.
>
> Secondly, he advanced a theory of wages which was adopted by Ricardo.
>
> Thirdly, he discovered the law of comparative cost, the credit of which is usually ascribed to Ricardo.
>
> Fourthly, he advanced a theory of profits which differed from that of Ricardo, and which was considerably nearer the truth.

Before discussing these four points, we may notice that there is a fifth one which Seligman mentions, without giving it great importance, that is Torrens's plea (put forward in 1834 in the tract *On Wages and Combination*, but to some extent traceable even to his first economic work, *The Economists Refuted*, of 1808) for 'a national insurance fund to be applied to the alleviation of [the] misery' caused to workers when they are (temporarily) thrown out of employment by the deployment of 'new and improved machinery' (Seligman 1903, p. 343). While this point is not given great prominence in Seligman's article (where it is made as a collateral point on Torrens's theory of profits), Seligman came later to regard it as a 'great point', and put it on the same plane as the other four listed above (Seligman, 1927–1928, p. 127). About this last point we may notice that state intervention for the relief of workers' distress was not unknown in the first half of the nineteenth century – indeed, 1816–1817 saw what Smart has called 'the first experiment of the century in what are now called Relief Works' (Smart, 1910, p. 543). But most economists were against them, their position being thus put forth by Ricardo: 'the raising of funds for the purpose of employing the poor ... diverts those funds from other employments which would be equally if not more productive to the community' (Ricardo to Malthus, 3 January 1817).[16] Torrens's position compares favourably with this *ante litteram* 'Treasury View', but while it is true that it was interesting and almost unique among economists, it was not backed by any original theoretical position, and appears to be based rather on common sense and a desire to redress an injustice to the workers: it is not in the name of the principles of political economy that Torrens advocated the measure, but in the name of 'Humanity and justice'. Moreover, Torrens appears clearly to think that the problem of unemployment was only partial and temporary,[17] therefore his position was not so unorthodox as it could appear at first sight. We can therefore turn to the more specifically economic arguments for which Seligman put forward the four claims listed above for Torrens's 'neglected' originality.

TORRENS ON RENT

On rent, Seligman's claim is based on the fact that in the first edition of the *Essay on the External Corn Trade* (1815) Torrens conceives rent as a 'net surplus', which is undoubtedly true, but not in itself very significant: Adam Smith had already written of rent as surplus produce,[18] and following Smith the same conception is to be found in a number of authors, for instance in Spence's 1807 tract *Britain Independent of Commerce*, which Torrens certainly knew, having written *The Economists Refuted* against it in 1808. Spence in fact speaks of rent as 'the surplus produce paid to [the class of land proprietors] under the denomination of rent' (Spence, 1807, p. 17).[19]

Seligman however adds that Torrens 'explains later ... that cultivation proceeds from the better lands to inferior lands, the difference in the produce of "soils of first rate" and of "second rate or third rate quality" "appearing in the form of rent"' (Seligman, 1903, p. 342). This is more significant (and nearer to Malthus's and Ricardo's conceptions), but the problem is that the words Seligman seems to quote (putting them in inverted commas) are not to be found in the pages of the edition of *External Corn Trade* he refers to, nor indeed have I been able to trace them at all in the whole book.[20] They seem in fact to come from the 1826 edition of the book, where Torrens writes:

> In the First Edition of the Essay on the Corn Trade, which was written in 1814, and published early the following year, before the Author was acquainted with the very able and original disquisitions of Mr. Malthus and Mr. Ricardo, it was stated, that the difference between the returns to capital upon the worst, and upon the best lands under tillage appears in the form of rent; and that when we increase the cost of obtaining subsistence, a greater portion of the produce of labour will be required for wages, and a less proportion will remain for profits. (Torrens, 1826, p. ix)

But Torrens's assertion is not substantiated by the text of the 1815 *External Corn Trade*. I think it can be said that in 1826 Torrens, being keen to distance himself from Ricardo, and to claim priority with respect to him on a number of points (also taking advantage of the fact that Ricardo was dead), asserted that in 1815 he had written something which he had not really written. Indeed, as Robbins rightly recalls,[21] Torrens himself (rather inconsistently with these bold claims in the 1826 *External Corn Trade*) in the second edition (1820) of the book, had written about its first edition that

> with respect to the influence of the Corn Trade upon the distribution of wealth, there were defects in his [1815] work which, in the existing state of economical science, it would have required much patient investigation to supply. (Torrens, 1820, p. xvii)

In fact the 1815 edition of the *External Corn Trade* is marred by the pervasive presence of the Smithian idea that wages profits and rent are 'constituent parts of the price of commodities', or 'original sources' of value, so that if rent rises this would be paid for by increased prices, not diminished profits. And conversely, 'the component parts of natural price are rent, profits, and wages, and a free external corn trade would have a powerful effect in lowering them all' (Torrens, 1815, p. 298).

The best approximation to Malthus's theory of differential rent one can find in the 1815 *External Corn Trade* is in a passage where Torrens writes:

> Competition perpetually tends to equalize the rate of profit upon stock; and whatever enables inferior lands to be cultivated, necessarily increases the rent due from the superior ... the increased value added to land ... will go to augment the revenue of the proprietor. (Torrens, 1815, pp. 219–220)

This is certainly consistent with the Malthus/Ricardo theory of rent,[22] but it must be just with reference to passages like these that Robbins (by no means a detractor from Torrens's merits) writes that on rent 'There is not the same edge to Torrens' first tentatives ... as there is to the statements of West or Malthus or Ricardo' (Robbins, 1958, p. 42). Indeed, they compare poorly with the sharp formulations that we find in those authors – especially West and Ricardo.

As for priorities, although it is true that as Seligman writes (following Torrens himself) the *Essay on the External Corn Trade* was mainly written in 1814 (it was published in February 1815), it is certainly wrong to say that 'in all probability' Torrens's *Essay* 'antedated them [the essays by West and Malthus]' in publication (Seligman, 1903, p. 342).[23] In particular, Malthus's two 1815 rent pamphlets (*Inquiry into Rent* and *Grounds of an Opinion*) were certainly published before Torrens's *Essay*, so much so that Torrens quotes *Grounds of an Opinion* (undoubtedly the later of the two pamphlets)[24] in the preface to the *Essay* (Torrens, 1815, p. x), and in the text (1815, p. 281);[25] even if one argued that Torrens did not know them when (undoubtedly in 1814) he wrote the bulk of the *Essay*, we would be at most discussing a case of simply *subjective* originality for Torrens.[26]

It must also be remembered that although in the Preface to the 1826 edition, as already mentioned, Torrens declares his agreement with the proposition that 'the difference between the returns of capital upon the worst, and upon the best lands under tillage appears in the form of rent', later in the text of this very book Torrens criticises 'Ricardo and his followers' for having maintained that 'rent is the difference of produce obtained with equal capitals, and with equal labour, on the same, or on different qualities of land' (1826, p. 138).[27] This criticism was partly based on rather silly numerical examples, which it is not necessary to discuss here. Torrens believed he had added to the theory of rent the point that '[n]either the gradations of soil, nor the successive applications of capital to land, with decreasing returns, are in any way essential, either to the appearance or to the rise of rents'. Rent could according to him be generated by the surplus profit that increasing demand of agricultural produce would generate, by causing a rise in the price of agricultural produce. Rent would absorb this surplus profit so as to bring the agricultural rate of profits to the same level as that of the manufacturing sector (1826, p. 137ff). But of course the idea that the price of agricultural produce would rise just because demand was rising, and without a rise in its cost of production, was in utter contradiction with the theory of value espoused by Torrens, which made price depend on cost of production,[28] not supply and demand.[29] If cost of production did not rise,[30] the surplus profit due to the excess demand would disappear with the increased agricultural production which this very surplus profit would call forth.[31] It must here be recorded that Torrens withdrew his criticism of Ricardo on the theory of rent in the 1844 introduction to *The Budget*, where he blames himself for having in the past criticised Ricardo on this subject, stating that he 'mistook an extension for a refutation of Mr. Ricardo's theory of rent' (Torrens, 1844, p. xvi). He then inserts a long quotation from the 1826 edition of the *External Corn Trade*, where he had put forward that 'refutation', and where the basic point was that rent could manifest itself irrespective of the existence of decreasing returns. We may simply notice that Torrens is not really disowning the (wrong) point he had made in 1826, but merely saying that his point was an 'extension', not a 'refutation', of his 'great master' – whose definition of rent however Torrens still declares to find 'defective' (Torrens, 1844, p. xxi).

TORRENS ON WAGES

On the theory of wages, Seligman (1903, p. 342) states that 'Torrens first put forward the theory of the natural rate of wages as influenced by the standard of life, and it is this theory that soon became the stock-in-trade of the classical school'. The truth of the first half of Seligman's sentence can hardly be doubted, but the second half is highly problematic.

It is certainly true that Ricardo mainly adopted ideas on wages which Torrens had formulated in the 1815 *External Corn Trade*. As Seligman recalls, Ricardo himself, in the chapter 'On Wages' of his *Principles*, quoting in full a paragraph from Torrens's book, added: 'The whole of this subject is most ably illustrated by Colonel Torrens' (Sraffa & Dobb, 1951–73, Vol. 1, p. 97n).[32] Indeed, before Seligman, Cannan (1893, p. 246) had already noticed that 'Ricardo ... in the opening paragraphs of his chapter "On Wages" follows Torrens very closely'.[33] Although Cannan then starts one of his hair-splitting disquisitions on some minor differences between Ricardo's and Torrens's treatment of wages, there can be no doubt that Torrens influenced Ricardo, and that even to a modern reader some of Torrens's points are remarkable, as the one where he notices the importance of social influences in the determination of the 'natural' (i.e. the subsistence) level of wages:

> That the labourer must, usually, obtain for his work, a sufficient quantity of those things, which the climate may render necessary to preserve himself, and such a family as

> may keep up the supply of labour to the demand, in healthful existence, is self-evident; and, when we consider that things not originally necessary to healthful existence, often become so from use, and that men will be deterred from marriage, unless they have a prospect of rearing their families in the mode of living to which they have been accustomed, it is obvious, that the labourer must obtain, for his work, not only what the climate may render necessary, but what the *habits of the country, operating as a second nature*, may require. (Torrens, 1815, p. 63; emphasis added)

The problem with Seligman's position is that this theory, although adopted by Ricardo and recognised by him as due to Torrens, rather than becoming 'the stock-in-trade of the classical school' as Seligman writes, was swiftly abandoned – *not least by Torrens himself*. Indeed, the case of the theory of wages is particularly illuminating on the point I have made above, that the neglect of Torrens came rather from his being a Classical – and to a good extent a *Ricardian* – economist than from his *opposing* an alleged Ricardian Orthodoxy. As I have argued above, the whole structure of the Ricardian theory was soon submerged and forgotten, and Torrens with it. Very soon (already in the mid-1820s)[34] the conception of a natural wage determined by the level of subsistence, which Torrens had 'most ably' illustrated, and Ricardo shared with him, was completely superseded by the theory of the Wage Fund, where the level of wages is determined by the ratio between the amount of capital which pays the wages and the number of workers employed – the subsistence wage now becoming only the minimum level below which wages cannot fall. Torrens himself by the late 1820s espoused this conception (see the appendix to Torrens, [1829] 1972), which he more fully expounded in his 1834 tract on *Wages and Combination*. He no longer distinguishes (as he had done in the 1815 *External Corn Trade*, and Ricardo did in *Principles* two years later) a *market* and a *natural* rate of wages, the former determined by 'the proportion ... between the demand and the supply', the latter '*by other laws*', being equal to the workers' subsistence (Torrens, 1815, p. 62; emphasis added). In *Wages and Combination* the level of the workers' subsistence is only '[t]he minimum below which wages cannot permanently fall' (Torrens, 1834, p. 11) – the maximum being fixed on the other hand by the amount that would absorb all net product (1834, p. 7ff). Within this interval the 'actual level of wages' is determined by 'the proportion between the number of labourers and the quantity of that component part of our farmer's capital, which he exchanges for labour' (1834, p. 15).[35] Irrespective of what one thinks of the relation between this conception and the theory of the natural rate of wages which Torrens had advocated in 1815, there can be no doubt that by the early 1830s the latter had been quietly discarded by Torrens himself.

TORRENS ON COMPARATIVE COSTS

Seligman's claim that Torrens arrived at formulating the principle of comparative costs before Ricardo is one which has been widely accepted in the literature. This merit would be sufficient for probably ensuring immortality to Torrens, the principle of comparative costs (or comparative advantage) being considered, as *The New Palgrave* put it in the entry devoted to it (Findlay, 1987, p. 514) 'the deepest and most beautiful result in all of economics'. Yet this very entry attributes the paternity of the principle to Ricardo ('first clearly stated and proved' by him: Findlay, 1987, p. 514) rather than to Torrens.[36] We must here distinguish two questions. One is the precedence in formulating the principle, the other the fullness with which the principle is illustrated, the uses to which it is put etc. From the latter point of view, I think one should agree with Jacob Hollander rather than with Seligman. In a famous discussion they had in the September 1911 *Economic Journal*, following the publication of Hollander's (1910) study of Ricardo, Hollander forcefully spelled out his denial that it was possible to ascribe to Torrens the paternity of the principle of *comparative* advantage in production – as distinguished from the much less important principle of the *absolute* advantage of the territorial division of labour, which can certainly be found in Torrens's early economic work (e.g. his 1808 *The Economists Refuted*). Hollander rightly argued that the principle of the *absolute* advantage accruing from the territorial division of labour is not only different but certainly much less sophisticated and less important than that of gains deriving from specialisation according to *comparative* advantage. We may quote Hollander's argument in full:

> The theory of international trade set forth in Torrens's [1815] *Corn Trade* is, with a single exception, the principle of territorial division of labour as propounded in the *Economists Refuted*: Commerce is advantageous in that it enables a country to obtain a greater quantity of other goods in exchange than the same labour and capital could have produced at home .... In the latter part of the *Corn Trade*, detached from the earlier statements of the theory, with neither antecedent nor consequent, and figuring only as an explanation of the possible importation of corn by a country before lands of superior quality have been brought under the plough – occurs the single paragraph upon which Torrens's claim rests. (Seligman & Hollander, 1911, p. 460)

Hollander therefore added that saying – as Seligman had done – that Torrens had provided a treatment of comparative advantage 'as full as that by Ricardo' meant to wrongly identify the principle of the advantages of territorial division of labour with that of comparative costs, because the treatment of the latter in the 1815 *Essay on the External Corn Trade* was much less than full – let alone 'as full as that by Ricardo'. Indeed, it was only a rather casual and very limited formulation, and the principle was far from being understood by Torrens in all its important implications. The point could not be better put than in the words of Jacob Viner, an author who is not only one of the highest authorities on the subject, but also far from unsympathetic to Torrens:

> Torrens clearly preceded Ricardo in publishing a fairly satisfactory formulation of the doctrine [of comparative costs]. It is unquestionable, however, that Ricardo is entitled to the credit for first giving due emphasis to the doctrine, for first placing it in an appropriate setting, and for obtaining general acceptance of it by economists. Hollander, moreover, appears to be justified in his contention that the doctrine was never an integral part of Torrens's thinking. (Viner, 1937, pp. 442–443)

Indeed, as pointed out by Hollander and Viner,[37] it is only *in a single passage* of the 1815 *External Corn Trade* that Torrens spelled out the principle of *comparative* advantage. We may quote it in full:

> If England should have acquired such a degree of skill in manufactures, that, with any given portion of her capital, she could prepare a quantity of cloth, for which the Polish cultivator would give a greater quantity of corn, than she could, with the same portion of capital, raise from her own soil, then, tracts of her territory, though they should be equal, nay, *even though they should be superior*, to the lands in Poland, will be neglected; and a part of her supply of corn will be imported from that country. (Torrens, 1815, p. 264; emphasis added)

So we may say that Seligman's claim that Torrens has to be given precedence with respect to Ricardo for a formulation of the principle of comparative advantage was formally right – but virtually void of substance. The story however cannot really end here. Strangely enough, an acknowledgement of indebtedness made by Torrens in the Preface to the 1815 *External Corn Trade* has passed virtually unnoticed. Torrens wrote:

> The author conceives that several of the disquisitions, particularly those relating to the indirect operation of internal taxation, upon the importation of foreign articles, were never before presented to the public. He believes, however, that one or two of the arguments contained in the Second Part, may have been suggested by a pamphlet of considerable merit, entitled 'Observations on the Importation of Foreign Corn', and an excellent article which appeared in the Eclectic Review. (Torrens, 1815, p. xiv)[38]

As a matter of fact this pamphlet contains a formulation of the principle of comparative costs no less clear than Torrens's *External Corn Trade* of the following year, but it has to this day been completely ignored.[39] Here we have a really neglected economist, of whom even the name is unknown.

No author writing on Torrens seems to have taken the trouble of following his (admittedly rather vague) hint. As far as I know the only person who actually knew the pamphlet Torrens was referring to, and realised that it contained the principle of comparative costs, was Piero Sraffa.[40] The pamphlet was published anonymously and to the best of my knowledge no hypothesis has ever been formulated on the identity of its author. Indeed, I have never seen it mentioned in the secondary literature at all. An extended quotation from this anonymous author may be in order:

> The blind conception, that if in a trade between two countries, it was beneficial to one, it must therefore be in as much disadvantageous to the other, no longer misleads; at least in Britain. We have become sensible that all commerce, although perhaps in some instances more beneficial to one country than to the other, is, however, necessarily beneficial to both. Climate, soil, a more perfect skill, or other accidental circumstances, may give to one country advantages which another cannot, or does not possess. Their exchanges must consequently be mutually beneficial. If two countries can exchange one with the other any articles, whether of manufacture, or raw material, or sustenance ... for other articles, whether of manufacture, raw material or sustenance, which have relatively been produced with less labor and capital, the mutual advantage must be evident. If England exchanges with Germany a piece of cotton cloth, which has been made with the labor of ten persons, for ten days, (allowance being made for the value of the cotton wool imported), for a quantity of iron or wheat, which could not have been produced in England, but with the labor of double the number of persons for the same time, it must be evident, that England is more advantaged than she could have been in the application of her own double labour to its production: and consequently, that English capital must be augmented by the exchange, beyond what it would have been by the direct application of its labour and means to the production of the iron or wheat. Also, if on the other hand, Germany could produce with ten days' labor of the ten persons, the iron or wheat she exchanges for the piece of cotton cloth, which, although made in England with the ten days' labor of the ten persons, the iron or wheat she exchanges for the piece of cotton cloth, which, although made in England with the ten days' labor of the ten persons, could not have been made in Germany but with double the labor and capital, or at double the price of them, Germany too is in this manner advantaged. Also, if one of the two countries, equally capable of producing the same things by means of the same labor and capital, should however be able to direct that labor and capital to more advantageous pursuits, the advantage to that country in so doing must be not less apparent, although it should thereby be obliged to receive from the other country the things which it could otherwise have produced within itself. Supposing England and Germany both capable of producing the iron and wheat at the same expense of labor and capital, yet if England at the same time can by superior ingenuity, convert this labor and capital to the manufacture of cotton cloth, producing a quantity of it greatly beyond what Germany might be able to produce by the similar application of its labor and capital, then must both countries still be benefited by the exchange ... Germany obtains more cotton cloth than it could have fabricated for itself, by means of the same labor and capital employed in the fabrication of the cotton cloth. (Anon., 1814, pp. 7–9)

There is no doubt that (a) this is a fuller statement than the rather cursory one we find in Torrens's 1815 *External Corn Trade*, (b) it was made and published the year before the publication of the *External Corn Trade* and (c) Torrens himself – a rather unreliable source as far as acknowledgement of priorities are concerned, inclined to overstate his own originality and importance[41] – acknowledged that the 1814 pamphlet had suggested 'one or two of the arguments' of the *External Corn Trade*. The fact that Torrens's acknowledgement refers to Part II of the *External Corn Trade*, whereas his own formulation of the comparative cost principle appears in Part III is rather irrelevant, and cannot cancel the facts which, to sum up, are the following:

(1) Torrens did formulate, but rather casually and in only one passage of the 1815 *External Corn Trade*, the principle of comparative advantage, before Ricardo's (by far fuller and deeper) formulation in his 1817 *Principles*.
(2) The year before the publication of *External Corn Trade* the principle had been formulated in the anonymous pamphlet entitled *Considerations on the Importation of Foreign Corn*, a formulation that was certainly known to Torrens when he wrote *External Corn Trade*.
(3) Therefore, the earliest known formulation of the principle of comparative advantage (or comparative costs) is the one by the anonymous author of the *Considerations on the Importation of Foreign Corn* (even though it is by no means impossible that there were earlier – but still unearthed – formulations of the principle).

One is even tempted to speculate that, given that the principle of comparative advantage is only so cursorily formulated by Torrens in the 1815 *External Corn Trade*, and that the rest of the book does not rely on it at all, Torrens – when he had more or less fully conceived his book, coming across the principle of comparative advantage as formulated in that anonymous pamphlet, and having seen the important point (Torrens certainly had a sharp mind, and was analytically inclined) – did not resist introducing it in his own book, feeling however duty bound to acknowledge the influence of what he had read in that pamphlet. With the passing of time, especially given that Ricardo entered the scene shortly afterwards with his powerful formulation in the *Principles*, the earlier formulations of Torrens's *External Corn Trade* and of the 1814 anonymous pamphlet were forgotten. But the unknown author of the 1814 pamphlet has in any case priority over Torrens.

TORRENS ON PROFITS

As has been mentioned above, Seligman maintains that Torrens 'advanced a theory of profits which differed from that of Ricardo, and which is considerably nearer the truth' (Seligman, 1903, p. 341). As a matter of fact, when Seligman (very briefly) illustrates the point he appears to be saying something different. He writes that the really important contribution made by Torrens is 'a criticism rather than … a piece of constructive work' (1903, p. 346). This would be Torrens's criticism of Ricardo's famous point that profits vary inversely with wages, or that 'profits depend on wages'. According to Torrens (as reported by Seligman) 'profit … depends, not only on the rate of wages, but to a much more important extent upon the quality of the soil under cultivation, and above all upon the degree of skill with which labour is applied' (Seligman, 1903, pp. 346–347).

Seligman's account of Torrens's point is not wholly adequate. Torrens's position is in fact the following. He argues that 'the doctrine that profits depend on wages' is 'equally untenable, whether the terms, alteration of wages, alteration of profits, are employed with reference to proportions, or whether they are used in relation to quantities' (Torrens, 1826, pp. xv–xvi). Torrens illustrates the point with one of his numerical examples: he first assumes that to produce 60 units of corn it is necessary to employ 20 units of corn as wages, and 20 units as seed, so that the rate of profits in the production of corn would be 50%. Supposing then that the conditions of production improve, he assumes that the same 60 units of corn are produced employing only 10 units as seed, with the same number of workers, whose wages however are raised so as to consist of 25 units of corn as a whole. The rate of profits would have risen to 71%, but wages would also have risen, both as a quantity of commodities and as a proportion of the product. This partially disproves a point of Ricardo's, who had himself shown in the *Principles* that *commodity* wages may well rise without the rate of profits declining, if the conditions of production improve (see Ricardo, 1821, p. 48ff), but had not apparently seen that wages as measured as a *proportion of the product* – the way they had to be measured according to him (see Sraffa & Dobb, 1951–73, Vol. 1, p. lii and de Vivo, 1987a, p. 190) – need not decrease to allow a rise in the rate of profits. In Marx's terms, a reduction in the 'organic composition of capital' (the ratio of non-wage to wage capital) may accommodate a higher rate of profits with undiminished 'proportional wages'. Ricardo's oversight derives from his basic neglect of non-wage capital in the determination of the rate of profits. So Seligman is right, but we must notice that in making his point Torrens was not original; the same point had already been made in McCulloch's *Principles*, published the year before, and Torrens was undoubtedly aware of it (see Torrens, 1826, p. xiii). Besides, Torrens's point, though valid, was not of such importance as to invalidate Ricardo's theory of profits, but only a specific proposition. In fact Torrens himself in the introduction to *The Budget* (1844) presented his criticism from another angle, more favourable to Ricardo: he stated that Ricardo's point was valid, provided one kept to Ricardo's own hypotheses: that 'the whole of the advances of the capitalist consist of wages', and that wages be 'estimated by the quantity of labour required to produce them'; that is by the proportion of the product paid to the workers as wages (Torrens, 1844, pp. xxv and xxvii, respectively).

As far as Torrens's own theory of profits is concerned, we may notice that the only consistent theory of profits Torrens was ever able to expound was taken from Ricardo. Torrens in fact never went beyond Ricardo's 'corn-ratio' theory of profits (in the example just given it is clear that the rate of profits is determined assuming that both product and capital only consist of corn), or its generalisation; that is a theory of profits based on the assumption of physical homogeneity between the *aggregate* of commodities composing the product and the *aggregate* of commodities composing the capital (see Sraffa & Dobb, 1951–73, Vol. 1, pp. xxxi–xxxiii and de Vivo, 1996).[42] As Torrens himself acknowledged in the Preface to the second edition of the *External Corn Trade*, he only got to have an acceptable theory of distribution – and in particular a theory of profits – after reading Ricardo's *Essay on Profits* (Torrens, 1820, pp. xvi–xvii),[43] when – as Ricardo put it in a letter to Malthus – Torrens became 'quite a convert to *all* what you have called my peculiar opinions on profits, rent, &c. &c.' (Ricardo to Malthus, 28 May 1816, in Sraffa & Dobb, 1951–73, Vol. 7, p. 36). And we may add that the idea that profits are a surplus is reached by Torrens only after reading Ricardo's *Essay*. Torrens's 1815 *External Corn Trade* followed Smith very closely, and the idea that profits are a surplus does not really appear in it: indeed, the work is marred by the Smithian idea that wages profits and rent are the 'original sources of value', that is the 'adding-up theory of price' (Sraffa & Dobb, 1951–73, Vol.1, p. xxxv), which makes Torrens (as it had Smith) loose sight of the connection between the level of wages and the level of profits. As a matter of fact, in the 1815 *External Corn Trade* the rate of profits is determined *à la* Smith 'by the proportion ... between the supply of capital and the demand for it' (Torrens, 1815, pp. 58–59). No relationship being seen between the level of wages and that of profits, the nature of profits as a surplus is lost, as indeed in Adam Smith. But, with Ricardo's 'agricultural' theory of profits, their surplus nature is impossible to be lost sight of, and it is grace to it that Torrens arrives at stating with great clarity that 'Profit is that net surplus which remains with the capitalist after the complete re-placement of all his advances' (Torrens, 1820, p. 384).[44] No comparable statement can be found in the 1815 edition.

NOTES

1. This preface was dropped when the content of the appendix was incorporated in the main body of the dictionary, and is little known.

2. We may notice that these words of Palgrave's spell out the anti-Ricardian position which in Seligman's article is very much kept in the background.

3. It is however to be noticed that Lloyd was the Drummond Professor at Oxford. Longfield was the first incumbent of the economics chair founded by Archbishop Whately at Trinity College Dublin. Longfield's *Lectures* were praised by Torrens in his Introduction to *The Budget* (Torrens, 1844, pp. li–lii).

4. Torrens was born in 1780, and died in 1864; he was 8 years younger than Ricardo (who died very young, in 1823), and 18 years younger than Malthus (who died in 1834).

5. Torrens tabled one of the first three questions to be discussed at a meeting of the Club. He tabled at least another 18 questions in his years as member (see Higgs, 1921, p. 5ff). In 1851, Torrens boasted to have been the person who had originally suggested the creation of the Club (Torrens to Lord Overstone, 6 February 1851, in O'Brien, 1971, p. 506), but this (very late) claim must be taken with some reserve. It is generally thought that it was mainly Thomas Tooke who inspired the foundation of the Club. Lord Overstone described Torrens as one of the Club's 'great guns' (Higgs, 1921, p. 306). Regarding his departure from the Club, see the letter to Lord Overstone quoted above, and Moore (2004, p. 55). Moore's essay is an important source of biographical information on Torrens.

6. Sir Robert Peel (the younger) was the Prime Minister. Many years before, in 1819, he had caused another famous act to be passed, which re-established the Bank of England's specie payments after the suspension of the Napoleonic period. The Act of 1819 was also often referred to as 'Peel's Act'.

7. Torrens attributed the intellectual paternity of the proposal to Lord Overstone, whom he loved to flatter (Overstone was one of the richest men in England, and Torrens often made recourse to his help when in trouble). The intellectual ancestor of the proposal was really Ricardo's *Economical and Secure Currency* (1816), and his posthumously published *Plan for the Establishment of a National Bank* (1824).

8. Indeed, Torrens receives not little attention in Fetter's work. Torrens's positions on money – as on many other topics – underwent wide changes: from the extreme anti-Bullionism of his 1812 *Essay on Money and Paper Currency* to full orthodoxy. The *Essay on Money* Torrens himself many years later described as his 'original sin' (see the letter to Lord Overstone of 24 January 1848, in O'Brien, 1971, p. 414).

9. On Wakefield and his 'modern theory of colonization', see Marx ([1887] 1977, chap. 33).

10. The charge was that of having (indirectly) bought land in the colony, contrary to an 1835 ruling that Commissioners must not engage in commercial dealings with their Commission.

11. It must however be mentioned that the most important study of classical theory in the second half of the nineteenth century, Cannan's *History of the Theories of Production and Distribution in English Political Economy from 1776 to 1848* (1893), devoted not little attention to Torrens.

12. Harris claimed that '[Torrens's] works took usually the form of letters to the ministry of the day' (Palgrave 1899, p. 550), thus showing he was mainly taking into account Torrens's pamphlets such as those collected in *The Budget*, and overlooking his more important works, published mostly in the 1810s and 1820s, which often took the form of (rather bulky) treatises.

13. Torrens is mentioned two or three times in Mill's *Principles*, but his ideas had been given much more prominence in Mill's *Unsettled Questions*, where from the very preface Mill declares himself to be a follower of Torrens's ideas as put forward in *The Budget* (see J. S. Mill, [1844] 1967, p. 231).

14. Torrens formulated his critique of Ricardo's labour theory of value in the late 1810s, but by the beginning of the 1830s in his *Address to the Farmers* (1831), and in *Letters on Commercial Policy* (1833) he went back to the labour theory of value (see the present writer's editorial introductions to the reprints of these works in de Vivo, 2000, Vol. 8).

15. In the twentieth century, decades after Seligman's article, Torrens has attracted the attention of important authors such as Robbins (1958), Viner, who devotes much attention to him in *Studies in the Theory of International Trade* (1937), and Sraffa (see the 'Introduction' in Sraffa and Dobb, 1951–73, Vol. 1). In *Production of Commodities*, Sraffa (1960) resuscitated Torrens's treatment of fixed capital as a joint product, which after Marx had fallen into total oblivion.

16. In his reply, Malthus agreed that 'the funds raised for the support of the poor ... essentially interfere with other employments' (see Sraffa and Dobb, 1951–73, Vol. 11, p. xi). In his *Principles*, however, he wrote that 'the employment of the poor in roads and public works ... are the means most within our power and most directly calculated to remedy that disturbance in the balance of production and consumption, which has been occasioned by the sudden conversion of soldiers, sailors, and various other classes which the war employed, into productive labourers' (Malthus, 1989, Vol. 1, p. 512).

17. Torrens in fact writes: 'whenever a new application of mechanical power throws a *particular class of operatives* out of employment, a national fund should be provided, to aid them *in betaking themselves to other occupations*' (Torrens, 1834, p. 44; emphasis added).

18. For example, Smith ([1789] 1922, Vol. 1, p. 147) writes: 'land, in almost any situation, produces a greater quantity of food than what is sufficient to maintain all the labour necessary for bringing it to market.... The surplus ... is always more than sufficient to replace the stock which employed that labour, together with its profits ... [and it] remains for a rent to the landlord'.

19. Also, D. Buchanan in his comments on the *Wealth of Nations* had written of rent as a 'neat surplus' (Buchanan, 1814, p. 134).

20. Seligman refers the reader to pages 212, 256 and 325 of Torrens (1815).

21. We may mention however that strangely enough Robbins, in his book on Torrens, although quoting Seligman more than once, never really discusses Seligman's claims about Torrens.

22. I believe that Sraffa's attribution to Torrens's 1815 *External Corn Trade* of 'the principle of rent based on diminishing returns from the extension of cultivation to inferior qualities of land' (Sraffa and Dobb, 1951–73, Vol. 4, p. 6) was rather overgenerous. It is also surprising that they should call *External Corn Trade* a pamphlet when it was a 350-page book.

23. The point was reiterated by Seligman (Seligman & Hollander, 1911, p. 455) in his discussion with Jacob Hollander, who (1911, p. 467) retorted that Torrens quotes *Grounds of an Opinion* in the *External Corn Trade*, and that this is the later of the two pamphlets by Malthus.

24. It was in fact conceived as an appendix to *An Inquiry* (Malthus, 1815a), as stated in its title: *The Grounds of an Opinion on the Policy of Restricting the Importation of Foreign Corn; Intended as an Appendix to 'Observations on the Corn Laws'* (Malthus, 1815b).

25. This was noticed by Sraffa and Dobb (1951–73, Vol. 4, p. 6), and had been noticed earlier by J. H. Hollander (Seligman & Hollander, 1911).

26. West's *Essay*, according to the chronology of publication established by Sraffa and Dobb (1951–73, Vol. 4, p. 5), was published immediately after Malthus's pamphlets, and about ten days before the *External Corn Trade* and Ricardo's *Essay on Profits*, for both of which Sraffa and Dobb give the date of publication as 24 February 1815.

27. The same principle of Ricardo which he was criticising is shortly afterwards summarised by Torrens as follows: 'rent is the difference between the quantity of produce obtained by a given capital from lands of superior quality, and the quantity obtained by the same given capital from the worst quality of land resorted to' (p. 143).

28. In *External Corn Trade* Torrens often used the expression 'price of production' (made later famous by Marx) instead of 'natural price' (on this, see de Vivo 1987b).

29. It could be thought that the mechanism described in the text was simply the short run rise in market prices of agricultural produce which in the end would cause land of inferior quality to be brought into cultivation (or capital yielding a lower return be applied to land of first quality). But if this was so, Torrens's claim to have added something new to the theory of rent would be even less justified.

30. This must be what Torrens is assuming, because it is only if cost of production does not rise *pari passu* with the increase in price that a surplus profit arises. Also, a rise in the cost of production would have implied diminishing returns, whereas Torrens wanted to show, against Ricardo, that rent could arise even when there were no diminishing returns.

31. It should be mentioned that in this same year T. Perronet Thomps on published his *True Theory of Rent*, where he criticised Ricardo's theory of rent on much the same lines as Torrens. Torrens felt that Thompson had borrowed from him without acknowledgement (on this, see also the present writer's editorial introduction to the reprint of Torrens's *Letters on Commercial Policy*, in de Vivo, 2000, Vol. 8).

32. It is rather strange however that Ricardo acknowledged Torrens's contribution only in the second edition, and rather grudgingly, after complaints by Torrens for not having been quoted. Ricardo seems to have had reservations about Torrens as a person, and this may explain Ricardo's aversion to quoting him.

33. Following Cannan, Sraffa and Dobb annotated these opening paragraphs in their edition of Ricardo to the effect that they 'appear to be derived from Torrens's *Essay on the External Corn Trade*, 1815' (Sraffa & Dobb, 1951–73, Vol. 1, p. 93n).

34. A pioneer in this was McCulloch, with his 1826 *Essay on Wages*, of which Section I is entitled: 'Rate of wages in any given country at any particular period, dependent on the magnitude of the fund or capital appropriated to the payment of wages, compared with the number of labourers' (McCulloch, 1826, p. 112).

35. We may notice that as already mentioned Torrens is basing himself on a 'corn-ratio' theory of wages.

36. The entry on 'International Trade', on the other hand, makes a cursory reference to the 1815 *External Corn Trade*, apparently attributing priority to Torrens with respect to Ricardo (Chipman, 1987, p. 937).

37. According to Viner the same point had been made not only by Hollander, but, before him, by Leser (see Viner, 1937, pp. 441–442).

38. Torrens has the title of the pamphlet wrong, but there is no doubt as to what pamphlet he is referring to. The article mentioned must be one on the Corn Laws, published in July 1814 in the *Eclectic Review*. The author of the article, as Torrens almost certainly knew, was James Mill.

39. It is not listed for instance in the extensive bibliography of Viner's 1937 book, one of the most learned works on the subject. The pamphlet being 'printed for the author' almost certainly did not have a wide circulation, but it is not excessively rare, especially in Britain. Major British universities (Cambridge, Oxford, LSE) have a copy, as do the British Library and the Goldsmiths' Library. Seligman had a copy in his collection (now at Columbia University) and there is a copy in the Kress Library at Harvard. There is no copy in the Library of Congress. No copies are recorded by Black (1969) as present in Irish libraries.

40. Sraffa actually owned two copies of the pamphlet, one of which he read and annotated to the effect that it contained the principle of comparative cost (see the entry relative to this pamphlet in the catalogue of his library forthcoming under the present writer's editorship).

41. As Sraffa (1930, p. 543) put it, Torrens is 'always an unreliable guide in questions of priority'. A detailed reconstruction of all the claims and counterclaims on different points of doctrine which Torrens put forward for himself would require a paper by itself.

42. This generalization seems to be entirely due to Torrens. Seligman was completely unaware both of Ricardo's 'corn-ratio' theory of profits and of its presence (and generalization) in Torrens.

43. Acknowledging the defects of the theory of distribution he had expounded in the first edition of the *External Corn Trade*, Torrens attributes it to the fact that at the time of writing it he had not read Ricardo's *Essay on Profits* (1815) and also Malthus's *Inquiry into Rent* (1815a). However, he writes that 'the whole' of the work

had been written and printed before the appearance of Ricardo's *Essay*, and 'the greater part' before Malthus's *Inquiry*.

44. Also, in *Production of Wealth* Torrens writes '[t]he profit of stock ... is essentially a surplus – a new creation – over and above all that is necessary to replace the cost of production, or, in other words, the capital advanced' (Torrens, 1821, p. 54). From this however Torrens also derives the idea that the natural price (which he equates to cost of production *excluding* profits) is different from the market price (which includes profits as well), and that the latter does *not* gravitate towards the former (1821, p. 55). This point was criticised by Malthus in the manuscript of the revisions to his *Principles*, which have only recently been published in its *variorum* edition (Malthus, 1989, Vol. 2, p. 53). We may notice that in *External Corn Trade* Torrens had adhered to the view that the market price tends to equality with the natural price (see Torrens, 1815, pp. 60–61).

REFERENCES

Anon. (1814). *Considerations on the importation of foreign corn; arising out of the Proceedings, at a Meeting of the Heritors of Fifeshire, proposing to petition the legislature for further restriction, as published* in *The Courier Newspaper of 10th December 1813*, London (printed for the author).

Black, R. D. C. (Ed.) (1969). *A catalogue of pamphlets on economic subjects published between 1750 and 1900 and now housed in Irish libraries*. Belfast: The Queen's University Press.

Buchanan, D. (1814). *Observations on the subjects treated of in Dr. Smith's inquiry into the nature and causes of the wealth of nations*. Edinburgh: Oliphant, Waugh & Innes.

Cannan, E. (1893). *A history of the theories of production and distribution in English political economy from 1776 to 1848*. London: Percival & Co.

Chipman, J. S. (1987). International trade. In: J. Eatwell, M. Milgate & P. Newman (Eds), *The new Palgrave dictionary of economics* (Vol. 2, pp. 922–955). London: Macmillan.

De Vivo, G. (1987a). David Ricardo. In: J. Eatwell, M. Milgate & P. Newman (Eds), *The new Palgrave dictionary of economics* (Vol. 4, pp. 183–198). London: Macmillan.

De Vivo, G. (1987b). Prices of production. In: J. Eatwell, M. Milgate & P. Newman (Eds), *The new Palgrave dictionary of economics* (Vol. 3, pp. 960–961). London: Macmillan.

De Vivo, G. (1996). Ricardo, Torrens, and Sraffa: A summing-up. *Cambridge Journal of Economics*, *20*(3), 387–391.

De Vivo, G. (Ed.) (2000). *The collected works of Robert Torrens* (Vol. 8). Bristol: Thoemmes.

Fetter, F. W. (1965a). The relation of the history of economic thought to economic history. *American Economic Review*, *55*(1/2), 136–142.

Fetter, F. W. (1965b). *Development of British monetary orthodoxy, 1797–1875*. Cambridge, MA: Harvard University Press.

Findlay, R. (1987). Comparative advantage. In: J. Eatwell, M. Milgate & P. Newman (Eds), *The new Palgrave dictionary of economics* (Vol. 1, pp. 514–517). London: Macmillan.

Foxwell, H. S. (1899). Introduction. In: A. Menger (Ed.), *The right to the whole produce of labour: The origin and development of the theory of labour's claim to the whole product of industry*. London: Macmillan.

Gordon, B. J. (1967). *Non-Ricardian political economy: Five neglected contributions*. Boston, MA: Baker Library.

Higgs, H. (Ed.) (1921). *Political economy club: Founded in London, 1821; minutes of proceedings, 1899–1920; roll of members and questions discussed, 1821–1920; with documents bearing on the history of the club* (Vol. 6). London: Macmillan.

Hollander, J. H. (1910). *David Ricardo: A centenary estimate*. Baltimore, MD: Johns Hopkins Press.

Malthus, T. R. (1815a). *An inquiry into the nature and progress of rent, and the principles by which it is regulated*. London: John Murray.

Malthus, T. R. (1815b). *The grounds of an opinion on the policy of restricting the importation of foreign corn*. London: John Murray.

Malthus, T. R. (1989). In: J. Pullen (Ed.), *Principles of political economy: Variorum edition* (Vol. 2). Cambridge: Cambridge University Press.

Marx, K. (1969–72). *Theories of surplus value* (Vol. 3). London: Lawrence & Wishart.

Marx, K. ([1887] 1977), *Capital: A critique of political economy* (Vol. 1). Moscow: Progress Publishers.

McCulloch, J. R. (1826). *An essay on the circumstances which determine the rate of wages, and the condition of the labouring classes*. Edinburgh: Black and Tait.

Mill, J. S. ([1844] 1967). *Essays on some unsettled questions of Political Economy*. Vol. 4, *Collected Works of John Stuart Mill* (Vol. 4). Toronto: University of Toronto Press.

Moore, P. L. (2004). Robert Torrens (1780?–1864). In: H. C. G. Matthew & B. Harrison (Eds), *Oxford dictionary of national biography* (Vol. 55, pp. 55–58). Oxford: Oxford University Press.

O'Brien, D. P. (Ed.) (1971). *The correspondence of Lord Overstone* (Vol. 3). Cambridge: Cambridge University Press.

Palgrave, R. H. I. (Ed.) (1899). *Dictionary of political economy* (Vol. 3). London: Macmillan.

Palgrave, R. H. I. (Ed.) (1908). *Dictionary of political economy. Appendix*. London: Macmillan.

Ricardo, D. (1815). *An essay on the influence of a low price of corn on the profits of stock; showing the inexpediency of restrictions on importation*. London: John Murray.

Ricardo, D. (1816). *Proposals for an economical and secure currency: With observations on the profits of the Bank of England, as they regard the public and the proprietors of Bank stock*. London: John Murray.

Ricardo, D. (1821). *On the principles of political economy, and taxation* (3rd ed.). London: John Murray.

Ricardo, D. (1824). *Plan for the establishment of a national bank*. London: John Murray.

Robbins, L. C. (1958). *Robert Torrens and the evolution of classical economics*. London: Macmillan.

Seligman, E. R. A. (1903). On some neglected British economists. *Economic Journal, 13*(51 and 52), 335–363 and 511–535.

Seligman, E. R. A. (1927–1928). *Lectures on the history of economics: Stenographic notes taken by P.S. Allen*. Mimeo, Columbia University, New York.

Seligman, E. R. A., & Hollander, J. H. (1911). Ricardo and Torrens. *Economic Journal, 21*(83), 449–468.

Smart, W. (1910). *Economic annals of the nineteenth century. 1801–1820*. London: Macmillan.

Smith, A. ([1789] 1922). In: E. Cannan, E. (Ed.), *An inquiry into the nature and causes of the wealth of nations* (2 Vols.). London: Methuen.

Spence, W. (1807). *Britain independent of commerce; or, proofs, deduced from an investigation into the true causes of the wealth of nations, that our riches, prosperity, and power, are derived from resources inherent in ourselves, and would not be affected, even though our commerce were annihilated.* London: T. Cadell and W. Davies.

Sraffa, P. (1930). An alleged correction of Ricardo. *Quarterly Journal of Economics, 44*(3), 539–544.

Sraffa, P. (1960). *Production of commodities by means of commodities: Prelude to a critique of economic theory*. Cambridge: Cambridge University Press.

Sraffa, P., & Dobb, M. (Eds). (1951–73). *The works and correspondence of David Ricardo*. Cambridge: Cambridge University Press.

Torrens, R. (1808). *The economists refuted, or, an inquiry into the nature and extent of the advantages derived from trade*. London: S.A. Ody.

Torrens, R. (1812). *An essay on money and paper currency*. London: J. Johnson.

Torrens, R. (1815). *An essay on the external corn trade; containing an inquiry into the general principles of that important branch of traffic; an examination of the exceptions to which these principles are liable; and a comparative statement of the effects which restrictions on importation and free intercourse, are calculated to produce upon subsistence, agriculture, commerce, and revenue*. London: J. Hatchard.

Torrens, R. (1820). *An essay on the influence of the external corn trade upon the production and distribution of national wealth; containing an inquiry into the general principles of that important branch of traffic; an examination of the exceptions to which these principles are liable; and a comparative statement of the effects which restrictions on importation and free intercourse, are calculated to produce upon subsistence, agriculture, commerce, and revenue* (2nd ed.). London: J. Hatchard.

Torrens, R. (1821). *An essay on the production of wealth; with an appendix, in which the principles of political economy are applied to the actual circumstances of this country*. London: Longman, Hurst, Rees, Orme, and Brown.

Torrens, R. (1826). *An essay on the external corn trade* (3rd ed.). London: Longmans, Rees, Orme, Brown, and Green.

Torrens, R. ([1829] 1972), *An Essay on the external corn trade* (5th ed.). Reprint of Economic Classics, Clifton, NJ: Augustus M. Kelley.

Torrens, R. (1831). *Address to the farmers of the United Kingdom: On the low rates of profit in agriculture and in trade*. London: Longman.

Torrens, R. (1833). *Letters on commercial policy*. London: Longman.

Torrens, R. (1834). *On wages and combination*. London: Longman, Rees, Orme, Brown, Green, and Longman.

Torrens, R. (1837). *Letter to Lord Melbourne on the causes of the recent derangement in the money market, and on bank reform*. London: Longman, Rees, Orme, Brown, and Green.

Torrens, R. (1844). *The budget: On commercial and colonial policy*. London: Smith, Elder, and Co.

Viner, J. (1937). *Studies in the theory of international trade*. London: George Allen and Unwin.

JOHN CAZENOVE (1788–1879) ON SAY'S LAW AND BANK CREDIT: A WORTHY RECRUIT FOR THE 'BRAVE ARMY OF HERETICS'?

John Pullen

In 'On some neglected British economists', Edwin Seligman (1903) referred briefly to an anonymous work entitled *Considerations on the Accumulation of Capital and Its Effects on Profits and on Exchangeable Value*, published in 1832. His reference to the *Considerations* was mildly complimentary, describing it as of 'somewhat more than ordinary interest'. In his view, the *Considerations* was designed to enforce the doctrine that 'gluts are possible and can be averted only by an increase of luxurious or unproductive consumption' (Seligman, 1903, p. 351). He did not say whether he agreed or disagreed with this doctrine, and it could be argued that his was a less than adequate summary of the *Considerations*.

Seligman was apparently not aware that the author of the *Considerations* was John Cazenove, and that Cazenove was the author of at least ten other books and pamphlets in political economy (see the appendix for a complete list of Cazenove's economic writings).

Cazenove was born in London, of French Huguenot origin. He worked for a time in his father's commercial firm, and in 1832 described himself as 'late a continental merchant' in 'a large commercial firm' with 'some sixty or seventy foreign correspondents'. The present London stockbroking firm

English, Irish and Subversives Among the Dismal Scientists
Research in the History of Economic Thought and Methodology, Volume 28-B, 111–136

ISSN: 0743-4154/doi:10.1108/S0743-4154(2010)000028B008

Cazenove & Co. was founded by his brother, but Cazenove seems not to have been involved.

Cazenove was a supporter and particular friend of Malthus, who proposed his name in 1821 for the membership of the Political Economy Club at its second meeting. In its debates he sided with Malthus against Ricardo and James Mill. He was asked (by Malthus) to review Malthus' *Principles of Political Economy* (1820), but declined (as reported by Malthus) 'on the grounds of modesty and want of time' (in Malthus to John Murray, 26 January [1821], John Murray Archives). Malthus, in recommending Cazenove to Thomas Chalmers, described him as 'a very clever man, and good political economist' (T. R. Malthus to Thomas Chalmers, 6 February 1833, Thomas Chalmers Papers).[1] After Malthus' death in 1834, Cazenove applied (unsuccessfully) for Malthus' position as professor at the East India College. The position was given to Richard Jones.

In January 1821, Malthus told John Murray that Cazenove was making 'remarks' on Malthus' *Principles* 'for his own satisfaction and amusement' (Malthus to John Murray, 26 January [1821], John Murray Archives). Malthus thought that Cazenove might offer them to Murray for publication, perhaps as a review in the *Quarterly Review*, or perhaps as a book or pamphlet to be published by Murray. There is no record of any such involvement by Murray. However, textual evidence suggests the possibility that Cazenove might have been the author of a two-part review of Malthus' *Principles* in the *British Critic* in 1820. He is also known to have been the anonymous author of a review in 1824 in the *British Critic* of J. R. McCulloch's *A Discourse on ... Political Economy* (1824), as well as the 1832 review in the *British Critic* of Thomas Chalmers' On Political Economy.[2]

In the same letter to Murray, Malthus spoke highly of Cazenove's *A Reply to Mr Say's Letters to Mr Malthus on the Subject of the Stagnation of Trade* (1820),[3] stating that: 'It appears to me to be so good, and to shew so much knowledge of the subject generally'.

Cazenove, for his part, was very complimentary towards Malthus,[4] whom he once described 'the most sagacious commentator on the great work of Adam Smith, and the safest guide in tracing the various relations of political and commercial life' (Cazenove, 1824, p. 614). In contrasting the Malthusian school of political economy with the 'Ricardoite' school, he declared that 'the disciples of Ricardo appear to us somewhat in the light of heretics',[5] and described the Malthusian school as a 'sage and modest sect':

> The pupils of Mr Malthus never try to startle mankind by strange, enigmatic propositions; never set a value upon their opinions merely because they are incapable

> of being reconciled with those of other people: but, on the contrary, take pleasure in using the language of common life in their deepest investigations, and think themselves most successful when they are most fully understood. (Cazenove, 1824, pp. 623–624)

In addition to publishing at least 11 books and pamphlets of his own, and several reviews, Cazenove was extensively engaged in editorial work. He was almost certainly the anonymous editor of the second (posthumous) edition (1836) of Malthus' *Principles of Political Economy*,[6] and he edited a second edition (1853) of Malthus' *Definitions in Political Economy* (final edition, 1827). He was also mainly responsible for editing the Literary Remains (1859) of Richard Jones, although he declined the offer of the editor, William Whewell, to be formally recognised as editor.

Cazenove might also have been the author of a paper entitled 'Letters to David Ricardo', criticising Ricardo's theory of value. The paper, in the form of three 'Letters', appears to be in Cazenove's hand. (See Malthus, 2004, pp. 292–302. The fact that Cazenove's Ms. is amongst Malthus' papers could mean that he had asked for Malthus' comments with a view to publication.)

Cazenove's publications contain comments on a wide variety of topics, such as the nature of value; the measure of value; the incidence of taxation; capital; wages; profits; interest; rent; national debt; machinery; foreign trade; productive and unproductive labour; productive and unproductive consumption; tithes and population. A complete summary of his ideas on all of these topics is beyond the scope of this chapter. Some of the topics were treated by Cazenove in depth, but some only in passing, and they vary in doctrinal significance. The chapter concentrates on two issues – Say's Law and Bank Credit – which he analysed in detail and which continue to be of interest and relevance today.

SAY'S LAW

If a reason is sought for not neglecting Cazenove, we need look no further than to his views on demand, consumption, saving and gluts, and to his criticisms of what he called 'Say's principle' and 'Say's new theory'.

The Evidence of Experience

Contrary to the theory of Say, James Mill and Ricardo[7] that a general glut would not and could not occur, Cazenove in his *Reply to Say* (1820) appealed first of all to experience.

> Experience, however, incontestibly [sic] proves that from some circumstance, or combination of circumstances, a general stagnation of trade may and frequently does take place, while the funds for the maintenance of labour and the means of production are in the greatest abundance. (1820, p. 45)

He believed Europe in general, and England in particular, provided at that time an example of a general glut. Thus experience, he argued, proves that there can be an over-supply of capital relative to the demand for the products of capital, and that the supply of products does not create its own demand.

> If, frequently or occasionally, there be a difficulty in employing capital profitably, how can it be said with any truth that it can never accumulate too rapidly. (1820, pp. 44–45)

The argument from experience was repeated in Cazenove's (1832) *British Critic* review of Thomas Chalmers, in his *Elementary Treatise* (1840), and in his *Thoughts* (1859). In the review he stated:

> that multitudes may be seeking for employment, while capital is lying idle for want of profitable investment, is a fact but too well authenticated to leave its existence doubtful; and it is readily admitted as well as felt by all practical men. (Cazenove, 1832, p. 315)

In the *Elementary Treatise* (Cazenove, 1849, p. 146) he claimed that experience has shown that an alteration can occur in the proportion between demand and supply, not only for one particular commodity, but for all commodities, leading to a reduction in the general rate of profit and a glut; and in the *Thoughts* (Cazenove, 1859, p. 90) he used the existence of government loans as further evidence against Say's position: the facility with which loans are raised is empirical proof that accumulation can often get ahead of the means of employing it profitably.

The Role of Demand in the Progress of Wealth and the Dependence of Capital Accumulation in Demand

The key argument used by Cazenove in rejecting Say's Law centred on the essential role of revenue or demand in the progress of wealth.[8] This can be seen in statements such as:

> employing revenue in the purchase of commodities, appears to me so absolutely necessary to the growth of opulence, that without it, I do not see how it is possible that the employment of productive labour by capital can be carried to any extent. (Cazenove, 1820, p. 36)

This clear endorsement of the role of demand reappeared in the *Considerations* (Cazenove, 1822), where he argued 'it is very possible for capital to increase faster than the demand for its products', and denied that supply of itself would create an adequate demand. If demand does increase at the same time as supply, and in the same proportion, 'that must be from causes very different from those which have led to the increased supply' (Cazenove, 1822, pp. 2–3).

His criticism of Say for neglecting the role of demand can also be found in his review in the *British Critic* (Cazenove, 1824) of J. R. McCulloch's *Discourse on … Political Economy*. McCulloch had just been appointed the first professor of an institute set up in 1823 in London to honour the memory of Ricardo, and to provide a course of lectures in which the 'leading principles and conclusions [of political economy] should be briefly, popularly and clearly explained' (McCulloch, 1824, quoted in Cazenove, 1824, p. 598). In his strongly worded review, Cazenove referred to 'the nonsense of Macculloch's lectures'.[9] He predicted that the theory of profits of Ricardo and McCulloch 'is doomed, at no distant period, to encounter the neglect and derision which never fail to punish every remarkable deviation from the boundaries of common sense', and declared that 'the peculiar notions of Mr Ricardo … as far as they are peculiar, are either erroneous or unintelligible' (Cazenove, 1824, pp. 615, 619). In criticising Say's view that there can be no glut, he quoted McCulloch's 'hence it is that the true and only genuine encouragement of industry consists *in the increase of production*!' and responded with the following satirical comment on 'the sage of the Ricardo Institute':

> If you have ten millions of quarters of corn more than the country requires, there is an acknowledged glut of that one article; but you are not to think of remedying the evil by getting the superfluous grain eaten up; you are to have all things increased in the same degree; you are to encourage production in every department to the same extent; have ten millions of every thing more than you want, and the glut will forthwith cease and determine! (Cazenove, 1824, p. 621; original emphasis)

Cazenove's idea that a glut could be remedied, or by implication prevented, by 'getting the superfluous grain eaten up' could be interpreted as an argument for raising the level of effective demand, rather than the level of production.

He returned to the question of gluts in his *Outlines of Political Economy* (1832), Chapter XIX, 'On the Nature and Causes of Demand', where he explicitly stated his disagreement with Say and James Mill:

> It is with regret that I find myself, on this subject, compelled to differ from such eminent authorities as Mons. Say and Mr. Mill, who hold that the market can never be overstocked with all descriptions of goods at the same time – that the superabundance of some sorts implies a deficiency of others – that the total demand is always equal to the total production, and that, consequently, the grand concern is only how to increase the supply. (Cazenove, 1832b, p. 110)

He believed that the error of Say and Mill lay in their not recognising that a source of demand is necessary, independently of the production process.

> The error obviously originates in regarding every commodity, as soon as it is produced, as the cause of demand for others, whereas it only becomes so under certain circumstances. A previous condition is necessary – that of its being itself in demand; a consumer must, in the first instance, be found for it. (1832b, p. 108)

Cazenove accused Mill of confusing 'supply' in the sense of quantity, with 'supply' in the sense of value.

> The supply of each man depends upon the *quantity* which he brings to market; his demand for other things depends upon the *value* of his supply ... How is it possible, then, to assert that in individual cases the demand and the supply are always equal to each other, and to found upon such an assertion the doctrine of the universal equality of supply and demand? (1832b, pp. 111–112; original emphasis)

The role of demand is also emphasised in Chapter XXV of the *Outlines* (1832b), 'On the immediate cause of the progressive increase of wealth',[10] where he argued that an increase of capital alone is not sufficient to ensure a permanent increase of wealth, and that a continued increase of capital requires an increase of demand.

> Although, therefore, the accumulation of capital is all that is necessary to the increase of production, it is not all that is necessary to its profitable or permanent increase. In order to secure this permanence, and render the accumulation an *effectual* one, there must be a contemporaneous increase in the demand. (1832b, p. 145; original emphasis)

Once again he argued that the production of a commodity does not, of itself, create a demand for it.[11]

> it is incorrect to regard every commodity, as soon as it is produced, as being a demand for other commodities, because there must first of all be a demand for it, and this demand for the produced commodity must come from a source extraneous to the commodity's production. (1832b, pp. 112–113)

The argument was supported with a quotation from Richard Jones:

> The object of all production ... is consumption, and the possibility of consumption rests upon ... the existence of revenues in other hands, co-extensive with the value of the goods produced through capital employed. (Cazenove, 1857, p. 95; quoted in Whewell, 1859, p. 452)

Cazenove's emphasis on demand in the progress of wealth is also to be seen in his criticism of the 'fallacy' of McCulloch's optimistic views on the introduction of machinery. He interpreted McCulloch as saying that the substitution of machinery for labour necessarily occasions an equal or greater demand for the disengaged labourers in some other employment. According to Cazenove:

> This can never happen unless there be an augmentation of the value as well as the quantity of what that machinery produces, a circumstance which entirely depends upon the extension of the market, or the increase of the amount of demand for its products. (1832b, p. 121; see also, pp. 144–145)

Cazenove was aware that Say and Ricardo had argued that income used as capital creates demand just as when used as revenue. But his response was to stress the primacy of consumer demand: 'The former species of demand is wholly subservient to the latter, is limited by it, and must ultimately terminate in it' (Cazenove, 1820, p. 23).[12] While not denying or even diminishing the importance of capital in economic growth, Cazenove repeatedly gave priority to demand, rather than to capital, stressing capital's dependence on demand.

> The means of the producers for replacing their capital, and continuing their trade, can only be procured by exchange; and there can be no exchange without consumers who are disposed to expend their revenue in the purchases of those [produced] goods. (Cazenove, 1861, p. 24)

The expenditure of revenue in this way is said to be 'an indispensable condition of capital being used at all' (1861, p. 24), so that production is not merely *dependent* on demand, but also *limited* by demand. '[T]he capital employed in production must be limited by the revenues that are given in exchange for its produce, and by which exchange that capital is replaced' (1861, p. 47). In his *Remarks* (1873), at 85 years of age, Cazenove persisted in attacking 'Say's principle' and 'Say's new theory', and in promoting the role of demand. He argued that the employment of capital in production will depend on sales of the products, and that sales will depend on, and will be limited by, the amount that buyers are able and willing to spend on the products (Cazenove, 1873, p. 11). He stated, 'it would clearly have been useless for any one to have accumulated capital in order to produce that for which there would have been no demand' (1873, p. 17). And two years later, in his *Remarks* (1875), he insisted that, far from being injurious to capital and industry, the spending of money on consumption is beneficial to production.

> the expenditure of revenue in exchange for other commodities that are the produce of capital, so far from being injurious to industry, is calculated to promote it, by furnishing a fund for the support and maintenance of those who have produced them, and without which their special trade would come to an end. (Cazenove, 1875, p. 307)

Thus, for over 55 years, Cazenove maintained a persistent attack on the idea that production or supply would of itself generate sufficient demand.

Cazenove accused Say of adopting an inconsistent[13] and contradictory position on the question of gluts. Say had argued that capital cannot accumulate too quickly, and that a general glut is due to a deficiency, not a superabundance, of capital. But Say also said that investments can become scarce and that a great deal of capital can remain unemployed, 'locked up in the coffers of its proprietors' (Say, *Traité d'Econome Politique*, as quoted in Cazenove, 1820, pp. 43–44). This, according to Cazenove, is a self-contradiction by Say:

> We have here Mr. Say's own authority against himself, for these admissions absolutely contradict the whole of his previous reasoning on the subject. (Cazenove, 1820, p. 44)

He also accused Say of begging the question, by defining 'production' in a way that reduces his principle to a tautology.

> Mons. Say has, indeed, in his last new publication, qualified his opinion upon this subject by confining the term productions (*produits*) to such commodities only as do repay the cost of bringing them to market. But this is begging the whole of the question. No one ever imagined that of such commodities there ever could be a superabundance; but in the ordinary sense of the term, experience fully proves what the true theory teaches, – that, as any particular commodity may, from over-supply or from want of sufficient demand, fall below its cost, so the whole number of commodities which are brought to market, collectively taken, may in like manner fail to fulfil the condition of their supply, and fall below the cost of their production. The demanders want either the will or the power to give the producers the means of putting into motion all the labour which they have cost, and a portion of their capital is in consequence absorbed and destroyed. (Cazenove, 1932b, p. 113)

In this emphasis on the tautological nature of Say's theory, Cazenove's argument against Say was very similar to Malthus'.

There was also a close similarity in their use of the distinction between the power and the will, or the means and the motives, in their theories of demand. Like Malthus, Cazenove argued that a deficiency of demand, relative to supply, can be due to a discrepancy between the power to consume and the will to consume.

> It, therefore, frequently happens that the supply of commodities increases faster than the demand for them; not, indeed, that there are not many who would willingly consume them if they had the means, but because those who alone have the power to consume, have not always the will to do it. (Cazenove, 1822, p. 14)

J. S. Mill on the Demand for Commodities and the Demand for Labour

In his *Supplement* (1861) and *Remarks* (1873), Cazenove made some critical comments about J. S. Mill's view that the demand for commodities is not a demand for labour. According to Mill:

> What supports and employs productive labour, is the capital expended in setting it to work, and not the demand of purchasers for the produce of the labour when completed. Demand for commodities is not demand for labour. The demand for commodities determines ... the *direction* of the labour; but not the more or less of the labour itself ... the demand for labour is constituted by the wages which precede the production, and not by the demand which may exist for the commodities resulting from the production. (Mill, [1849] 1909, pp. 79, 80; original emphasis)

Mill believed that 'among political economists of reputation', hardly any, except Ricardo and Say, have kept this theorem 'constantly and steadily in view' (Mill, [1849] 1907, p. 80). At first, Cazenove appears to have agreed with Mill's statement – 'This is quite true' – because 'the mere fact of purchasing commodities does not of itself give employment to labour'. But he then proceeded to the following argument:

> Nevertheless, the demand for commodities is the sole cause of the demand for productive labour. It would clearly be of no use to employ such labour unless there existed a demand for what it produced. (Cazenove, 1861, p. 24)

Cazenove seems to have argued that, although a demand for commodities is not in itself a demand for labour, it creates a demand for labour and is an essential cause of the demand for labour. He developed the criticism more forcefully in his *Remarks* (1873), where he began by stating that Mill's statement is 'unquestionably true', because 'The purchaser of commodities does not maintain the labour that has produced them, nor indeed does he maintain any future labour'; but then accused Mill of overlooking the fact that what the purchaser does not do is done by the person who produces the commodities or sells them to the purchaser:

> Mr. Mill has unaccountably shut his eyes to the fact, to which the experience of every tradesman bears witness, that those to whom he sells his goods, supply him, in exchange for them, with a fund which replaces the capital that has been consumed in their production, and which he accordingly employs *in the maintenance of productive labour*; it being his clear interest to make this profitable use of it. (1873, p. 16; original emphasis)

Cazenove thus appears to have accused Mill of failing to distinguish between the demand for commodities as a *sufficient* cause of the demand for labour and as a *necessary* cause.

The Balance between Saving and Consumption

Because of the importance of revenue and demand in the economic system, Cazenove argued that it is undesirable for too much money to be saved and used as capital, and too little used as revenue for consumption.

> Whatever is added to capital is taken from revenue; and it follows, that the less that is taken from it the larger will the revenue remain, and the greater will be the demand. (Cazenove, 1820, p. 25)[14]

He argued that demand would be encouraged by the spending of the wealthy on luxuries and superfluities,[15] and that the beneficial effects of luxury spending would be curtailed if saving by the wealthy became excessive and 'if the habits and structure of the society incline them to be too parsimonious' (Cazenove, 1822, p. 14). A fall in the demand for luxuries would have repercussions on employment, and on the demand for necessaries, resulting in a universal glut.

> More luxuries being produced than the community is willing to consume, they fall below their cost, labour is thrown out of employment, which diminishes the demand for necessaries, and renders the whole mass of commodities excessive in relation to the demand for them. (1822, pp. 16–17)

The level of profits would also be affected by the balance between saving and spending; 'the proportion in which the net revenue of a country is saved and spent must be practically the great regulator of profits': (1822, p. 30). Excessive saving, therefore, would endanger profits – 'accumulation beyond a certain point must not only absorb all profit, but cause a certain loss' (Cazenove, 1820, p. 33).

Cazenove's theory of growth was essentially a theory of balance.[16] The level of demand and growth, he argued, will depend on a correct balance or proportion between saving and spending.

> any circumstances which alter the proportions in which revenue is saved and spent, must have a great effect in widening or narrowing the whole amount of demand. (Cazenove, 1822, p. 10)

And general stagnation will occur if there is 'a disproportion between capital and revenue, or between commodities and the demand for them' (Cazenove, 1820, p. 50). The remedy, he believed, was 'to augment revenue, not only without unpairing the actual capital, but so as to afford an adequate stimulus to its progressive increase', but he recognised that such a remedy would not be easy to implement: 'To effect this is the grand difficulty' (1820, pp. 46–47). He conceived of this optimum balance between saving and consumption not as a fixed and universal position, but as dependent on the circumstances of each country. It was a relativist, rather than an absolutist, concept.

> What, indeed, is the precise proportion between what should be spent and saved, so as to create the greatest demand for labour, and cause the most rapid increase of wealth, must, in every particular country, depend upon its situation and circumstances generally, but more particularly upon the fertility of the land. (Cazenove, 1822, p. 19)

The *Considerations* (1822) concluded with a strong restatement of his opposition to the idea that supply creates demand, and with strong support for the need to search for an optimum balance, even though it cannot be accurately fixed.

> experience seems fully to confirm what theory teaches us to expect – that the disposition to consume is not co-extensive with the power to produce, that demand and supply depend on different causes, and are not always equal to each other, and that there is a point, between the saving and spending of revenue, though we cannot accurately fix it, in which, under the actual circumstances of every country, the whole amount of produce, the demand for labour, and the progressive increase of wealth are at their maximum. (1822, pp. 63–64)

In his *Thoughts* (1859),[17] Cazenove resumed the theme of balance, arguing that there must be a balance between the amount of money destined to be saved and invested as capital and the amount of money destined to be spent on consuming the products of industry. If the latter increases without a corresponding increase in the former, 'there would be an increased demand for the products of capital without an increased supply of them'. If the former increases without a corresponding increase in the latter, 'there would be an increase in the supply of the products of capital, but no increase in the demand for them' (1859, p. 42), and consequently 'a superabundance of capital seeking employment, side by side with labourers standing all the day idle in the market-place' (1859, p. 90). His warning in the *Reply to Mr. Say* and the *Considerations* of the dangers of excessive saving were repeated in the *Supplement* (Cazenove, 1861), where he enunciated the principle that has become known in modern textbooks as the paradox of saving. In commenting on Adam Smith's statement that what is saved is consumed, as well as what is spent, he said:

> If every one were bent upon saving his revenue to the utmost, in order to capitalise it, the object would necessarily defeat itself ... without a corresponding expenditure of revenue, there would be no scope for the employment of additional capital. A country cannot therefore convert into capital the whole of its surplus revenue, but only so much of it as

> will leave a sufficient remainder to create a demand for the products of this new capital, and render possible its profitable employment. (1861, pp. 22–23)

On this question of the importance of balance in economics, Cazenove was advocating the principle that Malthus called the 'doctrine of proportions', now more commonly known as the concept of the optimum.

Redistribution

In the following statement from Cazenove's *Reply to Mr. Say*, there is a faint suggestion that a remedy for general stagnation might lie in the redistribution of income:

> The progressive increase of wealth depends very much upon the portions of the value of the annual produce of the land and labour of the country, which fall to the share of the landlord, the capitalist, and the labourer, in the shape of rents, profits, and wages. (Cazenove, 1820, p. 49)

A suggestion that a more equal distribution of income might be a remedy for general stagnation – and that excessive saving can be harmful – is implicit in the quotation from the Old Testament on the title page of the *Reply to Mr. Say*: 'There is that scattereth, and yet increaseth; and there is that with-holdeth more than is meet, but it tendeth to poverty' (Proverbs 11:24, King James Bible).[18]

There is also a hint of a redistributionist remedy in Cazenove's statement that demand could be increased through the inheritance of subdivided properties. He argued that this has a tendency to lessen accumulation, because 'when a large income is divided among several, more is usually spent and less saved' (1820, p. 26) – which could be seen as an implicit recognition by Cazenove of the Keynesian concept of diminishing propensity to consume.

But an anti-cyclical policy of redistribution was not pursued by Cazenove, except in stressing that the capitalist must have an adequate share of the whole produce if society's wealth is to increase. This pro-capitalist, pro-profits stance is evident in the statement:

> The main object is to increase profits, which are not only the chief source of accumulation, but without which it is impossible there can be any effective stimulus to industry. (1820, p. 51)

If Cazenove advocated redistribution as a remedy for stagnation, it seems to have been mainly a top-down, trickle-down, form of redistribution. If to be a Keynesian means to emphasise the role of demand in economic growth, then Cazenove was clearly Keynesian. But if to be a Keynesian means to advocate a redistribution of income from rich to poor in order to stimulate growth, then Cazenove was not Keynesian. He argued that the transfer of a larger share of the produce of a country to the labouring classes would reduce the fund available for taxation or enjoyment, because 'it would not command the same quantity of labour as before: its real power and efficiency would be diminished' (Cazenove, 1832b, p. 94). This suggests that Cazenove cannot be categorised as an underconsumptionist.

Government Expenditure, the National Debt and Public Wealth

Another non-Keynesian feature of Cazenove's anti-stagnation policy was his opposition to expenditure by government in public works in order to create employment. He referred to 'the folly and absurdity of attempting by legislative enactments to find employment for the labouring classes beyond what the funds destined for their maintenance can be reality employ' (Cazenove, 1840, p. 143).[19] He recognised, however, that wartime expenditure financed by government loans was desirable and necessary. Through government loans during the late war large sums of money which would have been capital in the hands of individuals were employed as revenue by the government, resulting in a great increase in demand in proportion to supply. This wartime reduction in capital and increase in demand stimulated industry – 'the prodigious stimulus it gave to industry is too notorious to be denied' (Cazenove, 1820, p. 36) – and led to a very high level of wealth and profits, and also to savings (1820, pp. 26–27). The reduction in spending at the end of the war led to a reduction in demand, and to a reduction in production and wealth,[20] even though more capital was available for use in production. This phenomenon, he said, is 'inexplicable upon Say's principle' (Cazenove, 1859, p. 91). In terms frequently used by both Malthus and himself, Cazenove argued that capitalists at the end of the war had the power to invest and to produce, but not the will. They lacked the will because, although consumers had the will to demand and consume, they lacked the power, with the result that producers lacked profitable production opportunities and expectations.

However, his justification for public expenditure in wartime did not lead him to advocate public expenditure based on government loans as a general policy. He argued on the contrary that 'the system of borrowing on public credit' creates 'an artificial stimulus, which is ultimately more prejudicial than it is beneficial'. In this respect he therefore differed from a Keynesian-type policy of peacetime pump-priming by means of public works financed by public loans. He also opposed public loans on the grounds that 'such a national debt as ours ... throws such a vast power into the hands of the Crown, as is highly dangerous to the constitutional liberties of the country' (Cazenove, 1820, p. 27).

His opposition to government loans and expenditure in peacetime was based on sociological grounds (fear of corruption) and political grounds (fear of despotism), rather than economic grounds (stimulus to demand). A critic might ask why the economic arguments for public expenditure in wartime ceased to be applicable in peacetime, and whether the benefits from preventing or curing stagnation in peacetime by means of an increase in the national debt might not outweigh the possible sociological and political dangers.

Free Trade and Laissez-Faire

The main remedies that Cazenove prescribed for stagnation – perhaps his only remedies apart from the faint hints on redistribution – were free trade and foreign investment. In the *Reply to Mr. Say*, he stated that a cure for stagnation 'will probably never be brought about on an extensive scale in any other way than by the removal of the restrictions on trade' (1820, p. 47).

By 'restrictions on trade' in this context he seems to have meant 'restrictions on foreign trade'. He argued that 'undoubtedly the most effectual means' of augmenting revenue (and, hence, effective demand) without reducing capital was to remove 'all unnecessary restrictions upon our commercial intercourse with other nations' and to give 'every possible encouragement to foreign trade' (1820, p. 52).[21] And in the *Considerations*, he added that the only stagnation cure he could envisage would be a lower value of commodities arising from an increase in foreign trade, and from capital investment in new and hitherto unexplored countries (Cazenove, 1822, p. 63).

This laissez-faire policy approach is evident in his discussion of the need for a balance between saving and spending. His statement that 'Every one is the best judge of what it suits him to spend, and what it suits him to save' (Cazenove, 1820, p. 38), if taken literally, appears to rule out any government involvement in the balancing process. He also ruled out any government intervention to cure a deficiency of demand: 'To this state of things, however, no legislative remedy can be applied' (Cazenove, 1822, p. 63). Logically, the laissez-faire stance would also rule out any intellectual attempt by critics such as himself to alter the *status quo*.

Conclusion on Universal Gluts

Cazenove summarised the two schools of thought on the question of universal gluts as follows:

> That of Malthus, Chalmers, Sismondi and Storch, distinguishes between the commodities that constitute capital, and the revenues which constitute the power of purchasing them ... The school of Say and Mill, on the other hand, confounds commodities with the means of purchasing them. (Cazenove, 1859, p. 92)

His arguments on the importance of demand, and on the need for a balance between saving and spending or between production and consumption, appear to be worthy contributions to the former school, but whether or not he provided a complete and satisfactory answer to the questions of how to achieve the best balance between saving and spending, and of how to avoid or cure stagnation, will depend on how much trust can be placed in his mainly laissez-faire solution.

BANK CREDIT

The most notable, and potentially the most radical, of Cazenove's contributions on questions other than Say's Law was his discussion of the role of banks, the effects of paper money and, in particular, the issue of bank credit or bank loans. These discussions can be found in the *Evidence* (1832a), the *Outlines* (1832b), the *Money Crisis* ([1847]) and the *Thoughts* (1859).

In the *Evidence* (1832a), he presented himself with the following question which might have been put to him if he had been giving evidence before the Committee enquiring into the renewal of the Bank Charter Act:

> In what respect do the loans of a banker differ from the loans of any other individual?

His reply was:

> The difference between them is material. When a loan is made in the ordinary way between individuals, the lender foregoes in favour of the borrower a certain right or power of purchase; it is a mere transfer of money from A to B. But it is, otherwise, in respect to the advances, which are made by a banker out of the funds which are deposited with him. In that case the power of purchase conferred on the borrower, does not deprive the original depositor of any part of his power, – which remains in force, just as if no such borrower had existed. In the one case, the total amount of demand remains the same as before. In the other case, an entirely new demand is created. Two parties have a right over the same parcel of money, and the result is precisely the same as if that parcel of money had been doubled. (Cazenove, 1832a, p. 4)

He added that 'the same money is lent over and over again' and 'every fresh loan gives rise to a new deposit' (1832a, p. 7).

Cazenove believed that the idea that bank credit is a form of money was first pointed out by Thomas Tooke in his *Thoughts and Details on the High and Low Prices of the Last Thirty Years* (Tooke, 1823; 2nd edition, 1824), and subsequently in *Considerations on the State of the Currency* (Tooke, 1826).[22] He also noted that this idea had been 'ably explained' by James Pennington in a note that Tooke had appended to his *Letter to Lord Grenville on the Currency* (Tooke, 1829; in Cazenove, 1832b, p. 42n). In his *Money Crisis* (Cazenove, [1847], pp. 7–8) Cazenove gave greater emphasis to Pennington's contribution, stating that the function performed by the book credits of banks 'was first made known' in 'the very valuable paper' by Pennington appended in Tooke's letter to Grenville. And in his *Thoughts* (Cazenove, 1859, p. 81), he again credited Pennington with having first explained the nature and effects of banking credits, adding that the subject 'is generally very little understood' and 'was quite unknown to Ricardo, and all the economists of his day'. He referred to Macleod's *Dictionary of Political Economy* (1863) as a recent publication that has some correct views of the subject.[23]

Cazenove also had some interesting comments on the limits that should apply to the creation of credit by the banks. He said that it is 'generally supposed' that bank loans could be extended 'without imprudence' to about two-thirds of the amount of their deposits[24] – a figure somewhat different from the cash reserve ratios in the modern banking system – but he added,

> it is almost impossible to say what a *safe* proportion is: what it would be safe to do under certain circumstances, might not be safe under others. A safe proportion may be instantly converted into an unsafe one by a panic or an unusual drain of gold. (Cazenove, 1832a, p. 7; original emphasis)

In answer to further supposed questions, he stated that bank credit has the same effect as the coining of more metallic money or the issuing of more paper money – viz. 'general prices are raised by it' – but he believed that the inflationary tendency would be only temporary, and would be corrected by international currency movements: when prices 'get to a certain point, the exchanges fall and money is exported, which restores the prices to their natural level' (1832a, pp. 4–5). The export of gold and silver would reduce the deposits of gold and silver in the banks of the exporting country, and would contract their creation powers (1832a, p. 6). There should be an obligation on banks never to exceed the safe proportion. However, if the proportion deviated from this safe level, it should be left to adjust itself.

He recognised that the power to issue bank credit is 'an engine of vast power, and one which might be productive of the greatest mischief' (1832a, pp. 20–21), but he was happy with the current system, because it is in the hands of a body of men,

> who from their property, their integrity, their ordinary habits of prudence, and their high character, are deservedly esteemed and looked up to by the whole commercial community. (1832a, p. 22)

His support for the private creation of bank credit thus presupposed high moral standards on the part of those responsible for the running of the banking system.

His belief that the free market, by means of exporting gold and silver, possesses the power to correct any inflationary tendency of bank credit might however be questioned on practical grounds. He did not consider the possibility or the probability that the issue of bank credit and the ensuing inflation might be just as prevalent in other countries as in England.

Because of his confidence that the personal morality of bankers would ensure a self-correction for any over-issue of currency, Cazenove did not draw any radical policy proposals from his analysis of bank credit. He did not, for example, agree with the view of William Anderson (fl. 1797–1832) that the issue of paper money (and, by implication, the issue of bank credit) should be the prerogative of the state or of a state-owned bank.[25] His proposal, though radical, was less radical than Malthus' idea that the profits of the Bank of England should be shared with the public; and even less radical than Ricardo's proposition that the issue of paper money should be the exclusive privilege of the state, and that there should be a National Bank (in Sraffa & Dobb, 1973, letters of 10 September 1815, 1 October 1815, 6 October 1815 and 3 August 1823). Cazenove did not suggest that the creation of bank credit by private individuals is an anti-social and criminal activity equivalent to counterfeiting. Nor did he advocate the policy, later to be developed by C. H. (Major) Douglas that for moral and economic reasons private banks should be restricted to the distribution of bank credit, and its creation should be reserved to the state. It could, however, be argued that Cazenove's idea that the issue of bank credit should be limited to a certain ratio of external deposits is similar to Irving Fisher's idea of '100% money', but whereas Fisher proposed regulation, Cazenove merely put forward a recommendation.

His views on bank credit were developed further in his *Outlines of Political Economy* (Cazenove, 1832b), where he said that the currency of a country consists of three kinds of money: real money, or the gold, silver and copper coins; paper money or promissory notes and credit money, or 'that which is borrowed or created to serve a temporary purpose' (1832b, p. 42). He repeated, from the *Evidence* (Cazenove, 1832a), the idea that '*credit* money operates as *real* money in adding to the circulating medium and raising prices' (Cazenove, 1832b, p. 42n; original emphasis). He regarded paper money and bank credit as substitutes for real money, and recognised that they have certain advantages. They are cheap, more portable, less liable to loss or theft, more traceable and are 'national gains' because the profit derived from their issue adds to the annual wealth of the country. Any tendency for an over-issue to raise prices would be counteracted, as noted above, by the export of precious metals.

But he nevertheless recognised that these money substitutes have disadvantages:

> The facility wherewith they are created has a continual tendency to lead to an abuse of them. They are very apt to engender a spirit of speculation and overtrading, which by raising prices gives a fictitious appearance of prosperity, which cannot be durable, but must in the end lead to a contrary state of things. (1832b, p. 126)

A further disadvantage is that as they depend wholly on credit, a loss of credit from political or commercial causes will cause 'a rapid extinction … with the most ruinous effects'. His conclusion therefore was that 'there are evils inseparable from the use of these substitutes, which, perhaps, nearly counterbalance the advantages derived from them' (1832b, pp. 126–127). His attitude towards bank credits thus appears to have been more circumspect and less sanguine in the *Outlines* than in the *Evidence*.

In *The Money Crisis* ([1847]),[26] Cazenove reiterated the idea that the English currency system consists of three elements: metallic money, paper money and 'book credits' (the last being also called 'bank credits'). He explained that the great bulk of monies deposited in the banks is lent out by the banks at interest, on the basis of securities taken by the banks as a guarantee of the repayment of the loans. He stated that 'every loan made by a banker out of the deposits in his hands … has all the effect of an addition to the existing mass of floating currency', adding that the question whether those bank credits 'are to be regarded as money or not, is purely verbal. If not money, they are a substitute for it – since more money would be required if they did not exist'. He described these bank credits as 'an integral and important part of our Currency' ([1847], pp. 4–6).

In his *Thoughts* (Cazenove, 1859), he defined bank credits as 'the loans granted by bankers out of the deposits that are placed in their hands ... on such securities as they may deem satisfactory'; and, as in the *Evidence* and the *Outlines*, he described bank credits (and bank notes) as substitutes for gold and silver, adding now that they are 'virtually money' and a 'privilege' enjoyed by banks. He again noted that bank credits have 'precisely the same effect on the currency, as if a fresh supply of money had been received from abroad' (1859, pp. 22–23).

But unlike the *Evidence* and the *Outlines*, the *Thoughts* contained a significant reservation about bank credits. He argued that there is an important distinction between the different kinds of substitutes for metallic money. If paper money or promissory notes are issued to excess, their convertibility to gold and silver 'will soon pare them down to their proper dimensions'. But if Banking Credits swell the currency beyond its 'due amount', prices will rise, the exchanges will fall and metallic money will be exported, but the Banking Credits will not be simultaneously reduced, because a sudden reduction would cause great distress and numerous failures in the mercantile community, as happened in 1825, as a result of the over expansion of the currency in 1824, with the result that the Bank of England was 'gradually drained of nearly all her treasure' (1859, pp. 24–25).

Conclusion on Bank Credit

Cazenove's comments on bank credit are significant and radical because of his insistence that when banks issue credit they are in effect creating money (or money substitutes) just as surely as if they minted coins or printed notes. He recognised that the practice had both advantages and disadvantages. It was an essential part of the English economic system, with vast power, but with the potential for great mischief. He even went so far as to say that the evils inseparable from credit creation by banks 'perhaps nearly counter-balance' its advantages (Cazenove, 1832b, p. 127). Unlike some critics, he did not condemn outright the practice of credit creation by private banks, and did not, with moral and economic outrage, call either for its abolition or nationalisation, but it is obvious that he had serious concerns and reservations. He recommended strict observance of a 'safe' proportion of loans to deposits, relying for its implementation on the probity of the banking community.

CAZENOVE AND THE 'BRAVE ARMY OF HERETICS'

If Seligman had been aware of the number and range of Cazenove's publications, and of his standing amongst political economists of the time,[27] he would surely have given him more than an eight-line comment.

Cazenove's preference for anonymity probably contributed to his neglect, during his lifetime and subsequently. Seven of his eleven books and pamphlets were anonymous, as well as the bulk of his editorial work. His reviews in the *British Critic* were also anonymous, in accordance with the usual practice. He was not included in the first edition of Palgrave's *Dictionary of Political Economy*, nor in the second edition (1925–1926) revised by Henry Higgs, and modern standard works in the history of political economy rarely if ever mention him. But he would not be classified today as a 'neglected' British economist if Keynes had been aware of his views on effective demand and Say's Law. Keynes would surely have recruited him into the 'brave army of heretics', alongside Mandeville, Malthus, Gesell, Hobson and Major Douglas 'who, following their intuitions, have preferred to see the truth obscurely and imperfectly rather than to maintain error' (Keynes, 1936, p. 371).

NOTES

1. Malthus referred in the letter to Cazenove's review in the *British Critic* (1832) of the second edition of Chalmers' *On Political Economy* (1832a); and to Cazenove's recent anonymous publication, *Outlines of Political Economy* (1832). Malthus also enclosed, with his own letter, a letter from Cazenove to Chalmers, written after Cazenove had seen a pamphlet by Chalmers. The (unnamed) pamphlet was presumably Chalmers' *The Supreme Importance of a Right Moral to the Right Economical State of the Community* (1832b). Chalmers replied in this pamphlet to McCulloch's critical review of his *On Political Economy*, but praised the review in the *British Critic* – 'whose perfect concurrence with us in the main lessons of our work, could not fail, amid the general lack of English sympathy, to be exceedingly agreeable' (Chalmers, 1832b, p. 99). Malthus' letter of 6 February 1833, revealed to Chalmers that the author of the *British Critic* review was Cazenove. The location and content of this enclosed letter from Cazenove to Chalmers are unknown, although presumably it responded to Chalmers' praise. Another letter, dated 11 June 1833, from Cazenove to Chalmers, thanked Chalmers for sending, through Malthus, a copy of his Bridgewater Treatise.

2. It has been argued that further reviews in the *British Critic* might possibly have been written, at least partly, by Cazenove. Rashid (1982, pp. 11–15) suggests that ten

economic articles in the *British Critic* between 1815 and 1824 either were written by Malthus or directed by Malthus who 'exercised the role of an editor', and that Malthus either wrote or directed the review of his own *Principles* (*British Critic*, 1820, Vol. 14, pp. 118–138, 275–293). But Rashid also believes that 'it is quite possible that some of these articles were partly written by John Cazenove'. Rashid does not claim to have direct evidence of the authorship of the articles, but cites indirect evidence from their style and content.

Gordon (1985) also considered the connection between Cazenove and the economic articles in *British Critic*, and suggested that 'he could have well been the author in a number of instances, but it is unlikely that he was responsible for others'. Gordon believed there is 'very strong textual evidence to suggest that he contributed at least five times between September 1820 and May 1822'. Gordon (1985, pp. 17, 18, 22) also quoted a personal communication from Patricia James (22 September 1979) in which she said: 'I imagine that Le Bas roped in Cazenove to write the economic articles in the *British Critic*, but there's no hard evidence'.

The only *hard* evidence known to the present writer that links Cazenove with articles in the *British Critic* is his 1824 review of McCulloch's *Discourse on … Political Economy*, and his 1832 review of Chalmers' *On Political Economy*.

3. A presentation copy to Ricardo contains manuscript annotations by Ricardo. The annotations, with the relevant passages of the *Reply to Mr. Say*, are in Sraffa and Dobb (1973, Vol. 10, pp. 405–410; Vol. 11, p. xxx).

4. However, Cazenove's support for Malthus did not prevent him from taking a critical and independent position on some issues; see Pullen (1978).

5. Cazenove used 'heretics' here in a derogatory sense, not as a commendation in the sense used by Keynes in his reference to 'the brave army of heretics'.

6. The evidence for Cazenove's authorship is presented in Pullen (1989, pp. lxi–lxiv).

7. It is interesting to note that although Cazenove grouped Ricardo and Say together in his criticisms, Ricardo was not always in complete agreement with Say on Say's Law. In an MS. note added to Cazenove's *Reply to Mr. Say*, Ricardo said: 'I am as much dissatisfied as the author, with Mr Say's defence of the principle which both he and I maintain to be true' (Sraffa & Dobb, 1973, Vol. 10, p. 28).

8. By 'revenue' Cazenove appears to have meant money which is destined for spending on the products of industry, as distinct from 'capital' which is money destined for spending on production, either as wages or materials. 'Revenue' thus seems to be equivalent to demand for the consumption of consumer goods, and 'capital' seems to be equivalent to saving and/or investment. The connection between 'demand' and 'revenue' can be seen in the statement: 'The demand for commodities must always be limited by the actual revenue existing at the time' (Cazenove, 1820, p. 34). However, the terms 'consumption' and 'consume' appear to be sometimes used in a broad sense to include both the consumption of consumer goods and the consumption of production or capital goods.

9. Cazenove seems to have later changed his opinion of McCulloch. In editing the second edition of Malthus' *Definitions in Political Economy*, Cazenove removed Malthus' critical chapter on McCulloch, stating that Malthus' 'strictures on the writings of a highly estimable and talented living author have been altogether omitted' ('Editor's Preface', in Malthus, 1853, p. viii).

10. The title is similar to that of Chapter VII, 'On the immediate causes of the progress of wealth' in Malthus (1820), reflecting a similarity between Malthus and Cazenove in their concern for 'immediate' causes.

11. These statements by Cazenove can be compared with Malthus' statement that 'a very serious error' of Say, Mill and Ricardo 'consists in supposing that accumulation ensures demand' (Malthus, 1989, Vol. 1, p. 359). Cazenove's use of the concept of 'effectual' accumulation is also very reminiscent of Malthus.

12. A manuscript note at this point by Ricardo in his copy of Cazenove's *Reply to Mr. Say* states: 'Parsimony does not diminish revenue, it only transfers it to another class. No other evil c[an] arise from parsimony than a fall of profits which…' (Sraffa & Dobb, 1973, Vol. 10, p. 408; note incomplete).

13. According to Cazenove (1820, p. 44n), Ricardo was as erroneous as Say, but was consistent. A letter (in French) from Cazenove to Say, currently pending publication, will probably provide further insights into their arguments for and against the law of markets.

14. A note added by Ricardo at this point states: 'This is a great error it supposes that a reven[ue] saved does not give as great a stimulus to demand, as a revenue expended as such' (Sraffa & Dobb, 1973, Vol. 10, p. 409).

15. At one point Cazenove appears to argue that unproductive consumption (on luxuries and superfluities) will be more effective in stimulating demand than productive consumption (on necessaries). He said that if income is saved, that is employed as capital, it will create a demand for necessaries, but if it is spent as revenue it will create 'two demands instead of one' (1822, pp. 42–43). The argument is difficult to follow and to sustain. It does not recognise that money spent on the direct maintenance of labour in production will indirectly lead to an increased demand for commodities.

16. See Gordon (1985, p. 11): 'The critical feature of Cazenove's analysis … is his emphasis on the need to establish a balance between saving and consumption expenditure to ensure the continuance of steady growth'.

17. The *Thoughts* contained (pp. 5–65) ten short chapters on a wide variety of topics, followed by a lengthy appendix (pp. 67–102), containing 33 notes on points raised in the ten chapters.

18. Cazenove could also have quoted Proverbs 11:26, which continues the anti-withholding theme: 'He that withholdeth corn, the people shall curse him: but blessing shall be upon the head of him that selleth it' (King James Bible).

19. The *Elementary Treatise* (Cazenove, 1840) contains 17 chapters in 97 pages on a wide variety of topics at a fairly introductory level. But it also includes an appendix of 17 notes, pp. 99–150, of more advanced material.

20. In his *Questions Respecting the National Debt and Taxation* (1829), Cazenove disagreed with those who attributed the post-war depression and stagnation to the burden of the national debt and taxation. He argued that the want of demand that characterises stagnation 'cannot fairly be ascribed' to the pressure of loans and taxes (1829, pp. 4–6).

21. Cazenove's attitude to the Corn Laws was therefore significantly different from Malthus'.

22. Tooke's *Considerations* (1826) is presumably what Cazenove refers to when he mentions Tooke's '*Tracts on the Currency*'.

23. Macleod (1863, pp. 73, 75) argued that modern banking is 'equivalent to a creation of currency, or to an increase of capital', and that those who think that banking does not add to capital, that it only distributes existing capital, and that bankers are merely agents between lenders and borrowers, are guilty of an 'enormous error'.

'Of all the fallacies that beset Political Economy at the present day this is one of the most mischievous and pestilent ... It is an entire misconception of the nature and effects of banking, and no sound progress can be made in Political Economy, until it is entirely extirpated from the subject' (Macleod, 1863, p. 75).

24. *Evidence* (Cazenove, 1832a, p. 6). However, his view on the precise level for a safe proportion of loans to deposits was not clear. Later in the *Evidence* he stated that in his opinion the amount of loans issued on securities could be safely fixed at five-eighths (rather than two-thirds) of the 'average issues' of the banks (1832a, p. 20).

25. See, for example, Anderson (1797, pp. 15, 17): 'the banker as certainly robs every other man in the society, by circulating his notes, as by levying a tax, or putting his hands into their pockets and taking out a part of their money'. According to Anderson, the only difference between robbing by issuing bank notes and ordinary robbing is that the former is effected with 'much greater ease'.

26. *The Money Crisis* was intended for the *Quarterly Review*, as a review of two works: Lord Ashburton, *The Financial and Commercial Crisis Considered* and R. Torrens, *On the Operation of the Bank Charter Act of 1844*, as it affects commercial credit (1847), but Cazenove explained in an introductory note that he had a few copies printed, to send to some members of Parliament, in time for the expected debate on the Bank Charter Act rather than wait for the next number of the Review.

The Money Crisis was anonymous and undated, but in the British Library copy, 'By John Cazenove', in Cazenove's hand, is written on the title page.

27. His known surviving correspondence, though not extensive, includes letters to and from Jean-Baptiste Say, William Stanley Jevons, James Pennington, William Whewell and Thomas Chalmers, as well as the publisher John Murray (Malthus, 2004, pp. 292–302).

28. It is said that Cazenove was president of the London Chess Club, and published (anonymously), in addition to his works in political economy, *A Selection of Curious and Entertaining Games of Chess That Have Been Actually Played* (1817), London.

ACKNOWLEDGMENT

The author gratefully acknowledges the permission granted by the John Murray Archives and Special Collections at the University of Edinburgh Library for use of material from their collections.

REFERENCES

Private Papers

Thomas Chalmers Papers, Special Collections, New College Library, Edinburgh University, Edinburgh, UK

John Murray Archives, National Library of Scotland, Edinburgh, UK

Anderson, W. (1797). *The iniquity of banking: Or, bank notes proved to be an injury to the public, and the real cause of the present exorbitant price of provisions.* London: J.S. Jordan (two further editions were published in 1797, with a fourth in 1800, and a fifth in 1801).

Cazenove, J. (1824). Macculloch's discourse on political economy (Review of McCulloch, J. R. (1824), A discourse on the rise, progress, peculiar objects, and importance of political economy). *British Critic, 22*, 598–624.

Cazenove, J. (1832). Chalmers – on political economy (Review of Chalmers, T. (1832), On Political Economy, in Connexion with the Moral State and Moral Prospects of Society, 2nd ed.). *British Critic, 24*, 306–347.

Chalmers, T. (1832a). *On political economy, in connexion with the moral state and moral prospects of society* (2nd ed.). Glasgow: W. Collins.

Chalmers, T. (1832b). *The supreme importance of a right moral to a right economical state of the community: With observations on a recent criticism in the Edinburgh review.* Glasgow: W. Collins.

Gordon, B. J. (1985). John Cazenove (1788–1879): Critic of Ricardo, friend and editor of Malthus. Conference paper, History of Economic Thought Society of Australia, La Trobe University, Victoria, Australia.

James, P. (1979). *Population Malthus: His life and times.* London: Routledge & Kegan Paul.

Keynes, J. M. (1936). *The general theory of employment, interest and money.* London: Macmillan.

Macleod, H. D. (1863). *A dictionary of political economy: Biographical, bibliographical, historical, and practical* (Vol. I). London: Longman, Brown, Longmans, and Roberts.

Malthus, T. R. (1820). *Principles of political economy: Considered with a view to their practical application.* London: John Murray.

Malthus, T. R. (1836). *Principles of political economy* (2nd ed.), (The 'Advertisement to the Second Edition', pp. vii–xii, and some footnotes, are attributable to Cazenove, who may also have made textual alterations.). London: William Pickering.

Malthus, T. R. (1853). *Definitions in political economy.* Second edition edited by John Cazenove with a Preface, Notes and Supplementary Remarks. London: Simpkin and Marshall.

Malthus, T. R. (1989). In: J. Pullen (Ed.), *Principles of political economy: Variorum edition* (Vol. 2). Cambridge: Cambridge University Press.

Malthus, T. R. (2004). In: J. Pullen & T. H. Parry (Eds), *T.R. Malthus: The unpublished papers in the collection of Kanto Gakuen University* (Vol. II). Cambridge: Cambridge University Press.

McCulloch, J. R. (1824). *A discourse on the rise, progress, peculiar objects, and importance of political economy: Containing an outline of a course of lectures on the principles and doctrines of that science.* Edinburgh: Constable.

Pullen, J. (Ed.). (1978). The editor of the second edition of T. R. Malthus' *Principles of Political EconomyHistory of Political Economy, 10*(2), 286–297.

Pullen, J. (1989). Introduction. In: T.R. Malthus (Ed.), *Principles of political economy* (Variorum ed., Pullen, J. (Ed.), Vol. 2, Vol. I, pp. lxi–lxiv). Cambridge: Cambridge University Press.
Rashid, S. (1982). Malthus and the *British Critic*. *History of Economics Society Bulletin*, *3*(2), 11–15.
Seligman, E. R. A. (1903). On some neglected British economists. *Economic Journal*, *13*(51 and 52), 335–363 and 511–535.
Sraffa, P., & Dobb, M. (Eds). (1973). *The works and correspondence of David Ricardo* (Vol. 11). Cambridge: Cambridge University Press.
Tooke, T. (1823). *Thoughts and details on the high and low prices of the last thirty years* (2nd ed). London: John Murray. 1824, with slightly different title.
Tooke, T. (1826). *Considerations on the state of the currency*. London: John Murray.
Tooke, T. (1829). *A letter to Lord Grenville on the effects ascribed to the resumption of cash payments on the value of the currency*. London: John Murray.
Whewell, W. (Ed.). (1859). *Literary remains: Consisting of lectures and tracts on political economy of the late rev. Richard Jones*. London: John Murray.

APPENDIX. CAZENOVE'S ECONOMIC PUBLICATIONS[28]

Books and Pamphlets

Works published anonymously are indicated by asterisks.*

(1820) * A Reply to Mr. Say's Letters to Mr. Malthus on the Subject of the Stagnation of Trade, London, J.M. Richardson, 60 pp.

(1822) * Considerations on the Accumulation of Capital and Its Effects on Profits and on Exchangeable Value, London, J.M. Richardson, 64 pp.

(1829) Questions Respecting the National Debt and Taxation Stated and Answered, London, J.M. Richardson, 44 pp.
(A copy with MS. notes in Cazenove's hand suggests that he at one time envisaged a second edition.)

(1832a) * The Evidence That Would Have Been Given by Mr. _____ , Late a Continental Merchant, Before the Committee of Secrecy Appointed to Inquire into the Expediency of Renewing the Bank Charter, London, P. Richardson, 22 pp.
(The British Library copy has the name 'John Cazenove' inserted in Cazenove's hand in the space after 'Mr.' on the title page, and contains a number of corrections in Cazenove's hand.)

(1832b) * Outlines of Political Economy: being a plain and short view of the laws relating to the production, distribution, and consumption of wealth; to which is added, a brief explanation of the nature and effects of taxation; suited to the capacity of every one, London, P. Richardson, 151 pp.

(1840) An Elementary Treatise on Political Economy: or a short exposition of its first and fundamental principles, London, A.H. Baily, 150 pp.

[1847] * *The Money Crisis*, 16 pp. No date, no place of publication, no publisher. Printed by Bradbury and Evans, London.
(In the British Library copy, 'By John Cazenove' has been inserted in Cazenove's hand on the title page.)

(1859) *Thoughts on a Few Subjects of Political Economy*, London, Simpkin, Marshall and Co., 102 pp.

(1861) Supplement to Thoughts on a Few Subjects of Political Economy, London, Simpkin, Marshall and Co., 54 pp.
(A letter from James Pennington to Cazenove is printed on pp. 48–54.)

(1873) * *A Few Remarks upon Certain Practical Questions of Political Economy*, London, Simpkin, Marshall and Co., 23 pp.; (1873) 2nd ed., 24 pp; (1874), 3rd ed., 24 pp.

(1874) * A Few Remarks on Professor Cairnes' Recent Contribution to Political Economy. By a former member of the Political Economy Club, London, Simpkin, Marshall and Co., 18 pp.

Publications Edited by Cazenove

Malthus (1836, 1853).

Reviews

Cazenove (1824, 1832).

SELIGMAN ON 'E.R.': A CONTRIBUTION TO THE HISTORY OF MATHEMATICAL ECONOMICS

James P. Henderson

The efforts to develop the history of mathematical economics in Britain date back to William Stanley Jevons who prepared a 'List of Mathematico-Economic Books, Memoirs, and Other Published Writings'. He published this list in the second edition of his *The Theory of Political Economy* (Jevons, 1879). Irving Fisher updated and revised Jevons's 'List', publishing it first as an appendix to his 1892 doctoral dissertation (Fisher, 1926), and as a 'Bibliography of Mathematical Economics', which he appended to Nathaniel T. Bacon's translation of Augustin Cournot's *Researches into the Mathematical Principles of the Theory of Wealth* (Fisher, 1927). Jevons and Fisher identified the first and second contributions to mathematical economics in Britain: Major-General Henry Lloyd's *An Essay on the Theory of Money* (1771) and Samuel Turner's *Letter Addressed to the Right Hon. Robert Peel with Reference to the Expediency of the Resumption of Cash Payments at the Period Fixed by Law* (1819). But neither discovered the third publication to employ mathematics in economic analysis. That discovery was made by Edwin R. A. Seligman in his 'On Some Neglected British Economists' (1903, p. 352). *An Essay on Some General Principles of Political Economy, on Taxes upon Raw Produce, and on Commutation of Tithes* was

English, Irish and Subversives Among the Dismal Scientists
Research in the History of Economic Thought and Methodology, Volume 28-B, 137–151

ISSN: 0743-4154/doi:10.1108/S0743-4154(2010)000028B009

published anonymously in 1822. The author who identified himself only as 'E.R.' in the 'Preface' was Edward Rogers (1794?–1824). Seligman noted that Rogers's mathematical *Essay* had escaped the notice of both Jevons and Fisher. This pamphlet was the first mathematical critique of Ricardo's *Principles* and Seligman called its mathematical elements 'worthy of note' and discerned the 'extreme simplicity' of Henry Lloyd's mathematics when compared with Rogers's pamphlet (Seligman, 1903, p. 352).

Edward Rogers entered Gonville and Caius College, Cambridge in 1810 where he earned a bachelor of arts degree in 1814 and a master of arts in 1817 (Venn, 1898, Vol. II, p. 155). Seligman noted that the *Essay* was Rogers only known publication. His discovery of Rogers's *Essay*, when added to the Jevons–Fisher bibliography of mathematical economics works, completed the list of mathematical publications authored by the Whewell Group of Mathematical Economists. Six authors published mathematical economics works in Britain between 1822 and 1850: Rogers, William Whewell, Colonel T. Perronet Thompson, John Edward Tozer, Sir John William Lubbock and Dionysius Lardner. These six are linked together and form the Whewell Group of Mathematical Economists, an important subset of the Cambridge Network of Science (see Henderson, 1996).[1]

Ross M. Robertson, in his article 'Mathematical Economics before Cournot', specifies two characteristics common to the early mathematical economists: 'first, they use mathematical notation, and second … conscious functional thinking characterises [their] work' (Robertson, 1949, p. 524). Applying Robertson's criteria to the early British mathematical economists eliminates works that employed arithmetic examples rather than 'conscious functional thinking'. The Whewell Group authored all of the known mathematical economics works published in Britain between 1822 and 1850.

The relationships and linkages within and around the Whewell group are clear cut. William Whewell was the central figure to whom the others in the group were linked. They all shared a commitment to the inductive methodology. All had achieved some distinction in mathematics as students: Rogers was third wrangler in 1814, and Whewell was second wrangler in 1816. In addition, Cambridge served as a common base for the Whewell group. Those whom Whewell saw as opponents – Jeremy Bentham, James Mill, David Ricardo, John Stuart Mill and Richard Whately – were neither mathematicians nor graduates of Cambridge.

Two historians of mathematical economics – Ross M. Robertson (1949) and Reghinos D. Theocharis (1983) – explored the early development of mathematical economics after Seligman (1903). Jevons and Fisher had concluded that Jevons's mathematical predecessors 'suffered complete oblivion'

(Jevons, 1879, p. xlvii; Fisher, 1926, p. 109). Robertson concurred, claiming that the early mathematical economists stand 'as more or less isolated figures who cannot be said to have contributed to a current of thought because there is no discernable flow' (Robertson, 1949, pp. 535–36).[2] Yet with Seligman's rediscovery of Rogers's *Essay*, a 'current of thought' becomes clear – That 'current flows' from Edward Rogers to William Whewell to John Edward Tozer. All three formulated mathematical models of several doctrines set forth by David Ricardo. Furthermore, their objective was to employ mathematics to uncover the logical flaws in Ricardo's *Principles.* A simple review of their mathematical treatment of Ricardo's *Principles* reveals the similarities in their mathematical models. A search of Whewell's correspondence confirms that after reading Rogers's *Essay*, Whewell decided to attack Ricardo mathematically in two papers read before the Cambridge Philosophical Society and published in that Society's *Transactions* – 'Mathematical exposition of some doctrines of political economy' (1829) and 'Mathematical exposition of some of the leading doctrines in Mr. Ricardo's *Principles of Political Economy and Taxation*' (1831). This flow of thought continues on to John Edward Tozer's two mathematical economics papers – 'Mathematical investigations of the effect of machinery on the wealth of a community in which it is employed and on the fund for the payment of wages' (1838) and 'On the effect of the non-residence of landlords, &c. on the wealth of a community' (1840). Like Whewell, Tozer read these papers before the Cambridge Philosophical Society and they too were published in the Society's *Transactions.* In his introduction to the reprint of Tozer's two mathematical economics papers, David A. Collard emphasises the deliberate association, asserting that in his mathematical economics works 'Tozer was a disciple of William Whewell' (Collard, 1968, p. xvii).

Rather than recounting the contributions made by all of the members of the Whewell Group of Mathematical Economists, here we will focus attention on Edward Rogers and William Whewell. We are interested in Seligman's treatment of Rogers's *Essay* and the consequences of Seligman's discovery on the subsequent efforts to write the history of early mathematical economics in Britain.

The mathematical works of the Whewell Group of Mathematical Economists fall into two categories: First, those aimed at refuting certain doctrines promulgated by Ricardo and his school, whose highly rationalistic and *a priori* methodology had little in common with the intellectual traditions of Whewell and the Cambridge network. The second category included those employing mathematics to develop original economic analyses. Included in the first category are the works by Rogers, Whewell and Tozer. By specifying certain Ricardian doctrines in mathematical terms, these authors opened the way to a serious consideration of the empirical relevance of these theories.

Rogers formulated mathematical statements of the idea that price is determined by the interaction of demand and supply and he created a mathematical model to analyse the economic effects of Ricardo's treatment of a commutation of the tithe. Whewell formulated mathematical statements of demand elasticity, drawing on Rogers's analysis. He also developed mathematical models of several of David Ricardo's theories, including his growth model, his analysis of the incidence of various forms of taxation, his fixed capital concepts and his treatment of specie flows and foreign trade prices. Whewell also analysed mathematically John Stuart Mill's reciprocal demand model of foreign trade. He read two mathematical economics papers before the Cambridge Philosophical Society in 1850 – 'Mathematical exposition of some doctrines of political economy, second memoir' and 'Mathematical exposition of certain doctrines of political economy, third memoir'. As their titles point out, Tozer's two papers examine the effects of the introduction of machinery on wealth and the wages fund and he analysed the effects of the non-residence of landlords on a nation's wealth when such rent payments are sent out of the country.

DEMAND ANALYSIS

Seligman noted four topics that Rogers investigated in this pamphlet: the principles that regulate the exchange value of commodities; the wage theory; the incidence of taxes on agricultural products and an analysis of the economic consequences of a commutation of the tithe. This last topic Rogers treated mathematically. Seligman asserted that the

> appearance of Malthus's *Principles of Political Economy* in 1820 ... [gave] rise to an active discussion on some of the fundamental topics in dispute between Ricardo, Say and Malthus... . Most of the essays of the time, however, were concerned with the discussion of the nature and measure of value, and of these the majority based themselves on the theory advocated by Ricardo and McCulloch. (1903, pp. 351–352)

Yet Rogers claimed in the preface to his *Essay* that he wrote it before he had seen Malthus's *Principles of Political Economy*.

Seligman identified Rogers's pamphlet as the first significant attack on the Ricardian labour theory of value. He quoted Rogers's strong claim that

> Commodities are not sold because they are produced, but because they are demanded. Neither does their exchangeable value arise from the cost of producing them, but from

the demand for them when produced ... The quantity of labour only affects the value as it affects the supply. (Rogers, 1822, p. 8, quoted in Seligman, 1903, p. 352)

Seligman explained that Rogers 'proceeds with his argument to show that high wages do not necessarily mean low profits, but may mean high prices; and he then applies this doctrine to the subject of taxation' (Seligman, 1903, p. 352). Rogers then formulated the first known attempt to express mathematically the idea that price is determined by the interaction of supply and demand (Rogers 1822, p. 62).

$$\text{Price} \propto \frac{\text{Demand}}{\text{Supply}}$$

The symbol $\propto$ is one of proportionality, and the equation is read: 'the price will vary as the demand directly, and the supply inversely' (1822, p. 19).

Rogers' analysis of demand directly influenced William Whewell's mathematical formulation, in particular his concept of demand elasticity. Rogers examined the labour theory of value as put forth by both Adam Smith and David Ricardo. After reviewing and rejecting the 'high authority' of Smith and Ricardo, he asserted 'that the real and permanent exchangeable value of a commodity is not dependent *immediately* either on the quantity of labour which is condensed in it, or on the quantity of labour which is condensed in the object given for it' (1822, p. 7). Demand plays a much more prominent role in the determination of exchange value than either Smith or Ricardo was willing to attribute to it. Rogers's commentary bears a remarkable similarity to the famous argument put forth later by Richard Whately: 'It is not that pearls fetch a high price *because* men have dived for them; but on the contrary, men dive for them because they fetch a high price' (Whately, 1832, p. 253). In Rogers's words: 'Commodities are not sold because they are produced, but because they are demanded. Neither does their exchangeable value arise from the cost of producing them, but from the demand for them when produced' (Rogers, 1822, p. 8).

Rogers offered two alternative concepts of demand and he spoke of the two senses in which he used the term.

The term demand may be employed either as a measure of the quantity of produce which would be purchased, if the price remained the same, or of the whole sum which persons are willing to expend in the purchase of that produce rather than diminish their consumption, if the price rises, or with an actual increase of consumption, if the price falls. (1822, p. 12)[3]

The first part of Rogers's definition implies demand in the schedule sense of the term – a relationship between the quantity demanded, 'the quantity of produce which would be purchased', and the demand price. When used in this sense, the price is stable.

Rogers made a clear distinction between functional relationships and proportional relationships, a distinction not made by those British writers who had made earlier efforts in mathematical economics.

> Mr. Say lays it down as a rule, that 'the value of every commodity rises always in a direct ratio to the demand, and in an inverse ratio to the supply'. This, however, is not correct, if the word demand be employed in the former of its two senses; for though the price may depend upon the demand, it will not be proportional to the demand... . One thing, it is clear, may depend upon another without being proportional to it. (1822, pp. 12–13)

He proposed to use a proportional demand relationship, when 'we employ that word in the latter of the two senses' (1822, p. 15.). Given his distinction between functional and proportional relationships, this is clearly a simplifying assumption used only to facilitate the analysis of the effects of a price change. Rogers's 'conscious functional thinking' here meets Robertson's second criteria of truly mathematical economics.

Rogers's second concept of demand was expressed in terms of total consumer expenditure – 'the whole sum which persons are willing to expend in the purchase of that produce'. In his second sense of the term 'demand', he focused on the effects that price changes have on total consumer expenditures. He developed a crude demand elasticity concept from this meaning of demand. It was this concept of demand that was most influential. In particular, this offers a way to directly quantify demand, something that neither Smith's definition – the quantity of labour that could be purchased with said commodity – nor that of Ricardo's – the labour employed to produce the commodity – could measure. Moreover, Rogers's concept gave William Whewell a tool that he used in his own analysis of demand and demand elasticity.

Rogers's second demand definition enabled him to develop a rough concept of demand elasticity. He employed demand elasticity in his analysis of the incidence of a tax on raw agricultural produce. First, he analysed the incidence of this tax assuming that the demand was perfectly inelastic – 'consumers would rather pay the necessary increase of price than diminish their consumption in any degree'. He realised that this was not necessarily always true, for the raw produce might be 'so little desirable that its purchasers would choose to diminish their consumption rather than to increase their expenditure in any degree'. Next, he considered the tax incidence when the demand was unitarily elastic – 'the consumers completely defend their income from the exactions of the tax-gatherer'

(1822, pp. 31–32). This, too, was a simplifying assumption about the demand elasticity. His own best estimate of the elasticity of the demand for corn was this:

> Suppose the price of corn to rise one-tenth, it is probable that many persons, rather than pay eleven shillings for flour in place of ten, would prefer to consume something less; not, indeed, one-tenth less, for they would divide the matter; they would spend in flour perhaps ten shillings and six pence instead of ten shillings, and consequently consume about one-twentieth less. (1822, pp. 33–34)

What is particularly interesting about this passage is Rogers's halting effort approximate a more realistic estimate of consumers' reaction to price changes. Whewell did this too using 'Gregory King's Law of Demand', as we shall see. Though Rogers's conception of demand elasticity is crude, it had important implications for his analysis of the incidence of a tax on raw produce. It was also used by Whewell to create his own more sophisticated analysis of demand elasticity.

On 2 and 14 March 1829, Whewell read his first memoir, 'Mathematical exposition of some doctrines of political economy', before the Cambridge Philosophical Society. This paper reviewed a dispute over the incidence of various taxes levied on 'the produce of land, as tithes, land-tax, rates, &c'. The disputants were 'the followers of Mr. Ricardo, &c. [who] maintain that all taxes on the produce of land are ultimately paid by the consumers' and Colonel T. Perronet Thompson who 'hold[s] it demonstrable that they fall principally upon the landlord' (Whewell, 1829, pp. 205, 196). Whewell sided with the position Thompson took in his *True Theory of Rent* (1826). As Edward Rogers had employed mathematics to analyse the consequences of a commutation of the tithe in his *Essay*, Whewell too developed mathematical models to settle the questions of tax incidence.

Each of the parties to the dispute started with a common set of assumptions. Since Whewell limited himself to elementary mathematics, so that Cambridge honours students could follow his arguments, he took a 'Euclidian' approach to economics in this paper and specified six postulates on which his mathematical economic analysis would be founded.[4] He himself disagreed with these six axioms because they had been asserted rather than developed by a careful inductive process. His fourth and fifth postulates are interesting because they express his view of the relationships of supply, demand and value. These two postulates read:

(4) Increase of price is proportional to the diminution of supply.[5]
(5) Price = cost of production + profits[6] (Whewell, 1829, pp. 201, 203, 205, and 230).

In the 'corrections' that he added to this paper, Whewell noted that the fourth axiom: 'comprehends only *one* of the elements of a change of price, the alteration of the supply. Any causes which affect demand directly, affect price through it; but such causes are not considered here' (1829, p. 230).

Whewell prefaced the fourth axiom with a discussion of 'the subject of *prices*, as influenced by *demand* and *supply*'. He stated his concept of demand in an obscure way that requires careful reading to understand fully all that is implied. Since supply is a quantity, it 'offers us no difficulty in measuring it theoretically'. Demand posed a different problem, since it 'is of a more intangible and fugitive nature. It consists originally of moral elements as well as physical: of the vehemence of desire, and the urgency of need which men have, as well as their extent of means'. The problem was how to treat this demand concept mathematically. He reviewed the approach taken by Edward Rogers, who assumed that people set aside a fixed sum of money to purchase a given commodity and that this sum measured their demand for that commodity. This is Rogers's second concept of demand. 'The price therefore will vary *inversely as* the supply (not speaking with popular laxity, but in mathematical strictness)'. Whewell believed that this was a good beginning, 'but probably the approximation is a very loose and inaccurate one' (1829, pp. 199–200). He specifically rejected the notion that demand elasticity was always unity, as had Rogers in his *Essay*.

Whewell's mathematical formulations of demand elasticity are far more sophisticated than Rogers's simple verbalisations. In his first paper, Whewell's (1829) measure was

$$w = eu$$

where $w = \partial p/p$ and $u = \partial p/p$ so that

$$e = \frac{w}{u} = \frac{\partial p/p}{\partial q/q}$$

Whewell's e measures the inverse of demand elasticity, that is, price flexibility. That is a tool most often used in agricultural cases where changes in crop production causes price fluctuations, and it was Ricardo's analysis of taxes on agriculture that both Rogers and Whewell treated mathematically.

Whewell then turned to an empirical estimate of demand, reproducing a version of 'Gregory King's Law of Demand' (more accurately called the 'King-Davenant Law of Demand' for the crucial role that Charles Davenant played in developing the concept). Whewell found this in Thomas Tooke's

Table 1

A Defect in the Harvest of	Raises the Price of Corn
1/10	3/10
2/10	8/10
3/10	16/10
4/10	28/10
5/10	45/10

Note: Tooke (1824, p. 285); quoted in Whewell (1829, pp. 200–201).

book *Thoughts and Details on the High and Low Prices* (1824).[7] This table estimated the increases in corn prices resulting from various reductions ('defects') in the harvest (Table 1).

Tooke used the table as the basis for refuting the claim that all demand curves must be of unitary elasticity – the view of those who 'take it for granted that the variations in price must be in exact proportion to the variations in the quantity' (Tooke, 1824, p. 283; Tooke, 1838, p. 10). Whewell, too, wished to refute that assertion and introduced the 'King-Davenant Law' after reviewing Rogers's statement to that effect. Remember too that Rogers had formulated his own rough estimate of demand, supposing 'the price of corn to rise one-tenth', he claimed that consumers 'would prefer to consume something less; not, indeed, one-tenth less', but perhaps 'about one-twentieth less' (Rogers, 1822, pp. 33–34). Whewell, using the King-Davenant table, estimated that a *one-tenth decrease in quantity* yields a *three-tenths increase in price*. Rogers had estimated that a *one-tenth increase in price* yields a *one-twentieth decrease in the quantity demanded.* Whewell estimated price flexibility and Rogers demand elasticity.

When Whewell discovered the King-Davenant table in Tooke's 1824 book, he sent a letter to his friend, the economist Richard Jones, dated 5 March 1829. Here Whewell explained that he was presenting this paper at the Cambridge Philosophical Society.[8] He asked Jones about the demand table: 'I have been putting on paper & reading & I found a memorandum which I had made of the dependence of price on supply but without the name of the book in which it is given' (Whewell to Jones, 5 March 1829, Whewell Papers, Add. Mss.c51[62]). Whewell described the King-Davenant law and then confessed that he intended to make use of such 'facts' that were allegedly obtained inductively. He told Jones that 'Any facts or even assertions of this kind will be useful to me & their accuracy not very important'. Rogers's crude estimate was an 'assertion' of the kind that Whewell found 'useful to me'. Whewell's mathematical economics papers were not directly concerned with demonstrating the inductive approach to economics, which, he said, 'belongs to you [i.e., to Jones]'. His concern was to use empirical data to illustrate 'the *mode* of applying mathematics' to political economy and to expose the defects in Ricardo's deductive logic, which 'may, I am sure, be managed best by my implements' – mathematics. After reproducing the King-Davenant table, in his 1829 paper, he remarked:

> There can be little doubt that this table is at least so far true, that the increase of the price is much more rapid than the diminution of supply. And according to this table the increase of the price varies according to no simple power of the defect of the supply. It would be easy to find the law by which the increase of price may depend on the defect and the square of the defect of the supply, so as nearly to satisfy the above data; but it is not necessary for our purposes to go into this detail. (Whewell, 1829, p. 201)

Notice how he dodged the issue of the inductive accuracy of the table – 'it is not necessary for our purposes to go into this detail' – since the table was merely intended as an illustration – 'to shew the *mode* of applying mathematics'. This completed his preliminary discussion, and he stated his fourth axiom – 'Increase of price is proportional to the diminution of supply'.

Then Whewell considered this axiom in terms of the King-Davenant table:

> Accordingly the fraction which expresses the deficiency must be multiplied by some constant number, in order to give us the fraction which expresses the increase of price. In the table just mentioned, 1/10 defect of supply gives 3/10 increase of price. It may therefore perhaps be assumed, that up to the magnitude of 1/10, the increase of price is three times the deficiency of supply. Thus a deficiency of 1/60 would increase the prices 1/20 and so on. I shall however use the general number e instead of 3 in most cases. It is manifest that whatever more accurate data we may hereafter obtain for establishing the law of dependence, the increase of price *ceteris paribus* must be a function of the defect of supply, and may in this manner be introduced into the calculation (1829, p. 201).

Several things must be said about this remarkable statement. Firstly, his use of the term 'supply' here seems to convey the meaning of changes in 'quantity demanded' – that is, movements along the demand curve. That Whewell was analyzing a demand curve is clear from comments found in one of his notebooks (Whewell Papers, R.18.8[10]). In that notebook, is a crude diagram, based on the King-Davenant table. Though that notebook is undated, it contains his notes for the 1829 mathematical economics paper. The diagram appears on the same page as the King-Davenant table. That page also contains several calculations employing his price flexibility equation, $w = eu$, where u is set equal to the table's price rises and w is set equal to the table's 'defects' in the corn crop.[9] We know of no earlier drawings of a 'demand' curve. Next, in the statement quoted above, Whewell referred to a simplifying notion that he used again, and that Jevons also employed – the simplest way to express the price–quantity relationship shown in the King-Davenant table is to assume that the change in price equals 'the square of the defect of the supply'. Thirdly, Whewell recognised that the elasticity of the demand curve for corn varies with the degree of the 'defect of the crop', yet chose to make the *simplifying assumption* that 'the increase of price is proportional to the deficiency of the supply'. This simplifying assumption applies only as long as the 'deficiency of supply' is held to small changes, 'up to the magnitude of 1/10'. Finally, there is a clear statement made by a competent mathematician, that the price–quantity relationship in the King-Davenant table establishes 'the law of dependence, the increase of price *ceteris paribus* must be a function of the defect of' the quantity demanded. Whewell's 'law of dependence' – Law of Demand – reverses the neoclassical statement by making price the dependent variable and quantity demanded the independent variable. That is the appropriate conclusion given the nature of the King-Davenant table, which was an example drawn from agriculture where changes ('defects') in crop production will affect prices.

ANALYZING THE INCIDENCE OF AGRICULTURAL TAXES

As Seligman pointed out, Rogers examined the incidence of taxes on agricultural production. Where the demand for these products was perfectly inelastic, agricultural production was unaffected by the tax and the whole tax fell upon the consumer. Whewell analysed this same case in his 1829 paper and concluded that such a tax fell not only upon the consumer, but also on the landlords' rent and the capitalists' profit. Clearly, Whewell's model of Ricardo's tax was more inclusive than Rogers's, including as it did the incomes of landlords and capitalists.

Where the demand for agricultural products was unitarily elastic, Rogers concluded that there was no change in total revenue as output was reduced, so that the tax fell wholly on the farmers. Whewell's analysis of this case concluded that the whole tax fell on the landlords' rent and the capitalists' profit. Again, the Whewell model was more inclusive than Rogers's simpler model. Moreover, Whewell having formulated a more sophistical measure of demand elasticity, his price flexibility equation $w = eu$, was able to analyse additional cases beyond Rogers's treatment of perfectly inelastic and unitarily elastic demand curves. Yet it is clear that Rogers's *Essay* influenced Whewell's mathematical models in his first mathematical economics paper (1829).

In a letter to Richard Jones, dated 21 May 1821, Whewell remarked: 'I have been reading Rogers' pamphlet which seems very tolerably clear-headed, though not very striking as to general views – but it is no small merit as it keeps him out of mischief which cleverer men get into' (Whewell Papers, Add. Mss.c.51[11]). Whewell's 1829 paper concerned problems similar to those dealt with by Rogers in his earlier pamphlet; in particular, Whewell used Rogers's concept of measuring demand for his own more sophisticated analysis. Before deriving his own mathematical statement of demand, Whewell described Rogers's analysis and pointed out the weaknesses in that approach:

> A member of this University who formerly applied mathematical reasoning to some questions of this kind, proposed to measure demand by considering the latter element (the means of purchasing) as constant, the desire and the difficulty balancing each other so as to preserve this constancy. He supposed (merely as a means of reducing questions to calculation) that men set aside a certain sum to purchase a given article, and that this sum measures the demand. If the article increases in price they may buy just so much less, if it becomes cheaper they purchase so much more. The price therefore will vary inversely as the supply, (not speaking with popular laxity, but in mathematical strictness). Now this mode of reasoning, answers extremely well the purpose of avoiding all indefiniteness, and offers a kind of approximation to the law which obtains as to changes of prices; but probably the approximation is a very loose and inaccurate one. (Whewell, 1829, pp. 9–10)

Whewell's reference to 'a member of this University who formerly applied mathematical reasoning to questions of this kind', his description and use of Rogers's approach to measuring demand, the fact that both treated mathematically Ricardo's analysis of taxes on agriculture, and Whewell's comments to Jones in the 21 May 1822 letter all establish the link between Rogers and Whewell. Moreover, the first time that Whewell ever mentioned his interest in applying mathematics to economic analysis was his reference to Rogers's *Essay* in his 21 May 1822 letter to Richard Jones. Thus, it seems fair to conclude that Edward Rogers's *Essay* inspired Whewell's own interest in this effort.

Without Seligman's discovery of Edward Rogers's 1822 pamphlet – *An Essay on Some General Principles of Political Economy, on Taxes upon Raw Produce, and on Commutation of Tithes* – the history of early British mathematical economics was incomplete. The clear-cut flow of ideas from Rogers to Whewell to Tozer had not been discerned before Seligman's discovery. The importance of Rogers's influence on William Whewell's decision to apply mathematics to Ricardian economics now becomes clear. Whewell's growing stature at Cambridge gave him enormous influence in academic circles. We see this influence most clearly in the sciences, where his interest in applying mathematics to economic analysis conveyed the impression that political economy could become a science. Moreover, his willingness to join Richard Jones and others to grant economics entrance into the most influential scientific institution of the day – the British Association for the Advancement of Science – offered the discipline a type of scientific respectability that the leading political economists of that era could not match (see the chapter entitled 'The Attempt to Make Economics a Science: The Statistical Section and the Statistical Society', in Henderson, 1996). Seligman's discovery of Edward Rogers's mathematical economics pamphlet was the key to understanding how William Whewell came to apply the tools of mathematics to economics.

NOTES

1. It should be made clear from the start that the Whewell Group of Mathematical Economists was not a 'school'. Fairly general agreement defines the sociological characteristics of a school of economic thought. Henry W. Spiegel, for instance, notes that a school consists of 'a recognised leader, a closely knit group of followers to exalt and spread the doctrines of the master, and a periodical to help in their dissemination'. Such schools frequently have a geographic base, institutional links, and access to or control over a journal. Finally, 'the founders of influential schools devoted many years to their nurture' (Spiegel, 1971, pp. 183–184). Though the Whewell Group meets several of these criteria, key elements are missing. Thus, we have something akin to a 'school' which I have chosen to call a 'group' of mathematical economists.
2. Only Theocharis (1983, p. 1) detected 'certain currents of thought' that link 'Ceva... to Spinelli, Beccaria to Silio, Frisi through Ortes, Ferroni, Venturi and others to Valeriani and Fuoco, Gioja and Cournot, Kroncke to Thunen, [and] Isnard to Lang'. Theocharis missed the Whewell Group of Mathematical Economists in Britain because he focused on Cournot and ends his study at 1838 when Cournot's work first appeared.
3. Note also that in each meaning, the definition is framed in *ex ante* terms.
4. In Henderson (1996), I devoted a chapter to the target audience of Whewell's applications of mathematics to economic issues. There were two audiences: Cambridge students and political economists. That he wished to attract Cambridge students explains why his models are relatively simple and avoided the use of calculus

at points where it would be a most useful tool. He used mathematics to attack the deductive analysis of David Ricardo and his followers, while relying on inductivists like Richard Jones and Charles Babbage to provide an inductive alternative for the political economists.

5. On page 205, the six axioms were summarised, Whewell wrote the fourth axiom this way: 'Increase of price $\propto$ diminution of supply'.

6. When he introduced this axiom, Whewell stated it in these words: 'The rate of price of any article will be such that the whole price of any portion is equal to the capital employed to produce it together with the usual profits' (Whewell, 1829, p. 202).

7. Thomas Tooke (1774–1858) employed the King-Davenant table in a chapter titled 'Effect of Quantity on Price', which is found in both *Thoughts and Details on the High and Low Prices of the Thirty Years, from 1793 to 1822* (1824) and in his *A History of Prices and the State of the Circulation from 1793 to 1837* (1838). These are impressive collections of data and analyses of prices and money, exactly the kind of inductive study that Whewell and his friend, Richard Jones, wished to promote.

8. Richard Jones and William Whewell set about to 'partly find and partly form' an inductivist school of economics. Whewell was to use mathematics to attack the deductive economics of the Ricardians, while Jones was to develop a series of alternative inductive studies on economic topics (see Henderson, 1996).

9. These calculations and the fact that all of the books referred to in the notebook appeared before 1829 lead to the conclusion that the notebook dates from 1829.

REFERENCES

Private Papers

Papers collection. Trinity College Library, Cambridge.

Collard, D. (1968). Introduction to the work of John Edward Tozer. In: J. E. Tozer (Ed.), *Mathematical investigations of the effect of machinery on the wealth of a community in which it is employed and on the fund for the payment of wages* and *On the effect of the nonresidence of landlords, &c. on the wealth of a community* (pp. v–xxi). New York: Augustus M. Kelley.

Fisher, I. (1926). Bibliography of mathematical economic writings. In: *Mathematical investigations in the theory of value and prices* (pp. 120–124). New Haven: Yale University Press, Appendix 4.

Fisher, I. (1927). Bibliography of mathematical economics. In: A. Cournot (Ed.), *Researches into the mathematical principles of the theory of wealth* (pp. 173–209). New York: Macmillan. Bacon, N.T. (Trans.).

Henderson, J. P. (1996). *Early mathematical economics: William Whewell and the British case*. Lanham, MD: Rowman & Littlefield.

Jevons, W.S. (1879). List of mathematico-economic books, memoirs, and other published writings. In: *The theory of political economy* (pp. 301–310). London: Macmillan, Appendix I.

Lloyd, Maj.-Gen, H. (1771). *An essay on the theory of money*. London: J. Almon.
Robertson, R. M. (1949). Mathematical economics before Cournot. *Journal of Political Economy*, *57*(6), 523–536.
Rogers, E. (1822). *An essay on some general principles of political economy, on taxes upon raw produce, and on commutation of tithes*. London: Henry Butterworth.
Seligman, E. R. A. (1903). On some neglected British economists. *Economic Journal*, *13*(51 and 52), 335–363 and 511–535.
Spiegel, H. (1971). *The growth of economic thought*. Englewood Cliffs, NJ: Prentice-Hall.
Theocharis, R. D. (1983). *Early developments in mathematical economics*. London: Macmillan.
Thompson, T.P., Col. (1826). *The true theory of rent, in opposition to Mr. Ricardo and others, of fallacies of rent, tithes, &c. in the form of a review of Mr. Mill's elements of political economy*. London: Effingham Wilson.
Tooke, T. (1824). *Thoughts and details on the high and low prices of the thirty years, from 1793 to 1822*. London: John Murray.
Tooke, T. (1838). *A history of prices and the state of the circulation from 1793 to 1837* (6 vols.). London: Longman, Orme, Brown, Green, and Longmans.
Turner, S. (1819). *A letter addressed to the right Hon. Robert Peel with reference to the expediency of the resumption of cash payments at the period fixed by law* (2nd ed.). London: J. Hatchard.
Venn, J. (1898). *Gonville and Caius Bibliographical History, 2 vols.*, Cambridge: Cambridge University Press.
Whately, R. (1832). *Introductory lectures on political economy*. London: Fellowes.
Whewell, W. (1829). Mathematical exposition of some doctrines of political economy. *Transactions of the Cambridge Philosophical Society*, *3*(1), 192–230.
Whewell, W. (1831). Mathematical exposition of some of the leading doctrines in Mr. Ricardo's *Principles of Political Economy and Taxation*. *Transactions of the Cambridge Philosophical Society*, *4*(1), 155–198.

SAMUEL BAILEY AND THE QUESTION OF HIS 'INFLUENCE': A SCEPTICAL VIEW

Samuel Hollander

Edwin Seligman, in his study of 'neglected' British economists, represented Samuel Bailey – author of *A Critical Dissertation on Value* (1825), written anonymously in reply to the formulation of Ricardian theory in De Quincey's *Templars' Dialogue* (1824) – as one of the 'more acute critic[s] of Ricardo' who 'exerted considerable influence at the time' (Seligman, 1903, p. 352). Seligman intended '[t]he opposition to the labour theory of value, the emphasis put on time as an element in value, the broadening of the rent concept, the criticism of the statement that rent does not enter into price, and the importance assigned to productivity in affecting value – all these constitute doctrines of importance in the recent phases of the science' (1903, p. 355; also p. 534). Particular mention is made of Bailey's insistence on value as relative and his objections to the notion of a commodity possessing invariable value, and also his position that value 'although often spoken of as a quality of external objects, really implies "a feeling or state of mind"' (Seligman, 1903, p. 353, quoting Bailey, 1825, p. 180). The broadening of the rent concept refers to an analogy between land rents and labour rents: 'The extraordinary profit out of which rent arises is analogous to the extraordinary remuneration which an artisan of more than common dexterity obtains beyond the wages given to the workman of ordinary skill .... In the one case this monopoly is bounded by the existence of inferior

English, Irish and Subversives Among the Dismal Scientists
Research in the History of Economic Thought and Methodology, Volume 28-B, 153–198

ISSN: 0743-4154/doi:10.1108/S0743-4154(2010)000028B010

soils, in the other of inferior degrees of dexterity' (Bailey, 1825, pp. 196–197). As for the function of time, Seligman (1903, p. 218) cites Bailey's Böhm-Bawerkian theme, that '[w]e generally prefer a present pleasure or enjoyment to a distant one, not superior to it in other respects'. Beyond this, Bailey was 'the first to put his finger on the real fallacy of the doctrine that wages and profits must vary inversely. ... "If the productive power of labour be augmented ... labour may rise in value without a fall, nay, even with a rise of profits"' (Seligman, 1903, pp. 354–355; quoting Bailey, 1825, pp. 65–66). This insight, Seligman maintained, 'virtually contains the whole of the modern theory of the economy of high wages'. He makes no mention of Bailey's varieties of imperfect competition and barriers to entry that impressed other commentators.

In concluding his summary of Bailey's achievements Seligman remarked '[t]hat they should have been enunciated in 1825 and then seemingly forgotten is eloquent testimony to the power which is sometimes exerted by a few great names in silencing for a time all criticisms, however sound they may be' (Seligman, 1903, p. 255; see also, p. 355).[1] At one time, Lionel Robbins – impressed by the significance accorded *relative* valuation – similarly took this rationale for granted: 'It was one of the few real injuries done to the progress of Economic Science by the solidarity of the English Classics that, presumably because of its attacks on Ricardo and Malthus, Bailey's work was allowed to drop into neglect' (Robbins, 1935, p. 60n). The Seligman–Robbins position had, of course, been suggested earlier by Jevons: 'Economists such as Malthus and Senior ... were driven out of the field by the unity and influence of the Ricardo-Mill school' (Jevons, [1924]1879, pp. li–lii).

J. A. Schumpeter (1954, p. 464) welcomed Seligman's 'justly famous article', and took the same positive view of Bailey, who 'attacked the Ricardo-[James] Mill-McCulloch analysis on a broad front and with complete success. His *Dissertation*, which said, as far as fundamentals are concerned, practically all that can be said, must rank among the masterpieces of criticism in our field, and it should suffice to secure to its author a place in or near the front rank in the history of scientific economics' (1954, p. 486).[2] R. M. Rauner starts his specialist study of Bailey on value by observing that 'the many things that Bailey said so well so much earlier had to be re-discovered all over again. Professor Seligman, in his memorable article, was amongst the first to start the re-discovery' (Rauner, 1961, p. 1; also 1987, p. 174). And similarly D. P. O'Brien (1988, pp. 180–182, 186–188 and 198) gives Seligman an excellent press, taking on board much of his position on Bailey.

Schumpeter deduced from Cotterill's (1831, p. 8) comment that there are 'some Ricardians still remaining' that 'the decay of the Ricardian School must have become patent' soon after 1826 (Schumpeter, 1954, p. 478). But he hedged his account of Bailey: 'though but few contemporaries did justice to him, it became clear in time that he had turned the tide and dealt a fatal blow' (1954, p. 599). And that Bailey's attack was not decisive, Schumpeter opined in line with Seligman and Robbins, could be partly explained by 'the henchmen who continued to stand by their guns and to teach exploded doctrine as if nothing had happened' (1954, p. 478).

Seligman's evaluation that Bailey's contributions 'constitute doctrines of importance in the recent phases of the science', and his reference to 'the modern theory of high wages', suggest that he attributed to Bailey the construction of an alternative paradigm to Ricardo's. He is, however, more cautious when summarising his position at the outset of Part II of his paper: 'In the controversy that arose during the early twenties on the subject of value we found that important criticisms of the Ricardian theory were advanced by Bailey and Cotterill, and that the foundation stones for an entirely different theory was laid by Lloyd, the originator of the marginal utility doctrine of value' (Seligman, 1903, p. 511).[3] And similarly at the end of his paper, the focus is on the contributions by Lloyd, Read and Longfield, 'above all the theory of marginal utility as the basis of value, and the marginal productivity theories of wages and interest ...' (1903, p. 534), with Bailey assigned to the second rank of dissenters, making a contribution of a critical rather than positive nature.

Marian Bowley, writing a generation after Seligman, regretted that 'economists who criticized Ricardo, as for example Senior and Bailey, have been considered simply as critics who perhaps added some improvements by the way but who did not differ from him on fundamental doctrine', her own view being that 'the developments of the theory of value between 1823 and 1862' revealed 'two different and more or less contemporary schools even in England' – the Ricardian and the utility schools (Bowley, 1937, pp. 16–17). However, when it comes to evidence regarding Bailey, she (like Seligman) offered little justification for designating him a 'utility' theorist, focusing rather on his rejection of any sort of 'intrinsic' value, and his emphasis on the exceptions to a cost theory which fall under the rubric of cases of 'monopoly' (1937, p. 93). She subsequently altered her position on the broader issue, arguing that in fact '[n]o revolutionary significance' was attached by contributors in the British literature to the law of diminishing marginal utility, or the concept of intensity of demand or utility measurement, since these all stemmed from the '*Wealth of Nations*' (Bowley, 1972, p. 27).

What, however, was indeed 'inherently revolutionary' was '[t]he analysis of the limited validity of the pure cost of production theory of natural price by Bailey, Senior and Cournot in terms of market structures' (1972, p. 28).

Mark Blaug maintained that 'Bailey's criticism of Ricardo contained the germs of a far-reaching reconstruction of basic economic concepts', though he adds that Senior alone realised it (Blaug, 1958, p. 58; see also below). Rauner is more definite in his estimate of a paradigmatic breakthrough on Bailey's part: 'like Jevons, Bailey understood that Ricardo's determination to use "absolute" or "real" cost concepts was bound to bring him to untruths. On his essentially relativist foundation Bailey appreciated that a valid theory of value proceeded from more complex causes than simple labour quantity. He understood that a theory of value depended on "mental states", on "estimations", on "scarcity", and on "time" and so on' (Rauner, 1961, p. 94; also p. 101). Similarly, Rauner's later contribution to the *New Palgrave* points to a paradigmatic breakthrough, albeit an 'incomplete' one. Essentially, 'Bailey's work freed analysis from the need to link production and distribution to socioeconomic class relationships. It pointed instead towards relationships between individual needs and perceptions, and the material goods that can satisfy them' (Rauner, 1987, p. 174).

D. P. O'Brien opens his discussion of 'Classical reassessments', dealing with the contributions by Longfield, James Mill, Senior, Bailey, Torrens and Say, by declaring that these writers 'were men of independent mind and independent spirit' (O'Brien, 1988, p. 179). Bailey's independence from Ricardo is supported by reference to Rauner's 1956 doctoral dissertation, treating Bailey's philosophical orientation (Bailey, 1821), whereby 'Bailey placed the rationale of economic activity in mental phenomena ... reject[ing] the physical material conceptions of classical economics ...'. Bailey, in brief, 'saw economics as a science of mind – it was not concerned with technology. His basic philosophical position is extraordinarily "Austrian" and is much more post-1870 than the recently received interpretation would suggest, in this respect at least' (Rauner, 1956, p. 200; see also Bowley, 1937, p. 93; Rauner, 1961, pp. 5–6 and Black, 1988, p. 224). Notwithstanding all this, O'Brien plays down Bailey's originality in economics by denying that he was 'part of a separate tradition of economic thought, contemporary with mainstream classical economics, [for] it now seems clear that Bailey was in the main classical tradition insofar as his positive value theory was concerned and that he did not provide material either for a separate tradition or for a revolution in value theory' (O'Brien, 1988, p. 199).[4] Similarly, in making his case for a reappraisal, O'Brien cites an opinion to the effect that '[t]he weight of "the Ricardian errors" was so strong that even the critics and outspoken opponents of Ricardo came under their spell' (O'Brien, 1988, p. 179, quoting Blaug, 1958, p. 227).[5]

Seligman and later participants in the debate neglect the advice offered by Jacob Viner that any investigation of the extent and nature of the early dissension requires that attention be accorded to the replies of the Ricardians to their critics, for 'some of the criticisms against the Ricardian analysis were either based on misinterpretations of it or would have been accepted by the Ricardians' (Viner, 1958, pp. 419–420). In what follows, we shall follow Viner's recommendations with respect to Bailey. It emerges that in many cases Bailey's criticisms constitute misunderstandings of Ricardo's position, while others would have been considered wholly acceptable by Ricardo. Our analysis in effect dots the i's and crosses the t's of the position stated briefly by Elie Halévy, shortly after Seligman but to precisely the opposite effect, that 'all the elements of [Bailey's] criticism are borrowed from Ricardo's book' (Halévy, [1904] 1955, pp. 353–354).[6] Bailey's failure to achieve a paradigmatic breakthrough, recognised in the commentaries, is attributable neither to roadblocks erected by the authorities nor to a failure to exert sufficient pressure, but to the fact that the doctrines he propounded were essentially Ricardo's.

A second set of issues relates to Bailey's 'influence' on other 'dissenters' (Cotterill, Read, Senior, Lloyd and Torrens), on the 'Ricardians' (James Mill, McCulloch and J. S. Mill) and on Malthus. Here we have in mind Seligman's representation of Bailey as an 'acute critic' of Ricardo on value who 'exerted considerable influence at the time', and also the evaluation that '[t]he impact of Bailey's attack upon contemporary thinking was profound, judging by the number of references to it in an age not given to crediting sources' (Blaug, 1958, pp. 55–56). Our analysis finds little to justify this view of Bailey's influence.

A brief section will be devoted to Bailey's 'obligations' to others. The Conclusion summarises the Bailey–Ricardo nexus. And an appendix discusses the disputed authorship of two contributions of 1821.

BAILEY AS RICARDIAN *MALGRÉ LUI*

Elie Halévy essentially expressed the view recorded by James Mill in his anonymously written 'On the Nature, Measures, and Causes of Value'[7] that the first chapter of the *Critical Dissertation* relating to the nature of value 'contains not an assertion, who which, as far as *ideas* politico-economical are concerned, Mr. Ricardo would not have assented; it contains, not indeed, as far as such ideas are concerned, an assertion which is not implied in the propositions which Mr. Ricardo has put forth. It is a criticism on some of Mr. Ricardo's forms of expression ...' ([J. Mill], 1826a, p. 157). The justification for the Ricardian reaction is clear enough, as I shall now show.[8]

Bailey charged that Ricardo's notion of an invariable standard is self-contradictory: 'It would be an absurdity to suppose, that the value of A to B could alter, and not the value of B to A; that A could rise in value to B, and B remain stationary in value to A ...' (Bailey, 1825, p. 5; also pp. 17, 103). And '[t]he specific error of Mr. Ricardo on the subject of invariable value', he found, 'consists ... in supposing, that if the causes of value affecting one commodity remained the same, the value of that commodity could not vary, overlooking the circumstance, that value denotes a relation between two objects, which must necessarily alter with an alteration in the causes affecting either of them' (1825, p. 121). But that this objection is purely terminological emerges when we take account of Ricardo's objective in the quest for an 'invariable' measure, and of Bailey's repeated concessions that the exercise was in fact valid.

Ricardo's statement of objective in no way indicates an incomprehension of the relative value concept; to the contrary: 'When commodities varied in relative value, it would be desirable to have the means of ascertaining which of them fell and which rose in real value, and this could be effected only by comparing them one after another with some invariable standard measure of value, which should itself be subject to none of the fluctuations to which other commodities are exposed' (Sraffa & Dobb, 1973, Vol. 1, p. 43).[9] And this exercise Bailey fully allowed throughout his book. Thus at the outset: 'The truth intended by saying that B remains of the same value is, that the cause of the altered relation between A and B is in the former, and not in the latter; and to determine where the change originated is in fact the whole object of those who endeavour to show what commodities have remained stationary in value and what have varied' (Bailey, 1825, p. 12; also p. 6). And subsequently, a commodity produced with a constant labour input would permit one to establish where observed fluctuations had 'originated' (1825, p. 121); for such a commodity 'would enable us to ascertain, not the fluctuations in value between two or more commodities (for these are facts to be gathered from appropriate evidence), but the fluctuations in the quantity of labour which produced them' (1825, p. 124). And yet a further undermining of his own critique is the following footnote which frankly allows that the Ricardian programme seeking the source of variation in observed exchange rates was a 'rational, and might prove a useful inquiry' (1825, p. 127n). As a final instance of Bailey's concession: 'If A is equal in value to B, this must be owing, not only to causes operating on A, but also to causes operating on B .... [Yet] it may not be useless to recollect, that although value must in every instance arise from the combination of two sets of causes, any alteration, any rise or fall of value, may proceed from only one. The value of A and B is the effect of causes acting on both, but a change in their mutual value may arise from causes acting on either' (1825, pp. 183–184).

In the light of these concessions, it is difficult to understand why Bailey insisted so strenuously that invariability of 'value', in the sense of exchange rather than real value, is 'absurd' (1825, p. 18).[10] No one denied it. Equally problematic are his assertions that Ricardo and his followers were unaware of what it was that they were seeking to do. In fact, he conceded the game: 'Many of the strictures, which have been made on Mr. Ricardo's writings ... would be in some degree obviated if two things were conceded, namely, if we assumed that he was constantly speaking of real value, and if we were to grant him the absurdity which we have shown this expression to imply; or, in other words, if we were to consider it as importing cost of production, without relation to the power of commanding in exchange' (1825, p. 253). Bailey must have forgotten that he himself represented Ricardo's concern to be precisely the isolation of the source of an observed change in exchange rates.

That Bailey conceded the validity of the Ricardian exercise, only to proceed as if the concession had never been made by concentrating solely on the use of the term 'value' as synonymous with exchange value rather than allowing for the alternative sense of real costs, is also apparent when he cites Ricardo's own belief regarding 'the impossibility of finding any commodity of invariable value' (1825, p. 19), yet insists on a fundamental difference between their positions. For Ricardo, Bailey points out, invariability could not be satisfied since 'no commodity could be found, which is not itself exposed to the same causes of fluctuation as all other commodities', whereas for Bailey himself, even 'if all commodities were produced under exactly the same circumstances, as for instance, by labour alone' – the very simplest case – 'any commodity, which always required the same quantity of labour, could not be invariable in value, while every other commodity underwent alteration: [Ricardo] asserts, on the other hand, that such a commodity would be invariable ...' (1825, pp. 20–21; also p. 119).

As he expressed the matter in *A Letter to a Political Economist* – responding to the *Westminster Review* strictures on the *Critical Dissertation* – he had never said of Ricardo, and various others including Lauderdale and Torrens, that 'they deny the impossibility of an invariable measure';

rather, 'they maintain ... invariableness to be necessary to constitute a measure of value, while I contend that invariableness has nothing to do with it' (Bailey, 1826, pp. 14–15). Once again, Bailey can only be understood here if one adopts his usage of the term *exchange*, rather than *real*, value and understands its 'measurement' correspondingly.[11] But this in no way negates the fact that he recognised the 'truth' and 'usefulness' of Ricardo's quest for a commodity that is 'invariable' in its own costs, as a means of discerning the source of a change in observed exchange rates.

Strikingly, Bailey's *Money and its Vicissitudes of Value* (1837) follows precisely these Ricardian lines by distinguishing between, and evaluating the effects of, a change in the 'value of money' originating in circumstances affecting money alone, and those affecting commodities alone, such as general productivity increase not pertinent to the precious metals, in which case 'the prices of other commodities must necessarily fall as the facility of supplying such commodities increases' (Bailey, 1837, p. 17).[12]

James Mill was therefore justified in his reaction. That Ricardo would have responded to Bailey in the same manner is clear from his response to the anonymous *Observations on Certain Verbal Disputes* (Anon., 1821a), which in its essentials is so similar to the *Critical Dissertation* that Bailey feared he might be accused of plagiarism (see the appendix). Writing to Trower in August 1821, Ricardo observed: 'With respect to our difference of opinion on the subject of exchangeable value it is more an apparent difference than a real one. In speaking of exchangeable value you have not any idea of real value in your mind – I invariably have. Your criticisms on passages in my book are, I have little doubt, correct, because they are also the criticism of others on the same passages. A pamphlet has appeared "On Certain Verbal Disputes in Polit. Econ". where the same ground of objection is taken as you take; the fault lies not in the doctrine itself, but in my faulty manner of explaining it' (Sraffa & Dobb, 1973, Vol. 9, p. 38).

Not only is it the case that Bailey himself presented no alternative model, but of this he was well aware –'the science cannot yet be exhibited as a regular and perfect structure' (Bailey, 1825, p. xii) – although he did express a methodological preference for greater 'generality' than characterised the Ricardians. For all that, he frankly admitted in the concluding chapter 'On the Causes of Value' that Ricardo himself was not a guilty party:

> Mr. Ricardo, indeed, explicitly allows the influence of other causes [than labour embodiment], such as time, differences in the proportion of fixed and circulating capital, and inequalities in the durability of capital, by which he admits the value of commodities is liable to be affected. Notwithstanding these modifications, however, his followers

continue to lay down the position of quantity of labour being the sole cause of value in the most precise and positive terms. (Bailey, 1825, p. 230)

Even his objection to the 'followers' is somewhat watered down: 'not that they deny the exceptions, but they appear to lose sight of their existence, and frequently fall into language incompatible with their admission; while they altogether overlook the source of value to be found in partial or incomplete monopolies, and the intermixture in production of commodities which are indebted for their value to different causes' (1825, pp. 230–231).

These allowances regarding Ricardo come as a surprise since Bailey had earlier noted that '[t]he only place in Mr. Ricardo's work, where I have been able to find the expression of the general rule properly qualified is the Index'. He there says, 'the quantity of labour requisite to obtain commodities, the *principal* source of their exchangeable value' (1825, pp. 213–214n).[13] In any event, he also recognised elsewhere Ricardo's position that a wage variation will influence relative prices assuming non-uniform factor proportions (1825, p. 217); similarly, with respect to 'the effect of time on value', he allows that '[t]he influence of this cause is admitted by Mr. Ricardo, but Mr. Mill contends, that time can do nothing'. The book closes in surprisingly weak terms. His purpose had not been to decide whether or not Ricardo had 'really enriched the science of political economy with any new and important truths', but he did feel it safe to 'pronounce that – whatever those achievements might be – they are not inferences from the doctrine, that the quantity of labour employed in the production of commodities is the sole determining principle of their value. It may be affirmed, without any hazard of error, that there is not one of them, whatever they may be, which would not equally flow from the more accurate proposition, that it is the principal cause' (1825, p. 232) – which, of course, is precisely Ricardo's position.

The complaint cited above that Ricardo's followers had neglected the implications for pricing of 'partial' or 'incomplete' monopolies requires attention.[14] Bailey is using the standard early nineteenth-century term for less than infinitely elastic supply, covering the increasing-cost case characterising agriculture. And he has Ricardo in mind, and not only the followers. For though Ricardo formally classified commodities according to the 'source' of their exchangeable value, namely 'scarcity' and quantity of labour, focusing on the latter because it was quantitatively the most significant, he in fact 'enters into the consideration of the value of labour, of corn, of gold, and of other articles, in the production of which competition certainly does not operate without restraint', whereas the labour theory did not apply in these three cases: 'the value of labour can in no sense be said to be determined by the quantity of labour necessary to produce it; the value of corn in general is determined, on his own principles, by the quantity of labour required to raise corn on the worst soils in cultivation, and not by the quantity of its own producing labour; and in the same way the value of gold itself depends, not on the labour necessary to produce every individual portion of it, but on the labour necessary to extract it from the least fertile mines that are worked' (1825, pp. 228–229). Here we have Bailey giving a lesson on marginal labour cost, but turning it against Ricardo on the irrelevant grounds that the price of an *average* corn unit is not determined by 'the quantity of its own producing labour'.

The deduction from all this is that the value of intra-marginal units of corn is determined not by cost, but by 'the state of the supply and demand, or the competition of the purchasers', which 'might raise the price to an indefinite height, if it were not for the existence of other lands, which although they could produce corn only at a greater cost, would be brought into cultivation as soon as the price had risen sufficiently high to pay the ordinary profits on the capital required' (1825, p. 194). Their existence established 'the limit beyond which its value cannot rise', but 'cannot be said to the cause of its value. It is the cause of its being no higher, not the cause of its being high' (1825, p. 195).

Now despite his anti-Ricardo posturing, Bailey seems to have appreciated that he was merely restating Ricardian doctrine, for he even commends Ricardo's form of expression: 'We accordingly find that the expression used by Mr. Ricardo on this subject is, not that the value of corn is *caused*, but that it is *regulated* by the cost of production on the least fertile lands. The owners of land of superior fertility enjoy a monopoly, which, however, does not enable them to raise their commodity indefinitely, according to the varying wants and caprices of mankind, but which is bounded by the existence of inferior soils' (1825, p. 195).

Bailey goes on to point out that perceiving rent as a 'monopoly' return or an 'extraordinary profit which is obtained by the possession of an instrument of production, protected up to a certain point from competition', it followed that such 'extraordinary profit might exist, although the land in cultivation were all of the same quality; nay, must exist before inferior land was cultivated; for it could be only in consequence of extraordinary gains obtained by the monopolizers of the best land, that capital and labour would be expended on soils of a subordinate order. Rent, therefore, might exist, while all the land under cultivation was of equal fertility' (1825, p. 196). But not one word of all this is in any way novel. Ricardo himself had shown that differential rent is but a special case of a more general phenomenon – scarcity value. Thus in his discussion of early settlements, he observed: 'no one would pay for the use of land, when there was an abundant quantity not yet appropriated, and therefore, at the disposal of whosoever might choose to cultivate it' (Sraffa & Dobb, 1973, Vol. 1, p. 69); conversely, '[if] air, water, the elasticity of steam; and the pressure of the atmosphere, were of various qualities; if they could be appropriated, and each quality existed only in moderate abundance, they, as well as the land, would afford a rent, as the successive qualities were brought into use' (1973, Vol. 1, p. 75). The extension of this statement runs explicitly in terms of demand-and-supply: 'On the common principles of supply and demand, no rent could be paid for such land, for the reasons stated why nothing is given for the use of air and water, or for any other of the gifts of nature which exist in boundless quantity ...; as the supply is boundless, they bear no price' (1973, Vol. 1, p. 69). And there is his recognition of rent as a pure demand-determined surplus, generated even on marginal units of output, in the case of zero-elastic supply, referred to by Ricardo as a case of 'monopoly' price (1973, Vol. 1, pp. 250–251). Bailey had added nothing.

We return to Bailey on pricing, and a concession – confirming all that we have said above – that '[t]here is at the bottom, little actual difference among economists as to [the] causes [of value], but they do not agree either in their methods of explanation, or in the language they employ' (1825, p. 199). At this point, however, Bailey adds a proposition that has struck some readers – including Seligman – as particularly significant: 'It has been shown [1825, pp. 1–2, 180, 183] that the immediate causes of value are the considerations which act on the minds of human beings, and that the circumstances, which form or furnish those considerations, must be the causes into which the economist has to inquire. Our present object, therefore, is to find those circumstances which act upon the mind with certainty and precision, in the interchange of commodities of the class under our notice'. But we are cautioned to keep the 'philosophical' background in proper perspective, for Bailey in this very context focuses on costs of production as the main consideration in the case of commodities 'which can be increased by industry, and on which competition acts without restraint' (1825, p. 198), to illustrate the role of states of mind: 'No man, who bestows his time and attention on the production of a commodity, will continue to produce it for the purpose of exchanging it against another commodity, which he knows costs less to the producer than his own: and, on the other hand, every producer will be willing to sell as large a quantity of his commodity as he can dispose of at the same price as his fellow producers' (1825, pp. 199–200). But this sort of proposition is, of course, wholly orthodox,[15] terminology suggestive of 'states of mind' appearing in Ricardo's discussion of the tendency to cost price: 'It is then the desire, which every capitalist has, of directing his funds from a less to a more profitable employment, that prevents the market price of commodities from continuing for any length of time either much above, or much below their natural price' (Sraffa & Dobb, 1973, Vol. 1, p. 91).

Similarly orthodox is Bailey's further contention that 'if we do not aim at undue generalization, but are content with a simple statement of facts, the value of objects, in the production of which competition operates without restraint, may be correctly stated to arise principally from the cost of production; and that cost of production may be either labour or capital, or both' (1825, p. 205). We need but recall Ricardo's clarification in his third edition that even to maintain a strict labour theory of value is not to deny that profits enter into costs (Sraffa & Dobb, 1973, Vol. 1, pp. 46–47). And finally, Bailey's references to non-monetary characteristics, such as '[t]he discredit, the danger, the disagreeableness of any method of employing capital' (in addition to time of investment) to illustrate influences on value acting via 'the minds of men' (1825, pp. 206–207) obviously rehearses a celebrated Smithian theme which was standard canonical fare.

The terminological penchant of Bailey's book is apparent in comments upon Ricardo's identification of a change in the 'value' of wages – wages in terms of his invariable measure – with a change in the proportion of wages in aggregate output, that is the representation of labour as rising or falling in value 'only when a larger or smaller proportion of the commodity produced goes to the labourer' (1825, p. 56). For Bailey restricted the term 'value' to exchange value, so that the 'value of labour' indicates *commodity* wages (1825, p. 46); on the other hand, he perceived profits as a rate of return – 'the gain of the capitalist' relative to the 'capital employed' (1825, p. 63), such capital comprising wage payments: 'a rise of profits and a rise of labour are essentially distinct in their nature, the one signifying an increase of proportion, the other an increase in the quantity which a definite portion of labour will command' (1825, p. 64; also p. 70). Not surprisingly, on this usage only in the case of constant output must an increase in the commodity wages paid to a given work force involve a decline in the profit share (Bailey's rate of profit), whereas allowing for increase in output (and neglecting rent) wages and profits may both vary in the same direction. As Bailey pointed out, his contention was simply 'that in cases of improved productive power, the product might be so divided, that the rate of profits [identified with the profit share in output] should be increased while the value of labour [the commodity wage] was enhanced' (1825, p. 241).

Nothing in all this conflicts with Ricardian analysis. To the contrary, a feature of Ricardo's growth model is the increase of the commodity wage with no reduction, even conceivably an increase, in the profit rate, in early stages before manifestations of land scarcity, that is, when production is subject to increasing returns (Sraffa & Dobb, 1973, Vol. 1, p. 98). By the same token, in the course of subsequent expansion subject to declining marginal productivity, both the wage and profit rates tend downward simultaneously (Sraffa & Dobb, 1973, Vol. 1, p. 101; see Hollander, 1992, pp. 194–202, 2001, 2007). Bailey, however, failed to spell out this latter feature.

Bailey's criticisms of the inverse profit–wage relation were evidently not directed at Ricardo's position as Ricardo understood it, namely as a theorem entailing the 'real' wage or cost of producing the wage measured in terms of his hypothetical 'gold' which also indicated the proportional wage. And in fact Bailey conceded that 'Mr. Ricardo's inference is a legitimate deduction from his premises, if we concede certain postulates. Grant him the kind of value called *real*, which has no relation to the quantity of commodities commanded, but solely to the quantity of producing labour, and it inevitably follows, that there could be no alteration in the *real* value of labour, but from an alteration in the proportion of the product which went to the labourer' (1825, p. 58). So far, so good. Unfortunately, he errs when he adds: 'Neither, if money were always produced by a uniform quantity of labour, could there be any alteration in the money value of labour' (1825, p. 58n). For Ricardo's money wage is, of course, not a constant; Bailey seems to have confused Ricardo's with Malthus's measure.

Also to be noted is the fact that Bailey's recognition that the profit rate falls when commodity wages rise (given labour productivity) runs along strictly Ricardian lines (Sraffa & Dobb, 1973, Vol. 1, pp. 28–29), involving as it does the proposition that – *pace* Adam Smith – capitalists cannot pass on the higher wage costs to consumers in the form of higher prices, since the prices, that is the exchange values, of *all* commodities cannot logically be raised simultaneously: '[I]t is a contradiction to maintain, that a universal rise in the value of labour can increase the value of commodities' (1825, pp. 64–65).[16]

BAILEY'S INFLUENCE ON OTHER 'DISSENTERS': COTTERILL, READ, SENIOR, LLOYD, TORRENS

Seligman, we have seen, represented Bailey as an 'acute critic' of Ricardo on value who 'exerted considerable influence at the time'. The justification for this assertion turns largely on an alleged impact on C. F. Cotterill: '... the views of Bailey were in part repeated and developed by Cotterill (1831) in his *Examination of the Doctrines of Value*. Cotterill makes short work of the labour theory of value, which he deems to have been completely refuted by Bailey, the author of the *Critical Dissertation*, of whose name he seems to be ignorant.... Like Bailey, he opposes to the labour theory the cost of production theory of value' (Seligman, 1903, p. 355). There is Cotterill's broadening of the rent concept to labour, on which matter 'Senior as well as Cotterill was preceded ... by Bailey' (1903, p. 356). Seligman is unclear whether in his estimation either Senior or Cotterill owed a positive debt to Bailey. He also makes mention of Samuel Read who 'confesses that in his main point of theory he has been anticipated by Bailey', referring to the proposition that wealth is not the result of accumulated labour, but of labour and capital (1903, p. 517; also p. 353), which again does not necessarily imply influence.

Seligman's reading of Cotterill neglects Cotterill's own recognition of the need for an 'invariable standard', and his belief in the possibility of its construction; indeed, amongst the most important features of his pamphlet Cotterill counted the statement of 'the conditions necessary to a standard of value' and the refutation of 'the erroneous doctrine that the supposition of such a standard involves contradictory conditions' (Cotterill, 1831, p. v). And it was Bailey (as well as Torrens) whom he largely had in mind when making this latter statement (Cotterill, 1831, p. 99). His main objection as far as concerned Ricardo himself was to the specific character of Ricardian 'money' as an invariable standard, but not to the principle of the matter. Indeed, Cotterill provided illustrations of the 'correct' procedure designed to guarantee that aggregate money value remains unchanged in the face of an alteration in distribution (Cotterill, 1831, p. 76) – Ricardo's primary concern, as Sraffa has taught us. And he candidly recognised Ricardo's contribution to the proposed solution: 'The conditions, however, essential to an invariable standard, do appear to me so very obvious, especially upon Mr. Ricardo's own principles in opposition to Adam Smith'.[17]

Cotterill, moreover, expressed his dissatisfaction with Bailey's performance regarding the 'causes' of value. The analysis in *A Critical Dissertation* was 'extremely unsatisfactory: notwithstanding many parts of that work cannot but be admired by everyone friendly to the science of political economy' (Cotterill, 1831, p. 53), nor did he think that Bailey's work constituted 'a performance likely to set the controversy at rest; on the contrary, I consider the Author's use of the term value, on many occasions, inconsistent with its obvious meaning, and the chapter on the causes of value, in my opinion leads to nothing less than complete scepticism' (Cotterill, 1831, pp. 40–41). If Cotterill was critical of Ricardo in the context of the causes of value, he was equally dissatisfied with Bailey, whose explanation of long-run exchange value in terms of cost of production was 'defective': 'it does not include profit, and therefore never can determine value, because, though the labour or capital should not vary, the profit may vary, and consequently the value of any commodities'. This objection is noted by Seligman (1903, p. 355) who regards it as 'a regression'.

Seligman's linkage of Read's book to Bailey, and similarly a comment by Schumpeter (1954, p. 488) that Read's work 'bears witness to the influence of Bailey whom Read followed in his Ricardo criticism' are open to question. For Read in fact took Bailey to task regarding the key feature of the 'Critical Dissertation': 'It appears to me that the fundamental error in that work, and that from which all the others to be found in it flow, consists in his treating of value as if it were *a mere* relation *of commodities between themselves*; whereas it appears to me that the idea of value in commodities *cannot even be conceived* without being mingled with the idea of their relation to mankind and to human labour, of which *some portion* must always be employed in producing or procuring them originally' (Read, 1829, p. viii).[18] Professor Meek, in his study of the 'decline of Ricardian economics in England', mistakenly understands this passage relating value to 'mankind and human labour', as a position rejected by Read who attributed it to Ricardo, rather than one maintained by Read himself, and observes that 'it was this vital concept which virtually vanished from English political economy after Ricardo's death' (Meek, 1967, p. 67). The evidence to the contrary speaks for itself at least as far as concerns Read.[19]

I return to Seligman's comment regarding the generalisation of the rent doctrine, that 'Senior as well as Cotterill was preceded ... by Bailey'. As we mentioned, this does not necessarily imply *influence*. Bowley (1937, p. 94) too is somewhat reticent: 'It is tempting to consider Bailey as ... of some importance [in the development of Senior's economics] although Senior never referred to the Dissertation in connection with the theory of value ...'; again, 'the bearing of the existence of different wage rates on the labour theory of value ... played some part in Bailey's criticism of Ricardo [and] may have indirectly influenced [Senior]' (1937, p. 193). Regarding the 'extension of the rent concept' by Senior in *Political Economy* (1836, pp. 129–30), Bowley (1937, p. 131; also p. 70n) remarks only that 'Bailey had already extended it to wages in 1825'.[20] And with respect to abstinence, she allows no more than that '[i]is possible to put forward a claim for Samuel Bailey as an anticipator of the theory ...' (1937, p. 144n).

Blaug (1958, p. 58; also p. 157), we have seen, does discern a strong obligation: 'Nassau Senior seems to have been the only writer to have realized that Bailey's criticism contained the germs of a far-reaching reconstruction of basic economic concepts'. In particular, in his appendix to Whately's (1826) *Elements of Logic* 'he adopted Bailey's generalization of the concept of rent as only a "*species* of an extensive genus"' (see Senior, [1836] 1951, p. 236). 'One need only glance at Senior's earlier economic writings' – the reference is to Senior's 'Report on the State of Agriculture' for the *Quarterly Review* of 1821[21] – 'to realise how much he had learned from Bailey'.

This perspective is problematic. In the first place Senior makes no specific reference to Bailey in his appendix, although it reviews the literature. As for the 'Report' (1821), it contains material suggesting that it is Bailey who in 1825 may well have been initially inspired by Senior. Particularly noteworthy are Senior's representation of differential rent as a monopoly return and its exclusion from price; his insistence that it is not the cultivation of inferior land that is the 'cause' of a high corn price, but the high price itself, due to high demand, that is the 'cause' of the cultivation of inferior land and the emergence of rent; and his observation that 'when we say that the price of a thing is governed by the cost of production we mean the cost of its own production, not of the production of something else' (Senior, 1821, pp. 474–476). All of this, we have seen, is to be found rehearsed in Bailey (1825).

I shall allow myself brief comments on Lloyd and Torrens, both highly praised by Seligman as competent dissenters. As for Lloyd, Seligman perhaps implied that Bailey, by clearing away the undergrowth by his criticism of Ricardo, allowed Lloyd to proceed more readily to a marginal utility exposition (see above). Whether or not this was the case, it may be argued that Lloyd in no way depended on Bailey. For while his definition of 'value' focused on utility, his purpose was to demonstrate the legitimacy of 'the notion of absolute as distinguished from comparative or exchangeable value … without any reference to other objects' (Lloyd, 1834, p. 28). Thus he rejected the assertion as expressed anonymously by J. S. Mill in the *Westminster Review* in 1825 – there is no mention of Bailey's formulations of this theme – that 'value is a relative term: if it is not this, it is nothing: if any one talks about absolute value, or any other kind of value than exchangeable value, we know not what he means' (1834, p. 34). He similarly took Say to task for his proposition that 'the valuation of an object is nothing more or less than the affirmation, that it is in a certain degree of comparative estimation with some other specified object' (1834, citing Say, [1819] 1880,

p. 284), and he objected to that proposition as elaborated in *Verbal Disputes* (Anon., 1821a, pp. 10–11), which, as we have noted earlier, closely resembles Bailey's *Critical Dissertation*.

Other complexities arise in the case of Torrens, whose praise of the *Critical Dissertation* as a 'masterly specimen of perspicuous and accurate logic' exerting an 'already perceptible influence' (Torrens, 1826, pp. xii–xiii) is said to be 'typical, perhaps, of the average reaction' to Bailey (Blaug, 1958, p. 57). More specifically, Torrens is reported in Mallet's celebrated account of the Political Economy Club's meeting on 13 January 1831 as opining, regarding the status of Ricardian value theory, that 'the dissertation on the Measure of value published in 1825 by Mr. Baillie of Leeds, has settled that question' (Political Economy Club, 1921, p. 223).

Two points are in order regarding Torrens's reaction as an adequate index of Bailey's influence. Firstly, Torrens intended by the general abandonment of Ricardian value theory, the replacement of the pure labour theory by a cost of production theory, which we know to have been Ricardo's own position all along. (On this matter, see Bowley, 1937, pp. 90–91.) Secondly, Torrens entered a very strong defence of Ricardo's proportions – measuring 'gold' in his later writings, basing himself on Longfield's position that all non-labour inputs may be reduced to labour so that the only payments to consider ultimately are wages and profits (Longfield, 1834, p. 172f). Accordingly, Ricardo's linkage of the profit rate to the proportionate shares held good; moreover, Longfield (1834, pp. 266–267) also justified Ricardo's isolation of the conditions required to assure that changes in money wages reflect changes in proportionate wages (1834, pp.). This defence of Ricardo Torrens accepted both in *Colonization of Southern Australia* 1835 and *The Budget* 1844. Any positive influence by Bailey on Torrens in the 1820s would have been only temporary.

BAILEY AND THE 'RICARDIANS': JAMES MILL AND MCCULLOCH

J. S. Mill refers in his *Autobiography* to changes introduced by James Mill into the third (1826) edition of the *Elements* with respect to the profit theory based (in some unstated way) on 'Conversations' held at Grote's house ([1873] 1981, p. 125). Since the *Critical Dissertation* was one of the books examined by the study circle, the question of Bailey's possible influence on James Mill naturally arises.

We take as a base the first and second editions of the *Elements* (Mill, 1821, 1824). When considering the contention by some critics of Ricardo 'that profits of stock depend not solely upon the share received of that which is divided, but also upon the magnitude of the whole that is to be divided', Mill distinguishes between 'profits' as a quantity of commodities and its more common meaning as a rate of return on capital (including food, raw materials and tools) – a ratio of values – asserting that only in the latter case do 'profits depend wholly upon wages', since technical progress (or diminishing returns) raising (or lowering) output yielded by given capital and labour will not affect the aggregate value of that output, so that 'the proportion of that value which goes as profits of stock depends wholly upon that which goes as wages. The rate of profits, therefore, or the ratio which the value of that which is received by the capitalist bears to the value of the capital depends wholly upon wages' (1821, pp. 57–60; 1824, pp. 73–76).

It is thus Mill who – before Bailey – pointed to the more usual sense of profits as a rate of return, though he insisted that on this usage the inverse wage–profit relation held good despite changing productivity; only with the uncommon usage of profit as an absolute quantity of commodities did the inverse relation require qualification.

Much of this is reworked in the third edition of the *Elements* and Rauner (1961, p. 114) suggests that here the influence of Bailey is discernable. It is doubtless true that the revisions were made in the light of the *Critical Dissertation*, and it is only to be regretted that Mill nowhere mentions Bailey (see Winch, 1966, p. 191). But we find no substantive retractions in the new version; to the contrary, Mill sought to strengthen the Ricardian case, as I shall now show.

When the sense of Ricardian or 'real' value is adopted, Mill explains in his new edition, whatever the output to be shared, its value – if produced 'by an invariable quantity of labour' – remains constant, so that should wages rise in 'value' the remainder or profits falls, and '[i]n this sense of the word value ... it is strictly and undeniable true, that profits depend upon wages so as to rise when wages fall, and fall when wages rise' (Mill, 1826b, p. 75). This is to restate what had been affirmed earlier, namely that aggregate value remains unchanged with an altered distribution (1821, p. 82; 1824, pp. 107–108). Now at this point Mill reverts – as in the earlier editions – to 'the common mode of expressing profits' as a rate of return on capital 'including the wages, which it is necessary to advance', for in practice profits are expressed not 'per cent of the produce but per cent upon his capital'. But this potential objection is played down: 'It is only, however, the language which here is different; the thing expressed is precisely the same ... whether the capitalist says he receives 10 per cent upon his capital, or 28 ½ per cent of the produce, he means in both cases the same amount ...' (1826b, p. 76). The rate-of-return perspective as the usual mode of expressing profits so much insisted upon by Bailey – for which James Mill himself had precedence – is thus, as before, identified with the proportionate share of net produce, and the inverse wage–profit relation holds good unreservedly. Bailey had exerted no effect whatsoever.

Torrens's part in this episode bears mention. In the preface to the third edition of his *Essay on the External Corn Trade* he controverted Mill's 1826 defence of Ricardo's inverse relationship, maintaining that proportional wages might remain unchanged while the profit rate increased when account is taken of *non-labour* inputs (Torrens, 1826, pp. xvi–xviii), in effect putting his weight behind Bailey. But this was only temporary, for (as mentioned above) Torrens later withdrew the objection, basing himself on Longfield's defence of Ricardo.

There remains to note the conditions required of a measure of value, as Mill had it.[22] These were that money be produced by a constant quantity 'of labour and capital' – formally identified in an addition made to the second edition with 'immediate' and 'hoarded' labour (Mill, 1824, pp. 108–110), and that it be produced 'under the medium circumstances', and this 'because by far the greater number of commodities are produced under circumstances more nearly approaching to the medium than any of the extremes' (1824, p. 111).[23] Mill points to real-world gold as most closely approximating the latter condition, that is as 'less imperfect as a measure of value than any other commodity, perhaps which could be taken' (1824, p. 112). A mean-proportions measure is required to minimise the variations in relative prices upon a change in the wage rate (1824, p. 109). Such effects, Mill allowed – though, as we have seen, for Mill aggregate value remains unaffected – despite his extreme formulation of a labour theory (1821, p. 74; 1824, p. 94), a formulation actually reinforced in the second edition by reference to McCulloch (though without citing a specific text), who had 'most pertinently and conclusively remarked ... that time does nothing'. 'How then', Mill continues, 'can it create value? Time is a mere abstract term. It is a word, a sound' (1824, p. 99). For this he was taken to task by Bailey (1825, pp. 207, 217–219).[24]

Since these distinctive principles remain unchanged in the third edition (Mill, 1826b, pp. 105–117), Bailey's objections evidently left no impression. But there is one qualification. The commendation of McCulloch was deleted in 1826, and this was possibly in reaction to Bailey's animadversions. On the other hand, a more elaborate justification is offered for conceiving capital as 'hoarded labour' (compare Mill, 1824, pp. 97–99 with Mill, 1826b, pp. 101–104), so what to make of the deletion is not self-evident.

In his specialist study of McCulloch, O'Brien makes the point that Bailey's 'famous onslaught [on Ricardo] might have been expected to have a significant impact on McCulloch', but it failed to do so partly because 'his main fire was directed against the invariable measure; McCulloch was with him there' (O'Brien, 1970, p. 137). O'Brien is correct to point out that Bailey had little to teach McCulloch on the matter at hand. His correspondence with Ricardo of 1823 might – except for the accompanying labour theory element – easily have been written by Bailey himself so close are the formulations on the matter of principle: '... there neither is nor can be any real and invariable standard of value; and if so it must be very idle to seek for that which can never be found. The real inquiry is to ascertain what are the circumstances which determine the exchangeable value of commodities at any given period – and these I think are all clearly reducible to one – the comparative quantities of labour bestowed on their production' (11 August 1823; in Sraffa & Dobb, 1973, Vol. 9, p. 344; also 24 August, p. 369). But O'Brien loses sight of the fact that in his *Principles* McCulloch proceeds along purely Ricardian lines. He seems to have taken to heart Ricardo's position, as we now briefly show.

McCulloch cites Bailey favourably at one point in his *Principles*: 'The conditions essential to the production of an invariable measure of exchangeable value were first clearly pointed out in the *Dissertation on the Nature, Measures, and Causes of Value*, p. 17' (McCulloch, 1825, p. 214n).[25] We reiterate, however, that Ricardo needed no convincing since his quest had been rather to isolate the 'source' of an observed change in exchange values.[26] And this quest is reflected in McCulloch's *Principles*. Certainly he writes that an invariable measure – of *real* value or costs – is in practice unattainable since all commodities are subject to 'perpetual variations' in labour input reflecting diminishing returns and/or technical progress (1825, p. 221), but the requirements in principle – which are all Ricardo sought to define – are spelled out. Thus, as a conspicuous instance, McCulloch distinguished conceptually between a nominal wage change and a 'real' wage change; the latter reflected by a change in terms of money of 'invariable value', or money produced with constant labour input, which also implies a change in proportional wages (1825, p. 295); and it is the latter that concerned him with an eye to profit-rate determination (1825, pp. 365, 380). A second condition is that money be produced by a process entailing mean factor proportions (1825, p. 310). Yet more important, McCulloch demonstrated that a rise in the wage leaves aggregate value unchanged though the price structure will be affected, implicitly applying a mean-proportions measure (1825, pp. 312–313). However, disturbances to the price structure are played down on the empirical grounds that they are 'confined within comparatively narrow limits', since 'a very large class of commodities are produced by means of nearly equal portions of fixed and circulating capital ...' (1825, p. 311). Here McCulloch was following Ricardo, but he may also have benefited from James Mill's formulations, since various examples devised to indicate the impact on the price structure of a change in the wage are said to be 'substantially the same' as those in Mill (1824) and McCulloch (1825, p. 309n). McCulloch went even further, in a later edition, by referring to the feature that real-world money, 'which is all but universally taken as a standard by which to estimate price, is usually produced by capitals of about the medium degree of durability' so that 'the influence of variations of wages on prices, will, on the whole, be confined within very narrow limits, the rise in those mainly produced by hand labour being balanced by the fall in those principally produced by machinery' (McCulloch, 1864, p. 292). And particularly significant is McCulloch's reinforcement of the Ricardian structure by providing an allocative rationale – later adopted by Marx – for the price restructuring created by a wage increase, turning on the correction, by way of resource transfers, of profit-rate inequalities (1825, pp. 303–304). All of this is properly represented by McCulloch as a confirmation of Ricardo's position (1825, pp. 298–299, 313).

McCulloch's adoption and indeed reinforcement of the Ricardian perspective is scarcely in the nature of 'lip service', as O'Brien has it (1970, p. 146). And only with this in mind can we properly appreciate his stance 20 years later when he repeated *verbatim* his 1825 position that '[t]he conditions essential to an invariable measure of exchangeable value were first clearly pointed out in [Bailey's] dissertation', but adding 'but however ingenious and acute, Mr. Bailey does not appear to have properly appreciated the Ricardian theory of value, or to have succeeded in any degree in shaking its foundations' (1845, p. 33). Bailey had no effect on McCulloch not because McCulloch sided with Bailey on the invariable measure but, to the contrary, because he rejected Bailey's 'famous onslaught'.

McCulloch had other objections to the *Critical Dissertation*. One entails a strong defence of De Quincey 1824 against Bailey (McCulloch, 1825, p. 220n).[27] A second relates to the rent theory where McCulloch makes appeal to Ricardian marginal costs against Bailey's contention 'that because the value of that corn which is raised on lands paying rent, is not, after inferior lands are taken into cultivation, proportioned to the cost of its production, it is incorrect to represent the value of the aggregate quantity of produce raised in a country where cultivation has been extended over inferior lands, as depending on that principle' (1825, p. 285).

There remains to discuss a further aspect of the Bailey–McCulloch relationship perceived in the literature, entailing an alleged transition by McCulloch from the pure Ricardianism, with respect to profit-rate determination, of his 1823 contribution to the *Encyclopaedia Britannica*, to a qualified version appearing in his *Principles* 1825 under the influence of Bailey's *Critical Dissertation* (Rauner, 1961, pp. 113–114). For 'McCulloch himself had not freed profits from dependence on "proportional wages" until after the *Critical Dissertation* had appeared' (1961, p. 113). We shall consider this assertion.

Consider first McCulloch's exposition in 1823 of the inverse wage–profit relation in the context of secular growth, indicating the joint incidence of diminishing returns: 'profits' – the context specifies concern with the *profit rate* though leaves the denominator of the expression undefined – 'do not depend on wages estimated in money, in corn, or any other commodity, but on *PROPORTIONAL wages, that* is, *on the share of the commodities produced by the labourer, or of their value, which is given to him*' (McCulloch, [1823]1825, p. 149). In the 1825 version by contrast the matter is more complex: 'there are very many exceptions to Mr. Ricardo's theory' (1825, p. 368). In an example entailing a doubled return given labour and non-wage capital, McCulloch shows that 'both parties will still obtain the same proportions of the [net] produce of industry as before; and if we look only to them, we must say that neither profits nor wages have risen. But, when we compare, as is invariably done in estimating profits, the return obtained by the capitalist with the capital he employs, it will be found, notwithstanding proportional wages have remained constant, that the *rate* of profit has increased ...' (1825, p. 374).[28]

Rauner makes his case for a positive influence exerted by Bailey by comparing McCulloch's insistence on perceiving profits as a ratio of net produce to 'the capital employed in its production' with Bailey's definition of profits as the 'gain of the capitalist [relative to] the capital employed' and also his insistence that the inverse relationship held good only with productivity constant. And he points to Torrens's fulsome praise for Bailey, which is followed immediately by reference to McCulloch's *Principles* (Torrens, 1826, p. xiii). It is certainly true that while James Mill insisted on the inverse profit–wage relation even when 'profit' in the sense of a rate of return on capital is intended, McCulloch was prepared to qualify the principle in that case. Yet his argument is not identical to that of Bailey. For Bailey's rate of return relates to absolute profits relative to wage capital alone – Marx's rate of exploitation, s/v, whereas McCulloch took the profit rate as net profit relative to capital including non-wage items – Marx's $s/(c+v)$.[29]

It is also instructive to trace out McCulloch's treatment in the *Principles* of the course of the real-wage and profit rates during the course of secular expansion given technology in order to confirm the extent of his continued adherence to this key feature of Ricardianism. '*The decreasing fertility of the soil is … the great and only necessary cause of a fall of profits*. The *quantity* of produce forming the return of capital and labour would never diminish, but for the diminution that uniformly takes place in the productiveness of the soil: nor is there any other physical cause in existence why the *proportion* of wages to profits should be increased, and the rate of profit diminished, as it uniformly is, in the progress of society' (McCulloch, 1825, pp. 380–381). So we revert after all to the profit rate as a function of the proportionate shares – as in 1823 – despite all the *mea culpas* to the effect that the Ricardian theory breaks down except when output is constant. Indeed, McCulloch goes yet further in confirming his Ricardian *bonâ fides* by insisting – again as in 1823 – on a necessary increase in the proportionate wage even in the complex case of a declining commodity wage in the course of secular growth assuming land scarcity, a trend represented as one 'uniformly found' (1825, pp. 362–363).[30]

Rauner (1961, p. 118) is right when he concluded that 'Bailey's *Critical Dissertation* did not make much headway with the Ricardians' – that though McCulloch 'flirted with some of Bailey's notions … when it came to the point, he was unable to carry out the full implications of his dalliance'. My only qualification is that Bailey too remained in Ricardo's camp, though certainly unwillingly.

BAILEY AND THE RICARDIANS: J. S. MILL

Seligman made no mention of J. S. Mill in his paper. But much of Schumpeter's case for the early demise of Ricardianism turned on the alleged influence of Bailey's *Critical Dissertation*, and he certainly implies that J. S. Mill represented the pattern. For, so runs his argument, Mill rejected the conception of a measure of absolute value; only relative price mattered, and since value was a ratio all values could not vary simultaneously (Schumpeter, 1954, p. 589). Similarly, there was no such thing as 'the total value of all the services of wealth (or of all wealth) taken as a whole' in contrast to the position adopted by Ricardo and Marx. Indeed, 'the energy with which Mill insisted on the relative character of [exchange value] completely annihilated Ricardo's Real Value and reduced other Ricardianisms to insipid innocuousness' (1954, p. 603). Similarly, O'Brien (2004, p. 110): Mill's 'inverse relationship of wages and profits is not derived from the invariable measure, as ... it was for Ricardo'. And particularly relevant for us is his attribution to Bailey of a potent impact on Mill: 'It is ... clear that [Bailey] influenced J. S. Mill in a number of areas, including the treatment of rent, the abstinence theory of profit, the inverse relationship of wages and profits, the hierarchy of wages as affecting exchangeable value, and the rejection of the invariable measure – this despite Mill's failure to credit Bailey' (O'Brien, 1988, pp. 198–199).[31]

Let us first of all look closely at the foregoing contentions regarding the inverse relationship and its derivation by Mill. We shall keep before us a statement by Mill on the relativity of value appearing in an early article of 1825: 'Value is a relative term: if it is not this, it is nothing: if any one talks about absolute value, or any other kind of value than exchangeable value, we know not what he means. One commodity may rise or fall in value with respect to another; all commodities cannot rise or fall in value, with respect to themselves' (Mill, [1825] 1967, p. 36). Now this appeared in the January issue of the *Westminster Review* and could not possibly have been drawn from Bailey's *Critical Dissertation*. Moreover, Mill by his assertion was denying Malthus's conception of aggregate demand, not challenging the Ricardian position regarding absolute value. Unfortunately Lloyd (1834, p. 34) – and so many since – took the statement out of context and applied it to the latter. As for Bailey himself, in *A Letter to a Political Economist* (1826) he applauded the sentiment of the article but expressed surprise at finding an insistence upon value as a relative conception in the *Westminster Review* which in 1826 had published an attack – which we know to be by James Mill – upon his own *Critical Dissertation* (Bailey, 1826, p. 37). If the respective contexts are taken into account the apparent inconsistency of position between the journal volumes creates no difficulty whatsoever.

What then was J. S. Mill's position regarding the value issue? In his *Principles*, he rejected – as in January 1825 – the notion of a measure of exchange value as a conceptual impossibility but insisted upon that of a measure of cost of production ([1848] 1965, Vol. 3, p. 579). Now although such a measure of cost 'though perfectly conceivable, can no more exist in fact, than a measure of exchangeable value', because of the likelihood of changes in the production cost of any commodity chosen, yet gold and silver 'are the last variable' and, if used, the results obtained must simply be 'corrected by the best appearance we can make for the intermediate changes in the cost of production itself'. This represents precisely the position adopted by Ricardo, who had laid down the requirements for an *ideal* measure fully aware of its impractibility.

Mill also provides a full Ricardian analysis of the effects of wage-rate changes, and concludes: 'If money itself undergoes no variation in cost, the money price of labour is an exact measure of the Cost of Labour, and may be made use of as a convenient symbol to express it' ([1848] 1965, Vol. 3, p. 696). Assuming money to be such an invariable measure, the rate of money wages will depend upon both the commodity wage and the prices of wage goods and accordingly productivity in the wage-goods sector. It is upon the 'cost of labour' that the rate of profit depended, the cost of labour identified with 'money' wages. Mill thus defined an inverse relation between the profit rate and the money wage rate, adopting the 'proportions-measuring' money in terms of which a rise of wages implies an increased share of the labourer in the 'value' of his output and a reduced profit share, and accordingly rate of return on capital. There is no basis for the case that Bailey converted J. S. Mill from Ricardo on the inverse wage–profit relation and its derivation in terms of an invariable measure.

At this point we turn to a suggestion by Rauner that Bailey's influence on J. S. Mill was of another sort, his criticisms of Ricardo inducing Mill to enter a stronger defence in his essay 'On Profits and Interest', published in 1844 but written in 1829–1830 (in Mill, [1844] 1967), entailing – according to Rauner – a reinforcement of the proportionality property by emphasising the wage rate as referring to the *value* of the wage not the commodity or absolute wage (Rauner, 1961, pp. 113–117, 135–137).

The objection to Ricardo appearing in the essay on profits related to his reducing capital entirely to labour, on the grounds that the repayment of *profits* entered into the outlay of a capitalist upon produced means of production, and not merely wages (Mill, [1844] 1967, p. 295). Accordingly, the profit rate is not given simply by the ratio of current surplus after replacing outlay to an outlay amounting solely to the wages of direct and indirect labour, as Ricardo had it ([1844] 1967, p. 297). For all that, '[i]t is remarkable how very slight a modification will suffice to render Mr. Ricardo's doctrine completely true'. This was to relate the rate of profit to the '*cost* of wages' – which includes the profit of the capital-goods producer – as distinct from the '*value* of wages' or the labour embodied in the wages bill. But the identity between the cost of wages (the strategic wage variable) and labour's proportionate share in output was no longer tenable: 'the interpretation which some economists have put upon Mr. Ricardo's doctrine, when they explain it to mean that profits depend upon the proportion which the labourers collectively receive of the aggregate produce, will not hold at all' ([1844] 1967, p. 299).

Rauner's view of Mill as seeking to reinforce Ricardo after reading Bailey's criticisms is in fact unconvincing. For it reads Mill's essay as championing the proportionality thesis in answer to Bailey's criticisms, whereas Mill was in fact here denying its validity. (In any event, Bailey himself had accepted the proportionality thesis on Ricardo's use of terms, as we showed earlier). Mill's 'slight modification', namely the replacement of the '*value* of wages' by the '*cost* of wages', seems to be quite independent of Bailey's commentary. Rather, in this episode can be discerned the possible influence of Robert Torrens, who had insisted that the profit rate depends not only on the proportionate share of wages which governed the ratio of profits to wages, but also on the non-wage capital required, a technological improvement permitting the relinquishing of fixed capital or materials – Marx's 'constant' capital – implying a rise in the profit rate (Torrens, 1829, pp. xv–xviii).[32] Even McCulloch is a candidate considering the inclusive character of his 'capital' (see above).

Mill's qualification to the Ricardo doctrine was, however, adopted only temporarily. In the *Principles*, as we have seen, he once again championed the proportionality theorem. His argument is simply that since 'our supposed capitalist is not meant to represent a single employment, but to be a type of the productive industry of the whole country, the advances may after all be reduced in the last resort entirely to wages' ([1848] 1965, Vol. 2, p. 412).

So much for the inverse wage–profit relation. As for abstinence, we recall the brief formulation by Bailey noted by Seligman at the beginning of this essay. But *influence* is another matter. No evidence is provided to show that Mill 'derived' or 'borrowed' the abstinence theory from Bailey who, as maintained by Bowley, is better seen as an 'anticipator' of the theory. By contrast, an indisputable 'influence' was exerted by Rae's *New Principles* (1834). 'In no other book known to me' – Mill wrote in his chapter 'Of the Law of the Increase of Capital' – 'is so much light thrown, both from principle and history, on the causes which determine the accumulation of capital' ([1848] 1965, Vol. 2, p. 162; also to Rae himself, 19 September 1855; in Mineka & Lindley, 1972, p. 240).[33]

We turn to Mill's alleged 'derivation' or 'borrowing' from Bailey of the generalisation of Ricardo's rent concept.[34] The Mill analysis relates presumably to his account of 'cases of extra profit analogous to rent' such as the extra return to a patent holder allowing production at low cost in the event that demand is high enough to require the continued contribution of high-cost firms (Mill, [1848] 1965, Vol. 2, pp. 494–495). And '[t]he extra gains which any producer or dealer obtains though superior talents for business, or superior business arrangements, are very much of a similar kind' ([1848] 1965, Vol. 2, p. 495; see also p. 490). Oddly enough, in his discussion of relative wages ([1848] 1965, Vol. 2, pp. 380–399) Mill (like Adam Smith) says nothing of natural differences of 'talent' or 'genius' which might give rise to rent – the particular generalisation specified by Bailey (see above). There is every reason to believe that this sort of extension was acceptable to Mill, but its absence suggests little reliance on Bailey.

Beyond this, it would be an error to exaggerate the novelty of Bailey's principle, since aspects of the generalisation of the rent doctrine had already been set in motion by Ricardo himself when he spelled out the conditions for the emergence of rent in industry. Also pertinent is his analysis of a contemporary case where certain *industrial* firms had their labour costs subsidised, thus generating a (discrete) increasing-cost supply schedule. The appropriate margin and corresponding marginal labour cost are explicitly assumed to be governed by 'the quantity of produce required', that is, by the level of demand. Should that level be sufficiently low for the output of the subsidised firms alone to be 'equal to all the wants of the community', the unsubsidised, or high-cost firms would be excluded and the equilibrium determined by the low-cost firms, but at higher demand the higher marginal cost becomes pertinent (Sraffa & Dobb, 1973, Vol. 1, p. 73). This analysis is found in the chapter 'On Rent' and the unstated implication for rent is self-evident; it is an exact parallel to Mill's analysis of the case of a patentee, mentioned above.

Rauner (1961, p. 139) sees an apparent influence of Bailey on Mill with respect to the implications for price of qualitative differences in labour. I see no evidence for this linkage, though it cannot be ruled out. I would point out that recognition of heterogeneous labour led both Adam Smith and Ricardo to abandon the pure labour theory, even prior to allowance for capital and land, and have recourse to a labour-cost theory, Ricardo taking James Mill to task for neglecting the implications for the labour theory of a wage change not common to all types of labour (Sraffa & Dobb, 1973, Vol. 9, p. 127). Bailey's (1825, pp. 209–210) charge that Ricardo refused to draw the implications of the formal recognition of heterogeneity is unjustified.

Bowley complained that Mill, by his organisation and weight of emphasis, unjustifiably played down the role of demand in price formation. Thus he made 'no attempt to point out the difference in importance of demand in determining price in [the increasing-costs] case compared to the constant cost case' with the result that the theory of value is made to 'look simple' (Bowley, 1973, p. 168). In this, she argued, he followed Ricardo rather than Bailey (1825) or Senior (1836).

There is limited justification for this evaluation. As early as 1828, Mill defended the differential-rent theory against the strictures of those 'who affect to suppose that Sir Edward West, Mr. Malthus, and Mr. Ricardo considered the cultivation of inferior land as the *cause* of a high price of corn' ([1828] 1967, Vol. 4, p. 174). He mentions no names, but doubtless Senior (1821), Bailey (1825) and Thompson (1826) were intended. Rather, that 'the cultivation of inferior soils' is the effect of high price 'itself the effect of demand' was a doctrine 'explicitly laid down by the distinguished authors previously referred to, and particularly by Mr. Ricardo'. Similarly in the *Principles*: 'Mr. Ricardo does not say that it is the *cultivation* of inferior land' [that is the 'cause of rent on the superior'], 'but the *necessity of cultivating* it from the insufficiency of the superior land to feed a growing population' ([1848] 1965, Vol. 2, p. 428). This is a wholly justified defence of the Ricardian position with its full allowance for demand (see Hollander, 1979, p. 665). Also relevant is Mill's appreciation that it was 'distinctly a portion of Ricardo's doctrine' that 'the land of a country supposed to be of uniform fertility would, all of it, on a certain supposition, pay rent: namely, if the demand of the community required that it should all be cultivated, and cultivated beyond the point at which a further application of capital begins to be attended with a smaller proportionate return' ([1848] 1965, Vol. 2, p. 428). These episodes reveal the illegitimacy of according to Bailey and Senior a perspective on demand foreign to the orthodox classicists.

Also to be found in the secondary literature is the attribution to Bailey and Senior of a positive influence on J. S. Mill regarding 'the classification of types of "imperfect competition"' (Blaug, 1958, p. 167). On the other hand, Bowley (1973, p. 169) regards the barriers-to-entry classification of Bailey and Senior more sophisticated than Mill's fixed- and elastic-supply classification of monopoly and competition respectively.[35] Yet, as I have argued elsewhere, 'Mill's analysis both of price and non-price competition turns strategically on the absence of barriers, whereas that of "monopoly" (strictly defined) and of imperfect competition requires them; in fact Mill took a major step forward by recognising the implications for market structure of the "natural" barriers generated by scale economies. And all this apart from the adjustment of prices to cost in the standard (constant cost) case where potential entry plays a key role, and from the analysis of the wage-rate structure where barriers are of the essence' (Hollander, 1985,

p. 304). How much Mill may have learned from Bailey and Senior regarding this issue remains an open question.

BAILEY AND MALTHUS

Malthus is frequently classed amongst the 'dissenters'. There is Jevons's view to that effect, mentioned earlier. Blaug (1958, p. 227) refers to 'the critics and outspoken opponents of Ricardo', intending 'men like Malthus, Bailey, Scrope, Jones, Longfield and Senior ...'. Rauner describes Malthus's reaction in the *Definitions* to the *Critical Dissertation* as 'most striking', considering that 'Malthus had something in common with Bailey in being generally out of step with the Ricardians' (Rauner, 1961, p. 118), but he goes on to explain that 'Malthus actually proved just as inhospitable to Bailey's message as the others', though not because Malthus and the Ricardians were in the same theoretical boat but because Malthus founded his own measure of value 'on a conception of value dependent on causes of an absolute and inherent nature'.

I would say that while Rauner is right to focus on Malthus's defence of an 'absolute' measure in responding to Bailey in Chapter 8 of his *Definitions*, he underplays the degree of common ground between Malthus and Ricardo. McCulloch, in brief, was perfectly correct when he observed that while '[s]ome of the subordinate doctrines respecting value advanced by Mr. Ricardo in the first and second editions of his *Principles* ... were opposed by Mr. Malthus in his recent publication' (i.e. Malthus, 1820), yet 'Mr. Malthus does not attempt to invalidate the leading principles established by Mr. Ricardo; and the alterations and corrections which the latter has made in the third edition of his work, have gone far to remove the objections of Mr. Malthus' (McCulloch, 1823, p. 135). That this is indeed so is clearly revealed not only by Malthus's total rejection of Bailey's position on 'absolute' value, but also by his adoption of the Ricardian inverse wage–profit relation in the growth context in terms of his own labour-commanded measure of absolute value.

Malthus found particularly objectionable Bailey's belief that 'the only use of a measure of value, in the sense of a medium of comparison, is between commodities existing at the same time', no relation being conceivable between the value of commodities over time ([1827] 1986, p. 75f.; citing Bailey, 1825, p. 117).[36] In fact, those who made such comparisons did so with two possible ends in mind: 'They obviously mean either to compare the esteem in which a commodity was held at one period with the esteem in which it was held at another, founded on the state of its supply compared with the demand, and ordinarily on its costs of production; or to compare the general power of purchasing which a commodity possessed at one period with its general power of purchasing at another period' ([1827] 1986, p. 77; also p. 81). By this reference to 'esteem' Malthus did not intend 'utility'; esteem is indicated by the *cost price* of a commodity and it made sense to compare cost price in period t with cost price in period $t+1$, both expressed in terms of an invariable measure, or a commodity whose cost price – labour and profits – can be presumed not to have changed.

A striking feature of the response to Bailey is Malthus's *defence of Ricardo*. His differences with Ricardo are represented as differences of detail, not of principle, and the defence is prologue to a justification of his own measure. His primary concern at this stage was simply to undermine Bailey's contention that the Ricardo measurement procedure – entailing a commodity produced by a constant labour input – conflicted with the notion of value in exchange ([1827] 1986, p. 82; citing Bailey, 1825, p. 122). Furthermore, Malthus maintained in his defence of Ricardo that Ricardian silver served better than real silver over secular periods as an index of general purchasing power, for it 'would be secured from that greatest source of variation in the general power of purchasing occasioned by the variation in its own producing labour; and an ounce of such silver would command much more nearly the same quantity of labour and commodities, for four or five hundred years together, than an ounce of silver derived from mines of greatly varying fertility'. The same held good of the function of a measure in indicating changes in 'estimation' over time of any *given* commodity – an allusion to cost price ([1827] 1986, p. 83). From an example that follows, it emerges again that, by 'esteem', Malthus refers essentially to the *cost price* of the commodity in question, doubtless because its cost price reflected the conditions of supply in the sense of the 'sacrifice which people were willing to make in order to obtain it'. Malthus adds that variations of the Ricardian-money price of X would also show precisely variations of X's command over other commodities 'which had not altered in the conditions of their supply, or the elementary costs of production'.

Malthus recognised that even Bailey, in dealing with 'the causes of value', found himself obliged 'to estimate the causes affecting one commodity as distinct from the causes affecting another; although, according to his previous doctrine' – an allusion to his formal insistence on relativities – 'the value of one commodity might be just as powerfully affected by causes operating upon another commodity as by causes operating upon itself' ([1827] 1986, p. 85). Bailey had to concede 'that to confine the term value ... to the mere relation of any one commodity to any other, is to render it pre-eminently futile and useless' ([1827] 1986, p. 86).

We will not elaborate the response made to Bailey's chapter 'On the Measure of Value Proposed by Mr. Malthus', other than to say that it constitutes the wholesale rejection of Bailey's attack on the notion of absolute value. The rejection is important for us because it reinforced Malthus's support for Ricardo's inverse wage–profit theorem, as we shall now see.

Malthus's adherence to the theorem is spelled out in his *Quarterly Review* article for 1824 treating McCulloch's *Encyclopaedia Britannica* contribution of the previous year: 'Of all the truths which Mr Ricardo has established, one of the most useful and important is, that profits are determined by the proportion of the whole produce which goes to labour. It is, indeed, a direct corollary from the proposition, that the value of commodities is resolvable into wages and profits; but its simplicity and apparent obviousness do not detract from its utility' ([1824] 1963, p. 189; also [1823]1957, pp. 28–29).

These references are to observations made before the appearance of the *Critical Dissertation.* But there is nothing to suggest that Malthus ever abandoned this position. Indeed, new support is offered for the inverse theorem in proportionate terms in the modifications introduced into the projected second edition of the *Principles*: 'whether the productive powers of labour are great or small, increasing, stationary, of diminishing ... profits depend upon the proportion of the value of the whole produce, which goes to pay the wages of the labour employed to obtain them' (Malthus, 1836, p. 267), and 'if labour be the measure of value, which I trust has been shown, this is the same as saying that profits are determined by the proportion of the value of the produce which goes to pay the labour which has obtained it' (1836, p. 291).

It also emerges from all this that Bailey's insistence that the inverse relation only applies *given* labour productivity left no impression on Malthus. This is further confirmed by his adherence to the 'shared incidence' principle whereby the profit rate declines during growth subject to increasing land scarcity despite a contemporaneous decline in the commodity wage, since proportionate wages necessarily rise. On Malthus's own reading, linguistic differences alone distinguished his own from Ricardo's formulations: 'When a given portion of labour and capital [in 1836: a given value of capital] yields smaller returns whether on new land or old, the loss is generally divided between the labourers and capitalists, and wages and profits fall at the same time. This is quite contrary to Mr. Ricardo's language. But the wages we refer to are totally different. He speaks of the cost [in 1836: mere labour cost] of producing the necessaries of the labourer; I speak of the necessaries themselves' (Malthus, 1820, p. 154; 1836, p. 152).[37]

A NOTE ON BAILEY'S OBLIGATIONS

Our evaluation of Bailey's obligations to Ricardo will be made in our concluding section. Other candidates must include Ricardo's 'votaries', pre-eminently perhaps De Quincey whose *Dialogues* discuss the character of *relative*, as distinct from *absolute*, value from which Bailey might have benefited (e.g. [1824] 1970, p. 80). There is too McCulloch's rejection of an invariable measure of exchangeable value: 'If you are to measure the value of any one commodity, you must measure it by the agency of some other commodity possessed of value. ... But as the circumstances under which every commodity is produced are always liable to perpetual change, it is clear to demonstration that none can be selected which can ever form an invariable measure or standard of value; though, as some commodities are much less variable than others, they may be used as rude approximations' (McCulloch, 1824, p. 114).[38] It is also conceivable that Bailey drew from J. S. Mill's '[v]alue is a relative term ...', for Mill's formulation appeared in the January 1825 issue of the *Westminster Review* and *A Critical Dissertation* was only published in June.

We turn to predecessors actually noted by Bailey himself – apart from the anonymous *Verbal Disputes* (see the appendix). These include Lauderdale, whose *Inquiry* (1804) is cited approvingly: 'We cannot express value, or a variation of value, without a comparison of two commodities' (Bailey, 1825, p. 4, citing Lauderdale, 1819, p. 19; see also, Lauderdale, 1804, p. 21). And in *A Letter to a Political Economist* we find: 'The impossibility of a measure of invariable value has been ... maintained by the Earl of Lauderdale, Col. Torrens, and others ...' (Bailey, 1826, p 14). In this context, it will be recalled, Bailey also cites Ricardo on the 'impossibility of finding any commodity of invariable value', reminding James Mill that this had been explicitly recognised in the *Critical Dissertation* itself, as we have seen is indeed the case.

By his mention of Torrens, Bailey intended the case made out in Torrens' *Essay on the Production of Wealth* (1821) regarding the inconceivability of a measure of exchange value. This is clear from the *Critical Dissertation*: 'After these critical strictures [against Ricardo, Malthus and De Quincey], it is a pleasure to cite a passage from an author, whose views as to the nature of value appear to me to be sounder than those of any other writer' (Bailey, 1825, p. 32). The passage in question entails the proposition that 'even if a commodity could be found which always required the same expenditure for its production, it would not therefore be of invariable exchangeable value, so as to serve as a standard for measuring the value of other things. Exchangeable value is determined, not by the absolute, but by the relative cost of production.... In the very term, exchangeable value, a relative and not an absolute quantity is implied' (Torrens 1821, pp. 56–57). There is, however, no formal expression here of 'debt' on Bailey's part.

Bowley draws attention to Craig's (1821) extension of the rent concept to the income from fixed capital (Bowley, 1937, p. 131n; see also Williams, 1978, p. 48); and, more generally, she maintains that '[t]hroughout his criticisms the influence of Say is very marked, and Bailey was in fact criticizing certain sections of Ricardo's system in the light of Say's general results' (Bowley, 1937, p. 93).[39]

Of potential importance as a 'source' – though not formally recognised by Bailey as such – is Senior's 'Report on the State of Agriculture' (1821), which contains several propositions close to those found in *Critical Dissertation* including differential rent as a 'monopoly' price, an emphasis on demand–supply as 'cause' of a high corn price with the corn raised at greatest cost only 'regulating' the price of all corn units, and – in particular – the observation that the price of a random unit of corn will not reflect its 'own' labour input.

CONCLUDING REMARKS

It has not usually been observed that Bailey's *Questions in Political Economy* (1823) is very positive towards James Mill and his *Elements*, which is described there as an 'excellent elementary work on Political Economy', with reference to foreign trade; the Corn laws ('a most able discussion ... the summing up of a luminous mind'); the general glut issue; paper currency (in the 'excellent Sections on Money'); the impact of monetary expansion on production and colonies (an 'excellent' discussion) (Bailey, 1823, pp. 21, 31, 39, 69, 73, 89). Beyond all this, Mill's analysis of exchange value, representing 'demand–supply' as accounting for short-run price and 'costs' for long-run price, is said to be 'so clear and concise, that it will be generally considered as a satisfactory solution to the problem' (1823, p. 99). The issue, Bailey adds, 'applies to "such commodities only", to borrow the words of Mr. Ricardo, "as can be increased in quantity by the exertion of human industry, and on the production of which competition operates without restraint". Monopolised commodities are acknowledged, on all hands, to depend upon the principle of supply and demand' (1823, p. 100).

What may have induced Bailey's transformation in attitude between 1823 and the *Critical Dissertation* of 1825? Although regarding the essentials of value theory, including the passage admired in 1823, the second edition of the *Elements* (1824) is identical to the first, there is this formal difference that the labour theory is reinforced by the commendation of McCulloch's notion that 'time does nothing', for which Mill was taken to task by Bailey. And there is too the appearance in 1824 of De Quincey's *Dialogues* – designed 'to draw into much stronger relief than Ricardo himself had done' the labour theory – which Bailey himself cites as providing the stimulus to compose the *Critical Dissertation* (see note 27).

Bailey's formal crusade of 1825 against Ricardo faced considerably more hostility than Seligman, Schumpeter and other commentators imagine, even amongst the so-called 'dissenters' – Malthus himself, so frequently classified uncritically as such, was positively hostile towards Bailey – and *a fortiori* amongst Ricardo's 'votaries' including McCulloch who some moderns imagine to have been non- or even anti-Ricardian. The Seligman–Robbins–Schumpeter view that the orthodox Ricardians had stifled the criticism, it also follows from our demonstration, is unjustified. These positions cannot account for the strong defence of Ricardo by Malthus, and the acceptance by Bailey and other dissenters of so much of the Ricardian doctrine.

Our results thus support James Mill's judgment that Bailey's analysis of the 'nature of value' 'makes profession, or rather ostentation, and parade, of being a controversy with Mr Ricardo', while it contained nothing of substance with which Ricardo would not have assented, and it provides the justification for Halévy's judgment that 'all the elements of [Bailey's] criticism are borrowed from Ricardo's book'. Yet caution is advised in this regard, for to 'borrow' might be understood in the pejorative sense of blatant plagiarism, though one cannot be sure that Halévy intended to be so understood. And it may not be a justified charge, since there is always the possibility that Bailey did not read Ricardo carefully enough to appreciate the richness of the *Principles*. Fortunately, we can to some extent go beyond surmise regarding these difficult matters, for there are some specific indications in our opening section regarding the character of the Bailey–Ricardo relation.

As for the charge that an invariable measure of exchange value is an inherently illogical conception, Bailey himself recognised in *Critical Dissertation* that Ricardo had taken the same view, and pointed this out in responding to his *Westminster* reviewer (James Mill). A related issue (not mentioned by Seligman) is Bailey's rejection of Adam Smith's proposition that a general wage increase is passed on in higher prices, namely that since *all* capitalists are subject to the same disturbance no single capitalist can raise the rate of exchange of his commodity relative to any other. Now this result is conspicuously established in the first chapter of Ricardo's *Principles*, and it is difficult to imagine that Bailey could have been unaware of, or could have forgotten, this fact. (He would, in any event, have been reminded by De Quincey [1824] 1970, pp. 62–63.) Yet the matter is more complex. The Ricardian objections to Smith turn on the contrast drawn between disturbances such as a general wage change affecting all products uniformly and those affecting products differentially, the latter including wage changes pertinent to specific categories of labour (or specific taxes) or to general wage changes which have a differential impact because of non-uniform factor ratios, which Ricardo himself reduced to differential investment periods. And in fact Bailey explicitly recognised that Ricardo had allowed modifications to a pure labour theory. Plagiarism thus does not enter the picture, which in fact must modify the impression left by the discussion of Smith.

Bailey, unfortunately, continued to leave an impression of a breakaway from Ricardo even in the present context – *vide*, for example, his unjustified complaint that only in his Index did Ricardo qualify the general rule that products exchanged in strict proportion to relative labour inputs. And, similarly, we have Bailey's formal denial that goods exchange according to relative labour inputs in the increasing-cost case, considering that intra-marginal units of corn do not sell at their 'own' costs. Now Bailey spells out that the marginal cost principle itself is pure Ricardo, and he even praises Ricardo's expression that value is not *caused* but *regulated* by marginal costs. Yet, notwithstanding, he directs the argument against the labour theory as if he were thereby striking out into virgin territory. And there is a second device. Thus Bailey concedes that Ricardo 'indeed, explicitly allows the influence of other causes' than labour quantity acting on relative value, but then deflects the criticism to apply to Ricardo's followers.

We turn to rent doctrine, first that rent emerges as a scarcity payment even should 'all the land under cultivation [be] of equal fertility'. Did Bailey not then realise that Ricardo had spelled this out explicitly as well as the proposition that rent under certain conditions might be paid in industry? One cannot tell in this particular case whether Bailey was simply unaware that he was expounding Ricardian principles – for which there is little excuse, although he would be in good company – or simply chose to remain silent.

Of particular interest is Bailey's insistence on what Seligman refers with admiration to something akin to, or consistent with, 'the modern theory of the economy of high wages', namely that if output is rising, a high wage is consistent with a high profit rate, the inverse profit–wage relation holding good only with output held constant. Here Bailey was expounding Ricardian doctrine, for Ricardo had sought to establish that it is the proportionate share of wages in the (marginal) product and not the absolute wage that mattered in profit-rate determination, particularly in establishing the inverse wage–profit theorem. Now since Bailey recognised the validity of the fundamental theorem assuming Ricardo's terminological usage, it might appear unlikely that he was unaware of the obvious implication for simultaneous increase or decrease in absolute returns depending on alternative assumptions regarding output. On the other hand, we must allow the possibility that he believed himself to be stating a novel proposition absent from the Ricardian canon. That, at least, is the most favourable construction to place on the episode.

Without question, the secondary literature – Seligman included – view Bailey as an anti-Ricardo 'dissident'.[40] We have shown the matter to be far more complex. Though Bailey frequently sought – somewhat in the manner of J.-B. Say (see Hollander, 2005) – to leave an impression of hostility towards the canon, when one attends to the details of the texts it emerges that he did appreciate that most of his major propositions were already to be found in Ricardo's *Principles*. Indeed, his claims to fame in some contexts – including the perception of value as implying a 'state of mind' – are surprisingly muted.

NOTES

1. A further suggestion for the long-term ineffectualness of the 'dissenters' is their failure to enter into practical policy issues (Seligman, 1903, pp. 534–535).

2. See also Sowell: 'If there is a classic of criticism in economics, it must be Samuel Bailey's *A Critical Dissertation* ...' (1970, p. 402).

3. On this matter alone Schumpeter takes issue with Seligman: 'Professor Seligman was in error when he allocated to Lloyd the proud position of having been the first thinker in any country to advance what is known today as the marginal theory of value, and to explain the dependence of value on marginal utility' (1954, p. 1055).

4. See O'Brien (2004), where Bailey is referred to as 'author of a brilliant if negative survey of value theory' (2004, p. 7), and as 'provid[ing] a damaging critique

of Ricardo's value theory, though, it must be said, he had relatively little of value to contribute himself" (2004, pp. 55–56).

5. Blaug (1958, p. 227) opined that '[t]he short-comings of anti-Ricardian economics – its eclectic character, its failure to carry through – far more than the dogmatism of Ricardo's disciples was the factor responsible for its lack of success'.

6. We shall elaborate specific features of two earlier papers, Hollander (1977 and 1998), devoted to the dissenting literature as a whole.

7. For the attribution to Mill, see Rauner (1961, pp. 149–157); Fetter (1962, p. 584); and O'Brien and Darnell (1982, pp. 108–128).

8. By contrast, Schumpeter (1954, p. 599) found Mill's contribution to be 'pathetically inadequate', and O'Brien (1988, p. 200) sees it as a reflection of Mill's 'fury'.

9. This is precisely the point made in 'Absolute Value and Exchangeable Value', when discussing Torrens on value, namely that his 'language may be correct as he uses it to express only exchangeable value but in Political Economy we want something more [;] we desire to know whether it be owing to some new facility in manufacturing cloth that diminished power in commanding money is owing, or whether it be owing to some new difficulty in producing money' (Sraffa & Dobb, 1973, Vol. 4, pp. 374–375).

10. Sowell errs when he writes *tout court* that 'Bailey rejected the Ricardian notion of a measure of value as designating the original cause of a change in relative values' (1970, p. 404).

11. *A Letter*, on my reading, is characterised by a refusal to read Ricardian texts fairly in terms of 'value' as labour embodied or, more generally, costs. See, for example, the discussion of De Quincey (Bailey, 1826, pp. 12–13). For a discussion of *A Letter*, see Rauner (1961, Chapter 6).

12. Rosenstein-Rodan points out correctly that 'the classical distinction between changes in the value of money originating on its side and changes in its value originating on the side of commodities' reflects 'the theory of real value' (1936, p. 263). This theory, he opines, 'has been vigorously exposed in the brilliant book of S. Bailey… . But the distinction was so generally accepted that Bailey himself fell back into it in his otherwise very valuable book: *Money and its Vicissitudes in Value* (1837, pp. 16–17)'.

Bailey's *Money* – not mentioned by Seligman – is of high importance, especially for its analysis of 'accelerated circulation' as means of activating 'inert' or 'dormant' or 'unemployed' capital and labour (1837, pp. 55f.), appearing in print seven years before J.S. Mill's 'Of the influence of Consumption on Production' (in *Essays on Some Unsettled Questions in Political Economy*: Mill [1844] 1967, Vol. 4, pp. 262–279). Mill makes no reference to this analysis; Marx cites it at length in his *Grundrisse* ([1857–58] 1986, pp. 502–504).

13. The index was probably compiled by James Mill (see Sraffa & Dobb, 1973, Vol. 1, pp. xxi–xxii).

14. In his chapter dealing with the causes of value, Bailey distinguished between 'commodities which are monopolized, or protected from competition by natural or adventitious circumstances'; those 'in the production of which some persons possess greater facilities than the rest of the community, and which therefore the competition of the latter cannot increase, except at a greater cost'; and those 'in the production of

which competition operates without restraint' (Bailey, 1825, p. 185). The general notion is that 'their respective causes of value cannot be the same'.

15. Bailey adheres to the Torrens' position (Torrens, 1821, pp. vi–vii; also 1818, p. 336), when he writes that '[i]n a civilized country … the mass of commodities are determined in value by the capital expended upon them' (Bailey, 1825, p. 206).

16. See the Appendix on the *Inquiry* (1821) where the joint-incidence principle is spelled out, though to this day it is uncertain whether or not Bailey is the author.

17. Rauner (1961, p. 129) writes that Cotterill's book 'clearly contained a debt to the *Critical Dissertation*', but his account raises similar issues to those in our text. For a denial of significant influence, see O'Brien (1988, p. 199).

18. Extraordinary as it may seem, Read objected to the 'Ricardo School' for following Lauderdale 1804 in *emphasising* utility and scarcity or supply–demand rather than cost analysis (Read, 1829, pp. 220–221).

19. For a downplaying of Bailey's influence on Read, see also Rauner (1961, p. 128), and O'Brien (1988, p. 199).

20. Bowley (1973, pp. 161–167) provides a detailed comparison of the two writers.

21. For the attribution to Senior, see Fetter (1958, p. 159), and also *The Dictionary of National Biography* (see Bowley, 1937, p. 344).

22. Bailey commended Mill for introducing in his second edition (even before De Quincey) the contrast between a *measure* and *cause* of value, but charged him with inconsistent usage, referring to Mill (1824, p. 108; see Bailey, 1825, pp. 171n, 205n). Mill made no adjustment in his third edition (1826b, p. 113).

23. The conditions were already formulated in the first edition of the *Elements* (Mill, 1821, p. 82), but the 1824 version is extended, and one suspects that Mill benefited from Ricardo's draft 'Absolute Value and Exchangeable Value', the language of which resembles that adopted by Mill: 'By far the greatest number of commodities which are the objects of exchange are produced by the union of capital and labour rather than by the 'extremes' (Sraffa & Dobb, 1973, Vol. 4, p. 405).

24. It did not escape Bailey that the 'credit of this argument … is due to Mr. McCulloch, whose authority is cited by Mr. Mill' (Bailey, 1825, p. 217n). For Ricardo's objections to Mill in this regard in 'Absolute Value and Exchangeable Value', see Sraffa and Dobb (1973, Vol. 4, pp. 375–376).

The proposition that profits are compensation for time was denied by McCulloch in correspondence with Ricardo, 24 August 1823 (Sraffa & Dobb, 1973, Vol. 9, pp. 266–68). Mill's reference of 1824, one supposes, is to McCulloch's formulation of this theme in his 1823 *Encyclopaedia Britannica* contribution regarding maturing wine (1825 [1823], pp. 141–142). Although no specific mention is made in this context of 'time', it is implied, and Mill might well have appreciated the implication. Very shortly thereafter, in the *Principles* (which is directly based on the earlier article), McCulloch spelled out – politely distancing himself from Ricardo – that 'the additional value, acquired by the wine during the period it has been kept in the cellar, is not a compensation or return for time, but for the effect or change that has been produced on it. Time cannot of itself produce any effect; it merely affords space for really efficient causes to operate, and it is therefore clear it can have nothing to do with value' (McCulloch, 1825, p. 314).

25. The *Principles* appeared in December 1825 and the *Critical Dissertation* in June (see Rauner, 1961, p. 86n). The point at hand is that 'how constant or uniform so ever a cause affecting one commodity may be, it cannot make that object of

constant value, without the concurrence of other invariable causes acting upon the commodity with which it is compared' (Bailey, 1825, p. 17).

26. Ricardo's paraphrase in the 1823 correspondence of McCulloch's position reveals his own position, that to understand the 'law' of exchange value was a necessary preliminary to specifying the invariability conditions required of a measure of value (letter of 31 August 1823, in Sraffa & Dobb, 1973, Vol. 9, p. 377).

27. De Quincey's *Dialogues of Three Templars* (1824) had stimulated Bailey to compose his *Critical Dissertation* (1825, pp. xxiv–xxv). The object of this early work, De Quincey later observed, had been 'to draw into much stronger relief than Ricardo himself had done that one radical doctrine as to value by which he had given a new birth to Political Economy' (De Quincey, 1844, p. 119). And while he had been pleased with the attention given to the work by Bailey, nevertheless 'with all his ability, that writer failed to shake any of my opinions. I continue to hold my original ideas on the various aspects of this embarrassing doctrine'.

28. With capital = 1,000 qs (or £1,000), of which wages = 500, non-wage capital (seed etc.) = 500 yielding 1,200, then profits = 200 or 20% and profit/wages = 2/5. With a doubled yield but retaining a 2/5 profit–wage ratio of the *additional* output, profits rise by 2/7 (1,200) = 343 to 543 and wages by 5/7 (1,200) = 857 to 1,357. As *shares of net output* (output less constant non-wage capital = 500), wages remain at 71%, and profits at 29%, but the *rate of profit* estimated on total capital rises from 20% to 543/1,000 = 54%.

29. In elaborating his numerical illustrations in the chapters 'On Wages' and 'On Profits', Ricardo allowed that the capital stock in the denominator of the profit-rate expression should be understood as including non-wage items (Sraffa & Dobb, 1973, Vol. 1, p. 117). But this was as an afterthought and adds nothing to the basic analysis.

30. In this context, McCulloch uses the term 'real wages' to indicate the commodity wage as distinct from proportional wages, and formulates a standard Ricardian theme: 'If the productiveness of industry were to diminish, proportional wages might rise, notwithstanding that real wages, or the absolute amount of the produce of industry falling to the share of the labourer, might be diminished: and if, on the other hand, the productiveness of industry were to increase, proportional wages might be diminished, while real wages might, at the same time, be increased' (McCulloch, 1825, p. 365).

31. O'Brien cites for support: Blaug (1958, pp. 167, 173; and 1985, p. 220); Bowley (1973, p. 167); and Rauner (1961, pp. 135–140). See also, Blaug (1997, p. 212) on Mill's deriving the abstinence principle from Bailey and Senior.

32. On this linkage between Bailey and Torrens, see Tucker (1961, p. 96).

33. Mill explains that 'I first heard of [*Some New Principles*] from Mr. Senior who recommended it to me as a book of which he had a high opinion …' (in Mineka & Lindley, 1972, p. 241). When the information was conveyed is not specified, but evidently it was sometime before 1848.

Senior's influence on Mill's *Principles* appears to be limited to terminology. For example: 'As the wages of the labourer are the remuneration of labour, so the profits of the capitalist are properly, according to Mr. Senior's well-chosen expression, the remuneration of abstinence' (Mill, [1848] 1965, Vol. 2, p. 400). No mention is made of Senior in the chapter 'Of the Law of the Increase of Capital', and none in 'Of Profits' apart from the above-cited definition.

34. Rauner, while claiming an apparent influence by Bailey upon Mill, is cautious. He points out that 'Bailey had not been alone in seeking the generalization of the rent concept. But he had been among the first and foremost advocates of it in England. And if Mill, perhaps, drew more directly from Senior than Bailey, this is not to say that Senior himself was unaware of the *Critical Dissertation*, although he never explicitly referred to it' (Rauner, 1961, p. 140).

35. On this classification, see Bowley (1973, pp. 161–169); and Williams (1978, pp. 62–67).

36. For criticism of this feature, see Bode's reference to Bailey's Chapter V, 'On Comparing Commodities at Different Periods', as deficient in 'attempt[ing] to show that any *intertemporal* comparison of the value of a commodity must be meaningless .... [I]n all cases where the periods in question fall within the scope of one plan, intertemporal comparison of value is not only possible but is essential to the rationality of this plan' (Bode, 1935, p. 344). The deficiency is ascribed in part 'to the fact that Bailey did not recognize the essence of subjective value as that of an index of degree in the subjective economic scale ....' Also see Robbins: 'Bailey overstates his case to this extent, that he does not mention *prospective* value relations through time' (1935, p. 60n). This is to be generous, since Bailey positively denied the meaningfulness of intertemporal value comparisons.

37. See Ricardo's agreement with Malthus on the falling commodity wage in his Note 61 (Sraffa & Dobb, 1973, Vol. 2, p. 124). He insisted, however, that the *money value* of the lower commodity wage necessarily rises only with his own measure.

38. See also McCulloch (1825, pp. 212–214) for a corresponding formulation made after the appearance of *A Dissertation*, which pays some tribute to Bailey.

39. As an example of the complexities involved, consider the fact that despite Say's representation of the invariable standard as a 'pure chimera', he nonetheless actually adopted Malthus's measure – which Bailey, of course rejected. On this matter, see Hollander (2005, p. 43).

The analogy between land rents and payments to skilled labour exceeding reimbursement of training costs is also to be found in Storch 1823 (see Williams, 1978, p. 48).

40. This view has filtered down, a New School web site (http://cepa.newschool.edu/het/schools/anti.htm) having the following under *Samuel Bailey*: 'Pointed out the logical difficulties of both the labor theory of value and Ricardo's "invariable measure". An early promoter of the theory of scarcity and the generalisation of the Ricardian theory of rent, thus, can be considered a precursor of the Marginalist Revolution'.

41. Schumpeter does add a reference to Bailey's *A Letter to a Political Economist* (1826), as responding to 'a grossly unfair criticism in the *Westminster Review*', the review now known to have been written by James Mill.

42. It is not clear that Seligman read the pamphlet carefully; see the comment by Sraffa (Sraffa & Dobb, 1973, Vol. 9, p. 27n), regarding Seligman (1903, p. 351).

REFERENCES

Anon. (1821a). *Observations on certain verbal disputes in political economy, particularly relating to value, and to demand and supply*. London: R. Hunter.

Anon. (1821b). *An inquiry into those principles respecting the nature of demand and the necessity of consumption lately advocated by Mr. Malthus*. London: R. Hunter.

Bailey, S. (1821). *Essays on the formation and publication of opinions*. London: R. Hunter.

Bailey, S. (1823). *Questions in political economy, politics, morals, metaphysics, polite literature, and other branches of knowledge*. London: R. Hunter.

Bailey, S. (1825). *A critical dissertation on the nature, measure and causes of value*. London: R. Hunter.

Bailey, S. (1826). *A letter to a political economist, occasioned by an article in the 'Westminster Review' on the subject of value*. London: R. Hunter.

Bailey, S. (1837). *Money and its vicissitudes of value: As they affect national industry and pecuniary contracts*. London: Effingham Wilson.

Bailey, S. ([1825] 1967), A critical dissertation on the nature, measure and causes of value. London: Frank Cass.

Black, R. D. C. (1988). Commentary. In: W. O. Thweatt (Ed.), *Classical political economy: A survey of recent literature* (pp. 221–225). Boston: Kluwer Academic.

Blaug, M. (1958). *Ricardian economics*. New Haven: Yale University Press.

Blaug, M. (1985). *Economic theory in retrospect* (4th ed.). Cambridge: Cambridge University Press.

Blaug, M. (1997). *Economic theory in retrospect* (5th ed.). Cambridge: Cambridge University Press.

Bode, K. (1935). Review of A critical dissertation on the nature, measures and causes of value. *Economica, n.s.*, *2*(7), 342–344.

Bowley, M. (1937). *Nassau senior and classical economics*. London: George Allen and Unwin.

Bowley, M. (1972). The predecessors of Jevons – the revolution that wasn't. *Manchester School*, *40*(1), 9–29.

Bowley, M. (1973). *Studies in the history of economic theory before 1870*. London: Macmillan.

Cotterill, C. F. (1831). *An examination of the doctrines of value*. London: Simpkin Marshall.

Craig, J. (1821). *Remarks on some fundamental doctrines in political economy*. Edinburgh: Archibald Constable.

Dennis, K. (1973). The Bailey notebooks and authorship of 'Verbal Disputes'. *History of Economic Thought Newsletter*, *11*(Autumn), 17–18.

De Quincey, T. ([1824] 1970). Dialogues of three Templars on political economy. In: D. Masson (Ed.), *Political Economy and Politics* (pp. 37–112). New York: A.M. Kelley.

De Quincey, T. (1844). *The logic of political economy*. Edinburgh: Blackwood.

Fetter, F. W. (1958). The economic articles in the Quarterly Review and their authors, 1809–1852 – II. *Journal of Political Economy*, *66*(2), 154–170.

Fetter, F. W. (1962). The economic articles in the Westminster Review and their authors, 1824–1851. *Journal of Political Economy*, *70*(6), 572–596.

Halévy, E. (1904/1955). *The growth of philosophic radicalism*. Boston: Beacon Press.

Hollander, S. (1977). The reception of Ricardian economics. *Oxford Economic Papers*, *29*(2), 221–257.

Hollander, S. (1979). *The economics of David Ricardo*. Toronto: University of Toronto Press.

Hollander, S. (1985). *The economics of John Stuart Mill*. Toronto: University of Toronto Press.

Hollander, S. (1992). *Classical economics*. Toronto: University of Toronto Press.

Hollander, S. (1998). The canonical classical model: Content, adherence and priority. *Journal of the History of Economic Thought*, *20*(3), 253–277.

Hollander, S. (2001). Classical economics: A reification wrapped in an anachronism? In: E. Forget & S. Peart (Eds), *Reflecting on the classical canon in economics* (pp. 7–26). London: Routledge.

Hollander, S. (2005). *Jean-Baptiste Say and the classical canon in economics: The British connection in French classicism*. London: Routledge.
Hollander, S. (2007). Ricardo as a 'classical economist': The 'new view' reexamined – a reply to Peach. *History of Political Economy*, *39*(2), 307–312.
Jevons, W. S. ([1924] 1879). Preface to 2nd ed. In: H. S. Jevons (Ed.), *Theory of political economy* (4th ed., pp. xi–lii). London: Macmillan.
Lauderdale, J. M. (1804). *An inquiry into the nature and origin of public wealth*. Edinburgh: Archibald Constable.
Lauderdale, J. M. (1819). *An inquiry into the nature and origin of public wealth* (2nd ed.). Edinburgh: Archibald Constable.
Lloyd, W. F. (1834). *A lecture on the notion of value*. London: Roake and Varby.
Longfield, M. (1834). *Lectures on political economy*. Dublin: Richard Milliken and Son.
McCulloch, J. R. (1824). Principles which determine the exchangeable value of commodities and the rate of profit. *The Scotsman*, *8*(430), 113–114.
McCulloch, J. R. ([1823]1825). Political economy. In: J. McVickar (Ed.), *Outlines of political economy*. New York: Wilder & Campbell.
McCulloch, J. R. (1825). *The principles of political economy* (1st ed.). Edinburgh: William and Charles Tait.
McCulloch, J. R. (1845). *The literature of political economy: A classified catalogue*. London: Longman, Brown, Green and Longmans.
McCulloch, J. R. (1864). *The principles of political economy* (5th ed.). Edinburgh: Adam and Charles Black.
Malthus, T. R. (1820). *Principles of political economy*. London: John Murray.
Malthus, T. R. ([1823] 1957). *The measure of value stated and illustrated*. New York: Kelley and Millman.
Malthus, T. R. ([1824] 1963). Political economy (Quarterly Review). In: B. Semmel (Ed.), *Occasional papers of T.R. Malthus* (pp. 71–104). New York: Burt Franklin.
Malthus, T. R. ([1827] 1986). In: E.A. Wrigley & D. Souden (Eds), *The Works of Thomas Robert Malthus, Vol. 8: Definitions in Political Economy*. London: William Pickering.
Malthus, T. R. (1836). *Principles of political economy*. London: William Pickering.
Marx, K. ([1857–58] 1986). *Karl Marx – Frederick Engels collected works*, Vol. 28: *Grundrisse*. New York: International Publishers.
Marx, K. ([1861-63] 1989). *Karl Marx – Frederick Engels collected works*, Vol. 32: *Theories of surplus value*. New York: International Publishers.
Meek, R. L. (1967). *Economics and ideology, and other essays*. London: Chapman & Hall.
Mill, J. (1808). *Commerce defended*. London: C. and R. Baldwin.
Mill, J. (1821). *Elements of political economy*. London: Baldwin, Cradock, and Joy.
Mill, J. (1824). *Elements of political economy* (2nd ed.). London: Baldwin, Cradock, and Joy.
Mill, J. (1826a). On the nature, measures, and causes of value. *Westminster Review*, *5*(9), 157–172.
Mill, J. (1826b). *Elements of political economy* (3rd ed.). London: Henry G. Bohn.
Mill, J. S. ([1825] 1967). The Quarterly Review on political economy. In: J. M. Robson (Ed.), *Collected works of John Stuart Mill*, Vol. 4, *Essays on economics and society, Part I* (pp. 23–43). Toronto: University of Toronto Press.
Mill, J. S. ([1828] 1967). The nature, origin, and progress of rent. In: J. M. Robson (Ed.), *Collected works of John Stuart Mill*, Vol. 4, *Essays on economics and society, Part I* (pp. 161–180). Toronto: University of Toronto Press.

Mill, J. S. ([1844] 1967). Essays on some unsettled questions in political economy. In: J. M. Robson (Ed.), *Collected works of John Stuart Mill, Vol. 4, Essays on economics and society, Part I* (pp. 229–339). Toronto: University of Toronto Press.

Mill, J. S. ([1848] 1965). Principles of political economy. In: J. M. Robson (Ed.), Collected works of John Stuart Mill, Vols. 2–3, *The principles of political economy with some of their applications to social philosophy*. Toronto: University of Toronto Press.

Mill, J. S. ([1873] 1981). Autobiography and literary essays. In: J. M. Robson & J. Stillinger (Ed.), *Collected works of John Stuart Mill*, Vol. 1, *Autobiography and literary essays*. Toronto: University of Toronto Press.

Mineka, F. E., & Lindley, D. N. (1972). *Collected works of John Stuart Mill, Vol. 14: The later letters of John Stuart Mill: 1849–1873*. Toronto: University of Toronto Press.

O'Brien, D. P. (1970). *J.R. McCulloch: A study in classical economics*. London: George Allen & Unwin.

O'Brien, D. P. (1988). Classical reassessments. In: W. O. Thweatt (Ed.), *Classical political economy: A survey of recent literature* (pp. 179–220). Boston: Kluwer Academic.

O'Brien, D. P. (2004). *The classical economists revisited*. Princeton: Princeton University Press.

O'Brien, D. P., & Darnell, A. C. (1982). *Authorship puzzles in the history of economics: A statistical approach*. London: Macmillan.

Political Economy Club. (1921). *Political Economy Club, centenary volume, Vol. 6, minutes of proceedings*. London: Macmillan.

Rae, J. (1834). *Statement of some new principles on the subject of political economy*. Boston, Hilliard: Gray and Co.

Rauner, R. M. (1956). *Samuel Bailey and classical economics*. Ph.D. thesis, University of London.

Rauner, R. M. (1961). *Samuel Bailey and the classical theory of value*. Cambridge: Harvard University Press.

Rauner, R. M. (1987). Bailey, Samuel. In: J. Eatwell, M. Milgate & P. Newman (Eds), *The New Palgrave: A Dictionary of Economics* (1, pp. 173–175). London: Macmillan.

Read, S. (1829). *Political economy: An inquiry into the natural grounds of right to vendible property or wealth*. Edinburgh: Oliver and Boyd.

Robbins, L. C. (1935). *An essay on the nature and significance of economic science* (2nd ed.). London: Macmillan.

Rosenstein-Rodan, P. N. (1936). The coordination of the general theories of money and price. *Economica, n.s., 3*(11), 257–280.

Say J.-B. ([1819] 1880). In: C.R. Prinsep (Trans.), *A treatise on political economy: Or the production, distribution & consumption of wealth* (4th ed.). Philadelphia: Claxton, Remsen & Haffelfinger.

Schumpeter, J. A. (1954). *History of economic analysis*. New York: Oxford University Press.

Seligman, E. R. A. (1903). On some neglected British economists. *Economic Journal, 13*(51 and 52), 335–363 and 511–535.

Senior, N. W. (1821). Report on the state of agriculture. *Quarterly Review, 25*(July), 466–504.

Senior, N. W. ([1836] 1951). *An outline of the science of political economy*. London: George Allen & Unwin.

Sowell, T. (1970). Samuel Bailey revisited. *Economica, 37*(148), 402–408.

Sowell, T. (1972). *Say's law: An historical analysis*. Princeton: Princeton University Press.

Sowell, T. (2006). *On classical economics*. New Haven: Yale University Press.

Sraffa, P., & Dobb, M. (Eds). (1973). *The works and correspondence of David Ricardo, 11 vols*. Cambridge: Cambridge University Press.

Stigler, S. M. (1983). Review of Authorship puzzles in the history of economics, by D.P. O'Brien and A.C. Darnell. *Journal of Economic History, 43*(2), 547–550.
Storch, H. (1823). *Cours d'Économie politique*. Paris: Bossange & Aïllaud.
Thompson, T. P. (1826). *An exposition of fallacies on rent, tithes, &c.* London: Hatchard, Rivington.
Torrens, R. (1818). Strictures on Mr. Ricardo's doctrine respecting exchangeable value. *Edinburgh Magazine*, October, pp. 335–338.
Torrens, R. (1821). *An essay on the production of wealth*. London: Longman, Hurst, Rees, Orme and Brown.
Torrens, R. (1826). *An essay on the external corn trade* (3rd ed.). London: Longmans, Rees, Orme, Brown, and Green.
Torrens, R. (1829). *An essay on the external corn trade* (new ed.). London: Longman, Rees, Orme, Brown, and Green.
Torrens, R. (1835). *Colonization of South Australia*. London: Longman, Rees, Orme, Brown, Green, and Longman.
Torrens, R. (1844). *The budget: On commercial and colonial policy*. London: Smith, Elder, & Co.
Tucker, G. S. L. (1961). *Progress and profits in British economic thought: 1650–1850*. Cambridge: Cambridge University Press.
Viner, J. (1958). *The long view and the short: Studies in economic theory and policy*. Glencoe, IL: The Free Press.
Whately, R. (1826). *Elements of logic*. London: Mawman.
Williams, P. L. (1978). *The emergence of the theory of the firm: From Adam Smith to Marshall*. London: Macmillan.
Winch, D. (1966). *James Mill: Selected economic writings*. Edinburgh: Oliver & Boyd.

APPENDIX

Samuel Bailey and Two Anonymous Contributions of 1821

The authorship of *Observations on Certain Verbal Disputes in Political Economy* (1821a) remains to be ascertained. Marx noticed similarities between this pamphlet and Bailey's *Critical Dissertation* and charged Bailey with plagiarism ([1861–63] 1989, pp. 299, 312, 347). Bailey himself feared he might be subjected to such accusation: 'This Book exhibits some striking coincidences with my Treatise on Value – so striking that I might possibly incur the charge of plagiarism if any one compared the two works. The truth is however that I did not see this pamphlet till my own book was published' (Dennis, 1973, p. 17, citing Bailey's private notes, held in the University of Edinburgh, undated). Dennis (1973, p. 18) gives cogent reasons to accept Bailey's disclaimer.

The Cass edition of Bailey's works ([1825] 1967), however, includes the pamphlet, and Sowell (1970) makes out a positive case for Bailey as author, which applies also to the *Inquiry into Those Principles Respecting the Nature of Demand and the Necessity of Consumption Lately Advocated by Mr. Malthus* (1821b):

> Comparing the *Observations* and the *Inquiry* with other works known to have been written by Samuel Bailey, there is a remarkable range of similarities and no significant differences. These similarities may be grouped in four broad categories: (1) discussions of the role and importance of words in economics, (2) value theory, (3) methodology, and (4) opinions of economics and of particular economists. There are also certain stylistic similarities between these two anonymous works and Bailey's other writings. (Sowell, 1970, p. 402; also 1972, pp. 131–134)

Sowell (2006) reaffirms this attribution with respect both to *Verbal Disputes* (2006, p. 233 n89; p. 234 n91, n102; p. 239 n26; p. 247 n124, n129; and p. 248 n143) and to the *Inquiry* (p. 141; p. 216 n61; p. 230 n44; p. 248 n137; p. 267 n50, n51; and p. 269 n81).

Sowell does not take into account either the evidence by Dennis entailing Bailey's private denial of plagiarism and, by obvious implication of authorship, with regard to the *Observations*, or the case against Bailey as author convincingly elaborated in O'Brien and Darnell (1982, pp. 86–89). (O'Brien and Darnell propose Brougham as probable author.) Rauner (1961, p. 89 n43) had, in any event, long before cast doubt on Bailey as author of the *Observations*.

More challenging is the *Inquiry* (1821b). As mentioned, Sowell (1970, 2006) make out a case for Bailey. So too in this case do O'Brien and Darnell (1982, Ch. 5). But their conclusion turns on an application of a statistical analysis (1982, pp. 91–107), called into question by Stigler (1983). O'Brien and Darnell write of a 'widespread belief that Bailey was the author of this work [the *Inquiry*]' ((1982, p. 90), but this surely is to exaggerate. Rauner (1961, 1987) make no such attribution and – like *Verbal Disputes* – it remains unattributed in the Kress and Goldsmiths' collections. Seligman himself made no attempt at attribution. Schumpeter takes no note at all of the *Inquiry*, and while *Verbal Disputes* is described as a 'main contribution' it is not ascribed (1954, p. 599n). As for Bailey: 'The only publication of his that needs to be mentioned is *A Critical Dissertation* …' (1954, p. 486n).[41]

Two considerations point away from Bailey's authorship of the *Inquiry*. Firstly, Dennis contrasts Bailey's denial in his notebooks of authorship with respect to the *Verbal Disputes* with the (apparent) absence of references to the *Inquiry*: 'the presumption of Bailey's authorship of the latter should thereby be weakened inasmuch as the textual linkages between the two pamphlets of 1821 are at least as strong as those between the *Inquiry* and Bailey's accredited works' (Dennis, 1973, p. 17). Secondly, Sowell – who argues for Bailey's authorship of both 1821 pamphlets – himself allows that the fact that the *Verbal Disputes* and the *Inquiry* 'failed to appear in any of [the lists of selected earlier works which appeared in Bailey's later works] presents a difficulty' (1970, p. 408).

The present writer at one time accepted uncritically the attribution of the *Inquiry* to Bailey (Hollander, 1998, p. 261). But though, in the light of the foregoing complexities, it now seems unlikely that the *Inquiry* is by Bailey, it is desirable that the quest for authorship continue since Seligman (1903, p. 351) was unjustified in describing the pamphlet – along with *Verbal Disputes* – as 'of minor importance'.[42] As a conspicuous instance of its significance, we find expressed in the clearest terms the simultaneous fall in both wages and profits characterising the 'canonical' growth model, the shared incidence attributable to increasingly scarce land and a rising corn price (Anon., 1821b, p. 25). The author further clarifies that the profit rate varies with *proportionate* wages; simultaneously high (low) profit and wage rates are quite consistent in conditions of high (low) productivity (Anon., 1821b, p. 100).

PLACING WILLIAM FORSTER LLOYD IN CONTEXT

G. C. G. Moore and Michael V. White

> It is a trite saying that the history of political economy is still to be written.
>
> Edwin Seligman (1903, p. 335)

There are few historical records extant relating to William Forster Lloyd (1794–1852). It is known that he was the second surviving son of Thomas Lloyd, who was a rector of Aston-sub-Edge, Gloucestershire, but who actually resided at various villages immediately outside West Wycombe, Buckinghamshire, before becoming a private tutor of some note (and some calling prior to the rise of the public schools) at nearby Peterley House, Great Missenden, Buckinghamshire. William F. Lloyd's elder brother was Charles Lloyd (1784–1829), a tutor in mathematics at Christ Church, Oxford, and, through his influence over Sir Robert Peel (who he prepared for exams), rose rapidly in the church, eventually becoming Regius Professor of Divinity and Canon of Christ Church (1822–1829) and Bishop of Oxford (1827–1829). William F. Lloyd himself seems to have excelled as a child, becoming captain of Westminster in 1811, matriculating to his brother's college, Christ Church, in 1812, and graduating with first-class honours in mathematics and second-class honours in classics in 1815. He subsequently gained an MA and held posts at Christ Church as a Greek reader (1823) and mathematics lecturer (until the end of 1824). He then fell from view, before gaining the five-year term Drummond Chair in Political Economy (1832–1837), where he delivered lectures, many subsequently

English, Irish and Subversives Among the Dismal Scientists
Research in the History of Economic Thought and Methodology, Volume 28-B, 199–241

ISSN: 0743-4154/doi:10.1108/S0743-4154(2010)000028B011

published, which some scholars purport to contain theoretical concepts now dominant in the discipline of economics. Lloyd's position as Drummond Professor led to some belated advancement, including being elected a fellow of the Royal Society in 1834. However, he never became a member of the Political Economy Club and he is not mentioned in the many reminiscences of this age. He remained a 'student' of Christ Church from 1812 to 1837, and hence his time at Oxford seems to have ended with his last lecture as Drummond Professor. Although in holy orders, he held no preferment, residing on his property in Prestwood, Missenden and dying there on 2 June 1852.[1]

The enigmatic William F. Lloyd, an individual for whom there are no character sketches from the historical records to draw on, is the subject of this study. In particular, we wish to provide the context for those of Lloyd's ideas that, according to many, anticipated modern economic ideas. The two most famous declarations in which modern concepts are attributed to Lloyd are E. R. A. Seligman's (1903) conjecture that Lloyd anticipated the 'marginal utility' theory of value and Garret Hardin's (1968) assertion that Lloyd was one of the earliest scholars to recognise the tragedy of the commons. We argue that Lloyd deployed these theoretical tools at the end of an era in which political economy at Oxford was driven by two charismatic dons, Richard Whately and Charles Lloyd (brother of William F. Lloyd), who operated from power bases at the then two dominant Oxford colleges – Oriel and Christ Church respectively – and who wielded influence via their two most famous and more capable charges, Nassau Senior (who Whately prepared for exams) and Robert Peel (who Lloyd prepared for exams). There are eight sections to the chapter. In the second section, we describe how Whately and Senior subscribed to an intellectual tradition associated with the Oriel Noetics and drew upon this tradition to build an abstract-deductive political economy that yielded an optimistic vision of the market economy. In the third section, we describe how Lloyd's Christ Church heritage induced him to draw upon the abstract-deductive method that was championed by the Oriel Noetics to construct a far less optimistic vision of the market economy. In the fourth, fifth and sixth sections, we present the (non-marginalist) surplus model that Lloyd developed in his capacity as Drummond Professor. In the seventh section, we argue that Lloyd deployed his analytical model to challenge the Poor Law reforms that were then being championed by Whately and Senior. In the eighth section, we review the modern interpretations of Lloyd in the light of the context provided in the previous sections.

OXFORD POLITICAL ECONOMY: WHATELY, SENIOR AND THE ORIEL NOETICS

There is no exaggeration in the claim that abstract-deductive political economy in pre-Tractarian Oxford was driven by Richard Whately and hence centred at Oriel College. At this time Oriel was defined by a group of intellectuals now commonly referred to as the Oriel Noetics, of whom Whately was one, and the nature of Oxford political economy in the opening decades of the nineteenth century (including William F. Lloyd's contribution to it) cannot be understood outside the context of the intellectual tradition established by the Oriel Noetics. The Noetics were unconventional reformist clerics (one could not use the slippery mid-Victorian word 'liberal', as they were predominantly conservative Whigs or reform-minded Tories of the Pitt mould, in which order and tradition were maintained through moderate, but not radical, change); admired rational thought and absent-mindedly tested social conventions with their speech; were unafraid to question religious shibboleths if they deemed them bereft of scriptural foundation (such as Sabbatarianism); deployed logical processes to bolster their religious beliefs, which they held in an unsentimental fashion, and thereby to some extent practised that most contradictory of creeds, a logical faith; and, most importantly for this chapter, constructed a Christian Political Economy by dichotomising knowledge into a theological domain, in which they inferred from scriptural evidence that individuals should pursue the ends of attaining specific virtues (not utility!), and a scientific domain, in which they deduced scientific laws that would enable individuals to achieve the ends of attaining these virtues. They looked upon the rising Romantic Movement in general and the spiritualist yearnings of the Oxford Tractarians in particular with simple incomprehension, if not disgust. They deplored with equal measure the Evangelicals' enthusiasms, willing incogitency and lack of institutional anchor, yet sought to establish a broader national church that included dissenters (but not Catholics). They were most prominent in the 1810s and 1820s before colliding violently in the 1830s with, and being sidelined by, the Tractarians, many of whom they had, ironically enough, mentored and promoted.[2]

This Oriel Noetic tradition was established by two dominant Oriel provosts, John Eveleigh, who was provost from 1789 to 1814, and Edward Copleston, who was provost from 1814 to 1828 and who figures prominently in the narrative that follows. These two dominant personalities were instrumental in promoting the pedagogical and institutional reforms to the exam statutes over 1800–1809 that in many ways anticipated the more famous university reforms of 1854 and which slowly transformed Oxford from the indolent institution of Edward Gibbon's day (with its 'idle monks') to the more earnest institution of Matthew Arnold's day. Eveleigh's and Copleston's reformist zeal and careful recruitment processes also raised Oriel from a state of mediocrity to one of the most respected colleges of Oxford. Fellows were chosen less on the basis of connections and patronage and more on the basis of character and intellectual spark. The latter strategy meant that men with double second-class degrees, but with character and first-class minds, were often chosen as fellows over men with double firsts. The first batch of recruits became the core of the Oriel tradition: John Davison became a fellow in 1800, Richard Whately in 1811 (as one of the disappointed double-second men), John Keble in 1811, Edward Hawkins in 1813 and Renn Dickson Hampden in 1814. These fellows, in turn, recruited younger men of the calibre of Thomas Arnold, Robert Wilberforce, Robert Hurrell Froude, John Henry Newman (who did not even get a second class) and Edward Pusey, with the last few ultimately betraying the Oriel tradition by forming the Oxford movement. Finally, for reasons discussed below, Nassau Senior of Magdalen College should also be considered an honorary Oriel Noetic. It was, however, Copleston and Whately who were the real leaders, especially in the second decade of the century when it was said that Copleston and Whately ruled the college and, indeed, threatened to conquer Oxford (Mozley, 1882, p. 22).

The manner in which this Oriel Noetic tradition shaped Oxford political economy as an abstract-deductive discipline is best seen in the way that it brought Whately, Copleston and Senior together to contemplate logic and, ultimately, to produce *Elements of Logic* (1826), which may be viewed as *their* most high-profile literary product and as the conceptual manifesto for *their* vision of political economy. This point requires some explanation, for although Whately's name correctly appears as the author on the flyleaf of this publication, it was in many ways a joint production of all three and, indeed, of the Oriel Noetic tradition itself, which largely revolved around resurrecting Aristotelian logic at Oxford and defending the role of logic in the Oxford curricula. The central role Copleston played in this tradition, and the way this tradition effectively made political economy an extension of logic, is easy enough to explain. Copleston was in the ascendancy at Oriel in 1811 when he took the newly appointed Whately under his wing. Copleston's reputation as a reasoner was more than a match for Whately's sharpness of mind, and a famous friendship was struck between the two. Indeed, Copleston surpassed even Whately in his preoccupation with definitions, the precision of language and logical processes. He was particularly fascinated by, and severe on those who practised, false terminology. Guests invited to Oriel, especially those who liked to relax after dinner over port, were put out by the sharpness of the post-dinner conversation: it was said that the 'Oriel Common Room *stunk* of Logic' (Fitzpatrick, 1864, p. 9). It also should be emphasised that although Copleston published little due to his numerous practical cares in his college (and later in his diocese), he did demonstrate his ratiocinating talents in 1809 by tearing apart a text on logic by a certain 'Horse' Kett and, in 1810–1811, by defending Oxford curricula (including the centrality of logic in this curricula) in the *Edinburgh Review* (Ward, 1965, p. 17). Copleston, moreover, entered his meditations on logic into a commonplace book, which Whately freely drew upon in his classes and in the preparation of the *Elements of Logic*. It is therefore not surprising that Whately publicly dedicated the book to Copleston, stating in the preface that, given the long gestation of the associated ideas in the Oriel common room, it was impossible to disentangle Copleston's contribution (Whately, [1826] 1890, p. vi). Finally, Senior became drawn into the Oriel environment of logomachies and syllogistic gymnastics by famously being failed in his first attempt at exams, which, in turn, forced him to look beyond his college (Magdalen) for a private tutor, namely Whately, to resurrect his career. Senior, subsequently gained a double first, became central member of Whately's Oriel circle and, as an outward sign of this allegiance, furnished an appendix for the *Elements* that illustrated ambiguities of terms in political economy (Whately, [1826] 1890, p. vii; Levy, 1970, p. 52).

The implications of (Copleston–Senior–Whately's) *Elements* for political economy were readily seen by their contemporaries. This was partly because of Senior's appendix on ambiguous terms in political economy and partly because of their publications in this discipline, both prior and subsequent to, the publication of the *Elements* in 1826. The Noetics' interest in political economy certainly dates from the previous decades (Corsi, 1987, p. 106; Waterman, 1991, p. 184ff). Copleston's commonplace book records his readings of political economy texts taken from the Oriel reading room, and, in his aforementioned 1810 response to criticisms of Oxford curricula in the *Edinburgh Review*, he drew upon this reading to state that political economy should not be privileged over other disciplines (especially his treasured logic), while at the same emphasising its inherent worth. John Davison (1817), one of Copleston's close friends at Oriel, also published a tract entitled *Considerations on the Poor Laws*, which called for the repeal of the Poor Laws, with respect to able-bodied men, over a 10-year period to minimise the ills that a sudden repeal would bring. Copleston (1819a, 1819b) then wrote two *Letters to the Rt Hon Robert Peel* during the bullion controversy of 1819, in which he articulated an abstract-deductive methodology for political economy (at least by demonstration) and, in support of the resumption of cash payments, attributed pauperism to the inflation caused by the absence of cash payments (by initially reducing real wages earned by the lower classes) rather than to the admittedly injurious Poor Laws, which he argued should be reformed rather than repealed (1819a, p. 34). Copleston's pamphlets were more than mere policy declarations, for he believed that when 'first principles are brought into question [within a policy debate], it is necessary to explain and vindicate the very elements of the science' (1819a, p. 2). This is an impressive output for a group of scholars whose primary objective throughout this period was not the promotion of political economy at all, but, as mentioned earlier, to impose logic as the centre of the liberal-arts curricula at Oxford. Indeed, one could say that modern political economy, in its abstract-deductive form, is partly the product of this institutional goal.

Any doubt about the arrival of a Copleston–Whately–Senior or 'Oxford' school of political economy with the publication of *Elements* was put to rest with the election of Senior as the first holder of the Drummond Chair of Political Economy in June 1825. His introductory lecture in 1826 was, following the Oriel line, devoted to defending political economy as an abstract-deductive science with a policy branch attached. The other 37 lectures delivered by Senior during his five-year tenure used this abstract-deductive method to explain and mitigate the calamitous state of the economy in the mean post-Napoleonic years. Specifically, the dislocation that ensued from the movement to a peace-time economy and the industrialisation process, gave rise to mass underemployment, periodic famines (especially in Ireland) and the threat of insurrection every three years or so. Any recovery seemed to quickly founder in the face of a bad season (1816–1817, 1823–1825 and 1828–1831) or a financial crisis (1825). Senior, like the London Utilitarians (but with his own twists), therefore drew upon the trilogy of T. R. Malthus's *Essay* (1798), Francis Horner's *Bullion Report* (1810) and David Ricardo's *Principles* (1817) to provide an account of the situation that is familiar to historians of the period: the old Poor Laws induced an escalation in the geometric progression of the population while agricultural produce continued to rise at an arithmetic rate; the corn laws further eroded the wage fund available for the resulting 'redundant population' by transferring excessive surpluses to the landlords; and inconvertible paper notes debased the currency and accentuated financial crises. The solution was to reform the Poor Laws, abolish the

Corn Laws and insist on convertibility (see Senior, 1828, 1830a, 1830b). Senior became particularly concerned with addressing the prevailing population problem (while providing his own optimistic qualifications to the unrelenting Malthusian logic) and the associated agricultural distress. The events of 1789 and the Reign of Terror that followed loomed large in the psyche of the Noetics, as it did for all Oxford dons, and Senior believed that it was essential to reform the Poor Laws before civil disobedience transformed into open rebellion. This was stated with particular apolocalyptic relish in his final lectures in 1830, where (in the year of the Swing Riots) he emphasised that labourers invariably suffer most from such revolts: 'Those who have property may escape with a portion of it to some country in which their rights will be protected; but the labourer must remain to enjoy his own works – to feel that the real rewards for plunder and devastation are want and disease' (1830b, p. xii). Senior saw it as a race against time.[3]

Senior, with this rather dire warning, passed the Drummond Chair to Whately when his five-year term came to an end in 1830. Their precise goals, however, were slightly different. Whately's quest to defend abstract-deductive political economy, as a Christian Political Economy, from its critics was more driven and manifest than Senior's and, indeed, it was the main reason for his acceptance of the Drummond Chair in 1829 (for taking it up in 1831) (Whately, 1866, p. 66; Anon., 1864, pp. 477–482). Whately was effectively shifting the emphasis of the Drummond lectures from Senior's quest to demonstrate how political economy could be used to solve the economic problems of the age to defending political economy from the charge that it was anti-religious (which was more specifically an Oxford problem).[4] Whately saw this defence as a duty given the ultra-Tory disparagement of political economy as anti-religious, especially in a year that was defined by an ultra-Tory backlash at Oxford. The anti-progressive turn of 1829 was driven by the Catholic emancipation debates and the ejection of 'Christ Church' Peel from the Oxford borough for reversing his position on this question by supporting the Emancipation Act of 1829. The importance of this event cannot be over-emphasised. Historians of economic thought correctly preoccupy themselves with those (aforementioned) flashpoints from this period that turn on bullion reports, Poor Law reforms and corn laws, but on occasion this leads to the neglect of the really divisive issues within what was effectively a theocracy (and England was then a slightly more civilised version of modern Iran), namely the state–religion nexus and the attendant issue of religious bigotry. Every Oxford reminiscence from this period focuses on the uncompromising stands taken on this issue. Whately was, of course, for reform and against what was called the bigoted 'two-bottle' orthodoxy of the die-hard Tories, although, surprisingly, some of the younger Oriel generation voted against Peel on the grounds that he should not have turned on a coin when it came to his principles. Even Newman, who later converted to Rome, turned on Peel for changing in mid-stream without warning. Whately never forgave Newman and, in revenge, invited the most pig-ignorant and bigoted Oxford dons to a dinner and placed Newman in the middle of them, and then asked: how do you like your friends? (Fitzpatrick, 1864, p. 65). It was, then, these religious debates that drove Whately's 1831 lectures, which were published as *Introductory Lectures on Political Economy* and happened to be the only lectures he managed to deliver before his early resignation from the Drummond Chair to become Archbishop of Dublin in 1831.

The historical narrative has reached a critical point, namely the departure of Whately for Dublin in 1831, to undertake a more critical inspection of Oriel political economy – a political economy that Lloyd both drew from and rejected in his own lectures. The published version of Senior's introductory lecture in 1827 (as well as the application of this method in his subsequent lectures) and Whately's 1831 lectures reinforced the methodological position that had already been articulated in Copleston's two letters to Peel in 1819 and which was implicit in Whately's *Elements* in 1826. Specifically, the Noetics had, by the end of the 1810s, drawn upon some of the leading theological trends of the day, as reflected in, for example, John Bird Sumner's *Record of Creation* (1816), to dichotomise knowledge into a theological domain, in which scriptures were taken on faith and then deployed to infer the virtues that one should pursue as ultimate ends, and a scientific domain, in which the scientific laws were constructed to enable one to achieve these virtuous ends (Mandler, 1990, p. 86; Waterman, 1991, p. 207). That dichotomy put an end to the then common belief that political economy was at odds with theology. The Noetics then further dichotomised the scientific domain into the construction of scientific laws and the application of those laws in a policy setting. Specifically, the laws of political economy in the scientific domain were to be deduced with syllogistic precision from sets of first principles that were generally regarded as true (such as 'men pursue wealth'), but sufficiently abstract to prevent them from being used to prescribe policies without first re-admitting the frictions and disturbing causes that were initially left out (see Senior, 1827, pp. 7–8; Corsi, 1987, p. 106). This now famous science–art dichotomy provided the required protective belt around the deduced laws, and thereby prevented them both from being dismissed as false (when their tendencies were offset by disturbing causes) and from being used hastily by decision makers to form inappropriate policies. The two dichotomies were the natural outcome of the Oriel tradition of prioritising logic. It also enabled the Noetics to use the discipline as a conservative tool in the face of the dislocation and deprivation in the decades after the defeat of Napoleon.

The more precise machinery by which the abstract-deductive political economy from the scientific domain did not challenge the theological domain was constituted by two main mechanisms. The first of these has been particularly emphasised by Mandler (1990). The Noetics believed that a nexus between virtue and commercial advancement was the means by which the construction of abstract-deductive laws of political economy in the scientific domain would allow policy makers to achieve higher levels of virtue in the theological domain. They believed that scarcity breeds brutish behaviour, whereas the pursuit of industry and prudence to overcome scarcity breeds virtuous behaviour and, finally, the attainment of commercial wealth (when guided by the virtuous who inhabit the established institutions of the Anglican ascendancy) would permit the further attainment of virtue. Senior made this point emphatically in his introductory lecture (1827, p. 12) and it is also discussed with great nuance and with many qualifications in the published versions of Whately's 1831 lectures (pp. 44, 51, 190 and 202). The abstract-deductive laws of political economy would therefore enable community leaders to make decisions that promote prudence and industry, and hence permit virtue to flourish. Thus, to take the issue that occupied the Noetics most in these years, the nightmarish laws of nature embedded in the first edition of Malthus's *Essay* of 1798, in which there seemed no solution to the redundant population in the hopelessly overpopulated agricultural districts, was re-phrased (as Malthus himself subsequently re-phrased it) with an escape clause: the pursuit of wealth via prudence and industry promotes virtue and hence, amongst other things, checks re-production. This increased virtue, in turn, makes the pursuit of wealth more likely, and hence a virtuous cycle is set afoot. The Noetics therefore called for the Poor Laws to be reformed to promote industry and prudence. The giving of alms to able-bodied labourers was certainly not the way to achieve this outcome, unless the alms (or the conditions under which they were given) fell short of what was earned by the able-bodied working labourer (the principle of 'less eligibility'). It is this vision, rather than some sort of London Utilitarianism, that drove the Noetic support for, and Senior's active role in, the Poor Law reforms of 1832–1834. In Mandler's (1990, p. 91) words: 'whereas the Benthamites began by asking how poor relief could be administered without sapping the wages fund, the Noetics began by asking how poor relief could be administered without sapping the virtue fund; but the outcome is the same'. The faith of the Noetics in the wealth–virtue nexus, however, was always qualified by the realisation that commercial success could lead to degeneration, especially if society was not guided by the virtuous in the established institutions and if misguided interventionist policies (such as the old Poor Laws) were allowed to sap industry and prudence. Political economy was, in short, given conservative credentials. The gaining of virtue was to be an individual act of character with, at most, virtuous men of wealth and the established order giving moral support.

The second Noetic 'defensive' mechanism to ensure the benign relationship between the scientific and theological domains is drawn out in Whately's lectures (but is not to be found in Senior's) and is more explicitly theological. This mechanism in some ways weakens the scientific–theological division as a strict dichotomy, as it makes the domains far more intertwined, and it has itself two parts. First, Whately grants that the scriptures are taken on faith and that moral principles are inferred from these scriptures. He adds, however, that individuals first need to have the independent moral and thinking capacity to apply these principles to concrete situations because the scriptures provide no clear guidance on every application to every situation. This argument is similar to the Oakeshott–Ryle–Polyani–Kuhn argument that principles cannot provide complete guidance to action until their applications are comprehended within a tradition (or paradigm). It allowed Whately to downplay the written word of the scriptures and to yield more ground to the abstract-deductive approach of the political economists: 'the scriptures enjoin charity to the poor; but give no directions as to the best mode of administering our charity' (1831, p. 38 and pp. 31–32). Second, Whately invokes the natural theology gambit that the study of the social system within the scientific domain sheds light on the designs of divine wisdom in the theological domain, and that the identification of the human folly that interferes with this design may explain away the calamitous events observed in the social system (1831, p. 97). Specifically, Whately believed that the coordination of the economic system via the price mechanism reflected God's design. Whately described the benevolent design of this coordination process in almost Hayekian terms, arguing that a central authority, or what he called a head commissioner, could not surpass the effectiveness of the market mechanism due to its lack of knowledge about the multitude of markets: 'Public spirit … implies not merely benevolent feelings stronger than, in fact, we commonly meet with, but also with powers of abstraction beyond what the mass of mankind can possess' (1831, p. 102). Only individuals pursuing wealth via decentralised markets can achieve the desired ends, and he grants (with much hedging to head off those who were hostile to such an un-Christian idea) that Mandeville was correct to the extent that such a system was often driven by individuals pursing their own interests rather than virtuous ends (1831, pp. 109 and 156). He also accepted that the market mechanism did not always work due to human follies, but this could be attributed to friction in the system: 'The character and direction of the moving principle of a machine, should be first understood generally, before we attend to the impediments of friction and the resistance of air' (1831, p. 172). The obvious tension in Whately's approach – that the pursuit of wealth leads to virtue, yet the gains from the pursuit of wealth are driven by the unvirtuous disposition of selfishness – perhaps could have been resolved, but Whately did not, in our view, so resolve it. Still, in Whately's eyes, abstract-deductive political economy shed light on God's design and hence was not hostile to theology.

This framework was recognised as an Oxford product, as opposed to a specific Oriel product specifically, by the non-Oxford contemporaries who were unaware of the subtleties of the Oxford college alliances, machinations and squabbles.[5] Unfortunately, the Oriel tradition came to an end almost immediately. Not only were the key Oriel exponents of political economy no longer attached to the college, but the effective leader, Whately, had (through Senior's Whig contacts in the new ministry) been appointed to the Dublin See and hence had left Oxford (Anon., 1864, pp. 477–478; Anon., 1867, p. 496). Whately's elevation, not surprisingly, was met with surprise and alarm amongst the Oxford Tories, but unbeknown to them it gave rise to the destruction of the Noetic tradition in Oxford. The tradition inside the walls of Oriel itself also imploded. Hawkins, who had succeeded Copleston as provost in 1828, engineered the resignation of the three tutors, Newman, Froude and Wilberforce, when he refused their request to reform the tutorial system in 1831–1832. The squabbles at Oriel were the ruination of the college, as men of that calibre are not easily replaced (Ward, 1965, p. 70). The younger Oriel men were then transformed into enemies of the Noetic tradition when they took to Tractarianism, apostolic succession, mystic spiritualism and so on (Anon., 1864, p. 478). Whately lived a stone's throw away from his old friend Newman (now Rector of the Catholic University of Ireland) in Dublin, but at no point did they ever again exchange greetings. To some extent the Noetics also failed to form a lasting school because they did not create the institutional machinery to do so: there were no clubs, societies and journals (Tuckwell, 1909, p. 258). Whately talked about establishing a political economy club at Oxford (perhaps as a counter to the London Political Economy Club), but nothing seems to have come of it, and, along with Arnold, Senior and Blanco White, he started the *London Review* as a radical-religious counter to the radical-secular *Westminster Review*, but this journal quickly folded (Mozley, 1882, p. 58). Thus, when Oriel ceased to be a breeding ground for Noetics, no second generation came through to dominate the university. The abstract-deductive method they championed (as opposed to their confidence in the markets of the machine age and the attendant liberal reforms) was, however, taken up by William F. Lloyd, who paradoxically emerged from a corporate tradition, Christ Church, which was hostile to all things Noetic, and who employed this method to reach entirely different conclusions.

THE CHRIST CHURCH ALTERNATIVE: WILLIAM FORSTER LLOYD

William Forster Lloyd, as a product of Christ Church, emerged from a 'traditional' institutional and intellectual framework which was in open competition with that constructed by the Oriel Noetics. Christ Church in the early nineteenth century was shaped by Dr Cyril Jackson, who was the dean of this House from 1783 to 1809. Jackson celebrated hard work and intellectual endeavour within the new examination framework ushered in with the 1800–1809 reforms. His manners, even the way he spoke, were imitated by the Christ Church men and it is generally agreed that he generated a certain Christ Church character type: a buoyant personality who accentuated his cynical aloofness on intellectual matters with a realist view of the world, sharp retorts at the high table, eccentric mannerisms and an arrogant pride in Christ Church. This last characteristic was particularly accentuated, as undergraduates were encouraged not to make friends outside of the college, which was the largest and richest in Oxford, and to dismiss the intellectual pretentions of the other colleges, especially Oriel. The Deans that followed Jackson were ineffective (leaving no mark other than successfully carrying on the Jackson tradition) and the House was thereafter effectively run by an oligarchy of tutors. The most charismatic and strongest of these was William F. Lloyd's brother, Charles Lloyd, who had matriculated from Eton in 1803, was awarded a studentship in 1804, embraced the Christ Church ethos of hard work, graduated with first-class honours in 1806 and became a mathematics tutor in 1807.[6] Charles Lloyd and his fellow tutors presided over a die-hard Tory House, the members of which were contemptuous of precious views of life. Some of the more priggish students from evangelical backgrounds were shocked at the rowdyish nature of Christ Church undergraduate life (for which it had a reputation) and to see senior members (even bishops, as Lloyd later became) play cards and drink to excess. Others mistook the no-nonsense and rowdyish environment for an anti-intellectual culture, which no doubt existed, but which must be qualified by the Jackson-inspired tradition of encouraging those with ability to pursue honours. This was reflected in the sheer quantity of first rate men that the college produced over this period, with Christ Church gaining 82 firsts to Oriel's 29 between 1814 and 1828 (Ward, 1965, p. 324).

The mix of good-natured competition and open animosity between Oriel and Christ Church is best seen in the way that the Oriel leaders, especially Copleston and Whately, vied with Charles Lloyd for influence over the students and the positions that were dispensed by the State. Lloyd invariably won these contests in the 1820s through his hold over the greatest of Christ Church products, Robert Peel (or 'Christ Church' Peel), who he prepared for exams in 1807 and subsequently counselled on affairs of state.[7] Peel's meteoric rise in the Tory ministries in the years that followed enabled him to assist his ex-tutor and occasional political confidante to gain institutional positions, such as the Chair of Divinity in 1823 and the See of Oxford in 1827 (for which Copleston openly canvassed). In the former office, Lloyd resurrected theological studies at Oxford and, through his famous post-graduate tutorials for both Christ Church and Oriel men, acted as an incubator for what became the Oxford Movement (although Lloyd was no Anglo-Catholic himself). Newman, one of the more prominent of those theological students, recalled in particular the antagonism between Lloyd and Whately at this time, and thereby indicated just how much the young Oriel fellows defied Whately and the Oriel tradition by attending Lloyd's classes. Newman wrote that the two were the respective representatives of an 'unnatural rivalry between Christ Church and Oriel' and, further, that '[s]harp words passed between them; they spoke scornfully of each other, and stories about them and the relation in which they stood towards each other were circulated in the Common-Rooms' (1903, Vol. 1, p. 96; and Faber, [1933] 1936, p. 121). Still, for all this, it must be emphasised that Lloyd was not the typical Christ Church 'ultra' or 'two-bottle' Tory that the Noetics really detested. He was, instead, a follower of the 'realist' Toryism of Pitt, in which reform was opposed until it was seen to be inevitable and in which the liberalism of the rising machine age was viewed with distrust. Peel took a similar (but not identical) path to Lloyd and hence caused generations of voters confusion, and on occasion a sense of betrayal, due to his tendency to reverse political positions, which he had previously steadfastly supported, once the conditions changed. His most famous *volte faces* were the Catholic Emancipation in 1829 and the Corn Laws in 1846. It was, in fact, the strain Lloyd experienced in his controversial support for Peel's Emancipation Act of 1829 in Parliament (as Bishop of Oxford) that induced his early death in that year.

It was in the shadow of this contest between the Oriel Noetics and Christ Church Tories that William F. Lloyd accepted the Drummond Chair and presented his lectures from 1832 to 1837. Although Whately had departed Oxford for Dublin and Charles Lloyd had died, the effects of their different visions (and those of their charges) can be seen in the younger Lloyd's depiction of the social framework. Lloyd drew upon the Oriel tradition of syllogistic, abstract and mechanistic model building, but did so to construct an alternative economic vision that was far less optimistic about the capacity of markets to deliver optimum outcomes. It was a mild Tory framework that was more akin to his brother's balanced outlook (and even then with distinct radical hues) than the more ultra-Tory views of some of his Christ Church colleagues, but distinctly anti-Oriel nonetheless. Specifically, the social constitution, although subject to change through time, was understood to be naturally hierarchical and inequitable, with the basis for wealth accumulation found in the agricultural sector of the economy. Poverty was not, as claimed by the Noetics, an inevitable result of inappropriate penalties and rewards which distorted otherwise well-oiled market mechanisms that reflected God's benevolent design. Rather, poverty was the result of the incentives facing the mass of the population in an economy where property ownership was highly concentrated and where it was difficult to calculate the likelihood of adverse future events. Property owners and their political representatives therefore had an obligation, using the Poor Law, to assist those at the mercy of disruptive economic forces in the short term and, in the long term, to address the extent of poverty by reducing population growth. Given this position, it is not surprising that Lloyd used his lectures to sharply criticise the 'new' Poor Law of 1834 with which his two predecessors in the Drummond chair were closely associated. Senior and Whately were not mentioned by name and they repaid Lloyd by failing to acknowledge the existence of his Drummond lectures in their own work.

This wider institutional and intellectual context has often been ignored in the history of economic thought literature – so much so, that Whately, Senior and Lloyd are often portrayed as being from a single Oxford set.

There is also a tendency to confine attention to Lloyd's lecture on value, first published in 1834, and thereby to marginalise the other lectures he presented in his five-year tenure. Specifically, following Edwin Seligman (Seligman, 1903), the 1834 lecture has generally been regarded as a 'precursor' account of marginal utility theory which, because it was an 'abstract' discourse, was analytically separate and, in that sense, disconnected from Lloyd's other work. Some historians, however, have also considered his lectures concerning the Poor Law, population growth and theory of distribution (Lloyd, 1968). Although it was initially suggested that some aspects of those lectures prefigured a Marxist analysis (Gordon, 1966), Richard Romano subsequently concluded that Lloyd was simply a 'paternalistic Tory', who was highly critical of changes in the British economy, particularly the effects of an expanding manufacturing sector, and the new Poor Law (Romano, 1977). Here, we offer a somewhat different perspective, showing that Lloyd's value lecture was an integral component of his project to defend a more liberal Poor Law and that his analytical framework was quite different from that of the later marginalist theory. Specifically, Lloyd presented a surplus theory of distribution, with the surplus originating in the agricultural sector. While the analysis was clearly directed against the proponents of the new Poor Law, such as Senior and Whately, his value lecture suggests that Whately was a particular target.

Lloyd's distribution theory explained the basic principles of the economic surplus and prices, with any long-period outcome constructed with a given set of 'data' ([1837] 1968, p. 78), including the population level, the real wage bundle per labourer (in effect, a natural wage),[8] techniques of production and level of output. The surplus was equal to total output minus necessary consumption and consisted of rent which was, in turn, equal to the sum of manufactured commodities ('conveniences and luxuries') or national wealth ([1837] 1968, p. 58n). A unit of unskilled labour was the numeraire in the system. While Lloyd discussed the effects of changes to his initial data, the explanations for the natural wage, changes in the techniques of production and the level of output were analytically separate from the value and distribution analysis. Although the latter could consider changes in wage rates and output levels, for example, the changes were taken as given in that no explanation was given for them. That explanation, which required reference to more complex institutional and historical features than was possible in the distribution theory, was referred to elsewhere in Lloyd's lectures. The discussion of the wage rate, for example, can be found in his first published lectures where Lloyd explained why the pressure of population would reduce the large class of labourers to near subsistence conditions (Lloyd, [1833] 1968). Some of the effects of changes in techniques of production on employment and incomes were also considered in lectures on the Poor Law (Lloyd, [1835] 1968), while the explanation for the long-period level of output was principally referred to in the value lecture (Lloyd, [1834] 1968). We begin with Lloyd's designation of the long-period wage, showing how its references to property rights prefigured a number of themes in his later lectures. The fifth section considers the distribution analysis, while the sixth section discusses Lloyd's treatment of value. The seventh section then explains how Lloyd's value and distribution theory was a critique of Senior and Whately.

THE LONG-PERIOD WAGE

Lloyd's explanation of a long-period wage, presented in a striking critique of T. R. Malthus' *Essay on Population*, depicted the behaviour of the mass of the population as a rational response, in conditions of ignorance and uncertainty, to the incentives created by contemporary institutions. That analysis underpinned Lloyd's references to the importance of property rights for understanding poverty and the role of the Poor Law, which he discussed in later lectures.

The Critique of Malthus

The principal purpose of Lloyd's lectures on population growth was to explain why the pressure of population on 'the means of subsistence' would reduce the class of landless labourers to near subsistence conditions. As Lloyd made clear, the broad terms of his argument were taken from Malthus' *Essay*. However, in explaining the absence of a 'preventive check', which was equated with 'moral restraint' in having children, Lloyd's account was quite different. He presented a stark account of a (historically specific) subsistence condition for the mass of the population, shorn of the qualifications that Malthus had introduced after the first edition of the *Essay* (Winch, 1996, pp. 374–376). In particular, Malthus had allowed that the preventive check could reduce population pressure. As he put it in part of a lengthy extract that Lloyd cited from the *Essay*, the preventive check

> is peculiar to man, and arises from that distinct superiority in his reasoning faculties, which enable him to calculate distant consequences… [M]an cannot look around him, and see the distress which frequently presses upon those who have large families … without

> feeling a doubt whether, if he follow the bent of his inclinations, he may be able to support the offspring which he will probably bring into the world ... [Such] considerations are calculated to prevent, and certainly do prevent, a great number of persons in all civilized nations from pursuing the dictate of nature in an early attachment to one woman. (Malthus, 1817, Vol. 1, pp. 18 and 19; cited in Lloyd, [1833] 1968, pp. 4–5)[9]

While Lloyd agreed with an analytical focus on the 'distinct superiority of human reasoning faculties', his critique of Malthus' argument regarding the ability to 'calculate distant consequences' led to a further difference in their respective explanations of poverty.[10] For Malthus, 'Though human institutions appear to be, and indeed often are, the obvious and obtrusive causes of much mischief to society, they are, in reality, light and superficial, in comparison with those deeper-seated causes of evil, which result from the laws of nature and the passions of mankind' (Malthus, 1817, Vol. 2, p. 246). Although Lloyd acknowledged that passions were important in explaining behaviour, he argued that the decision by the labouring class to have more children was the result of rationally weighing costs and benefits.[11] If the effects were dire, they were due, in large part, to the 'institutions and conditions of society' (Lloyd, [1833] 1968, p. 170).

Lloyd depicted human behaviour in a utilitarian fashion, driven by weighing a 'present pain or inconvenience' against a resultant 'future benefit' or the 'gratification of a present desire' against an 'eventual evil'. In a 'large society', however, the effects of each individual's behaviour in contributing toward a future event would become 'evanescent', so that, 'in the absence of any countervailing weight, the conduct of each person is determined by the consideration of the present alone ... [T]he effect is, that, though the reasoning faculty is in full force, and each man can clearly foresee the consequences of his actions, yet that conduct is the same as if that faculty had no existence' (Lloyd, [1833] 1968, pp. 7, 20 and 21). The phrase 'can clearly foresee the consequences' might suggest that each person was fully aware of the results of their actions. Lloyd's discussion indicates, however, that each person was acting in ignorance of their contribution to the aggregate effect. He explained that point by arguing that the ability to take all costs and benefits into account depended on an actor's 'motives' and 'disposition'. Motives were governed by events external to the individual and were due to the 'constitution of society'. Disposition, by contrast, was explained by factors 'internal to the mind', combining the 'strength of reasoning faculty' and a 'degree of self-command' or prudence ([1833] 1968, p. 46). Lloyd considered that prudence was non-existent in the relevant section of the labouring class, so that his explanation for the lack of a preventive check was principally concerned with motives.

In explaining motives, Lloyd argued that it was rational for each family to increase its numbers so as to increase total employment and income. Their only resort was to increased labour because property ownership was polarising under the impact of enclosures, coupled with:

> the revolution in manufactures, by which small capitalists have been thrust out of the market, the accumulation of farms, which in agriculture has produced a similar effect, the decay of monopolies, and the increased productiveness of land ... while the right of primogeniture has maintained nearly a stationary condition, or has perhaps caused even a retrogradation in the number of landed proprietors. ([1833] 1968, p. 68)

Family employment was available as 'the extended use of machinery ... [in the manufacturing sector], by performing those parts of operations requiring mere force, has opened a wider field for the employment of women and children, thereby, in a great measure, relieving the head of a family of the burden of its maintenance' ([1833] 1968, p. 69). Children could thus be employed from the age of eight or ten with the prospect of that age being lowered by further technological change. Making due allowance for the 'natural passions', the consequent lack of 'a prudential disposition' with regard to family size followed from the 'substantial benefits' of marriage and because it appeared that 'no individual [would] benefit from abstinence' ([1833] 1968, pp. 25, 48 and 35). Each labourer could not see the effects of aggregate behaviour and hence had no reason to restrict the size of his family:

> Each, therefore, will feel ill effects, corresponding precisely, in character and quality, with the consequences of his own conduct. Yet they will not be the identical effects flowing from that conduct; but being a portion of the accumulated effects resulting from the whole conduct of the society in general, would, therefore, still be felt, though the conduct of the individual should be changed. Thus it is that the universal distress fails to suggest to the individual any motive for moral restraint. ([1833] 1968, p. 22)[12]

With the mass of the population dependent on their labour for income and the incentive to have more children, it could not be concluded that population 'pressing too closely against the means of subsistence' was the result of a 'fault ... in the people themselves ... [rather than] with the constitution of the society, of which they form a part'. ([1833] 1968, p. 23)

Lloyd's emphasis on rational behaviour by the labouring class was reinforced by a further argument explaining the failure of moral restraint. He noted that 'In the actual business of life, we commonly find some labourers out of employment, and more at one time than another' ([1833] 1968, p. 26).[13] While the possibility of unemployment could potentially constrain the birth rate, the 'uncertainty' of the 'failure of employment' could only be calculated and acted upon if it was 'periodical, that is ... to recur at known intervals, and to continue during periods of known duration'. There was, however, no such periodicity. Hence it was not feasible to act 'on account of an obscure anticipation of a danger which is not near, which may perhaps never be realised, or which, on the contrary, may fall on them with such force, as utterly to overwhelm them, not withstanding their best precautions'. Given the 'vast degree of uncertainty in the prospects of a labouring man ... the natural consequence is that he must act at random' ([1833] 1968, pp. 41–42 and 45). In this regard, Lloyd had previously remarked that, when considering to have more children, a man taking into account the possibility of unemployment 'would reckon it hard, were he the person, on whom, in a particular instance, the lot should fall'. The situation was like a 'lottery [where], since the chances of all are equal, we must in idea consider them as divisible' (1968, pp. 29 and 30). This, then, was another reason for the absence of moral restraint.

Having discussed the motives for the behaviour of the labouring class, Lloyd turned to the effects of 'disposition', which combined the 'strength of reasoning faculty' and a 'degree of self-command' or prudence, that is 'the habit of attending to future consequences' ([1833] 1968, pp. 46 and 54). He argued that prudence was the result of a formal education or of 'experience' which was principally a function of age. Learning thus played an important role in Lloyd's explanation of human behaviour, which was consistent with his reference to the importance of 'habits' ([1833] 1968, p. 53). Education was, however, irrelevant for the labouring class because of 'constant labour at an early age'. Experience could play no role because labourers had families when they were in their twenties, decisions on which their elders could have no impact because the young were economically independent through paid work. This was quite different from the situation facing 'the higher and middling classes of society', where the older generation had 'command of wealth' in the family and could thus constrain the young ([1833] 1968, pp. 59, 61 and 63). Given the constitution of society, education and experience could play no role in constraining population growth.

Lloyd thus depicted economic behaviour as driven by passions, emulation and habits, which meant that behaviour could be altered by education and experience. With those characteristics, economic actors attempted to behave rationally in the sense of comparing the good and evil effects of behaviour. This suggests that Lloyd thought that people were basically the same in 'nature' and could thus be represented as reasoning individuals. However, different class behaviours were also crucial, where classes were defined in terms of property relationships and hence the ownership of the means of production. Different class behaviours were explained by different incentives and opportunities which reflected, in particular, the growth of the manufacturing sector and the way in which aggregate effects appeared to be untraceable to individual behaviour. The form of employment opportunities within the set of property relationships thus principally explained population pressure. As Lloyd put it, 'were capital as uniformly distributed, and as easily obtained, as is the ability to labour, then ... the capitalists would be as badly off as are at present the labouring classes' (Lloyd, [1833] 1968, p. 72).

Lloyd's position was consistent with Malthus' claim that 'the tendency of population to increase beyond the means of subsistence may be seen in almost every register of a country parish in the kingdom' (Malthus, 1817, Vol. 2, p. 85). It was a position that was unfashionable by the early 1830s with, for example, Nassau Senior arguing that there was no such inexorable tendency (Senior, 1829, Lecture II). That point was crucial in the formulation of the 1834 Poor Law, where Senior's role was pivotal (Dunkley, 1981). It should be emphasised, however, that Lloyd's analysis was quite different from that of Malthus, who attributed 'the greater part of the sufferings of the lower classes of society exclusively to themselves'. Malthus did acknowledge that part of the responsibility could be laid at the door of 'the higher classes of society', particularly because they had introduced the Poor Law which increased the birth rate and promoted 'that carelessness and want of frugality observable among the poor [who] ... seem always to live from hand to mouth. Their present wants employ their whole attention; and they seldom think of the future ... [A]ll that they earn beyond their present necessities goes, generally speaking, to the ale-house' (Malthus, 1817, Vol. 3, p. 142 and 108 and Vol. 2, pp. 332 and 334).[14] If the Poor Law encouraged fecklessness, drunkenness and dissipation, those effects did not 'entirely obscure the light of nature and reason on this subject ... [S]till they contribute to make it comparatively weak and indistinct' (1817, Vol. 3, pp. 140–141).

The key point, then, for Malthus was that the behaviour of the labouring classes was primarily driven by passions. As suggested in the title of the last chapter of his *Essay*, the only realistic basis for a 'rational expectation' of the preventive check becoming more widespread in the long term, so that 'the impulses of passion' could be 'in some degree modified by reason', was that the lower classes could be 'infused' with knowledge of the population principle (and, indeed, of political economy more generally) by means of a 'parochial' school system, coupled with a '*very gradual* abolition of the poor-laws' (Malthus, 1817, Vol. 3, pp. 106 and 200 and Vol. 2, p. 369;

emphasis in original). It was because the poor were ignorant and brutish, unable to register the significance of the evidence for their own behaviour, that they were subject to the blandishments of 'the most successful supporters of tyranny', that is, radicals such as William Godwin and Tom Paine, who attributed 'the distress of the poor ... to human institutions and the iniquities of governments' (1817, Vol. 3, p. 158). Reason was not completely absent, but it was in short supply.

While Lloyd was, like Malthus, critical of proposals for 'systems of equality',[15] his picture of the lower classes was quite different in that there was no mention of drunkenness and dissipation, no impression given of an ignorant and credulous mass subject to the blandishments of 'inflammatory and seditious publications' (Malthus, 1817, Vol. 3, p. 319). The different tone of Lloyd's account is indicated by his comment that:

> The late war ... was owing, in a very considerable degree, to the apprehension entertained by the aristocracy of the contagion of the French revolution. But they would have had less ground for apprehension, had the bulk of the people been easy in their condition. Few will deny that an easy command of subsistence is almost a panacea for discontent among the lower classes. (Lloyd, [1833] 1968, p. 9)

Indeed, Lloyd stood out in the contemporary debates for the way in which he depicted the labouring class rationally comparing costs and benefits in conditions of uncertainty and ignorance which were due to the 'institutions and conditions of society'. Assuming a uniform human nature and a utilitarian explanation of motivations, which sounds more like Jeremy Bentham than Malthus or William Paley, Lloyd explained different class behaviours by the institutional structure of property relationships. His argument, highly unusual for the time in British political economy, that probability calculations (if they could be made) would underpin behaviour, presumably reflected his previous lecturing in mathematics. In extending that point to the mass of the population, however, Lloyd went further than the probability pioneers of the French Enlightenment (Daston, 1988).

The Commons and Property Rights

Lloyd also used his analysis of why the aggregate effects of behaviour could be 'evanescent' in a discussion which, as mentioned in the introduction to this chapter, Hardin (1968) subsequently labelled 'the tragedy of the commons'.[16] Referring to the reasons for enclosures of common ground, he posed a series of questions: 'Why are the cattle on a common so puny and stunted? Why is the common itself so bare-worn, and cropped so differently from the adjoining inclosures?' The reason was that, if one person put more cattle in their own field which had only a 'sufficiency of pasture', there would be no net benefit. On a common, however, 'only a small part' of the food 'is taken from his own cattle', with a consequent net private benefit. All would behave in the same way, thereby going 'beyond [the point] which no prudent man would add to his stock' on enclosed ground. This story was a metaphor. In the 'existing state of things', 'the field for the employment of labour is in fact a common' because, in both cases, 'the commons ... must be constantly stocked to the extreme point of saturation' (Lloyd, [1833] 1968, pp. 30, 31 and 32). While Lloyd did not make clear whether people realised the cumulative effect of adding more cattle, his use of the 'field of employment' metaphor elsewhere in the lectures ([1833] 1968, pp. 29, 38, 65 and 69) indicates that the commons outcome was due to ignorance, rather than a conscious decision to pursue a self-destructive outcome.

Lloyd returned to the issue of the commons at the close of his population lectures, noting that the 'common reasons for the establishment of private property in land are deduced from the necessity, of offering to individuals sufficient motives for cultivating the ground, and of preventing the wasteful destruction of the immature products of the earth' (Lloyd, [1833] 1968, p. 71; for an example, see [Marcet], 1816, pp. 55–56, 154). If Lloyd produced his commons metaphor by reworking some well-known arguments for enclosures, the metaphor also entailed a more general point regarding property rights. Lloyd argued that the theory of population added another reason for private property which was that, 'since the earth can never maintain all who offer themselves for maintenance, it is better that its produce should be divided into shares of definite magnitude'. Landowners 'should be able to command definite shares [of food as] ... a necessary consequence of their ownership ... [It] is necessary that there should be a title to wealth without the labour of producing it. A state of perfect equality ... would bring back society to ignorance and barbarism'. There was, however, a 'limit' to the concentration of property. A marked concentration and a large class of landless labourers provided a rationale, analogous to that for property ownership, to 'justify the appropriation of the field of employment, and a monopoly of labour. But, since such a monopoly is not easily attainable, we are led to look for an equivalent in the diffusion of a sufficient degree of property throughout the whole fabric of society' (Lloyd, [1833] 1968, pp. 71, 72 and 74–75).

As these were the closing sentences of the lectures, they might, if read in isolation, suggest that Lloyd was a radical reformer, at least with regard to the existing concentration of landed property. His use of a phrase similar to 'an equivalent in the diffusion of a sufficient degree of property' in a later lecture indicates, however, that he was referring to a right of subsistence under the Poor Law.[17] Lloyd was thus part of a tradition, dating from the seventeenth century, which argued that there were two key sets of property rights. The first was a negative or exclusive right so that, for example, enclosures were justified on the basis that they increased agricultural productivity and hence the agricultural surplus. The second was a positive or inclusive property right, whereby the dispossessed landless labourers could claim a right to subsistence from the landowners and which could thus provide a rationale for the Poor Law (Horne, 1990). Lloyd argued in subsequent lectures that, while there was a definite right to subsistence, the population principle had compromised the domain of the application of the Poor Law, which should be restricted to the unemployed, as well as the sick, old and orphans.[18] However, a 'liberal' use of the Poor Law under those conditions would provide the 'true method of promoting moral restraint, or prudence with respect to marriage' (Lloyd, [1836] 1968, p. 70). Far from necessarily increasing the population growth rate, a Poor Law could reduce it.

Lloyd's first published lectures provide an example of how, in Classical political economy, a long-period wage could be explained using a framework which, at least in broad outline, owed a good deal to Malthus, while turning the analysis in unexpected directions. In particular, Lloyd presented the mass of the population as rationally responding to the incentives produced by the class structure and institutions of society. The decision to have more children took place in conditions of uncertainty, where it was not possible to calculate the probability of some events, and of ignorance, where the complexity of an event precluded the possibility of identifying a relationship of cause and effect. In the latter case, the requisite information could be obtained by learning but, because that possibility was erased by the 'institutions of society', Lloyd's discussion can be characterised as a theory of social ignorance. His explanation of behaviour thus reflected a Malthusian pessimism about the possibility of improvement in living standards, while reworking a key aspect of Enlightenment thinking about the possibility and extent of rational human behaviour. At the same time, Lloyd's subsequent lectures indicated that he thought it was possible to reduce population growth by a revamped Poor Law. Both his explanation for population growth and his defence of a right to relief under the Poor Law, referred to in his metaphors of the commons and the 'field of employment', indicate that he was clearly opposed to the analysis of his predecessors in the Drummond chair.

The Distribution Analysis

Lloyd provided a more elaborate defence of the right to poor relief in his distribution analysis. He began by depicting a simplified or 'imaginary' economy which had five principal characteristics:

(a) a high concentration of land ownership;
(b) two classes – landed proprietors and landless labourers;
(c) two sectors producing food ('corn') and manufactured commodities;
(d) zero food cultivation costs and negligible, although positive, harvesting costs, so that the output was a 'free gift of nature' (Lloyd, [1837] 1968, p. 62) and
(e) cottage industry production of manufactures.

An annual crop of ten million quarters provided 'the amount of food, which six million ... persons would only be just able and willing to consume' ([1837] 1968, pp. 86 and 89). This provided each labourer with a satiety food bundle which would always be consumed, provided that the labourer had the means to do so. In all situations, the landowners took a fixed bundle from the crop, so that their consumption of necessaries was a given. Labourers would only consume less than the satiety bundle if the total amount of food available was insufficient for them to do so. In that case, a state of 'scarcity' would exist. Any adjustment in their consumption thus occurred because of changes in the food/population ratio or in real incomes. With a population of ten million, an annual crop of ten million quarters would only provide labourers with a 'scanty maintenance'. This was the minimum possible long-period real wage, the subsistence amount necessary if the working population was to 'continue to exist'. While that wage appears at times to be a physiological minimum, Lloyd's comparison between Irish and English wages indicates that the subsistence level was historically and socially determined ([1837] 1968, pp. 88, 89 and 70).

Once the labouring population exceeded six million, each labourer's food bundle would begin to diminish and all would be 'stinted in their [food] allowances'. Some labourers would then 'offer a portion of their labour' to the landowners, by producing manufactures in exchange for a satiety bundle ([1837] 1968, pp. 92–93). Under 'necessity' all other labourers would do the same, otherwise their bundle would shrink further. A food price, measured in the labour units necessary to produce the manufactures, would then exist. (With a population of less than six million, any attempt by the landowners to impose a price and obtain a rent would be defeated by 'competition' between them ([1837] 1968, p. 91). While the numeraire of the system was a unit of labour time (for example, an hour; [1837] 1968, pp. 91, 93–94), the surplus could also be given a monetary equivalent as money was simply a unit of account ([1837] 1968, p. 31). Total ground rent (the surplus) thus equalled total manufacturing output in terms of both labour and monetary units.

The labour numeraire enabled Lloyd to posit a social division of labour and a concept of surplus labour time in the economy. Both hinged on the distinction between 'the amount of necessary and the amount of disposable labour'. Necessary labour was that 'required for the production or modification of the necessaries of life consumed by the whole population', while disposable labour was 'all the remaining part of the power of labouring' (i.e. the remaining hours worked). For 'each labourer considered individually', the ratio between total hours worked and the number of hours necessary to actually produce the wage bundle indicated the extent of surplus labour time worked ([1837] 1968, pp. 97 and 98).

With an increasing population, increased competition between labourers would take the form of increased hours and the resort to 'more dangerous, more unhealthy, or more unpleasant employments', until the maximum population level of ten million was reached. The long-period wage was now given in terms of the subsistence bundle. However, the price of food would continue to increase until it amounted to 'nearly the utmost labour ... of which human nature is capable [of providing], in exchange for a daily subsistence' ([1837] 1968, pp. 100 and 94). At this point, rent and national wealth were at a maximum, given the available techniques of production. It was the focal point of much of Lloyd's subsequent analysis and will be referred to here as the labour maximisation point (LMP).

To explain 'the actual state of things', Lloyd discussed a series of changes in the initial data, concerning agricultural production costs, the presence of a 'capitalist' class, techniques of production and some diversity of incomes within the labouring class. The modifications also explained how the amount of the surplus produced ('as estimated in labour') could vary ([1837] 1968, pp. 102 and 103). With regard to agricultural production costs, Lloyd emphasised that, once the LMP prevailed, labourers' real incomes and the food price would be the same in his initial 'imaginary' economy and in an economy where food had to be produced by the 'unceasing labour of the whole population' because the land was 'barren' ([1837] 1968, p. 12). He then introduced a third case, midway between the 'free gift' and barren ones, to characterise England ([1837] 1968, pp. 59–62). Here, costs of production rose with successive 'increments of produce' due to differential land fertility. Food was then sold 'at the highest price demanded by nature for this extreme part', although the last increments of output were 'scarcely more than adequate to the maintenance of labourers by whose agency they are raised' ([1837] 1968 p. 61). In the gift and the English cases, labourers' incomes would also eventually be the same because the LMP would prevail. The role of agricultural costs in the English case was thus to explain a differential rent or surplus, rather than the long-period food price:

> the pressure against the means of subsistence, all other things, being the same, the only effect of the diversity in the liberality of nature, will be a difference in the amount of rent ... [T]he condition of the people is the same ... In both [economies] they give all their labour, receiving in exchange only a maintenance. ([1837] 1968, pp. 60 and 61)

With the introduction of a 'class of capitalists', the economy changed from a 'feudal' to a capitalist one ([1837] 1968, pp. 104 and 106). Although Lloyd acknowledged that this class included farmers who laid out capital, he focussed on the manufacturing employers whose enterprises resulted in an 'increase in the efficacy [i.e. average productivity] of labour' ([1837] 1968, pp. 17 and 105). In an analysis reminiscent, in this respect, of Adam Smith's discussion of the natural wage (Smith, 1976a, pp. 84–85), Lloyd argued that 'Employers ... have a strong and direct interest in over-working their labourers; and the smallness of their number, joined to the superiority of their intelligence and other circumstances, gives to them a power which throws the workman entirely at their feet'. With the employers able to 'dictate' any 'degree of labour within the bounds of physical possibility', Lloyd argued that, even if there was no 'extreme pressure against the means of subsistence', the LMP would still prevail because of 'the power of the masters'. In that sense, the 'introduction ... of the class of capitalists' makes 'no difference ... so far ... as the labourers are concerned' (Lloyd, [1837] 1968, pp. 105–106).

Apart from extracting a maximum of surplus labour time with given techniques of production, employers also introduced new techniques in both the manufacturing and agricultural sectors. In manufactures it was the lowest cost techniques which raised labour productivity and set the price for particular commodities. In agriculture new techniques also raised average labour productivity, increasing the aggregate amount of surplus labour in the economy. It was the combined effects of the increase in the population and agricultural improvements that explained the increase of rent, as estimated in labour, in modern times' (Lloyd, [1837] 1968, p. 102).

Lloyd's final modification to the data was to allow for diversity in working class incomes. Although England was inexorably becoming a three class society, there were still artisans and small landholders, so that society was not completely 'fluid' and the processes of 'competition' between labourers (and capitalists) was not as 'perfect as the initial analysis had suggested ([1837] 1968, pp. 71–73 and 104). While the mass of the population received the natural wage, skilled or 'valued' workers received higher rates.

In Lloyd's distribution theory, the surplus produced in the agricultural sector was exchanged for manufactured commodities, an explanation that was consistent with his position on taxation policy.[19] With a unit of unskilled labour as the numeraire for the system, although nature was the source of the surplus labour produced all wealth:

> The actual sources of wealth being supposed to remain always equally fertile, national wealth will be proportional to the quantity of toil devoted to its production, and to the skill, dexterity, and judgement, with which the toil is applied. Assuming, therefore, these latter circumstances to remain the same, the wealth will then be proportional to the toil alone. (Lloyd, [1837] 1968, p. 58)

Two further aspects of the distribution analysis should be noted for their relevance in understanding Lloyd's treatment of value which will be considered below. The first concerns his explanation for why labourers would continue to work up to the LMP 'in exchange for a daily subsistence'. Lloyd argued that the 'leading principle' of their behaviour was as follows: 'The appetite of a hungry man for an ounce of food is great; after he has eaten one ounce, the appetite for a second ounce is less; for a third ounce still less than for a second; and so on, until, at length, he has no desire to eat any more. Let this limit be fixed at forty ounces'. The 40 ounces was the satiety bundle. With an increasing population, because 'the share of each individual is proportionally diminished, and, therefore, the unsatisfied desire more intense, a greater proportion of labour must be continually given in return for the diminished share' (Lloyd, [1837] 1968, pp. 94 and 95). This prioritisation of wants, so that the intensity of unsatisfied desire increased with 'every increase in the difficulty of obtaining' the full bundle, explained the labourers' behaviour in producing the surplus. It was the prioritisation that Lloyd termed 'value' and which was quite distinct from exchange value (see below). As Lloyd put it, his surplus theory depended on 'the effect of scarcity in giving a value to produce' ([1837] 1968, pp. 90 and 101), so that 'scarcity' and 'difficulty of attainment' became synonymous terms.

The second aspect of the distribution analysis which is relevant for understanding Lloyd's treatment of value concerns his criticism of the definition of value as a relative term, which thus referred to an exchange ratio and was restricted to meaning value in exchange (see below). One reason for that criticism is evident from the distribution lectures where Lloyd argued that a labourer had a 'right' to relief under the Poor Law as a matter of justice. This was a question of 'whether the law, under particular circumstances, ought not to impose to secure to him something more' than the wage paid when the labourer was employed ([1837] 1968, p. 11). Justice 'is the virtue which gives every person his due', which meant 'not what actually is, but what ought to be awarded to each person by the laws'. More specifically, the purpose of the Poor Law should be 'to secure ... a maintenance that they may not perish' ([1837] 1968, pp. 23–24 and 28). The rationale for this, where Lloyd cited the authority of 'all the writers on the theory of property' was that land was 'the common inheritance of all the inhabitants of the earth', rather than 'intended solely and absolutely for the use and benefit of a few appropriators [i.e., landowners]'. Where land was 'unequally, and very unequally, appropriated', and some inhabitants could not obtain a sufficient maintenance, the application of the Poor Law was a matter of justice. While poor relief could not solve the general problem of poverty, it could nevertheless be applied to 'a very large proportion of the people' ([1837] 1968, pp. 38, 40 and 69).

Lloyd thus criticised an argument, made in 'the *Communications* to the Commissioners under the late Commission of Poor Law Inquiry', that relief was a matter of 'charity' and not of justice. The argument was that, if people did not have the means to support themselves, it was due to them not having saved enough when they had been employed and had received 'an equivalent for their labour' in the form of wages ([1837] 1968, pp. 5–6 and 7). For Lloyd, this simply amounted to arguing that the labourer 'receives a full equivalent, so far as an exchange of equal values in the market is an exchange of equivalents', which was 'merely a truism' ([1837] 1968, pp. 9–10). The 'full equivalent' of labour had been defined, in effect, as labour's 'marketable value depending on the numbers and necessities of the labourers, and on the comparative scarcity of food and other articles of consumption which are given in exchange for it' ([1837] 1968, p. 34). To refer to an exchange of equivalents in that way did not, however, establish that the labourer 'receives in exchange for his labour, either a reasonable share of the produce of his own labour, or an amount of the produce of the labour of other persons proportional to the quantity of his labour which he gives in exchange for it' ([1837] 1968, p. 10; see also p. 56). Lloyd thus used his surplus analysis to show how defining value in terms of exchange could be deeply misleading.

VALUE AND UTILITY

Lloyd's lecture on value was dominated by two principal issues. The first was a defence of his concept of value where, claiming an analytical lineage from Adam Smith, he criticised the argument that value could only be defined as an exchange ratio (Lloyd, [1834] 1968, pp. 38–40). The distribution lectures indicated that Lloyd was opposed to the exchange ratio definition in part because it could be used to argue that wages constituted an equivalent exchange for the labour worked in obtaining a commodity. The second issue in the value lecture was the analysis of utility which Lloyd used to argue that generalised over-production was impossible, thereby explaining the determination of the level of output in a long-period, one of the givens in his distribution analysis. The analysis of value and utility will be considered first, followed by a discussion of the potentially confusing example Lloyd used in an attempt to clarify the difference between the concepts of utility and value.

Value and Utility

The complicated debates within Classical political economy regarding the conceptualisation of value usually took Adam Smith's *Wealth of Nations* (hereafter *WN*) as their point of analytical departure, extracting and reworking certain passages while ignoring or rejecting others. Lloyd continued in that vein by claiming, at the beginning of his lecture, that when Smith had discussed 'the real measure of exchangeable value', he had identified value in the same manner as Lloyd. On Lloyd's reading, *WN* did not conceptualise value as involving a comparison of, or ratio between, commodities but rather as referring to 'something positive and absolute ... belonging to a single object'. Furthermore, Smith referred to value 'in the sense of the real importance of an object to the person possessing it, and ... he made this importance to depend on the difficulty of attainment' (Lloyd, [1834] 1968, pp. 5 and 6).

For Lloyd, value depended on the possession of a commodity and indicated the relative importance an economic actor attached to a unit of that commodity: 'In the reasons which exist for preserving and for retaining the possession of an object, its value essentially consists. It has with great propriety been defined to mean the esteem in which an object is held' ([1834] 1968, pp. 10–11). Such esteem would decline with the acquisition of further units of the commodity until value became virtually negligible. At that point, 'it is a matter of indifference whether it [i.e., an extra unit] is parted with or retained ... In its ultimate sense, then, the term [value] undoubtedly signifies a feeling of the mind, which shows itself always at the margin of separation between the satisfied and unsatisfied wants' ([1834] 1968, pp. 12 and 16). This was consistent with his explanation for why labourers would work up to the LMP in the distribution lectures (see above).

While value depended upon individual possession, so that, at a time of famine, corn could become more valuable, utility was defined as an 'absolute' concept, to which possession was irrelevant:

> We estimate the utilities of objects by the importance of the wants they are capable of supplying, considered absolutely ... a difference in the degree in which any want is supplied makes no difference in the utility of the object which can supply it. Water is no more useful in a ship at sea, where it is scarce, than on land, where it is plentiful. The utility of corn is the same after an abundant harvest as in a time of famine. ([1834] 1968, pp. 12 and 16)

The crucial point here is that utility did not change according to the scarcity of 'plentifulness' of a commodity as possession 'is a matter of indifference' ([1834] 1968, p. 16)

In *WN*, Smith distinguished between value in use (utility) and value in exchange, using an analysis of utility and human behaviour which was clarified in the *Theory of Moral Sentiments* (Smith, [1776] 1976a, pp. 44–45 and [1759] 1976b, IV, p. i).[20] It was that analysis which underpinned Lloyd's argument that 'Utility ... is predicated of an object with reference to the wants of mankind' (Lloyd, [1834] 1968, p. 32). For Smith and the Classical political economists, an understanding of human nature and wants was necessary to explain the accumulation of wealth. Wants arose from human nature where it was essential to provide for particular material needs such as food and shelter. With the satisfaction of primary wants, secondary wants arose which had to be satisfied, thus leading to higher levels of wants. Certain material conditions were required if the want ratchet effect was to continue unimpeded. For example, as Lloyd argued in his lectures on population growth, it was only with private property and inequality that 'civilisation' could exist (see above). Nevertheless, it was still possible to explain quite different forms of behaviour, different in form and custom, by referring to them as economic behaviour in that they were directed to the satisfaction of wants.

As Lloyd indicated, the utility of a commodity remained unchanged because it was used to designate the components of output in a hierarchical ordering of wants and commodities, an ordering dependent on the importance of the wants the commodities satisfied. Hence the different utilities indicated different positions on the hierarchy, so that specific commodities could be classified according to their comparative usefulness. In this way, commodities could be categorised as necessaries, comforts or luxuries, the latter being dependent upon 'artificial wants' ([1834] 1968, pp. 25 and 13). The social classification of wants and commodities also made it possible to differentiate between consumption patterns in different types of social structures. Different societies would, according to their degree of 'civilisation', have different hierarchies of wants and desires. Even climate was important – in one climate clothing would be a necessary want, but quite unnecessary in another ([1834] 1968, pp. 8–9 and 32).

While utility could be posited in an absolute sense and the utility hierarchy could be established without any reference to value, the commodity composition of the hierarchy was not static. The composition could change in that new wants could be created by the production of new commodities under certain social conditions. Such changes did not indicate a change in the hierarchical designation of necessaries, conveniences and luxuries. Rather, the changes were used to explain why a certain type of society would not be satisfied with the accumulation of necessaries and would continue the accumulation process even if any new accumulation was simply of luxuries. As Lloyd argued, while the wants of 'savages' were confined to 'necessaries', the wants of 'civilised societies' were not. In the latter societies, wants were multiplied by expanding production, so that the accumulation of commodities itself could explain why wants were 'indefinite and insatiable'. The desire for the accumulation of specific commodities could be sated, but accumulation of wealth produced new wants so that the commodity composition of utilities continually expanded ([1834] 1968, pp. 8 and 9). This designation of the relation between accumulation and utility was then used to argue that general over-production was impossible. There could be no such barrier to the accumulation of wealth since, if a general glut occurred, it could only mean all wants were sated. Such an argument was refuted 'by philosophy' and the 'experience of mankind' ([1834] 1968, p. 8). Lloyd thus used the analysis of utility to argue that general over-production was impossible.[21] This was important for his analysis of the Poor Law which, Lloyd argued, was necessary to deal with unemployment. The latter, however, was not caused by a deficiency in aggregate demand (see below). It should also be noted that Lloyd's discussion entailed that the explanation of prices, with which value was concerned, was analytically separate from the determination of the level of output which was explained with reference to utility.

Special Utility and Value

In the analysis of utility and wealth accumulation, want variation for particular groups of commodities played an important role in creating a space for the demand for new commodities (Lloyd, [1834] 1968, p. 9). Since the analysis of value also depended on want variation, there was a danger of confusing the different domains of analysis with which utility and value were concerned and Lloyd thus attempted to explain the distinction with an illustration concerned with want satiation. The illustration consisted of a man who possessed six coats and who, when offered a seventh, would probably refuse it since, as Lloyd put it, he would have 'no use for it'. It was the analysis of the coat which provided a 'point of contact' and hence the possibility of 'confusion' between the two concepts. There were thus two sides of the analysis to be kept separate. On the one side, the coat had no value in the man's estimation and he had no reason to possess it. This was clearly an analysis of zero value. On the other side, in the analysis of utility, the man's reply would not be predicated on the coat's 'abstract utility', as given in the societal commodity hierarchy, but rather on the coat's 'special utility' to him. The latter term was defined as relevant only 'under the circumstance of his want of coats being already so far supplied' and was thus restricted to the situation where the satiation point had been reached for a commodity ([1834] 1968, pp. 17 and 18). This second side of the analysis, another 'way' of examining the same coat, was concerned with the analysis of wealth accumulation. The man had no want for the extra coat, but that did not mean his want for other commodities was zero. The concepts of utility and value could, as Lloyd had previously explained, be used to examine the same commodity or group of commodities; the concepts provided 'two ways' of analysing the same things ([1834] 1968, p. 14), as illustrated by the seventh coat. However, because the two sides of the analysis were concerned with the different concepts utility and value, Lloyd argued that the designation of 'special utility' though approaching 'very near to' the concept of zero value, was 'not quite the same' concept ([1834] 1968, p. 18). Concerned with different domains and questions of analysis, the discussion of value and utility had to be kept conceptually separate.

It should be noted here that Lloyd's example of the seventh coat played a crucial role in Seligman's depiction of Lloyd as a precursor of marginal utility theory. Seligman argued that Lloyd's discussion of 'absolute' utility was the same concept as the later marginalist concept of total utility and that Lloyd's 'special utility' was the same concept as the later marginal utility. On that basis, Seligman concluded that it 'would be difficult to put in clearer or happier language the substance of the modern theory of the relation between value and utility' (Seligman, 1903, pp. 360–361). The difficulty with this reading is twofold. First, Lloyd clearly distinguished between value and utility – they were quite different concepts, concerned with different analytical issues. Second, Lloyd's concept of special utility was restricted to a satiation point. It did not have the more general significance of applying to successive increments within a consumption bundle before the satiation point. Hence, there was no distinction between total and marginal utility in Lloyd's analysis.

LLOYD'S CONTEXT OF REFUTATION

Lloyd set out his defence of the justice in, or right to, poor relief in his long-period analysis of value and distribution. In two published sets of lectures which dealt with the specifics of the policy (Lloyd, [1835] 1968, [1836] 1968), he argued that the Poor Law could not solve the general problem of poverty, that is, the near to subsistence wage of the mass of the population, which was the result of pressure against 'the means of subsistence'. Instead, the Poor Law should be directed to helping two groups – the sick, orphans, widows and the aged on the one hand, and the 'unemployed' on the other (Lloyd, [1835] 1968, pp. 53 and 119; and [1836] 1968, p. 35). Expanding the explanatory factors mentioned in his population lectures (see above), Lloyd argued that unemployment was caused by seasonal fluctuations, the 'caprice of fashion, alterations in taxation, a transition from war to peace, or from peace to war, discoveries in manufacturing or agricultural science, new facilities in communication, such as the invention of steam-boats or steam-carriages'. Unlike poverty, unemployment was analysed as a market-period phenomenon which resulted in an 'irregularity in the distribution of food ... from time to time' (Lloyd, [1835] 1968, pp. 52, 53, 54 and 61). While his long-period analysis provided a rationale for the Poor Law in 'effecting' a 'qualified right of property in the earth' (Lloyd, [1836] 1968, p. 59),[22] the market-period analysis dealt in specific detail with the effects on employment of organisational and technological changes in both the manufacturing and agricultural sectors (Lloyd, [1835] 1968, pp. 66–79). In facilitating adjustment to changing employment conditions in a 'manufacturing society', the Poor Law acted 'as oil to its machines, and allow the force of the moving power, instead of being wasted by the friction and concussions of immediate obstacles, to operate, almost undiminished, on the remotest extremities' ([1835] 1968, p. 102; see also p. 126). Lloyd thus criticised the 'new Poor Law' for driving claimants into the workhouse, thereby failing to discriminate between them according to the causes of their distress (Lloyd, [1836] 1968, p. 57).[23]

As an integral part of his argument for the right to relief, Lloyd's value lecture was an intervention in the contemporary debates as to whether value should be understood as a 'relative' or 'absolute' concept. It has been suggested that the key figure in the discussion of value by the first three Drummond professors was Samuel Bailey (Bowley, 1937, pp. 94 and 109). In his anonymously published *Critical Dissertation on the Nature, Measures and Causes of Value* of 1825, Bailey had rejected Ricardo's and Malthus' conceptualisations of 'absolute' value, arguing that only a notion of relative value was satisfactory. He opened his critique with the statement that 'Value, in its ultimate sense, appears to mean the esteem in which any object is held' (Bailey, 1825, p. 1). It is possible that Lloyd had read Bailey as he remarked that value 'has with great propriety been defined to mean the esteem in which any object is held' (Lloyd, [1834] 1968, p. 11).[24] If Lloyd rejected Bailey's conceptualisation of value, he was following the critique in Malthus' *Definitions in Political Economy*, a text to which Lloyd also referred (Malthus, 1827; Lloyd, [1834] 1968, p. 30). For Malthus described Bailey's opening statement about value meaning esteem as 'just', while going on to defend his own notion of absolute value by arguing that, to obtain an estimate of esteem, it was necessary to 'refer each' commodity singularly to 'the desires of man and the means of production' (Malthus, 1827, pp. 128 and 208–209). That wording might suggest that, in part, Lloyd formulated his own solution to the problem of value by reworking Malthus' argument.

Considered overall, Lloyd's lectures can be read as a critique of his two predecessors in the Drummond chair and hence as another example of the ideological and cultural friction between Christ Church and Oriel that was described in the first part of this chapter. Both Senior and Whately were closely associated, in different ways, with the new Poor Law criticised by Lloyd (Mandler, 1990, pp. 96–102). By defending the right to or justice in relief, Lloyd's analysis was markedly different from his predecessors in explaining why labourers did not receive a full equivalent for their labour in the form of wages and why a more liberal Poor Law was necessary to deal with unemployment. His treatment of value was also clearly opposed to his predecessors, both of whom had followed Bailey in arguing that only a notion of relative value was valid (Senior, 1836, p. 134; Whately, 1832, pp. 6–8; 1853, pp. 30–33). Indeed, one component of Lloyd's analysis suggests that Whately was a particular target.

In his value lecture, Lloyd argued that, because the 'commercial intercourse ... to which we are accustomed' blended the concepts of value and exchange, 'it requires some effort of the imagination to form a distinct idea of value by itself, disengaged, on the one hand, from value in exchange, and, on the other, from the mere notion of utility'. Examples of the idea were thus difficult to extract 'from the facts and occurrences with which we are familiar', while 'cases purely hypothetical are less interesting and less instructive' (Lloyd, [1834] 1968, pp. 20–21). To illustrate how value could be identified not just in a society 'such as exists in England' but also in the behaviour of an 'isolated individual', Lloyd included two pages of quotations from Daniel Defoe's *Adventures of Robinson Crusoe* ([1834] 1968, pp. 22–23). The use of Crusoe as an exemplar in political economy was highly unusual at the time (White, 1982) and the space devoted to the quotations appears odd in that Lloyd acknowledged that he had 'not found any thing so much to the point as I could have wished' in Defoe's text (Lloyd, [1834] 1968, p. 21). A possible explanation for the illustration, however, is suggested by Whately's published lectures, where he argued that political economy should not be characterised as 'the science of national Wealth', but rather as 'CATALLACTICS, or the "Science of *Exchanges*"'. This meant that 'A man ... in a desert island, like Alex Selkirke, or the personage his adventures are supposed to have suggested, Robinson Crusoe, is in a situation of which Political-Economy takes no cognizance' (Whately, 1832, pp. 6, 7 and 8). The first detailed references to Robinson Crusoe as an illustrative device in British political economy were thus part of the contemporary debates over the meaning of value. Lloyd's lectures emphasise how those debates were integral components of different approaches to the conceptualisation of the economy which, in turn, were geared to considering contemporary policy questions.

CONCLUSIONS

Lloyd's analysis of value had a quite different role to that ascribed to it in the marginalist precursor readings initiated by Edwin Seligman. The analysis had no link to an explanation for a negative functional relationship between the quantity demanded and the price of a commodity, but was used instead to explain labourers' behaviour when producing wealth from the economic surplus in the agricultural sector. (It was only the behavioural mechanism, however, as the full explanation required specifying the particular type of the economy and the unequal power relationships between different classes). A rising food price, the mirror of the non-equivalent exchanges between labourers and employers, meant that increasing wealth was associated with grinding poverty for the mass of the population who produced the wealth.

If an analysis that clearly identifies the source of the surplus in the agricultural sector can be characterised as neo-physiocratic, Lloyd did not identify any sources for his analysis. He might have owed something to Thomas Chalmers' *Political Economy* (1832) which also presented 'the population principle in its starkest form', devoid of the significant modifications that Malthus had introduced (Winch, 1996, pp. 381–385; see also Meek, 1963, pp. 340–341, 359–362).[25] Lloyd might also have owed a debt to the second edition of Malthus' *Essay* on population where, in a sympathetic treatment of the French 'Economists', Malthus argued that 'the great position of the Economists will always remain true, that the surplus produce of the cultivators is the great fund which ultimately pays all those who are not employed upon the land' (Malthus, 1803, pp. 435–436; see also p. 433). Malthus, however, significantly changed his argument in later editions, such as the fifth which Lloyd cited (Gilbert, 1980). In any case, Lloyd produced his own distinctive account. In particular, while Lloyd paid homage to Malthus and the population principle in explaining a long-period wage rate, he switched the analytical focus for explaining an increasing population to the institutional structure of the economy and the consequent incentives for labourers' behaviour. Nor should Lloyd's arguments be dismissed as a throwback to the eighteenth century. His lectures were, in part, clearly designed as an intervention in the debates over value following Bailey's critique, while his familiarity with recent literature was signalled by his citation of Charles Babbage's *Economy of Machinery and Manufactures* (Babbage, 1832; Lloyd, [1833] 1968, p. 40n).

Lloyd was not alone in defending a more liberal Poor Law by the mid-1830s, joining those, such as George Poulett Scrope, who used 'the language of natural jurisprudence as the proper basis for a legally required welfare provision' (Horne, 1990, p. 197).[26] Nevertheless, Lloyd's approach was quite distinctive in combining a surplus distribution theory with the argument that labour created all wealth. Couple that with his claim that land was 'the common inheritance of all the inhabitants of the earth' and his lectures have a number of key points in common with contemporary radical analyses of the production and distribution of wealth (Ashcraft, 1995). While his defence of landed property indicates that Lloyd was no radical, his account is analytically too complex to be simply characterised as the reflection of a 'paternalistic Tory'.

In that context, it should also be noted that, while a number of the early 'under-consumptionists' presented their arguments in a framework which sounds distinctly like, or is reminiscent of, an agrarian surplus analysis (Meek, 1963, ch.3.), Lloyd rejected the possibility of a general glut. At the same time, he paid particular attention to the problem of unemployment. His lectures show that it was possible for a proponent of what later became known as 'Say's Law' to argue that unemployment was a significant problem which required legislative intervention. Although he analysed unemployment as a market-period phenomena, Lloyd was clear that the problem could last for a significant length of time. Its existence was largely due to the nature of the economy and, unlike subsequent neoclassical theorists, Lloyd did not argue that it could be solved by cutting real wage rates.

We have argued here that new light can be cast on Lloyd's political economy lectures by reading them in the context of the contest between the Oriel Noetics and Christ Church Tories. It is thus appropriate to conclude by noting that it has become common in the history of economics literature to group Lloyd with his predecessors in the Drummond chair, Senior and Whately, who are characterised as 'subjective value' theorists. This is highly misleading and not simply because Lloyd's lectures were, at least in part, directed against them as part of the Poor Law debates. Just as, if not more important, is that his analysis was quite different in presenting a surplus theory of value and distribution. In that regard, it is also misleading to characterise Lloyd as part of an 'anti-Ricardian reaction'. If Ricardo was virtually irrelevant in Lloyd's context of refutation, grouping Lloyd with the subjective value theorists distracts attention from the significance of his critique of value as a relative notion and the analytical role of the concept of value in his distribution analysis.

NOTES

1. The standard work on Lloyd is Romano (1977), which is of great merit. See also Seligman (1903), Romano (1971) and Gordon (1966, 2008). Valuable background information is also presented in Baker's (1981) biography of Charles Lloyd, but strangely there are only two cursory references to William F. Lloyd in this work. There is no entry on Lloyd in the old *Palgrave* and the entry by Clerk (1917) in the old *Dictionary of National Biography* and new *Oxford Dictionary of National Biography* is of no consequence.

2. Noetic is Greek for intellectual or reasoner. The modern popularisation of the phrase 'Oriel Noetics' may be traced to Tuckwell (1909). The term was, however,

commonly used by contemporaries as a means of bating the intellectual pretensions of the Oriel men (see Mozley, 1882, p. 19). The nexus between the religious and economic beliefs of the Noetics has already been the subject of admirable, but very different, studies by Corsi (1987), Mandler (1990) and Waterman (1991). For a more specific account of the Noetic's liberal theology see Brent (1997). For biographical accounts of the key Noetics see Copleston (1840, 1851), Whately (1854), Fitzpatrick (1864), Anon. (1864, 1867), Whately (1866) and Rigg (1917). Finally, even though the Noetics are not central to their studies, Hilton (1988) and Winch (1996) shed light on the wider context.

3. For the voluminous literature on the shift in thinking about the Poor Laws prior to the reforms of 1834, see the references in Mandler (1987).

4. This emphasis bemused some outsiders, such as J. S. Mill: '[Whately] contends at great length against what he terms the false and dangerous impression, that Political Economy is unfavourable to religion. But where, we ask, was such an impression ever entertained, except at Oxford? and who would have suspected that it was entertained even there, if the Professor had not betrayed the secret?' (*Examiner*, 12 June 1831).

5. See Corsi (1987) and Maas (2008) for the hostile response of the Cambridge Inductivists, namely Whewell and Jones and J. S. Mill's newspaper commentaries (especially the *Examiner* of June 1831) for the positive response of the London Utilitarians.

6. The studentship is unique to Christ Church (which is without Fellows). It is something between a scholarship and a fellowship, may be provided before gaining a degree, does not allow for the individual to participate in the governance of the college and is relinquished when an individual marries or becomes a cure of souls (Baker, 1981, p. 24). See Wordsworth (1891), Oakley (1855/1856), Ward (1965) and Baker (1981) for accounts of Christ Church and Charles Lloyd at this time.

7. The most important policy issue that Charles Lloyd and Peel considered in their correspondence, at least from an economist's perspective, was the currency question of 1819 (see Parker, 1899). Lloyd's role in this policy formation has been written out of the related secondary literature because Peel is incorrectly put down as Copleston's rather than Lloyd's student in an effort to support the associated claim that Copleston's 1819 publications on this question influenced Peel (Halévy, [1923] 1987, p. 52; Gordon, 1976, p. 192; Mandler 1990, p. 93). Others suggest, but do not explicitly state, that Copleston was Peel's tutor in their quest to emphasise Copleston's hold over Peel (Rashid, 1983, p. 250). The elimination of Charles Lloyd from the secondary literature in this way indirectly serves to dislocate William F. Lloyd from his institutional context, as it means that he is not singled out as a product of a tradition that stood in opposition to the Noetics. One of the few scholars to note the Lloyd–Peel connection, if only briefly, is Romano (1977). This issue is discussed in greater detail in the longer version of this chapter, which may be found at http://researchonline.nd.edu.au/bus_conference/14/.

8. Lloyd referred to a long-period outcome where the wage was 'at its natural level' (Lloyd, [1835] 1968, p. 87).

9. We have followed Lloyd in using the fifth edition of Malthus' *Essay*.

10. Lloyd defined poverty as 'misery produced by want' which was equated, in effect, with 'scarcity in the means of subsistence'. He argued that the English population doubled in 50 years (Lloyd, [1833] 1968, pp. 9 and 12).

11. Although Lloyd did not use the word 'rational', it will be used here to mean behaviour based on a comparison of perceived cost and benefits, using all available information in a consistent manner.

12. Lloyd clearly assumed that all relevant household decisions were made by the adult male.

13. Unemployment was not due to a deficiency in aggregate demand, but rather to more 'partial causes' such as shifts in the patterns of demand for particular commodities and 'oscillations in the currency' (Lloyd, [1833] 1968, p. 26).

14. The (old) Poor Law also reduced employment outside the workhouses and increased the 'price of provisions' (Malthus, 1817, Vol. 2, pp. 332–334 and 346).

15. Even here, however, there was a subtle difference. Malthus argued that the radicals' proposals would produce an unprecedented population problem, greater than 'in any society that has ever yet been known' (Malthus, 1817, Vol. 2, p. 252). While Lloyd argued that 'universal distress fails to suggest to individuals any motive for moral restraint' in a 'system of equality', the result would be the same as in 'the existing state of things' (Lloyd, [1833] 1968, pp. 18 and 23).

16. Hardin (1968), however, erased Lloyd's sophisticated analysis of behaviour in conditions of ignorance and uncertainty by depicting economic actions as based on full knowledge of all effects. For discussion of this and the treatment of Lloyd in the post-Hardin literature, see White (2009).

17. '[A] qualified right of property in the earth, such as that which can be effected by the Poor Laws, ought to be extended to as many families which inhabit it, as can be maintained in comfort out of the produce' (Lloyd, [1836] 1968, p. 59]. See also Lloyd, [1837] 1968, pp. 38 and 40.

18. Summarising his position, Lloyd argued that 'the principle of our proposed Poor Law becomes relief to the impotent and work for the able-bodied' (Lloyd, [1836] 1968, p. 7).

19. In an 1834 letter to Robert Peel, Lloyd argued that, 'With respect to the County rates, so far from wishing to see the landed interest relieved from any part of them, I should like to see it burthened with almost the whole weight of the national taxation'. He acknowledged that this was an 'extreme opinion' (Lloyd to Peel, 22 July 1834, Peel Papers, British Library, Add. Mss. 40.404).

20. Smith's discussion was subsequently reworked to construct the myth of a 'diamonds and water paradox' in *WN* (White, 2002).

21. While Lloyd discussed overproduction in terms of the gratification of existing wants, and the 'indefinite passion for wealth', he argued that the 'main question' in the glut analysis 'is concerned rather with the remuneration of the producers than with the disposition of consumption' (Lloyd, [1834] 1968, p. 7) This appears to be a reference to Malthus' analysis where although the 'disposition to consumption' created a problem of deficient demand, the deficiency was registered in the divergence of market from natural prices (Constabile, 1983).

22. Lloyd declared that Malthus' critique of the right to relief was 'absurd' (Lloyd, [1835] 1968, p. 38).

23. For a detailed discussion of Lloyd's Poor Law analysis, see Romano (1977, pp. 428–435).

24. In a subsequent anonymous pamphlet, Bailey mentioned an article in the *Westminster Review* which defended the use of value as a relative term (Bailey, 1826, p. 37). Although unsigned, the article was written by John Stuart Mill ([Mill], 1825, p. 224). Lloyd cited and criticised a longer version of the same passage from Mill's article (Lloyd, [1834] 1968, pp. 33–34).

25. Lloyd referred to Chalmers in his population lectures (Lloyd, [1833] 1968, pp. 36 and 65).

26. Lloyd was particularly taken with Scrope's Poor Law analysis (Lloyd, [1835] 1968, pp. 97 and 105–107).

REFERENCES

Anon. (1864). Memoirs of Richard Whately. *Blackwood Magazine*, October, pp. 472–491.

Anon. (1867). Art. vii – Life and correspondence of Richard Whately, D. D. Late Archbishop of Dublin (by E. Jane Whately, 2 Vols, Longmans 1866). *London Quarterly Review*, *27*(54), 449–504.

Ashcraft, R. (1995). Lockean ideas, poverty, and the development of liberal political theory. In: J. Brewer & S. Staves (Eds), *Early modern conceptions of property*. London: Routledge.

Babbage, C. (1832). *On the economy of machinery and manufactures*. London: Knight.

Bailey, S. (1825). *A critical dissertation on the nature, measures and causes of value*. London: Hunter.

Bailey, S. (1826). *A letter to a political economist: Occasioned by an article in the Westminster review on the subject of value*. London: Hunter.

Baker, W. J. (1981). *Beyond port and prejudice: Charles Lloyd of Oxford, 1784–1829*. Orono: University of Maine at Orono Press.

Bowley, M. (1937). *Nassau Senior and classical economics*. London: Allen and Unwin.

Brent, R. (1997). Note, the Oriel Noetics. In: M. G. Brock & M. C. Curthoys (Eds), *The history of the University of Oxford, Vol 6: Nineteenth-century Oxford, Part 1* (pp. 72–76). Oxford: Clarendon Press.

Clerk, A. M. (1917). Lloyd, William Forster. In: L. Stephen & S. Lee (Eds), *The dictionary of national biography* (Vol. 11, p. 1319). Oxford: Oxford University Press.

Constabile, L. (1983). Natural prices, market prices and effective demand in Malthus. *Australian Economic Papers*, *22*(40), 144–170.

Copleston, E. (1819a). *A letter the right honourable Robert Peel on the pernicious effects of a variable standard of value, especially as it regards the condition of the lower orders and the Poor Laws*. London: J. Murray.

Copleston, E. (1819b). *A second letter to the right Hon. Robert Peel, M. P. for the University of Oxford on the causes of the increase of pauperism, and on the Poor Law*. London: J. Murray.

Copleston, E. (1840). *Letters of the earl of Dudley to the bishop of Llandaff*. London: J. Murray.

Copleston, W. J. (1851). *Memoir of Edward Copleston, DD, Bishop of Llandaff. With selections from his diary and correspondence etc*. London: John W. Parker.

Corsi, P. (1987). The heritage of Dugald Stewart: Oxford philosophy and the method of political economy. *Nuncius: Annali di Storia della Scienza, 2*(2), 89–144.

Daston, L. (1988). *Classical probability in the enlightenment*. Princeton, NJ: Princeton University Press.

Davison, J. (1817). *Considerations on the Poor Laws*. Oxford: Parker.

Dunkley, P. (1981). Whigs and paupers: the reform of the English Poor-Laws, 1830–1834. *Journal of British Studies, 20*(2), 124–149.

Faber, G. ([1933] 1936). Oxford apostles: A character study of the oxford movement. London: Faber and Faber.

Fitzpatrick, W. J. (1864). *Memoirs of Richard Whately: Archbishop of Dublin: With a glance at his contemporaries & times*. London: R. Bentley.

Gilbert, G. (1980). Economic growth and the poor in Malthus' essay on population. *History of Political Economy, 12*(1), 83–96.

Gordon, B. (1966). W.F. Lloyd: A neglected contribution. *Oxford Economic Papers, 18*(1), 64–70.

Gordon, B. (1976). *Political economy in parliament: 1819–1823*. London: Macmillan.

Gordon, B. (2008). Lloyd, William Forster (1794–1852). In: S. Durlauf & L. Blume (Eds), *New Palgrave dictionary of economics* (2nd ed.). New York: Palgrave Macmillan.

Halévy, É. ([1923] 1987). *The liberal awakening (1815–1830)*. London: Ark.

Hardin, G. (1968). The tragedy of the commons. *Science* (162), 1243–1248.

Hilton, B. (1988). *The age of atonement: The influence of evangelicalism on social and economic thought, 1785-1865*. Oxford: Oxford University Press.

Horne, T. A. (1990). *Property rights and poverty: Political arguments in Britain, 1605–1834*. Chapel Hill, NC: University of North Carolina Press.

Levy, S. L. (1970). *Nassau W. Senior 1790–1864: Critical essayist, classical economist and adviser of governments*. Plymouth, UK: David and Charles.

Lloyd, W. F. (1830). *Prices of corn in Oxford in the beginning of the fourteenth century: Also from the year 1583 to the present time*. (*To which are added some miscellaneous notices of prices in other places. Collected from the manuscripts at Oxford. With a full account of the authorities on which the several prices are stated*). Oxford: Oxford University Press.

Lloyd, W. F. ([1833] 1968). Two lectures on the checks to population. In: *Lectures on population, value, Poor-Law and rent: Delivered in the University of Oxford during the years 1832, 1833, 1834, 1835 & 1836*. Reprint of Economic Classics. New York: A.M. Kelley.

Lloyd, W. F. ([1834] 1968). A lecture on the notion of value, as distinguishable not only from utility, but also from value in exchange. In: *Lectures on population, value, Poor-Law and rent: Delivered in the University of Oxford during the years 1832, 1833, 1834, 1835 & 1836*. Reprint of Economic Classics. New York: A.M. Kelley.

Lloyd, W. F. ([1835] 1968), Four lectures on Poor-Laws. In: *Lectures on population, value, Poor-Law and rent: Delivered in the University of Oxford during the years 1832, 1833, 1834, 1835 & 1836*. Reprint of Economic Classics. New York: A.M. Kelley.

Lloyd, W. F. ([1836] 1968). Two lectures on Poor-Laws. In: *Lectures on population, value, Poor-Law and rent: Delivered in the University of Oxford during the years 1832, 1833, 1834, 1835 & 1836*. Reprint of Economic Classics. New York: A.M. Kelley.

Lloyd, W. F. ([1837] 1968). Two lectures on the justice of Poor Laws and one lecture on rent. In: *Lectures on population, value, Poor-Law and rent: Delivered in the University of Oxford during the years 1832, 1833, 1834, 1835 & 1836*. Reprint of Economic Classics. New York: A.M. Kelley.

Lloyd, W. F. (1968). *Lectures on population, value, Poor-Law and rent: Delivered in the University of Oxford during the years 1832, 1833, 1834, 1835 & 1836*. Reprint of Economic Classics. New York: A.M. Kelley.

Malthus, T. R. (1803). *An essay on the principle of population: Or, a view of its past and present effects on human happiness* (Rev. ed.). London: J. Johnson.

Malthus, T. R. (1817). 5th ed. *An essay on the principle of population: Or a view of the past and present effects on human happiness* (3 Vols.). London: Murray.

Malthus, T. R. (1827). *Definitions in political economy*. London: Murray.

Mandler, P. (1987). The making of the new Poor Laws redivivus. *Past and Present*, *117*, 131–157.

Mandler, P. (1990). Tories and paupers: Christian political economy and the making of the new poor law. *Historical Journal*, *33*(1), 81–103.

Marcet, J.H. (1816). *Conversations on political economy: In which the elements of that science are familiarly explained*. London: Longman.

Maas, H. (2008). A hard battle to fight': natural theology and the dismal science, 1820–1850. *History of Political Economy*, *40*, 143–167.

Meek, R. L. (1963). *The economics of physiocracy: Essays and translations*. Cambridge, MA: Harvard University Press.

Mill, J. S. (1825). Periodical literature – Quarterly review. *Westminster Review*, *3*(5), 213–232.

Mozley, T. (1882). *Reminiscences, chiefly of Oriel College and the Oxford movement*. London: Longmans Green.

Newman, J. H. (1903). In: A. Mozley (Ed.), *Letters and correspondence during his life in the English church, with a brief autobiography* (2nd ed., 2 Vols.). London: Longman and Green.

Oakley, F. (1855/56). Christ church under Dean Hall and Dean Smith. In: Q. Couch (Ed.), *Reminiscences of Oxford, by Oxford Men, 1559–1850* (pp. 301–345). Oxford: Clarendon Press.

Parker, C. (1899). *Sir Robert Peel: From his private papers*. London: J. Murray.

Rashid, S. (1983). Edward Copleston, Robert Peel, and cash payments. *History of Political Economy*, *15*(2), 249–259.

Rigg, J. M. (1917). Whately, Richard. In: L. Stephen & S. Smith (Eds), *Dictionary of national biography* (Vol. 20, pp. 1334–1340). Oxford: Oxford University Press.

Romano, R. (1971). W.F. Lloyd – A comment. *Oxford Economic Papers*, *23*(2), 286–290.

Romano, R. (1977). William Forster Lloyd: A non-Ricardian?. *History of Political Economy*, *9*(3), 412–441.

Seligman, E. R. A. (1903). On some neglected British economists-I. *Economic Journal*, *13*(51), 335–363.

Senior, N. (1827). *Introductory lecture on political economy. Delivered before the University of Oxford on the 6th of December 1826*. London: J. Mawman.

Senior, N. (1828). *Three lectures on the transmission of the precious metals from country to country and the mercantile theory of wealth. Delivered before the University of Oxford, in June, 1827*. London: J. Murray.

Senior, N. (1829). *Two lectures on population. Delivered before the University of Oxford in Easter term, 1828*. London: Saunders and Otley.

Senior, N. (1830a). *Three lectures on the cost of obtaining money; and on some effects on the effect of private government money, presented in June 1829*. London: J. Murray.

Senior, N. (1830b). *Three lectures on the rate of wages. Delivered before the University of Oxford in Easter term, 1830: With a preface on the causes and remedies of the present disturbances.* London: J. Murray.

Senior, N. (1836). *An outline of the science of political economy.* (Offprint from the encyclopaedia metropolitana). London: Clowes and Son.

Smith, A. ([1776] 1976a). In: R. H. Campbell, A. S. Skinner & W. B. Todd (Eds), *An inquiry into the nature and causes of the wealth of nations.* Oxford: Clarendon Press.

Smith, A. ([1759] 1976b). In: D. D. Raphael & A. L. Macfie (Eds), *Theory of moral sentiments.* Oxford: Clarendon Press.

Tuckwell, W. (1909). *Pre-Tractarian Oxford: A reminiscence of the Oriel Noetics.* London: Smith Elder.

Ward, W. R. (1965). *Victorian Oxford.* London: Frank Cass.

Waterman, A. (1991). *Revolution, economics, and religion: Christian Political Economy, 1798–1833.* Cambridge: Cambridge University Press.

Whately, E. J. (1866). *Life and correspondence of Richard Whately, D.D., late Archbishop of Dublin.* London: Longmans Green.

Whately, R. ([1826] 1890). *Elements of logic* (9th ed.). London: Longmans Green.

Whately, R. (1831). *Introductory lectures on political-economy: Being part of a course delivered in Easter term 1831.* London: Fellowes.

Whately, R. (1832). *Introductory lectures on political economy.* London: Fellowes.

Whately, R. ([1833] 1853). *Easy lessons on money matters; for the use of young people* (13th ed.). London: Parker.

Whately, R. (1854). *Remains of the late Edward Copleston.* London: John W. Parker.

White, M. V. (1982). Reading and rewriting: The production of an economic Robinson Crusoe. *Southern Review, 15*(2), 115–142.

White, M. V. (2002). Doctoring Adam Smith: The fable of the diamonds and water paradox. *History of Political Economy, 34*(4), 659–683.

White, M. V. (2009). *Mangling a metaphor: W.F. Lloyd and the tragedy of the commons.* Australia: Economics Department, Monash University.

Winch, D. (1996). *Riches and poverty: an intellectual history of political economy in Britain, 1750–1834.* Cambridge: Cambridge University Press.

Wordsworth, C. (1891). *Annals of my early life, 1806–1846: With occasional compositions in Latin and English verse.* London: Longmans Green.

JOHN ROOKE: RENT, DISTRIBUTION, MONEY AND REPEAL OF THE CORN LAWS

Nigel F. B. Allington

Since the publication of E. R. A. Seligman's (1903) celebrated articles, 'On Some Neglected British Economists', some of the epigones he so enthusiastically treated have found a permanent place in the history of economic theory. Several have been subject to full-length studies and the textbooks of O'Brien (1975), Sowell (1974) and Blaug (1985) contain many references to Torrens, Bailey, Longfield and Lloyd to mention only four. John Rooke, on the other hand, has been neglected again despite Seligman's praise, possibly because Schumpeter's influential *History of Economic Analysis* (1954, p. 475) describes him as having 'no case at all' with regard to the originality of his work. This summary dismissal, however, can only be attributed to his failure to consider the totality of his work that has considerable merit across a wide range of topics. Indeed some of his analysis is seen as precursory to contemporary debates in, for example, monetary economics. This reappraisal attempts to assess some of these topics by comparing Rooke with the Smithian and Ricardian legacies. After this short introduction, section two considers Rooke's place in the development of the marginal theory of rent, section three considers the rest of the distributive shares and section four analyses his contribution to value and the measure of value that excites modern commentators. This work received scant attention from Seligman, as did the subject matter of section five 'Rooke's

English, Irish and Subversives Among the Dismal Scientists
Research in the History of Economic Thought and Methodology, Volume 28-B, 243–302

ISSN: 0743-4154/doi:10.1108/S0743-4154(2010)000028B012

attack on the Corn Laws', which sparked parliamentary debate and helped to convince some of the protagonists of the merits of the case for repeal. The sixth section considers his analysis of capital accumulation and growth and the seventh section on public finance was again a subject missed by Seligman who devoted a considerable proportion of his academic career to the subject. The eighth section concludes.

What emerges from this assessment is the confirmation of the vigorous debate that ensued during the nineteenth century outside the London clique of major political economists, giving the work of those like Rooke a refreshingly original appearance. Any reassessment, of course, is heavily dependent upon possession of the complete *oeuvre*, but in this case, the greater part of what according to the extant evidence was a weighty volume of material, the Rooke–Graham Papers, were destroyed by a descendant of the Graham family. The difficulties that this presents cannot be resolved.

Rooke came to the study of political economy during the heady years of the nineteenth century, a period of monetary instability and agricultural distress. In this pursuit, he was fortunate to make the acquaintance of a number of influential people from Cumberland in the North West of England that subsequently had a profound influence on his thinking, but perhaps none more so than Sir James Graham, sometime First Lord of the Admiralty and Home Secretary in Peel's government, just prior to the repeal of the Corn Laws. Both Rooke and Graham had agricultural interests, Rooke as yeoman farmer and Graham as wealthy landowner. In their published work, in fact, both show a deep appreciation and realistic appraisal of the role of agriculture in the British economy.

It would appear from the major studies of Sir James Graham's political career that Rooke benefited the most from the association (Torrens, 1863; Erickson, 1952; Ward, 1967). In the build up to the repeal of the Corn Laws, an anonymously published pamphlet by Rooke, at first mistaken as the work of Graham, meant that the latter enjoyed some notoriety in the press and Parliament, more particularly when he switched his position in favour of repeal at a later date. However, various unpublished letters and other testimony cast an entirely different light on the matter. Specifically, Graham writes to Rooke, 'I am disposed to receive your lucubrations with the respect due to your private worth'; and, 'I hear from you, however, at all times with pleasure; and *I frequently derive very useful suggestions from the train of thought to which your speculations lead*'; and again 'I have received your letters and I am disposed to receive with *attention and respect* every suggestion which you may offer on the subjects of corn and currency' (Graham Papers, 1827, 1834, 1838; italics added). Finally, in a letter written shortly after the repeal of the Corn Laws, Graham makes some telling remarks on Rooke's analysis and influence: 'I am sincerely glad that the course which my sense of public duty has compelled me to adopt with respect to the Corn Laws meets with your entire approbation. *Your views on this subject have been consistent and uniform; and the necessity of no longer treating the trade in corn as an exception to general principles was obvious to you long before it had forced itself on my convictions.* I give you full credit for your foresight, and disinterested boldness and honesty in the early avowal and steady maintenance of these opinions' (Graham Papers, 1846; italics added).

This is not the place to document the full extent of Graham's indebtedness to Rooke, but in his biography of Rooke, Lonsdale captures the substance of the matter, contrasting the polar backgrounds of the two men:

> Rooke created in him a new force, if not a new direction of study… and excited his ambition to become a political writer and a man of the times. If Rooke, bucolic born and village-taught, untrained, and uncultivated, could dictate articles (and books) worthy of note on abstruse political subjects, why should not he (Graham), Oxonian in culture, the heir to an English baronetcy, and some diplomatic and parliamentary claim to boot, try to solve some of the problems affecting the financial interest and general welfare of the nation? The spirit of emulation was roused in Graham by Rooke's example, and gave to the stirrings of his own nascent ambition a powerful impetus political-wards. From this period a special feeling for the study of our monetary relations, and the arguments concerned in general political economy, gained possession of Graham, and not without giving a direction to his future statesmanship. (Lonsdale, 1868, pp. 45–46)

On the other hand, Graham encouraged Rooke to read Hume, Smith, Paley, Malthus and Ricardo amongst others, which he did with profit. The philosophical writings of Jeremy Bentham also seem to have been an influence on Rooke's work, particularly on his *Free and Safe Government* (1835). Nevertheless, it is the economics of Adam Smith that formed an important starting point for much of his analysis.

On the subject of neglect and Seligman's reappraisal, a number of points are important. Seligman correctly notes that Rooke, unlike some of the other economists he examined, produced a 500-page treatise on the whole spectrum of the subject rather than some specialised subset, publishing separate works on money, government and the national debt as well as a large tome on geology. What distinguished his *Inquiry* ((1824) was the inductive method with copious carefully collected statistics deployed and much practical analysis. Without having read the early articles of Rooke in the *Evans and Ruffy Farmer's Journal and Manufacturer's and Traders' Register*, Seligman accepts his claim to originality on the discovery of differential rent and praises his development of marginal cost 'as a universal principle' (p. 512). Seligman also thinks he comes close to making a correct distinction between interest and profits. His optimism over the prospects for economic growth in Britain set him apart from the more pessimistic views of many Ricardians 'the formation of capital is continually accumulating new stores of wealth, and thereby cheapening the means of living. Although population trends tend to increase, "capital is constantly setting free the means of subsistence faster than population has advanced" ' (p. 513). But somewhat ironically, Seligman neglected much of importance in Rooke's work.

ROOKE'S PLACE IN THE DEVELOPMENT OF THE THEORY OF RENT

One of the several claims that Seligman makes for Rooke is that he should be accorded priority in the discovery of the *correct*, that is Ricardian, doctrine of rent:

> there seems little doubt that the doctrine of rent was developed practically simultaneously by Malthus, West, Torrens and Rooke in 1814, but so far as the priority of actual publication is concerned, the above list should be reversed. And in the interests of historical accuracy, Rooke and Torrens must hereafter be accorded the position which they deserve. (Seligman, 1903, p. 512)[1]

He goes on to state that the essay of Rooke antedates that of Torrens. This assessment is rejected however by Hollander in his *David Ricardo: A Centenary Estimate* (1910), who supported the case of two other authors. First, Malthus, on the basis of prefatory remarks in his *Inquiry into the Nature and Progress of Rent* (1815) indicating that he developed the differential rent theory in lectures at Haileybury from 1805 onwards. However, even in his earlier *Observations on the Effects of the Corn Law* (1814), there is only a hint of the differential principle, indicating that Hollander is claiming too much; even his *Inquiry* is an unsophisticated mixture of Smithian and Physiocratic rent doctrines. The second case is that of West, who published his *Essay on the Application of Capital to Land* in 1815, and states its composition spanned a number of years. However, his primary concern was with the determination of profits, in the course of which the principle of diminishing returns does indeed play a part. In fact, nearly all of the authors of interest here seemed to arrive at an analysis of rent via this route, so that West is in good company with Ricardo, Torrens,

West and Rooke. What does emerge too is the fact that beyond considering Rooke's own *Claim to the Original Publication of Certain New Principles in Political Economy* (1825) on the matter of priority, neither Hollander nor Seligman actually considered the primary evidence examined here.

The classical theory of rent is important because it forms a central pillar of the classical theories of value and growth and in this context two strands of thought are to be found, one which may be described as Ricardian and incorporating the idea of differential costs and another, designated demand, which examines the role of excess demand in the determination of rent. The latter may be designated the quantitative form of analysis, while the former should be considered qualitative. The roots of classical rent theory are to be found in Smith's *Wealth of Nations* that served as a starting point for Anderson, Malthus, Ricardo, Rooke and others. Having noted this to be the case though, Smith cannot be acknowledged as the originator of the rent principle, on the grounds that his analysis is pluralistic and confused, viz, rent may arise out of monopoly, differential advantage or the bounty of nature (Gee, 1981).

Rent determination is limited to land used for productive output and is defined as a monopoly price, 'rent, considered as the price paid for the use of land, is naturally the highest which the tenant can afford to pay in the actual circumstances of the land' (Smith, 1977, Vol. I, p. 35). Smith is distinguishing here between scarce and unimproved land and that upon which the landlord has invested capital (that is 'neat rent') and total rent:

> The rent of land, it may be thought, is frequently no more than a reasonable profit or interest for the stock laid out by the landlord upon its improvement. This, no doubt, may be partly the case upon some occasions; for it can scarce ever be more than partly the case. The landlord demands a rent even for unimproved land, and the supposed interest or profit upon the expense is generally an addition to this original rent. Those improvements, besides, are not always made by the stock of the landlord, but sometimes by that of the tenant. When the lease comes to be renewed, however, the landlord commonly demands the same augmentation of rent, as if they had been made his own. (Smith, 1977, Vol. I, p. 8)

The greatest proportion of rent is 'neat rent', in fact, representing about one third of total produce and Smith considers this to be a hindrance to investment in land. It is the surplus that is left after the costs of production and average profit of the tenant have both been met and it is determined by the demand for corn and thereby price. The differential principle is also present, 'the rent of land not only varies with its fertility, whatever be its produce, but with its situation, whatever be its fertility' and the more distant the land from the marketplace the higher is rent, owing to transportation costs (Smith, 1977, *ibid.*).

Rent is not simply a residual payment in Smith's model either, for it is included as part of costs of production. This has led to some confusion, for rent cannot be price determined and price determining. The solution to this apparent dichotomy is simple, the rent on land used to cultivate corn determines the rent 'cost' on land used for other agricultural purposes – the cost of production, or adding-up theory of price, was not applied to corn. Hence the price of agricultural commodities in general must adjust to the price of corn which is determined by the supply and demand for silver (Smith, 1977, Vol. I, pp. 42–45).[2]

On the issue of the rental share, Smith is once again inconsistent, for on the one hand he argues that the rental share has increased, but that when improvements are considered, 'rent, though it increases in proportion to the extent, diminishes in proportion to the produce of the land' (Smith, 1977, Vol. I, p. 9). Wages rise faster than both profits and rent, although rapid capital accumulation raises *total* profits even if the rate of profits falls. Any increase in wage costs in the agricultural sector, however, will be automatically passed on to the landlord, whereas in manufacturing, the price of the product is raised.

Summarising Smith's rent analysis, his is essentially a demand-determined surplus arising out of the limited supply of land, although differing fertility plays a part when two producing units are compared. This involves no conflict, however, for the former relates quite clearly to demand conditions, while the latter refers to supply. The differential concept that is found in the work of Ricardo is also present, but unlike him, Smith does not consider marginal land to be rent free. In comparing the different uses of land, rent equalisation was also considered, but the important point is that not all land produces rent, thereby refuting the physiocratic notion of rent. In other words, in the early stages of development, land does not produce a rent because the competitive forces are too weak to ensure a positive return and later differentials can persist. The idea of rent as a transfer payment on the other hand is clearly present.

A serious challenge to any claim to priority of publication in 1815 now requires attention. James Anderson's much neglected *Observations on the Means of Exciting a Spirit of National Industry* was published in 1777, essentially as an attack on Smith's deductive method. That he worked out the concept of diminishing returns, demonstrating rent to be an intra-marginal surplus, is beyond doubt and ensures him priority of discovery. Despite this, his work remained undiscovered until the publication of

McCulloch's *Literature of Political Economy* in 1845. In Anderson's case, Hollander (1895) has claimed, on the basis of his second publication, *Calm Investigation* (1801), that he devalues his original conception through inconsistency of argument. However, once the short run and long run are separated and increasing returns allowed in the latter case, the charge is found to be incorrect (Hollander, 1895; Cannan, 1892).[3]

Assessing the explosion in pamphlets on rent in the single year 1815, it is appropriate to deal with Malthus, West and Ricardo before Rooke. Malthus' earliest work on population contains only vague references to the principle of diminishing returns, although by the third edition it is frequently referred to. In the course of that discussion Malthus criticises Anderson's claim in *Calm Investigations* that increasing population raises agricultural output, so that the latter's more sophisticated statement of rent remains unknown to him. Malthus merely recognised the intensive and extensive margin in his *Observations on the Effect of the Corn Laws* (1814) and a year later, in *The Nature and Progress of Rent* where rent is said to be 'the excess of price above the cost of production at which raw produce sells in the market' (Malthus, 1815, p. 180). He rejects Smith's explanation in terms of land scarcity as insufficient, preferring to explain the phenomena in terms of the pressure of population growth pushing up corn prices as a consequence of rising costs of production and variable fertility: 'diminish this plenty, diminish the fertility of the soil, and the excess (of price above cost of production) will diminish it still further, and it will disappear. *The cause of the high price of the necessaries of life above the cost of production, is to be found in their abundance, rather than their scarcity*; and is not only essentially different from the high price occasioned by artificial monopolies, but from the high price of those peculiar products…, not connected with food, which may be called natural and necessary monopolies' (Malthus, 1815, p. 210).[4] Later in this same essay, marginal land is said not to be able to pay more than the costs of production, so that rent is zero. The emphasis is on the decreasing cost case, but this is generalised to accommodate economic growth and subsequently the increasing cost case that formed the basis of Ricardo's analysis. This duality in Malthus' account is obviously the combination of an inadequately specified value theory and adherence to Smith's 'competition of capital' account of profit determination (Dobb, 1973).

The variable fertility of land, the no-rent margin of production and the role of population growth provide the common ground between Malthus and Ricardo on the theory of rent. Both argue that rent is price determined and that the price of corn is not high because rent is high, neglecting, according to Buchanan (1929), the competing uses for land. However, in his *Principles of Political Economy*, Malthus does extend his earlier rent analysis to incorporate competitive land usage, albeit somewhat modified in the posthumous second edition (Malthus, 1815, pp. 178–179). High prices, Malthus argued, led to high rents, and thereby to the cultivation of fresh soil and improvements to soil already under cultivation. As a net addition to national wealth, his rent concept has clear physiocratic overtones. From this he deduces his protectionist arguments in favour of the retention of the Corn Laws (for a contrarian interpretation, see Hollander, 1997).

Edward West also published in 1815. In attempting to explain the relative price of corn and thereby account for the determination of profits, he utilised the law of diminishing returns: 'each equal additional quantity of work bestowed on agriculture, yields an actually diminished return; – and of course if each equal addition of work yields an actually diminished return, the whole of the work bestowed on agriculture in the progress of improvement, yields an actually diminished proportionate return' (West, 1815, p. 6). As Brewer (1988) notes this is a statement of the incremental law of diminishing returns rather than the proportional one ascribed to West by Blaug (1985, p. 78). West continues a little later, 'the principle is simply this, that in the progress of the improvement of cultivation the raising of rude produce becomes progressively more expensive, or, in other words, the ratio of the net produce of land to its gross produce is continually diminishing' (West, 1815, p. 9).[5] And distinguishing between the extensive and intensive margin 'the additional work bestowed upon the land must be expended either in bringing fresh land into cultivation, or in cultivating more highly that already in tillage' (1815, p. 9). The problem here is that the productive powers of labour in agriculture 'improve less rapidly than the productive powers of labour in manufacturing' (1815, p. 9). Increasing population pressure, argues West, causes an expansion in agricultural production to take place by both extending the area under cultivation and the application of more capital to land already under cultivation. The fertility of the land was not thought to be highly variable by West, however, so that the supply curve for corn would be smoothly rising, whereas Ricardo believed fertility to be variable suggesting a stepped curve. The more capital that can be applied to the land without incurring diminishing returns, West argued, the lower the rent would be. The major difference between West and Ricardo involves the movement of the relative share of rent, for Ricardo stated that this share would *ultimately* rise, whereas West believed it would fall. Brewer (1988, p. 505) determined that West went on to develop a dynamic equilibrium model of economic growth that was consistent with the so-called 'new view' of Ricardo that can also be found in Rooke. This led West, like Rooke, to argue the case for the repeal of the Corn Laws as the more immediate way to benefit the landlord.

While Smith, Malthus and now West clearly recognised the differential principle, the major honours in this area must go to Ricardo, whose *Essay on the Profits of Stock* represents not only a succinct restatement and correction of the rent principle developed by Malthus, but a sophisticated application of it to the determination of profits. In this way, the concept is invested with new meaning and purpose. In the *Essay*, Ricardo established the inverse relationship between wages and profits, a division of income which in the *Essay*, but *not* in the *Principles*, is dependent upon the notion of a no-rent margin (Smith, 1977, Vol. I, pp. 328–329). There are two immediate results from this analysis. First, competition of capital, recognised by Smith as the determinant of profits is rejected (West also rejected it in his *Essay* although in different terms) and, secondly, when the role of the money supply is incorporated in the analysis at a later date, Ricardo perceives that a change in wages no longer *necessarily* causes an equal change in prices.

Ricardo defines rent using the extensive and intensive margin in examples which do not need to be repeated here, but an indication of the application of the principle is in order 'by bringing successively land of a worst quality, or less favourably situated into cultivation (due say to the progress of population and/or wealth) rent would rise on the land previously cultivated, and in precisely the same degree (as wages would therefore rise) would profits fall; and if the smallness of profits do not check accumulation, there are hardly any limits to the rise of rent and fall of profits' (Sraffa & Dobb, 1951b, Vol. II, 14; also Vol. I, 1951a, pp. 412–413n).[6] Like Smith, Ricardo subdivides rent and the division of most importance to him relates to the 'portion paid for the use of the original power of the land', and not 'that portion (which) is evidently paid for the use of capital' (Sraffa & Dobb, 1951a, Vol. I, p. 18). Rooke's concern is precisely the reverse of Ricardo's on this matter. However, in the *Essay*, the size of the distributive share, to which this distinction refers, does not concern Ricardo.

In assessing the contribution of Rooke the above comments make it clear that the 1815 pamphlets should be divided into two leagues, with only Ricardo's in the premier division. Rooke's first published essay in the *Evans and Ruffy Farmer's Journal*, however, which appeared in July 1814, does recognise the differential principle. Examining the effect of a greater demand for labour from manufacturers on costs, Rooke notices that returns will fall on inferior land. Also, as manufacturers competitively bid up wages a large demand for agricultural commodities is created and this 'statement will be sufficient to explain the rise of rents of corn' concludes Rooke (1814). The interpretation of this statement involves an increasing demand for corn with a short-run fixed supply of agricultural land, thereby giving rise to increasing rents. Another essay, written in October 1814 and published the following January, makes it clear that Rooke recognises the no-rent margin, but unlike the account in Ricardo's *Essay* the import of this fact is not understood. Rather, Rooke uses the analysis to argue the case for free trade on the grounds that agricultural prices would be much higher and the benefits to the landlord likewise greater.

The essays led to the Seligman–Hollander (Hollander, 1911; Seligman, 1911) debate that appeared in the *Economic Journal* in September in response to Hollander (1910). Again the origin of rent is discussed in the context of free trade and for the first time the supply of corn is linked specifically to technological improvements in agriculture. Rooke's view is that wealth will be advanced if excess labour is removed from agriculture, where its marginal productivity is zero and applied to manufacturing. The second part of the essay establishes that the price of corn is determined by the conjunction of a limited supply of land and the size of the population, so that: '... the association of these two factors require that soil should be cultivated which we consider only capable of returning the expense of cultivation, the remuneration of capital and a small value given by way of acknowledgement to the landlord for rent – so that, however more productive (after deducting expense and return of capital) any soils (other) than the worst class which demand brings under tillage, so much more valuable are they, the same demand which causes the tillage of inferior soils, also gives encouragement to the more careful cultivation and improvement of all those which have been previously cultivated' (Rooke, March 1815).

The earlier part of the essay had already made it clear that the landlord received his rent from the tenant after the latter has defrayed his charges and taken his wages. He goes on to state that money wages determine the price of corn, 'the same way as it regulates the ultimate money price of every other article', thereby confounding the special status accorded to corn in Smithian analysis. The Corn Laws should not be permitted, therefore, to destabilise the wages of labour in such a way that the cultivation of corn is curtailed. Their repeal would benefit not only labourers and manufacturers, but also the landlords.

The whole argument is summarised towards the end of the essay where Rooke denies that rent determines the price of corn, rather rent, the intra-marginal surplus, is determined by the price of corn and is a 'gift of nature':

> My opinion is, that all land will be tilled which is capable of returning the expense of cultivation and the due remuneration of capital; if there is any overplus, it makes little difference whether it belongs to the state, or Corporate Body or an individual. Rent, or the private contract between landlord and tenant, has no more connection with the price of corn than the bargain between a wholesale and retail dealer, for it does not matter at what price the latter buys; he sells his article to the public for all he can get, whether profit or loss. Poor Rates are of the same description as the Public Revenue, and are nothing more than a part of the neat rental, or that overplus produce, after deducting the expenses of husbandry and return of the due value of the employment of capital, which may properly be compared to the gifts of nature. (Rooke, March 1815)

Rooke's claim to priority can now be assessed more carefully. It should be recorded that Rooke merely stated that he had been the first to publish the 'true' theory of rent, as well as the price of labour as the regulator of money and that the price of corn is determined at the margin of cultivation, in a letter to the Member of Parliament, E. D. Davenport. Davenport suggested that the letter should be published and went so far as to give it a title, while at the same time protesting that Rooke's work had been plagiarised. In the event, Rooke claimed nothing more than independent and prior discovery of the principle of rent, amongst other things.[7]

Certainly Rooke's early essays contain similar building blocks to those found, to a greater or lesser extent, in the works of Smith and Malthus as well as West. That is to say, rent is an intra-marginal surplus arising from increasing demand factors given a limited supply of non-homogeneous land, recognising both the extensive and intensive margin. Despite the remarkable achievements of Rooke, West, Malthus and Smith, it is Ricardo's exposition, irrespective of its shortcomings, which is the single highest achievement amongst the 1815 pamphlets. But of course actual priority in 'Britain' goes to Anderson, of whom all the others were ignorant and who first described rent as a price-determined surplus arising from diminishing returns, even if this was mainly in terms of the extensive margin.

Rooke's major book, *An Inquiry into the Principles of National Wealth* (1824) contains a more fully integrated statement of the theory of rent and he had undoubtedly read the pamphlet literature of 1815. It also includes a long analysis of the effect of agricultural improvements on its progress over time. He notes that when land is abundant no rent is paid for the use of it, but that when it is assigned to particular individuals rent arises and this encourages capital investment on the land. He regards rent as a residual payment, as does Smith, so that labour is paid first, second a 'return to cover the costs of circulating capital', specifically 'seed and horse provender', third, profit, 'the rate of profits of moveable stock employed in the cultivation of land is open to general competition, (it) … is the usual rate of the profits of stock not laid out under the advantages of any peculiar monopoly' and finally, a return to the landowner for fixed capital investment (Rooke, 1824, pp. 30–31).[8] The return to fixed capital is designated as part of rent on the grounds that it cannot be withdrawn from the land, 'capital, when once embodied in the soil, or attached to it in the shape of roads, drains, hedges etc., cannot be withdrawn from it in the same way as moveable capital' Rooke (1824, p. 31).

Taxes falling on rent are consequently detrimental to the further accumulation of fixed capital and he attacks the early socialist claims that labour is entitled to the whole produce of industry. Whether the landlord should invest is determined by marginal principles involving a comparison of the cost and subsequent return, with the latter being set against the 'ordinary profit of stock'. Hence a tax on marginal land would deter investment and if revenue falls below costs, cultivation could cease. Taxing the consumer is also condemned, on the grounds that wages would rise and consequently profits would fall below the ordinary level. Thus, unknowingly, Rooke has made an application of Ricardo's core theorem of the inverse relationship between wages and profits found in the 'new view' or equilibrium model (Hollander, 1979a, 1979b; O'Brien, 1981).

In his chapter 'On Rent', Rooke also introduces competing uses for land and thus opportunity cost and concludes that a certain value for rent must inevitably be included in the price, if it is not to revert to its alternative and therefore more profitable use. Hence Rooke has established that a minimum supply price determines whether a particular type of cultivation will be undertaken (Rooke, 1824, pp. 49, 57).

Smith is somewhat ambiguous about the progress of the rental share and it should be noted that some authors have detected a similar, but unconnected ambiguity, in Ricardo (Barkai, 1966). Theoretically the difficulty has been solved by Hicks, but it is also possible to resolve the issue by careful textual exegesis of Ricardo's *Essay, Principles* and *Notes on Malthus* (Hicks, 1932, 1939).[9] The conclusion is that Ricardo did believe the rental share would rise in the long run, although improvements in agricultural technology would slow down its progress. This brings the argument back to Rooke, because he also claimed that the rental share would rise, but specifically that this *would be caused by agricultural innovations*. Clearly, therefore, he had in mind the return to fixed capital and not that to any 'gift of nature'.

The fundamental similarity between Malthus and Ricardo on rent determination did not lead to agreement on the effect of improvements in the short run. Ricardo believed that improvements would lower rent and raise profits, at least in the short run (O'Brien, 1975). The displaced capital and labour is reabsorbed in manufacturing for Ricardo, but Malthus maintained that it remains in agriculture; not only this, but increasing population pressure would certainly not permit rents to fall. Indeed in the long run, Ricardo felt that both were in agreement, 'improvements in agriculture never lowered rents ... and may be expected to be in the future, the *main* source of the increase of rents' (Sraffa & Dobb, 1951b, Vol. II, pp. 186–187).[10] Nevertheless, Malthus felt he was able to go much further than this, so that technological change not only reduced costs, but also increased output, a position that fully accords with that of Rooke. However, Rooke and Ricardo are at one in regarding rent as a transfer payment, whereas Malthus saw it as a net addition to wealth. The only rationale for this is that Malthus neglected to separate pure rent from the return on fixed capital.[11]

For Rooke and Ricardo, rent is a major source of investible funds although it would appear from the accounts in the secondary literature that Ricardo's long-term pessimism from growing rent and wages, accompanied by falling profits and impending stationarity, is very much at odds with Rooke's optimism. However, this is a gross distortion of Ricardo's position, for he is at pains to show that the stationary state is a long way off on account of improvements in particular (Sraffa & Dobb, 1951d, Vol. VI, pp. 94–95). Indeed the rate of capital accumulation is fundamentally affected by both the introduction of machinery and free trade, primarily because of their effect on the price of wage goods.

Technical change in agriculture increases rents in Rooke's account, not the resort to inferior land of Ricardo's account, but this does not occasion any reduction in profits or real wages. The only check to this expansion comes from a stationary population that would lead to increasing real wages and following Smithian procedures a reduction in rents and not profits, as Ricardo maintained. On the other hand, any surplus population can be readily absorbed in manufacturing industry. He concludes, 'Mr. Ricardo's doctrine of rent appears erroneous, as rent does not advance in consequence of the employment of less productive labour, but in consequence of the employment of more productive labour' (Rooke, 1824, p. 64).

Progress beyond the medium term however is likely to be impeded by trade restrictions that threaten to hold up the spread of specialisation in production. Britain's comparative advantage lies in manufacturing according to Rooke, but this does not represent a threat to agriculture or agricultural interest groups, for both would benefit from increased demand for their products. Even if there is some highly desirable contraction in that sector, it can still be highly efficient and profitable.

While the class antagonism argument has been overplayed in Ricardian analysis, Rooke more than Ricardo and Malthus and certainly long before Senior (1836, p. 138) wrote on the subject, recognised that there is a natural harmony between the three major groups in society. That harmony was vitally dependent upon high investment in agriculture, free trade and a prosperous manufacturing sector, giving due regard to the welfare of labour. Like Ricardo, Rooke had no sympathy for the protectionist arguments that stem from Malthus' analysis of rent (Hollander, 1977, pp. 25–29, 44; 1997).

THE DETERMINATION OF PROFITS AND WAGES

The analysis of profits and wages are less contentious than that of rent. All of the classical economists recognise that profit is the return on capital, which is split into circulating capital (a wage fund) and fixed components. Profit is one of the three distributive shares and its analysis requires that attention is paid to three aspects: the origin of profit, why it is paid and, finally, its determination.

Smith argued that profit was entirely separate from the wages of management and that it consisted of interest and a premium for risk taking in about equal proportions. He believed that it was paid because it was an important adjunct to the division of labour, thereby raising the level of productivity, although he failed to notice that this was dependent on a fixed supply of such capital. The secondary literature suggests that the problem of productivity – the use of more roundabout methods of production – was not resolved until Senior wrote on the subject. However, there are grounds for believing that Smith himself put forward an argument in terms of time-consuming processes:

> In that rude state of society in which there is no division of labour,… it is not necessary that any stock should be accumulated or stored up beforehand, in order to carry on the business of the society…. But when the division, of labour has once been thoroughly introduced, the produce of a man's own labour can supply but a very small part of his occasional wants. The far greater part of them are supplied by the produce of other men's labour … (these cannot be purchased) till such time as the produce of his own labour has not only been completed, but sold. A stock of goods of different kinds, therefore, must be stored up somewhere sufficient to maintain him, and to supply him with the materials and tools of his work, till such time, at least, as both these events can be brought about. (Smith, 1977, Vol. II, p. 1)

Both circulating and fixed capital are required in this process.

So much for the demand for capital. Turning to supply, there is a great deal of confusion in the classical period generally, that can only be resolved in terms of an abstinence explanation. This category, discussed above, includes a return to uncertainty and a surplus above this to accommodate risk, meaning a return to entrepreneurship and an interest payment. The net return must therefore be equated with the rate of interest, which Hollander has called 'the minimum supply price of loanable funds' (Hollander, 1973a, 1973b, p. 168). The fact that the accumulation of capital is not wholly dependent upon a particular rate of interest does imply, however, that Smith is unaware of the notion of abstinence.

It is the competition of capital which determines the rate of profit for Smith, a position that Ricardo subsequently rejected. In particular, Ricardo showed that an increase in wages cannot but affect the capitalist howsoever the increase may be caused. That is to say, an increase in wages, without an increase in the money supply, given the 'average' capital/labour ratio, will not be compensated for by an increase in prices. For Smith, rising wages do not necessarily lead to falling profits rather 'the increase of stock which raises wages tends to lower profit. When the stocks of many rich merchants are turned into the same trade, their mutual competition naturally tends to lower profit, and when there is a like increase of stock in all the different trades carried on in the same society, the same competition must produce the same effect on them all' (Smith, 1977, Vol. II, p. 8). This conception is later extended to take account not only of the quantity of stock, but also of the opportunities for investment (Smith, 1977, Vol. II). In this regard, the development of new products and the exploration of new markets are both to be encouraged. When these opportunities are exhausted, wages are at subsistence and net investment is zero.

Ricardo's position has already been alluded to and the determination of profit represents the very core of his analysis. After an initial period of uniformity with Smith's position, a radical departure occurs. Wages are competitively determined by the demand and supply for labour and may, for extensive periods, remain above subsistence. Leaving aside improvements and free trade, falling productivity in agriculture, rising food prices and consequently rising money wages lead to a reduction in profits. Contrary to accounts in the secondary literature, wage goods are also of the manufactured variety, so that a comprehensive summary of Ricardo's major thesis can be identified:

> I have been endeavouring to get you to admit that the profits on stock employed in Manufactures and commerce are seldom permanently lowered or raised by any other cause than by the cheapness or dearness of necessaries, or of those objects on which the wages of labour are expended. Accumulation of capital has a tendency to lower profits. Why? Because every accumulation is attended with increased difficulty in obtaining

> food, unless it is accompanied with improvements in agriculture; in which case it has no tendency to diminish profits.... I admit at the same time that commerce, or machinery, may produce an abundance and cheapness of commodities, and if they affect the prices of those commodities on which the wages of labour are expended they will so far raise profits: but then it will be true that less capital will be employed on the land, for the wages paid for labour form a part of that capital. (Sraffa & Dobb, 1951c, Vol. IV, p. 162)

This account of profit determination is to be found in the *Essay on Profits* and the *Principles* and is not in any way modified by, or dependent upon, a particular measure of value or capital/labour ratio.

Finally, it is maintained by Sraffa (1951c) in particular, that agricultural profits determine the general profit rate, giving authority to the view that the corn model epitomises Ricardo's economics (Eatwell, 1975). However, even as early as the *Essay on Profits*, the *two-way* influences on the determination of profit, as between agriculture and manufacturing, is made abundantly clear: 'in this state of society, when the profits on agricultural stock, by the supposition, are fifty per cent, the profits on all other capital, employed either in the rude manufactures ... or in foreign commerce ... will be also, fifty per cent. If the profits on capital employed in trade were more than fifty per cent, capital would be withdrawn from the land to be employed in trade. If they were less, capital would be taken from trade to agriculture' (Sraffa & Dobb, 1951c, Vol. IV, p. 12).

The greater part of Rooke's discussion of profit is to be found in his *Inquiry* (1824) so that the work of Smith and Ricardo was available before its publication, even if most of it had been composed before 1817. In the event, Rooke's treatment is not very inspiring, although there are flashes of insight. It should be noted though that he was more concerned with investment opportunities and the creation of profit and higher income levels rather than a detailed and theoretical assessment of the individual component parts of costs of production.

Rooke went to great lengths to distinguish fixed and circulating capital in his discussion of rent and that it was the return to fixed capital that engaged his attention. Capital is employed, as with Smith, to augment the powers of labour, 'when a capital stock has been laid up and the cultivation of the soil commenced, it is obvious that the purely natural relations of man are materially changed, and that a new source of income has been opened, namely, a reward is offered for labour laid by for future use, independent of its immediate value' (Rooke, 1824, p. 14). Capital is described as 'stored up labour' and the application of both fixed and circulating capital is necessary, for example, to the most conducive cultivation of the land. The amount of capital available for investment depends upon the prosperity of the society, 'the chief utility of capital is that it renders the immediate powers of each individual labourer more productive' (1824, p. 30). The order of the division of produce was rent first, followed by circulating capital and wages and, finally, the return to fixed capital as a residual. Given that there is a natural rate of profit, further investment of either kind is dependent upon the marginal return being greater than normal profits, 'as a general principle the application of fixed (and circulating) capital to the cultivation of land is limited by the last additional portion of it, which returns no more than the ordinary profits of stock, and the other expenses incurred by cultivation. Should a tax be levied upon that last additional portion ... the capital cannot be advanced which might have been called into operation' (1824, pp. 33–34). The outlay on new capital is therefore dependent upon a strong demand for the products of the industry concerned and in the case of land, benevolent landlords who give their tenants every incentive to invest in land.

Rooke deserves credit for distinguishing between interest and profits on capital. The return to fixed capital on the land, which is in the nature of a monopoly, is equivalent to the annual savings of labour. However, there is no monopoly in the production of most implements of circulating capital, the prices of which are dependent upon the market forces of supply and demand. The exchangeable value of a machine will not be the labour saved therefore, but the cost of its production. Whereas the return to fixed capital can vary widely, the return to circulating capital is influenced by supply and demand, but profit must, of course in some instances, take account of depreciation and risk. The return to the capital is profit and thus should be equated with the interest on money loans, determined by the demand and supply of loanable funds, in order to judge the worth of investment opportunities.

As with Smith, therefore, the level of profit is determined by the competition of capital: 'the several heads of cost, which enter into the component parts of manufactures, being almost wholly made up of the profits of capital and the wages of labour, and which are open to free competition, their exchangeable value naturally falls in proportion as more ready modes of obtaining them are discovered; and, in this way, their exchangeable value chiefly resolves itself into the common rate of the profits of capital and wages of labour' (1824, p. 84). Even though profits will fall with a greater supply of capital Rooke, again like Smith, believes that this will not inhibit further investment:

> it would then appear that the whole community is benefitted by the accumulation of capital and the fall of profits. The landowner gains by a rise of rent in consequence of

> being able to obtain cheaper capital to improve the soil; the active employer of capital gains by doing more business; the money lender has an advantage in augmented customers and a greater amount of loans; and the consumer is benefitted by being able to purchase at a cheaper rate. (1824, p. 40)

Eventually though increasing population reduces wages so that labour suffers, unless further rapid capital accumulation 'sets free new stores of production and thereby constantly cheapens the means of living' (1824, p. 40).

Rooke was optimistic that this would in fact be the case and, further, that the introduction of machinery, which sets labour free, would by the same means ensure its speedy re-employment avoiding unemployment. It ought to be recognised that Rooke's statement on supply and demand factors was really rather sophisticated and Austrian, because he had earlier noted that the use of capital meant that roundabout methods of production could be used (1824, p. 15; see Böhm-Bawerk, 1959). Also, that the expenditure of capital, stimulated by the final demand for the products, required in the first instance abstinence from present consumption, so that the supply of capital is limited – (it is also limited by the rate of interest on loanable funds and the level of taxation on capital itself). Rooke is therefore clearly stating the abstinence theory of profits in all respects before Senior. The level of savings was dependent upon the distribution of wealth which, Rooke argued, should be as equitable as possible, thereby noting one of Mill's amendments to Senior's exposition (Senior, 1836, p. 140). Thus, Ricardo's core theorem is not part of Rooke's mainstream analysis of profits.

As with the theory of profits, all of the elements of Rooke's theory of wages were to be found in Smith, but strictly speaking only two variants were sustained during most of the classical period; one a short-run theory based upon supply and demand (or the wage–fund), the other, long run and based on subsistence.

Smith's reference to working capital implies that a wages fund lies behind the demand for labour and therefore the growth of population. (Precisely how fixed and circulating capital was apportioned from total capital stock is not provided by Smith.) Market pressures will then ensure that a competitive wage is established – continuously expanding capital stock leads to a continually increasing wage rate. The wage rate is also influenced by consumption of the final product, although this analysis would not appear to have re-emerged during the classical period (Smith, 1977, Vol. I, pp. viii, 76). On the supply side of the equation, the population mechanism is the major factor and this is determined by infant mortality – the level of population follows with a lag from the demand for labour.

However, Smith did not really work out in a precise way either the demand or supply functions for labour – indeed only McCulloch really got to grips with this latter conception (O'Brien, 1970, pp. 360–366).

The view that Ricardo regarded wages as ultimately fixed at subsistence cannot be sustained, because he argued that for considerable periods of time, particularly during rapid capital growth and hence an expanding demand for labour, wages would be above the minimum (subsistence). Thus population will not automatically increase if there is a change in real wages. A representative example will suffice as evidence of Ricardo's position, 'notwithstanding the *tendency* of wages to conform to their natural rate, their market rate may, in an improving society, *for an indefinite period*, be constantly above it; for no sooner may the impulse, which an increased capital gives to a new demand for labour be obeyed, than another increase of capital may produce the same effect' (Sraffa & Dobb, 1951a, Vol. I, pp. 94–95; Caravale & Tosata, 2003). Finally, there is no evidence that Ricardo used a rigid wage fund to determine the demand for labour, when he extends Smith's view of the influence of final consumption on the demand for labour, which has implications for the capital/labour ratio. Wages also exert an independent influence on prices and impact on resource allocation, indicating a mutual interdependence between pricing and distribution, entirely consistent with general equilibrium procedures.

Rooke's discussion of wages does not represent an integrated explanation of their determination, mainly because he is more concerned with wages as a potential measure of value. The level of wages is determined by the demand and supply for labour and the supply is assumed to be fixed in the short run, so that the amount of fixed and circulating capital, together with the consumption of the final product, determines the demand function:

> Labour exerts its powers in proportion to its efficient demand, and capital accumulates accordingly, accompanied by a progressive development of knowledge and skill. The demand for labour arises from two distinct sources: first, from a natural desire to consume the necessaries and comforts of life; and, secondly, from an inclination to gratify a number of feelings and moral notions that arise out of acquired habits, and which prompt us to consume a number of marketable articles.... Consumption, in the two ways just stated, is therefore the cause of the formation of new income; and the new income, on being acquired, goes to supply additional funds, which may be either laid out in more extensive consumption, in the formation of new capital, or in the repair of that which had been previously realised. Consumption and production would therefore appear to excite each other reciprocally and to form the chief cause of their mutual advancement. (Rooke, 1824, pp. 104–105)

Although Rooke notes a tendency for population to expand towards new and higher levels of subsistence, he is ultimately optimistic about the prospects for capital expansion that would maintain real wages at a high level, 'the wages of labour (are) the highest where the powers of production are the greatest and population in excess' (Rooke, 1824, p. 179). The 'corn value' of money wages in Cumberland was stable in fact for long periods so that Rooke rejected Ricardo's pessimism (Rooke, 1835, p. 182).[12] The movement of the precious metals serves to bring prices and subsequently wages into line, via the mechanism of unrestricted trade *in the long run*.[13] Nevertheless, as with Ricardo, Rooke demonstrates that there is a sufficient interval during which labour is available to contribute substantially to the level of savings, particularly those without family responsibilities who collectively might contribute up to ten percentage points of the total level of income in the economy for capital investment (Rooke, 1824, pp. 88–89).

The greatest factor influencing wages apart from demand and supply is the variation in the value of money. What might be described as the 'natural level' of wages, balancing out supply and demand factors, was, Rooke argued, determined in the export sector of the economy. He analyses this as follows, 'it is the wages of labour expended in the production of those commodities that are sold abroad and bring in the precious metals with which every country is supplied ... which regulate the *money* wages of labour at home and as a matter of course, the natural value of productions along with it and the exchangeable value of money also' (1824, p. 81; italics added). It was therefore the relationship between gold flows and *money* wages that was important and while the money wage of agricultural labour was sticky, money wages in the export sector were more sensitive, making them a better and certainly a more immediate index of the value of money. The influence of the money supply would *eventually* be the same on all wages contracts. It was simply that until the demand for commodities increased (as a result of the augmented money supply working its way through the entire economy) its impact would not be felt equally in all sectors. This analysis confirms that the wages of labour were under the direct influence of the price of the final product, but it was not until the demand for export labour had risen that wages rose elsewhere. There was always, in fact, an inequality between export and agricultural wages.

Rooke's analysis is essentially a combination of Smithian wage fund elements reinforced by an assessment of the role of final consumer demand, but less fully worked out in comparison with Ricardo's own schema. Not being a fully integrated account therefore, it is not surprising that the shortfalls of the wage fund theory, in particular, escaped Rooke's attention.

VALUE AND THE MEASURE OF VALUE

If the accounts of value theory attributed to Smith and Ricardo in the secondary literature were accepted without reservation, then Rooke would join that small band of minor economists who developed value theory in terms of a supply and demand apparatus. However, the secondary literature has once again been rather dogmatic and oversimplistic in its approach.[14]

First, Smith has a rudimentary application of demand and supply analysis in his *Lectures* that is considerably refined in the *Wealth of Nations*. The chapter 'Of Natural and Market Price of Commodities' examines this relationship and gives some consideration to the elasticity of demand and supply (Smith, 1977, Vol. I, pp. 73–74). The notion of a negatively sloped demand curve is also to be found in Malthus' pamphlet, *An Investigation of the Causes of the Present High Price of Provisions* (1800), although the supply curve is assumed to be price inelastic. Malthus' account has been the subject of criticism, however, on the basis of his subsequent (unsatisfactory) treatment of demand in his *Principles of Political Economy* (Malthus, 1836, pp. 63–67; Hollander, 1997). Lauderdale, who published his *Inquiry Into the Nature and Origin of Public Wealth* in 1804, also examined the demand curve and showed it to be negatively sloped, distinguishing between a change in demand and a change in quantity demanded (Lauderdale, 1804, pp. 65–66). His notion of elasticity derives from a consideration of consumer tastes, habits and preferences and also commodity substitution, which is clearly an advance on Malthus' simple treatment in terms of income alone. However, Malthus was able to achieve the integration of cost of production with supply, which, when further integrated with demand, represents a considerable advance over Lauderdale's exposition.

Perhaps the most surprising finding, however, is that Ricardo also had a highly sophisticated value theory in terms of demand and supply, which extended beyond the short period, as part of his general equilibrium model. For example:

> Does not (corn) ... vary, on the one hand, from improvements in agriculture (supply), from improved machinery (supply) and implements used in husbandry, as well as from the discovery of new tracts of fertile land, which in other countries may be taken into cultivation, and which will affect the value of corn in every market where importation is free? Is it not on the other hand subject to be enhanced in value from prohibitions of importation (supply) from increasing population and wealth (demand), and the greater difficulties of obtaining the increased supplies, on account of the additional quantity of labour which the cultivation of inferior lands requires? Is not the value of labour equally variable; being not only affected, *as all other things are, by the proportion between the supply and demand,* which uniformly varies with every change in the condition of the

community, but also by the varying price of food and other necessaries, on which the wages of labour are expended? (Sraffa & Dobb, 1951a, Vol. I, p. 15)[15]

Examples of the appropriate market-clearing process are given in these terms in the case of both the corn market and the labour market. In the case of the goods market the point is also made that demand determines the level of supply, which does not, of course, conflict with Say's Law of markets, provided hoarding is ruled out (Sraffa & Dobb, 1951a, Vol. I, pp. 405–406). Ricardo goes beyond this sort of anaemic statement, however, and tackles the elasticity of both functions in remarkable terms. Ricardo's negative statements on supply and demand should therefore be interpreted as an attack on the 'proportions approach' that leaves out of consideration costs and elasticity (Smith, 1951, 1956).

Rooke's work contains an early and not totally inadequate statement of demand and supply analysis, albeit rather brief – once again it is not central to his procedures. Value is distinguished under three headings in the following terms: '(1) the natural value, which agrees with the cost of production; (2) the market value, which is regulated by the immediate supply of and demand for any commodity; (3) the market price of commodities, which is inclined to fluctuate, according to the fluctuating value of the money, or universal pledges which represent them' (Rooke, 1822, p. 18).[16] Market price is therefore determined by three distinct principles all of which operate at the same time and maintain a continuous action and reaction upon one another. His analysis then proceeds on two levels providing an interesting treatment of the perennial price dichotomy in classical economics. The first is concerned with the determination of price through the mechanism of supply and demand and the second involves a detailed discussion of the destabilising effect of changes in the quantity of money. This is followed by precise plans for regulating the value of money with the intention of stabilising the long-run price level that has excited some favourable debate on Rooke's position in the secondary literature recently.

There is very little detailed discussion of supply and demand relations and the first account is contained in a letter to the *Evans and Ruffy Farmer's Journal*, published in July 1816: 'supply and demand regulates ultimately the price of commodities. If an increased supply of any article be brought to market, without a corresponding demand, the price of such article will fall; if the demand increase, without an increase in supply, the price will rise', and he follows this by saying that 'the prices of all articles are determined by three separate causes – ultimate value, supply and demand and speculation. Ultimate value is that proportion of money prices which would eventually be the cost of all commodities, should the two last cease to operate; the united influence of all the three produce the present money price or value. (As speculation is so intimately connected with supply and demand, I shall not in future call it in question)' (Rooke, July 1816). Changes in value are due therefore to temporary or incidental changes in supply or demand. And demand is emphasised by Rooke as the root cause of value and the governing factor behind it was necessity and the 'estimation' in which the good is held, 'estimation' being very similar to Malthus' concept of intensity of demand (Rooke, 1824, p. 72). The analysis becomes very Keynesian at this point, for demand is considered to determine supply, which accords where the new view of Ricardo with demand itself being regulated by the cost at which the commodity can be brought to market (1824, p. 71).

While Lauderdale may have conceived of the supply and demand explanation for value before Rooke and analysed it quite comprehensively, Rooke did achieve the integration of cost of production and supply *before* Malthus developed his synthesis. Lauderdale, of course, failed to do this and it is only when supply-cost is examined that the definition of 'natural price' (to use Malthus' term) and its dependence upon supply and demand can be achieved. Rooke proceeds in a remarkable statement – noted by Seligman (1903, p. 512) – to develop the concept of marginal cost, a concept he employed consistently throughout the *Inquiry*: 'it is a *general rule* in the production of every marketable article that the last additional portion, added to the whole supply, will do no more than repay the cost of labour and remuneration of the capital employed in its production. In case any commodity allows more than this, the supply will naturally increase; and if the market value does not, upon an average, allow these two component parts of cost, the supply will diminish'. Furthermore, 'it is this universal and active principle, diffusing and extending itself in every direction, which regulates the relations and proportions of political economy. Necessity marks out the natural bound of value, and consumption and production are universally accommodating themselves to this first law, constantly regulated by the last additional portion of production, in reference to demand' (Rooke, 1824, p. 26).[17] Hence, while production is obviously dependent upon an adequate demand, Rooke only failed to arrive at an integrated theory of value because his account lacked a fully worked-out demand schedule: although he comes equally as close as Malthus in formulating demand, when he considers how income regulates the 'intensity' of demand. He does however investigate the long-run supply curve in manufacturing, showing it to exhibit increasing returns to scale (1824, pp. 84, 230). Value is therefore a combination of 'demand factors' and cost of production at the margin; the latter being a wider application of the margin in agriculture, an application Ricardo achieved, but did not generalise (Sraffa & Dobb, 1951a, Vol. I, p. 73). In the final assessment, Rooke's analysis compares favourably with that of Smith, but his purpose is entirely different from that of Ricardo and much more neoclassical.

In his *Remarks on the Nature and Operation of Money*, Rooke repudiates cost of production as the determinant of exchangeable value, in this case the exchange value of the precious metals, arguing that exchangeable value determines the cost of production. Now although Rooke does not make use of this analysis in his *Inquiry* and therefore the full import of it was clearly not evident to him, the idea was taken up much later by Jevons (Blaug, 1985, pp. 324–325).[18] Rooke's argument was that the present value of any good depends on the quantity already in the market, a valuation which is disturbed by the level of credit. Hence in his example, the present market value of gold would determine its present cost of production, so that large quantities of credit or bank paper would affect the cost of production of gold by raising its present exchangeable value (Rooke, 1819a, p. 16; see also Marshall, 1887).

The second and major strand of Rooke's value analysis recognises the influence of the money supply on prices. Like many economists writing at the time of the return to convertibility, he was concerned that the value of gold should not fluctuate too widely because of its detrimental effects, particularly on stock holders. This concern also influenced his analysis of the national debt considered below.

His first published pamphlet, *Remarks on the Nature and Operation of Money*, contains an argument in favour of the regular depreciation of gold as a stimulant to trade and industry, which undeservedly earned him a 'crank inflationist' label in some of the secondary literature (Fetter, 1965, p. 210). But he subsequently recanted this view in *Supplement to the Remarks etc*., published in the same year, arguing for a convertible paper currency with gold circulating for denominations of less than one pound sterling. It is his intention to establish a circulating medium such that the fluctuations in market prices can be more accurately determined, 'the true standard of value requires that time contracts be fulfilled in a money unit which purchases equal quantities of commodities, given that the latter is subject to the pressures of supply and demand' (Rooke, 1824, p. 20).

The issue which Rooke analyses here is equivalent to the index number problem identified in the early twentieth century.[19] Fisher (1920) recorded that the United States only started to produce index numbers in 1890 and consequently was unable to improve the quality of the monetary unit. In his own plan, Fisher dedicated his book, *Stabilising the Dollar* to John Rooke, Simon Newcomb and Alfred Wallace, noting in an appendix that Rooke's proposal was 'substantially like that proposed in this book' (Fisher, 1920, p. 293, quoted in Patinkin, 1993).[20] Rooke, like Scrope (1833a, 1833b) after him,[21] devised a 'tabular standard' based not on a basket of commodities, because these are too variable and subject to non-monetary influences, but rather an index of wage rates so that the price level moves inversely with the marginal product of labour.[22]

The disadvantage of Rooke's method is that if employment is procyclical then nominal GDP targeting would also be procyclical. And yet 'under a wage targeting scheme, the monetary authority would allow the price level to increase enough so that wage bargaining units would negotiate new wage contracts at the (constant) aggregate nominal wage target. By targeting nominal wages, Rooke's plan would minimise the adjustment costs of moving the aggregate nominal wage rate to a new equilibrium value. By allowing the price level to fluctuate, real wages would be able to adjust smoothly to macroeconomic disturbances, even if nominal wages were sticky' (Sumner, 1991, p. 756). Even if the central bank maintained wage stability, short-term wage stickiness accompanied by deflation could lead to unemployment. This could be mitigated, in analysis 'surprisingly sophisticated for its time', by a 'monetary policy that precludes the need for such adjustments. In [Rooke's] view, the (presumably more flexible) price level would act as a shock absorber to accommodate required changes in the aggregate real wage rate. The nominal wages paid by individual firms would still be allowed to fluctuate according to local conditions' (Sumner, 1995, p. 206).[23] Before examining Rooke's plan the views of Smith and Ricardo on the measure of value are briefly examined.

Smith makes the labour commanded by a commodity his index on the basis of individual welfare being dependent upon his command of goods and services, 'The value of any commodity … to the person who possesses it and who means not to use or consume it himself, but to exchange it for other commodities, is equal to the quantity of labour which it enables him to *purchase or command.* Labour, therefore, is the real measure of the exchangeable value of all commodities' (Smith, 1977, Vol. I, p. v). Even in a complex economy with factors other than labour in play, Smith consistently applies this standard, recognising that labour, in particular, has to be reduced to common units of disutility.[24]

Now Ricardo rejected Smith's measure on the grounds that wages vary so that the measure itself is unstable. Nevertheless, he also wanted a reliable measure to determine the relative value of commodities. The problem labour embodied, for example, arose from the fact that no commodity always required the same labour input. Not only this, if wages changed, the price of the commodity would change depending upon the capital/labour ratio, the durability of capital and the period of production. However, Ricardo was prepared to overlook these problems as being of no great matter and to settle on constant quantities of labour *embodied* as the best measure available. Subsequently, he extended this to include an average capital/labour ratio as an additional requirement. On the basis of these two requirements, gold was chosen as the measure with one caveat, 'it was never contended that gold under the present circumstances was a good measure of value, it was only hypothetically, and for the purpose of illustrating a principle, supposed that all known causes of variability of gold were removed ... (so that) *we* may speak about the variations of other things in an unvarying measure without confusion' (Sraffa & Dobb, 1951a, Vol. I, p. 83). Ricardo's measure is therefore confirmed as a purely theoretical construction.

Unlike Thomas Attwood, with whom Rooke had an exchange in the *Farmer's Journal* and for whom he obviously had a great deal of respect, Rooke favoured the continued use of Bank of England notes rather than any other sort of national paper. Having admitted that, though, he saw the need to restore the value of money to what it was when the debts of Britain were contracted and that this could be achieved by manipulation of the convertibility of Bank of England notes into the precious metals (Rooke, 1819b, pp. 81–82). (In this way fluctuations in the value of both gold and silver would be confined to the demand and supply for the metals themselves.) The problem was therefore to define the rate of convertibility to maintain a predetermined level of prices.[25] To achieve this objective, the rise or fall in the value of the circulating pound sterling could be estimated in one of three ways: first by the price of farm labour, secondly the comparative relation between the wages of farm labour and export labour or thirdly the quantity of the circulating medium (1819b, p. 88).[26] Now the quantity of the circulating medium was in a quantity theory sense the prime factor in this part of his theory and the wages of farm labour and export labour are the indices by which to judge the change in the value of money. Of the two though, the wages of export labour were considered to be more sensitive to demand factors; in his *Remarks* Rooke explains that the export of manufacture brings a supply of the precious metals to the country and that this is instrumental in determining the wages of export labour and, with a time lag, agricultural labour. There is a clear link between wages in the agricultural and export sectors, although the latter always seems to move ahead of the former, with both exhibiting elements of downward rigidity (Rooke, 1819a, p. 8).

Rooke was very well aware of the fact that an invariable standard of value was not possible and he clearly rejected Ricardo's synthetic gold. Labour embodied or commanded were both rejected in favour of the price of farm labour, which he designated a 'natural standard of value', meaning the 'provisions capable of maintaining any given number of inhabitants' (Rooke, 1819b, p. 11). Likewise, the corn measure to be found in Smith's work was dismissed mainly because of the variability of the supply of provisions in general while farm labour on the other hand, 'is continually equalising itself with the natural intensity of cultivation, the wants of population and the expected demand and supply of the soil' (Rooke, 1824, p. 40). It therefore follows that, 'whenever the average price of farm labour has a natural tendency to either rise or fall, it may be concluded that the value of money has risen or fallen with the price of that sort of industry; because the same quantity of money will not set to work the same number of labourers' (1824, p. 216). After making this statement, Rooke refers again to the problem of the rigidity of wages in agriculture and he switches to the price of export labour as a more satisfactory index to operate as a check on the price of farm labour. (Precisely how export and agricultural wages adjust one with the other is not specified by Rooke, but competitive integrated labour markets are implied.) He produced data to show that wages had been stable in the agricultural sector whereas those of cotton weavers were 'extremely variable' (Rooke, 1835, p. 182, quoted in Grampp, 1956, p. 931).

The method of control was then quite simple. If the price of farm labour should rise, it is occasioned by the circulation of too much money, the supply of which should be reduced, although he does not quantify the extent of the reduction required to cause a finite reduction in the price of labour. To give more evenness to the results, however, a 10 per cent variation in the price of labour should be struck off. Next, if the wages of farm labour fell, but those of export labour were found to be higher, the fall in farm wages would be considered as temporary and ignored. Rooke in fact adopted 14 shillings a week as the 'standard' of agricultural wages, which he calculated by averaging the price of labour over the country during the years 1805–1815, a period when the currency was considered to be 'more perfectly regulated' (Rooke, 1824, p. 218). He further suggests the use of weaver's earnings as a surrogate for export wages. In summary, therefore, 'the regulation of the new system is, that in whatever proportion the general and annual price of farm throughout the kingdom, has a tendency to rise and fall, that rise or fall shall be countered by a reverse rise or fall in the current price of gold and silver' (1824, p. 221). This would leave gold coin, which should be withdrawn from circulation as 'the grand corrector of the value of bank paper' (1824, p. 222).

Besides regulation of the money supply in the way described, the price of gold and silver would be adjusted according to fluctuations in the value of farm labour. The following plan was recommended for immediate implementation, 'repeal of the Corn Laws the coining of gold into one ounce and half ounce pieces; and of silver into half ounce and quarter ounce pieces, in order to expedite the exchange of notes for gold. Silver to be legal tender for all sums below 20 shillings at the current prices fixed by government; free import and export of the precious metals; free import and export of the precious metals; country bank notes to be made payable at fourteen days' notice' (Rooke, 1819b, pp. 91–95).

Rooke is therefore no crude inflationist and his plan, given the predominance of agriculture in the British economy, does have some merit from a practical point of view (Corry, 1966).[27] The nuances of Ricardo's procedures are clearly not part of Rooke's concern; rather, his analysis is in the tradition of British index number formulations and highly regarded by Fisher (1911, 1922).

ROOKE AND THE REPEAL OF THE CORN LAWS

Rooke's appraisal of the Corn Law issue is closely linked with his analysis of the variable value of money and the appropriate remedial measures that government should implement to stabilise it. Indeed, a stable monetary standard is only possible, in Rooke's opinion, after genuinely free trade has operated for a number of years, 'the present (early eighteen twenties) is not, indeed, the most suitable moment for instituting a well regulated currency, since the various rates of prices may be expected to be more equally adjusted, after we have experienced a few years of free trade' (Rooke, 1824, p. 333).[28]

Free trade, particularly in corn, was advocated in Rooke's earliest writings, before Ricardo ventured into print and long before such views became fashionable on five grounds: first to promote faster population growth; secondly to encourage the reciprocal lowering of trade barriers; thirdly to further the division of labour and remove the check to the growth of national wealth; fourthly to establish the free circulation of the precious metals and stabilise prices making real wages more stable and finally fifthly to lower the growth of the rental share (clearly a reference to the 'neat' and not the fixed capital component). Emphasis is also placed upon an extension of Smith's vent for surplus argument as an adjunct to the third point above:

> Here then, is the chief cause why we must reverse the whole order of political economy, and occasion that market for labour which foreign and domestic commerce never fails to create; and in proportion as we shall, by such means, be able to find a more extensive market for labour, the efficiency of our farm labourers at home is augmented, the productive processes of cultivation of the soil are set free, and the whole combination of events requisite to public wealth is maturely formed. But how is this to be accomplished? By Corn Laws? No. Corn laws are inimical to commerce; and whatever restrains or destroys commerce restrains or annihilates the progressive influence of that scheme upon which national wealth depends. (1824, p. 341)

Rooke proceeds to make the case in rather more analytical terms utilising the theory of absolute advantage worked out earlier by Smith, so that ultimately unobstructed 'free trade accommodates all the natural relations of industry, harmonises the universal interests of society and extends the bounds of human happiness, so far as wealth is concerned' (1824, pp. 349–350; 1828, pp. 19–21). Manufacturer's profits are raised generally by productive and free trade, since they will benefit from larger markets. It is also in the interest of landlords to accept free trade since contrary to their beliefs this would raise, and not lower, the price of corn. (This occurs directly through the greater flow of precious metals into the country, but also indirectly via an expanded manufacturing sector which raises the domestic demand for subsistence goods.) The free export of capital is shown to have similar effects (Rooke, 1824, pp. 367–372).

Rooke's publishing fortunes took a dramatic turn when he published anonymously his *Free Trade in Corn: The Real Interest of the Landlord* in 1828 that gave the author as 'A Cumberland Landowner'.[29] The contents were proclaimed in Parliament by Colonel G. P. Thompson as affording 'opinions and sentiments, expressed in much better language and in a much more forcible manner' than his own (Hansard, 1834, pp. 294–295). In opposing Huskisson's views on the matter of the Corn Laws, Thompson (1834, p. 296) found this pamphleteer 'an able authority' when he required 'an answer to Mr. Huskisson' and he quoted from it quite generously during the course of his speech; he was, like many others, of course, under the misapprehension that Sir James Graham, also a Cumberland landowner, was the author (Lonsdale, 1868, p. 241).[30]

In this pamphlet, Rooke developed his earlier arguments on free trade in the *Inquiry* and various letters to the *Farmer's Journal.* The first section gives a detailed history of the Corn Laws and notes that when imports had been the freest, the price of corn had been relatively higher; 'had Lord Lauderdale's political economy not been exceedingly elusive, he must have perceived that a free trade in foreign corn is *advantageous to the whole British Community,* since every class of capitalists increased in opulence between the year 1765 and the year 1819, beyond any other period in our history' (Rooke, 1828, p. 7). In particular, if Lauderdale had correctly analysed the causal connection between the monetary standard and price instability, linked this to the incentive for a greater accumulation of capital from free trade, then the course of government legislation might have been entirely different. That is to say, the price of corn should not be perceived as determined by supply and demand alone because money represents a complication that undermines this 'real' relationship. In his explanation of the determination of corn prices, in fact, Rooke has clearly broken away from Smithian procedures, for the special place accorded to silver by Smith is not to be found here:

> The medium price of corn, in a series of years, seems to be regulated by principles very different from the opinions which have been commonly received as true. If corn be at any time unusually plentiful or scarce, in proportion to the natural demand for it (and its supply appears to be almost constantly in this predicament), the market price will either rise in the one case, or fall in the other, above or below the cost of its production. Every one possessing a common degree of observation perceives a commercial rule so obvious, and so continually in operation before him. (Rooke, 1828, pp. 9–10)

High and low prices, generally, are therefore indicative of the state of the money supply, and the productiveness of the (gold) mines should be viewed as part of the supply side of the price of corn equation. Given the state of the currency, Rooke proceeds to construct a number of tables to show the progress of British industry, the price of wheat and also the balance of trade, so that he is able to demonstrate conclusively that, in all respects, restricted trade has been detrimental to all interests:

> On casting the eye over the periods of time, in which England exported corn regularly, and when there was a constant excess of imports above exports, an obvious difference is observable in three respects. First, whether viewed in parts or collectively, the prices of wheat were uniformly lower during an excess of exports than when there was an excess of imports. Secondly, the disparity of the prices of wheat, between England and Dantzic, was uniformly greater in the export period, when its price was low, than during the period of importation, when its price was high. Thirdly, as the means of British industry entering into successful competition with foreigners would seem to depend materially on the price of corn in the home market being brought as nearly as possible to an equality with its price abroad, so a high price of corn has been exceedingly more favourable to British competition than a low price has ever been. The data, on which these important

> considerations rest, are so fully established ... that it is hoped no doubt can be entertained concerning the correctness of the inferences drawn therefrom. (Rooke, 1828, p. 36)

Foreign commerce, he continued, regulates the circulation of the currency so that this process is interrupted by impediments to trade: 'the true way to keep up a permanently high amount of currency and thereby to support high prices, is freely to buy foreign corn; and thereby to raise its price abroad, so as to increase the circulating medium there, and to prevent the gradual drain upon the currency at home, now in slow and certain progress' (1828, p. 59). Rooke believed that the dramatic fall in prices after 1819 was the result of the operation of Peel's Act and the subsequent accumulation of gold by the Bank of England that withdrew the precious metals and banknotes. The periodic fluctuations in prices both before and after 1819 were therefore due to the derangement of the currency and foreign exchanges and this was exacerbated by restrictions on 'reciprocal barter' without doubt. Consequently it would be impossible in the long run for Britain to maintain high prices at home while low prices prevailed abroad without serious consequences for the exchanges. High or low prices are to be judged not by corn, or labour commanded as with Smith, but by the price of agricultural labour 'being extremely regular in its annual supply and demand' (1828, p. 53).

Returning to the impact of Rooke's pamphlet, it was the prior publication of Sir James Graham's *Corn and Currency* in 1826 that heightened the level of political excitement in 1828. Like Rooke, Graham was at pains to show the interconnection between monetary and mercantile questions, believing that elaborate attempts to regulate the price of money and the price of food by legal enactment were generally detrimental; he favoured a sweeping reduction in government expenditure and freer banking and trade. The pamphlet, however, contains no new theories or policies, rather it draws attention to the failure of the dogmatic belief that higher corn prices raise the price of all the necessities of life to the benefit of landowners and that both of these are dependent upon effective Corn Laws. Indeed, indicating perhaps the influence of Rooke here, he pointed out that in the long run it was doubtful whether the landowner gained at all. He could say with greater certainty, however, that high duties would seriously damage manufacturing industry, upon which the continued expansion of British wealth depended (Graham, 1826, p. 13).

Graham did not propose the abolition of the Corn Laws at this juncture though, for he was aware of the need to achieve a balance between the opposing viewpoints in the county and Parliament. To achieve this objective he adopted Ricardo's recommendation that duties should be reduced to a level that subsidised the landlord for the taxes, poor rates and tithes imposed on them, the precise size of the subsidy being open to negotiation. In particular, 'it was difficult to fix a protecting duty with fairness when the standard of value was itself unfair. This was the core of the whole subject' (1826, p. 16). To eradicate this difficulty he considers the gold and corn standards, recommended by various political economists, but found these wanting on a balance of considerations. He personally favoured compensation for the burdens imposed by the 1819 Act for resumption and in particular:

> With the same standard we must have the same price; there is no escape from the dilemma: and if the Land Owners would preserve their estates, either the standard must be adjusted to their encumbrances, or their encumbrances to the standard. I have spoken with perfect freedom of the existing Corn Laws; their effect on the price of corn is now absolutely nugatory, excepting in years of inadequate supply; then their burthen becomes intolerable to the consumer, and fatal to the prosperity of the manufacturer. Public opinion is strongly opposed to them; in their present shape (and) ... on an average of years, while Mr. Peel's Act remains unaltered, the monopoly, which they give, must be abortive in raising prices. Land Owners (should) ... make a timely compromise with the public, and take an ample, but fair, protecting duty, with open ports, on the admission of foreign corn; a duty, equivalent to the burthens imposed on the producers of corn in this country, to which the consumers of corn are not equally liable. (1826, pp. 18–19)

As things stood in 1826, the labouring classes were impoverished by the combination of the Corn Laws and the 1819 Act, while there were no clear benefits to be observed elsewhere that might be set against these losses.

During the course of the years 1826–1828, Parliament occupied itself with the very issues raised in Graham's pamphlet.[31] However, considerable furore interrupted the languid debates when the anonymous pamphlet by Rooke appeared, for it was assumed to be the work of Graham and represented a much stronger attack on the Corn Laws. Intriguingly, Graham did not protest his innocence very widely. In a further debate on the Corn Laws in 1834 he gave even more ammunition to those now firmly convinced of his new position on the subject, by stating that he did debate the issues with the real author and assisted in finding a publisher (Hansard, 1834, pp.134–135). Indeed it was not until 13 years later in 1841 that Graham ventured into print to repudiate authorship.

The *Globe* published a long leading article in its edition of 3 August 1841 in which the 'ambiguities' in Graham's publications, including *Free Trade in Corn*, were brutally exposed. The leader was prompted in part by a speech Graham delivered in Dorchester to celebrate his re-election to Parliament. He is reported to have stated that an assured supply of bread is dependent upon protection to agriculture, but the editor goes on to report an excerpt from *his Free Trade in Corn* to the effect that '(restricted trade) more than (all the factors enumerated) will lead to the eventual ruin of the agricultural interest itself'. Not only this, while his speech showed the coincidence of the interests of the landlords and manufacturers, his *Corn and Currency* pamphlet argued exactly the reverse, once again championing the virtues of freer trade: 'the course, therefore, to be adopted is to consent to a revision of the Corn Laws, to consent to a free importation with a moderate protecting duty, but to force, at the same time, a revision of all other monopolies and to carry a reduction of taxes to a very large amount'. Such was the ferocity of the attack that Graham felt it necessary to give a public rebuttal to the charge, although there is a strong hint to the effect that this was directed more against the charge of inconsistency and implied dishonesty, than against the substance of the free-trade argument. Hence on the following day, the *Globe* published a letter giving Rooke's name as the author.

The key point here is that Sir James Graham was a crucial figure in the eventual repeal of the Corn Laws in the sense that his views were widely respected and influential (Hansard, 1830, p. 997).[32] That he was keenly aware of the social, political and above all the economic ramifications of the state of the corn and currency laws is beyond doubt. The important question is therefore in what circumstances did he change his opinion on the Corn Laws? In answering this question it might be claiming too much to argue that Rooke was the essential catalyst. But the strength of his economic argument and the gradual modification Graham's views underwent in the course of published and unpublished writings and Parliamentary Speeches, during which time he was in close contact with Rooke, suggest that he played some, if not exactly a major, role. An indication of this is given in Graham's letter to Rooke dated 4 September 1846, immediately after the repeal. It would appear that during the course of 1845, the prospect of a further derangement of prices due to impending crop failures finally convinced Graham that Rooke's arguments were absolutely sound (Beer, 1921, pp. 150–151).

CAPITAL ACCUMULATION AND ECONOMIC GROWTH

Rooke's optimism with regard to the potential for economic growth has been recorded earlier, providing certain fundamental changes occur in monetary and international commercial relations. The question arises, however, as to whether or not periodic crises that interrupt the progress of national wealth will occur and Rooke, amongst a number of critics, has some important points to make on the subject. The major thinkers here were Lauderdale (1819) and Malthus (Corry, 1959) so that some attention must be given to their respective positions.

Lauderdale's position was essentially that the decision to save is also a simultaneous decision to invest (Smith, 1977, Vol. I, Book II, Ch. 3), but that it was possible to undertake too much investment given a fixed capital/labour ratio, so that the rate of profit would fall. Higher savings might also reduce consumption and thus could depress further the prospects for future investment. Only if technology changed or new markets were exploited, could a higher level of investment be sustained. Alternatively, government could raise its expenditure and effect a change in the distribution of wealth in order that consumption and investment could be maintained. Malthus' position exhibits similarities on a number of counts, but more specifically he noted that over-investment through a high rate of savings would eventually lower the rate of profit. This analysis has a modern ring about it for Malthus has effectively applied the capital stock adjustment model with which modern macroeconomists are familiar (Matthews, 1955).

The problem Malthus envisaged was really the breakdown in the flow of information; high savings and low demand led to a glut, but it would not be until profits had fallen that this situation became apparent to capitalists, so that investment levels could be reduced. His solution was to keep up the level of demand through high levels of unproductive expenditure and to widen the market for goods by encouraging trade. If this turned out to be an insufficient stimulus, then public-works schemes were a necessary remedial measure and any consequent reduction in the level of capital, although insignificant, was to be welcomed. Ricardo, of course, objected to this proposal on the grounds that there was a single capital pool and any reduction occurring as a result of government expenditure (investment) would reduce private investment by a similar amount.[33] Malthus' more enduring argument, however, was really only deficient in one respect and that relates to the lack of a multiplier mechanism.

Rooke himself adopts an expenditure approach consistently in his analysis of production that has a very Keynesian ring (Corry, 1966, pp. 141–142). This becomes apparent in an early publication dealing with the national debt, in which three component parts of consumption are identified and related subsequently to income in the sense of a causal relationship. Consumption includes, 'the demand of the common wants of life; the repair of old capital and the creation of a new one; luxurious and unproductive (consumption)' (Rooke, 1822, pp. 17–18). The latter category is incorrectly stated to be productive of no new income, so that if this were large, then more resources would have to be devoted to capital accumulation to maintain income levels. While wealth would be stimulated by 'the free expenditure of individual income', saving would represent a leakage from the circular flow of income, 'savers, who are extremely anxious to accumulate fortunes, directly contribute to the prevention of that creation of income which a more liberal system of expenditure produces, and do much towards stopping the progress of public wealth' (Rooke, 1828, p. 18). Corry has argued that this 'only meant that investment led to a falling rate of profit'. However, the paradox of thrift phenomenon that the above extract conveys turns out to be a consistently recognised difficulty in Rooke's work (Corry, 1966, p. 140).[34] Profit earners are encouraged to spend their incomes to 'cause a demand for a new advance of capital' (Rooke, 1824, p. 92); the propensity of labourers and capitalists to consume causes the advancement of national wealth, 'consumption is therefore the cause of the formation of new income (that) goes to supply additional funds, which, may be either laid out in more extensive consumption, in the formation of new capital, or in the repair of that which had been previously realised. Consumption and production would therefore appear to excite each other reciprocally and to form the chief cause of their mutual advancement' (1824, p. 105). Expenditure, he goes on to state, does not reduce the capital stock as some economists had maintained, but simply redistributes it.

The problem of hoarded savings is also discussed and placed in its proper context; Rooke gives a particular example noting that over-production of various items would be the result of saving, 'a general inclination to save income … would cause more work-tools, more workshops, and more of the rude materials of manufacture to be provided than were demanded, and a general decay of capital and industry would follow as a necessary consequence' (1824, p. 109).[35] (The example used relates to manufacturing industry simply because Rooke is at pains to point out that the demand for and supply of the necessities of life are more closely aligned, so that a shortfall of demand is more likely for periods of time in manufacturing.) In the context of events causing great uncertainty, for example war, the propensity to hoard is particularly noticeable, and the disastrous consequences reveal themselves in a large number of bankruptcies (1824, p. 194). The danger inherent in large hoards also led Rooke for a time to recommend depreciation of the currency as a way of encouraging the spending of these sums (1824, p. 235). Even government should be invoked if hoarding becomes too great by either taxing hoards directly, 'income that is not positively necessary to him who possesses it, and the use of which is optional' (1824, p. 255) or through a more equal distribution of wealth, 'national wealth can never be too generally diffused among the various ranks of the people, while that diffusion does not interrupt the collection of capital into masses sufficiently large to carry on the processes of production' (1824, p. 233).

This argument is separate from, but related to the capital stock adjustment model, that Rooke also employs. In his *Inquiry* he notes that the level of income is dependent upon a stable and high average propensity to consume. Should the level of saving increase and consumption fall, the level of investment, which depends not on the availability of savings, *but the level of previous consumption*, will subsequently be too high and unsustainable. The rate of profits and income will fall until such time as the capitalist has adjusted the level of investment or consumption has revived:

> As expenditure is the chief cause that excites the accumulation of national wealth, the people of every prosperous county must have a tendency to spend more than their former income. Were this not the case, a new income could not be formed by the employment of a larger capital, since capital must uniformly tend to increase the supply, and unless that supply meet with an adequate demand, no accumulation of public wealth can take place; because that portion of the capital stock which is annually drawn away by consumption, is more than counterbalanced by the powerful means of production which capital and labour are attaining. (1824, p. 106)

Clearly, if income is increasing then the level of consumption out of that new income must be maintained – or increased. The link between the level of investment and the expected level of consumption is quite explicitly made, 'had the additional capital realised in 1821 in expectation of a greater demand in 1822, not met with a greater consumption in the latter year, the supply would have exceeded the demand, profits would have fallen and income would have had a tendency to diminish' (1824, p. 106). The tendency of innovations to reduce the price of goods encourages wider consumption – certainly there is no shortage of investible funds to achieve this result – and, of course, free trade would provide a number of new markets for British goods. At one point he goes so far as to argue that spendthrifts and government could borrow money from savers, 'without ever repaying it (so that) public wealth would be continually stimulated by consumption' (1824, p. 235). However on the whole he feels that this would be a dangerous step to take and eventually result in 'the annihilation of the public wealth'. Depreciation of the currency is also rejected as an incentive to borrowing for similar reasons, but additionally because of the derangement to monied contracts generally that this would bring.

Rooke therefore has some stimulating discussion of the determination of income that has clear Keynesian overtones – indeed at two stages he is on the verge of expounding the multiplier mechanism. His theoretical analysis has clear overlaps with that of both Lauderdale and Malthus, particularly the capital stock model. On the policy implications of deficient consumption, Rooke does not foresee anything more than short-term deficiencies and does not discuss in any great detail possible remedial measures beyond those mentioned above. The greatest emphasis is upon free-trade that might remove any excess labour (unemployment) created by new methods of cultivation in agriculture by encouraging manufacturing to expand. But more controversially, through a policy of colonisation might serve to promote manufacturing and therefore economic growth (1824, p. 372; Wagner, 1931, p. 261).[36] Public works, for example, discussed in the context of a 'real' sinking fund, are not linked to the under-consumptionist analysis. Malthus and Lauderdale, on the other hand, do emphasise public works in such a counter-deflationary context.

PUBLIC FINANCE – TAXATION AND THE NATIONAL DEBT

Taxation and debt creation represent the two major sources of government revenue and receive widespread attention from the classical economists. Rooke is no exception here and part three of his *Inquiry* is devoted to an analysis of these subjects on both of which he has interesting things to say. Once again a brief overview of the position of the major classical economists is provided for the purposes of comparison.

The classical economists adhere pretty well to Smith's well-known canons of taxation – equality, certainty, convenience and economy in the collection – although they may be expressed differently. O'Brien (1975, p. 241) has pointed out that Smith's equality maxim really embodies two notions as to how the tax burden should be distributed. First the benefit method, whereby the tax is paid according to specific benefits received, although this is acknowledged to be difficult to accomplish and, secondly, the ability to pay method that is really self-explanatory and incorporates the idea of a taxable capacity within the economy. Now Bentham, Say and Hume subscribed to the first and McCulloch and J. S. Mill, in particular, to the second view. In all cases, the most important consideration seems to be that the rate of economic growth should not be impaired by the level of taxation and this was certainly Rooke's feeling on the matter. The taxes were generally divided into indirect and direct, although there is some disagreement at the margin of this division is maintained below. Of the major figures, Ricardo favoured direct taxes, whilst Hume, Smith, Say and McCulloch preferred indirect taxes, with John Stuart Mill somewhere in the middle. The preference for indirect taxes is nicely summarised from Smith's arguments by O'Brien, 'they did not involve investigation of personal details, they had a useful sumptuary role, they encouraged accumulation (and hence the demand for labour) and they stimulated effort, ingenuity and saving, whereas direct taxes stimulated only savings' (1975, p. 245).

On wage taxation both Smith and Ricardo thought it was passed on, the former in higher costs via a subsistence mechanism and the latter through the core theorem and a concomitant reduction in profits. For Smith, a rise in wages in manufacturing would be passed on in the form of higher prices, but in agriculture rents would fall by an equal amount (Smith, 1977, Vol. I, p. vii); Ricardo rejected this, prices would only rise in labour intensive industries, otherwise profits would fall. Consequently only Ricardo favoured wage taxation (Sraffa & Dobb, 1951a, Vol. I, Ch. 16). Smith did not favour taxes on profits because they sent capital abroad and impeded entrepreneurship amongst other things (Smith, 1977, Vol. I, p. viif). Ricardo favoured a tax on profits through the taxation of wages as we have seen, but additionally a general profit tax would raise all product prices and via a long-term specie flow mechanism, prices would eventually be restored (Sraffa, 1951a, *Works*, Vol. I, Ch. 15). With regard to rent, the 'neat' or surplus and return on fixed capital investment is usually distinguished and taxes on the surplus portion were permissible. James Mill and Ricardo favoured the taxation of surplus rent (Sraffa, 1951a, *Works*, Vol. I, Ch. 10), but McCulloch rightly saw the two components as difficult to separate and therefore feared that agricultural investment might fall (O'Brien, 1970, pp. 251–253). Smith preferred the taxation of ground rents (Smith, 1977, Vol. I, p. viih). An income tax was generally felt to be a temporary expedient and the idea of an allowance set at subsistence implied progression that both McCulloch and J. S. Mill rejected (Seligman, 1908, p. 183). The taxation of houses was generally acceptable, though window taxes were not. Taxes on inheritance were favoured and both Bentham and Mill took progression to extreme lengths here (Stark, 1952, Vol. II).

Indirect taxes were popular with the classical economists, but they were aware of the need to maintain some sort of balance so as not annihilate expenditure (consumption). Most of these economists assumed that indirect taxes would raise the price of the product and furthermore that they would be passed on to the consumer. Mainly for this reason, taxes on necessaries were to be avoided since wages would rise followed by prices for Smith, while profits would fall for Ricardo (Smith, 1977, Vol. I, p. viik and Sraffa, 1951a, *Works*, Vol. I, Ch. 16). Taxes on luxuries, on the other hand, were widely recommended. Taxes on raw materials were unacceptable too, because they raised costs; Ricardo argued they raised prices in order that profit equality between agriculture and industry was maintained, so that money rents remain the same, but as the price of corn rose, corn rents would fall. Smith believed that tithes fell on the landlord, whereas Ricardo argued that they raised prices and hence fell on the consumer. Nevertheless, tithes were rejected by the classical economists for being a deterrent to agricultural investment.

Gordon (1979, p. 142) has generously noticed that Rooke offered, 'a strongly contrasting approach to taxation' that distinguishes him from mainstream classicalism; whether this is an appropriate assessment is now examined. In opening his discussion, Rooke distinguishes the general categories of taxation, direct and indirect and makes the distinction between luxuries and necessaries and proceeds to detail these considerations. The taxation of necessities is condemned, but the need to mobilise hoarded funds and encourage consumption is given greater consideration. Hence like McCulloch in particular, Rooke is concerned that taxation should promote growth whenever and howsoever it can (Rooke, 1824, pp. 255–256). To this end two classes of taxation are very important, 'the first class are such taxes as fall on articles the use of which is optional and do not administer to the common wants of life;[37] also second taxes levied on annual income, the disposal of which, with respect to its owner, is optional' (1824, p. 255). With reference to duties on wines and spirits alone, Rooke is convinced that a great increase in wealth is possible by five routes:

(1) They form a broader basis for capital to rest upon.
(2) They furnish a direct means of livelihood to those who gain a support from the duties arising from them.
(3) The means of spending they create is not only productive of a greater consumption of them and of an increase of these duties, but of taxes in general.
(4) They cause the wealthy to become greater spenders and greater purchasers of these luxuries, and, by that means, a demand for them is created abroad, which enables the foreigner to purchase our productions in return.

(5) As they assist foreign commerce materially, they tend to perfect the division of labour, improve the conveniences of water carriage, and of the inland roads of the country. (1824, p. 257)

The taxation of luxuries (providing their consumption is not greatly reduced) and the taxation of hoarded funds can only raise wealth if the revenue is judiciously expended. Rent, presumably excluding 'neat' rent, is exempt from the latter heading of taxation on the grounds that it would seriously impair the level of agricultural investment. Taxes which may impede the progress of national wealth generally are also to be avoided, although some may be permitted on a short-term basis. However, in this connection, Rooke notices that some taxes may have an incentive effect, 'in proportion, however, as the direct injury sustained from any particular tax is less, the indirect energy imparted to production by the expenditure of those taxes will be more likely to repair the evils it has occasioned' (1824, p. 259). Finally, in this introductory discussion, Rooke rejects an income tax that does not protect those with 'no spare income to dispose of' and particularly profit recipients, since once again this would reduce the rate of growth, 'the first of these would obstruct the natural increase of population;[38] and the second would be opposed to the accumulation of capital' (1824, p. 259). Taxes on necessaries would also reduce population growth.

Moving to specific taxes and their effects, Rooke determines whether or not they are acceptable according to three rules: (1) they shall not reduce necessary population growth; (2) they shall not reduce accumulation and (3) they should maintain the income of the community. First direct taxes. A tax on the rent of land cannot be passed on and in line with Rooke's whole approach to rent such a tax is condemned as detrimental to agricultural investment putting Rooke in opposition to Ricardo. But a low short-term tax of this type is not ruled out and Rooke further notes that a higher rate would, in point of fact, reduce expenditure on luxuries and in consequence the tax yield (1824, pp. 263–267). James Mill was the only whole-hearted supporter of this tax and Rooke's position accords with that of both Smith and McCulloch – Ricardo accepted the taxation of rent, but he does have reservations on the basis of the difficulty of separating the surplus and return on fixed capital, believing that a tax on the latter *would be passed on to the consumer* (Sraffa, 1951a, *Works*, Vol. I, p. 175).

Poor rates cannot be passed on either and also fall on the rent of land with the previously noticed results. The only evidence in favour of such expenditure Rooke can find relates to the fact that they may reduce hoards and increase consumption; that they may raise population is a serious danger. Ricardo, on the other hand, saw the need for a rising population if growth was to proceed and given that poor rates could, to a certain extent, be passed on, he did not condemn them altogether. Nevertheless, Rooke chose to deal at greater length with the abuse of the system of poor relief, where employers would pay lower wages and on that basis he argued for major reform (Rooke, 1824, pp. 269–271, and also pp. 380–388). Parochial assessments that led to investment in infrastructure on the other hand were welcomed by Rooke.

The taxation of profits is dealt with very briefly by Rooke without any of the complicating factors contained in Ricardo's assessment. He argued that the price of the product would be raised, but that if the tax were imposed mainly on profits in the agricultural sector, it could not be passed on so easily, in which case rent would fall so that the usual rate of profit could be earned – this would then impede agricultural investment. Where it is passed on, population would be held back and growth adversely affected. A tax on the interest of money would fall on the lender and this would reduce the level of lending in the future and again impede the progress of wealth (1824, pp. 271–273). In conclusion, therefore, Rooke's analysis is decidedly inferior to that of both Smith and Ricardo, but not without some merit.

Wage taxation does not form a separate heading for discussion in the *Inquiry*, but as noted earlier if such taxation reduces population growth and consumption, then national wealth would be reduced. Elsewhere in the *Inquiry* the fact that labour requires a minimum subsistence is noted and a tax on the wages of agricultural labour was thought to lead to a reduction in rent, making Rooke a follower of Smith and not Ricardo on this matter. His hostility to income tax has already been recorded, although even here he leaves room for a progressive income tax, without going into specifics, and the income from trades and professions is given separate treatment. In this context, progression is implied by the need for allowances and given these, income from such 'services' could be taxed in the short run, but not in the long run, since the cost of the services provided would rise (1824, p. 274).

Various other direct taxes are discussed briefly. A tax on the rent of mines, given that part of this is a return to fixed capital, can be partially offset through higher prices. In view of this, there is some scope here for taxation (1824, p. 274). A general tax on houses and industrial buildings does not, according to Rooke fall on the owner, but the occupier, reducing population and wealth although if they fall on the houses of the wealthy consumption would be stimulated. The owner expects the general rate of profit and will not build houses unless this rate is assured, however, as Edgeworth was able to demonstrate much later. This confirms Smith's position that the incidence of the tax, *vis a vis* the occupier and owner, is indeterminate (Edgeworth, 1925, Vol. 2, pp. 82–85).

Turning now to indirect taxes, Rooke, like Smith before him, was more favourably disposed towards these and spent much more time on them. As already noted, taxes on luxuries were particularly commended, providing they did not reduce consumption, 'taxes of this description (on malt, hops, spirituous liquors, wine, cider, foreign drugs, sugar, tobacco etc.) have the effect of putting that income in motion which might otherwise have remained stationary, to the detriment of the whole community, from a want of that consumption and reaccumulation of new income which generate wealth' (Rooke, 1824, p. 261). Rooke is at pains to show that the judicious expenditure of funds raised in this way can act as a very efficient generator of national wealth invoking a multiplier-type mechanism. He is less certain about the taxation of tea, coffee and sugar as these are to be regarded as necessities, but provided the tax is light no great harm would be done. As sugar comes from the West Indies, however, the need for a low tax is reinforced by the knowledge that its free purchase in Britain provides a fund for the purchase of British manufactures there (the notion of reciprocal trade). Of the classical economists, Ricardo was the least enthusiastic about taxes on luxuries (Sraffa, 1951a, *Works,* Vol. I, Ch. 16).

Rooke takes Ricardo to task for his analysis of taxes on raw produce, for while the latter argued that the consumer would pay through higher prices, Rooke maintained that the burden would be borne by rents. While Ricardo had shown that part of the tax would be borne by consumers as corn prices rose, wages would have to rise so that some portion was borne by capitalists through lower profits. The method employed by Rooke to counter this argument was to show that not only labour, but capitalists could resist the burden of the tax so that inevitably the landlord absorbs the tax. The long-term result would be a reduction in cultivation and a check to both population and national wealth. Rooke, of course, was noting the long-run consequences of the fall in profits in terms of an adjustment of production in those sectors where profits were consequently below the normal level (Rooke, 1824, pp. 284–287). Therefore, the difference between them is more apparent than real, for both had in their alternate ways failed to give adequate attention to the time lags for adjustment in respect of wages, profits and the level of production – although Ricardo did generalise his results to indicate that the precise response depended upon the particular commodity examined (Sraffa, 1951a, *Works*, Vol. I, pp. 157–171).

It is Rooke's opinion, as it was Smith's, that tithes fall on the rent of land and that the price of corn is not raised. Corn cannot be sold at a higher price, Rooke continues, for the progress of population would have been 'instantly' checked, thereby negating the increase. Tithes reduce the level of investment in land, particularly where it falls on the gross produce rather than the net and the demand for agricultural land falls (Rooke, 1824, p. 276). Hence tithes reduce the output from the land and this directly affects the welfare of labour. Thus, in common with the classical economists, Rooke argued for the commutation of tithes; he suggested a number of ways by which this objective could be achieved (Rooke, 1824, pp. 376–380).

One group of taxes were condemned by Rooke as being 'extremely unfair and oppressive' demonstrating his detailed empirical knowledge of individual taxes. These included taxes on salt, leather, soap and candles that fall upon consumers and represent the necessaries of life. Likewise a tax on imported clover-seed falls on rent and this reduces investment and is oppressive. Taxes on foreign corn limit population and foreign commerce and again restrict national wealth: they should not be imposed. If taxes are imposed on imports of raw materials this reduces the wages of export labour, because the value of the finished product must remain competitive. Less of the precious metals would come into the country if prices did rise at all and the general price level would fall. More importantly, they impede foreign trade and the production of national wealth: they should be removed. Rooke does approve of stamp and legacy duties because landed property is a less risky investment and property owners should make a contribution to the revenue of the state on this account. The taxing of legacies, a direct tax, is recommended because it helps to dissipate hoards and would raise consumption, 'the hoarder, being indebted to the laws of a well-regulated state of society for the security of the property he has enjoyed, and having avoided many of those contributions which tend to uphold the validity of that property during his lifetime, only pays back what he justly owes to the body politic by a tax upon the capital stock of the personal property he may die possessed of' (1824, p. 295). But this is not a confiscatory tax as it was for Bentham (Stark, 1952; Dome, 1999). The classical economists are not generally favourably disposed to stamp duties.

From this survey, it is clear that Rooke is closer to Smith on taxation, believing that the emphasis should be on indirect taxes with only a limited role for short-run direct taxes, other than legacies. Like McCulloch the emphasis is always on the need to maintain a high level of economic growth. On several important points of taxation there is little disagreement with Ricardo, except over the taxation of rent. To some extent, therefore, Gordon's view is vindicated.

Any shortfall of government revenue must be made up by government borrowing, more particularly during times of war. While the mercantilists saw the national debt as a redistribution of resources within the country, the classical economists, excepting Lord Lauderdale, argued that growing interest charges and the size of the debt itself imposed restrictions on national wealth. Both Rooke and Ricardo adopted this position, arguing that if the interest payments were expended unproductively, then national wealth would fall. Moreover, Rooke maintained that such government expenditure was unproductive itself, 'a sum of money laid out in the creation of a productive capital is quite different, as it is expected to replace itself with a profit, besides defraying the annual charge of use' (Rooke, 1824, p. 13). Although the classical economists generally feel that taxation to pay the interest on government bonds was a burden, Ricardo favoured taxation for this purpose to the extent that manufacturers and landowners might have to sell their property to meet their liabilities. However, he recognised that such taxes would be passed on as much as possible so that prices would rise and ultimately the wages of labour with the usual repercussions. In these circumstances the imposition of taxes at the time of expenditure to enforce accountability was proposed, together with an all-out effort to remove the existing debt even though capital might go abroad. Rooke too favoured direct taxation, even the imposition of temporary direct taxes, in order to remove the debt burden once and for all. And in all his deliberations, Rooke took account of the variable value of money and was particularly concerned to see that lenders were not repaid in a devalued currency. McCulloch went so far as to argue that post-war deflation had benefited the bond holders so that reductions in the rate of interest would be equitable. However, Mushet's analysis to the effect that bond holders had lost during the war inflation an amount equal to the gains thereafter persuaded McCulloch to repudiate this plan and for a time he supported Ricardo's capital levy scheme (Mushet, 1821). Rooke also quoted Mushet approvingly.

The size of the debt problem that the Government faced was calculated by Rooke as equivalent to a two million pound loan contracted in 1714 at an interest rate of five percentage points. This accounts for an annual interest charges of thirty million pounds in 1822 and he concluded that the existing arrangements were incapable of liquidating such a debt. Part of the problem in the past had been that interest payments were periodically suspended so that new loans had eventually to be contracted to pay for these until the point was reached where new loans became barely adequate to meet the current obligations of the government:

> There can be no doubt (that) by Government making a few real payments the system might go on to the end of time, without any one feeling inconvenienced by it. But ... sooner or later, human intelligence will be able to comprehend and develop the exact bearings of the principle, and will deal with it accordingly.... Nothing can place the *abuse* of the funding system in a more striking point of view, than the fact, that though the public expenditure in 1812, in civil and military purposes, exceeded £60,000,000 sterling, yet we now find the greatest difficulty to go on with an expenditure of £18,000,000 sterling. (Rooke, 1822, pp. 22–23)

Following Robert Hamilton, Rooke proposed a real sinking fund as the only remedy, whereby the annual interest charges can be met together with substantial surplus revenue to place the fund on a proper basis. From a theoretical point of view, Ricardo considered a sinking fund perfectly adequate to liquidate the national debt. He raised two objections, however, one related to the later period of liquidation, in which the stockholder finds he has surplus funds and inadequate investment opportunities and a second regarding the remission of interest, whereby expenditure falls and commodity prices fall with them. Ricardo answered his own objections to the effect that investment opportunities were widely available and desired by the stockholder and that there was no evidence to suggest that prices would fall. On a practical level, however, he was led to consider that the sinking fund was misapplied and positively encouraged the accumulation of further debt (Sraffa, 1951c, *Works*, Vol. IV, pp. 143–201). Between 1819 and 1823 in various Parliamentary speeches, Ricardo made his opposition to the sinking fund perfectly clear, moving towards a capital levy – a tax on property – to clear the national debt, with safeguards to prevent individuals concealing their property. He realised of course that such a scheme had little chance of being adopted.

In contrast to Ricardo's view, Rooke pursued the real sinking fund idea and put forward a novel scheme to permit the government to spend beyond its revenue without incurring further debt during periods of crisis, such as wars. Surplus revenue was a prerequisite, so that higher taxation was inevitable in the short run, involving the taxation of rent, profits and wages, 'but such taxes ought never to be made permanent, because they diminish the reward of individual industry, and keep back the accumulation of capital' (Rooke, 1822, p. 30). Wherever possible taxes on luxuries are to be preferred. Liquidation through a budget surplus would have commanded general approval from the classical economists, but Rooke went much further than this and recommended a permanent sinking fund that they had previously rejected.

Rooke notes Smith's view that saving during peacetime is required if debt is not to be incurred in a period of war, but that this could be avoided if the state had an immediate method of raising additional revenue as required making the issue of government securities unnecessary (see Hamilton, 1818, pp. 608–618). Increased taxation as suggested by Ricardo would not be forthcoming quickly enough to achieve this end. The only remedy was to raise extra revenue and invest this in profitable outlets such as 'the formation of harbours and canals, the construction of bridges and roads' or land reclamation, yielding five percentage points in rents, tolls or dues, which would then be reinvested (Rooke, 1822, p. 41). Should war break out, these public assets could be sold and new revenue raised for the government. Or, alternatively, they could be mortgaged and subsequently sold, if the price was deemed too low at the time of the sale. (If such a scheme had been instituted in 1721, Rooke estimated the available capital in 1822 would amount to eight and a half thousand million pounds with no debt outstanding.) The alternative to such a scheme seemed patently obvious to Rooke,

> The *abuse* of the Funding System, it would appear from the evidence of facts, and the clearest deductions of numbers, is calculated to enervate and finally destroy the power and revenues of states, to sow the seeds of civil discord, and to embarrass alike the governors and the governed. It is true, that so long as a system of borrowing from economists, and of throwing the funds *so borrowed* into the hands of extravagance can be carried on, the wealth of the country will be stimulated; but, it ought not to be forgotten, that this stimulus does not send a single bayonet into the field against an enemy, after the accumulations of compound interest have taken root. (Rooke, 1822, p. 44)

If the present system continued, future generations would have to make good the enormous sums of money required to service the national debt and again national wealth would be seriously impaired. It is to be regretted that unlike Ricardo's scheme, Rooke's appears to have gone almost unnoticed. The only major figure to see a place for state enterprise, albeit in a different context, was Jeremy Bentham, who argued that government should take over Friendly Societies, undertake deposit banking and issue paper money (Stark, 1952, pp. 8–20).

CONCLUSIONS

This chapter has shown that there was much more to Rooke's political economy than a simple reading of Seligman's reassessment alone would suggest. Rooke's *Inquiry into the Principles of National Wealth* and many pamphlets made an important contribution to the development of the subject, although it is difficult to determine what impact they had on other economists and politicians, beyond those referred to above, in an age where citations were uncommon. Much has been written about priority over who was the first to discover the differential principle governing agricultural rent in Britain. Anderson in the eighteenth century was clearly the first, but who 'rediscovered' it and, more importantly, incorporated it into a model of the determination of profits and economic growth in the nineteenth century has excited many economists. Certainly Rooke's contribution was not in the same league as that of Ricardo, but he developed the theory in letters to the *Farmer's Journal* in mid-1814 and then used it to argue the case for repeal of the Corn Laws. He recognised the no-rent margin and the inverse theorem, although the two propositions were not satisfactorily linked together: his emphasis was on policy rather than high theory. Rent was determined by price, but included in price when the opportunity cost of alternative uses for land were taken into account. Rooke also argued that technological improvements in agriculture (that raise the rental share) would free up labour which should be transferred to the manufacturing sector where its marginal product would be higher.

Turning to the distributive shares, Rooke's focus was on the creation of profits and the new investment opportunities these would support. The total product was distributed in the following order: first to land (rent), secondly to circulating capital (mainly wages) and, finally, as a residual (to fixed capital) profits. He distinguished between profits and interest with profits determined through competition, but with a minimum requirement if production was to continue. The discussion of wages is limited because the emphasis was more on the role of labour as a measure of value. Wages, however, depended on the demand for and the supply of labour, with demand governed by the consumption of final goods and services and the amount of circulating capital available. Despite rising population he does not anticipate wages falling to subsistence because of the growing level of investment expected in the British economy. And wages were sufficiently above subsistence for labourers to be able to save in addition to the recipients of rental income and profits. The 'so-called' natural level of wages depended on wages in the export sector and the inflow of the precious metals that governed the supply of money.

Value was determined by demand and supply and particularly demand without which there would be no supply. Natural value was equated with costs of production (and the long-run supply curve exhibited increasing returns) while the market price was influenced by the value of money, but in any case could rise above costs if demand exceeded supply in the short run.

The short-run price then acted as a signal for resources to move towards production having higher temporary profits. Seligman had earlier drawn attention to the fact that the cost of production was determined at the margin as a general rule. It was then Rooke's intention to eliminate the impact of changes in the value of money on market prices. In his *Remarks* (1819a), Rooke favoured convertibility of the currency with the rate of exchange to be determined by a tabular standard based on an index of wage rates in the agricultural sector, but with reference to wage rates in the export sector as an additional check. As several modern commentators have observed, this is equivalent to targeting nominal GDP to achieve price stability. The correction to the monetary standard should then take place within the context of free trade.

Free trade in goods and services is a common thread running through the work of Rooke. By publishing an anonymous pamphlet calling for free trade, for some time believed to have been written by Sir James Graham, a prominent Tory MP and landowner, Rooke helped to give wider currency to the arguments in favour of repeal of the Corn Laws. Not only this, he was instrumental in convincing Graham to support the case for repeal more vigorously.

Rooke had an optimistic view of the prospects for economic growth. Consumption plays an important role here and the detrimental effect of unproductive savings is examined in terms that are very Keynesian. Innovations that lower the price of goods and encourage higher levels of consumption together with free trade have a positive effect on growth. In analysing issues connected with public finance, Rooke is at pains to avoid any policy that might impede economic growth. The taxation of luxuries is therefore recommended rather than rent or necessary goods that, like incomes, should only be taxed very lightly. Some taxes, like those raised to fund poor relief, were acceptable if they led to productive investment in the process. Some profits might be taxed, but not those in agriculture because these could not be passed on in higher prices as those on profits in manufacturing could be. Imports, particularly of raw materials, should not be taxed as these might lead to retaliatory taxes and/or lower the demand for British-manufactured exports: these would impact on growth. Rooke favoured the commutation of tithes, and taxes on landed property that might reduce unproductive savings and raise consumption were to be welcomed. Where Rooke departed from the classical economists most was on the need to establish a real sinking fund to repay the national debt. And more radically he favoured temporary taxation to fund capital investment projects undertaken by the state that would yield a revenue stream and could be sold off (at a profit) at times of war. Thus essential government expenditure could be met without building up debt.

Rooke therefore provides a remarkable body of analysis that attempts to cover virtually the whole field of political economy with the overriding aim of promoting national wealth. Some areas that had been neglected were drawn to the profession's attention in 1903, but much remained buried inside his dense and prolix analysis that encompassed a considerable body of published work. Fisher first drew attention to his achievements in the field of indexation, but recently many more economists have rediscovered this part of his work and have been pleasantly surprised by the level of sophistication they found.

NOTES

1. Rooke worked out the theory over the period 1811–1812. All contributions apart from Rooke's appear to be inspired by the 1814 *Parliamentary Reports Respecting Grain and the Corn Laws*. The dates of publication are as follows: Rooke (1814, 1815); Malthus ([1815b] 1970); Malthus (1815b); West (1815); Torrens (1815) and Ricardo (Sraffa & Dobb, 1951a, Vol. 4).
2. Such a formulation is dependent upon a particular interpretation of Smith's 'Digression on Silver' (1977).
3. Cannan (1892) has done less than justice to Anderson and ignored Rooke.
4. The differential cost case is further explored towards the end of the pamphlet (see Malthus, 1815, p. 210).
5. Ricardo records in his copy of the *Essay* that 'this was published before my *Essay on Profits*, but it never came into my hands till after I had published my *Essay*' (Ricardo, *Works*, Vol. 4, p. 6).
6. Rent arises from the infertility of the soil and not, as with Malthus, from the abundance of nature, although in the *Principles* Ricardo uses the intensive margin model that avoids the requirement (Sraffa & Dobb, 1951a, Vol. 1, pp. 412–413n).
7. The evidence is contained in the Bromley–Davenport Muniments. A note in Davenports' hand suggests the title *Question of Plagiary – A Letter Addressed to E. D. Davenport Esq., of Calvely Hall, Cheshire by the Author of the Inquiry into the Principles of National Wealth as to who was the Original Publisher of Certain Modern Doctrines in Political Economy*. In the event, Rooke's title became *Claim to the Original Publication of Certain New Principles in Political Economy, Addressed in a Letter to E. D. Davenport Esq*. In a further letter to Davenport (8 August 1825), Rooke considers the claim of Malthus in detail and also that of Torrens. He points out the similarities between his early essays and the former's pamphlet on rent and concludes that his claim is legitimate.
8. Fixed investment is also governed by the 'normal rate' of profit.
9. The only early socialist to publish before 1824 was P. Ravenstone, but Rooke does not refer to him. Therefore W. Godwin, who is mentioned, is more likely to be the source of this argument on behalf of labour (1796, 1797). It is possible too that Rooke saw R.

Owen's, *Observations* (1815) and through Graham's offices, George Mundie's three letters to D. Ricardo entitled 'Mr. Owen's Proposed Arrangements' and written in 1818.

10. Improvements are both capital and labour saving for Ricardo, but their unemployment does not lead to two profit rates as O'Brien (1975, p. 129) suggests because of the principle of profit equalisation and the role of Say's Law of markets.

11. Rooke is at pains to point out that Ricardo particularly and Malthus to a lesser extent, ignored the important second category, and he deduces figures from a sample survey to quantify its size (see Table 1 here). Had he compared Ricardo's *Essay* with Malthus' *Principles*, he would have been harder on Malthus (see Malthus, 1836, pp. 421–422).

Table 1. The Sample Survey Rooke Cites Regarding Fixed Capital.

Years/Category	1790 (%)	1804 (%)	1813 (%)
Labour	26	27	24
Seed etc.	29	25	29
Profit	11	11	12
Rent or surplus	32	35	32

Source: Board of Agriculture Returns.

12. Grampp (1960, chap. 2) has a fuller analysis of this point.

13. This is the mechanism by which Heckscher–Ohlin demonstrate the tendency of factor returns to converge to equality.

14. The evidence is surveyed in Bharadwaj (1978).

15. This argument would be no surprise to Alfred Marshall (1890).

16. This was written before the *Inquiry* was published in 1824 and represents a proportion of that manuscript.

17. Rooke must therefore be recognised as the first economist to use marginal cost, although his contribution was clearly unknown to J. H. von Thünen ([1842] 1996) who was previously thought to have priority. For further applications, see Rooke (1824, pp. 73–75, 204, 210–211, 225).

18. The curious point to note here is that neither Jevons, nor indeed Menger, both early marginalists, integrated marginal cost with supply, making Rooke's achievement all the more remarkable.

19. Several authors have dealt with the index number problem, one of the earliest was Bishop Fleetwood (1707), and then, contemporaneously with Rooke, were Sir George Shuckleburgh-Evelyn (1798), John Wheatley (1803), Lowe (1822) and, finally, G. P. Scope (1833b). Even Bagehot (1892) missed Rooke.

20. Newcomb (1879) anticipated the equation of exchange and Fisher dedicated his book the *Purchasing Power of Money* to him. Wallace ([1898] 1900) is considered by many to have co-discovered the theory.

21. On Scrope's plan, see Opie (1929, pp. 120–122).

22. Viner (1937, chap. 5) noted that Rooke's scheme also took explicit account of the need to regulate the quantity of paper money so that its quantity rose when the purchasing power of paper money increased. Sumner (1990, p. 115n) has argued

that Rooke's scheme is 'surprisingly … in some ways actually more "modern" than the Williams–Fisher plan in that it would be accommodative toward supply shocks'.

23. Attwood (1818) provided a similar solution.

24. It is in the context of the relationship between silver and corn that Smith discusses corn as the standard of value.

25. There has been renewed interest in aggregate nominal GDP targets for monetary policy since the 1990s following in the tradition of Fisher (1920). Fisher argued that the price of gold should periodically be adjusted to offset changes in the price level to maintain stable purchasing power for the currency. Rooke and others were earlier if neglected pioneers of this methodology (Sumner, 1991, p. 755).

26. Rooke considered at one point using the price of silver as a measure (Rooke, 1824, p. 482, reported in Haig, 2006, p. 362).

27. Corry (1966, p. 142) failed to notice that Rooke recanted his earlier view that the currency should be constantly depreciated when he calls him 'one of the more extreme inflationists'.

28. Precisely the same point is made by Graham (1826, p. 17). Rooke's biographer Lonsdale (1868, p. 240) notes that before the publication of *Corn and Currency*, Graham had discussed it with him and 'benefitted no little from the extent of his information'. Lonsdale's report is substantiated by a letter from Graham to Rooke, dated 29 June 1827, in which he writes, 'every day's additional experience convinces me more and more of the soundness of *our* views respecting the currency; the bill of 1819 lies at the foundation of all our difficulties: Corn Laws, custom regulations, emigration reports, and relief to the manufacturers, all are but the fringes of this one great first cause, on which our difficulties and our fate depend. We must come to the discussion of it at last; it will be forced upon us; but the Legislature is not yet ripe for it, and the ignorance still prevalent on the subject exceeds your belief of possibility' (Graham Papers, Bodleian Library, Oxford University).

29. This is a year before Thompson's *Free-Trade Catechism* appeared, large portions of which were pre-empted by Rooke. Ricardo published his *On Protection to Agriculture* in 1822, but did not achieve the integration of the monetary and trade factors that lay behind the contemporary distress in the same way that Rooke and, later, Graham did.

30. Lonsdale (1868) notes that the pamphlet gained great notoriety in political circles, although even this tribute needs to be put into perspective, because he goes on to say that: 'for at least fifteen years subsequently to the issue of Rooke's brochure, the anti-Corn-Law league of 1845 would have had no *locus standi* if the practical views of the Cumberland laird had taken deeper root and got more fair play at the hands of the press in 1825' (p. 241). Nevertheless, it did go to a second edition.

31. Gordon (1979, p. 52) has described the debates of this period as an anticipation of those during the late 1830s when the anti-Corn Law League was formed. In view of this the doctrines promulgated in this period assume even greater importance.

32. The landlord interest in Parliament was not in the mood for the arguments of political economists. Indeed, Sir James Graham utterly repudiated them when he stated that he 'had heard so much of political economy as connected with the corn question, that without any objection to the men, he was heartily sick of political economists altogether and he wished them no further harm than that a clause should be inserted in the present bill, enacting that every vessel laden with foreign corn

destined for this country should take back, instead of ballast, a cargo of political economists' (Hansard, Volume XVII, p. 997).

33. Pigou (1908) in his inaugural lecture took a similar stance.

34. In the very next paragraph to the one cited in the text above, Rooke (1822, p. 18) makes his position abundantly clear on this issue, 'The way in which the funding system has been managed during the last eight years, has had a strong tendency to promote the dissipation of these hoarded incomes, through the mechanism of a private channel, and to give free scope and action to the creation of capital in agriculture, manufactures, and commerce, as well as in Houses, Roads, Canals etc'.

35. An alternative view denying the paradox of thrift is to be found in Corry (1966).

36. In this sense Rooke's liberalism should be read as nationalism. Policy makers who supported free trade did so not because it would benefit the economic welfare of the world, but because 'it would bolster British wealth and international power and give the country a manufacturing monopoly' (Helleiner, 2002, p. 320).

37. But likely to have an elastic demand.

38. And thus raise wages.

REFERENCES

Private Papers:

Attwood Papers, Mrs. P. Williams, London.

Bromley-Davenport Muniments, John Rylands Library, Manchester.

Sir James Graham Papers, Netherby Hall, Longtown.

Sir James Graham Papers, Bodleian Library, Oxford University (microform).

Senhouse Papers, Carlisle Record Office, Carlisle.

Anderson, J. (1777). *Observations on the means of exciting a spirit of national industry*. Edinburgh: C. Elliot.

Anderson, J. (1801). *Calm investigation of the circumstances that have led to the present scarcity of grain in great Britain; suggesting the means of alleviating that evil, and of preventing the recurrence of such a calamity in the future*. London: J. Cumming.

Attwood, T. (1818). Observations on currency, population and pauperism. In: *Two letters to Arthur Young, Esq*. Birmingham: R. Wrightson.

Bagehot, W. (1892). A new standard of value. *Economic Journal*, *2*(7), 472–477.

Barkai, H. (1966). Ricardo's second thoughts on rent as a relative share. *Southern Economic Journal*, *32*(3), 285–293.

Beer, M. (1921). *History of British socialism*. London: Bell & Sons.

Bharadwaj, K. (1978). *Classical political economy and the rise to dominance of supply and demand theories*. Calcutta: Orient Longman.

Blaug, M. (1985). *Economic theory in retrospect* (4th ed.). Cambridge: Cambridge University Press.

Böhm-Bawerk, E. von (1959). *Capital and interest*. Translated by G. D. Huncke. South Holland: Libertarian Press.

Brewer, A. (1988). Edward West and the classical theory of distribution and growth. *Economica (n.s.)*, *55*(220), 505–515.

Buchanan, D. H. (1929). The historical approach to rent and price theory. *Economica*, *26*, 123–155.

Cannan, E. (1892). The origin of the law of diminishing returns. *Economic Journal*, *2*(5), 53–89.

Caravale, G. A., & Tosata, D. A. (2003). *Ricardo and the theory of value, distribution and growth*. London: Routledge.

Corry, B. (1959). Malthus and Keynes – A reconsideration. *Economic Journal*, *69*(276), 717–724.

Corry, B. (1966). *Money, saving and investment in English Economics*. London: Macmillan.

Dobb, M. (1973). *Theories of value and distribution since Adam Smith*. Cambridge: Cambridge University Press.

Dome, T. (1999). Bentham and J. S. Mill on tax reform. *Utilitas*, *11*(3), 320–339.

Eatwell, J. (1975). The interpretation of Ricardo's *Essay on Profits*. *Economica (n.s.)*, *42*(166), 18–87.

Edgeworth, Y. (1925). *Papers relating to political economy* (3 vols.). London: Macmillan.

Erickson, A. B. (1952). *The public career of Sir James Graham*. Oxford: Basil Blackwell.

Fetter, F. W. (1965). *The development of British monetary orthodoxy*. Cambridge, MA: Harvard University Press.

Fisher, I. (1911). *The purchasing power of money: Its determination and relation to credit, interest and crises*. New York: Macmillan.

Fisher, I. (1920). *Stabilising the dollar: A plan to stabilise the general price level without fixing individual prices*. New York: Macmillan.

Fisher, I. (1922). *The making of index numbers: A study of their varieties, tests and reliability*. Boston, MA: Houghton Mifflin.

Fleetwood, W. (1707). *Chronicon preciosum: Or an account of English money, the price of corn and other commodities, for the last 600 years*. London: Charles Harper.

Gee, J. M. A. (1981). The origin of rent in Adam Smith's *Wealth of Nations*: An anti-neoclassical view. *History of Political Economy*, *13*(1), 1–18.

Goodwin, W. (1796). *Enquiry concerning political justice and its influence on general virtue and happiness*. London: G. and G. Robinson.

Goodwin, W. (1997). *The enquirer, reflections on education, manners and literature*. London: G. and G. Robinson.

Gordon, B. (1979). *Economic doctrine and Tory Liberalism, 1824–30*. London: Macmillan.

Graham, J. (1826). *Corn and currency*. London: J. Ridgway.

Grampp, W. D. (1956). Malthus on money wages and welfare. *American Economic Review*, *46*(5), 924–936.

Grampp, W. D. (1960). *The Manchester School of Economics*. Stanford: Stanford University Press.

Haig, B. (2006). Sir Timothy Coghlan and the development of national accounts. *History of Political Economy*, *38*(2), 339–375.

Hamilton, R. (1818). *An inquiry concerning the rise and progress, the redemption and present state and the management of the national debt of Great Britain and Ireland*. Edinburgh: Oliphant, Waugh and Innes.

Hansard Parliamentary Debates. (1830). Volume XVII, Irish Universities Press.

Hansard Parliamentary Debates. (1834). Volume XXI, Irish Universities Press.

Helleiner, E. (2002). Economic nationalism as a challenge to economic liberalism? Lessons from the 19th century. *International Studies Quarterly*, *46*(3), 307–329.

Hicks, J. (1932). *The theory of wages*. London: Macmillan.

Hicks, J. (1939). *Value and capital: An inquiry into some fundamental principles of economic theory*. Oxford: Clarendon Press.

Hollander, J. (1895). The concept of marginal rent. *Quarterly Journal of Economics*, *9*(2), 175–187.

Hollander, J. (1910). *David Ricardo: A centenary estimate*. Baltimore, MD: Johns Hopkins University Press.

Hollander, J. (1911). Ricardo and Torrens. *Economic Journal*, *21*(83), 455–468.

Hollander, S. (1973a). Ricardo's analysis of the profit rate, 1813–15. *Economica (n.s.)*, *40*(159), 260–282.

Hollander, S. (1973b). *The Economics of Adam Smith*. Toronto: University of Toronto Press.

Hollander, S. (1977). Ricardo and the Corn Laws: A revision. *History of Political Economy*, *9*(1), 1–47.

Hollander, S. (1979). *The economics of David Ricardo*. Toronto: University of Toronto Press.

Hollander, S. (1997). *The economics of Thomas Robert Malthus*. Toronto: University of Toronto Press.

Lauderdale, J. M. (1804 [1819]). *An inquiry into the nature and origin of public wealth* (2nd ed.). Edinburgh: Archibald Constable.

Lonsdale, H. (1868). John Rooke. In: *Worthies of Cumberland*. London: George Routledge & Sons.

Lowe, J. (1822). *The present state of England in regard to agriculture and finance*. London: Longman, Hurst, Rees, Orme, and Brown.

McCulloch, J. R. (1845). *Literature of political economy: A classification catalogue of select publications in the different departments of that science with historical, critical and biographical notices*. Fairfield, NJ: A.M. Kelley.

Malthus, T. R. (1800). *An investigation of the causes of the present high price of provisions*. London: J. Johnson.

Malthus, T. R. (1814). *Observations on the effects of the Corn Laws, and the rise or fall in the price of corn on the agriculture and general wealth of the country*. London: J. Johnson.

Malthus, T. R. (1815a). *The grounds for an opinion on the policy of restricting the importation of foreign corn*. London: J. Murray.

Malthus, T. R. ([1815b] 1970). An inquiry into the nature and progress of rent. In: *Pamphlets of Thomas Robert Malthus*. New York: A. M. Kelley.

Malthus, T. R. (1836). *Principles of political economy* (2nd ed.). London: J. Murray.

Marshall, A. (1887). Remedies for fluctuations of general prices. *The Contemporary Review*, *51*(March), 355–375.

Marshall, A. (1890). *Principles of economics*. London: Macmillan.

Matthews, R. C. O. (1955). Capital stock adjustment theories of the trade cycle and the problem of policy. In: K. Kurihara (Ed.), *Post Keynesian economics* (pp. 170–191). London: George Allen & Unwin.

Mundie, G. (1818). *Mr Owen's proposed arrangement*. London.

Mushet, R. (1821). *A series of tables exhibiting the gains and loss to the fundholder arising from the fluctuations in the value of the currency from 1800 to 1821*. London: Baldwin & Co.

Newcomb, S. (1879). The standard of value. *North American Review*, *129*(274), 223–237.

O'Brien, D. P. (1970). *J. R. McCulloch: A study in classical economics*. London: George Allen & Unwin.

O'Brien, D. P. (1975). *The classical economists*. Oxford: Oxford University Press.

O'Brien, D. P. (1981). On Ricardian economics and the economics of Ricardo. *Oxford Economic Papers*, *33*(3), 352–386.

Opie, R. (1929). A neglected English economist: George Poulett Scrope. *Quarterly Journal of Economics*, *44*(1), 101–137.

Owen, R. (1815). *Observations on the effect of the manufacturing system and report to the county of Lanark*. London: R. & A. Taylor.

Patinkin, D. (1993). Irving Fisher and his compensated dollar plan. *Federal Reserve Bank of Richmond Economic Quarterly*, *79*(3), 1–34.

Pigou, A. C. (1908). *Economic science in relation to practice*. London: Macmillan.

Rooke, J. (1814). Examination of the rise of the price of corn. *Evans and Ruffy Farmer's Journal and Manufacturer's and Traders' Register*, London.

Rooke, J. (1815). The appreciation of the value of money considered. *Evans and Ruffy Farmer's Journal and Manufacturer's and Traders' Register*, London.

Rooke, J. (1819a). *Remarks on the nature and operation of money*. London: Baldwin, Craddock and Joy.

Rooke, J. (1819b). *A supplement to some remarks on the nature and operation of money*. London: Baldwin, Craddock and Joy.

Rooke, J. (1822). *An essay on the national debt showing the use and abuse of the funding system*. London: J. Richardson.

Rooke, J. (1824). *An inquiry into the principles of national wealth*. Edinburgh.

Rooke, J. (1825). *Claim to the original publication of certain new principles in political economy, addressed in a letter to E. D. Davenport, Esq. by John Rooke, author of An Inquiry into the Principles of National Wealth*. London.

Rooke, J. (1828). *Free trade in corn and the true policy of the state*. London: J. Ridgway.

Rooke, J. (1835). *Free and safe government traced from the origin and principles of the British constitution*. London: J. Ridgway.

Schumpeter, J. A. (1954). *History of economic analysis*. London: George Allen & Unwin.

Scrope, G. P. (1833a). *An examination of the bank charter question, with an inquiry into the nature of a just standard of value, and suggestions for the improvement of our monetary system*. London: J. Murray.

Scrope, G. P. (1833b). *Principles of political economy deduced from the natural laws of social welfare and applied to the present state of Britain*. London: Green and Longman.

Seligman, E. R. A. (1903). On some neglected British economists. *Economic Journal*, *13*(51 and 52), 335–363 and pp. 511–535.

Seligman, E. R. A. (1908). *Progressive taxation in theory and practice*. Princeton, NJ.

Seligman, E. R. A. (1911). Ricardo and Torrens. *Economic Journal*, *21*(83), 448–455.

Senior, N. (1836). *Outline of the science of political economy*. London: Richard Griffin and Co.

Shuckleburgh-Evelyn, G. (1798). An account of some endeavours to ascertain a standard of weight and measure. *Philosophical Transactions of the Royal Society of London*, *88*, 133–182.

Smith, A. (1977). Glasgow edition. *An inquiry into the nature and causes of the wealth of nations*. (2 vols.). Oxford: Oxford University Press.

Smith, V. E. (1951). The classicists 'use of demand'. *Journal of Political Economy*, *59*(3), 242–257.

Smith, V. E. (1956). Malthus' theory of demand and its influence on value theory. *Scottish Journal of Political Economy*, *33*(3), 205–220.

Sowell, T. (1974). *Classical economics reconsidered.* Princeton, NJ: Princeton University Press.

Sraffa, P., & Dobb, M. (Eds). (1951a). *Works and correspondence of David Ricardo. Vol. I, Principles of political economy and taxation*. Cambridge: Cambridge University Press.

Sraffa, P., & Dobb, M. (Eds). (1951b). *Works and correspondence of David Ricardo. Vol. II, Notes on Malthus*. Cambridge: Cambridge University Press.

Sraffa, P., & Dobb, M. (Eds). (1951c). *Works and correspondence of David Ricardo. Vol. IV, Pamphlets and papers, 1815–1823*. Cambridge: Cambridge University Press.

Sraffa, P., & Dobb, M. (Eds). (1951d). *Works and correspondence of David Ricardo. Vol. VI, Letters and correspondence 1810–1815*. Cambridge: Cambridge University Press.

Stark, W. (1952). Introduction. In: W. Stark (Ed.), *Works of Jeremy Bentham* (Vol. II). London: George Allen and Unwin.

Sumner, S. (1990). The forerunners of 'new monetary economics': Proposals to stabilise the unit of account. *Journal of Money, Credit and Banking*, *22*(1), 109–118.

Sumner, S. (1991). The development of aggregate economic targeting. *Cato Journal*, *10*(3), 747–759.

Sumner, S. (1995). Using monetary policy to target a nominal wage index. *Journal of Economics and Business*, *47*(2), 205–215.

Thompson, P. (1834). *Catechism on the Corn Laws: With a list of fallacies and the answers: To which is added the article of free trade from the Westminster review, no. xxiii: With the article on the silk and glove trades, from no. xxxii: and the supplements from no. xxxiii, xxxiv, and xxxv: With a collection of objections and the answer by a Member of the University of Cambridge*. London: Robert Heward.

Torrens, R. (1815). *Essay on external corn trade*. London: Hatchard.

Torrens, T. M. (1863). *Life and times of the Rt. Hon. Sir James Graham*. London: Saunders, Otley & Co.

Viner, J. (1937). *Studies in the theory of international trade*. New York: Harper and Brothers.

Von Thünen, J. H. ([1842] 1996). *The isolated state*. Translated by C. M. Wartenberg. Oxford: Pergamon Press.

Wagner, D. O. (1931). British economists and the Empire, I. *Political Science Quarterly*, *46*(2), 248–276.

Wallace, A. R. ([1898] 1900). Paper money as a standard of value. *The academy*, Vol. 31. Reprinted in *Studies scientific and social* (Vol. II). London: Macmillan.

Ward, T. J. (1967). *Sir James Graham*. London: Macmillan.

West, E. (1815). *An essay on the application of capital to land, with observations showing the impolicy of any great restriction of the importation of corn, and that the bounty of 1688 did not lower the price of it*. London: T. Underwood.

Wheatley, J. (1803). *Remarks on currency and commerce*. London: Cadell and Davies.

APPENDIX. REPOSITORIES FOR THE PUBLICATIONS OF JOHN ROOKE

Key to Repositories:

British Museum	BM
British Museum (Colindale)	BMC
Jackson Library, Tullie House, Carlisle	JL
Kress Library, Harvard University	Kress

1814	July 4	'Examination of the Rise of the Price of Corn', *Evans and Ruffy Farmer's Journal and Manufacturer's and Traders' Register* (hereafter *ERFJ*), *London.* (BMC)
1815	February 13	'On the Proper Measures of the Value of Labour', *ERFJ.* (BMC)
	February 20	'On the Same Subject', *ERFJ.* (BMC)
	February 28	'On the Same Subject, in continuation', *ERFJ.* (BMC)
	April 3	'In Answer to Mr. Young and Mr. Farey on Corn Rents; and on Regulating Rents and Money Securities, so as their value may be least affected by the increase or depreciation of the value of Money', *ERFJ.* (BMC)
	June 19	'An Inquiry into the Probable Future Price of Farm Produce', *ERFJ.* (BMC)
	October 30	'In Answer to a Political Economist on the Present Prices of Farming Produce', *ERFJ.* (BMC)
1816	January 13	'Difficulties of the Times', *Carlisle Patriot*, Carlisle. (JL)
	February 17	'Present Difficulties', *Carlisle Patriot.* (JL)
	February 26	'On the Nature and Necessity of Introducing a New Money System', *ERFJ.* (BMC)
	April 27	'On the Commutation of Tithes', *Carlisle Patriot.* (JL)
	June 10	'On Political Economy Being a Fit Subject for this Journal', *ERFJ.* (BMC)

APPENDIX (*Continued*)

	July 29	'The Appreciation of the Value of Money Considered', *ERFJ.* (BMC)
	August 10	'The Appreciation of Money', *Carlisle Patriot.* (JL)
	September 14	'Thoughts on the Present System of Economy', *Carlisle Patriot.* (JL)
	September 30	'Public Difficulties', *ERFJ.* (BMC)
	October 21	'Overabundance', *ERFJ.* (BMC)
	December 30	'On the Causes of the Depreciation of the Current Corn', *ERFJ.* (BMC)
1817	January 13	'On the Nature and Use of a Political Barometer', *ERFJ.* (BMC)
	April 7	'On the Comparative Financial Resources of the Kingdom', *ERFJ.* (BMC)
	April 14	'On Taxation', *ERFJ.* (BMC)
	September 18	'On the Interest of Money', *Carlisle Patriot.* (JL)
	November 27	'To the Inquirer', *Carlisle Patriot.* (JL)
1819		*Remarks on the Nature and Operation of Money with a View to Elucidate the Effects of the Present Circulating Medium of Great Britain Intended to Prove that the National Distresses are Attributable to our Money System*, London. (JL)
	September 30	'Mr. Rooke on Relieving the Distress', *ERFJ.* (BMC)
	October 18	'Mr. Rooke on Rent', *ERFJ.* (BMC) *A Supplement to the Remarks on the Nature and Operation of Money etc.*, London. (JL)
	November 22	'Mr. Rooke on Currency and Cash Payments', *ERFJ.* (BMC)
1820	January 20	'On the Standard of Value', *ERFJ.* (BMC)
	March 13	'Currency versus Corn', *ERFJ.* (BMC)
	April 3	'On the Standard of *Value*', *ERFJ.* (BMC)
	April 17	'On Currency', *ERFJ.* (BMC)
	April 24	'On the Question of Currency', *ERFJ.* (BMC)

APPENDIX (*Continued*)

	June 26	'On Currency and the Standard of Value', *ERFJ.* (BMC)
	September 25	'On Currency', *ERFJ.* (BMC)
	October 30	'On the Currency Question', *ERFJ.* (BMC)
	December 4	'On Currency', *ERFJ.* (BMC)
1821	January 8	'On the Real Price of Wheat', *ERFJ.* (BMC)
	January 15	'On the Question of Currency', *ERFJ.* (BMC)
1822		*An Essay on the National Debt, Showing the Use and Abuse of the Funding System*, London. (JL)
	October 28	'Corn and Currency', *ERFJ.* (BMC)
	December 16	'Mr. Rooke on Attwood', *ERFJ.* (BMC)
1823	January 20	'To Thomas Attwood on Relieving Distress', *ERFJ.* (BMC)
1824		*An Inquiry into the Principles of National Wealth Illustrated by the Political Economy of the British Empire*, Edinburgh. (BM)
	October 25	'On the Value of Manufactures in Scotland', *ERFJ.* (BMC)
	November 15	'On Free Trade', *ERFJ.* (BMC)
1825		*Claim to the Original Publication of Certain New Principles in Political Economy, addressed in a letter to E. D. Davenport, Esq., by John Rooke, author of An Inquiry into the Principles of National Wealth*, London. (Kress)
1828		*Free Trade in Corn, the Real Interest of the Landlord and the True Policy of the State*, London. (JL)
1835		*Free and Safe Government Traced from the Origin and Principles of the British Constitution*, London. (BM)

APPENDIX (*Continued*)

1838	*Geology as a Science Applied to the Reclamation of Land from the Sea,* London. (JL)
1851	'Geology of the Lake District', in *History, Topography and Directory of Westmorland ... together with a descriptive and geological view of the Lake District,* Beverley. (JL)
1852	'An Appendix on the Geology of the Lake District', in *A Description of Scenery in the Lake District Intended as a Guide for Strangers.* (JL)

PIERCY RAVENSTONE: TORY DEMOCRAT AND PHYSIOCRATIC ANTI-CAPITALIST

Noel W. Thompson

Seligman's treatment of Ravenstone was brief (Seligman, 1903, pp. 514–515); on the grounds that his concern in the *Economic Journal* articles was really with 'the economists proper, rather than with their Socialist critics' (1903, p. 515). In his discussion he contrasted Ravenstone's inherently critical and pessimistic view of contemporary society with that of '[John] Rooke and the dominant school of economists'. He elided any discussion of his position on Malthus and population, 'which [does] not materially differ from…other works of the kind' (1903, p. 515), even though that was articulated at some considerable length in Ravenstone's *A Few Doubts as to the Correctness of Some Opinions Generally Entertained on the Subjects of Population and Political Economy* (1966 [1821]). No note was taken at all of *Thoughts on the Funding System and its Effects* (Ravenstone, 1966 [1824]). Instead, Seligman concentrated on his views on property and capital, rent and profit, where Ravenstone was placed in the company of Marx and those whom H. S. Foxwell (1899) had identified as the 'Ricardian socialists'. In particular he was seen by Seligman as 'the first predecessor of Marx to advance the surplus value theory' though differing from Marx in seeing rent as the primary and profit as 'the derivative form of exploitation' (Seligman, 1903, p. 515). More generally, Ravenstone was seen as a member of 'the earliest of that group of

English, Irish and Subversives Among the Dismal Scientists
Research in the History of Economic Thought and Methodology, Volume 28-B, 303–327

ISSN: 0743-4154/doi:10.1108/S0743-4154(2010)000028B013

writers who, during the twenties, sought to undermine the basis of the edifice so carefully erected by the economists' (1903, p. 515).

Where, and if, we should locate Ravenstone in that group is something that is discussed at length later in text. However, before doing so it is necessary to address one issue that has certainly ensured that a number of commentators continued to evince an interest in Ravenstone after the publication of Seligman's article, namely that of his true identity.

IDENTITY

Joseph Dorfman in his introduction to the 1966 edition of Ravenstone's *A Few Doubts on the Subjects of Population and Political Economy* argued that Ravenstone was Rev. Edward Edwards, a major contributor on political economy to the *Quarterly Review* and *Blackwood's Magazine*. The case Dorfman made was circumstantial but nonetheless a strong one. First there was the fact that 'articles in these Tory organs [were] roughly speaking in accordance with the views of "Ravenstone"' (Dorfman, 1966). Both Ravenstone and Edwards were, for example, strongly critical of Malthusian population theory and its implications. Furthermore, on the basis of a reading of the 1821 work, Dorfman opined that Ravenstone was a trained theologian, something consistent with Edwards' clerical status, and that both had a predilection for historical reflection. Dorfman also believed he had found evidence in the files of John Murray, the publisher of the *Quarterly Review*, to substantiate his identification. Thus he cites a letter from Murray to William Gifford, a member of the publishing house, dated 3 November 1820, which makes reference to a manuscript sent to Murray shortly before *A Few Doubts* was published by another house. Moreover, Murray's correspondence files show that Edwards thought highly of Henry Brougham, and there is a copy of *A Few Doubts* in the Goldsmiths' Library in London, which is inscribed from the author to him (Dorfman, 1966, p. 20).

In the early 1970s, Dorfman was in correspondence with Piero Sraffa about this matter: the latter's papers contain a letter from him dated 9 January 1970 stating, 'I have been tracking down leads that Piercy Ravenstone may be Richard Puller', but that he had 'found nothing substantial that casts doubt on my hypothesis that "Piercy Ravenstone" was "Edward Edwards"'. And a month later (4 February), still clearly fired by the thrill of the chase, he wrote – 'What intriguing detective work' (both letters in Sraffa Papers, D3/11/203). Surprisingly, though, while Dorfman clearly considered there were sufficiently marked similarities between the political economies of Ravenstone and Edwards to suggest that the authors were one and the same person and while such similarities undoubtedly exist, he did not furnish any detailed comparative analysis of the work of the two. This is an omission that is addressed later in the chapter as it throws light on both the issue of identity and also the political economy, or rather political economies of Tory radicalism, extant in early-nineteenth-century Britain to which Ravenstone and Edwards made a significant contribution. What can be said at this juncture is that while, by the early 1970s, some basis had been provided for believing that Ravenstone was Edwards, there was no obviously smoking gun.

Piero Sraffa also became intrigued by the issue of identity while working on his edition of the *Works and Correspondence of David Ricardo*. His preferred candidate was Richard Puller, the son of a merchant family whose father, Christopher was noted as a Director of the South Sea Company in *Kent's Directory* for 1780 (see Sraffa Papers, D3/11/203). In 1791, the same *Directory* noted that his son Richard Puller had been elected a director of the South Sea Company in 1790; Richard was identified with that position in each subsequent annual edition of the *Directory* until 1809. Sraffa also identified this Richard Puller as a Fellow of Oriel College, Oxford, and found his likely obituary in an 1826 *Gentleman's Magazine*, which gave his death as 5 December and his age as 80 (Sraffa Papers, D3/11/203). However, it is Richard Puller, his son, whom Sraffa suggests as the author of *A Few Doubts* in Ricardo's *Collected Works* (Sraffa & Dobb, 1973, Vol. 11, p. xxviii). As to Dorfman's identification of Ravenstone as Edwards, Sraffa wrote that there 'appears to be no evidence to support this conjecture' (1973, Vol. 11, p. xxviii). As evidence of Ravenstone as Puller, he noted that

> A copy of *A Few Doubts* has come to light, on the title-page of which 'Piercy Ravenstone, M.A.' has been crossed out and 'Richard Puller' written in, 'Puller on Political Economy' is lettered on the spine of the binding, which is contemporary; this may well have been the author's own copy. Another copy, which is in the Fetrinelli Library in Milan is inscribed on the fly leaf: 'the real author of this book was Richard Puller, brother of Sir Christopher Puller, member for Hertfordshire about 1858'. (Sraffa & Dobb, 1973, Vol. 11, p. xxviii)

Sraffa's Ricardo was published in 1973. However, in October 1970, an article had appeared in the *La Trobe Journal*. The article related to the papers of Charles Pearson, 'a leading, nineteenth-century English medieval historian', who 'helped to pioneer the study of historical geography, and contributed regularly to London reviews'. Pearson had been a lecturer in history at the University of Melbourne in 1874, an educational reformer, a member of the Victoria legislative assembly from 1878–1892, and a Minister of Public Instruction in the state government from 1886–1880. As the author of this article – John Tregenza – wrote 'he belonged to that rare species, the Australian politician who is also an intellectual' (Tregenza, 1970, p. 45).

In a collection of Pearson's papers that had recently come to light, Tregenza noted that there was 'a manuscript in Pearson's own hand of his autobiographical fragment "The Story of My Life"', which ends with his arrival in Australia in 1871. When Tregenza compared it to a version printed in William Stebbing's (1900) memorial to Pearson, he noted that passages had been altered and excisions made. And, 'one of the passages so omitted was a casual remark that an uncle, Richard Puller, "wrote a book on Population, as Percy [for Piercy] Ravenstone"' (Tregenza, 1970, p. 46).

Taken together with the evidence cited by Sraffa, Tregenza's find would seem to be conclusive against the Dorfman hypothesis and convincing as regards the identification of Ravenstone as Puller. And yet a lingering concern remains. For Richard Puller, the elder, died in 1826. Moreover, in a highly critical review of *A Few Doubts* in the *British Critic*, the reviewer referred to its author as 'an old man and a Master of Arts' (Anonymous, 1821, p. 421). Richard Puller the younger could hardly have been so described in 1821; he was probably in his late 30s or early 40s. Also, given his age, if he were the author, it seems strange that he should have written in *A Few Doubts*: 'At my time of life and in my retirement I do not seek fame' (Ravenstone, 1966 [1821], p. 4). One might also add that as a Director of the South Sea Company, Richard Puller, the elder, would have been well-placed to discourse critically on the financial system in the manner of *Thoughts on the Funding System and Its Effects* (Ravenstone, 1966 [1824]). The intriguing possibility arises therefore that the author was the father and not the son.

However, this does not square with Pearson's reference to Puller as an uncle unless he was, for some reason, hopelessly confused as to the generation of the Richard to whom he referred. Also the inscription in the Fetrinelli copy of *A Few Doubts*, which refers to Richard Puller's brother Christopher as 'a member for Hertfordshire about 1858', points clearly to Richard Puller the younger as the author. Unless, again the author of the inscription is confusing this Christopher with the brother, of the same name, of the elder Richard, who was a Chief Justice of Bengal and died in 1824. It therefore seems relatively safe to conclude that, since the Seligman article, the authorship of Ravenstone's work has been established and that this issue is now unlikely to exercise the minds of future scholars

Sraffa also sought to identify the script of the author. Noting three possible examples of this he went to the lengths of using right-angled triangles to establish the slope of different signatures. The signatures he used were those of the 'author' on a copy of *A Few Doubts* (Goldsmiths' Library) and an affidavit sworn in connection with Puller's sister Charlotte. However, the signature on the volume could not be established as the same as that on the affidavit, though another putatively authorial signature on a copy of *Thoughts on the Funding System* in the University of London, Library is not unlike it.

CATEGORISATION

In paying tribute to H. S. Foxwell's retrieval of early-nineteenth-century British anti-capitalist and socialist political economists from the neglect that they suffered in the period after 1850, Seligman noted 'one exception, who seems to have escaped' Foxwell's 'notice...and that one curiously enough, the earliest advocate of the theory of surplus value subsequently adopted by Marx, "Percy [sic] Ravenstone"' (Seligman, 1903, p. 514). As Seligman also remarked this was all the more surprising as he was 'the earliest advocate of the theory of surplus value subsequently adopted by Marx' (1903, p. 514). For Seligman, Ravenstone was, therefore, 'the earliest of that group of writers who, during the twenties, sought to undermine the very basis of the edifice so carefully erected by the economists', and *A Few Doubts* was put in the company of 'other Socialist publications' (Seligman, 1903, p. 514).

Other writers have categorised Ravenstone as a socialist. G. D. H. Cole, in listing early British socialists, mentions in passing 'such unknowns as Ravenstone' and places Ravenstone's works amongst 'the most important works of the British socialists of the 1820s and 1830s' (Cole, 1953, pp. 219 and 323). More specifically he has also been labelled a 'Ricardian socialist'. So, for Blaug (1958, p. 141), 'the school of Ricardian socialists begins with "Piercy Ravenstone"' and, for Viner (1933, p. 117), 'Ravenstone was the first of the so-called Ricardian socialists' having 'a marked influence on Thomas Hodgskin and also, probably, William Thompson' (see also Burkitt, 1984, p. 129; O'Brien, 1987, p. 96).

Certainly both Ricardo and Marx took favourable cognisance of Ravenstone. Sraffa noted that Ricardo, in correspondence with James Mill and Malthus, 'refers several times with interest to the book', (Sraffa & Dobb, 1973, Vol. 11, p. xxviii) although the references are brief. To Mill, he wrote that he had 'looked with some interest at a work on Polit. Econ. by Mr. Piercy Ravenstone. Which though full of errors has some good things in it ... he is a strenuous and able advocate of Reform' (Ricardo to J. Mill, 28 August 1821, in Sraffa & Dobb, 1973, Vol. 9, p. 45). In his letter to Malthus,

Ricardo also commented that what Ravenstone had to say on the 'cause of the state of the working classes' was 'well stated'. Although, for Ricardo, 'he appear[ed] not to be aware of the difficulty of providing a remedy' (Ricardo to Malthus, 10 September 1821, in Viner, 1933, p. 119).

Furthermore, in a later letter, also to Mill, he notes a similarity between some of Ravenstone's views on population and those of William Godwin; views which he saw Francis Place's work on population as having effectively rebutted (Ricardo to J. Mill, 9 September 1821, in Sraffa & Dobb, 1973, p. 59). He also drew the attention of Malthus to the work, the latter responding that 'it is certainly, as you say, full of errors, but I believe he is a well-meaning man and I will look at it again' (Malthus to Ricardo, 13 September 1821, in Sraffa & Dobb, 1973, p. 64). Thereafter, Ravenstone is not remarked upon by either writer.

Marx is a different matter. Ravenstone is mentioned at a number of points in the *Grundrisse*; Marx's primary focus being on what he saw as Ravenstone's conception of absolute and relative surplus value. In this regard he quoted Ravenstone's view that the origin of property lay in the advancing productivity of labour and the growing surplus which that produced. For Marx, Ravenstone had grasped that 'the whole development of wealth rests on the creation of disposable time' and that the ratio between 'necessary' and 'superfluous' labour time varied 'with the different stages of the development of productive forces' (Marx, 2000a [1857]); a point Marx was to make again in *Capital* (Marx, 1974, Vol. 1, p. 479). Engels also noted Ravenstone's contribution to a British anti-capitalist and socialist literature of the 1820s and 1830s, which saw various formulations of a concept of surplus value; a literature which he admits with 'a certain mortification' was, despite Marx's reference to it in the *Poverty of Philosophy* and elsewhere, almost 'totally unknown in Germany' (Marx, 1974, Vol. 2, p. 14).

In addition, in the *Grundrisse* Marx made reference to Ravenstone's view that machinery was only deployed 'when it acts on great masses; when a single machine can assist the labours of thousands'. 'It is not called into action by a scarcity of men, but by the facility with which they are brought together' (Marx, 2000a [1857]).[1] Expatiating on and agreeing with this view, Marx argued that 'only in the imagination of economists does it leap to the aid of the individual worker. It can be effective only with masses of workers, whose concentration relative to capital is one of its historic presuppositions.... Machinery enters only where labour capacity is on hand in masses' (Marx, 2000b [1857]). Marx stopped short of crediting Ravenstone with anticipating machinery's role in creating an industrial reserve army and yet he might have gone on to do so as such a concept is indeed articulated in

Ravenstone's *A Few Doubts*, where he wrote that 'every particular branch [of industry] must ... be provided with more hands than it can constantly employ. It could not otherwise satisfy extraordinary demands. There must then be alternately in every branch a number of persona without employment' (Ravenstone, 1966 [1821], p. 270). In short a reserve of labour was necessary to cope with the cyclical nature of demand in the contemporary economy.

Marx also picked up on Ravenstone's work in the *Theories of Surplus Value*. Here, however, the focus was exclusively upon his *Thoughts on the Funding System*, which was seen by him as a 'most remarkable work', 'an original piece of work', and was discussed under the heading of 'Opposition to the economists (based on Ricardian theory)' (Marx, 1972, Vol. 3, pp. 257, 252): a view of Ravenstone also expressed in the 'Afterword' to the second German edition of *Capital* and which was integral to a particular reading of the history of early-nineteenth-century political economy as being characterised by a degeneration from social science to apologetics – 'the bad conscience and evil intent of apologetic' (Marx, 1974, Vol. 1); a degeneration precipitated by a reaction against a putative socialist/anti-capitalist appropriation of Ricardian value theory for a critique of the capitalist system.[2]

In the *Theories of Surplus Value* too, as in the *Grundrisse* and *Capital*, Marx once again focused on Ravenstone's concept of surplus, noting on this occasion that he had a tendency to conceive of it in physical terms as a 'form of surplus product'. That said he also averred that in the *Thoughts* Ravenstone 'define[d] relative surplus value' with a fair degree of precision as 'being dependent on the development of the productive power of labour' (Marx, 1972, pp. 258, 266). But, as regards Ravenstone's alternative to existing economic and social arrangements, Marx saw him as one of those anti-capitalist writers who were 'determined to sacrifice the fruits which have developed within the antagonistic [capital/labour] form, in order to get rid of the contradictions' (1972, p. 261).

Yet favourable notice by Ricardo and Marx does not make Ravenstone either a Ricardian or a socialist. Ravenstone certainly advanced a labour theory of value but it does not underpin his theory of surplus value which, as Marx noted, tended to be articulated in essentially physical terms. What it does inform is his critique of what he saw as the metaphysical conception of capital deployed by many contemporary political economists and it is certainly used to critique the reward accruing to capital in a manner similar to that to be found in Thomas Hodgskin's *Labour Defended Against the Claims of Capital* (1825). Such a similarity was noted by Halévy (1956) in his biography of Hodgskin when he locates Ravenstone amongst those in this period who may legitimately be termed 'anti-capitalist'. Indeed, in relation to Hodgskin, Halévy goes further, writing that 'in a curious pamphlet written in 1821, Piercy Ravenstone had tried to make plain the illusions of the political economy of capitalism, and Hodgskin, to strengthen the working-class cause, took up Ravenstone's thesis and completed it' (Halévy, 1956, p. 89). However, while there are marked similarities between Ravenstone and Hodgskin as regards their critique of the concept of capital deployed by some classical writers; while Ravenstone, like Hodgskin, saw impoverishment and inequity as rooted in an 'artificial right' of property; and while both were highly critical of Malthusianism and the Corn Laws, there is no acknowledgement in Hodgskin's works of any indebtedness. *A Few Doubts* is noted in Hodgskin's (1966 [1827]) *Popular Political Economy*, but only in passing and only in relation to Ravenstone's views on the impact of knowledge on production (Hodgskin, 1966 [1827], p. 77n). In this regard there is no direct evidence that, as Halévy suggests, Ravenstone's was 'a criticism of the concept of capital from which Hodgskin has borrowed extensively' (Halévy, 1956, p. 89n). Nor does Hodgskin's *Natural and Artificial Rights of Property Contrasted* (1832) make any reference to Ravenstone and in terms of their concept of labour as the basis of property, the similarity of the views on natural and artificial rights would seem to derive from a common root in Locke.

Ravenstone is noted briefly in Stack's substantial study of Hodgskin but to emphasise that 'despite' his 'efforts' and those of others, it was only with *Labour Defended* that 'radicalism found a coherent response to the political economists' (Stack, 1998, p. 33). Furthermore, Ravenstone's critique of capital is referred to as one of the 'older, cruder, versions of labour as a power relation' to which 'radicalism' reverted *after* Hodgskin's work.

That said Stack rather overeggs the pudding. For even if, as he has argued, Ravenstone only dealt with 'merchant and usury capital' and while profits certainly were seen as derived ultimately from the surplus produced by agricultural labour, Ravenstone's critique of capital and discussion of the origins of surplus value anticipates in important respects what Hodgskin had to offer. Nor can Marx's approbatory comments be so easily ignored (Stack, 1998, pp. 134, 136). For, in Ravenstone's view, amongst those who share in the surplus that agriculture alone can create and which initially accrues to the landowner, is the 'master manufacturer': 'No sooner has the land-owner established his claim to share in the earnings of all those who exercise their industry in the cultivation of the soil, than the master-manufacturer sets up a similar claim to share in the earnings of those whose industry is employed in wool, or cotton, or iron or any of the other productions of human ingenuity' (Ravenstone, 1966 [1821], pp. 199–200). And, of course, the basis of that claim, the basis of the profits accruing to the master manufacturer was control over access to the means of production – namely fixed capital. Hodgskin may have more 'explicity ... separate[d] the capitalist and the landlord'. And it is certainly the case that, 'as conceived of by Ravenstone the origins of capital had agrarian roots', but Ravenstone clearly understood what allowed the woollen and the cotton manufacturer and the ironmaster to secure their share of the economic surplus (Stack, 1998, pp. 134–35).

So where should we locate Ravenstone in relation to the variegated tapestry of early-nineteenth-century anti-capitalist and socialist political economy? That he may legitimately be categorised as anti-capitalist is beyond dispute. Indeed Ravenstone is one of the first writers to attempt to subject capital and capitalists to sustained critical scrutiny. In that regard, *A Few Doubts* represents a qualitative change in the character of early-nineteenth-century radicalism while, in Ravenstone's case, as will be noted below, retaining at least elements of its critical political economy.[3] However this leaves open the nature of his anti-capitalism and how it relates to that of other writers. This has already been touched on in relation to the views of Stack but more might be said and although considerations of space prevent its exploration here, it is a question that might usefully be pursued in relation to the anti-capitalism of writers other than Hodgskin.

However, what will be considered is the more general question of the nature of Ravenstone's anti-capitalism. And here it is important to give further consideration to his concept of capital. For certainly with writers such as Ravenstone and Charles Hall a new social category entered the radical demonology. 'Capitalists [were] a species of vermin not easily thrown off' while 'capital when it has got its legs round the neck of a nation, never loosens its hold till it has strangled its victim' (Ravenstone, 1966 [1821], pp. 356, 357). And for Ravenstone it originated with rent and taxes. In relation to these: 'Capital [was] their child, their confederate, their constant ally, in all their encroachments on industry. It is indeed the pioneer who opens the way for their approaches. It is their great operative cause in swelling the numbers of idle men, in loading society with their burthen' (1966 [1821], p. 352).

However, to understand how Ravenstone perceived the nature of the relation between capital, taxes and rent, it is necessary to consider his position on the question of productive and unproductive labour, and also on the *fons et origo* of the surplus generated by economic activity. On these issues his position is essentially physiocratic. As he saw it, the 'pretension of the land-owner' to the ownership of the economic surplus in the form of rent,

> is, indeed, the basis of the property of every description which is seen to multiply so rapidly with the growth of civilization. On it are built the pretensions of the master-manufacturer, of the tradesman, of the capitalist. All are founded on the same principle. No sooner has the land-owner established his claim to share in the earnings of all those who exercise their industry in the cultivation of the soil, than the master-manufacturer sets up a similar claim to share in the earnings of those whose industry is employed in wool, or cotton, or iron or any of the other productions of human ingenuity. From this moment labour ceases to be free. (Ravenstone, 1966 [1821], pp. 199–200)

Only agricultural labour was productive. The surplus it produced when appropriated as rent created both a class of idle men – landowners – and those who looked for opportunities to enable them to consume that surplus. It was this latter group that sought to stimulate and satisfy a demand for manufactured goods and services; something that in turn produced an expansion of domestic and international trade. And it was in satisfying such adventitious wants that those involved in manufacture, commerce and service provision were able to acquire a share of the surplus which agriculture produced. So profits were derived from rental income; as were taxes which represented the share of that income stream which accrued to the state and to fundholders.

So idle men, in their expenditure of rents, generated a displacement of resources and effort to unproductive activity: 'Traders and artificers, in one sense, equally come within the class of idlers. If they are not idle themselves, they only assist others in being so. They are not less dependent for their subsistence on the cultivator. It is only because others produce more than they consume that they can exist at all'. Or again, 'Every one who is supported by rent, is a person taken from the class of producers, to be added to the class of consumers' (Ravenstone, 1966 [1821], pp. 223, 225)[4] The idle begat the unproductive.

Ravenstone did seek to make a distinction between those who were unproductive and those who were both unproductive and idle. Artisans and traders, for the most part, were the former but not the latter. They were unproductive in that they functioned as the dependents of the consumers of rental income. On the contrary, they gave a service or an artefact to the community. Nevertheless the desires they satisfied were those of the idle and their activity a transfer of resources to activity that often did little or nothing to meet the real needs of the community. In that sense they aided and abetted the indolent at the expense of the active.

So what role did capital and capitalists play in all this? First, it is important to note that capital was a term frequently applied by Ravenstone to government stocks and bonds and that the category of 'capitalist' undoubtedly encompassed what Cobbett would have termed stock jobbers and moneymongers, whose number and wealth had multiplied during the Revolutionary and Napoleonic Wars. Ravenstone's anti-capitalism was therefore often articulated, particularly in *Thoughts on the Funding System*, in terms of Cobbetian 'Old Corruption' and can be seen as consistent with the contemporary political economy of radicalism.

Yet, for Ravenstone, the concept of capital entailed something more than was dreamt of in the economic philosophy of William Cobbett. For 'capital' was seen as 'turning away to the maintenance of idlers the labours of the industrious' (1966 [1821], p. 40); a view of things which implies a capacity to command resources; to command both labour and what labour required for the productive activity necessary to satisfy the demands of the idle. In effect capital gave command over the means of production. As noted above, Stack suggests that Ravenstone had in mind mercantile and financial but not industrial capital, but if that were consistently so, how then did the manufacturers of wool, cotton and iron share in the rental surplus as Ravenstone clearly believed they did. In this regard when he wrote that capital effected 'a new distribution of the property of society', he surely had industrial as well as financial and mercantile capital in mind (1966 [1821], p. 23). Moreover, in the same work, he intimated that capital grew 'not by encouraging industry but by appropriating to itself its earnings' (1966 [1821], p. 40). Here, of course, the term 'industry' may be broadly defined but it is legitimate to suggest it encompassed the notion of manufacturing industry and, therefore, the idea of capital as a product and the *modus operandi* of an exploitative relationship between the 'master manufacturer' and his workforce. Elsewhere Ravenstone (1966 [1824], p. 3) also wrote of 'capital everywhere fastening on labour to share in the produce of labour'.

Like Hodgskin, Ravenstone also condemned the notion of the productivity of capital. As he wrote in *A Few Doubts*,

> How absurd ... is the pretension that has been set up by the capitalists, that to their capital is owing all the income of the nation; that without the aid of this imaginary wealth, the labours of men would be without effect, the fertility of the soil would produce no fruits. How ridiculous the alarm which has been attempted to be raised, that if the interests of the capitalists were not sufficiently attended to, they would abandon the country, and carry with them their capitals, would deprive it of the advantages afforded to industry by their protection. (Ravenstone, 1966 [1824], p. 352)

Conceived of in that way, as it was by many contemporary writers, 'the doctrine of capital and its effects is indeed the most injurious to society that ever was broached. To teach that the wealth and power of a nation depend on its capital is to make industry ancillary to riches, to make men subservient to property' (1966 [1824], p. 7). *Per contra*, for Ravenstone, it was agricultural labour alone that created wealth; it was it alone that had the capacity to produce surplus value. And again, implicit in this critique of the putative productivity of capital is a concept of it as being applied to a *range* of productive activity and therefore with generalised 'pretensions' – not just something that lived and moved and had its being within the mercantile and funding system.

In relation to what Ravenstone had to say on capital, capitalists, productive and unproductive labour and the economic surplus, some other points can be made. To begin with, perhaps in consequence of a particular reading of some of the classical economists, or extrapolating from his own conception of a reserve of labour, Ravenstone saw wages, or the reward of labour, as gravitating, under the existing system, to a basic subsistence level. Thus the 'the wages of the labourer will be restricted to what can procure him the necessaries of life, and the necessaries will be reduced as low as possible by the reluctant bounty of the contributor' (1966 [1821], p. 201). Existing social and economic arrangements had 'reduced the labourer's earnings to the lowest sum on which he can subsist, when in health and employ' (1966 [1821], p. 70). Moreover the relationship between those to whom the economic surplus accrued and those who produced it was essentially, and necessarily, antagonistic, based as it was on a zero sum game. So 'the idle man is richer only because the industrious one is worse paid. Wealth of the one is the poverty of the other' (1966 [1821], p. 223). And again, 'in the ordinary intercourse of individuals, the property one man acquires another as surely loses' (Ravenstone, 1966 [1824], p. 8); though it should be noted that Ravenstone also had a concept of increased surplus value as deriving from improvements in the productivity of labour.[5] But even here, even assuming that there was an ongoing increase in wealth, even if it was the case that the living standards of labour could rise, there was still the phenomenon of relative immiseration, and all that followed from that in terms of the unequal nature of the relationship between landowners and capitalists and those whom they employed. For 'wealth and power are wholly relative terms, they have no positive existence; all their power is derived from the poverty and weakness of others' (1966 [1824], p. 10).

In another sense too the interests of the producer and those who acquired and consumed the economic surplus were necessarily opposed, for 'everyone who is supported by rent, is a person taken from the class of producers, to be added to the class of consumers' (Ravenstone, 1966 [1821], p. 225). In consequence output would be diminished and wages further squeezed. Demand would be increased while supply would be correspondingly reduced.

Ravenstone also made a close connection between ownership of the economic surplus and legislative authority. As regards those to whom it accrued, he wrote that 'their interests will be considered as the interests of the whole community; they will frame its laws, which of course will sanction all their usurpations' (1966 [1821], p. 225) So 'the very form of government, the mode in which power is exercised, are dependant, whatever may be the laws, on the distribution of property' (1966 [1821], p. 434). In similar vein, Ravenstone established a powerful causal connection between the control of economic activity and the disposition of political power. As he wrote in *A Few Doubts*, 'All the disposable power of the state must reside with those who have the command of all its disposable industry… . Where there is but one species of property, the government, whatever be the form in which it is administered, must virtually reside in that property' (1966 [1821], p. 435). Whatever the institutional form assumed by the political system, whatever its putative political character, the fact was that those who wielded political power had to exercise their authority in harmony with the interests of those who wielded economic power. So parliament would 'only be allowed to exercise its pageant of power so long as it exercises it in obedience to the will of its master'. In contemporary circumstances therefore 'the spirit of such a government must be aristocratical' (1966 [1821], p. 435). So, for Ravenstone, the economic base most assuredly determined the political superstructure.

TORY DEMOCRAT

On the basis of his critical analysis, as it has been outlined earlier, it would be legitimate to term Ravenstone a physiocratic anti-capitalist, with a marked susceptibility to radical, Cobbettian discourse and a particular sense of how economic connected with political power. He was also a political economist with a clear conception of social antagonism underpinned by a concept of surplus value and its appropriation; and a clear sense too as to how that appropriation shaped the political system, political processes and the utilisation of political power.

Yet where does this leave his categorisation as a Tory. After all, commentators such as Claeys, Halévy and Stack have not only put Ravenstone in the company of Hodgskin but also those whom the former terms 'other radical, *Tory* and miscellaneous critics of the economic system'. On similar lines Dobb saw him as a '*Conservative traditionalist*' (Claeys, 1986, p. xxv; Dobb, 1973, p. 139; emphasis added) and, in the same vein, Dorfman categorised him as a 'radical *Tory*' and '*Tory* democrat' (Dorfman, 1966, emphasis added).

Certainly in his critique of the social impact of the growth of the funding system there is much that could legitimately be designated 'Tory'. Thus in his response to the 'new' money, the new monied classes and the social mobility and dislocation their emergence produced in the Napoleonic and post-Napoleonic War periods, there is much that, again, is consistent with the kind of Tory radicalism articulated by Cobbett and a number of other nineteenth-century writers. In *Rural Rides* Cobbett (1930) frequently lamented the extent to which the scions of the ancient aristocracy had been swept aside by the *nouveau riche* of the Great Wen and Ravenstone, similarly, highlighted the threats to social stability that stemmed from the new order of things which had emerged during this period of conflict and as a consequence of the manner in which it had been financed. In Ravenstone's work, these threats assumed a number of interconnected forms.

To begin with there was 'the display of upstart wealth that assails us on every side, the many of many millions, whose footsteps none can trace in the paths of regular commerce' (Ravenstone, 1966 [1824], p. 34). The wealth that had in some measure been sanctified by the passage of history; the wealthy who had long occupied a pre-eminent position within society had diminished in number and had been joined by those whose social roots and riches did not enjoy the sanction of a comparable longevity; those also who did not see wealth as carrying with it a moral onus to consider in their dealings the well-being of the community of which they were a part. Specifically, and in particular, the growth of funded debt in connection with the wars, had

> raise[d] up from the lowest and most worthless of the people a new set of patricians; to rob of a proportion of their property *the ancient gentry of the land*, to whose ancestors a whole nation owes its renown in arts and arms, and to transfer it to those new fangled hidalgos as a reward of their skills in the arts of fraud and peculation. (Ravenstone, 1966 [1824], p. 51)[6]

Where, in times of difficulty, the rich did support the poor; where they fulfilled, at least minimally, their social obligations, this was usually with resentment and from fear of social disorder. The growing exactions of the rich; their appropriation, whether as capitalist, landowner or trader, of an increasing fraction of the economic surplus, was exacerbating the sufferings of labour. And 'when property endeavours to exact more than it is possible for industry to give, the alliance is dissolved between the wants of the one and the superfluities of the other'. In such circumstances 'nothing is given but from fear' (Ravenstone, 1966 [1821], p. 471). And it was with a view to mitigate such fears that minimal social obligations were fulfilled by the *nouveau riche*. However, 'as the rich give only from fear, it is only from fear that the poor yield obedience'. Consequently, 'the true bonds of society, mutual affection and mutual interest are entirely destroyed' (1966 [1821], p. 290). So the relief furnish by the newly enriched was yielded from fear fuelled by their greed, grudgingly bestowed and resented by its recipients.

For Ravenstone, like many Tory radicals, Britain teetered on the brink of social revolution. The foundations of the old order of mutuality and respect had been eroded. The ancient gentry who had furnished them were in decline; the grasping *noveau riche* who threatened it in the ascendant. But, new or old, all 'land-owners' would now 'do well to consider that the vengeance of the mob is not always enlightened-that their judgement is not likely to be the most correct when suffering the torment of hunger' (1966 [1821], p. 426). When the social revolution came the mob would make no distinction between those who could trace their ancestry back to the Conqueror, and who had fulfilled their social obligations, and those the origins of whose social position lay in the recent expansion of the National Debt.

This evocation of the bogey of social revolution is integral to much of the political economy of *Tory* radicalism, and certainly to its purchase on the early-nineteenth-century mind. What is less apparent in such literature, though one can find it elsewhere in early-nineteenth-century radicalism, is the positive celebration of the impact of the French Revolution; and the juxtaposition of its favourable consequences with the economic and social circumstances prevailing in the British *ancien regime*. So, for Ravenstone, 'the French Revolution [had] entirely altered the relative condition of the inhabitants of the two countries. The misery which was formerly the characteristic of the French people is now transferred to their rivals… . In their anxiety to uphold old institutions, Englishmen have taken to themselves cast-off abuses of all other nations' (1966 [1821], p. 283). At the root of this relative transformation was the elimination of the idle in France and their multiplication in Britain. Thus 'the destruction of the idle classes removed her misery, but whilst the number of unproductive persons has been greatly diminished in France, it has greatly increased in England' (1966 [1821], p. 286). In short the French Revolution had swept away the impoverishment of the Ancien Regime by 'restor[ing] the rights of industry' and 'by curtailing the rights of property' (1966 [1821], p. 287). If this was Tory radicalism, it was with an emphasis on radicalism rather than Toryism.

Here it should also be noted that for Ravenstone the justification for the existence of property was a social one. There were no absolute rights of property. 'Property is the creature of convention; it owes its birth, its origin to society. It can have no rights but what it derives from its will, none but what are conducive to its benefit' (1966 [1821], p. 204). Given this, failure on the part of property owners to use their power in a socially-responsible manner had profound implications; implications which Ravenstone spelt out clearly in *A Few Doubts*. For, 'so far ... as the operation of property is beneficial to society', but only so far, 'it is lawful; when it becomes injurious, it is an usurpation; whilst it calls forth industry, and gives it a better direction, whilst it promotes civilization, and adds to the happiness of society, its claims must be admitted, when it oppresses industry ... [it] must be resisted' (1966 [1821], p. 204). Such a view of things again places Ravenstone within the ranks of Tory radicalism but very much on the radical wing of that particular political spectrum.

It is also clear that if Ravenstone was a Tory he was, as Dorfman suggested, a Tory democrat, and in this regard too sits easily in the company of Cobbett,[7] although in his understanding of the necessary preconditions for democracy he has probably more in common with Marx. As noted earlier Ravenstone saw the distribution of economic power and the consequent distribution of the economic surplus as defining the nature of the political system. Thus, 'where there are no rent, no taxes, where none share in the earnings of the industrious, the government by whatever name it may be called must be in fact a democracy, all power must reside in the people' (Ravenstone, 1966 [1821], p. 434). However, 'where there is but one species of property', to which the economic surplus accrues, 'the government, whatever be the form in which it is administered, must virtually reside in that property' (1966 [1821], p. 435). Of course, where such property bore the burden of taxation, then such a distribution of political power might be defensible. But, 'the introduction ... of taxes on consumption, by making a divorce between representation and taxation', undermined the legitimacy of the location of political authority in the hands of the landed aristocracy which had characterised the 'English Constitution' (1966 [1821], p. 438). 'If the right of representation were vested in property, when property was the only subject of taxation, it is unjust that it should continue to be vested when taxes are levied entirely on industry. Rights always imply duties. Property lost its privilege when it threw off its obligations' (1966 [1821], p. 443).

If the connection between taxation and representation were to be restored, therefore, all those who were taxed should have the opportunity of choosing their representatives. Until that occurred 'the rights of the people will be neglected, so long as the people has no share in choosing the House of Commons' (1966 [1821], p. 443). In that regard 'the cry against democracy was senseless' (1966 [1821], p. 444) and given what had occurred since the outbreak of the Revolutionary Wars it was certainly indefensible. The right to representation should reside with those who assumed the fiscal burdens of the state and as indirect and other forms of taxation now encompassed the greater part of the population, the franchise should be extended to all who consumed the produce upon which taxes were levied.

Ravenstone was no socialist. He made clear his opposition to the abolition of private property. He also denied that though value was derived from labour and labour furnished an entitlement to property, that there was any right to the whole produce of labour. 'To abolish property, to leave every man in full possession of his own earnings would only destroy industry… . To leave every man to the full fruits of his industry would not increase the amount of produce, it would only diminish the quantity of each man's labour' (1966 [1821], p. 226).

His justification for such a position lay in the need for a measure of coercion, if only the coercion of need, if labour was to work long hard and productively. Thus 'some force on the industry of individuals seems necessary to bring out all their powers… . This invasion of the natural rights of man seems justified by the advantages it produces'. Yet even if it did not add to a nation's economic strength and well-being, Ravenstone still considered it to be justified in that it 'add[ed] to its grace and dignity and ornament' (1966 [1821], p. 228).

Moreover a hierarchic society made for greater political strength and social stability as long as it was predicated on a distribution of property that was not excessively skewed in favour of those at the top. 'The pyramidal form of society is that which contributes most to its strength; is that which most assures its stability … it is the excess of rents, not their existence, which overthrows society' (1966 [1821], p. 228). So a society of measured, responsibility-bearing inequality; with power checked too by the existence of democracy; one where adventitious wants were reduced and where the profits of traders and capitalists were correspondingly circumscribed and a society from which the evils of credit and the funding system had been excised. Such was Ravenstone's ideal: the ideal of a physiocratic anti-capitalist and Tory democrat.

One other aspect of this vision is worthy of note: in part because it exemplifies the Toryism that celebrated a strong, cohesive, stable hierarchic society; in part too because it bears a remarkable similarity to the socialist literature of the period. This is perhaps unsurprising as this aspect of Ravenstone's political economy evinced that celebration of society and community which finds expression in public consumption. Thus in the same way that socialist writers such as Owen envisioned the architectural magnificence of their imagined communities (see Whitwell, 1972 [1830]), so Ravenstone believed there could be 'no better application of the surplus funds of society than in public works of splendour and magnificence which, giving to all a feeling of property, render men proud of their country and ennoble vanity into patriotism' (Ravenstone, 1966 [1821], p. 235). Such works would be a social expression of wealth and power; they would express the creativity and strength of the community. They would in a very real sense be communal property and they would correspondingly strengthen the commitment and loyalty of the populace to the community which produced them. Where, in private hands, such magnificence would embody and express the vices and social divisiveness associated with greed and ostentation; so as public monuments it would engender and reflect the virtues of solidarity and social progress. With such public consumption, 'The humble citizen' would 'place his glory in the splendour of the first magistrate of his state'. He would 'lavishly open the stores of his frugality to give magnificence to the public buildings of his city. What he denies himself, he freely gives to his country. As he is too poor to be vain in his own person, his vanity takes another direction; he is content to be vain of his city' (1966 [1821], p. 215).

So a hierarchic, pyramidal order is further strengthened by the physical expression of the ideal of social opulence. A frugality born of the demands of the state is acceptable where what is saved is expended in ways from which all could derive both pleasure and pride. Social consumption made for social commitment and thence social coherence and stability. For Ravenstone, it informed and expressed the ideals of his Tory democracy.

THE TORY RADICALISM OF EDWARDS AND PIERCY RAVENSTONE

So how does to the Tory radicalism of Ravenstone compare with that of Edwards and are there sufficient grounds for Dorfman's contention that, given their respective positions on key theoretical and policy issues, it is legitimate to believe that they may have been the same author? Here the most obvious similarity is their shared physiocratic conception of what constituted productive labour and the fact that both used it as the basis for a critique of the contemporary distribution of income and wealth. Thus, for Edwards, 'The fruit and vegetable productions of the earth constitute the fundamental riches of any country ... all states owe infinitely more to agriculture than to any other profession of life ... the manufacturer merely exercises his industry upon the productions of the cultivator ... art stands indebted to the husbandman for materials to work upon, and what it adds to nature establishes only a species of wealth subsisting by mutual convention or compact' (Edwards, 1827, p. 394). In effect manufacturing activity transmuted the form but did not add to the value which agricultural activity alone created.[8] Like Ravenstone too this led him to see the size of the manufacturing sector as governed by the surplus extracted from agricultural labour, while it was 'also evident that the commercial operations, and the foreign trade of the country, are equally dependent with our manufactures upon the surplus produce of our internal agriculture' (1827, p. 422).

On this basis Edwards formulated a critique of those who saw the burgeoning of manufacturing as driving the growth in the nation's wealth (1827, pp. 391–392), who privileged the role played by capital in this expansion and who sought and supported policies which prioritised both.[9] In this context he was, in Tory radical vein, protective of the interests of the labouring classes in relation to what he saw as the depredations of the manufacturing capitalist and the idle consumer more generally. And he was critical too of those 'economists' who furnished ideological support for a 'system' that 'set the working men down as animated machines, from the use of which it is sound policy to draw the greatest amount of profit at the least cost' (Edwards, 1830a, p. 56).

As with Ravenstone, the monied interest too came in for particular criticism and their gains in the turbulent economic circumstances of the war and post-war period were seen as socially destabilising. Thus the restoration of cash payments in 1819, which created a 'new standard of value of the same weight and fineness of the old standard abolished in 1797, gave the Jews, stock jobbers and attorneys of the country an enormous advantage, at the expenses of the classes connected with the land'. The deflationary pressures it produced and the increase in the real value of debt and indebtedness, allowed the realisation of 'profits' which 'enabled [them] to possess themselves of princely estates belonging to ancient families, whom this alteration of the standard ruined and beggared' (Edwards, 1830b, p. 63). 'The change in the currency forced an immense number of proprietors to part with their paternal inheritances,' which 'together with the leases under which they were let out, came into the possession of the race of Jews, stock jobbers and money-lenders' (1830b, p. 65). So social mobility, amounting to systemic instability, was a consequence of the funding system and its post-war effects. And this in turn had made for a discontent amongst the labouring classes that represented both the material loss and impoverishment which they were suffering in this period but also the fact that they were no longer insulated from its consequences by their natural protectors – the landowners whose social pedigree could be traced back through the centuries.

These classes represented the foundation of the social pyramid. They formed 'the base on which all the institutions of the country rest for support' and 'if this base become deteriorated – cankered to its very core, the whole political and social fabric must inevitably be exposed to dangerous, perhaps even fatal convulsions' (Edwards, 1829, p. 256). All should therefore be interested in the well-being, and associated character, of the labouring classes. Where that class enjoyed the independence that a reasonable level of subsistence bestowed, then social harmony and stability were the result. Where, as was the case, the well-being and thence the independence of many were undermined, that was a fundamental cause for concern. And, as Edwards saw it, while 'the cottage' in which many were previously 'trained was once the seat of simplicity, honesty and fidelity'; in contemporary circumstances 'it has been converted into a nursery of discontent, insubordination and profligacy' (1829, p. 280).

So there is much in Edwards' political economy, which is replicated in that of Ravenstone. Given the lineaments of their social and economic thinking, both may legitimately be denominated Tory radicals. Yet there is in the work of the latter a degree of radicalism not to be found in the *Quarterly* and *Blackwood's* articles of the former. Specifically there is no critique of rental income in Edwards' work. On the contrary he is scathing as to what had 'lately become the fashion to represent rent as an extortionate exaction, wrung, under the colour of law, and the arbitrary institutions of society, from the pockets of the poor; and the landlords themselves as a set of useless, selfish and greedy drones whose only service to the state is the consumption of a large and increasing revenue, which would otherwise be added to the earnings of the industrious classes ... But the doctrine is as palpably absurd as it is malignantly fallacious' (Edwards, 1827, p. 411). 'How malignant, then, how basely malignant is the conduct of those who systematically hold up the landowners of this country to public obloquy, as useless drones, fastening from generation to generation, upon the industry of the people!' (1827, p. 412).

The contrast with Ravenstone's position on rents and rental income could not be more stark, condemning as he did, throughout *A Few Doubts*, 'the avarice of landlords' that had 'not allowed for the free and full development of the powers of production. The improvement of the management of industry has been entirely lost to the nation.... The increased produce, instead of being shared with the cultivator, has been entirely reserved for the landlord.... To increase rents is to diminish produce' (Ravenstone, 1966 [1821], p. 223). For Ravenstone rents were correlated with the size of the unproductive component of the population and, beyond a certain level, with a psychologically and socially corrosive idleness. For Edwards they were an income stream vital to the social stability and economic prosperity of the country.

Moreover while Ravenstone clearly saw the extension of the franchise as a means of removing, by legislative means, some at least of the evils that afflicted the nation and, in particular, the labouring classes, no such notion is aired by Edwards. His ideal is that of a benevolently paternal landowning interest whose relatively untrammelled power would be exercised in the public interest; not a democracy where that power could be circumscribed and challenged from below. In this regard and in the manner noted earlier, Ravenstone's radicalism was qualitatively different from that of Edwards.

Finally, there is their respective position on protectionism. In *A Few Doubts*, Ravenstone is clear that protectionism in general and the corn bills in particular can do little to improve the economic situation. Edwards, in contrast, supported protection in general and agricultural protection in particular. As he put it in an article in *Blackwood's Magazine*,

> The laws which protected particular manufactures, and prohibited the free importation of corn, gave employment to the general body of the people, and security to the capital which set their industry in motion. These laws gave to every man a full scope for the exertion of his skill, or the application of his property to any pursuit or occupation which held out to him the promise of the greatest return of profit; exacting from him no condition in return except that he should consent to share his advantages with his fellow-citizens. These laws secured profitable employment to the poor, and restrained the rich from seeking enjoyments to be derived from foreign sources, when these could have been supplied at home. They ministered to the wants of the needy rather than the craving desires of the affluent. (Edwards, 1830a, p. 564)

In contrast Ravenstone did 'not anticipate any consequences from the Corn Bill; its effects must be entirely temporary. It may occasionally create a famine but it cannot permanently raise the price of corn' (Ravenstone, 1966 [1821], p. 277). Corn bills 'increased fluctuations in the price of corn', they tended to 'encourage ruinous extravagance in the landowners, by flattering them with hopes that can never be realized' and in so far as the landowner did benefit, it was 'by diminishing the share of the labourer. His nominal wages are to remain unaltered; where he formerly received two bushels of corn he is now to receive one' (1966 [1821], pp. 405, 405, 418).

On the basis of this textual evidence alone, therefore, and leaving aside the documentary evidence noted earlier, there seems very little to sustain Dorfman's opinion that Edward Edwards and Piercy Ravenstone are one and the same; though in their own ways they do represent a genre of political economy – that of a physiocratic, Tory anti-capitalism-that has been too little discussed by subsequent commentators. In so far as future scholars will evince an interest in Ravenstone and his distinctive contribution to early-nineteenth-century political economy; in so far as he will not, for the future, suffer the kind of neglect which Seligman noted in the past, it is with reference to this tradition that his work is likely to be most usefully discussed.

NOTES

1. A reading of Ravenstone on this issue which is reiterated in *Capital* where Marx cites specifically Ravenstone's *Thoughts on the funding system and its effects* (Marx, 1974, Vol. 1, p. 405n).

2. A reading also favored by some twentieth-century Marxist commentators. See, for example, Meek (1950, pp. 43–62). Of Ravenstone's critical use of Ricardian value theory Meek wrote that "the work of men like Charles Hall and Piercy Ravenstone might be safely ignored; but Hodgskin's *Labour defended*...could not be so easily passed over" (1950, p. 59). A contrary view has come from Hollander (1980). Hollander's argument is essentially that writers such as Ravenstone did not make use of Ricardian value theory. This is a view that is technically correct but rather misses the point; namely that writers such as Ravenstone and Hodgskin both utilised a labor theory of value to counter contemporary notions about the productivity of capital and the justification of profit as capital's legitimate reward. Whether such use of a theory associated with Ricardo precipitated a reaction of the kind identified by Marx and reiterated by other writers is another matter; but one that need not concern us here.

3. Even if it was anticipated in some measure by Charles Hall and Thomas Spence. See Hall (1970 [1805]), Spence (1795), and Thompson (1998, pp. 12–14).

4. There are strong parallels here between Ravenstone and Charles Hall's (1970 [1805]) analysis of trade and manufacturing in relation to agriculture.

5. Ravenstone (1966, p. 201): "The condition of the labourer received no improvement from the skilful employment of his industry, the greater amount of his product only adds to the income of the idle."

6. As Ravenstone (1966, p. 37) saw it "*the old gentry* ... had in reality given up one third of their property to form the endowment of their newly created brethren."

7. Although, surprisingly, there is no mention of Cobbett in Ravenstone's work nor, for that matter, reference to Thomas Paine's *Decline and Fall of the English System of Finance* (1797).

8. Edwards (1827, p. 423): "It should be recollected that the manufacturer does not create wealth: he merely modifies that which has already been produced by the labours of the agriculturist."

9. Thus Edwards was critical of free trade and, in particular, free trade in agricultural produce, as something which benefitted the manufacturing interest, the affluent and non productive classes, by diminishing the cost of the commodities which they consume; but this advantage is purchased solely at the expense of the productive classes, by diminishing their wages, and adding to their toil. This system is admirably calculated to minister to the luxury and enjoyments of the idle and opulent portion of the community; to foster the dissipation and augment the splendour of the palace and the hall.... What it adds to the enjoyment of bloated wealth, it takes from the scanty earnings of pining industry. In order that the votary of fashion and extravagance may purchase luxuries at a cheap rate, it trenches with ruthless severity upon the remuneration of productive industry. (Edwards, 1830a, p. 560)

ACKNOWLEDGMENTS

The author gratefully acknowledged the permission of Trinity College Library, Cambridge University, for use of materials from the Piero Sraffa Papers.

REFERENCES

Private Papers

Piero Sraffa Papers, Trinity College Library, Cambridge University, Cambridge, UK.

Anonymous. (1821). Article X, *British Critic*, Vol. 16, October.

Blaug, M. (1958). *Ricardian economics*. New Haven: Yale University Press.

Burkitt, B. (1984). *Radical political economy*. Brighton: Wheatsheaf.

Claeys, G. (1986). *Machinery, money and the millennium*. Cambridge: Polity Press.

Cobbett, W. (1930). *Rural rides* (Vol. 3). London: Peter Davies.

Cole, G. D. H. (1953). *A history of socialist thought, Vol. 1: socialist thought: The forerunners, 1789–1850*. London: Macmillan.

Dobb, M. (1973). *Theories of value and distribution since Adam Smith, ideology and economic theory*. Cambridge: Cambridge University Press.

Dorfman, J. (1966). Introduction. In: P. Ravenstone (Ed.), *A few doubts on the correctness of some opinions generally entertained on the subjects of population and political economy*. New York: Augustus M. Kelley.

Edwards, E. (1827). On agriculture and rent. *Quarterly Review*, Vol. 36, October, pp. 391–437.

Edwards, E. (1829). Condition of the English peasantry. *Quarterly Review*, Vol. 21, July, pp. 240–284.

Edwards, E. (1830a). The influence of free trade upon the condition of the labouring classes, *Blackwood's Edinburgh Magazine*, Vol. 27, No. 165, April, pp. 553–568.

Edwards, E. (1830b). The effects of variations in the currency. *Blackwood's Edinburgh Magazine*, Vol. 27, No. 161, pp. 59–71.

Foxwell, H. S. (1899). Introduction. In: A. Menger (Ed.), *The right to the whole produce of labour: The origin and development of the theory of labour's claim to the whole product of industry*. London: Macmillan.

Halévy, E. (1956). *Thomas Hodgskin*. London: Benn.

Hall, C. (1970 [1805]). *The effects of civilization on the people in European states*. New York: Augustus M. Kelley.

Hodgskin, T. (1825). *Labour defended against the claims of capital*. London: Knight and Lacey.

Hodgskin, T. (1966 [1827]). *Popular political economy*. New York: Augustus M. Kelley.

Hodgskin, T. (1832). *Natural and artificial rights of property contrasted*. London: B. Steil.

Hollander, S. (1980). The post-Ricardian dissension: A case study in economics and ideology. *Oxford Economic Papers*, n.s., *32*(3), 370–410.

Marx, K. (2000a [1857]). *Grundrisse der Kritik der Politischen Ökonomie*, Notebook 3. Available at http://www.marxists.org/archive/marx/works/1857-gru/g7.htm.

Marx, K. (2000b [1857]). *Grundrisse der Kritik der Politischen Ökonomie*, Notebook 4. Available at http://www.marxists.org/archive/marx/works/1857-gru/g13.htm

Marx, K. (1972). *Theories of surplus value* (Vol. 3). London: Lawrence and Wishart.

Marx, K. (1974). *Capital: A critical analysis of capitalist production* (Vol. 3). London: Lawrence and Wishart.

Meek, R. L. (1950). The decline of Ricardian economics in England. *Economica, n.s., 17*(65), 43–62.

O'Brien, D. P. (1987). Piercy Ravenstone. In: J. Eatwell, M. Milgate & P. Newman (Eds), *The new Palgrave: A dictionary of economics* (Vol. 4). London: Macmillan.

Paine, T. (1797). *The decline and fall of the English system of finance*. London: Hartley, Adlard and Son.

Ravenstone, P. (1966 [1821]). *A few doubts on the correctness of some opinions generally entertained on the subjects of population and political economy*. New York: Augustus M. Kelley.

Ravenstone, P. (1966 [1824]). *Thoughts on the funding system and its effects*. New York: Augustus M. Kelley.

Seligman, E. R. A. (1903). On some neglected British economists-II. *Economic Journal, 13*(52), 511–535.

Spence, T. (1795). *Description of spensonia*. London: Courier Press.

Sraffa, P., & Dobb, M. (Eds). (1973). *Collected works of David Ricardo* (vol. 11). Cambridge: Cambridge University Press.

Stack, D. (1998). *Nature and artifice: The life and thought of Thomas Hodgskin, 1787–1869*. London: Boydell.

Stebbing, W. (1900). *Charles Henry Pearson…memorials by himself, his wife and his friends*. London: Longmans, Green.

Thompson, N. (1998). *The real rights of man: Political economies for the working class, 1775–1850*. London: Pluto.

Tregenza, J. (1970). The Pearson papers. *La Trobe Journal*, *6*, 45–47.

Viner, J. (1933). An unpublished letter of Ricardo to Malthus. *Journal of Political Economy*, *41*(1), 117–120.

Whitwell, S. (1972 [1830]). *Description of an architectural model from a design by Stedman Whitwell, for a community upon a principle of united interests, as advocated by Robert Owen*. New York: Arno.

A DISSENTER FROM RICARDIAN COMPLACENCY: THE CONTRIBUTION OF GEORGE RAMSAY

Jan S. Prybyla

Among the British economists who wrote in the Ricardian shadow of the 1830s, Sir George Ramsay (1800–1871) is prominent by his failure to establish contact with his contemporaries and to impress later generations of economists. Ramsay ranks among the most neglected economists with the exception of Marx in the nineteenth century and in the twentieth century by all except three writers on the history of economics. Two of the exceptions – Seligman (1903) and Schumpeter (1954) – are sufficiently significant to cast serious doubt on the correctness of this omission. And later in the century, in a comprehensive treatment of classical economics from a modern Austrian perspective, Rothbard (1995) found matters of interest in Ramsay's *An Essay on the Distribution of Wealth* (1836), but confirmed that the book had been largely 'unknown and unremarked' upon (p. 136). A few scholars have found merit in some novel features in Ramsay's work, but he clearly did not warrant more detailed study. Other writers of the post-Ricardian decades in Britain had also been ignored or underrated by historians of economic thought (see Seligman, 1903; Smith, 1935; Black, 1945; Shields, 1955); some of them, notably Bailey, Longfield, Lloyd and

English, Irish and Subversives Among the Dismal Scientists
Research in the History of Economic Thought and Methodology, Volume 28-B, 329–349

ISSN: 0743-4154/doi:10.1108/S0743-4154(2010)000028B014

Torrens, were later rehabilitated and the contribution of each of these is assessed in this volume. But Ramsay has not shared to anything like the full extent in this revival. And yet if it be admitted that 'a science develops by small accretions that create a common fund of ideas' (Schumpeter, 1954, p. 480), the contributions of Ramsay to this reservoir deserve a more careful consideration than they have hitherto.

References to Ramsay and his work are few and far between. Marx deals with him fully, but in a somewhat critical vein, in *Theorien über den Mehrwert* (1863) and on several occasions refers to Ramsay's work in *Das Kapital* (Vol. 1, 1867 and posthumously Vol. 2, 1885 and Vol. 3, 1894) and in *Grundrisse der Kritik der Politischen Ökonomie* (1857). Seligman (1903, pp. 521–525) in his essay 'On some neglected British economists' brings out a number of salient features in Ramsay's work, Schumpeter (1954) in his *History of Economic Analysis* refers on several occasions to Ramsay's writings with considerable respect, and Rothbard (1995) is impressed by his distinction between gross and net profits, the role of time and the discussion of the entrepreneur. In addition to these more important signs of recognition, an article on Ramsay by Karl W. Bigelow is to be found in the *Encyclopaedia of the Social Sciences* (edited by Seligman, 1930–1935). It repeats substantially the major points brought out by Seligman in the article already mentioned. A two-line reference to Ramsay's economic writing is to be found also in the *Dictionnaire de l'Economie Politique* (1864), and there is a brief note in the *Dictionary of National Biography* (1871) and the new *Oxford Dictionary of National Biography* (2004). An equally brief resume appears in *The Biographical Dictionary of British Economists* (2004). Also, Sraffa (1951b) in his 'Note on Fragments on Torrens' has a paragraph on Ramsay's interpretation of fixed and circulating capital. The British Library is in possession of 12 of Ramsay's works.

George Ramsay[1] was born in 1800, the second son of Sir William Ramsay of Bamff in Perthshire. The family tree has its roots deep in the soil of that county, the lands of Bamff having been granted in 1232 by Alexander II, King of Scotland, to Neis de Ramsey, his principal physician. These lands 'have ever since continued in possession of the family by direct descent in the male line' (*Burke's Peerage*, 1949, p. 1656). George Ramsay was educated at Harrow and Trinity College, Cambridge, where he studied medicine (he gained a BA in 1823 and an MB in 1826). Upon the death of his elder brother in 1859, he succeeded to the title as ninth baronet. Married in 1830, he had three sons, of whom the youngest, George, became professor of humanity in the University of Glasgow in 1863, a Chair formerly occupied by his uncle and Sir George Ramsay's younger brother, William Ramsay

(1806–1865). Sir George Ramsay was a prolific writer in the fields of philosophy, psychology, politics and aesthetics.

On most of his works, the verdict of historians has been harsh. Bigelow (1930–1935) sums this up when he describes Ramsay's work as 'lacking in originality', and points to the author's limited success in 'synthesising the often new and important ideas eclectically borrowed from others' (p. 100). Seligman too, considers Ramsay's contributions as 'of considerably less originality' than those of Read and stresses the author's indebtedness to the French writers as well as his 'meagre results' in introducing into England the conceptions current among the French economists (1903, p. 521). Only Schumpeter's voice rises in dissent; while admitting Ramsay's debt to the French economists, Schumpeter notes the quality of Ramsay's synthesis and the 'many suggestive details' contained in the *Essay*. Ramsay's pen, though often mistaken, is lucid and his grasp of contemporary economic doctrine, both English and Continental, thorough and extensive.

THE CREATION AND VALUE OF WEALTH

The *Essay on the Distribution of Wealth* consists of a preface, 16 chapters divided into two parts (Part I, Preliminary, 4 chapters; Part II, Distribution of Wealth, 12 chapters) and a note on the union with Ireland. In the preface, Ramsay strikes a note of refreshing dissent from the growing complacency of the Ricardians who at this time were riding high on the prestige of Ricardo, the unstinting labours of James Mill, the popular treatise of McCulloch and the refined logic and fine zeal of De Quincey (while Mrs. Marcet had even invaded the finishing school). Although he fully recognises Ricardo's contributions to the science, Ramsay points out that 'the subject is far from being exhausted' and that in view of the incomplete and controversial state of the science, he has 'been induced to combat some errors supported by high authority' (Ramsay, 1836, p. vii).[2]

Following Adam Smith – whom he resembles in the frequent use of colourful, real-life example to support an essentially deductive argument – Ramsay pinpoints the study of wealth as the proper object of political economy and how 'it may be distributed most advantageously among the different classes of society' (*Ibid*., p. 143). This wealth, again in the Smithian tradition, but more rigorously stated, 'embraces material objects only' (*Ibid*., p. 11) and includes fixed capital. Ramsay comes out vigorously against attempts by J.-B. Say and others to inject into the definition of political economy a consideration of immaterial products

(Say, 1821, pp. 2–3; Chalmers, 1832, chap. 11; Whately, 1832, lecture 1, p. 10n). In the Ricardian manner, he excludes from the definition all material objects that are not in some way subservient to the various wants of men. Having gone so far, he stops and the problem of utility to the consumer so ably formulated two years earlier by Longfield (1834, pp. 110–115) and W. F. Lloyd (1834, pp. 15–31) finds no echo in Ramsay, interested as he is principally in 'natural' value.[3] Excluded from the definition of wealth are also those material objects that are provided by nature in unlimited abundance, without, that is, the aid of human exertion. Wealth, in short, the proper object of political economy, consists in 'those material objects necessary, useful and agreeable to man, which are not provided spontaneously by Nature in unlimited abundance.... Thus the only ideas essentially comprehended in the notion of wealth, are those of Matter, Utility and some degree of Scarcity' (Ramsay, 1836, pp. 12–13). Since utility is for all practical purposes shelved, the inquiry into the nature of wealth is launched in the direction of scarcity understood as the struggle of human exertion – as effort or sacrifice – against the Ricardian niggardliness of nature. The emphasis is on the creation of material goods or production.

Production thus becomes the first division of political economy. Blending the suggestions contained in Turgot's *Réflexions* and made explicit by J.-B. Say in his *Traité,* with Adam Smith's insistence on the significance of the propensity to truck, barter and exchange, Ramsay recognises four major divisions of the science of political economy: production, distribution, exchange and consumption of wealth. The division had earlier been made by James Mill in his *Elements of Political Economy* (1821). On the last of the four categories, Ramsay hardly touches, although there is some discussion of 'unproductive' consumption.

Ramsay's analysis of production is a curious blending of error and fruitful suggestion. The essence of production consists in 'the creation of utility in material objects through the aid of human exertion' (Ramsay, 1836, p. 14). Utility is brought in as a Ricardian precondition of exchangeable value, but the preoccupation is rather with the material envelope of the wealth produced. This is in sharp contrast with J.-B. Say's interest with the precondition as the essence of wealth. Such a formulation of the problem leads Ramsay to reject Say's inclusion of 'immaterial' services in the productive category and to adopt Adam Smith's distinction between productive and unproductive labour as outlined in Chapter III, Book II, of the *Wealth of Nations* (1776) and reiterated by Read (on whom Ramsay appears to be heavily leaning) in Chapter IV of his *Inquiry* (1829).

The criticism directed by Bigelow against Ramsay's inconclusive efforts to synthesise 'the often new and important ideas eclectically borrowed from others' (p. 100) is apparent in Ramsay's introduction of time into his discussion of value (Whittlesey, 1930, p. 232). Borrowing from Destutt de Tracy (1817, chapters IV and V) and from J.-B. Say (1821, chapter II, p. 5), Ramsay regards production as a change of form or a change of place, the former constituting the business of agriculture, the latter that of commerce. To these two changes in material objects, he later adds a third: change of time (Ramsay, 1836, p. 43), although Rothbard (1995, p. 141) notes that Ramsay deals with time in a less sophisticated manner than Senior does. By tying in these three elements into his discussion of value, Ramsay becomes the first British writer to formulate a distinction later rendered famous by Karl Knies (1853) into form, place and time value. The contribution is, however, not without its drawbacks aptly pointed out by Schumpeter in his discussion of Destutt de Tracy: 'by stressing what may be termed the physical aspects of production, it obscures the economic one' (1954, p. 499n19). The extraction, fashioning, transportation and holding of goods, although related to the satisfaction of human wants, loses much of its potential significance by being primarily related to the material mechanics of production rather than to an analysis of utility, a distinction certainly made more explicit in Knies.

Flowing from the discussion of production and closely related to the distinction between productive and unproductive labour, was the problem of productive and unproductive consumption that engaged, among others, the energies of Malthus and Senior. The idea at issue, present in Leontief's (1986) productive consumption by households, consisted in determining how far goods used up by the consumer, continued in the economic process by making productive labour possible or by directly giving rise to further goods. To Ramsay consumption implies a destruction of form only (again the emphasis is on the physical aspect of economic processes). Consumption is unproductive when the destruction of the form in which a commodity is serviceable to human wants is not followed either immediately, or at not too remote a time, by the production of a new material commodity. When, however, as in the case of fixed capital, consumption is 'immediately replaced by a new result' or when, as in the case of circulating capital, consumption 'maintains labourers who by their own hands actually give rise to some material object constituting wealth' (Ramsay, 1836, p. 30), the process of consumption may be regarded as productive. Since Ramsay accepts Say's Law without misgivings (1836, p. 159, see also p. 163), he feels no special compulsion to justify the existence of unproductive consumers on economic grounds (as Malthus did). He appears to be wavering here between the doctrine that unproductive consumption is, to say the least, not harmful because it provides employment to the labouring classes and Senior's view that 'it is not employment, but food, clothing, shelter and fuel – in short, the materials of subsistence and comfort, that the labouring classes require' (Senior, 1831, p. 52). Ramsay considers, therefore, that in the matter of unproductive consumers, 'the fewer [a nation] can do with, the better for the riches of the country' (Ramsay, 1836, p. 31). His defence of the landlords (in whom he perceives a strong tendency towards unproductive consumption) and of protection to agriculture stems largely from ideological premises.[4]

Ramsay prefaces his discussion of value with an examination of cost of production. In this he widens the wedge driven by Ricardo in his discussion of the element of time that must elapse before goods can be brought to market, whether due to differences in the durability of fixed capitals, in the rate of turnover of circulating capital, or in the proportions in which the two sorts of capital are combined. Where Ricardo admits the lack of purity in his labour quantity theorem of equilibrium value, but persists in treating the disturbances as of slight effect, convinced of the fundamental nature of human labour in the process of value formation, Ramsay (unlike Smith) rejects the claim of labour to be the exclusive source of value and insists 'that capital is a source of value independent of labour' (*Ibid.*, p. 55). He likewise rejects labour as a measure of value (*Ibid.*, p. 39). In all this there is more than a shade of Torrens who was at the origin of the wedge driven by Ricardo into the labour theory of value.[5] In rejecting labour as a measure of value, Ramsay follows Torrens in the footsteps of Lord Lauderdale (1804, chap. 2), but stops short of the formulation of Samuel Bailey (1825, pp. 180–220). It may be conjectured that Read's disagreement with Bailey on this point had some influence on Ramsay's position.[6]

'Thus as soon as a commodity will exchange for any quantity of one or more other commodities or of labour, it is said…to possess the quality of value in exchange…' (Ramsay, 1836, p. 37). Value estimated in gold and silver, the least variable of commodities, is called 'price'. Although utility is a precondition of value, the latter is not proportional to utility. In proof of this, Ramsay has recourse to the thread-bare paradox of value, resolved by Bernardo Davanzati as far back as 1588 (in his *Lezione delle moneta*), as well as by a host of other writers including John Law (in 1705) and Galiani (in *Della Moneta*, 1751, Book I, chap. II). The paradox was taken up by Adam Smith and Ricardo who saw in it an obstacle to a theory of value based on value-in-use. In the case of freely reproducible goods, value, argued Ramsay, must depend on the sacrifices required to produce the goods. These sacrifices are of two kinds: first, a sacrifice of ease; secondly, by the capitalists withdrawing their private consumption from their individual stock of wealth. Value, therefore, comes to depend upon the sacrifices of labour and capital. These are the elements of cost of production and are essentially psychic costs. Ramsay is careful to distinguish these 'costs' from wages and profits which are to him 'portions of the total product totally distinct from the cost of raising it' (1836, p. 143, see also p. 41).

In arguing that 'value does not even ultimately depend upon quantity of labour alone' (*Ibid.*, p. 66), Ramsay makes use of his definition of fixed capital to include raw materials (1836, p. 21).[7] This distinction between fixed and circulating capital (approvingly commented on by Marx who used a similar distinction for his constant and variable capital) was earlier made by Torrens in an unpublished (or at least lost) note to Ricardo (Marx, 1867, p. 64). It was, however, the first occasion on which the distinction was made by a British writer in a published work. Such a definition of fixed capital introduces a source of variation in the relative values of commodities (as expounded by Ricardo), which is not covered by that portion of Ricardo's paragraph in the second edition of the *Principles* relative to different proportions of fixed and circulating capitals and fixed capitals of unequal durability. Ricardo's published solution was an additional distinction introduced into the *Principles* relative to circulating capitals of unequal durability, but as Sraffa demonstrated (1951a, pp. 305–315, especially 312, paragraph 1), he had at one point envisaged an alternative solution – inconsistent with his distinction between fixed and circulating capital as one of degree only – which, in effect, conceded the Torrens–Ramsay formulation.

To show that value does not depend on the quantity of labour alone, Ramsay uses various devices from Torrens' arsenal of arguments: equal fixed capitals of differing durability and differing fixed and circulating capital structures. In the former case, he introduces the notion of time into the discussion of value by insisting that 'the longer a capital remains engaged, the more will the product when at last completed deviate in its value from that which it ought to have, were it in proportion merely to the labour bestowed. Because the greater will be the profit in the value of the whole' (Ramsay, 1836, p. 47). While all these variations do indeed shake the foundations of Ricardo's theory of value, they are congenial to Ramsay's argument that value does not even ultimately depend on the quantity of labour alone.

Ramsay, however, attenuates his conclusions relative to the influence of cost of production on value. 'Cost of production...is only the remote regulator, or cause of value, the immediate being the proportion between the supply and demand' (1836, p. 60). It would seem that Ramsay is merely restating here the classical distinction between natural and market value, and there is some evidence that this was, in fact, what he thought he was doing (*Ibid.*, p. 63, note). However, his discussion of how cost of production fits in with supply and demand reveals a groping towards the concept of supply and demand schedules, shifts in demand and supply and the notion of elasticity.[8]

The bulk of Part II of the *Essay* is devoted to the problem of 'primary distribution' of the whole produce among the owners and users of the different sources of wealth. Here, at the very outset, Ramsay introduces 'masters', eschewing Say's more precise use of the word 'entrepreneur', because of the terminological poverty of the English language. He wrote, 'the French call them entrepreneurs. For want of a proper term, I shall beg leave to style them masters' (*Ibid.*, pp. 78–83, 217–219). Masters have a claim to a share in the total produce distinct from the owners of capital or capitalists. The claimants in the process of distribution thus resolve themselves into labourers, landlords, capitalists and masters. The last 'may be looked upon as another and higher order of labourers, whose remuneration, however, is regulated very differently from the latter' (*Ibid.*, p. 86). Although the identity of the entrepreneur had been perceived as far back as the scholastics and although Cantillon mentioned them explicitly in his *Essai sur la nature du commerce en general* (written c. 1730, published 1755), it was J.-B. Say (1821) (rather than Saint-Simon, see Robbins, 1958) who first assigned to the entrepreneur a separate and distinct place in the capitalist process as a risk-taker or undertaker under conditions of uncertainty (Koolman, 1971). Although Blaug (1958) points out that William Ellis (1826) had made much the same distinction as Ramsay between 'the person who owns the capital and he who directs the work' (p. 82) referring to 'the remuneration for the productive employment of savings' designated 'neat profit' and 'the remuneration for time and skill, which remuneration may be called agency for superintendence' in an article in the *Westminster Review* (p. 107).

The Ricardians almost completely ignored the figure, making no distinction between profits and interest or, indeed, the entrepreneur and the capitalist. And as Koolman points out, it was Senior who first introduced the word into English political economy, having been inspired in this direction by the work of Say (1821) and von Storch (1815). The entrepreneur was not, however, totally absent from post-Ricardian English economic literature. Read, for one, makes a distinction between interest as a payment for the use of capital and business gains over and above the ordinary rate of interest that he identifies with wages or else describes as the result 'of fortune or accident...properly to be considered as compensation for risk' (Read, 1829, p. 263). Whereas Read does not pursue the matter much further, having assimilated entrepreneurial gains with wages or 'secret and unknown causes...without the pale of science, or at least political science' (*Ibid.*, p. 263), Ramsay does try to analyse this type of income and his attempt to introduce the whole concept into English political economy is, to say the least, noteworthy.

THE DISTRIBUTION OF WEALTH

In tackling the distributive shares that go to the four major claimants, Ramsay distinguishes between wages, profits and rent. Profits present certain specific problems in view of the distinct claims on them by the capitalist and the master. For ex-positional purposes, Ramsay sometimes combines the two claimants into what he terms 'master-capitalists'.

Wages

The discussion of the problem of wages in general follows Ricardian lines. It contains, however, a number of interesting suggestions and reservations. Ramsay pushes Ricardo's hesitations on the long-run equilibrium level of wages to their logical conclusion. Ricardo realised that for the long-run theorem to be meaningful required both a strict interpretation of the Malthusian principle of population and an equally strict formulation of the physical level of subsistence. Ramsay, however, recognised that neither was in fact possible. With Torrens he substituted for the physical minimum, a social minimum and with Malthus of the second edition of the *Essay on Population* he allowed a weakening of the population principle through the introduction of the prudential check which, in effect, rendered it inoperative. By the time these adjustments had been made, the long-run equilibrium level of wages had become indeterminate, and was overshadowed by a very long short-run in which the supply of labour was represented by a given number of labourers over a period of years, and the demand for labour by a given quantity of wage goods. Ramsay made use of these admissions to reject outright (as did Read) the concept of a natural or necessary price of labour (Ramsay, 1836, p. 133, see also pp. 135–136). He shows that wages may remain 'for a long time' below subsistence level (as determined by climate and opinion) and adroitly stresses Ricardo's admission that in an improving society wages may remain for an indefinite period above their natural rate, concluding that 'it is singular enough that what is called the natural price of labour should be of all the most uncommon' (*Ibid.*, p. 135).[9]

It is in this vein that he comes out strongly in favour of efforts directed at fostering among the labouring classes an appreciation of the benefits of a rising standard of living. Wage rates depend immediately on the supply of and demand for labour and ultimately on the 'productiveness' of those branches of industry that produce the necessaries of life and upon the 'style of living rendered necessary by the nature of the climate, or considered by opinion as necessary to the existence of the labouring population' (*Ibid.*, p. 86).[10] Although the ultimate improvement in the condition of labour must be sought in an increase in the productiveness of industry, immediate improvement should be achieved through limiting the supply of labour. Thus supply resolves itself into two elements: the total number of labourers and the customary length of the working day and year thereby anticipating Marx. By a judicious exercise of the preventive check, the first element may be set to work. To bring this about, it is necessary to 'raise the ideas of the labouring class as to what is necessary to their well-being' (Ramsay, 1836, p. 126).[11] The second means of restricting the supply of labour is to exercise control over the duration of the working day and year. Here, Ramsay comes out unequivocally in favour of factory legislation. Like Ricardo he also saw the possible negative effects on the working classes of the introduction of machinery, being described by Blaug (1958) as 'one solitary voice...raised on behalf of Ricardo's position' (p. 72). But by reducing the length of the working day chronic unemployment would be avoided.

His argument on this score is interesting. It stems in part from economic analysis,[12] in part from humanitarian considerations as well as from a certain interventionist temper that pervades the *Essay*. It is in sharp contrast with Senior's *Letters* (1837) and rather representative of what Mitchell has described as the attitude of landlords who 'subjected to...capitalist attack, responded by viewing with grave disapprobation pretty much all the abuses that were characteristic of the capitalist system' (Mitchell, 1949, p. 219).

Profits

Uninhibited by any concept of a natural rate of wages, Ramsay makes the amount of gross profit (of the master-capitalist) vary directly as the productiveness of labour and capital engaged in the production of articles of necessity and inversely as the amount of wages. Thus, while adopting Ricardo's statement that profits vary inversely with wages, he does not accept Ricardo's implication that this exhausts the matter. He seems to discern in Ricardo's analysis an ideological danger as well as faulty reasoning. The inverse variation of profits and wages will hold on the assumption of an unchanged productiveness of capital and labour. 'Quantity of labour is compounded partly of its intensity, partly of its duration. These remaining constant, real wages will vary with every increase or diminution in the amount of necessaries and comforts which such exertions enable [the labourer] to command' (Ramsay, 1836, p. 178). Hence, if productivity increases while the supply of labour remains constant, both real wages and profits will rise. This, incidentally, is another reason for some regulation of the duration of labour. He points to the economy of high wages. High profits resting not on high productivity, but on low wages, are harmful to the nation which is 'injured in its most numerous class' (*Ibid.*, p. 144).[13]

In editing the *Works and Correspondence of David Ricardo* for publication, Sraffa (1951a, p. xxxi) argued that Ricardo had developed a corn model to determine the rate of profits, a surplus conception of the problem, which has been the subject of vigorous debate since Hollander (1973) published an article on the subject. This was the prelude to his monumental reinterpretation of Ricardo as a general equilibrium theorist (Hollander, 1979). It is a highly contentious issue, where the resolution hinges on unfortunate ambiguities in the extant texts by Ricardo, not least the *Essay on Profits* ([1815], see Sraffa, 1951b). The corn model implies that the profit from capital employed on the marginal unit of land determines the rate of profit on all capital in the economy. In that debate, Skourtos (1991) approached the subject by examining whether contemporaneous writers with Ricardo had used the same model with the inference that by so doing, the model could be described as 'Ricardian', or at the very least 'classical'. Whether the model represented a useful construction is not the issue, but rather if and in what context, it was used by Ricardo (for earlier versions of the model see Groenewegen, 1986). If the corn model is correct, then value is determined sequentially by adding the various costs of production together instead of simultaneously, as Hollander (1979) maintains, with factor returns and the value of the final product determined together within a general equilibrium framework. Skourtos adds to the debate by arguing that the search for textual evidence supporting the corn model should be abandoned in favour of 'accruing documentation that most classical writers were acquainted with the theoretical possibility of using material-produce comparisons in estimating the agricultural rate of profit. Some of them integrated this procedure in their analysis, for others it was only a relic. Only a few grasped its implications fully; the majority used it very superficially' (p. 217). Torrens and Malthus according to this view used it (see Schefold, 1981; Langer, 1988; de Vivo, 1985, 1986; Prendergast, 1986), but Ramsay and Simonde de Simondi utilised fully the surplus approach.

Ramsay discusses the issue in a chapter entitled 'On Gross Profits' and following Torrens attempts to use the model to determine the relative price of commodities. Profits are a surplus and the primacy of the agricultural sector in their determination is apparent, until Ramsay introduces fixed capital into the sector as Ricardo had previously done. Now 'there must be some other way of comparing produce with expenditure, at least in individual instances. With regard to the whole nation, however, the case is different' (Ramsay, 1836, p. 128). From a microeconomic perspective the rate of profit (the surplus) determines the value of the whole product, but from a macroeconomic view point, the application of fixed capital makes profit depend on the gross produce.

Ramsay's investigation of the component parts of profits merits particular attention. Following J.-B. Say and von Storch (whose *Cours d'economie politique*, 1823/24, is frequently referred to), Ramsay distinguishes within gross profits: net profits of capital (or interest) and profits of enterprise, or profits of the master, the 'trouble and risk incurred and the skill exerted in the business of direction and superintendence' (1836, p. 193). Analytically, therefore, 'entrepreneurs receive the profits of enterprise, while capitalists receive interest or "profits" on capital', although the two are usually combined as 'the gross profits of the capitalist entrepreneurs' Rothbard (1995, p. 137).

Ramsay gives careful thought to the pivotal position of the entrepreneur in the capitalist process: 'he acts a most important part in the economy of society' (1836, p. 219). Not only are direction and superintendence among the entrepreneur's functions: 'he is the general distributor of the national revenue' (1836, p. 218–219; see also von Storch, 1823/24).

Despite the careful distinction that Ramsay draws between the capitalistic and the entrepreneurial functions – which may be viewed as another attempt to link the Cantillon–Say tradition with the dominant English school of political economy – his analysis of the respective incomes of the entrepreneur and capitalist tends to be set in the English classical mould. To him, as to other writers of the period (and beyond, in fact until Irving Fisher's *Rate of Interest*, 1907) who made a similar distinction, interest is essentially a return on physical capital expressed in monetary terms for reasons of convenience. It is not a separate problem arising in the market for money loans.

The net profits of capital (interest), according to Ramsay, are determined by the supply of persons having capital to lend and the demand of borrowers (including consumption borrowing) having good security to offer. This proportion and the intensity of competition between them depend on 'how much may reasonably be expected to be made by the use of capital in conjunction with the skill and industry of the master that is on the amount of gross profits supposed likely to be realized' (Ramsay, 1836, p. 200). Because of the existence of a rentier class of capital suppliers and of unproductive borrowers, however, interest may vary without any change in the rate of gross profits (*Ibid.*, p. 201). Gross profits, in turn, depend on the productiveness of those branches of industry that produce the necessaries of life consumed by the labourers and the various elements of fixed capital, as well as on the competition between master-capitalists and labourers.

The rate of interest being thus determined, the surplus of gross profits over interest constitutes the profits of enterprise (or profits of the master/entrepreneur). These profits of enterprise consist of three elements: the salary of the master – which he carefully distinguishes from wages – insurance for risk involved in entering upon the business and surplus gains (*Ibid.*, p. 226). The whole reasoning is curiously reminiscent of the treatment of entrepreneurial gains by Hufeland (1807) and F. von Hermann (1832, pp. 204–208)[14] which in Germany culminated in the work of von Mangoldt (1855) and in England that of John Stuart Mill (1848).[15] Elsewhere, Ramsay recognises also a temporary surplus entering into entrepreneurial income from the introduction of new machinery. Differences in the residual as between different branches of trade are due to differences in the degree of risk[16] and to differences in the amount of capital involved. As regards the former, where risk is high 'only the expectation of unusual gains will induce masters to embark on such undertakings', while this very uncertainty 'narrows competition in such branches' (1836, p. 222). Assuming, however, equal degrees of risk and equal remuneration for management, Ramsay believes that the surplus gains (i.e., the third element of enterprise profits) will rise in a greater proportion than the capital employed, for 'the larger the capital vested in any business, the smaller must be the proportion of the profits of enterprise which goes for the master's salary and insurance together and consequently the greater must be his surplus gains, not absolutely, but relatively to the capital engaged' (*Ibid.*, p. 227). This result follows, of course, from the assumption of equal returns to management, about which Ramsay is not too happy (*Ibid.*, p. 228).[17]

The analysis of the progress of the entrepreneur's surplus gains leads Ramsay to examine in the French manner the question of the concentration of capital, in the course of which he touches briefly upon economies of scale (*Ibid.*, p. 234). Given the assumption with regard to managerial returns, he arrives at the conclusion that 'the concentration of capital in the hands of a comparatively small number of masters is more favourable to its rapid accumulation and the increase of national wealth, than its subdivision among a larger body of persons; and hence that a great equality of fortunes, however desirable it may be in other respects, is not the state of things most conducive to the augmentation of the riches of a country' (*Ibid.*, p. 240). Here, confusedly perhaps, is the voice of large-scale industry and of the driving force of big capital, tempered throughout by a clear recognition of the social implications.

Rent

Ramsay's treatment of rent begins on the familiar West-Malthus-Ricardo lines, but branches off into considerations that foreshadow the Marshallian analysis. The elimination of rent from price was essential for the integrity of Ricardo's theory of value. Ramsay labours under no such necessity and consequently introduces rent into prices, though not without some qualms. Essentially, however, he follows the Ricardian detour in his attempt to explain the formation of rent by considerations of differential fertility rather than by stopping at scarcity and productiveness (Ricardo's 'original and indestructible powers of the soil') and recognising location and fertility differentials merely as permanent advantages linked to a material factor in inelastic supply. On this score, therefore, Ramsay does not advance much beyond the Ricardian analysis, nor could he, devoid as he was of the marginal concept. The Ricardian obstacle, moreover, by its insistence on the uniqueness of rent in land, prevented Ramsay from generalising the rent element beyond agriculture, the extractive industries and inland fishing. He thus concludes that 'no branches of industry except agriculture afford this revenue' (1836, p. 460) although at times he comes near to formulating a quasi-rent concept (*Ibid.*, pp. 481–482).

It is the manner in which Ramsay injects rent into price that is particularly interesting. In effect, his labours amount to defining the rent surplus in terms of a vaguely understood opportunity cost concept. 'Although rent unquestionably owes its origin to a high price of corn, or whatever may be the principal vegetable food of the people, yet when once created, it prevents the supply of other productions of the soil, such as animals and grass from becoming immediately equal to the demand and so keeps up their price until they rise sufficiently to give as good a rent as corn. In this manner the rent paid for one species of produce becomes the cause of the high value of others' (*Ibid.*, pp. 278–279; see also Marshall, 1920, pp. 299–300). The full implications of this analysis are, of course, obscured by Ramsay's Ricardian preoccupation with whether or not rent enters into value formation. This was not essential to his formulation of the theory of value, though it was to Ricardo's. He logically, therefore, admitted the former possibility, but in the process failed to explore the vistas presented by his excursions into rent as a cost of the opportunity type.

One further point should be disposed of in connection with Ramsay's analysis of rent. Influenced as he was by his reading of Adam Smith, he frequently speaks of rent as a monopoly return. This may indeed fit in with his conclusion that rent enters price, but this is not what he means. His use of the term is similar to that of Senior. It merely refers to the pricing of a 'costless' (in the sense of effort or sacrifice) agent, the supply of which is fixed. The monopoly idea in this case arose simply from the inadequacy of his analytical apparatus.

CONCLUSION

A substantial part of the *Essay* is taken up with a discussion of the economic, political and moral consequence of the division of landed property. The whole is of but limited interest, though it is marked by occasional flashes of insight and provides a link to the corn model interpretation of Ricardo's theory of profits. Ramsay points out, for example, some obstacles in the way of mobility of labour (*Ibid.*, p. 360) and with many qualifications looks favourably on legislative intervention to prevent an excessive parcelling out of landed property (*Ibid.*, p. 395, but see also pp. 438 and 442). In the teeth of a rising clamour for Corn Law repeal, he pronounces himself in favour of agricultural protection at existing levels. The grounds for this position are interesting: Ramsay looks with apprehension at what he considers a lop-sided development of the British economy. He sees a grave danger for the future from being an industrial economy heavily dependent on foreign markets. 'It is quite clear that unless there be some extraordinary natural advantages peculiar to Great Britain, it cannot have any right to suppose that it shall always supply the greater part of the world with manufactures at a cheaper rate than that at which they can be raised in their respective countries' (*Ibid.*, p. 496).

It is not improbable that Ramsay's failure to impress his contemporaries was due in large measure to the curious combination of classicism and anti-classicism that he reveals both in his theoretical arguments and in his policy recommendations. Possibly, he was ignored by both camps because of this. It is true, as Grampp (1960) has forcefully argued, that the doctrines of the dominant school had no lasting connection with the Corn Law repeal campaign and that a careful reading of Ricardo, McCulloch and William Thornton shows that their advocacy of free trade was qualified on grounds of military security, injustice to legitimate vested interests and (sometimes) economic logic (see also Nicholson, 1904). However, what really mattered was that the general tenor of their work was against protection and that in the popular, simplified form in which it reached the general public, the qualifications were forgotten (see McCord, 1958). McCulloch was cited as an authority by the Anti-Corn Law League lecturers and so, for that matter, was Senior. Torrens wavered between demand for immediate repeal and a programme of reciprocity. Yet both Senior's and Torrens' positions were essentially within the rising current of anti-protectionist sentiment. Ramsay's very consistency – his interventionist attitude vis-a-vis industry and agriculture – tended to weaken his case. His advocacy of factory legislation and of protection to agriculture did not particularly endear him to the manufacturing interest. The *Essay on the Distribution of Wealth* was published in the very year in which the Anti-Corn Law Association of London was founded. In the polarisation of contemporary thought, Ramsay's eclecticism was bound to obstruct his influence, neither contestant in the debate being satisfied with his analysis, even though it may have been, in some respects, superior to both.

The *Essay* though by no means a path-breaking work, represents a landmark in the development of English economic thought which it would be rash to pass by without more than a cursory glance. Though its direct influence was small, it did strive to incorporate into English classical economics ideas that were not native to it, but for the absence of which English political economy was so much the poorer. It represented, moreover, a reaction against the growing rigidity of Ricardian economics that Seligman himself attacked and that brought Ramsay to his attention in the first place. From all these standpoints it deserves the attention that for so long has been and continues to be, withheld by historians of economic thought and which this volume seeks to redress.

NOTES

1. See the obituary notice in *The Times*, London, February 27, 1871.

2. It is perhaps not irrelevant to recall here Schumpeter's interpretation of the "high authority of Ricardo: more than the neglected economists of the period, Ricardo contributed usable argument to the great issues of his time, that was at once free of (even essential) qualifications and analytically rigorous enough to satisfy high intellectual standards. He was skilled in polemics without that brashness which deters but does not convince. Not least, people took to his theory because they agreed with his recommendations" (Schumpeter, 1954, p. 473). This was most certainly not the lot of Ramsay. See also Mitchell (1949, pp. 177–183), Checkland (1949, pp. 40–52) and Samuelson (1962, pp. 8–10).

3. In this, Ramsay remains well within the Ricardian tradition and seems also to follow directly Samuel Read. In his *An Inquiry into the Natural Ground of Right to Vendible Property, or Wealth*, Read (1829, p. viii) refuses to go along with Samuel Bailey in the latter's interest in the forces determining market value. See note 6.

4. "Both theory and experience prove that aristocracy and *that alone* can give stability and therefore that *some portion* of it, at all events, is an indispensable ingredient in every government which can hope for permanence" (Ramsay, 1836, p. 418).

5. For Torrens' "wedge," see Sraffa (1951a, pp. 305–318). For a fuller statement of the capital theory of value see Torrens (1821) and also Robbins (1958, pp. 60–70).

6. See note 3 above. In his *Inquiry*, Read writes in reference to Bailey's approach to value: "Notwithstanding the very high respect I entertain for this author...I find occasion to differ from him very widely in his main positions in the *Critical Dissertation*. It appears to me that the fundamental error in that work...consists in his treating of value as if it were *a mere* relation *of commodities between themselves;* whereas it appears to me that the idea of value in commodities *cannot even be conceived* without being mingled with the idea of their relation to mankind and to human labour, of which *some portion* must always be employed in producing or procuring them originally" (Read, 1829, p. viii, emphasis in the original). See an interesting discussion of this problem by Daniel Raymond (1820, chapter 5, p. 77): "the word value in political economy has but one meaning, which is, the relation that one thing bears to another in regard to price."

7. Ramsay's definition of capital is quoted by Senior in his *Lectures* of 1847–1852, Course II (see Bowley, 1937, p. 59, note 2).

8. The relevant passage, though not outstanding for clarity, is worth quoting: "What is that sort of demand which influences value?...If by this phrase be meant simply the quantity demanded then this alone does by no means regulate value. For if a vast quantity be consumed, solely because the price is very low and the moment this begins to rise, should the quantity sought decline, then value cannot maintain itself and must instantly sink to its former level. Thus when there has been a superabundant crop of wheat, for instance, the consumption increases perhaps fully in proportion to the supply and yet the price does not rise, nay, is much lower than usual. The reason of which is that people consume more, only because corn has fallen and were it to rise ever so little, would content themselves with less. They are willing to spend as much on bread as formerly, but no more; so that if they can get a larger quantity for their money, well and good; if not, they will do with a smaller. So long

as this disposition of mind lasts, the whole wheat in the country will not exchange for more of other things, than it did when the crop was an ordinary or very deficient one. Before the price can rise, it is necessary that the buyers be both able and willing to purchase a greater quantity than usual even although at an advanced rate. If this determination holds, their eagerness will enable the sellers to increase the price of their grain. Therefore the intensity of the demand must be taken into account" (Ramsay, 1836, p. 61). See also "though the intensity be the only cause which at last determines value, yet as this cause is itself greatly modified by the quantity demanded, this circumstance also must be included in our notion of that demand which regulates the value, of commodities. It is composed then of two elements, Extent and Intensity" (1836, p. 6). In a somewhat more obscure passage, Ramsay tries to apply the same reasoning to supply.

9. "If we are persuaded that wages can never for any long period fall below what is necessary for the support not only of the labourer but also of his family, our sympathies will cease to be so warmly engaged on behalf of the most numerous part of the population" (Ramsay, 1836, p. 134).

10. The productiveness of industry, according to Ramsay, depends on (a) the fertility of the soil (and of "its bowels whence are derived metals and minerals") and (b) on the degree of skill with which labour and capital are applied (which, in turn, comes to depend on the rate of saving). Manufacturing industry, he believes, is subject to increasing returns. Agriculture, on the other hand, is in a progressing country subject to diminishing returns. There will thus tend to be a conflicting pull on both profits and wages arising from these two opposite forces.

11. Nothing could be more prejudicial to the labouring class than "the prevalence of the system of 'content.'...The fewer their wants, the lower their standard of comfort, the less will be the prevalence of the preventive check on population" (Ramsay, 1836, p. 128). Ramsay includes emigration in his argument in favour of a restriction in the supply of labour. See also Senior's *coloniam deducere* and his argument in favour of raising "the moral and intellectual character of the labouring population (Senior, 1831, p. v).

12. The "economic" argument is that given the ratio between capital and population, the labourers who work short hours will receive the same wages as those who work long hours (Ramsay, 1836, pp. 100–102). Ramsay's keen practical sense rebels against the emergence in theory of the economic man. He links welfare considerations to the very definition of political economy

13. See Senior(1959 [1831], p. iv): "The principal means by which the fund for the maintenance of labourers can be increased, is by increasing the productiveness of labour." Of interest in this connection is his discussion of machinery in Lecture III and in his *Political Economy* (Senior, 1872, pp. 162–168).

14. von Hermann had read both von Storch and Read.

15. John Stuart Mill (1848) distinguishes between wages of management, the premium for risk-taking, interest on the capital owned by the entrepreneur and sometimes a temporary return due to the introduction of new machinery or some other innovation. The last of these had been identified by Ricardo (1957, p. 263) in his chapter on Machinery, but he assimilated it in capitalist returns.

16. On the inappropriateness of including risk-taking among entrepreneurial functions, see Schumpeter (1954, p. 556, note 6).

17. "The modifications in the degree of superintendence required may afterwards be imagined as creating some little variety in the result, though, of course, it must always be exceedingly difficult, if not impossible, to determine with accuracy the quantity of labour which any head of an establishment is called upon to perform" (Ramsay, 1836, p. 228; but see also p. 225).

REFERENCES

Bailey, S. (1825). *A critical dissertation on the nature, measures and causes of value: Chiefly in reference to the writings of Mr. Ricardo and his followers.* London: R. Hunter.

Bigelow, K. W. (1934). Ramsay, Sir George (1800–1871). In: E. R. A. Seligman & A. Johnson (Eds), *Encyclopaedia of the social sciences.* New York: Macmillan.

Black, R. D. C. (1945). Trinity College, Dublin, and the theory of value, 1832–1863. *Economica, n.s., 12*(47), 140–148.

Blaug, M. (1958). *Ricardian economics: A historical study.* New Haven: Yale University Press.

Bowley, M. (1937). *Nassau Senior and classical economics.* London: George Allen and Unwin.

Burke, B. (1949). *A genealogical and heraldic dictionary of the peerage and baronetage of the British Empire* (78th ed.). London: Harrison.

Chalmers, T. (1832). *On political economy in connection with the moral state and moral prospects.* Glasgow: William Collins.

Checkland, S. G. (1949). The propagation of Ricardian economics in England. *Economica, n.s., 16*(61), 40–52.

de Tracy, D. (1817). *A treatise on political economy.* Georgetown: Joseph Milligan.

de Vivo, G. (1985). Robert Torrens and Ricardo's 'corn-ratio' theory of profits. *Cambridge Journal of Economics, 9,* 89–92.

de Vivo, G. (1986). Torrens on value and distribution. *Contributions to Political Economy, 5,* 23–36.

Dictionnaire de l'Economie Politique. (1864). Edited by Guillaumin and Charles Coquelin. Paris: Guillaumin.

Dictionary of National Biography. (1871). London: Smith Elder and Co.

Ellis, W. (1826). Effects of the employment of machinery &c upon the happiness of the working class. *Westminster Review, January,* 101–130.

Fisher, I. (1907). *The rate of interest.* New York: Macmillan.

Grampp, W. D. (1960). *The Manchester School of Economics.* Stanford, CA: Stanford University Press.

Groenewegen, P. D. (1986). Professor Porta on the significance of understanding Sraffa's standard commodity and the Marxian theory of surplus: A comment. *History of Political Economy, 18*(3), 455–462.

Hollander, S. (1979). Ricardo's analysis of the profit rate, 1813–15. *Economica, 40*(159), 260–282.

Hollander, S. (1979). *The economics of David Ricardo.* Toronto: Heineman.

Hufeland, G. (1807). *Neue Grundlegung der Staatswirthschaftskunst.* Gießen, Wetzlar: Tasché and Müller.

Knies, K. (1853). *Die politische Ockonomie vom Standpunkte der geschichtlichen Methode.* Braunschweig: Neue vermehrte Auflage.

Koolman, G. (1971). Say's conception of the role of the entrepreneur. *Economica, 38*(151), 269–286.
Langer, G. F. (1988). Corn: A classical landscape. *Economic Notes, 17*(1), 5–21.
Lauderdale, J. M. (Lord). (1804). *An inquiry into the nature and origin of public wealth and into the means and causes of its increase*. London: T.N. Longman & O. Rees.
Leontief, W. W. (1986). *Input-output economics* (2nd ed.). New York: Oxford University Press.
Lloyd, W. F. (1834). *A lecture on the notion of value as distinguishable not only from utility, but also from value in exchange*. London: Roake and Varty.
Longfield, M. (1834). *Lectures on political economy*. Dublin: Richard Milliken and Son.
Marshall, A. (1920). *Principles of economics* (8th ed.). London: Macmillan.
Marx, K. (1857). *Grundrisse der Kritik der Politischen Ökonomie*. Berlin: Dietz Verlag.
Marx, K. (1863). *Theorien über den Mehrwert*. Berlin: Dietz Verlag.
Marx, K. (1867). *Das Kapital* (Vol. I). Hamburg: Verlag Meissner.
Marx, K. (1885). *Das Kapital* (Vol. II). Moscow: Progress Publishers.
Marx, K. (1894). *Das Kapital* (Vol. III). Moscow: Progress Publishers.
McCord, N. (1958). *The Anti-Corn Law League, 1838–1846*. London: George Allen and Unwin.
Mill, J. (1821). *Elements of political economy*. London: Henry G. Bohn.
Mill, J. S. (1848). *Principles of political economy*. London: John W. Parker.
Mitchell, W. C. (1949). *Lecture notes on types of economic theory*. New York: A.M. Kelley.
Nicholson, J. S. (1904). *The history of the English corn laws*. London: Swan Sonnenschein.
Oxford Dictionary of National Biography. (2004). Edited by B. Harrison. Oxford: Oxford University Press.
Prendergast, R. (1986). A comment on 'David Ricardo's early treatment of profitability: A new interpretation'. *Economic Journal, 96*(384), 1098–1104.
Raymond, D. (1820). *Thoughts on political economy*. Baltimore: Fielding Lucas.
Read, S. (1829). *Political economy: An inquiry into the natural ground of right to vendible property, or wealth*. Edinburgh: Oliver & Boyd.
Ricardo, D. (1957). *The principles of political economy and taxation, everyman's library*. London: Dent.
Robbins, L. (1958). *Robert Torrens and the evolution of classical economics*. London: Macmillan.
Rothbard, M. N. (1995). *An Austrian perspective on the history of economic thought* (Vol. 2). Edward Elgar Publishing.
Samuelson, P. A. (1962). Economists and the history of ideas. *American Economic Review, 52*(1), 1–18.
Say, J.-B. (1821). A treatise on political economy, or the production, distribution and consumption of wealth (C. R. Princep, Trans.). Boston: Wells and Lilly.
Schefold, B. (1981). *Nachfrage und Zufuhr in der klassischen Ökonomie, in Studien sur Entwicklung der ökonomischen Theorie 1*. Berlin: Duncker and Humblot.
Schumpeter, J. A. (1954). *History of economic analysis*. London: Oxford University Press.
Seligman, E. R. A. (1903). On some neglected British economists. *Economic Journal, 13*(51–52), 335–363 and 511–535.
Senior, N. W. (1959 [1831]). *Three lectures on the rate of wages*. New York: A.M. Kelley.
Senior, N. W. (1837). *Letters on the Factory Act, as it affects the cotton manufacture*. London: B. Fellowes.
Senior, N. W. (1872). *Political economy* (6th ed.). London: Charles Griffin.

Shields, M. S. (1955). *Some Irish contributions to the history of economics*. Ph.D. Dissertation, Catholic University of America, Washington, DC.

Sir Ramsey, G. (1836). *An essay on the distribution of wealth*. Edinburgh: A. and C. Black.

Skourtos, M. (1991). Corn models in the classical tradition: P. Sraffa considered historically. *Cambridge Journal of Economics*, *15*, 215–228.

Smith, A. (1776). *An inquiry into the nature and causes of the wealth of nations* (Critical edition, edited by R. H. Campbell and A. S. Skinner, Oxford: Oxford University Press, 1976). London: W. Strahan and T. Cadell.

Smith, J. G. (1935). Some nineteenth century Irish Economists. *Economica, n.s.*, *2*(5), 20–32.

Sraffa, P. (1951a). *Works and correspondence of David Ricardo. Vol. 1, Principles of political economy and taxation*. Cambridge: Cambridge University Press.

Sraffa, P. (1951b). *Works and correspondence of David Ricardo. Vol. IV, Pamphlets and papers, 1815–1823*. Cambridge: Cambridge University Press.

The Biographical Dictionary of British Economists. (2004). Edited by D. Rutherford. Bristol: Thoemmes Continuum.

Torrens, R. (1821). *Essay on the production of wealth*. London: Longman, Hurst, Rees, Orme and Brown.

von Hermann, F. (1832). *Staatswirtschaftliche Untersuchungen*. Munich: Anton Weber.

von Mangoldt, H. (1855). *Die Lehre vom Unternehmergewinn*. Frankfurt: Sauer and Avermann.

von Storch, H. F. (1815). Considérations sur la Nature du Revenue National, Paris.

von Storch, H. F. (1823/24). *Cours d'Economie Politique*. Paris: Aillaud.

Whately, R. (1832). *Introductory lectures on political economy*. London: Fellowes.

Whittlesey, C. R. (1930). Value changes: The growth of a concept. *American Economic Review*, *2*(2), 231–234.

MOUNTIFORT LONGFIELD

Renee Prendergast

'One who is in some respects the most remarkable of all'. Thus Seligman opened his discussion of the work of Mountifort Longfield, the first incumbent of the Whately chair of political economy at the University of Dublin. The chair was founded in 1832 by Richard Whately following his appointment as Archbishop of Dublin. Whately, who had been Drummond professor of political economy at Oxford, was well known for his opposition to the labour theory of value and his view that the name Catallactics (science of exchanges) should be substituted for political economy.

Born in 1802, Longfield graduated from Trinity College, Dublin, with a first class degree in Science in 1823. Afterwards he specialised in law taking the degree Doctor of Laws in 1831 (Black, 1971, p. 6). Following a two-day examination into which both Whately and Nassau Senior had input, Longfield was appointed to the new chair of political economy at Trinity in November 1832 (Murphy, 1984, pp. 17–24).[1] He resigned in 1836 having already been appointed to the Chair of Feudal and English law at the University in 1834. Afterwards, he made his career in law rather than economics. He was a prominent property lawyer and judge and came to be regarded as the leading expect on land tenure systems in Ireland.

Under the terms of his appointment to the Whately chair, Longfield was required to deliver no less than nine lectures each year and publish at least one of these. His first set of lectures on the topic of value and distribution was delivered in the Trinity and Michaelmas terms of 1833. These were published in their entirety in following year under the title *Lectures on Political Economy*. In 1834, Longfield lectured on the poor laws in the

English, Irish and Subversives Among the Dismal Scientists
Research in the History of Economic Thought and Methodology, Volume 28-B, 351–374

ISSN: 0743-4154/doi:10.1108/S0743-4154(2010)000028B015

Trinity term and published these as *Four Lectures on the Poor Laws* (1834). In the Michaelmas term, he lectured on the topic of international trade. These lectures were published in 1835 as *Three Lectures on Commerce and one on Absenteeism*. Following his resignation from the chair of political economy, Longfield's main interest was the law. Nonetheless, he contributed four anonymous articles on money and banking to the *Dublin University Magazine* in 1840. In 1847, Longfield became one of the original vice-presidents of Dublin Statistical Society (later the Statistical and Social Inquiry Society of Ireland) and on Whately's death in 1863, succeeded him as president of the society (Black, 1971). In 1870, Longfield wrote the chapter on Ireland for the Cobden Club volume, *Systems of Land Tenure*. His final paper 'The Limits of State Interference with the Distribution of Wealth in Applying Taxation to the Assistance of the Public' was read before the Statistical and Social Inquiry Society of Ireland in 1872 and subsequently published in the society's journal.[2]

SELIGMAN'S EXPOSITION

Seligman's evaluation of Longfield's work concentrated exclusively on his views on value and distribution as set out in the *Lectures on Political Economy*. He noted that Longfield adopted many of the doctrines of the classical school but dissented from it in his treatment of distribution above all in his theory of profits (Seligman, 1903, p. 526). Seligman began with an examination of Longfield's 'noteworthy' theory of value which takes into account 'the influence of cost of production upon the supply side of the equation' as well as calling attention to the demand side (Seligman, 1903, p. 526). In discussing the demand side, Longfield pointed out that although the intensity of demand varies with different persons, all will affect their purchases at the market price. If an attempt was made to raise price above this level, the demanders whose intensity of demand was measured by the former price would cease to be purchasers. 'Thus the market price is measured by that demand, which being of the least intensity leads to actual purchases' (Longfield, 1834, p. 113; Seligman, 1903, p. 526). Seligman went on to note that, for Longfield, not only did intensity of demand vary between persons but also that 'the same person may be said to have in himself several demands of different degrees of intensity'. Longfield wrote:

> Each individual contains as it were within himself, a series of demands of successively increasing degrees of intensity; that the lowest degree of this series which at any time

> leads to a purchase, is exactly the same for both rich and poor, and is that which regulates the market price and that in the case of the rich man, the series increases more rapidly, that is to say, the intensity of his demand increases more rapidly in proportion to the diminution of his consumption than in the case of the poor man. (Longfield, 1834, p. 115)

Seligman concluded that in these passages, Longfield virtually expounded 'the doctrine of marginal demand', and he added that it was this marginal idea which Longfield applied to the supply side of the schedule as well, and which resulted in his most characteristic contribution to economics (Seligman, 1903, p. 527).

In support of the latter point, Seligman turned to pages 34–35 of the *Lectures* where Longfield discussed the use of labour as a measure of value. There, Longfield argued that in order for labour to be a measure of the value of any commodity, it was not necessary that the whole supply of the commodity should have its value entirely derived from the labour expended in its production. It was sufficient if some part, of equal value with the rest could be resolved into the labour which created it. 'The portion of every commodity whose value admits of being thus measured is that part which is produced under what I shall call the most disadvantageous circumstances; that is, under those circumstances which require the greatest expenditure of labour in order to produce any certain quantity of the commodity' (Longfield, 1834, pp. 34–35). With that Seligman concluded his discussion of Longfield's theory of value and turned his attention to Longfield's application of the marginal idea in the sphere of distribution (Seligman, 1903, p. 527).

In the preface to the *Lectures on Political Economy*, Longfield had highlighted both his acceptance of the 'Ricardian' theory of rent and his rejection of the view that profits were regulated by the fertility of the worst soils under cultivation (Longfield, 1834, p. vii). Longfield saw capital as being useful in two ways: first, by advancing to the workman the value of his labour before the produce of that labour was sold to the consumer and secondly, by supplying the labourer with tools and machinery that raised the productivity of his labour (Longfield, 1834, p. 187). Both mechanisms implied that at the end of a certain period, labour would have produced goods of greater value than it could have without the assistance of capital (1834, pp. 189–190). Longfield stressed the fact that the labourer who produces goods cannot wait for his wages until those goods are ready to be consumed. The difficulty is solved because the employer pays the wages to the labourer and in return for his work. The value of the labour transferred to any article is greater than the wages of the labour with the difference being the profit made by the capitalist for his advances. This profit can be viewed as the discount that the labourer pays for the prompt payment of his wages (1834, pp. 169–170). In considering what regulated the size of the discount that labour was obliged to accept, Longfield focused his attention on the addition to output that results from the employment of capital. The profits of the capitalist are the difference between the quantity of work produced with and without capital by that portion of capital which is employed with least efficiency (Seligman, 1903, p. 529). This was a consequence of the principle of competition, for if 'the owner of one machine could obtain more for its use than the owner of another of equal value and durability, people would purchase…the former rather than the latter , until the profits of each were reduced to their level' (Longfield, 1834, p. 187).

As Seligman noted, the matter was explained further using the analogy between the price of goods and the profits of capital. No matter how intense any man's desire for something, he would not pay a high price for it if he could procure it on cheaper terms (Longfield, 1834, pp. 194–195; Seligman, 1903, p. 529). In like manner, the addition to the value of a labourer's output as a result of the employment of some amount of capital compared with what he could produce unassisted could be regarded as a measure of the intensity of his demand for the capital in question. But this amount would not be paid because, given the abundance of capital, much of it would be employed in ways such that, in proportion to its quantity, it was not so capable of multiplying the efficiency of the labourer (Longfield, 1834, p. 195).

Seligman concluded that Longfield's work contained a clear and unequivocal statement of the marginal productivity doctrine of interest that was usually ascribed to Von Thunen (Seligman, 1903, p. 530), and he went on to say that Longfield's theory of wages also marked a decided advance on the classical theory according to which wages depended on the customary standard of life. Longfield had argued that this cost of production theory of wages was inappropriate because labour was not in fact produced for what it could earn. The wages of the labourer depended on the value of his labour and not on his wants. Like the value of everything else, wages depended on the relation between supply and demand. The supply was given at any point in time but the demand depended on the value of the work the labourers were capable of performing. Having noted Longfield 's statement that '*The wages of labour depend upon the rate of profit and the productiveness of labour employed in the fabrication of those commodities in which the wages of labour are paid*' (Longfield, 1834, p. 215, emphasis in original), Seligman suggested that the exact relation between profits and wages was left unclear. Still it was clear that Longfield's theory of wages was a productivity theory – though not actually marginal productivity theory (Seligman, 1903, p. 531).

Having outlined Longfield's theory of distribution, Seligman argued that his approach to distribution led to conclusions with regard to the effects of social progress on rent profits and wages which were different from those of the Ricardian school. Longfield accepted that an increase in population tended to diminish the productiveness of agricultural labour, to raise profits and lower wages. However, he argued that, as capital in general tended to increase, the rate of profit tended to decline and the impact of resorting to poorer soils was neutralised by improvements in agriculture. Above all, an improved system of division of labour and the extension of machinery in manufactures 'enables the labourer to live more comfortably than before' (Longfield, 1834, p. 238). He will gain more by the diminished prices of all other articles than he will lose by the dearness of food. Means of communication will improve and the part of the cost production which relates to the distribution of commodities will diminish. 'If life and property are secured, the rate of profits will diminish, and labour will become more productive, and the relative value of each man's labour will increase' (1834, p. 239).

Seligman concluded his discussion of Longfield by noting that the productivity theory of wages and the marginal productivity theory of interest as expounded by Longfield went unnoticed outside Ireland. However, Longfield's successor as Whately professor, Isaac Butt regarded his predecessor's conclusions as an accepted part of economic theory. Seligman credits Butt with having generalised Longfield's marginal productivity theory and extending it to all productive agents and not just capital.

LONGFIELD AFTER SELIGMAN

While Seligman's paper may be credited with establishing Longfield's reputation as an early marginalist (Moss, 1976, p. 22), it does not appear to have given rise to any immediate sustained study of Longfield's work by historians of economic thought. However, the 1930's brought a number of important developments. In 1931, Longfield's *Lectures on Political Economy* were reissued by the London School of Economics as part of a series of Reprints of Scarce Tracts in Economics. *Three Lectures on Commerce and*

One on Absenteeism was also re-issued in 1938 as part of the same series. Although the *Lectures on Commerce* had not been discussed in Seligman's article, it was these rather than the *Lectures on Political Economy* that attracted attention of Jacob Viner (1932, 1975 [1937])[3] who credited Longfield with one of the earliest attempts to extend the Ricardian theory of comparative advantage from the two-commodity case to the multi-commodity case. As Viner explained, in the two-commodity case, given the comparative costs, it is easy to identify which commodity each country will import and which it will export. However, matters are not so clear cut when there are many commodities (Viner, 1975 [1937], p. 454). According to Viner, Longfield was the first to examine the many commodity case and came close to a correct solution.

> if a nation enjoyed an immense superiority in the production of two or three articles of very general demand, the wages of her labourers might be, in consequence, so high that she could not compete with the rest of the world in any other manufacture under a system of free trade. Let us suppose that the productiveness of English labour to be ten times as great as that of any other nation, in the production of tin, calico, coals, cutlery, and pottery. The wages of her labourers will, in consequence, be much greater than those of any other nation; suppose them eight times as great and suppose English labour is only twice as productive as foreign labour, in the manufacture of other commodities. These latter, therefore, will be fabricated in the rest of the world, at the fourth part of the price which it will cost to make them in England. (Longfield, 1835, pp. 69–70)

In this passage, Longfield identifies which commodities are likely to be exported and which imported and indicates that the precise dividing line is determined by the comparative money wage rates in the two countries. While Longfield did not have a satisfactory theory of how the ratio of the wages in the two countries was to be determined, Viner regarded his contribution as an 'important step forward' albeit one that did not attract the attention of other leading writers on trade. (Viner, 1975 [1937], pp. 455–456).

In addition to his contribution to the theory of international trade, Viner also noted Longfield's contribution to the currency controversies of the mid-nineteenth century. On the one side, there was the currency school which argued that a mixed currency would operate properly only if it were regulated in such a way that it mimicked the operations of a purely metallic currency (Viner, 1975 [1937], pp. 220–222). On the other side, the banking school denied that any regulation was necessary because the amount of paper in circulation was adequately controlled by the ordinary processes of competitive banking (Viner, 1975 [1937], pp. 222–223). Part of the argument of the banking school was that volume of bank credit depended on the willingness of business to borrow but they also argued that any bank issuing notes in excess of its usual amount would eventually loose reserves to other banks thus being forced to contract its lending. Longfield accepted that this was true where there was a single bank but, by constructing a two bank model, he was able to show that for a multibank system 'the evil costs of over-issue of one are partly shared among its rivals. Thus the stimulus of overtrading is found to be almost irresistible' while prevention requires a degree of tact and skill rarely found among bankers (Longfield, 1840, p. 219). Longfield concluded that competition between note-issuing banks contributed to cyclical tendencies in the economy. In line with members of the currency School, his proposed solution involved the monopolisation and regulation of note issue (Moss, 1976, p. 166–168).

Longfield's contribution to international trade theory was also commended by Bertil Ohlin who credited him with anticipating his own factor proportions account of trade and specialisation (Ohlin, 1967). Ohlin's attribution was based on passages from the *Lectures on Political Economy* in which Longfield had argued that

> independent of every difference of soil or climate, the exchanges between two countries ... will consist principally of articles produced by that species of labour which in each country is relatively cheapest. The one will export articles where skill and integrity are required on the part of the workman, and where intelligence and capital are required on the part of his employer.... But the case will be different in the less civilised country where life and property are insecure, and capital therefore scarce, and profits high, and the labourer needy, ignorant and dishonest. The exports of this country will consist of articles produced by the most unwholesome and disagreeable labour. (Longfield, 1834, p. 240–241)

On the basis of this and similar passages, Ohlin interpreted Longfield's attempt to explain the pattern of trade on the basis of differences in relative factor prices as an attempt to overturn the Ricardian model with its emphasis on labour quantities. Moss[4] suggests, however, that had Ohlin consulted the *Lectures on Commerce*, it would have been clear to him that this was not the case and that Longfield's objective was to modify rather than replace the simple Ricardian model (Moss, 1976, pp. 130–131).

While Longfield's observations on international trade were the main focus of attention in the 1930's, mention should also be made of Marian Bowley's assessment of Longfield in her *Nassau Senior and Classical Economics* which was published in 1937. There was no doubt, Bowley wrote, that Longfield's 'explanation of both the marginal utility and marginal productivity analyses was worked out independently' (Bowley, 1937, p. 109). Bowley argued that Longfield's application of the marginal analysis was far more complete that either Senior's or Lloyd's. Elsewhere in her book, she referred to Longfield as having expounded a definite marginal productivity theory of wages (1937, p. 185). Bowley's assessment went considerably beyond that of Seligman who nowhere suggested that Longfield was an exponent of marginal utility theory and who referred to Longfield's theory of wages as a productivity theory but not a marginal productivity theory.

Bowley may have been the first to brand Longfield as an early exponent of marginal utility theory but in this she was no means the last. Similar assessments have been attributed to other authors including Roll and Schumpeter (Moss, 1976, p. 193; White, 2009). In his influential history of economic thought, Roll (1938, pp. 341–344) provided a clear and concise summary of Longfield's discussion relating to both utility and value as set out in the *Lectures*. Referring to the detail of Longfield's discussion of the intensity of demand, Roll concluded that no modern exponent of the marginal utility theory could object to Longfield's formulation (Roll, 1938, p. 339). As far as distribution was concerned, Roll described Longfield theory of wages as 'another anticipation of the marginal productivity theory' though later he allowed that 'that the principle is applied to capital with much greater clarity' (Roll, 1938, pp. 343–344). In his *History of Economic Analysis,* Schumpeter wrote that Longfield's merits could be summed up by saying that 'he overhauled the whole of economic theory and produced a system that would have stood up well in 1890' (Schumpeter, 1954, pp. 464–465). Schumpeter identified Longfield's two most original contributions as his anticipation of the essentials of Bohm-Bawerk's theory by making 'roundabout' processes of production the pivot of his analysis of capital and his development of a reasonably correct theory of distribution based on the marginal cost principle. Although Moss (1976, p. 29) holds that Schumpeter perpetrated the myth that 'Longfield was the archenemy of the labour theory of value and set out to establish a marginal utility tradition at Trinity College, Dublin', the evidence is not quite so clear cut. It is true that Schumpeter regarded Longfield as an effective critic of the labour theory of value but there is no evidence that Schumpeter attributed to Longfield a marginal utility theory of value or even a utility-based theory as White (2009, p. 85) alleges. In the course of a discussion of Austrian economics, Schumpeter refers to Dupuit and Gossen as 'forerunners' of marginal utility theory but to Longfield and Thunen as forerunners of marginal productivity theory (Schumpeter, 1954, p. 915n).

BLACK'S ASSESSMENT OF LONGFIELD'S CONTRIBUTION

The first major twentieth-century study of Longfield was a PhD thesis written at Longfield's *alma mater* Trinity College, Dublin by a young graduate of the University, RDC Black. As an undergraduate Black's interest in Longfield had been aroused by Ohlin's references to Longfield's work on trade (Murphy and Prendergast, 2000). With perhaps an element of youthful enthusiasm[5] for the achievements of his fellow countryman, Black claimed that Longfield set out the whole theory of marginal utility with extraordinary completeness. In a subsequent article, Black argued that something closely approaching to a 'subjective value school' existed in Dublin in the mid-nineteenth century (Black, 1945, p. 140). He also referred to Longfield's 'extraordinarily complete marginal value theory' and suggested that that Longfield's references to the same person having in himself several demands of different degrees of intensity is striking in its anticipation of marginal utility theory (1945, p. 142).

Black made a further assessment of Longfield's contribution in his introduction to *The Economic Writings of Mountifort Longfield* (Black, 1971). There, he argued that although Longfield's treatment of value and distribution in *his Lectures on Political Economy* is fundamentally different from that of Ricardo, the validity of this assertion is not immediately evident. This is because the contents of the first five chapters (corresponding to the lectures delivered in the Trinity term of 1833) do not deviate substantially from orthodox classical doctrine. Longfield's original contributions are in the sixth and later lectures which were delivered in the Michaelmas term of the same year. Black hypothesised that Longfield was initially uncertain about the direction which his analysis would take and that it was during the long vacation between the Trinity and Michaelmas terms that his thinking became clear (1971, p. 13). Accordingly, in his treatment of value from Lecture six onwards, Longfield develops a theory of price determination based on the interaction of demand and supply. Black acknowledged that the main emphasis is placed on demand and referred to Longfield building up the notion of a demand schedule as composed of a ranking of individual demands according to their intensity.[6] Having noted that Longfield's analysis moves from the market demand schedule to the individual demand schedule, Black commented that, while the individual demand schedule has been interpreted as a statement of marginal utility theory, such an interpretation is literally not correct (1971, p. 14). Black pointed out that although the same approach was adopted in the case of distribution, it was only in his treatment of profits that Longfield developed a strictly marginal technique. Schumpeter had incorrectly attributed a marginal productivty theory of wages to Longfield though Cannan[7] had correctly identified Longfield's wage theory as a produce less deductions theory (1971, p. 15). Black concluded that, while it would be wrong to represent Longfield's analysis as a complete anticipation of neoclassical pricing and distribution theory, the fact remained that whatever classical elements were left incompletely integrated within it, it was fundamentally and systematically a different analysis from the Ricardian one and reached radically different conclusions on how economic progress affects the division of the social product (1971, p. 160). The remainder of Black's Introduction relates to Longfield's lectures on the poor laws, commerce and absenteeism as well as his anonymous articles on Banking and Currency none of which were covered in Seligman's evaluation.

Black's final paper on Longfield addressed the question of Longfield's relationship with classical and neoclassical economics. In so doing , he drew attention to the relativity of history of economic thought itself and showed that the place of the early Whately professors as dissenters or otherwise depends crucially on the view taken of orthodoxy itself (Black, 1984, pp. 120–121). Black referred to the role of Seligman's 1903 articles in breaking up (with a lag) an earlier consensus that there was a single classical orthodoxy and replacing it with the notion of two competing schools – one Ricardian and one proto- marginalist emphasising supply and demand as determinants of price. Bowley and Black himself had contributed to the elaboration of this point of view which was reflected also in Schumpeter's *History of Economic Analysis*. A further re-assessment came with the appearance of the first volume of *The Works and Correspondence of David Ricardo* in 1951 (Sraffa & Dobb, 1973). This also led to a two traditions view but a different one. The dividing line was now between those who subscribed to the view that the value of a commodity was determined by the sum of the expenses required for production, these expenses/factor payments having been determined by supply and demand and those who anchored exchange relation in the conditions of production. Senior and Longfield belong to the former group together with John Stuart Mill and ultimately Marshall. In this view, Longfield is seen as a harmony theorist defending the *status quo*. Even so, as Black acknowledged, this did not prevent Dobb from seeing Longfield as a forerunner of the later marginal theory and crediting him with a marginal efficiency theory of profit (Black, 1984, p. 124). The final re-assessment of orthodoxy was that of Samuel Hollander[8] which, as Black notes, harks back to Marshall's view of the essential continuity of the classical and neoclassical approaches. According to this view, Longfield is seen as following Ricardian orthodoxy and developing it to some extent. Black's own view was that Hollander's position could not be sustained. He agreed with Professor Moss that it was Longfield not Ricardo that had made the concept of the demand schedule an integral part of the theory of price (1984, p. 129). On the more controversial question of whether or not Longfield could be regarded as a pre-cursor of the marginal utility approach, Black accepted the answer had to be negative if this meant providing an explicit statement of diminishing marginal utility (1984, p. 130). However, his own view was that taking all the evidence into consideration, it was still reasonable to classify Longfield as a marginal utility theorist.[9]

BOWLEY'S RE-EVALUATION

Bowley's initial assessment of Longfield as a forerunner of marginal utility theory was made in the course of her study of Nassau Senior. Thirty-five years later, following perhaps a closer study of Longfield's work, she significantly modified her position. In an article published in 1972, she accepted that Longfield did not provide a statement of the doctrine of declining marginal utility though she suggested that such a doctrine was required by Longfield's statement of the way in which the individual distributes his expenditure between goods so as to maximise his utility (Bowley, 1972, p. 20). Bowley was referring here to Longfield's rather opaque discussion of the relationship between utility and value. Longfield argued that antithetical contrasts between value and utility are in general fallacious and suggested that 'perhaps for all practical purposes the best measure of utility is value' (Longfield, 1834, p. 27). He went on to say that to be considered of any importance, this proposition must be understood in a sense different from that in which it is proved.

> In fact the utility of any particular article to the possessors must vary according to their circumstances and situation and exchanges serve the purpose of providing that the goods possessed by each individual shall in proportion to their value be of the greatest utility to him; that is, that they shall contribute more to his happiness, and to the satisfaction of his wants and the gratification of his desires, than any other possessions of equal value. The same cause that prevents a person from giving anything for that which does not have some power of satisfying his wants or gratifying his wishes – that is has not *some* utility – will also prevent him from making any exchange, unless what he receives will conduce at least as much to his happiness as what he gives. When an exchange is made therefore it may be fairly presumed that each party has gained something, by receiving for the article he disposed of something which is, *relative to him*, of more utility, according to the extended signification which I have given to the word. (1834, p. 27–28)

Referring to the passage quoted in full above, Bowley remarked that the passage can be interpreted in a manner consistent with marginal utility theory but that it is difficult to reconcile with the earlier statement that value, i.e. price, measures utility. Bowley suggested that the confusion that beset Longfield in this passage helps to explain why Longfield later adopted Malthus's concept of intensity of demand. The latter has the merit of 'explaining the shape of the demand curve and movements along it, without having to revert to the difficult problem of utility in relation to value' (Bowley, 1972, pp. 24–25). Elsewhere, Bowley compared Longfield's degrees of intensity of demand with Dupuit's maximum sacrifice which was used by him as the measure of utility and the reflection of diminishing marginal utility but she acknowledged that Longfield did not take this final step of showing the relation of the concept of the intensity of demand to the concept of utility (Bowley, 1973, p. 152–153).

While, on her own admission, Bowley's interpretation of Longfield underwent considerable modification (Bowley, 1972, p. 19), she was not prepared to accept that there was any essential change in her view about Longfield's place in the development of political economy. Thus, in her review of Moss' *Mountifort Longfield: Ireland's First Professor of Political Economy*, Bowley rejected Moss' suggestion that both she and Black had changed their views in any fundamental way. For Ricardo, except in a few unimportant cases and during temporary disturbances, 'demand *could not* affect exchange value, *only the quantity produced*' (Bowley, 1978, pp. 176–177). By contrast, the utility and demand and supply theorists, among whom she numbered Longfield, started from the presumption of the importance of demand in determining exchange value. In their scheme, costs were a limiting and not the determining factor of price (1978, pp. 176–177). Only those economists who needed to use the demand curve in the theory of value examined the nature of the demand curve as such, though they found the precise relation of utility to the demand curve baffling (1978, p. 178).

NON-RICARDIAN IN DISTRIBUTION BUT NOT IN VALUE?

Lawrence Moss' book on Longfield, the review of which is referred to above, offers a comprehensive evaluation of all of Longfield's economic writings. Moss saw himself as dismantling some of the myths surrounding Longfield's theory of value but he was willing grant that Longfield's lectures provided 'the most significant improvements in supply-and-demand theory that can be found in the pre-Marshallian literature' (Moss, 1976, p. 49). Despite this Moss argued that Longfield's development of a supply and demand theory of market price did not supply sufficient grounds for classifying him as non-Ricardian since Longfield seems to have been willing in principle to retain the Ricardian labour quantity approach for the analysis of secular trends in relative values (1976, p. 24).[10] This argument rests heavily on the Moss' view that Ricardo's theory of income distribution 'is substantially independent of the whole question of measuring value and its variations over time' (1976, p. 24).While it is true that the essential relationships of Ricardo's distribution theory as set out in his 1815 *Essay* on profits, did not depend on a theory of value, Moss' position does not take adequate account of Ricardo's rejection of Malthus's supply and demand approach as well as his continuing preoccupation with the theory of value in the last years of his life. Moss argued that the non-Ricardianism of the Dublin School is to be found not in their theory of value but 'in their rejection of the English account of wages and profit and their willingness to embrace the alternative theory that Longfield had developed' (1976, p. 25). In this, Moss argued, Longfield's motivation was to develop a more optimistic account of the laws governing the distribution of income and teach workers that their interests were best served by the existing social order.

Moss argued that, in the second of his lectures on political economy, Longfield had found the existing theory according to which the proportion between demand and supply determined market prices 'vague and indefinite' and 'apt to mislead' (Longfield, 1834, pp. 37, 247; Moss, 1976, pp. 29, 49). Instead, Longfield had proposed that exchangeable value be defined as that price which will produce an equality between supply and the effective demand where the meaning of effective demand was the demand of those who are willing to give the price in question for the article (Longfield, 1834, p. 37). Moss hypothesised that Longfield realised that something more was required to make the market price determinate and that it was for this reason that he returned to the topic of price determination in his first lecture of the Michaelmas term (lecture VI) and introduced the marginal demand concept of intensity of demand (Moss, 1976, p. 33). As Moss notes, this concept had originally been developed by Malthus who distinguished between two aspects of demand: extent and intensity. The extent of demand was of little use in explaining how demand and supply affected price. The intensity of demand had to do with the will combined with the power to purchase a commodity. Regardless of the intensity of their demand, no one would give a high price for something he could obtain for a low one. Consequently, the whole intensity of demand did not normally show itself. However, the fact that some demand existed at a higher price than the prevailing one was evidence of a greater intensity of demand (Malthus, 1820, pp. 61–83). In arguing that the demand side of the market is composed of individuals some of whom are willing to pay more than cost but do not have to do so as long as the market remains competitive, Malthus was able explain the shape of the demand curve and movements along it (Moss, 1976, p. 34). Moss, however, noted that Malthus's use of his innovation was in explaining how demand could be said to raise prices rather than in the determination of prices *per se* (Malthus, 1820, p. 68).

When Longfield introduced the concept of intensity of demand at the start of his lectures on distribution, he referred to it as if it were a well known concept and made no reference to Malthus (Longfield, 1834, p. 111). He explained that demand could affect prices even if it were not sufficiently intense to lead to an actual purchase. An example was the demand of those who did not purchase at existing prices but who would do so if a slight reduction in price took place. The demand of this group had the effect of keeping up prices in the same way as that of the second highest bidder at an auction. Moss suggested that this point was original to Longfield[11] as also was the view that the same person may be said to have in himself several demands of different degrees of intensity (Moss, 1976, p. 368). Moss also noted Longfield's argument that for a given decline in the quantity consumed, a rich man's intensity of demand increases more rapidly than that of a poor man thereby suggesting that the former was likely to have more inelastic demand (1976, p. 380). Moss saw Longfield's discussion of intensity of demand as an explanation of the downward slope of the individual and market demand curves and he suggested that Longfield's account of the market pricing refers to what Marshall called the market period where the supply of the commodity is fixed so that the price is determined by the marginal demand. In this, Moss differed from Seligman who attributed to Longfield an upward sloping rather than a vertical supply schedule (1976, pp. 34–35; Seligman, 1903, p. 527).

Whereas Seligman attributed to Longfield a theory of marginal cost as well as marginal demand, Moss argued that Longfield's account of market pricing assumes that quantity is given (Moss, 1976, p. 35–37). Still, Moss recognised that, even in the market period, supply is not a fixed magnitude since Longfield had acknowledged that a scarcity of food might cause farmers and dealers to withhold stock with a view to obtaining still higher prices (Longfield, 1834, pp. 51–52; Moss, 1976, p. 35–37). While Moss argued that Longfield was unclear about how to embody the idea of a supply schedule of varying elasticities into his supply-and-demand theory, he acknowledged that Longfield identified important differences between the behaviour of supply in manufactures and in agriculture (1976, p. 31). Longfield accepted that in the case of manufactured goods, there was a strong tendency for exchangeable value to equal the natural value or cost of production (Longfield, 1834, pp. 36–37, 47, 49–50) and he went as far as to suggest that even a considerable disproportion between the demand and supply would exercise little if any influence over the price (1834, p. 50). If there was excess supply in any period, both retailers and manufacturers would tend to temporarily withhold stock rather than reduce the price. Consequently, a temporary derangement of the usual proportion between demand and supply would not exercise any considerable influence over price. Moreover, any such derangement could only be temporary since manufacturers will not continue to produce goods which they can only dispose of at a loss. No great increase in price can take place either since customers can in general wait for a new supply. Things were different in the case of raw materials and especially in the case of food. In both of these, substantial variations in price were likely to take place. A new supply cannot be procured until the following harvest and consumers cannot dispense with the use of the article simply because of its high price (1834, pp. 50–51).

WHY DID LONGFIELD INTRODUCE THE CONCEPT OF INTENSITY OF DEMAND IN LECTURE VI?

As noted above, Moss hypothesised that Longfield returned to the issue of demand in Lecture VI because he was aware that his earlier statement of the condition for market equilibrium did not provide an explanation of how prices were determined (Moss, 1976, p. 33). Black, on the contrary, took the view that in the early lectures Longfield was uncertain about how his analysis would develop. He suggested that, having had the long summer vacation to think over matters, Longfield clarified his own views and decided to break away from the classical distribution theory. Thus, having proceeded along somewhat orthodox lines in the early lectures, from Lecture VI onwards, Longfield proceeded with impressive originality (Black, 1971, p. 13). A third perspective, as already noted, was offered by Bowley who argued that Longfield wished to explain the shape of the demand curve without dealing with the difficult issue of the relationship between utility and value. A fourth perspective is that offered by White 2009 who argues that intensity of demand was a means of providing a 'clear analysis of the relevance of distribution of wealth in explaining demand' (White, 2009, p. 75).

White rejects the characterisation of Longfield as a marginalist precursor of any kind and he argues that those who have interpreted Longfield in this manner have been using the later marginalist framework both to organise their reading of his lectures and to adjudicate on their successes and failures (2009, p. 66). White's focus is on Longfield's theory of value. He not only objects to the now discredited reading of Longfield as a marginal utility theorist but also the more temperate one of Longfield as a marginalist precursor in the sense that he provided an explanation for the downward slope of the individual and market demand curves. An objection to the latter is that, in Longfield's account, there is no suggestion that the relationship between demand price and quantity is a continuous function rather than a series of points (2009, pp. 88–89). White goes further than this, however, and argues that the terms of Longfield's analysis preclude a functional relationship between price and quantity demanded. This is because 'Longfield's explanation for the different intensities of demand and price was the distribution of wealth' (2009, p. 90). Consequently, White argues, the shape of any posited demand curve would depend on that distribution so that the curve would be perfectly elastic over the relevant range if the distribution of wealth was equal. It is true, as noted earlier, that Longfield argued that, in the case of a rich man, the intensity of his demand increases more rapidly in proportion to the diminution of his consumption, than in the case of a poor man (Longfield, 1834, p. 115) so that the shape of any posited demand curve would be more inelastic in the case of a poor man. It is also true that Longfield referred in a footnote to the possibility that increased wealth of the population would lead to increased intensity of demand (1834, p. 258). Since intensity of demand is intended to reflect both the power and will to purchase, the latter is hardly surprising. Moreover, White nowhere explains how he reconciles his view that the intensity of demand depends on the distribution of wealth with Longfield's view that the intensity of demand varies not only among different individuals but also within each individual.

There is much to be said for Black's argument that Longfield's innovations in distribution theory also motivated the development of his demand theory. This was Longfield's own explanation. As he put it 'I have made those preliminary observations [on intensity of demand] in the hope that they may render more intelligible to some a species of reasoning which I shall probably have occasion to employ once or twice in the course of this term' (1834, pp. 115–116). In Lecture IX, the lecture in which he introduced his theory of profit, Longfield had no difficulty explaining that the maximum profits which a capitalist or owner of an instrument could potentially reap would be the difference between the quantity of work which the labourer could do with and without its assistance. However, it was more difficult to explain why the maximum that would be paid at any time was determined by 'that portion of capital which is employed with least efficiency, which I shall call the last portion of capital brought into operation' (1834, p. 194). Longfield suggested that this 'subject may perhaps be made clearer, if we pursue a little farther the analogy between the price of goods and the profits of capital' (1834, p. 194) and, at this point, he re-introduced the concept of intensity of demand to useful effect. Apart from its explanatory value, Longfield's use of the analogy between the price of goods and the profits of capital also had the advantage of connecting a radical innovation by an unknown economist with a concept associated with a well-known figure like Malthus and which had also been endorsed by Sir Edward West (West, 1826, pp. 20–21).

LONGFIELD'S MARGINAL THEORY OF DISTRIBUTION

In his introduction to the *Economic Writings,* Black (1971, p. 14–15) noted that no less an authority than Schumpeter had written that Longfield had explained both wages and profits using marginal productivity theory. Having pointed out that only the theory of profits could be regarded as a marginal productivity theory, Black then posed the question, why had Longfield a marginal productivity theory of capital and not of labour? Black suggestion was that the way in which Longfield developed his theory made it difficult to generalise. Longfield did not derive the marginal product of capital through the addition of successive homogenous units of capital while other factors are held fixed. Rather, he began with the assumption that 'machines are of various degrees of efficiency'. He then considered the case of the capitalist supplying labour with identical machines (spades) this time assuming that the labourers are of varying efficiency (1971, p. 15). Black suggested that this treatment made it natural for him to think of wages as being neither more nor less than 'the amount of what he produces minus the profits of the capitalist' (Longfield, 1834, p. 214).

While Black's solution is a possible one, it is also worth bearing in mind that had Longfield sought to develop a marginal productivity explanation of wages as well as of capital, it would have been necessary for him to confront the question of whether, at equilibrium, the sum of the factor incomes would equal the total product or, at least, the total product less rent. We have no evidence that Longfield considered this issue but had he done so, it would have been reasonable for him to conclude that there was no necessity for this to be the case. As Pasinetti (1999, p. 13) has noted, the assumptions required to make this happen are quite stringent and have no obvious basis in either observation or logic.

In the Preface to his *Lectures*, Longfield declared himself unable to acquiesce in the theory of profit adopted by most English writers in political economy (Longfield, 1834, p. vii). As Moss (1976, p. 96) has pointed out, by the time that Longfield was writing he was by no means unique in criticising of the West/Ricardo theory of profit although he may not have been aware of this.[12] What makes Longfield stand out is the fact that in addition to criticising the most widely accepted theory, he offered an alternative to it. According to the West/Ricardo theory, the productiveness of the worst land under cultivation together with an exogenously determined wage regulates the rate of profit.[13] Longfield accepted that the productiveness of agricultural labour had a tendency to diminish with the advance of population. However, he was unwilling to accept that the wage was exogenously given or that the application of capital to land plays any special role in the determination of the general rate of profit.

'We must take care', he wrote, 'not to confound the last capital applied to land, with the last or least efficient capital, considered with a view to its efficiency in superseding labour...when inferior soils are brought under cultivation, some of the capital employed for that purpose is of the most efficient kind in superseding labour, and it is its efficiency in this respect that regulates profits'. (Longfield, 1834, p. 228)

Like those he criticised, Longfield accepted that the rate of profit tended to decline as capital increased. However, he saw this as being counteracted by a number of factors including agricultural improvements, an improved system of division of labour, increasing skill and discipline in the workforce, the extension of machinery in manufacturing and greater scope for the employment of capital as population increased (1834, p. 228–238). Longfield predicted that if freedom, security and education were carefully promoted, there was 'every reason to hope, that with the progress of society, population and wealth will increase together, and that more human beings will be supported in greater comfort than hitherto' (1834, pp. 235–235).

Seligman argued that Longfield's productivity-based theory of distribution must necessarily arrive at conclusions on the course of social progress which is different from those of the Ricardo School. In his Preface, the only general point highlighted by Longfield was that his analysis showed how impossible it is to *regulate wages generally* either by combinations of workmen or legislative enactments (1834, p. vii). In the body of the text, he argued that the only means by which the condition of the labourer could be effectively ameliorated was through an increase in productivity.[14] Longfield's emphasis in the preface on the ineffectiveness of combinations as a means of raising wages is consistent with Moss' (2010) view of Longfield as speaking up for the benevolent nature of the market process thereby countering the rantings of the radicals. Be that as it may, it would be wrong to give the impression that Longfield was an uncritical defender of the existing order. He devoted the whole of his fourth lecture on commerce to the impact of absenteeism and showed that it was prejudicial to the welfare of the community by worsening Irish terms of trade (Longfield, 1835, pp. 72–94). Murphy (1984, p. 18) has shown that a conservative member of his appointment panel at Trinity College described Longfield as a 'radical politician', Moreover, as Black (1984, p. 133) notes, although Longfield shared with his contemporaries a concern that the poor laws would promote idleness amongst the able-bodied and neglected to attend sufficiently to the problems of unemployment in the Ireland of his time, he also advocated that '*every individual is entitled to the means of support from the society which is determined to compel him to obey its laws*' (Longfield, 1834, p. 19; emphasis in original). These apparently contradictory views can be reconciled by noting that, as a Whig-free trader, Longfield would have been viewed as a dangerous radical by the landed aristocracy while, at the same time, he saw himself as devising economic arguments to combat the trade union militancy of the 1830s.

Ricardo's belief that with the progress of society and wealth, the natural tendency of profits was to fall. However, this tendency was checked by improvements which reduced the cost of production of wage goods.

> This tendency, this gravitation as it were of profits, is happily checked at repeated intervals by the improvements in machinery, connected with the production of necessaries, as well as by discoveries in the science of agriculture which enable us to relinquish a portion of labour before required, and therefore to lower the price of the prime necessary of the labourer. (Ricardo, 1821, para. 6.18)

For Ricardo, however, the accumulation of capital per se had no tendency to lower profits as it had for Longfield.[15] Although most commentators follow Seligman in arguing that Longfield's productivity-based theory of distribution necessarily gives rise to more optimistic conclusions on the course of economic development, it is not obvious that an extension of diminishing returns from land to other factors of production should, of itself, lead to this prognosis.[16] Longfield provided some analytical support for his views emphasising the positive effects of population growth on market size and positive effects of a low discount rate in increasing the attractiveness of durable improvements in infrastructure, in building and in education (Longfield, 1834, p. 229–233).[17] Ultimately, however, much of his optimism about the course of development under capitalism relied on the countervailing effect of improvements in agriculture and the improved system of division of labour and extension of machinery in manufactures (1834, p. 238).

CONCLUSION

Seligman identified Longfield's main innovations as his supply and demand theory of price determination and his productivity approach to distribution. He credited Longfield with expounding the doctrine of marginal demand and with applying the marginal idea to the supply schedule as well. On the distribution side, he attributed to Longfield a marginal productivity theory of profit and a productivity theory of wages.

In the first half of the twentieth century, there was a tendency to build on Seligman's claims and to regard Longfield's demand theory as a precursor of the marginal utility theory. While the validity of this claim depends to some extent on what being a precursor is taken to mean, the claim seems to involve reading into Longfield's work more than he actually states. Seligman's own view that Longfield provided a reasonable exposition of the doctrine of marginal demand has been accepted by all commentators with the exception of White. However, the same cannot be said for his claim that Longfield also applied the marginal idea to the theory of supply. The evidence on which Seligman based his claim was not entirely convincing and no other commentator has provided stronger evidence in support of that point of view.

As with the theory of value, in the first half of the twentieth century, there was a tendency amongst authors commenting on Longfield's theory of distribution to elaborate on Seligman's original claims and attribute to Longfield a marginal productivity theory of wages as well as a marginal productivity theory of profit. In most cases, however, this seems to have been done by those commenting on Longfield's work as part of a wider endeavour and does not appear to have been a feature of the more detailed studies of Longfield's work.

Most authors have followed Seligman in suggesting that Longfield's innovations in the theory of distribution led to a more optimistic prognosis for the capitalist system than that of the Ricardo/West school. While there is no doubt about Longfield's greater optimism, it has been suggested here that, just as in the Ricardian model, Longfield's predictions of a better future rely on the countervailing effects of technical change and institutional development.

Seligman's exposition of Longfield's work focused entirely on the theories of value and distribution in the *Lectures on Political Economy*. Other authors notably Viner and Ohlin and more recently Black and Moss drew attention to Longfield's important innovations in the theory of international trade. Viner also drew attention to Longfield's contribution to the monetary debates of the mid-nineteenth century while Moss noted Longfield's anticipation of Abba Lerner's symmetry theorem according to which it makes no essential difference to the pattern of international trade whether a nation puts its tax on its own exports to foreigners or instead puts a tax of similar magnitude on the foreigner's imports.

Taken together, Longfield's contributions to the marginal theory of price and distribution and to the theory of international trade were an outstanding contribution to political economy, and no exaggeration of his achievements is required to merit Seligman's characterisation of him as the most remarkable of all. Nowadays, Longfield is mentioned as an important pioneer in most histories of the subjects he wrote on. At least in part thanks to Seligman, he is no longer a neglected economist.

NOTES

1. The examination questions had been set by Whately, Senior and the registrar, Dr Robert Phipps. Although Whately agreed to review rather than examine the essays written by the candidates, it appears that he not only pointed out the three candidates from which the selection of Professor should be made but also the order of his preference without knowing the names of the candidates (Murphy, 1984, pp. 17–18).
2. Black (1971) contains a facsimile edition of the lectures on political economy, on the poor laws and on commerce. The volume also contains reprints of the articles on banking and currency and on the limits of state interference.

3. Viner's chapter on the doctrine of comparative costs in *Studies in the Theory of International Trade* (1975 [1937]) was a revised version of Viner (1932).

4. Moss (1976, p. 138) also noted that Longfield's *Lectures on Commerce* contain the first attempt to work out a theory of tariff incidence consistent with a Ricardian two country two good model. If incentives for international trade were created by differences between relative prices in each nation, then tariffs should be analysed in terms of altering these price ratios. Longfield concluded that 'as far as commerce is concerned, it is just the same thing whether we impose a duty all things imported from abroad, or foreign nations impose a duty on our commodities' (Longfield, 1835, p. 24).

5. Black was 19 when he began work on his dissertation and twenty one when he graduated with a PhD.

6. In this context, Black referred to a reprint of Vol. 1 of Mitchell's *Types of Economic Theory*. Mitchell noted that Longfield had not connected his analysis of demand closely with his remarks on utility (Mitchell, [1913] 1967, pp. 521–522).

7. In his *Theories of Production and Distribution*, Cannan ([1893] 1917) commended Longfield (along with West) for refusing to accept McCulloch's wage-fund theory. He described Longfield's theory as 'a produce theory' (pp. 266–267).

8. See Hollander (1979). In a review for *Oxford Economics Papers,* O'Brien (1981, p. 352) described it as 'a full scale frontal attack on the existing body of Ricardo Scholarship'.

9. Black seems to have continued to maintain this position. When asked in interview in 2000 whether or not he was still happy to regard Longfield as one of the main precursors of the marginal revolution, Black responded he was not as happy as he was at the time he wrote his thesis but that while willing to modify his position in light of additional research he still felt that Longfield was striking out on a line of his own (Murphy & Prendergast, 2000).

10. Longfield put the matter as follows in the second of his lectures on political economy: 'labour, from its concern in the cost of production, has an indirect influence over the exchangeable value that often makes it a convenient measure, especially as it is by reference to the labour employed in production that the source of any permanent variation in the relative exchangeable value of commodities can be found' (Longfield, 1834, pp. 38–39).

11. In *Price of Corn and Wages of Labour*, Edward West (1826, p. 21) provided an extended discussion and critique of Malthus's concept of intensity of demand in the course of which he made the point that the bidding of the second highest bidder in an auction enhances the price at which the item is sold. It is possible that Longfield was familiar with this work although he cites only West's 1815 work *On the Application of Capital to Land.*

12. For a discussion of early critiques of Ricardian economics, see Meek (1950); Fetter (1965, 1969); Gordon (1969), and O'Brien (1970).

13. The theory was attributed by Longfield to Sir Edward West, who he also credited with being the originator of the correct theory of rent (Longfield, 1834, p. xi). On West's opposition to the wage fund theory, see Grampp (1970). On his theory of distribution, see Brewer (1988).

14. Longfield (1834, pp. 217–218) argued that the condition of the labourer could also be ameliorated through a fall in the rate of profit. However, he went on to argue

that even a large reduction in profit would not be an effective means of increasing the wages of labour.

15. 'No accumulation of capital will permanently lower profits, unless there be some permanent cause for the rise of wages' (Ricardo, 1821, para. 21.1).

16. For a discussion of this issue, see Pasinetti (1999, p. 11).

17. Longfield's discussion indicates a clear understanding of the impact of the discount rate on the present value of future cash flows that is consistent with the fact that towards the end of his life he published a book entitled *An Elementary Treatise on Series*.

REFERENCES

Black, R. D. C. (1945). Trinity college, Dublin, and the theory of value, 1832–1863. *Economica, n.s., 12*(47), 140–148.

Black, R. D. C. (1971). *The economic writings of Mountifort Longfield.* New York: Augustus M. Kelley.

Black, R. D. C. (1984). The Irish dissenters and nineteenth-century political economy. In: A. E. Murphy (Ed.), *Economists and the Irish Economy from the eighteenth century to the present day* (pp. 120–137). Dublin: Irish Academic Press.

Bowley, M. (1937). *Nassau senior and classical economics.* London: George Allen and Unwin.

Bowley, M. (1972). The predecessors of Jevons: The revolution that wasn't. *Manchester School, 60*(1), 9–29.

Bowley, M. (1973). *Studies in the history of economic thought before 1870.* London: Macmillan.

Bowley, M. (1978). Review of *Mountifort Longfield: Ireland's first Professor of Political Economy* by L.S Moss. *Economic Journal, 88*(349), 176–178.

Brewer, A. (1988). Edward west and the classical theory of distribution and growth. *Economica, n.s., 55*(220), 505–515.

Cannan, E. (1917). *A history of the theories of production and distribution in English political economy from 1776 to 1848.* London: P.S. King and Son.

Fetter, F. W. (1965). Economic controversy in the British reviews, 1802–1850. *Economica, n.s., 32*(128), 424–437.

Fetter, F. W. (1969). The rise and decline of Ricardian economics. *History of Political Economy, 1*(1), 67–84.

Gordon, B. J. (1969). Criticism of Ricardian views on value and distribution in the British Periodicals, 1820–1850. *History of Political Economy, 1*(2), 370–387.

Grampp, W. D. (1970). Edward West reconsidered. *History of Political Economy, 2*(Fall), 316–343.

Hollander, S. (1979). *The economics of David Ricardo.* Toronto: University of Toronto Press.

Longfield, M. (1834). *Lectures on political economy.* Dublin: Richard Milliken and Son.

Longfield, M. (1835). *Three lectures on commerce and one on absenteeism.* Dublin: William Curry Jun.

Longfield, M. (1840). Banking and currency part II. *Dublin University Magazine,* February, pp. 218–233.

Malthus, T. R. (1989 [1820]). *Principles of political economy* (variorum ed., J. Pullen, Ed.). Cambridge: Cambridge University Press.

Meek, R. L. (1950). The decline of Ricardian economics in England. *Economica, n.s., 17*(65), 43–62.

Mitchell, W. C. (1967 [1913]). *Types of economic theory* (J. Dorfman, Ed.). New York: Augustus M. Kelley.

Moss, L. S. (1976). *Mountifort Longfield: Ireland's first professor of political economy*. Ottawa, IL: Green Hill Publishers.

Moss, L. S. (2010). Value and distribution theory at Trinity College Dublin, 1831–1844. In: T. Boylan, R. Prendergast & J. Turner (Eds), *Ireland and political economy: Toward a history of Irish economic thought*. London: Routledge.

Murphy, A. E. (1984). Mountifort Longfield's appointment to the chair of political economy in Trinity College, Dublin, 1832. In: A. E. Murphy (Ed.), *Economists and the Irish economy from the eighteenth century to the present day* (pp. 13–24). Dublin: Irish Academic Press.

Murphy, A. E., & Prendergast, R. (2000). *Contributions to the history of economic thought: Essays in honour of R.D.C. Black*. London: Routledge.

O'Brien, D. P. (1970). *J.R. McCulloch: A study in classical economics*. London: Allen and Unwin.

O'Brien, D. P. (1981). Ricardian economics and the economics of David Ricardo. *Oxford Economic Papers, n.s., 33*(3), 352–386.

Ohlin, B. (1967). *Interregional and international trade*. Cambridge: Harvard University Press.

Pasinetti, L. (1999). Economic theory and technical progress. *Economic Issues, 4*(Part 2), 1–18.

Ricardo, D. (1821). *On the principles of political economy and taxation*. London: John Murray.

Roll, E. (1938). *A history of economic thought*. London: Faber and Faber.

Seligman, E. R. A. (1903). On some neglected British economists-II. *Economic Journal, 13*(52), 511–535.

Schumpeter, J. A. (1954). *History of economic analysis*. Oxford: Oxford University Press.

Sraffa, P., & Dobb, M. (Eds). (1973). *The works and correspondence of David Ricardo, 11 vols*. Cambridge: Cambridge University Press.

Viner, J. (1932). The doctrine of comparative costs. *Weltwirtschaftliches Archiv, 36*(2), 356–414.

Viner, J. (1975 [1937]). *Studies in the theory of international trade*. New York: Augustus M. Kelley.

West, E. (1903 [1815]). *On the application of capital to land*. Baltimore: Lord Baltimore Press.

West, E. (1826). *The price of corn and the wages of labour*. London: John Hatchard and Son.

White, M. V. (2009). Hunting a pre-cursor: The limits of Mountifort Longfield on utility and value. *European Journal of the History of Economic Thought, 16*(1), 65–96.

ISAAC BUTT AND NEGLECTED POLITICAL ECONOMISTS

Alan O'Day

> The very best theories were but useless until made practical and public.
>
> Whately (1848, p. 3)
>
> We may feel the satisfaction that we are entering on inquiries of vast practical importance to the human race – we are attaining knowledge, which once attained, the common sense of mankind can easily apply.
>
> Butt (1837a, p. 48)
>
> Questions of economical legislation will be gradually redeemed from the province of passion and declamation, and brought with that of argument and reason.
>
> Butt (1838, p. 8)

Edwin R. A. Seliman in 1903 took up the theme of neglected British economists, including John Cairnes, Mountiford Longfield and Isaac Butt from Ireland. To subsequent generations, many of his economists remained 'neglected'; Seligman's explanation for his subjects being in the shadows was that these figures did not conform to the then prevailing economic orthodoxy. Although his observation applies to most of his subjects, it is not quite accurate as far as Butt is concerned. As well, there has been a growing academic appetite for political economy and economic development in Ireland. Still it remains true that for the most part both in Great Britain and Ireland discussion centres on the ideas of major economic thinkers; Butt is not enumerated among these (see Gray, 2004; O'Day, 2006, 2009). However, a recent four volume collection of Irish writings on political economy edited by Tim Boylan and Tadhg Foley (2003) has made the subject, and especially 'neglected' economists more accessible. Three

English, Irish and Subversives Among the Dismal Scientists
Research in the History of Economic Thought and Methodology, Volume 28-B, 375–401

ISSN: 0743-4154/doi:10.1108/S0743-4154(2010)000028B016

excerpts from Isaac Butt's lectures while holding the Whately Professorship of Political Economy at Trinity College Dublin are included in their important series. Serious modern reflection on Irish political economists was really begun in the 1940s and 1950s by R. D. Collison Black; he terms Butt as one of the 'Irish dissenters', that is political economists who took exception to the pre-eminent *laissez-faire* doctrine and in his view constituted a school (Black, 1983). Butt, he points out, detected the limitation to economic theory based on full employment assumptions. Instead Butt condemned the economic evil of landlord absenteeism and exalted the virtues of protectionism for Ireland (Black, 1983, p. 134; 1960, pp. 141–42).[1] Laurence S. Moss ([1973] 1991) also assigned Butt a meaningful place among Irish political economists, crediting him with 'presenting an embryonic version of the marginal utility theory of imputation'.

The Dublin 'School' is a recently challenged designation (McGovern, 2000), to the extent it centred solely on the development of utility theory. In the estimation of Boylan and Foley (2003, Vol. 4, p. 3), Butt 'provided a symbolic link between two major sets of critics of *laissez-faire* and free trade, the conservative landed interest and Irish nationalism'. Butt's best-known writings on economics resulted from lectures delivered between 1836 and 1841 when he succeeded Longfield as Whately Professor in Trinity College, becoming the second holder of the office. The professorship had been founded by the Church of Ireland Archbishop of Dublin, Richard Whately, in emulation of the similar Drummond Professorship at the University of Oxford which he had held, and was not part of the academic curriculum but created to popularise understanding of economics both within and outside Trinity College. The position was part-time with the occupant receiving £100 per year, then a considerable sum, and required to give nine lectures annually and to publish at least one. Whately, who enjoyed a long tenure in the sea of Dublin (1831–1963) guided by Nassau Senior, exercised immense influence over the appointment, though Butt's selection was against his wishes (McGovern, 2000, pp. 9–10). As Boylan and Foley point out, the years between 1816 and 1848 were the 'age of Ricardo' but Whately was a critic of the dominant ideology. Thus, unsurprisingly, the early holders of the Whately Professorship were anti-Ricardo although Butt may have been less susceptible to Whatley's influence than other occupants of the Chair. The first five holders form what is termed the Dublin School.

Butt's contributions during his spell as the occupant of the Chair, though deemed less important that those of Longfield and William Neilson Hancock, are recognised as helping shape debate about Ireland's economy

(Moss, 1976). Mark Blaug (1991, p. ix) sounds the usual note that 'Butt wrote no economics after his five-year appointment to the Whately Chair'. His judgement stems from a tradition of separating theory and practice, something Blaug implies when concluding that 'with the appearance of the Irish famine, he turned to the question of English policy towards Ireland, becoming a famous early advocate of Irish Home Rule' (1991, p. ix). It is suggested, in contrast, that much of Butt's later writing and public career, continued to expand, often from a concrete perspective on his set of ideas about political economy. As seen above, Butt, saw his role in the Chair as contributing to the stock of practical ideas on political economy: 'We may feel the satisfaction that we are entering on inquiries of vast practical importance to the human race – we are attaining knowledge which once attained, the common sense of mankind can easily apply' (Butt, 1838, p. 48). These, it will be argued, also, led him to advocate home rule or home government for Ireland as a means to implement economic remedies for specifically Irish wants. Butt fits R. D. Collison Black's (1960, p. 13) description of a political economist who sought to influence public opinion by making contributions to newspapers, through speeches and political participation.

Distinguishing Butt from many of Seligman's 'neglected' economists is his long and varied public life. Born in Donegal in 1813, son of a Church of Ireland clergyman and related to Bishop George Berkeley through his mother, he entered Trinity College, Dublin in 1828, aged 15, where he amassed a formidable academic record. The Berkeley lineage was to prove a major, perhaps the most decisive, influence on his economic perspective. Involved in most of the major public controversies of the day, Butt was successively a leading Irish Tory, a Conservative party MP and ultimately the founder of the Irish self-government movement. Butt was a prodigious writer, essaying topics ranging over the classics, Bishop Berkeley, political economy, the Irish land question, education in Ireland, amnesty of political prisoners and he authored the scheme of federal home rule which in one form or other was at the heart of the national demand until after 1914. Additionally, he turned his hand to writing histories of Italy and novels. Butt was a towering part of the circle around the *Dublin University Magazine* in the 1830s; to the detriment of his own legal earnings, he was an eloquent counsel for William Smith O'Brien and other Young Irelanders of 1848; in the mid-1860s he defended many Fenians gratis; he was the leading force in the Amnesty Association's efforts to free imprisoned Fenians at the close of that decade; he was chief political spokesmen for the tenant-right interest in the late 1860s and 1870s; and above all Butt was the inspiration behind the movement for Irish home rule in the 1870s. Added to this he was a renowned legal advocate and a major figure in the Westminster House of Commons. As an MP and also outside Parliament he voiced views on the leading public issues, which as suggested already, were grounded in his economics. Thus, he should be seen as a practitioner of political economy in the sense articulated by Archbishop Whately. The lion's share of attention, though, has focused on Butt's later nationalist career. Yet, too many in Ireland Butt came to epitomise Irish subservience to British rule; a man who, in the words of an early supporter, 'would not strip to fight' (quoted in Feingold, 1984, p. 96).

Despite extensive personal papers and a huge volume of reports in newspapers, the *Parliamentary Debates* and similar sources, only one biography of this intriguing man has appeared. Terence de Vere White's graceful, *The Road of Excess* (1946) traced Butt's journey from Protestant Orangeism and personal immorality to advocacy of Home Rule and acceptance of the Victorian notion of familial relations (see also Brown, 1972, p. 190). His analysis establishes the standard interpretation. Other works, typically concentrating on the later years, treat segments of his life and offer useful vignettes but usually are brief and embedded inside biographies of other figures or in monographs on the period.[2] R. Barry O'Brien's influential biography of Charles Stewart Parnell saw Butt overshadowed by the great Chief; nevertheless he 'will always stand in the front rank of Irish political leaders of the nineteenth century' (O'Brien, 1898, Vol. 1, p. 181). Michael Davitt's *The Fall of Feudalism in Ireland* painted a sympathetic portrait of Butt, viewing him as the reforming link between the Tenant League of the 1850s and the Land League formed in 1879. Davitt claimed that the spirit of Fenianism acted through him, dismissing Butt's record in the 1850s and early 1860s because he then 'had not yet received the 'call' which comes to men destined for a great work' (Davitt, 1904, pp. 79, 85, see also, pp. 81, 86, 90). John Redmond in 1913 saw Butt 'as the great link in the chain of success' (quoted in MacDonagh, 1946, p. 4). J. G. Swift MacNeill, a not inconsiderable Protestant home ruler of a subsequent generation, comments, 'the story of Mr Butt's gravitation is part of the history of Ireland' (MacNeill, 1925, p. 120).

However, some contemporaries and later historians are less generous, contributing to what has proved a contested legacy. In 1865, Lord Kimberley noted with approbation 'a drunken speech from Butt'; William Gladstone was reported to consider him 'a drunkard, a swindler, and devoid of principle' (Hawkins & Powell, 1997, p. 152; Bahlman, 1972, Vol. 2, p. 702). Butt's financial problems constantly dogged his political work, moving one member of his party to comment in November 1875, 'I would trust him with my cause but not my money. You might as well put water in a colander as money in Butt's pocket' (Joseph Royayne to John O'Leary, 8 November 1875, quoted in Larkin, 1996, p. 421). Butt's obituary in *The Times* on 6 May 1879 deftly caught the tenor of his life; 'when the choice was between the pleasure of the moment and the fulfilment of a duty, we will not say to others, but to the higher gifts of his own nature, pleasure was sure to gain the day'. Justin McCarthy who knew him well in the home rule years proclaimed that Butt 'did not prove quite equal to the work; he was sinking in years; he had wasted his iron constitution between over-work and over-relaxation' (McCarthy, 1899, p. 329).

Later writers have echoed these verdicts. R. B. McDowell (1952, p. 114) dismisses him and the group of writers of the *Dublin University Magazine* in the 1830s and 1840s as men who 'expressed crude prejudices in decent prose and tried to combine narrow and aggressive Toryism with the literary enthusiasms of the Romantic Movement'. Lawrence J. McCaffrey, while commending Butt's labours in the 1870s, maintains that he lacked toughness and political realism yet acknowledges that he 'deserves the credit for formulating and articulating the home rule demand and for creating a nationalist opinion willing to accept federalism as a satisfactory solution to the Irish question' (McCaffrey, 1962, p. 50). D. A. Thornley considered Butt's efforts to mould a self-government movement, maintaining that by later 1878 he was 'an anachronistic survival, a barrier to the development of the national movement...' (1964, p. 379). F. S. L. Lyons repeatedly characterises him as 'ineffectual' pointing to his 'inadequacies', and refers to 'Isaac Butt's fumbling home rulers' (1977, pp. 612, also, 52–53, 60, 76, 86). R. V. Comerford depreciates the sincerity of Butt's later adoption of popular causes for 'little can be taken for granted about his motivation on particular issues' (Moody, 1981, pp. 120–121, 128; Comerford, 1979, pp. 170, 174), an opinion replicated by R. F. Foster (1988, pp. 397–98). Foster's image of Butt in the 1870s is at odds with his more sympathetic treatment for the 1830s and 40s. Emmet Larkin focuses on Butt's 'inability at the critical moment to continue to articulate the emerging Irish political consensus.... The problem was less that Butt did not represent the sense of the party as it was constituted in 1874 than he did not understand the real state of Irish public opinion' (Larkin, 1996, p. 390).

Robert Kee (1972, pp. 353, 357) has proved a harbinger of the more nuanced appreciation, arguing that Butt deserves to be counted as a one of the personalities who changed the course of Irish nationalism; his contribution was to organise public opinion to reject the principle of piecemeal justice from a British Parliament and marshal it behind the demand that only an Irish Parliament could give the country the full justice required. The famine, according to Kee, was the beginning of Butt's disenchantment with the Union. He insists, 'Butt has been much disparaged by latter-day nationalists, and was indeed left behind by events even in his own lifetime. But the credit for first coordinating the movement from which latter-day nationalism was to draw its strength must be his' (Kee, 1972, p. 359). Still Kee subscribes to the usual view of Butt's limitations, noting that the performance of the home rulers under his leadership was ineffective 'partly because Butt himself, caught in the personal trap of trying to lighten a long accumulated burden of heavy debt by increasing burden of work at the bar, could not give the party more than part-time leadership' though seeing the quality of personnel at his command to be an even larger liability (1972, p. 361). Alvin Jackson (1998, p. 105) tellingly adds 'Butt occupied a political position of great strategic importance, standing at the intersection of several Irish political traditions'.

The growing tendency to view Butt's activities as an integrated whole is epitomised by W. J. McCormack; he reveals Butt as possessing an 'enormous capacity for adaptation' though broadly consistent over time in his outlook (McCormack, 1994, p. 152). His re-evaluation of Butt's writings places him as a transition figure functioning in the context of a cultural diagnosis the Irish professional classes (McCormack, 1989, p. 121). McCormack maintains that his

> biography does not so much demonstrate transformation and development as it exemplified a curious prolific range of stances, each obstructing or obscuring the central aspect of his identity – its immobility, its persistent concentration on the problem of the relation between inner and outer worlds, its ultimate...scepticism on the reality of a categorical distinction between the inner and the outer. (McCormack, 1989, pp. 124–25)

He makes the important observation, expanded upon here, that Butt's mentor was Bishop George Berkeley who possessed a unified view of reality in which economics, optics and metaphysics are aspects of one central argument (McCormack, 1994, p. 323). Butt was proudest of *The Irish Querist* (1967) based on his lecture on Berkeley in 1865 (1866; see McCormack, 1989, p. 195). Indeed this pamphlet was a vital reiteration of his early writings on political economy and a practical extension of those ideas. Butt, McCormack believes, sought to present some integral entity – a client in court, a denominational monopoly, an entire people (McCormack, 1989, p. 129). He was particularly concerned with the issue of class, writing in his final issue as editor of the *Dublin University Magazine* in November

1838, 'the Protestants of Ireland must inevitably be finally extinguished as a church in Ireland...unless...they enjoy some conservative, or ascendant protection by which, as a minority, they must be defended' (quoted in McCormack, 1994, p. 147). Thus, McCormack (1989, p. 131) sought to resolve the paradox of Butt's evolution from Orange Toryism to nationalist in the 1870s because home rule emphasised a domestic and middle-class locus. Three further scholars – John P. McBride (1987), Joseph Spence (2001) and Wayne E. Hall (1999) – amplify McCormack thesis, stressing Butt's essential consistency. Spence contests White's interpretation, highlighting continuity in Butt's outlook over time. He points to the importance of his literary output and writings on economics and places Butt's novels in the context of politics. Wayne E. Hall's analysis of the *Dublin University Magazine* stresses both Butt's formative influence over intellectual life in the 1830s and his ultimate political consistency. He suggests that especially during Butt's stewardship the journal 'expressed a complex brand of Irish national identity that defined itself partly in cultural and partly in political terms, and that helped create a position for Protestant Ascendancy in some ways self-contradictory and self-defeating, in other ways surprisingly consistent and resilient' (Hall, 1999, p. 13). Amplifying Hall's thesis, it is suggested that the greater portion of his considerable output of writing and speeches were rooted in the social condition of Ireland which was intimately linked to a particular vision of political economy. It was the unitary nature of the Union of Great Britain and Ireland, Butt believed, that pressed doctrines upon Ireland that jeopardised prospects for prosperity and effective employment of human resources. In the 1870s he argued for autonomy in domestic affairs mainly from the vantage point of his ideas concerning Ireland's economic needs.

WHATELY PROFESSORSHIP AND OTHER WRITINGS TO 1849

Butt can be placed within the framework of what George Boyce (1995, pp. 18–19) terms colonial patriotism. Butt's analyses of Ireland's economy and development during the next years brought together the several strands that marked out an Ireland of citizens, an Ireland of sort which has emerged at the turn of the present millennium. What were the influences on Butt and what is his place in the development of political economy? His position is best characterised as eclectic and distinct from the other early holders of the

Whately Chair. Drawing upon but not endorsing classical political economy, Adam Smith, Longfield, Jean-Baptiste Say and others, Butt defies pigeonholing. His economic analysis emerged slowly, and initially, there was little hint that he would expand on Longfield's position which essentially was a theory of profit (McGovern, 2000, p. 5). However, Butt moved beyond Longfield's analysis and whereas the latter remained in the classical tradition on free trade, he did not. He expanded Longfield's approach that crucial to the determination of the price of goods was the importance of applying a unit of whatever resource to its marginal use, concluding that the factors of production were remunerated in relation to the utility they created in their least efficient, marginal employment (Boylan & Foley, 2003, Vol. 2, p. 10). His importance, it has been observed, was in drawing attention to the potential resource mobilisation and distribution aspects of protection and in assessing the benefits and weaknesses of protection in relation to the complexity of specific circumstances (Boylan and Foley, 2003, Vol. 3, p. 5). Butt's Whatley lectures have received most attention although it will be suggested that certain of his other writings were as important or even more significant as indicative of his ideas on political economy. In his first Whatley lecture (Butt, 1837a), appropriating the title 'Introduction', Butt outlined somewhat verbosely the scope of what he intended to address and adopted the high ground about the purpose of political economy. He declared it was 'to teach certain truths connected with the social condition of man – it attempts to explain the nature of the causes by which is brought about that singular machinery of society by which Providence has set man to supply each other's wants, and thus receive and confer a mutual benefit' (1837a, p. 23). Butt addressed the question of production and the creation of 'utility'. Employing the illustration of cotton stockings, Butt demonstrated the complex interchange required to produce even the most mundane of articles (1837a, pp. 25–26). 'When you purchase your pair of cotton stockings', he noted, 'you are positively commanding for your own personal comfort and accommodation, not only the services of thousands of your cotemporary fellow creatures, but the accumulated results of the labours of generations that have long since passed away' (1837a, p. 28). Thus, he maintained, political economy 'teaches the laws which regulate the production, distribution and consumption of wealth' (1837a, p. 30).

In the preface to the pamphlet Butt (1837a, p. 6),

> endeavoured completely to distinguish between that relation of things to our nature, by which minister to our wants, or satisfy our desires, and that relation to each by which

> they are mutually exchanged in certain proportions – the one is utility, and the other value; the first is evidently the basis of the second; and it is utility, and not value, which is the end and object of all human effort, and of the act of exchange itself.

He defined wealth to be 'all those things which minister to the wants or satisfy the desires of man, and which, from their nature are *capable* of being transferred' (1837a, p. 32). 'Under the term wealth then', Butt stated, 'we include all things material or immaterial which are useful or agreeable to man, and the nature of which is such as to render them susceptible of transfer' (1837a, p. 38). His rejection of the old distinction between productive and unproductive labour won particular praise from the commentator on the lecture in the *Dublin University Magazine*. The reviewer, though, cast doubt on Butt's exclusion of value from the definition of wealth (Anonymous, 1837).

Adopting a lofty plateau, Butt urged the separation of political economy from 'the disturbing and exciting influence of general politics' (Butt, 1837a, p. 41). In his estimation 'the proper business of science is to supply the knowledge, not to dictate its application' (1837a, p. 44). The published lecture was accompanied by a long appendix in which Butt explained his terminology, and this probably is the most valuable portion of the pamphlet. Overall, there was little remarkable in his initial foray into the minefield of political economy.

Butt devoted only a portion of his time to the Whatley Professorship, explaining the long gap between delivery of the later lectures and their publication. Until being called to the Irish Bar in November 1838, he remained editor of the *Dublin University Magazine*. After 1835 when he went to London to give evidence before a parliamentary committee, Butt began spending part of each year in the capital in order to keep terms at the Inns of Court [Inner Temple], then a prerequisite for a call to the Irish Bar. During this time he frequented the gallery of the House of Commons, nurturing an ambition to enter Parliament. He married Elizabeth Swanzy (died 1897) the daughter of a Monaghan solicitor in February 1837. During this time Butt also wrote for a number of periodicals including the *Evening Mail* and a bevy of British newspapers. A founder of the *Protestant Guardian* he served as it editor until amalgamated with the *Warder* in early 1839 Butt also was editor of the *Ulster Times* from November 1836 until sometime in mid-1838.

In March 1837 the *Dublin University Magazine* published an article, thought to be by Butt, on the condition of literature in Ireland (Butt, 1837b). Whether by his hand or not, it expressed Butt's view and is notable for the interconnection between culture and all other aspects of the country's life, an affirmation of his refusal in the Whatley lectures to distinguish between productive and unproductive labour. Moreover the article stressed 'the vast capabilities of Ireland for the literary pursuit, which, in fact, was concealed by the overpowering demand of the English marts. Whatever is produced here is consumed there' (1837b, p. 371). It went on to note that the pull of England 'drains wealth, knowledge, and commercial enterprise from our shore – which makes the emigration of our talent a necessary thing, that justifies the absentee' (1837b, p. 372). Calling for the retention of home produced talent, the article links intellectual life to 'national amelioration' (1837b, p. 375).

In May 1837, writing from London, Butt issued an important pamphlet, *The Poor-Law Bill for Ireland Examined*, criticising the measure being introduced for his country. This publication foreshadowed thinking in subsequent Whatley lectures, later writings and public pronouncements, meriting closer attention than it has received. The pamphlet can be compared with his more famous, *Rent, Profits, and Labour* (Butt, 1838). He made one of his long-standing observations that

> any one acquainted with Ireland must feel, upon perusing this bill, that it has not grown naturally out of a knowledge of the wants and circumstances of the country, but has been framed to meet a particular exigency in legislation. The truth is, that it has been brought in to meet the desire on the part of the public, that some remedial measure should be applied to the destitution which is known to exist in Ireland. The necessity of meeting this desire determined the Cabinet to prepare some Poor-law. (Butt, 1837c, pp. 4–5)

He bemoaned the scheme as alien to Irish circumstances 'a plan utterly and miserably inefficient as a measure of relief, and just as foreign to the real character and causes of destitution in Ireland, as it is possible for any measure to be' (1837c, p. 6). For him,

> the fatal mistake is this…the assumption that destitution in Ireland…[is] the accident of individuals, instead of considering it as the essential and general condition of a class. It is this which…instead of suggesting a measure by which we might endeavour to find sufficient food for one-third of the population who have not enough to eat. (1837c, p. 8)

He went on:

> the evidence collected by the Poor-inquiry Commission, if it proves any thing, proves this, that generally throughout whole districts of Ireland, penury, and almost starvation, are the general condition of those classes who are called, by a mockery of their misery, the labouring classes, – which means the classes that are willing to labour, and can get no employment: it proves that the labourer cannot, by the utmost exertion of his industry, procure sufficient to support himself and his family throughout they year; that he can make no attempt to supply them with comforts, since he has not even wherewithal to supply them with a sufficiency of necessaries; and that the result of this state of things is a

> hideous and appalling mass of misery and destitution, amid which human beings, degraded by wretchedness to almost the scale of savage life, barely drag out a precarious existence in hovels that can scarcely be said to shelter them from the rains and winds of heaven. (1837c, p. 9)

Moreover, he believed, 'what we want in Ireland is not a shelter in a workhouse from the pressure of temporary penury: we want something that will raise the condition of an entire class.... We want, in a word, not relief for occasional want, but a remedy for general and permanent destitution' (1837c, p. 11). He prophesied that the duty of determining who should receive relief will render the 'name of Guardians' 'hateful to the people', 'the system they administer relieves the poor, it still punishes poverty as a crime; those whom they exclude will hate them, because they have been the instrument of denying them the assistance to which they feel or fancy themselves entitled' (1837c, p. 15). Moreover, he was cognisant that by compelling the local magistracy to be members of the boards, it would 'alienate the confidence of the people from the class of magistrates that comprise the resident gentry, for whom it should be the first object of a wise statesman to conciliate it' (1837c, p. 16). Butt also maintained that 'the rate to be levied is a local one; and nothing could more unjust than to make these prosperous districts pay for the maintenance of the paupers of the others' (1837c, p. 17). The poor would migrate to districts where they could obtain relief; refusal of relief would not mitigate the problem for they would come anyway and 'thus create a mass of pauperism in their own vicinity' (1837c, pp. 17–18). The outcome would to reduce the few improving districts 'to the level of the rest' (1837c, p. 18). He wrote,

> Justice demands that you should not tax the good landlord of a well managed district, to support, during his months of mendicancy, the cottier who is impoverished by the rackrent of a bad. Expediency demands that you should restrain, and not encourage the spread of pauperism; it is *contagious*, and the less it is diffused the better. (1837c, p. 18)

Instead Butt insisted 'that there is uncultivated and half cultivated land in Ireland, far more than sufficient, if cultivated, to make up the deficiency; and that there are labourers unemployed, more than sufficient to cultivate that land, as to raise the required supply' (1837c, p. 19). Part of the current difficulty he noted was that 'that every acre of cultivated ground in England yields, on the average, nearly twice as much as one in Ireland, – while at the same time, for each two labourers that any given quantity of ground maintains in England, the same quantity in Ireland ministers to five' (1837c, p. 20). 'It is not the disease for which alone the warmest admirers of the workhouse prescription offer it as a remedy; it is not the existence of occasional and accidental distress – it is the presence of permanent and general destitution' (1837c, pp. 24–25). 'In losing sight of this, you have made the bill nugatory for the purpose of relief – effective only for the purposes of mischief' (1837c, p. 25). 'There are 5,000,000 of uncultivated acres in Ireland, amounting to a third of the land now under cultivation. Here are the resources from which you can supply the wants of the poor' (1837c, p. 27). Butt's stress on uncultivated and under-cultivated land was a common theme in his own time and for later nationalists, notably, Parnell. His concept of the just rent found expression in his proposal

> That the holders of land, (the pauper cottiers of these impoverished districts,) reserve as their own share of the produce, barely what will give themselves and their families a miserable subsistence; all the produce beyond this goes to the landlord's share: perhaps it is exported to pay the absentee landlord's rent. But this matters not: the occupier of land, – the man whom in England you would call a farmer, but whom here we will more correctly denominate a pauper, – he pays for his land almost as much as the entire produce is worth; the share he reserves for himself yields him but a miserable subsistence. He has nothing then to give for the assistance of the labour that would multiply the produce of the land. (1837c, pp. 29–30)

Similarly, the just rent reverberated through contemporary and later nationalist circles. The outcome, he proclaimed, 'originates in the forced and unnatural competition for land, which raises its price beyond its fair limits – and the evil reproduces itself: since the occupier of land cannot afford to employ labourers, there is no market for the labourer who is not himself an occupier' (1837c, p. 30). 'The possession of land, then, is the first necessary of life', Butt asserted. 'The starving people bid for it, in their desperation, far beyond their means of paying: and thus the whole country is divided into miserable holdings – ill-cultivated and wretched pieces of ground – from which the unhappy occupier can barely supply himself with a scanty subsistence' (1837c, pp. 30–31).

> To dwell upon that state of things by which a large proportion of our produce is exported, without any return whatever, to pay the rent of the absentees; for unfortunately it is in produce that these rents are paid. Just in the same way, we do not now supply ourselves with manufactures. The manufactured articles, which are used by those of us who are in the condition to obtain them, come from abroad, and we have nothing to give in exchange for them but food. (1837c, p. 32)

'Literally, we ask for bread, and you give us a stone: we want an increase of the quantity of eatables in the country, and you build workhouses' (1837c, p. 33). 'They will regard your workhouses as only a specious contrivance for immuring them in prisons without compelling them to go through the formality of a crime' (1837c, p. 34).

Butt's trenchant analysis of the chief deficiencies of the Irish economy – namely sparse employment, excessive competition for scarce resources, low productivity, misallocation of land entailing ensuing poverty and starvation all exacerbated by Irish expenditure abroad and an absence of home manufactures – and the inappropriate means by which the British government meant to remedy the problem had a theoretical base. His theme would find outlets at both levels.

It is, however, two of Butt's published Whately lectures that bolster his claim to be a 'neglected economist': *Rent, Profits and Labour* (1838) was the published version of his lecture in autumn 1837 and *Protection to Home Industry* (1846) was delivered at Trinity College in autumn 1840. In the first lecture, Moss (1991 [1973], p. 35) points out, Butt forged a union of Say's utility approach and Longfield's theory of profit. His main point was that

> The product of any given quantity of labour will exchange for the product of so much of the powers of capital as render to production an assistance equivalent to that labour, at the lowest rate of assistance to which capital is forced by its abundance to have recourse.
>
> It will exchange for as much of the produce of the soil as could be raised by that labour, or the equivalent powers of capital, at the least productive expenditure to which the demand for produce has compelled the community to resort. (Moss, 1991 [1973], p. 32)

To Moss, this analysis represented an early attempt to explain how utility created by factors employed in combination can be imparted to each separately and that the insight that resources are rewarded in accordance with the utility they create in their least efficient applications is a notable attempt to work out a marginal utility theory of imputation.

> Butt argued in *Protection to Home Industry* that while he did not intend a general defence of protective duties these may answer one or both of two great ends.
>
> First – They may bring into action and play sources and powers of production, in a country, which but for their existence, would lie utterly wasted and unproductive.
> Second – They may act the part of the most wise and wholesome poor law, setting the poor to work at a cost of some little self-denial to the rich; and by compelling a particular distribution of the wealth of the country, they may insure a certain amount of comforts to the condition of its labouring classes. (Butt, 1846, p. 15)

The crux was 'to secure to all within the country the means of earning, by their labour, a comfortable independence, is an object to which, if it be attainable, all other objects should be subordinate' (1846, p. 31). To that end he maintained that those who had only their labour should enjoy some portion of the country's riches (1846, p. 37). He found

> no difficulty in arriving at the conclusion that in a country like Ireland exporting articles of food, while many of her own people have not enough to eat, every importation from other countries must tend to increase that exportation; and if it be produced by withdrawal of employment and wages from our labourers at home, is a direct withdrawal from them of the support of human life. (1846, p. 41)

From this he argued, 'the effect of our using Irish instead of imported manufacture would be, to leave all the present ability of paying for labour undisturbed – to leave, therefore, the amount of our produce the same, but to turn that produce from exportation to feeding our own people' (1846, p. 43). For Butt, 'the true test of the prosperity of a country is not what is sent out of it, but what is used in it. I mean by the prosperity of a country, the comforts which the great mass of its inhabitants enjoy' (1846, p. 53). 'That nation deserts its duty, in which there are people willing to work, who cannot, by any exertion, earn their bread' (1846, p. 62).

Directly assaulting Cobdenites, he declared,

> Let us have the artisans and the peasantry of our own country comfortable and prosperous, before we weigh the chances of feeding those of the world at large. The man who cares for no one in particular, has very little affection for his species at all; and the economical philanthropy that cares for the comforts of the workmen of all countries alike, assuredly, end in an equal disregard for all. (1846, p. 75)

In linking the problem of landlord absenteeism to free trade he maintained, 'it is impossible to distinguish the question of absenteeism from that of the use of foreign commodities' (1846, p. 92). 'Were all our people fed', he wrote, 'it then might be both true and applicable to assert, that we exported agricultural produce, because it was that which our country's resources naturally led us to raise. The exportation of agricultural produce is now an evil, because it is so grievously wanted at home' (1846, p. 95). Though scarcely a social revolutionary, Butt, nonetheless believed that the wealthy had a fundamental obligation to the poor. For him, 'inequalities of property we must have; but it is open to us to control the effects of these inequalities, so far as they affect the means of existence of any portion of our people' (1846, pp. 105–6). The connection between economics and politics was punctuated by his reflection, 'how deeply does the condition of too many of our peasantry reprove the unprofitableness of our politics; and how bitterly, although silently, does it rebuke the rancour of our disunion and the littleness of our feuds!' (1846, p. 108).

In due course Butt's defence of protection drew forth a sharp critique by William Neilson Hancock who, in contrast, argued that with free exchange both parties gain; protection interferes with production; wealth creates demand for labour and that the interests of classes were reciprocal (Boylan and Foley, 2003, Vol. 4, pp. 3, 63–73). By the time Butt got around to publishing *Protection to Home Industry* the Great Famine had Ireland in its grips. Many of his earlier observations on poverty and unemployment reaped a bitter harvest. Butt, wrote two pamphlets in reaction to the catastrophe. The first, *A Voice for Ireland: The Famine in the Land* (Butt, 1847) was published initially in the *Dublin University Magazine* in April 1847. The second was *The Rate in Aid* (Butt, 1849). Together these pamphlets, like the earlier, *Poor-law Bill for Ireland Examined* and later *Irish Querist* (Butt, 1837c, 1867), are fundamental to Butt's economic stance. *Famine in the Land* may be seen as a declamation against the failure to employ proper principles of political economy. He decried, 'we cannot support our population as agricultural labourers – no conceivable increase in our agricultural produce will enable us to do so. The choice is, whether we will support a portion of them as manufacturers or as paupers' (Butt, 1847, p. v). However, the issue was never simply about economics but had a moral dimension for, as Butt repeated, 'the moral crime which has been committed in Ireland, of leaving our poor without a legal right to support, has entailed upon us the consequences of a pauperised population, and of the deterioration of their character' (1847, p. vi). He implored, 'if Irishmen combine to forget party, and obtain for their country measures of practical advantage, there are elements enough of wealth in the country to supply all the demands that even this unprecedented crisis makes upon our resources' (1847, pp. vii–viii). Taking to task once more the *laissez-faire* orthodoxy, he wrote, 'the folly of relying on private enterprise to supply the deficiency is proved incontestably by the result' (1847, p. 11). To Butt it appeared obvious that

> if ever there was an occasion upon which practical proof could be given of the value to every member of the stated of the association of men into states, that permits the government to wield mighty powers for the common good – if ever there were a time when men in the remotest corners of Ireland might have been taught the lesson that they have a deep interest in the strength and greatness of the United Empire, this famine presented that occasion…and Britain is now branded as the only civilised nation which would permit her subjects to perish of famine, without making a national effort to supply them with food. (1847, p. 11)

Certainly the kernel of Butt's later nationalism can be detected in this commentary, but the problem went beyond mere British indifference for 'it is the misfortune of every movement in Ireland, that each class looks to what immediately affects itself, and forgets the interest that all have in the common prosperity of the whole' (1847, p. 17).

To meet the challenges, Butt's goal's was to secure harmony between classes and creeds which receives emphasis in *The Rate of Aid*. This relatively overlooked broadside is a testament to Butt's mixture of economics with its practical applications or more accurately the absence of these under the current governing arrangements. 'I contend – that Ireland must, notwithstanding the Union, be, under existing circumstances, for some purposes still treated, as a separate state' (Butt, 1849, p. 3). Furthermore, he argued,

> if the rate in aid teaches any lesson, it teaches that the interests of all creeds, and classes, and districts of Ireland, are inseparable. Accept the lesson, and that which was intended as the pretext of division becomes the bond of union, and the proposition of a rate in aid may be met, as it only can be met, by a unanimous demand from all ranks and classes of Irishmen, for justice to this noble but misgoverned country. (1849, p. 7)

In Butt's opinion:

> There is one way, and but one way, of meeting this proposal; it is, to prove that the whole system of poor-law legislation in Ireland is based in error – that the attempt to support the labouring population of the country without increasing the activity of the productive powers of the country, involves a problem that admits but of one solution, and, persevered in, must lead to but one result – the confiscation of the little property our island has, without any real or substantial benefit to the poor. (1849, p. 9)

According to Butt,

> the one expedient is to tax – its miserable sameness unvaried by a single effort to raise the condition of the people – to increase the fund from which they must be fed – to find profitable employment for the thousands of strong arms that belong to it willing to work – to bring into action those unworked resources that need but the labour of those arms to produce sustenance for those strong men, without being a burden to any one. (1849, p. 14)

He blamed free trade for the reduced value of the produce of the land (1849, p. 16). The consequence was,

> as the pauperism of the country increases, the produce of the land is diminished, and the little fund that, in the hands of the employers of labour, constituted at once the chief support of the labouring population and the capital of reproductive exertion, is transferred, under the name of poor-rate, to the expensive sustenance of the same population as idle paupers; and producing nothing in return, it perishes in the transfer. (1849, pp. 17–18)

The crux of the misunderstanding, he believed, was that

> they legislated as if they had to deal with isolated instances of occasional distress – as if their only object should be to provide temporary relief for those who might happen to

> fall below the ordinary condition of the people; whereas, in truth and in fact, to deal with the destitution of Ireland was, in many of its districts, to deal with a whole population sunk in misery; to provide the means of decent and adequate living for a labouring class that had not enough to eat. (1849, pp. 18–19)

He asserted that, as the means to relief the distress,

> our first step must be to raise the condition of the mass of her people; until they are made comfortable, all hope of building up the superstructure of society is vain.... To support our people in the same condition as the people of England, we must at least double the productiveness of the cultivated land, and we must find some other employment for, at least, half of our agricultural labourers than what is afforded in the present cultivation of the soil. (1849, p. 32)

'This must be done by the virtue and determination of our people themselves', he insisted, for 'I am tired of the cant of the necessity of the introduction of English capital. Capital lies around us – it lies in our uncultivated wastes – it lies in our teeming fisheries – it lies in the sinews of the men that famine is wasting from our land. These things are the capital of a country' (1849, p. 32).

To Butt it was axiomatic that

> the prosperity of every country depends upon the exertions and the enterprise of the people themselves. It is possible for governments to encourage them – so, unfortunately, is it possible to depress them; and it is difficult to conceive a course of legislation more calculated to effect the latter – to discourage industry, and make individual exertion hopeless – than that by which one million of people have been made a burden, in idleness, upon the industry and the capital of Ireland. (1849, p. 35)

Specifically, he urged a slat of action: 'As the beginning of national improvement, there ought to be afforded from the Imperial exchequer speedy and effectual assistance to the completion of railway communication in Ireland.... But a measure that would make Ireland the highway to the Atlantic would, at no distant period of time, attract trade to our deserted western harbours' (1849, p. 36); 'a packet-station on western coast and dockyards' (1849, p. 38); 'Irish Board of Trade and Plantations devise measure to encourage fisheries, instructors in unpractised departments of industry; reclamation of waste lands and similar undertakings; liberal powers of compulsory purchase of reclaimable lands' (1849, p. 45); 'new plantation on estates encumbered with debt' (1849, p. 49); 'principle that to elevate Ireland from her present condition there should be national interference with the improvement of the soil – an interference carried to the extent of the state, assuming for the purposes of that improvement its ownership' (1849, p. 50); 'the growth of manufacturing industry in a country is the natural, the almost inevitable attendant upon agricultural activity' (1849, p. 53); 'emigrants should go to a British settlement' (1849, p. 56); 'taxation upon all property of absentees; small tax upon all articles of manufactures imported into Ireland' (1849, p. 57); 'a tax, equivalent to the income-tax, on all official salaries in Ireland, and on all realised property not otherwise liable to the poor-rate' (1849, p. 58); and 'diminish present imperial contribution' (1849, p. 58). Also, there were many other measures which Ireland needs. 'A better adjustment of the law of landlord and tenant; some measures by which encumbered estates might be more easily and expeditiously transferred from the ruinous control of the Court of Chancery to the care of resident proprietors.... But all these measures must be vain until you recognize the right of every man who is willing to work to be fed, and you meet that right by purchasing his labour, and applying it to increase the resources of the country' (1849, p. 64). The principle of a poor-law for Ireland should be to give every man 'A FAIR DAY'S WAGES FOR A FAIR DAY'S WORK' (1849, p. 64).

In most respects Butt's two pamphlets reiterated his thoughts on the Irish economy and in that regard are not theoretical increments. But, they should be treated in the light of his earlier observations and his emphasis on state intervention, especially in the instance of an under-developed economy, were point of departure from many of his contemporary political economists.

AFTER THE 1840S TO 1865 THE PRACTICE OF POLITICAL ECONOMY

In the second phase of his public career he was an MP, first and briefly for the English constituency of Great Yarmouth in 1852 and then for the parliamentary borough of Youghal, County Cork, from 1852 until his defeat at the general election in 1865. Between 1852 and 1865 Butt was less active as a pamphleteer – merely four appeared during the 1850s (1853, 1854, two in 1857) and only one more (1863) until 1865. His main political thrust during the next 13 years was the forum of the House of Commons where he was one, perhaps the most consistently active Irish member. Much of his labour there affirmed the positions he had enunciated earlier in speeches, pamphlets and in the *Dublin University Magazine*.

Until 1859, his term as an MP coincided with the existence of the Independent Irish Party and his record compares favourably with its most active members (see Knowlton, 1991, pp. 246).[3] Butt's speeches in the House of Commons comprise his main corpus of ideas for the period and merit close attention. In 1852 he spoke on the Encumbered Estates bill and in November made a careful speech attacking free trade (*Hansard's*, 122 (18 June 1852), c. 986; 123 (26 November), cc. 676–680).[4] This second incursion was abstracted in *The Times*. During 1853 he spoke on a range of issues including education, income tax and the over-taxation of Ireland (*Hansard's*, 126 (26 April 1853), 611; (2 May), cc. 730–731, 741, 749–753, 754, 756, 808–809, 810, 819–820, 938–955 (2 June), cc. 1040–1043, 1046, 1055, 1060, 1061). He was never invariably opposed to harmonisation of practice between Great Britain and Ireland. A case in point was his argument for assimilation of English and Irish affairs where appropriate; in the debate on the income tax in 1853, Butt stated that he 'wanted nothing for Ireland that England had not got' (*Hansard's*, 127 (27 May 1853), cc. 747–748). He followed a similar pattern during 1854, 1855 and 1856 though the topics varied and legal questions began to receive emphasis. In March 1854 he spoke briefly on the Irish Fisheries bill, 6 April on emigration, 6 July on the Encumbered Estates Commission and on 14 and 17 July on the Poor Law Commission (*Hansard's*, 131 (16 March 1854), cc. 346, 350, 351, 354; 132 (6 April), cc. 579–581; 134 (6 July), cc. 1309, 1310; 135 (14 July), c. 298; (17 July), c. 359). Although by no means confining his participation to Irish matters, these certainly constituted Butt's main preoccupation. Yet, in spite of being a nominally a Tory he supported Lord Palmerston over the Crimean War.

Butt was returned unopposed as a Liberal at Youghal in the general election of 1857, claiming as a recommendation the procurement of a railway for the borough. In the new Parliament he continued to make regular interventions, supporting, for instance, the conditions for workers in the bleaching industry and Irish railways (*Hansard's*, 145 (18 May 1857), c. 478; 146 (14 July), cc. 1505, 1506).

From his student days onwards, Butt found himself chronically in debt. During the 1850s his fiscal difficulties mounted. He had an established liaison in London, resulting in at least one illegitimate son; Butt fathered eight children by his wife and at least two others out of wedlock. Questionable financial dealings were exposed publicly and one such occasion led to an enquiry into a breach of privilege of the House of Commons on 22 February 1858 (*Hansard's*, 148 (22 Feb. 1858), cc. 1856–58).[5] Although escaping formal censure, Butt's personal reputation was in tatters. He did not speak in the House again until late May when once more he criticised the Irish Poor Law Board and in June on the Sale and Transfer of Land (Ireland) bill (*Hansard's*, 150 (4 June), cc. 1562–1564, 150 (14 May), cc. 2065–2066, 151 (24 June), c. 1502–1505). Overall, though, his participation for the remainder of the session fell below previous years. He did not reappear again before the general election in 1859 at which Butt now standing as a Liberal was triumphantly returned by 128 votes to 54 (White, 1946, p. 183).

From 1860 his rhetoric took on a populist and national turn. On 19 June, for example, during the committee stage of the Tenure and Improvement of Irish Land bill he burst out, 'the very worst form of Government for a country was Government by Boards, and a country more miserably 'be-boarded' than Ireland did not exist on the face of the earth' (*Hansard's*, 159 (19 June 1860), c. 668). Butt supported local control, a position later advocated by Parnell. On 29 June he argued that tenant insecurity caused emigration and pronounced 'emigration would end in the extinction in Ireland of the old Celtic race' (*Hansard's*, 159 (29 June 1860), cc. 1196–1197). During 1861 Butt reprised many of these themes, supporting state sponsored railway construction and defended the evicted tenants on the Derryveagh estate (*Hansard's*, 161 (7 May), cc. 1720, 1721; (14 May), cc. 2065–2066; 163 (17 June), cc. 1809–1810; (24 June, c. 1502–1505; 164 (2 July), cc. 1195–11996). On 8 July during discussion of the Irish estimates Butt objected to the administration of the Poor Law (*Hansard's*, 164 (8 July), c. 566–567). He complained that all members of the board were English; in his view there should be one Irish Catholic and one Protestant. During 1862, Butt tread the now familiar course. On two occasions he insisted that Irish laws should be harmonised with those in England, stating on 24 July during discussion of the Poor Relief (Ireland) bill that 'outdoor relief should be no more denied in Ireland than it was in England' (*Hansard's*, 168 (24 July 1862), cc. 781–782; also see, (4 August), cc. 1195–1196). In the next session he complained about the removal of Irish paupers, 'the English got the advantage of Irish absentees both rich and poor, and ought to bear the corresponding disadvantages' (*Hansard's*, 171 (22 June 1863), c. 1285). These and other staple themes were repeated in 1864. On 25 April and 21 June Butt spoke for the assimilation of legal procedures between England and Ireland; on 23 June he supported financial aid to convent schools (*Hansard's*, 174 (25 April 1864), c. 1557; 176 (21 June), c. 30; (23 June), cc. 216–218). He only spoke once in 1865 before the dissolution.

From the evidence of *Hansard*, White's allegation that Butt neglected his parliamentary duties must be dismissed; in fact, he was one of the most active Irish members. His work at the Irish Bar had ceased for many years though he appeared briefly in 1857; he was called to the English Bar at the Inner Temple on 17 November 1859. Reappearing at the Four Courts in Dublin in 1864 at a low point in his finances, he quickly re-established a lucrative practice, spending most of his last year as MP for Youghal in Dublin. Despite declaring himself in favour of tenant right and denominational education he was defeated by another Liberal, the wealthy Catholic, Joseph Neale McKenna, at the general election of 1865 by 122 votes to 106 and found himself out of Parliament.

BUTT AS A NATIONALIST, 1865–1879

Loss of his seat occurred just when there was a sea-change in Irish politics. Fresh opportunities emerged in the second half of the 1860s. He produced five pamphlets between 1865 and 1867 (1865, two 1866, two 1867), including *The Irish Querist*. Between 1869 and 1877 he produced another 14 pamphlets. From 1865 he wrote on the land question, Irish railways and fisheries though some of the other work also had an economic perspective.

Alarmed at the Fenian conspiracy, the Government began in 1865 to arrest and try the conspirators. Although largely unable to save Fenians from prison, he earned their respect and gratitude, in the process being transmuted into a national icon. His defence of Fenians, including in 1865 of John O'Leary, earned the wrath of creditors and Butt found himself imprisoned for debt for 18 months. According to White (1946, p. 218), '1867 saw the beginning of his work as a national statesman', but, as his writings and speeches reveal, this is to ignore an early long stream of labours that merit the description of patriotic that date back to the 1830s.

The Irish Querist that examined Ireland's social condition can be seen as Butt's summation of his position on political economy. It was written as a series of questions numbering 328 plus a further 23 queries of Bishop Berkeley which remained unanswered. It took up the issues of poverty that is assessed from various angles and concludes with the query 'whether seven centuries be not a sufficient time for a fair trial of the experiment of governing a country by coercion? And whether it may not at the close of them be worth while to try the experiment of another system for seven years?' (Butt, 1867, p. 40). This and Butt's other pamphlets of the mid-1860s seem to put him firmly on the path to advocating national self-government.

In 1869, Butt re-emerged in political life to head the budding national movement. He pronounced, 'I mean a self-government which gives us the entire right to manage our own affairs' (*Nation*, 20 November 1869). He spoke at many demonstrations across Ireland and wrote with telling effect on tenant right, social and economic conditions, denominational education and above all else, in favour of amnesty for Fenian convicts. These issues he saw as inexorably intertwined. William Gladstone secured a Liberal victory in the general election of 1868 on the specific platform of remedying Irish disaffection. In 1869 he pushed through legislation disestablishing the Church of Ireland. Rather than staying grievances, it raised Irish expectations. Moreover, although the Government released a number of Fenian prisoners in late 1868, this merely heightened demands to free the remainder. In June 1869, Butt announced that he was glad to serve on the committee to establish an amnesty organisation and shortly afterwards he accepted the office of President of the Amnesty Association (*Nation*, 12 June 1869). He thought they should work for the release of the Fenians 'in a temperate, moderate, yet firm manner, and leave nothing for their enemies to catch a hold on for rejecting their purposes' (*Nation*, 21 August 1869). In September 1869 Butt, who was already head of the Amnesty Association, assumed the leadership of the new Irish Tenant League. There were many divisions within the patriotic community with amnesty, tenant right and education vying for priority. During autumn 1869 tenant farmer meetings were broken up by Fenians who resented any diversion from the amnesty campaign.

In a letter to the Secretary of the Central Amnesty Association in November 1869, Butt attempted to assuage the rivalry between these movements, stating 'I believe the two objects, so far from being antagonistic, help each other. Everything that calls out a national spirit in Ireland tends to create a power that forwards the redress of every Irish wrong' (*Nation*, 13 November 1869). The national question held a number of attractions, including the possibility of submerging these differences under a common banner. The self-government ideal might be fashioned into a tool capable of bridging divisions and advancing Irish political and economic claims across a broad front. Butt told one audience, 'it is a mere question of time when we…ought to strain every nerve to achieve for Ireland national independence. And when I say national independence I don't mean separation. I mean a self-government which gives us the entire right to manage our own affairs' (*Nation*, 20 November 1869). At an Irish Tenant League meeting on 13 December in Dublin he was reported to believe,

> that behind every question, whether it be tenant right, the church question, the amnesty question, or whatever other national question they might take up, there lay behind them

> a greater and deeper question, that would one day assume its proper place before the world; and he thought that all men who had the idea ought to shape their conduct and be guided in every action of political life by a reference to the day the demand he alluded to would be made by the Irish people. Entertaining that conviction strongly as he did, so far from compromising nationality by coming forward and joining in earnest, energetic demand for the emancipation of the Irish occupiers of the soil, they render the best service to the national cause. If they succeeded in obtaining a proper measure, they created an Irish nation out of the men who were now struggling into liberty from dominion of the landlords. (*Nation*, 18 December 1869)

As if to reinforce the linkage of issues, he spoke at an Amnesty meeting the same evening. When Gladstone introduced the Irish land bill in February 1870 tenant farming interests were disappointed. Butt gave voice to this feeling (*Nation*, 26 February 1870, 5 March 1870), thereby encouraging those who saw Ireland's best hope in the formation of a new patriotic organisation forged on the anvil of a revived self-government agitation.

On 19 May 1870, 49 gentlemen, a majority being Protestants, met in Dublin to discuss the future governing arrangements of their country (*Nation*, 28 May 1870).[6] Those present agreed to promote Butt's plan of federal home rule and the gathering became the nucleus of the Home Government Association. Butt was the guiding light although he never intended it to become a popular body modelled on the Repeal Association; for its object 'they should accustom the public mind to take in the project they had formed; and after showing that their aims were practical, they could organise the whole of Ireland, and English Ministers would think twice before they refused their demands' (Nation, 15 October 1870). Towards the end of the year Butt published *Irish Federalism*, which outlined what home rule entailed, distinguishing it from Repeal. In his view 'federalism' would offer Ireland an opportunity for 'independence without breaking up the unity of the empire, interfering with the monarchy, or endangering the rights or liberties of any class of Irishmen' (Butt, 1874, p. iv). Under it 'Ireland could enjoy all of [the] self-government and distinct national rights which would be necessary for full development of her national life'. Butt envisaged self-government as the means of reconciling competing interests: 'It is from the joint deliberations of all classes of Irishmen that we may most confidently hope to present a plan of a national legislature, in which the just influence of property and education, and rank may be harmoniously combined with popular privileges and power, so as to make the legislature the real representative of the nation' (1874, p. viii). Butt's vision set him apart from the bulk of Catholics who took up home rule in the 1870s.

CONCLUSION

The fusion of economic and political ideas was evident all phases of Butt's career. Like Parnell and later Sir Horace Plunkett, but also significantly Gladstone in 1886, Butt was searching for a means to reconcile the different groups in Ireland. However, he had the clearest economic analysis. Many concerns he articulated were part of the debate of his day: the drive by European empires to harmonise and centralise, the impact of post-mercantilist economics, and the particular vulnerabilities of agricultural regions. In the contemporary European Union the argument continues between centralisers and those who prefer a Europe of Nations. Butt would feel at home were he here to participate in the discussion. For him home rule offered the prospect of his panacea – full-employment. Although he did not rule out the goal of economic growth, Butt's main thrust lay elsewhere. Indeed, what Butt witnessed was the considerable de-industrialisation of much of Ireland in the face of the widening impact of British competition. Butt was not the most original of political economists but he made a contribution to its fund of ideas and he tried to implement a concrete programme or at least inform the British Parliament of that which it did not know while at the same time educating opinion in his native land. He addressed the pressing issues of the day, the land system, absenteeism, the care of the destitute, the role of private and public funding, public works, industrialisation and emigration.

ACKNOWLEDGMENTS

I am grateful to N. C. Fleming and Carla King who commented on an earlier version of this article and Col. Helen E. O'Day for her continued encouragement.

NOTES

1. Curiously, the only mention of Butt by Cormac Ó Gráda is in reference to his views on protection. See Ó Gráda (1995, p. 410).
2. See Collins (1913, pp. 179–94) for an appealing sketch of the man who's 'generosity was proverbial'.
3. Knowlton (1991) confines his attention to voting. For a comparison with Irish MPs in the 1830s see, Brian D. Crowe (1995, pp. 61–62, 93, 136, passim).

4. All citations to *Hansard's Parliamentary Debates*, 3rd series, are simply identified as *Hansard's*, followed by the volume, (date), and section number(s).

5. See also the articles about Butt's financial and parliamentary issues in *The Times* on February 24, 25, 26, and 27, and March 1, 2, 3, 4, 5, 6, 8, and 11, 1858.

6. See the letter from Butt to P. J. Smyth, 23 May 1870, in the Smyth Papers (MS 8215/2), National Library of Ireland.

REFERENCES

Anonymous. (1837). Comments on Butt's 'Introductory Lecture'. *Dublin University Magazine*, May 9, pp. 599–600.

Bahlman, D. W. R. (Ed.) (1972). *The diary of Sir Edward Walter Hamilton, 1880–1885*. Oxford: Clarendon Press.

Black, R. D. C. (1960). *Economic thought and the Irish question, 1817–1870*. Cambridge: Cambridge University Press.

Black, R. D. C. (1983). The Irish dissenters and nineteenth-century political economy. In: A. E. Murphy (Ed.), *Economists and the Irish economy: From the eighteenth century to the present day* (pp. 120–137). Dublin: Irish Academic Press.

Blaug, M. (Ed.) (1991). *James Wilson (1805–1860), Isaac Butt (1813–1879), T.E. Cliffe Leslie (1827–1882)*. Aldershot, UK: Edward Elgar.

Boyce, D. G. (1995). *Nationalism in Ireland* (3rd ed.). London: Routledge.

Boylan, T., & Foley, T. (Eds). (2003). *Irish political economy, 4 vols.* , London: Routledge.

Brown, M. (1972). *The politics of Irish literature: From Thomas Davis to W.B. Yeats*. London: George Allen & Unwin.

Butt, I. (1837a). *Introductory lecture*. Dublin: William Curry.

Butt, I. (1837b). Past and present state of literature in Ireland. *Dublin University Magazine*, *9*(March), 365–376.

Butt, I. (1837c). *The Poor-law bill for Ireland examined*. London: B. Fellowes.

Butt, I. (1838). *Rent, profits, and labour: A lecture*. Dublin: William Curry.

Butt, I. (1846). *Protection to home industry: Some cases of its advantages considered*. Dublin: Hodges and Smith.

Butt, I. (1847). *A voice for Ireland: The famine in the land; what has been done and what is to be done*. Dublin: J. McGlashan.

Butt, I. (1849). *The rate in aid: A letter to the right hon. The earl of Roden, K.P.* Dublin: J. McGlashan.

Butt, I. (1866). Berkeley. In: *The afternoon lectures on literature and art: Delivered in the theatre of the museum of industry, St. Stephen's Green, Dublin, in April and May, 1865*. London: Bell and Daldy.

Butt, I. (1867). *The Irish querist: A series of questions proposed for the consideration of all who desire to solve the problem of Ireland's social condition*. Dublin: John Falconer.

Butt, I. (1874). *Irish federalism: Its meaning, its objects and its hope* (4th ed.). Dublin: Irish Home Rule League.

Collins, J. (1913). *Life in old Dublin*. Dublin: J. Duffy.

Comerford, R. V. (1979). *The Fenians in context: Irish politics and society, 1848–82*. Dublin: Wolfhound Press.

Crowe, B.D. (1995). *The parliamentary experience of the Irish members of the house of commons, 1833–41*. Ph.D. dissertation, Queen's University Belfast.

Davitt, M. (1904). *The fall of feudalism in Ireland*. London: Harper & Bros.

Feingold, W. L. (1984). *The revolt of the tenantry: The transformation of local government in Ireland, 1872–1886*. Boston: Northeastern University Press.

Foster, R. F. (1988). *Modern Ireland, 1600–1972*. London: Allen Lane.

Gray, P. (2004). The making of mid-Victorian Ireland: Political economy and the memory of the great famine. In: P. Gray (Ed.), *Victoria's Ireland: Irishness and Britishness, 1837–1901* (pp. 151–166). Dublin: Four Courts Press.

Hall, W. E. (1999). *Dialogues in the Margin: A Study of the Dublin University Magazine*. Washington, DC: Catholic University of America Press.

Hawkins, A., & Powell, J. (Eds). (1997). *The Journal of John Wodehouse, first earl of Kimberley for 1862–1902*. Cambridge: Cambridge University Press.

Jackson, A. (1998). *Ireland 1798–1998: Politics and war*. Oxford: Blackwell.

Kee, R. (1972). *The green flag: A history of Irish nationalism*. London: Weidenfeld and Nicolson.

Knowlton, S. R. (1991). *Popular politics and the Irish Catholic Church: The rise and fall of the independent Irish party, 1852–1859*. New York: Garland.

Larkin, E. (1996). *The Roman Catholic Church and the emergence of the modern Irish political system, 1874–1878*. Dublin: Four Courts Press.

Lyons, F. S. L. (1977). *Charles Stewart Parnell, 1846–1891*. London: Collins.

MacDonagh, J. C. (1946). *Isaac Butt 1813–1879: Lecture delivered at the vocational schools, Stranarlor Co. Donegal*, December 14, 1945. Ballybofey, IR.

MacNeill, J. G. S. (1925). *What I have seen and heard*. Boston: Little Brown.

McBride, J. P. (1987). *The Dublin University Magazine: Cultural nationality and Tory ideology in an Irish literary and political journal, 1833–1852*. Ph.D. dissertation, University of Dublin.

McCaffrey, L. J. (1962). *Irish federalism in the 1870s: A study in conservative nationalism*. Philadelphia: American Philosophical Society.

McCarthy, J. (1899). *Reminiscences* (2nd ed.). London: Harper & Bros.

McCormack, W. J. (1989). Isaac Butt (1813–79) and the inner failure of Protestant home rule. In: C. Brady (Ed.), *Worsted in the game: Losers in Irish History*. Dublin: Lilliput Press.

McCormack, W. J. (1994). *From Burke to Beckett: Ascendancy tradition and betrayal in literary tradition*. Cork: Cork University Press.

McDowell, R. B. (1952). *Public opinion and government policy in Ireland, 1801–1846*. London: Faber and Faber.

McGovern, S. (2000). *When is a school not a school? The case of utility theory in early Irish political economy*. Dublin City University Business School Research Papers, no. 39. Available at http://doras.dcu.ie/2225/

Moody, T. W. (1981). *Davitt and Irish revolution, 1846–82*. Oxford: Clarendon Press.

Moss, L. S. (1976). *Mountifort Longfield: Ireland's first professor of political economy*. Ottawa, IL: Green Hill Publishers.

Moss, L. S. (1991 [1973]). Isaac Butt and the early development of the marginal utility theory of imputation. In: M. Blaug (Ed.), *James Wilson (1805–1860), Isaac Butt (1813–1879), T.E. Cliffe Leslie (1827–1882)*. Aldershot, UK: Edward Elgar, pp. 33–54.

O'Brien, R. B. (1898). *The life of Charles Stewart Parnell, 2 vols*. New York: Harper & Bros.

O'Day, A. (2006). Nationalism and political economy in Ireland: Isaac Butt's analysis. In: R. Swift & C. Kinealy (Eds), *Politics and power in Victorian Ireland* (pp. 119–132). Dublin: Four Courts Press.

O'Day, A. (2009). Three visions of economics and nationality: Butt, Parnell and Davitt. In: F. Lane & A. Newby (Eds), *Michael Davitt: New perspectives* (pp. 48–61). Dublin: Four Courts Press.

Ó Gráda, C. (1995). *Ireland: A new economic history, 1780–1939*. Oxford: Clarendon Press.

Seligman, E. R. A. (1903). On some neglected British economists. *Economic Journal, 13*(51–52), 335–363 and 511–535.

Spence, J. (2001). Isaac Butt, Irish nationality and the conditional defence of the union, 1833–70. In: D. G. Boyce & A. O'Day (Eds), *Defenders of the union: A survey of British and Irish unionism since 1801* (pp. 65–89). London: Routledge.

Thornley, D. A. (1964). *Isaac Butt and home rule*. London: MacGibbon and Kee.

Whately, R. (1848). Report of the address on the conclusion of the first session of the Dublin Statistical Society. Dublin, Hodges and Smith. Available at http://www.tara.tcd.ie/bitstream/2262/7720/1/jssisiVolI1_11.pdf

White, T. deV. (1946). *The road of excess*. Dublin: Browne & Nolan.

Printed and bound by CPI Group (UK) Ltd, Croydon, CR0 4YY

16/09/2026

14963402-0002